FORENSIC ASSESSMENTS IN CRIMINAL AND CIVIL LAW

FORENSIC ASSESSMENTS IN CRIMINAL AND CIVIL LAW

A Handbook for Lawyers

EDITED BY

RONALD ROESCH

PATRICIA A. ZAPF

OXFORD
UNIVERSITY PRESS

OXFORD
UNIVERSITY PRESS

Oxford University Press is a department of the University of Oxford. It furthers the
University's objective of excellence in research, scholarship, and education by publishing
worldwide.

Oxford   New York

Auckland   Cape Town   Dar es Salaam   Hong Kong   Karachi
Kuala Lumpur   Madrid   Melbourne   Mexico City   Nairobi
New Delhi   Shanghai   Taipei   Toronto

With offices in

Argentina   Austria   Brazil   Chile   Czech Republic   France   Greece
Guatemala   Hungary   Italy   Japan   Poland   Portugal   Singapore
South Korea   Switzerland   Thailand   Turkey   Ukraine   Vietnam

Oxford is a registered trademark of Oxford University Press in the UK and certain other
countries.

Published in the United States of America by
Oxford University Press
198 Madison Avenue, New York, NY 10016

© Oxford University Press 2013

Published by Oxford University Press, Inc.
198 Madison Avenue, New York, New York 10016
www.oup.com

Library of Congress Cataloging-in-Publication Data
Forensic assessments in criminal and civil law : a handbook for lawyers / edited by Ronald Roesch, Patricia A. Zapf.
p. cm. — (Best practices in forensic mental health assessment)
Includes bibliographical references and index.
ISBN 978-0-19-976685-7
1. Evidence, Expert—United States.   2. Forensic psychology—United States.   3. Forensic psychiatry—United States.
I. Roesch, Ronald, 1947-   II. Zapf, Patricia A., 1971-
KF8965.F69 2012
345.73'06—dc23
2012002447

1 3 5 7 9 8 6 4 2
Printed in the United States of Americaon acid-free paper

CONTENTS

PREFACE

The Oxford series edited by Kirk Heilbrun, Tom Grisso, and Alan Goldstein, entitled *Best Practices in Forensic Mental Health Assessment*, is an outstanding series directed toward forensic practitioners. *Best practice* evaluations are, as defined by the editors of this series, empirically supported, legally relevant, and consistent with applicable ethical and legal standards. The series comprises 20 books that provide a comprehensive coverage of assessment topics in both criminal and civil domains. The authors of these books are leading scholars and practitioners in forensic psychology. Each book follows a similar template, with chapters covering the legal context for a particular type of evaluation, forensic mental health concepts, empirical foundations, preparation for the evaluation, data collection and interpretation, and report writing.

The publication of the books in the series stimulated us to think that it might be worthwhile to pursue a similar project geared toward legal professionals. What we had in mind was a handbook that would provide lawyers and judges with what they need to know about forensic assessments. We believe that legal professionals would be interested in a single volume that covers psycholegal issues that arise in their practice. We believed that while judges and lawyers do not need to know the highly specific details of a mental health assessment, they do need to appreciate what to expect from an evaluation of a legal issue such as competence to stand trial, child custody, or jury selection.

Our goal was to prepare a standard reference that will be consulted by legal professionals as a highly authoritative resource for recommended practice in all of the major areas of forensic mental health assessment. To accomplish this, we invited the authors of each of the Best Practices books to take on the daunting task of condensing their book to a single chapter, and refocusing the text to provide legal professionals with the essentials that would allow them to make the most effective use of an expert conducting a forensic mental health assessment. We are grateful for their willingness to contribute to this handbook, and we believe the chapters they prepared accomplish our goal of informing the legal community about the best practices for evaluations of a range of civil and criminal forensic issues.

Each chapter follows a similar structure comprising five major sections. Section 1 (Legal Context) focuses on the relevant legal standards and procedures. This section provides an overview of how the relevant legal construct has been defined and refined in practice as well as a review of relevant landmark cases and discussion of the way in which these have shaped the evaluation objectives and process.

Section 2 (Forensic Mental Health Concepts) acknowledges that forensic examiners cannot proceed from legal definitions of mental conditions or capacities directly to data collection: the legal definitions first must be structured and translated using psychological and psychiatric concepts. Virtually every subfield of forensic assessment has developed "hybrid" concepts—*psycholegal constructs*—that employ psychological concepts to translate what it is that the law wants to know about examinees relevant to the legal question. These psycholegal constructs improve the ability of forensic practitioners to identify, operationalize, and measure legally relevant characteristics of examinees for the issue before the court. The purpose of this section is to describe for legal professionals the ways in which mental health professionals have come to conceptualize and translate the legal definitions into psycholegal constructs.

Section 3 (Empirical Foundations and Limits) provides a review of key empirical research that guides forensic evaluation in the subfield in question. This section identifies the *value* of various forensic assessment concepts and methods as well as the *limits* of those concepts and methods for interpretations and expert opinions. Assessment methods—no matter how well researched and strongly supported—are valid for some purposes and not others, and even their known validity is limited in a variety of ways. This section informs legal professionals about how research and empirically based methods can guide psychological practice as well as how psychological professionals can avoid making interpretations or claims that exceed the limits of their methods.

Section 4 (The Evaluation) briefly describes the evaluation process. This includes a brief summary of the evaluation process, the data to be collected as part of the evaluation, and the processes involved in the interpretation of that data. Legal professionals wanting more detail on the evaluation process for a given type of evaluation can refer to the relevant volume in the Best Practices series.

Section 5 (Report Writing and Testimony) provides the legal professional with an understanding of what constitutes appropriate and inappropriate report writing and testimony. The goal of this section is to provide legal professionals with a sense of what information a good evaluation report should contain as well as what information should be excluded.

We encourage legal professionals to seek out the relevant volume(s) in the Best Practices series, whenever necessary, for additional detailed information geared towards mental health professionals on the relevant areas of forensic mental health evaluation. These two resources should, together, serve to provide a well-rounded view of each of the relevant areas of practice.

Ronald Roesch
Patricia A. Zapf

ABOUT THE CONTRIBUTORS

Elizabeth W. Adams is a graduate student in the Clinical Child Psychology program at the University of Alabama. She completed her Bachelor's of Science at Furman University. Her research interests focus on the emotional processing and facial recognition of youth with callous-unemotional traits. She also examines the process of evaluating developmental maturity and broader assessment issues for youth who are being considered for transfer to adult court.

Xinying Ang is a graduate student in the Clinical Child Psychology program at the University of Alabama. She completed her Bachelor of Arts (Honors) in Psychology at the National University of Singapore. Her research interest focuses on understanding the etiology of conduct disorder, antisocial personality disorder, and psychopathy, specifically on examining how emotional processes (e.g., emotional regulation) and environmental factors (e.g., trauma, parenting style) contribute to the development of antisocial behaviors and psychopathic traits.

Curtis L. Barrett, PhD, ABPP, is a Fellow of the American Psychological Association, the American Academy of Forensic Psychology, and the Academy of Cognitive Therapy. He is Professor Emeritus, University of Louisville School of Medicine. He has board certifications from the American Board of Professional Psychology (Forensic Psychology) and the American Compulsive Gambling Certification Board (Compulsive Gambling). He has authored or co-authored over 100 book chapters, articles, brochures, and manuals. He consults on organizational and programmatic approaches to the evaluation and treatment of addictive and other behavioral disorders. (curtis.barrett@insightbb.com)

Stephanie Brooks Holliday, MS, is currently a graduate student in clinical psychology at Drexel University. Her research interests include forensic mental health assessment, risk and risk/needs assessment, risk reduction, and models of offender interventions. (sfb44@drexel.edu)

Karen S. Budd, PhD, is Professor of Psychology, Director of Clinical Training, and directs the Parent--Child Interaction Therapy Program at DePaul University in Chicago. She formerly directed a demonstration and research project at Cook County Juvenile Court on assessing parenting capacity in child protection cases. She has authored three books, conducts research on prevention and intervention programs for young children with disruptive behavior, and was a Fulbright Senior Scholar in Prague, Czech Republic. (kbudd@depaul.edu)

Jennifer R. Clark, PsyD, specializes in issues related to child abuse and neglect and assessment of parenting capacity in child protection cases; she is currently in private practice. She was previously the Clinical Director for the Child Protection Division at the Cook County Juvenile Court Clinic and Assistant Professor, Northwestern University Feinberg School of Medicine in Psychiatry and Behavioral Sciences. She is co-author of *Evaluation of Parenting Capacity for Child Protection* (2011). (JRClark1229@me.com)

Mary Connell, EdD, ABPP, is board certified in both Forensic Psychology and Clinical Psychology. She is in independent practice concentrating principally on sexual assault, child maltreatment, and child sexual abuse. She has authored or co-authored a number of books, chapters, and articles, including *Evaluation of Parenting Capacity in Child Protection*

(2011) and *The Evaluation of Child Sexual Abuse Allegations: A Comprehensive Guide to Assessment and Testimony* (2009). (mary@maryconnell.com)

Mary Alice Conroy, PhD, ABPP, is Director of Clinical Training for the Sam Houston State University Clinical Psychology Doctoral Program. She previously spent 20 years providing forensic services for the U.S. Bureau of Prisons. As Past President of the American Academy of Forensic Psychology she holds a Diplomate in Forensic Psychology. She remains active in providing forensic evaluation services for the courts in Texas. (maconroy@shsu.edu)

Mark D. Cunningham, PhD, ABPP, is a board-certified clinical and forensic psychologist who has testified at capital sentencing in over 170 cases. His practice is national in scope and he is licensed in 20 states. A prolific scholar and fellow of the American Psychological Association, Dr. Cunningham's research contributions have been honored with the 2006 American Psychological Association Award for Distinguished Contributions to Research in Public Policy and the 2005 Texas Psychological Association Award for Outstanding Contribution to Science. (mdc@markdcunningham.com)

Brian L. Cutler, PhD, is Professor of Social Science & Humanities at the University of Ontario Institute of Technology. Trained in Social Psychology at the University of Wisconsin-Madison, Professor Cutler conducts research on eyewitness identification, jury behavior, wrongful conviction, and related topics. He is a Fellow of the Association for Psychological Science and a Distinguished Member of the American Psychology-Law Society. Professor Cutler has served as editor of the journal *Law and Human Behavior* and as President of the American Psychology-Law Society. He has also served as an expert witness in various states and federal courts in the United States. (briancutler@mac.com)

Eric Y. Drogin, JD, PhD, ABPP, is a Fellow of the American Academy of Forensic Psychology and the American Bar Foundation (ABA), and a Diplomate and former President of the American Board of Forensic Psychology. He holds a faculty appointment with Harvard Medical School and has served as Chair of the American Psychological Association's Committee on Professional Practice and Standards, Chair of the APA's Committee on Legal Issues, and President of the New Hampshire Psychological Association. He is Chair of American Bar Association's Behavioral and Neuroscience Law Committee and the ABA's Section of Science & Technology Law. Dr. Drogin's multidisciplinary practice encompasses mental health law, expert witness testimony, and trial consultation. (edrogin@bidmc.harvard.edu)

Joel A. Dvoskin, PhD, ABPP, is an Assistant Professor in the Department of Psychiatry at the University of Arizona College of Medicine. Dr. Dvoskin is the former Acting Commissioner of Mental Health for the State of New York, and has been President of the American Psychology-Law Society and Psychologists in Public Service. He consults with mental health and criminal justice agencies across the United States, as well as Fortune 100 corporations, colleges, universities, and the NCAA. He is the lead editor of *Using Social Science to Reduce Violent Offending*, published by the Oxford University Press in 2011. (Joelthed@aol.com)

William (Bill) E. Foote, PhD, ABPP, has been a practicing forensic psychologist in Albuquerque, New Mexico, for over 30 years. He has been on the faculty of the University of New Mexico in the Departments of Psychology and Psychiatry and in the School of Law. Dr. Foote has served in many roles within the governance of the American Psychological Association, including leadership of the American Psychology-Law Society. He is a past-president of the American Board of Forensic Psychology. He is the author or co-author of a number of articles and book chapters and two books, many of which deal with the psychological aspects of employment cases. (forNpsych@aol.com)

Geri Fuhrmann, PsyD, is Clinical Professor of Psychiatry and Pediatrics and past Director of Child and Family Forensic Center at the University of Massachusetts Medical School. Currently, she serves as Manager of Juvenile Forensic Services for the Massachusetts Department of Mental Health. She co-authored *Evaluation of Child Custody and Parents Apart*®, a parent education program for separating parents, In 2001, she received the Manual Carballo Governor's Award for Excellence in Public Service. (geri.fuhrmann@massmail.state.ma.us)

Alan M. Goldstein, PhD, is Professor Emeritus at John Jay College of Criminal Justice—CUNY. His publications and practice focus on a range of psycholegal issues, including *Miranda* waivers, validity of confessions, trial competency, insanity, federal and capital sentencing, and malpractice. He is in independent practice in Hartsdale, NY. (alanmg@optonline.net)

Naomi E. Sevin Goldstein, PhD, is Associate Professor of Psychology at Drexel University and a member of the faculty of the J.D.-Ph.D. Program in Law and Psychology. Dr. Goldstein specializes in forensic psychology, and her research examines adolescents' abilities to make legal decisions. She focuses on suspects' capacities to waive *Miranda* rights and offer confessions during police interrogations. She also developed and is evaluating the efficacy of the Juvenile Justice Anger Management (JJAM) Treatment for Girls. (neg23@drexel.edu)

Jane Goodman-Delahunty, JD, PhD, is a Research Professor at Charles Sturt University in the Australian Graduate School of Policing and the School of Psychology (Manly Campus). She is a Commissioner with the New South Wales Law Reform Commission, a member of the NSW Administrative Decisions Tribunal, a mediator for the NSW Office of Fair Trading, and President of the Australian and New Zealand Association for Psychiatry, Psychology, and Law. Her research fosters evidence-based decisions to promote social, procedural, and distributive justice. (jdelahunty@csu.edu.au)

Thomas Grisso, PhD, is Professor of Psychiatry, Director of Psychology, and Director of the Law-Psychiatry Program at the University of Massachusetts Medical School. His research and clinical interests have focused on the use of psychological assessment in legal contexts, the range of legal competencies, and issues pertaining to mental health, juvenile justice, and public safety. (Thomas.Grisso@umassmed.edu)

Kirk Heilbrun, PhD, is currently Professor and Head, Department of Psychology, Drexel University. His research and practice interests include forensic mental health assessment, risk assessment and risk reduction, and community alternatives to prosecution of justice-involved individuals with severe mental illness. (kirk.heilbrun@drexel.edu)

Robert D. Hoge, PhD, is Professor Emeritus of Psychology and Distinguished Research Professor at Carleton University in Ottawa. His teaching, research, and consulting activities focus on child and adolescent psychology, forensic psychology, and psychological assessment. He has served as a consultant to government and private agencies on issues relating to the treatment of youth in mental health and juvenile-justice settings. He has published extensively in journals and authored numerous books relating to assessment and forensic issues. He is a Fellow of the Canadian Psychological Association and a registered psychologist in the Province of Ontario with a specialty in forensic psychology. (robert_hoge@carleton.ca)

Andrew W. Kane, PhD, ABAP, is a clinical and forensic psychologist in private practice in Milwaukee and a Diplomate of the American Board of Assessment Psychology. He is also a Professor at the Wisconsin School of Professional Psychology, and an Adjunct Clinical Professor at the University of Wisconsin-Milwaukee. He has authored or co-authored 10 professional books and over 70 articles. He is the Associate Editor for Psychology and the Chair of the Forensic Psychology Section of the journal *Psychological Injury and Law*. He served as a member of the Expert Panel on Psychiatric and Psychological Evidence of the ABA, which produced the *National Benchbook on Psychiatric and Psychological Evidence*. He is a former president of the Wisconsin Psychological Association and its Division of Forensic and Correctional Psychologists. (awkane@sbcglobal.net)

Christopher King, BS, is a student in the J.D.-Ph.D. program in law and clinical psychology at Drexel University. His research interests include forensic mental health assessment, risk assessment and reduction, and the application of law and public policy to offender subtypes. (chris.king@drexel.edu)

Margaret Bull Kovera, PhD, is a Professor of Psychology at John Jay College of Criminal Justice, City University of New York. She is a Fellow of the Association for Psychological Science, the American Psychological Association, the American Psychology-Law Society (APLS), the Society for Experimental Social Psychology, and the Society for the Psychological Study of Social Issues (SPSSI). She is a Past-President of APLS. She received the Saleem Shah Award for Early Career Achievement in Psychology and Law and the APLS Outstanding Teacher and Mentor in Psychology and Law Award from APLS. Her research has been published in *Law and Human Behavior*, *Journal of Applied Psychology*, *Applied Cognitive Psychology*, and *Psychology, Public Policy, and Law*. She regularly serves as a trial consultant and as an expert witness in cases involving eyewitness identification. (mkovera@jjay.cuny.edu)

Ivan Kruh, PhD, wrote this chapter based on his ten years of work as the Director of Forensic Services at the Child Study and Treatment Center (CSTC) in Tacoma, WA, where he conducted pre-adjudication evaluations of juveniles (competence to stand trial, mental state at the time of offense, and future violence risk), as well as provided competency remediation services to juveniles. He has provided training about the legal, clinical, and psycholegal aspects of conducting juvenile forensic evaluations to clinical trainees, seasoned clinicians, researchers, administrators, attorneys, and judges for many years. Currently, he is a forensic examiner for the New York State Office of Mental Health and offers forensic services and consultation privately. (ivankruhphd@gmail.com)

Casey LaDuke, MS, is a doctoral student in the clinical psychology program at Drexel University. His research interests include forensic mental health assessment, forensic neuropsychology, and the diversion of individuals with serious mental illness from the justice system. (casey.laduke@drexel.edu)

Douglas Mossman, MD, is Program Director for Forensic Psychiatry Training at the University of Cincinnati College of Medicine. In 2008, he received the Manfred S. Guttmacher Award from the American Psychiatric Association (APA) for his outstanding contributions to the literature in forensic psychiatry. He is a Distinguished Fellow of the APA, Treasurer of the American Academy of Psychiatry and Law, and past-president of the Midwest Chapter of the American Academy of Psychiatry and the Law. His 100-plus publications cover a wide range of topics, including legal and ethical issues, medical decision making, statistics, and psychiatric treatment. (douglas.mossman@uc.edu)

Erin M. Nelson, PsyD, is an Assistant Professor of Psychiatry at the University of Arizona College of Medicine—Phoenix, and is the Director of the Behavioral Sciences curriculum. Dr. Nelson is also a senior associate with Steven Pitt & Associates, a forensic psychiatric practice group that provides consultation and expertise to law firms and criminal justice agencies throughout the United States. (erinm.nelson@yahoo.com)

Ira K. Packer, PhD, ABPP, is Clinical Professor of Psychiatry at the University of Massachusetts Medical School (UMMS), and serves as director of the UMMS Forensic Psychology Postdoctoral Fellowship Program. He is Board Certified in Forensic Psychology, and has served as President of the American Board of Forensic Psychology. His publications include two books, *Evaluation of Criminal Responsibility* and *Specialty Competencies in Forensic Psychology* with Thomas Grisso, and he has published journal articles related to the insanity defense, expert witness testimony, and training and practice in forensic psychology. He is the recipient of the 2007 Distinguished Contributions to Forensic Psychology Award from the American Academy of Forensic Psychology. (Ira.Packer@umassmed.edu)

Lisa Drago Piechowski, PhD, is a clinical and forensic psychologist focusing on assessment and consultation in civil forensic matters, particularly those related to employment litigation. She is an associate professor of clinical psychology at the American School of Professional Psychology in Washington, DC. She is board certified in Forensic Psychology by the American Board of Professional Psychology. She has served as chair of the American Psychological Association's Committee on Professional Practice and Standards, as chair of the APA Office of the General Counsel, Committee on Legal Issues, and on the revision committee for the Specialty Guidelines for Forensic Psychology. She is a board member of the American Board of Forensic Psychology. Dr. Piechowski is a frequent conference presenter on matters related to disability and employment law. (lpiechowski@argosy.edu)

Debra A. Pinals, MD, serves as the Assistant Commissioner of Forensic Mental Health Services for the Massachusetts Department of Mental Health and is an Associate Professor of Psychiatry and Director of Forensic Education at the University of Massachusetts Medical School. She is the President-Elect of the American Academy of Psychiatry and the Law, and she has authored numerous publications, including work related to competence to stand trial, violence risk assessment, civil commitment, and stalking. (debra.pinals@umassmed.edu)

Steven E. Pitt, DO, is a Clinical Associate Professor of Psychiatry at the University of Arizona College of Medicine—Phoenix. Dr. Pitt is also the President of Steven Pitt & Associates, a forensic psychiatric practice group that provides consultation and expertise to law firms and criminal-justice agencies throughout the United States. (SEPitt@aol.com)

Kimberly M. Price is a graduate student in the Clinical Child Psychology program at the University of Alabama. She completed her Bachelor's of Science in Psychology at the University of Alabama at Birmingham. She examines the causes, correlates, and treatment of conduct-disordered youth. She also examines the self-report assessment of psychopathy and juvenile transfer to adult court.

Ronald Roesch, PhD, is Professor of Psychology and Director of the Mental Health, Law, and Policy Institute at Simon Fraser University. His research focuses on competency assessment of adults and youth, jail/prison mental health programs, and youth violence. He served as president of the American Psychology-Law Society (APLS) and the International Association of Forensic Mental Health. He has been the editor of the journals *Law and Human Behavior, International Journal of Forensic Mental Health*, and *Psychology, Public Policy and Law*. In 2010 he received APLS's Outstanding Contributions to the Field of Psychology and Law Award, and in 2009 received the APLS Outstanding Teaching and Mentoring in the Field of Psychology and Law Award. He has co-authored over 140 journal articles and book chapters, as well as 17 books and practice manuals. (roesch@sfu.ca)

Jill Rosenbaum is a graduate student in the Clinical Child Psychology program at the University of Alabama. She completed her Master of Arts degree at the University of Alabama and her Bachelor of Arts at the University of Massachusetts. Her research interests are on psychopathy in youth and the sexual behaviors of youth with this syndrome as well as the potential health outcomes that result from this personality style. In addition, she studies youth who are being considered for transfer to adult court.

Randall T. Salekin, PhD, is a Professor in the Department of Psychology at the University of Alabama. Dr. Salekin is Director of the Disruptive Behavior Clinic and Associate Director for the Center for the Prevention of Youth Behavior Problems. His research interests center on the examination of the risk and protective factors for young with oppositional defiant disorder, conduct disorder, and/or callous-unemotional traits. He also examines the treatment of disruptive behavior disorders including callous-unemotional traits. Dr. Salekin's work also entails the study of transfer to adult court. (rsalekin@as.ua.edu)

Kathryn E. Tant is a Research Assistant at the University of Alabama. She completed her undergraduate degree at the University of Alabama. Her research interests center on examining the causes and correlates of conduct disorder and callous-unemotional traits. Her research experience also involves the study of EEG in undergraduate students. Finally, Kathryn studies the process of evaluating youth who are being considered for transfer to adult court.

Philip H. Witt, PhD, ABPP, conducts a private practice in forensic psychology through Associates in Psychological Services, P.A., in Somerville, NJ. He also is a Clinical Associate Professor at Robert Wood Johnson Medical School. He is Past President of the American Academy of Forensic Psychology and serves on the examination faculty of the American Board of Forensic Psychology. He has a particular interest in the assessment of sex offenders specifically and assessment of risk more broadly. (phwitt@optonline.net)

Patricia A. Zapf, PhD, is an Associate Professor at John Jay College of Criminal Justice, The City University of New York. She is a Fellow of the American Psychological Association and a Distinguished Member of the American Psychology-Law Society (AP-LS). She is the Editor of the AP-LS Book Series and an Associate Editor for *Law and Human Behavior*. She has authored over 80 articles, chapters, and books on forensic psychology and forensic assessment, including the Oxford Best Practices book on the *Evaluation of Competency to Stand Trial*. She maintains a private practice in forensic psychology and provides continuing education and training in forensic psychology for licensed psychologists. (patricia.zapf@gmail.com)

Heather Zelle, JD, MS, received her law degree from Villanova University School of Law and will receive her PhD in clinical psychology from Drexel University in 2012. She is completing her clinical internship at the University of Massachusetts Medical School/Worcester State Hospital. Her research interests include juveniles' and adults' comprehension of *Miranda* rights, judicial interpretation of legal capacities, and clinical forensic assessment in juvenile and adult cases. (heather.zelle@gmail.com)

Robert A. Zibbell, PhD, is a psychologist in independent practice with Tananbaum & Zibbell, P.C., in Framingham, MA. He performs evaluations of families who litigate disputes over their children in family court. He also works as a parenting coordinator with divorced or never-married parents, assisting them to resolve ongoing child-related disputes. He has authored publications and presented in local and national conferences about issues relevant to these areas of professional practice. (razibbell@comcast.net)

FORENSIC ASSESSMENTS IN CRIMINAL AND CIVIL LAW

Foundations of Forensic Mental Health Assessment

KIRK HEILBRUN, THOMAS GRISSO, ALAN M. GOLDSTEIN,
AND CASEY LADUKE

Forensic mental health assessment (FMHA) refers to the practice of performing mental health evaluations to assist courts and attorneys in the process of deciding certain matters of law applied to criminal, civil, or juvenile cases. The legal system's use of FMHA—typically by psychologists and psychiatrists—has grown substantially during the past 25 years. It is important that both mental health and legal professionals understand the role these evaluations play in this process. Before focusing on specific legal questions in which FMHA may be useful, it is important to consider how FMHA is defined more broadly. It is also valuable to understand the relevant sources of authority that guide, allow for, and restrict the use of FMHA in legal decision making.

This chapter will describe foundational aspects of FMHA that are distilled for legal professionals. Unlike the other chapters in this volume, each of which focuses on a specific legal question, we address the broadly applicable considerations in FMHA. We begin by describing FMHA and defining key components. We also identify important sources of authority—law, science, ethics, and practice—that contribute to our focus on best practice. Broadly applicable principles of FMHA are described, as are other influences that can help attorneys to identify best practice (and good practitioners) in this area.

THE NATURE OF FMHA

What is FMHA? One way to describe it is to examine the types of cases for which FMHA is used. A second way is to describe how FMHAs differ from general clinical assessments.

Defining FMHA as a Domain of Assessments

As a practice, FMHA can be defined in part according to the types (or domain) of mental health assessments for courts. Modern texts have identified that domain (Appelbaum & Gutheil, 2007; Goldstein, 2003, 2007; Grisso, 2003; Heilbrun, 2001; Melton, Petrila, Poythress, & Slobogin, 2007; Rosner, 2003) and have provided two ways to describe it. One way is to classify assessments based upon their relevance for cases in *various systems of justice*. First are evaluations in criminal and delinquency cases, ranging from various criminal competencies (such as capacity to waive *Miranda* rights) to issues of insanity and questions arising in sentencing. The second category is evaluations for cases in civil courts, frequently requiring evaluations to determine the presence and relevance of mental disabilities for legal questions regarding individuals' care, protection of their rights, and adjudicating claims regarding injuries and illnesses. Some of these are civil evaluations pertaining to children and their welfare, such as evaluations for abuse and neglect or child custody. The third category includes issues involved in both criminal and civil systems (e.g., jury selection, eyewitness identification).

Another way to classify assessments in the FMHA domain involves the *nature of the tasks* required by the assessment. In this classification scheme, the first category includes assessments in which the task requires a discovery of the mental state, motivations, attitudes, and behaviors of individuals at some time *in the past* that is relevant for the legal question. Examinees' current mental conditions and abilities are relevant in these cases, but they are not determinative because often they do not directly address the legal question of mental states and abilities at a time in the past.

The second category involves assessments that describe an examinee's *current* mental status and abilities associated with a legal question about one's present capacities to function in some specific context. The third category focuses on estimates of the likelihood of behaviors, mental capacities, and functioning *in the future*. The objectives of assessments in the second and third categories are not always distinct. For example, while competence to stand trial focuses primarily on present functional abilities, the likelihood that those abilities will be sustained across the future duration of the trial enters into the assessment. This is even more the case for custody evaluations, where present parenting abilities are evaluated in order to make inferences about future parenting.

A Conceptual Definition of FMHA

Examining the term "forensic mental health assessment" offers another way to define FMHA that is more conceptual in nature. What is meant by "forensic"? What does the term "mental health" imply regarding the nature of FMHA? What makes FMHA different from general mental health assessment as a practice and a subspecialty?

"Forensic" Mental Health Assessment

The term "forensic" is often defined as pertaining to or employed in legal proceedings or argumentation. FMHAs are therefore assessments that are used in legal proceedings. Yet there are several ways one could interpret that assertion.

A first claim may be that the definition of forensic allows any assessment to be a forensic assessment as long as it is used in a legal forum. For example, if a clinical psychologist performs an assessment of a patient in the course of ordinary clinical treatment, and if the clinician is subpoenaed at some later time to describe that assessment in a legal proceeding involving the examinee, our dictionary definition could call this a FMHA. In contrast, many authorities in forensic psychiatry and psychology would not consider this to be a FMHA, as they limit the scope of the concept to assessments that were performed *with the intention* of being used in a legal proceeding. Specifically, FMHA consists of "an evaluation that is performed...as part of the legal decision-making process, for the purpose of assisting the [legal] decision-maker or one of the litigants in using relevant clinical and scientific data" (Heilbrun, 2001, p. 3). Using this second interpretation, an assessment is considered forensic not because its results *become* evidence in a court, but because the assessment was *undertaken specifically in order to produce* evidence that would be used in court. There is little to be said in support of the first interpretation, because it has no particular value. Calling any assessment "forensic" simply because it has been used in court does not advance our knowledge about how to do assessments that will maximize their usefulness to courts. Moreover, it creates a class of assessments based merely on where they are used, not what they are.

The fact that a FMHA is performed with the intention of assisting legal decision makers has significant implications. A forensic assessment is guided by the specific legal question facing the legal decision maker. For every type of FMHA, there is a body of law controlling the legal decision to be made. The examiner performing the assessment should know the relevant law within the jurisdiction in which the assessment is being performed, as well as the legal question. The examiner then determines the types of data that are relevant for that legal question and develops an assessment procedure that is designed specifically to obtain those data. Stated another way, the legal issue forms the referral question for a FMHA.

Most referral questions leading to forensic evaluations are quite different from the referral questions encountered in general clinical practice. General clinical assessments typically focus on identifying clinical needs and formulating interventions in the best interest of the patient. In contrast, forensic assessments focus on helping a legal decision maker decide whether an examinee has certain capacities, abilities, or behavioral tendencies that should be considered in order to decide how to resolve the legal question. Assessments for competence to stand trial, for example, may need to identify a defendant's clinical profile, but primarily for the purpose of identifying specific deficits in abilities that the law defines as relevant for participating as a defendant in a trial.

This definition has important implications for professionals who conduct FMHA (Melton et al., 2007). First, it requires knowledge and experience in translating the law's definitions of relevant abilities and conditions into concepts that are amenable to psychological and psychiatric investigation. For example, laws that define competence to stand trial refer to "the capacity to assist counsel." A FMHA that is designed to provide information related to that legal concept must first translate it into more specific abilities that the expert can observe and measure (see Chapters 2 and 16).

Second, the relation of the FMHA examiner to the examinee is different from that of the clinical examiner assessing a patient. General clinical assessments occur within a doctor–patient relationship directed toward the best interests of the patient. In contrast, the FMHA examiner's primary allegiance is to the legal process and its decision makers, not to the examinee. This distinction leads to many differences between FMHA and general clinical assessments in the ethical obligations of examiners. This is discussed further below.

Third, the distinction between forensic and clinical evaluations has implications for communication of one's assessment results. Clinical assessments typically are performed to inform other clinicians. Forensic assessments, however, must inform non-clinicians, often judges, attorneys, and jurors, who need the information translated for use in a non-clinical context. FMHA results must therefore be interpreted and described in very different ways than clinical evaluations, according to a set of legal rules that were not designed according to medical or psychological models for the description of human behavior.

Forensic "Mental Health" "Assessment"

The term "mental health" is used to distinguish forensic psychiatric and psychological assessments from other types of forensic assessments, such as forensic science and forensic accounting. The inclusion of "mental health" as a modifier does not restrict FMHA to assessment of the presence or absence of mental disorders. Included in FMHA are assessments of various mental states, psychological phenomena, and behavioral predispositions that are relevant for legal questions about human behavior but are not symptoms of mental illness. The term "psychological" would come closer to identifying the questions that FMHAs address, but its use would have the disadvantage of appearing to restrict FMHA to performance by psychologists, while the assessment of psychological phenomena is performed by psychiatrists and social workers as well.

The term "assessment" anchors FMHA in scientific and clinical methods of mental health professionals' evaluations of individuals. The forensic nature of FMHA involves different referral questions than those that direct general clinical assessment, but the two fields have a methodological similarity rooted in the essentials of assessment. Hallmarks of assessment in psychiatry and psychology have included a reliance on objective observation and the support of theory and empirical research when interpreting data to arrive at useful inferences. Historically, the general field of mental health assessment has evolved to favor systematic procedures designed to (a) obtain specific types of information, (b) use standardized methods that mitigate examiner bias, and (c) engage in interpretive processes guided by past research on the mental states or behaviors at the heart of the examiner's inferences. FMHA not only conforms to those values, but also tends to elevate those values to a higher standard than in general clinical practice, due in part to the gravity of the legal decisions for which FMHAs provide guidance.

In summary, FMHA is defined as a domain of assessments of individuals intended to assist legal decision makers in decisions about the application of laws requiring consideration of individuals' mental conditions, abilities, and behaviors. These schemes represent the most useful definitions for legal professionals wanting to understand the various types of assessments typically carried out by mental health professionals in the forensic context. Such assessments should be guided by a set of standards to which mental health professionals aspire, drawn from all relevant sources of authority involved. We turn now to that objective.

RELEVANT SOURCES OF AUTHORITY FOR DEVELOPING BEST-PRACTICE STANDARDS

Forensic psychology and forensic psychiatry have evolved over the past 100 years to the point that each is now recognized as a specialty. This evolution really began to crystallize in the 1960s, as it was during this time that a critical component for defining FMHA began to emerge—the notion that a general clinical assessment was not enough in forensic cases. Clinicians were beginning to assert that performing evaluations to inform legal decision makers required a logic and process that modified ordinary clinical methods in order to maximize their relevance for legal questions.

Forensic psychiatry and psychology have become specialties only relatively recently. Although there are no specific data, it is probable that most psychologists and psychiatrists performing FMHA today were not trained as forensic specialists. Postdoctoral training in forensic mental health practice emerged only in recent years. Thus it is not surprising that the quality of forensic evaluations has been to shown to vary widely (e.g., Borum & Grisso, 1995; Heilbrun & Collins, 1995; Heilbrun, DeMatteo, Marczyk, & Goldstein, 2008; Horvath, Logan, & Walker, 2002; Nicholson & Norwood, 2000; Ryba, Cooper, & Zapf, 2003; Skeem & Golding, 1998) and that the methods used by experts in conducting FMHA vary considerably (Heilbrun, 2001; Horvath, Logan, & Walker, 2002; Lally, 2003).

The ethics codes of the American Psychiatric Association and the American Psychological Association nevertheless make it clear that anyone practicing within a specialization must be competent to do so. All clinicians are expected to practice only within the boundaries of their expertise. Interpretation of this mandate, of course, requires standards that define necessary training, as well as what it means to practice competently. To describe those standards, one must consider the sources of authority that contribute to the development of a best-practice standard. These sources include the law, knowledge based upon the behavioral and medical sciences, professional ethics, and professional practice.

Law as a Contributor to Best-Practice Standards

A major factor that sets FMHA practitioners apart from clinical psychologists and psychiatrists working as treatment and assessment professionals is the need to rely on the legal system—statutes, case law, and administrative code—to shape the assessment itself and to structure the focus of the report and testimony. The law also determines who is an expert in legal cases, the admissibility of an expert's testimony, and the practices of experts conducting FMHA both within and across states (see Ewing, 2003, for a more comprehensive discussion of the relevance of law to FMHA).

The Law: Defining the Focus of FMHA

The law serves to regulate human behavior, and experts in the behavioral sciences may be called upon to assess a variety of concepts that may underlie, explain, or mitigate behaviors that result in a legal proceeding. The findings of these evaluations are used to provide information to the trier of fact, data that go beyond the scope of knowledge of the trial judge or the average juror.

As legal terms are not synonymous with psychological concepts, the FMHA expert cannot conduct an evaluation without a reasonable understanding of the elements of the legal referral question that has led to the referral. Forensic assessments must be relevant to the legal issue (Grisso, 2003), so the forensic mental health expert must collect data on mental health and behavioral concepts that are conceptually related to the legal standard. For example, in cases addressing legal competencies like competence to stand trial, testimony that describes only diagnoses or symptoms usually will not provide courts what they need to address forensic questions, especially since "the law does not presume that any psychiatric diagnostic condition is synonymous with any legal incompetency" (Grisso, 2003, p. 12). It is important, therefore, that the forensic mental health expert possess a thorough grasp of the legal underpinnings that drive the FMHA. It is also important for the attorney to seek to retain mental health professionals who have such knowledge of the applicable law and forensic process, typically acquired through training in and experience conducting such evaluations.

The Law: Deciding Who Is an Expert

To testify as an expert witness, the law requires that the mental health professional be accepted as such by the trial court judge. Although an attorney may retain a psychologist or psychiatrist as an expert, it is the court that determines whether this person can offer courtroom testimony. The designation of expert witness by a judge grants a special status to the mental heath professional. Unlike the fact witness or lay witness whose testimony is confined to knowledge usually acquired based upon what that individual has seen or heard directly, expert witnesses are permitted to offer opinions: they can testify to what they believe, interpreting the data and making use of their observations of the examinee in ways that go beyond a description of the facts.

In a landmark case decided in the D. C. Circuit Court of Appeals, *Jenkins v. United States* (1962), the court opined that an individual is not granted the status of expert merely because of his or her professional degree. What matters is whether the potential expert witness has the appropriate background, education, skills, training, or knowledge to address the question before the court. This is determined during the *voir dire* process. The concepts delineated in *Jenkins* have been incorporated into Rule 702 of the *Federal Rules of Evidence*, which states:

> If scientific, technical, or other specialized knowledge will assist the trier of fact to

understand the evidence or to determine a fact in issue, a witness qualified as an expert by knowledge, skill, experience, training, or education, may testify thereto in the form of an opinion or otherwise, if (1) the testimony is based upon sufficient facts or data, (2) the testimony is the product of reliable principles and methods, and (3) the witness has applied the principles and methods reliably to the facts of the case.

The Law: Determining Admissibility of Expert Testimony to a Specific Topic

Because the scope of FMHA encompasses a wide range of legal issues, the concept of a "generic" expert does not exist. A forensic mental health professional cannot possibly be an expert on every legal issue that the courts litigate. It must be demonstrated that the proposed expert possesses the *specialized* education, experience, knowledge, training, or skill relevant to the *specific* legal issue to be decided by the court.

If recognized by the court as an expert, the forensic mental health professional is likely to be required to indicate the nature of the testimony to be offered, and the methodology upon which the opinions are based. This is more likely if the proposed testimony would address a topic not usually considered by the court, or involves the use of a specialized tool used by the expert as part of the FMHA. The law sets requirements that must be met in order for testimony to be admissible, "to prevent unqualified experts from testifying in the courtroom on the basis of irrelevant or inadequate evidence" (Weissman & DeBow, 2003, p. 47). Attorneys must ensure that when they retain an expert, the approach taken by this expert to FMHA is such that his or her evaluation and oral testimony would meet the legal standard for admissibility, both in substance and methodology.

In *Frye v. United States* (1923) the court held that, in order for expert testimony to be admissible, the foundation on which it is based "must be sufficiently established to have gained general acceptance in the particular field in which it belongs" (p. 10). The *Frye* standard has been incorporated into federal and state jurisdictions, and served as the most influential standard for admissibility of expert testimony until 1993. In this year, the U.S. Supreme Court decided in *Daubert v. Merrell Dow Pharmaceuticals* (1993) that the more expansive

criteria for the admissibility of expert testimony described in the *Federal Rules of Evidence* superseded *Frye* in federal jurisdictions. The Court held that the *Frye* test was too restrictive, and should be replaced by a broader standard based upon whether such testimony would be likely to assist the trier of fact, and whether such testimony and the methods upon which it is based were reliable and relevant. As such, in all federal courts and in those states that have adopted the *Daubert* standard, testimony must be both substantively and methodologically consistent with scientific procedures. Unlike *Frye* jurisdictions, in which the court must only determine whether expert testimony is based on techniques that are generally accepted, judges in *Daubert* jurisdictions may be asked to consider a range of factors under *Daubert*. These may include whether the theory or technique in question can be tested; whether it has been tested; whether it has been subjected to peer review and publication; its known or potential error rate; the existence and maintenance of standards controlling its operation; and whether it has attracted widespread acceptance within a relevant scientific community. The consideration is flexible and must focus on principles and methodology rather than conclusions.

Subsequently, the U.S. Supreme Court (in *General Electric Co. v. Joiner*, 1997) held that the trial court judge's decision cannot be overruled by an appeals court (except in rare cases of abuse of judicial discretion). Preliminary hearings addressing the *Frye* or *Daubert* requirements are therefore critical to FMHA in any criminal or civil trial; if the legal standard is not met, the forensic expert will not be permitted to testify about any opinions that rely on the methods that did not meet the requirements. Whether practicing in a *Frye* or *Daubert* jurisdiction, it is therefore expected that forensic mental heath experts be aware of the specific evidentiary law that governs the admissibility of their testimony. Attorneys should also anticipate that experts' testimony on an unusual or controversial topic or the use of a specialized tool may be subject to legal challenge, so the expert should be well versed in both the practice and underlying science of all parts of his or her evaluations.

The Law: Setting Limits on Expert Testimony

In addition to the admissibility of expert testimony, the legal system also sets limits on the subject matter of testimony. Two limitations are particularly relevant for the testimony of forensic mental health experts: reliance on third-party information as a source of data in forming opinions, and whether experts can testify to the ultimate issue.

Forensic assessments differ significantly from traditional clinical evaluations in the presence of substantial external incentive to deceive the forensic examiner. To manage this challenge, experts must consider third-party information—reviewing records and interviewing collateral informants familiar with the examinee and the issue in question—to corroborate data provided by the litigant in testing and interviews. There are certain advantages provided by the use of third-party information in FMHA. Such information can (a) increase the accuracy of the findings; (b) increase the face validity of the evaluation and testimony; (c) improve communication with attorneys and judges regarding the assessment; and (d) provide information to the forensic mental health expert as to the role of deliberate distortion on the part of the examinee (Heilbrun, Warren, & Picarello, 2003; Otto, Slobogin, & Greenberg, 2007). Accordingly, attorneys should be prepared to facilitate experts' acquisition of relevant records and interviews with third parties who can provide useful information.

As attorneys are aware, third-party information is hearsay. The expert using such information relies on the indirect sources of records and interviews with collateral observers. While fact witnesses are not permitted to testify about hearsay information, the rules are somewhat different for forensic mental health experts. The *Federal Rules of Evidence* do allow the use and admissibility of third-party information, stating that "[i]f of a type reasonably relied upon by experts in the particular field in forming opinions or inferences upon the subject, the facts or data need not be admissible in evidence in order for the opinion or inference to be admitted" (FRE 703). Attorneys should be aware that this exception to the hearsay rule applies to the evaluations conducted by forensic experts.

In some jurisdictions the law also prohibits testimony on the ultimate issue (or even the penultimate issue) (see, e.g., Tenn. Code Ann. § 39-11-501 and FRE 704(b)), while in some states and in federal jurisdictions the rules on FMHA require experts to offer opinions on the ultimate legal issue (e.g., Mich. Stat. Ann. § 28.1043, 20a(6)(c); see also *United States v. Davis*, 1988; *United States v. Kristiansen*, 1990; *United States v. Salamanca*, 1993).

The ultimate issue refers to the legal question that the trier of fact—the judge or jury—is charged with answering (e.g., Was the defendant insane at the time of the crime? Should the defendant be put to death?). The penultimate issue refers to the statutory definition of the legal or ultimate issue (i.e., At the time of the crime was the defendant suffering from a mental disease or defect such that he did not know what he was doing or, if he did know what he was doing, that he did not know that what he was doing was wrong? What are the aggravating and mitigating factors in this capital sentencing case?). As well, there may be policy or practice considerations in some hospitals or court clinics in the public sector that require evaluators to express an ultimate-issue conclusion in order to trigger a certain response (e.g., a hospital report that did not give an opinion that the defendant was competent to stand trial might not result in the defendant's being transported back to court for disposition of charges). In most jurisdictions forensic experts are allowed to offer opinions on the ultimate issue (Ewing, 2003), although it should be noted that even within these jurisdictions a judge may exclude ultimate opinions if it is reasoned that (a) these opinions go beyond the expertise of the forensic clinician, and (b) such testimony represents legal conclusions that the trier of fact has been charged with deciding.

There is considerable debate among the psychological and psychiatric fields as to how directly the evaluator should answer the ultimate legal question (Grisso, 2003; Heilbrun, 2001). The debate goes beyond what is legally permissible, focusing on ethical and professional considerations. For instance, such testimony potentially usurps the role of the trier of fact by adding moral- and community-value-laden elements to the scientific and clinical expertise required of the forensic clinician, answering questions that cannot be answered without interjecting such values (Heilbrun, 2001; Morse, 1999; Melton et al., 2007; Tillbrook, Mumley, & Grisso, 2003). Several psycholegal scholars have argued in favor of providing ultimate legal opinions (e.g., Rogers & Ewing, 2003; Rogers & Shuman, 2000), reflecting the absence of consensus in the field on this question. Whether attorneys should seek to elicit experts' answers to the ultimate legal question remains an open question. What is clearer, however, is that they should attempt to retain experts who provide impartial, thorough, multi-sourced, legally relevant, and clearly communicated evaluations.

The Law Affecting the Regulation of FMHA Practice

State and provincial licensing laws regulate the practice of forensic mental health professionals in a number of ways. Each jurisdiction sets its own licensing requirements, and typically limits the practice of mental health professionals under applicable licensing regulations and ethics codes to activities that fall within the boundaries of the licensee's background and training. Licenses are largely generic and do not otherwise certify specific expertise, leaving such certification to specialty boards recognized by professional associations. While generally following these certification practices, certain jurisdictions (e.g., Massachusetts, Michigan, and Missouri) do offer limited specialty certification regarding specific forensic evaluations, and others (e.g., Alabama, Florida, and Virginia) provide periodic continuing education training that one must attend in order to be allowed to perform evaluations for the courts.

One controversial issue is whether mental health professionals can conduct FMHA in jurisdictions in which the practitioner does not possess a license (see, e.g., Drogin, 1999; Shuman, Cunningham, Connell, & Reid, 2003; Tucillo, DeFilippis, Denny, & Dsurney, 2002; Yantz, Bauer, & McCaffrey, 2006). Most states and provinces offer temporary, restricted licenses to clinicians who wish to conduct assessments outside of their licensed jurisdiction. Nevertheless, both attorneys and forensic mental health professionals should be familiar with the specifics of those provisions, because different states have somewhat different requirements for obtaining temporary licenses.

Behavioral and Medical Science Contributions to Best-Practice Standards

The behavioral and medical sciences include assessment methods that offer forensic mental health experts reliable and valid tools for forensic assessments. These tools provide an empirical basis for the interpretation of the data offered by experts in their reports and testimony. The science surrounding these tools provides the conceptual and empirical foundations on which FMHA is based.

Scientific Knowledge Providing the Theoretical Basis for FMHA

Behavior is complex and multi-determined, but forensic mental health professionals work within a legal system in which the decision options are typically dichotomous and forced-choice (e.g., sane vs. insane, competent to stand trial vs. incompetent to stand trial, liable vs. not liable). In the behavioral sciences, there is no concept of competence or incompetence, sane or insane. Not only do the terms have no clinical meaning, but they also imply that there is some line beyond which a person passes from one of these to the other. No such line exists on any behavioral measure in forensic mental health practice. The law may sometimes require that FMHA experts must say that the condition is "yes" or "no," but forensic mental health experts should always explain to what degree they believed the person possessed the relevant abilities, and therefore provide their logic for deciding whether the person did or did not meet the legal standard.

Theoretical Models for Conducting FMHA

Authorities in the field recommend that (a) FMHA be guided by the appropriate legal statutes and case law that underlie the referral question, (b) objective measures (including traditional tests and forensic assessment instruments) should be used in conducting evaluations whenever possible, and (c) evaluations should incorporate data from multiple sources of information (Goldstein, 2003, 2007; Grisso, 2003; Heilbrun, 2001; Heilbrun, Marczyk, & DeMatteo, 2002; Heilbrun, Marczyk, DeMatteo, & Mack-Allen, 2007; Heilbrun, Warren, & Picarello, 2003; Melton et al., 2007; Otto et al., 2007).

For over 20 years, the model communicated in *Evaluating Competencies* (Grisso, 1986, 2003) has provided the principal theoretical model that structures and guides FMHA. Grisso (1986) argued that most of the discontent with experts conducting FMHA resulted from (1) *ignorance* of the laws that drive the evaluation and the resulting irrelevance of the report and opinion; (2) *intrusion* into matters of the law, including opinions that address the ultimate legal question; and (3) *insufficiency* (reliance on inadequate information upon which to base opinions) and *incredibility* (speculation rather than data-based findings). To avoid these shortcomings, the model emphasizes the need to appropriately identify and understand the legal competency construct (the legal statute and case law relevant to the legal referral question) and to "operationalize" this construct so that its legal components are expressed in terms of "functional abilities" (that is, behaviors that forensic mental health professionals are qualified to evaluate). The model emphasizes the use of empirically based data whenever possible, rather than relying solely on observations and clinical impressions. Findings of the FMHA should be interpreted in terms of the degree to which the person's functional abilities are congruent with those required under the legal standard.

Principles, Guidelines, and Maxims for FMHA

Others have described principles, guidelines, and maxims for FMHA that provide theoretical contributions to a best-practice standard. Together these represent both broad theoretical components of FMHA and more specific and detailed guidelines that may be derived from them. Psycholegal scholars have generally followed two distinct approaches to considering the process of FMHA. The majority of scholars have identified a distinct form of FMHA, as defined by the legal question, and elaborated on the relevant law, ethical contours, supporting data, practice literature, and specialized tools (see, e.g., Grisso, 2003; Hess & Weiner, 1999; Melton et al., 2007; Weiner & Hess, 2005). An alternate approach begins with the assumption that all forms of FMHA share some common foundation, and then looks for the common elements of FMHA that occur across different kinds of forensic evaluations (see, e.g., Grisso, 2003; Morse, 1978).

Several leading scholars have merged these approaches into foundational sources of guidance for mental health professionals conducting FMHA. Works by Simon and Gold (2004) and Melton et al. (2007) include a description of different kinds of forensic assessment as well as a discussion of common guidelines and elements. Brodsky (1991, 1999, 2004) has described a series of maxims for forensic experts focused on delivering expert testimony. Heilbrun (2001) approached this discussion by focusing exclusively on foundational principles for conducting FMHA, which have subsequently been applied to specific forms of FMHA (Heilbrun, 2003; Heilbrun, DeMatteo, & Marczyk, 2004; Heilbrun et al., 2005; Heilbrun, Marczyk, & DeMatteo, 2002).

Hence, there are broad, foundational principles that guide FMHA regardless of the specific type of forensic evaluation involved. The considerable overlap in these broad principles, guidelines, and maxims allowed the authors of the book from which this chapter is derived (Heilbrun, Grisso, & Goldstein, 2009) to integrate the various attempts at describing broadly applicable aspects of FMHA

into a set of principles guiding FMHA (Table 1.1). This includes both general principles, applicable across the entire FMHA process, as well as principles specific to FMHA preparation, data collection and interpretation, and written and oral communication of results (see Heilbrun et al., 2009, for a detailed explanation of these principles). This integration appears to represent the most contemporary views of the nature of such principles serving to guide the field of FMHA. Accordingly, these principles should have value in describing the foundational aspects of FMHA for courts and attorneys as well as for mental health professionals.

Professional Ethics Contributing to Best-Practice Standards

Lawyers should be aware that forensic mental health professionals are guided by their respective codes of ethical conduct. For psychologists, the American Psychological Association's *Ethical Principles of Psychologists and Code of Conduct* (*Ethics Code*) (APA, 2002a) is written to apply to *all* areas of psychology. Specific to FMHA, the areas in which ambiguities may occur are those created by the marked differences between the role of treating mental health professionals and that of forensic mental health experts. These differences create special questions about identifying who really is the "client" to whom the professional owes a duty, the nature of the professional relationship with the client, the nature of confidentiality, demographics of the population of "clients" in forensic cases, competence of the expert, and trust in the client (Appelbaum, 1997; Appelbaum & Gutheil, 2007; Goldstein, 2003; Greenberg & Shuman, 1997; Rosner, 2003; Weissman & DeBow, 2003). Psychology ethics committees on the national and state levels frequently employ specialized guidelines endorsed by the American Psychological Association to interpret the broader *Ethics Code*. The *Specialty Guidelines for Forensic Psychologists* (*Specialty Guidelines*; American Psychological Association, in press) serve as a major source of ethics information for forensic psychologists. This document represents an *aspirational* model for forensic psychology practice. This means that the field recognizes that circumstances might not allow examiners to meet these higher standards in all cases, but that examiners should make every effort to strive to meet them. Like other ethical guidelines that are separate from the *Ethics Code*, this document is

---

TABLE 1.1 PRINCIPLES OF FORENSIC MENTAL HEALTH ASSESSMENT:
AN INTEGRATION.

GENERALLY

1. Be aware of the important differences between clinical and forensic domains.
2. Obtain appropriate education, training, and experience in one's area of forensic specialization.
3. Be familiar with the relevant legal, ethical, scientific, and practice literatures pertaining to FMHA.
4. Be guided by honesty and striving for impartiality, actively disclosing the limitations on as well as the support for one's opinions.
5. Control potential evaluator bias in general through monitoring case selection, continuing education, and consultation with knowledgeable colleagues.
6. Be familiar with specific aspects of the legal system, particularly communication, discovery, deposition, and testimony.
7. Do not become adversarial, but present and defend your opinions effectively.

IN SPECIFIC CASES

Preparation

8. Identify relevant forensic issues.
9. Accept referrals only within area of expertise.
10. Decline the referral when evaluator impartiality is unlikely.
11. Clarify the evaluator's role with the attorney.
12. Clarify financial arrangements.
13. Obtain appropriate authorization.
14. Avoid playing the dual roles of therapist and forensic evaluator.
15. Determine the particular role to be played within forensic assessment if the referral is accepted.
16. Select the most appropriate model to guide data gathering, interpretation, and communication.

Data Collection

17. Use multiple sources of information for each area being assessed. Review the available background information and actively seek important missing elements.
18. Use relevance and reliability (validity) as guides for seeking information and selecting data sources.
19. Obtain relevant historical information.
20. Assess clinical characteristics in relevant, reliable, and valid ways.
21. Assess legally relevant behavior.
22. Ensure that conditions for evaluation are quiet, private, and distraction-free.
23. Provide appropriate notification of purpose and/or obtain appropriate authorization before beginning.
24. Determine whether the individual understands the purpose of the evaluation and the associated limits on confidentiality.

Data Interpretation

25. Use third-party information in assessing response style.
26. Use testing when indicated in assessing response style.
27. Use case-specific (idiographic) evidence in assessing clinical condition, functional abilities, and causal connection.
28. Use nomothetic evidence is assessing clinical condition, functional abilities, and causal connection.
29. Use scientific reasoning in assessing causal connection between clinical condition and functional abilities.
30. Carefully consider whether to answer the ultimate legal question. If it is answered, it should be in the context of a thorough evaluation clearly describing data and reasoning, and with the clear recognition that this question is in the domain of the legal decision maker.
31. Describe findings and limits so that they need change little under cross-examination.

Written Communication

32. Attribute information to sources.
33. Use plain language; avoid technical jargon.
34. Write report in sections, according to model and procedures.

(continued)

TABLE 1.1 (CONTINUED)

Testimony

35. Base testimony on the results of the properly performed FMHA.

36. Prepare.

37. Communicate effectively.

38. Control the message. Strive to obtain, retain, and regain control over the meaning and impact of what is presented in expert testimony.

Reprinted by permission of Oxford University Press, Inc., Table 4.6 in Heilbrun, Grisso, & Goldstein (2009). *Foundations of Forensic Mental Health Assessment.*

not an enforceable code, but rather may be used by ethics committees to interpret the *Ethics Code*. The American Psychological Association also endorses a number of guidelines in such specialty areas as child custody assessments (APA, 2010), evaluations in child protective matters (APA Committee on Professional Practice and Standards, 1998), and record keeping (APA, 2007).

The American Psychiatric Association's *Principles of Medical Ethics with Annotation Especially Applicable to Psychiatry* (American Psychiatric Association, 2001) provides ethical standards that all psychiatric practitioners are expected to follow. The American Academy of Psychiatry and the Law has authored the *Ethics Guidelines for the Practice of Forensic Psychiatry* (*Ethics Guidelines*; 2005) to provide a more specific set of ethical guidelines for forensic psychiatrists. In setting standards of conduct for mental health professionals, ethics codes help define how the "reasonably prudent professional" should practice. As such, these codes of ethics represent an important influence on the behavior of forensic experts—and are potentially valuable for attorneys to consider.

Professional Practice Contributing to Best-Practice Standards

The professions of psychology and psychiatry have developed a number of standards for training and specialization. Attorneys should be familiar with these standards, which are summarized in this section, because a good forensic expert will have the training, specialization, and experience needed to satisfy many of them.

The substantial growth in professional organizations that focus on the intersection of the law and mental health, such as the American Psychology-Law Society, the American Board of Forensic Psychology, and American Academy of Psychiatry and Law, has contributed greatly to the development and dissemination of forensic research, scientific knowledge, ethics, and practice expertise. Formal practice guidelines provided by professional organizations have made important contributions to establishing a standard of practice both generally (Heilbrun et al., 2008; Otto & Heilbrun, 2002; Wettstein, 2005) and related to forensic subspecialties (American Academy of Child and Adolescent Psychiatry, 1997a, 1997b, 1997c, 1998, 1999; American Academic of Psychiatry and Law, 2002; APA, 1994, 1999, 2002b; APA, 2005; Association of Family and Conciliation Courts, undated, later 2006; Mossman et al., 2007; Society for Industrial and Organizational Psychology, 2003). Thus, both psychiatry and psychology have been active in the development of aspirational descriptions of the practice of various aspects of FMHA.

Another way of examining the elements that contribute to FMHA is to consider what is taught to those seeking to become experts or to those looking to expand their practice into relatively new areas. Training in FMHA occurs at a number of levels (Bersoff et al., 1997; Marczyk, DeMatteo, Kutinsky, & Heilbrun, 2007; Otto, Heilbrun, & Grisso, 1990; Rosner, 1983). At the graduate level in psychology, a number of colleges and universities now offer training in forensic psychology through master's-level degrees (M.A. or M.S.), doctoral training (typically as a forensic concentration or minor in clinical or counseling psychology programs), or joint degrees in law (J.D.) and psychology (Ph.D. or Psy.D.). Psychiatrists who eventually wish to be certified for forensic specialization must first acquire a specialty year of training in an accredited forensic psychiatry fellow program beyond their residency training. There are a number of forensic fellowships available in the United States, and continuing education is also viewed as an integral part of continued expertise.

Training in FMHA for those who have completed a doctorate in psychology usually occurs via postdoctoral fellowships (typically a single year of training, with some offering a second year; see Packer & Borum, 2003, for a sample curriculum), or as the result of participating in continuing education programs offered by an APA-approved sponsor and taught by individuals who are experts in specific areas of forensic research or practice.

Finally, board certification is often touted as a marker of specialized training in forensic psychology and psychiatry. The American Board of Professional Psychology (ABPP), the oldest and most rigorous of the organizations offering board certification in psychology, confers board certification in forensic psychology on those who meet the credentialing requirements of its member board, the American Board of Forensic Psychology (ABFP). Forensic specialization in psychiatry includes board certification through the American Board of Psychiatry and Neurology (ABPN), with added qualifications for a "Certification in the Subspecialty of Forensic Psychiatry."

TOWARD BEST PRACTICES IN FMHA

This chapter has provided a summary for legal professionals regarding standards of practice for forensic psychologists and forensic psychiatrists who perform FMHA. The focus has been on "best practices" as they have evolved within the relevant professions. In that sense, these are the standards with which the professions themselves evaluate the quality of FMHA practice when providing evaluations for courts. These best-practice standards provide mental health professionals with guidance in conducting informed, appropriate, sufficient, and credible assessments in the forensic context.

Legal professionals will use these professional best-practice standards when considering the appropriate standards of care for forensic practice. It would be presumptuous for mental health professionals or behavioral scientists to outline a standard of care in FMHA in general. Defining *standard of care* is the law's prerogative, typically done by the court, using the professions' standard of practice ("best practices") to inform but not to dictate what the standard of care should be (Heilbrun et al., 2008).

As the courts consider the forensic professions' best practices in the process of determining a standard of care, they should be aware of certain limitations and cautions when making that translation. We close by offering three of those cautions.

First, the best expressions of practice standards for a profession represent a consensus of those who protect, guide, and nurture the field. Yet who those protectors are, or should be, is not entirely clear. Sometimes they are a few authorities with senior status, and occasionally they are a committee of experts identified as such by their peers. However they are constituted, they will agree on some points and disagree on others. For many points of forensic practice, a well-established consensual standard may reasonably be challenged by a minority of highly qualified forensic professionals. Consensus about a practice standard does not mean unanimity; any definition of best practices in a field is far less than an absolute and infallible dictum. When these disagreements arise in legal deliberations about standards of care, the best that can be done is to be aware of alternative viewpoints so that one can explain to others the sources of controversy.

A second cautionary point about best-practice standards is their shelf life. As a dynamic ideal, standards of practice are always changing as a consequence of advances in the scientific base for the field and scholarly debate about issues of practice. Broad principles to guide the assessment process are likely to change less rapidly than, for example, recommendations regarding specific assessment tools. A published standard of practice, therefore, is always decaying in relation to the dynamic evolution of the field. Courts' use of practice standards in the context of standards of care needs to take this into consideration. Law tends to adhere to precedent, while forensic best practices are malleable in relation to the evolution of science and clinical methods. To some extent, the law's standards of care also must evolve with the professions' changing best-practice capacities.

A third caution about best-practice standards is difficulty in applying them to the diversity of cases, types of evaluations, and circumstances encountered in FMHA. Mental health professionals conduct FMHA across a variety of settings and contexts, each coming with its own set of facts, obstacles, and opportunities. Further, legal definitions of the forensic questions that these experts address may differ from one state to another, and judicial demands may differ between courts within a given state. Developing a single set of best practices for two different professions in a nation with 51 sets of laws is a daunting task. The success with which this can be done depends largely on recognizing how jurisdictions and professions may differ, then crafting the standard in a manner that accommodates to that diversity rather than offering a rigid set of rules. Therefore, the law will be challenged when attempting to apply a single, nationally referenced standard of practice to a standard of care within a particular jurisdiction, or a particular subtype of FMHA.

The remaining chapters of this book will incorporate the broad principles and practices discussed here, applying them more specifically to a variety of legal questions. This combination of broad principles in application to specific legal questions, seeking best practice whenever possible, should help attorneys and courts use these evaluations most effectively.

REFERENCES

American Academy of Child and Adolescent Psychiatry. (1997a). Practice parameters for child custody evaluation. *Journal of the American Academy of Child and Adolescent Psychiatry, 36,* 57S–68S.

American Academy of Child and Adolescent Psychiatry. (1997b). Practice parameters for the forensic evaluation of children and adolescents who may have been physically or sexually abused. *Journal of the American Academy of Child and Adolescent Psychiatry, 36,* 37S–56S.

American Academy of Child and Adolescent Psychiatry. (1997c). Practice parameters for the assessment and treatment of children and adolescents with conduct disorder. *Journal of the American Academy of Child and Adolescent Psychiatry, 36,* 122S–139S.

American Academy of Child and Adolescent Psychiatry. (1998). Practice parameters for the assessment and treatment of children and adolescents with posttraumatic stress disorder. *Journal of the American Academy of Child and Adolescent Psychiatry, 37,* 997–1001.

American Academy of Child and Adolescent Psychiatry. (1999). Practice parameters for the assessment and treatment of children and adolescents who are sexually abusive of others. *Journal of the American Academy of Child and Adolescent Psychiatry, 38,* 55S–76S.

American Academy of Psychiatry and the Law. (2002). Practice guideline for forensic psychiatric evaluation of defendants raising the insanity defense. *Journal of the American Academy of Psychiatry and the Law, 30,* S1–S40.

American Academy of Psychiatry and the Law. (2005). *Ethical guidelines for the practice of forensic psychiatry.* Bloomfield, CT: American Academy of Psychiatry and the Law.

American Psychiatric Association. (2001). *The principles of medical ethics with annotation especially applicable to psychiatry.* Washington DC: American Psychiatric Association.

American Psychological Association (1994). Guidelines for child custody evaluations in divorce proceedings. *American Psychologist, 49,* 677–680.

American Psychological Association. (1999). Guidelines for psychological evaluations in child protection matters. *American Psychologist, 54,* 586–593.

American Psychological Association. (2002a). Ethical principles of psychologists and code of conduct. *American Psychologist, 57,* 1060–1073.

American Psychological Association. (2002b). *Guidelines on multicultural education, training, research practice, and organizational change for psychologists.* Washington, DC: American Psychological Association.

American Psychological Association. (2005). Guidelines on effective behavioral treatment for persons with mental retardation and developmental disabilities: A Resolution by APA Division 33. Retrieved from http://www.apa.org/divisions/div33/effectivetreatment.html.

American Psychological Association. (2007). Record keeping guidelines. *American Psychologist, 62,* 993–1004.

American Psychological Association (in press). Specialty guidelines for forensic psychologists. *American Psychologist.* Revision approved by APA Council of Representatives on August 3, 2011. Accessed on May 16, 2012 from http://www.ap-ls.org/aboutpsychlaw/SpecialtyGuidelines.php.

American Psychological Association. (2010). Guidelines for child custody evaluations in family law proceedings. *American Psychologist, 65,* 863–867.

American Psychological Association Committee on Professional Practice and Standards. (1998). *Guidelines for psychological evaluations in child protection matters.* Washington, DC: American Psychological Association.

Appelbaum, P. (1997). A theory of ethics for forensic psychiatry. *Journal of the American Academy of Psychiatry and the Law, 25,* 233–247.

Appelbaum, P., & Gutheil, T. (2007). *Clinical handbook of psychiatry and the law* (4th ed.). Baltimore: Lippincott Williams & Wilkins.

Association of Family and Conciliation Courts. (2006). *Model standards of practice for child custody evaluation.* Milwaukee, WI: Author.

Bersoff, D., Goodman-Delahunty, J., Grisso, T., Hans, V., Poythress, N., & Roesch, R. (1997). Training in law and psychology: Models from the Villanova Conference. *American Psychologist, 52,* 1301–1310.

Borum, R., & Grisso, T. (1995). Psychological test use in criminal forensic evaluations. *Professional Psychology: Research and Practice, 26,* 565–473.

Brodsky, S. (1991). *Testifying in court: Guidelines and maxims for the expert witness*. Washington, DC: American Psychological Association.

Brodsky, S. (1999). *The expert expert witness: More maxims and guidelines for testifying in court*. Washington, DC: American Psychological Association.

Brodsky, S. (2004). *Coping with cross-examination and other pathways to effective testimony*. Washington, DC: American Psychological Association.

Daubert v. Merrell Dow Pharmaceuticals, 509 U.S. 579 (1993).

Drogin, E. Y. (1999). Prophets in another land: Utilizing psychological expertise from foreign jurisdictions. *Mental and Physical Disabilities Law Reporter, 23*, 767–771.

Ewing, C. P. (2003). Expert testimony: Law and practice. In A. M. Goldstein (Ed.), *Forensic psychology*. Vol. 11 of *Handbook of psychology* (pp. 55–68). Hoboken, NJ: Wiley.

Federal Rules of Evidence 702, 703 (2007).

Frye v. United States, 293 F. 1013 (D.C. Cir. 1923).

General Electric Company et al. v. Joiner et ux., 522 U.S. 136 (1997).

Goldstein, A. M. (Ed.). (2003). *Forensic psychology* . Vol. 11 of *Handbook of psychology*. Hoboken, NJ: Wiley.

Goldstein, A. M. (Ed.). (2007). *Forensic psychology: Emerging topics and expanding roles*. Hoboken, NJ: Wiley.

Greenberg, S. A., & Shuman, D. W. (1997). Irreconcilable conflict between therapeutic and forensic roles. *Professional Psychology: Research and Practice, 28*, 50–57.

Greenberg, S. A., Shuman, D. W., Feldman, S. R., Middleton, C., & Ewing, C. P. (2007). Lessons for forensic practice drawn from the law of malpractice. In A. M. Goldstein (Ed.), *Forensic psychology: Emerging topics and expanding roles* (pp. 446–464). Hoboken, NJ: Wiley.

Grisso, T. (1986). *Evaluating competencies: Forensic assessments and instruments*. New York: Plenum.

Grisso, T. (2003). *Evaluating competencies: Forensic assessments and instruments* (2nd ed). New York: Kluwer Academic/Plenum.

Heilbrun, K. (2001). *Principles of forensic mental health assessment*. New York: Kluwer Academic/Plenum.

Heilbrun, K., & Collins, S. (1995). Evaluations of trial competency and mental state at the time of the offense report characteristics. *Professional Psychology: Research and Practice, 26*, 61–67.

Heilbrun, K., DeMatteo, D., & Marczyk, G. (2004). Pragmatic psychology, forensic mental health assessment, and the case of Thomas Jefferson: Applying principles to promote quality. *Psychology, Public Policy, and Law, 10*, 31–70.

Heilbrun, K., DeMatteo, D., Marczyk, G., Finello, C., Smith, R., & Mack-Allen, J. (2005). Applying principles of forensic mental health assessment to capital sentencing. *Widener Law Review, 11*, 93–118.

Heilbrun, K., DeMatteo, D., Marczyk, G., & Goldstein, A. M. (2008). Standards of practice and care in forensic mental health assessment: Legal, professional, and principles-based considerations. *Psychology, Public Policy, and Law, 14*, 1–26.

Heilbrun, K., Grisso, T., & Goldstein, A. (2009). *Foundations of forensic mental health assessment*. New York: Oxford.

Heilbrun, K., Marczyk, G., & DeMatteo, D. (2002). *Forensic mental health assessment: A casebook*. New York: Oxford.

Heilbrun, K., Marczyk, G., DeMatteo, D., & Mack-Allen, J. (2007). A principles-based approach to forensic mental health assessment: Utility and update. In A. M. Goldstein (Ed.), *Forensic psychology: Emerging topics and expanding roles* (pp. 45–72). Hoboken, NJ: Wiley.

Heilbrun, K., Marczyk, G., DeMatteo, D., Zillmer, E., Harris, J., & Jennings, T. (2003). Principles of forensic mental health assessment: Implications for neuropsychological assessment in forensic contexts. *Assessment, 10*, 329–343.

Heilbrun, K., Warren, J., & Picarello, K. (2003). Third party information in forensic assessment. In A. M. Goldstein (Ed.), *Forensic psychology*. Vol. 11 of *Handbook of psychology* (pp. 69–86). Hoboken, NJ: Wiley.

Hess, A., & Weiner, I. (Eds.). (1999). *Handbook of forensic psychology* (2nd ed.). New York: Wiley.

Horvath, L., Logan, T., & Walker, R. (2002). Child custody cases: A content analysis of evaluations in practice. *Professional Psychology: Research and Practice, 33*, 557–565.

In re Gault, 387 U.S. 1 (1967).

Jenkins v. United States, 307 F.2d 637 (U.S. App. D.C., 1962).

Lally, S. (2003). What tests are acceptable for use in forensic evaluations? A survey of experts. *Professional Psychology: Research and Practice, 34*, 491–498.

Melton, G., Petrila, J., Poythress, N., & Slobogin, C. (2007). *Psychological evaluations for the courts: A handbook for mental health professionals and lawyers* (3rd ed.). New York: Guilford.

Morse, S. (1978). Law and mental health professionals: The limits of expertise. *Professional Psychology, 9*, 389–399.

Morse, S. (1999). Crazy reasons. *Journal of Contemporary Legal Issues, 10*, 189–226.

Mossman, D., Noffsinger, S., Ash, P., Frierson, R., Gerbasi, J., Hackett, M., Lewis, C., Pinals, D., Scott, C., Sieg, K., Wall, B., & Zonana, H. (2007). AAPL practice guideline for the forensic psychiatric evaluation of competence to stand trial. *Journal of the American Academy of Psychiatry and the Law, 35*, S3–S72.

Nicholson, R., & Norwood, S. (2000). The quality of forensic psychological assessments, reports, and testimony: Acknowledging the gap between promise and practice. *Law and Human Behavior, 24*, 9–44.

Otto, R., Heilbrun, K., & Grisso, T. (1990). Training and credentialing in forensic psychology. *Behavioral Sciences and the Law, 8*, 217–231.

Otto, R. K., & Heilbrun, K. (2002). The practice of forensic psychology: A look toward the future in light of the past. *American Psychologist, 57,* 5–18.

Otto, R. K., Slobogin, C., & Greenberg, S. A. (2007). Legal and ethical issues in accessing and utilizing third-party information. In A. M. Goldstein (Ed.), *Forensic psychology: Emerging topics and expanding roles* (pp. 190–208). Hoboken, NJ: Wiley.

Packer, I. K., & Borum, R. (2003). Forensic training and practice. In A. M. Goldstein (Ed.), *Forensic psychology.* Vol. 11 of *Handbook of psychology* (pp. 21–32). Hoboken, NJ: Wiley.

Rogers, R., & Ewing, C. P. (2003). The prohibition of ultimate opinions: A misguided enterprise. *Journal of Forensic Psychology Practice, 3,* 65–75.

Rogers, R., & Shuman, D. (2000). *Conducting insanity evaluations* (2nd ed.). New York: Guilford.

Rosner, R. (1983). Education and training in forensic psychiatry. *Psychiatric Clinics of North America, 6,* 585.

Rosner, R. (Ed.). (2003). *Principles and practice of forensic psychiatry* (2nd ed.). New York: Oxford.

Ryba, N. L., Cooper, V. G., & Zapf, P. A. (2003). Juvenile competence to stand trial evaluations: A survey of current practices and test usage among psychologists. *Professional Psychology: Research and Practice, 34,* 499–507.

Shuman, D., Cunningham, M., Connell, M., & Reid, W. (2003). Interstate forensic psychological consultations: A call for reform and proposal of a model rule. *Professional Psychology: Research and Practice, 34,* 233–239.

Simon, R., & Gold, L. (Eds.). (2004). *Textbook of forensic psychiatry.* Washington, DC: American Psychiatric Publishing.

Skeem, J., & Golding, S. (1998). Community examiner's evaluations of competence to stand trial: Common problems and suggestions for improvement. *Professional Psychology: Research and Practice, 29,* 357–367.

Society for Industrial and Organizational Psychology. (2003). *Validation and use of personnel selection procedures* (4th ed.). Bowling Green, OH: Society for Industrial and Organizational Psychology.

Tillbrook, C., Mumley, D., & Grisso, T. (2003). Avoiding expert opinions on the ultimate legal question: The case for integrity. *Journal of Forensic Psychology Practice, 3,* 77–87.

Tucillo, J., DeFilippis, N., Denny, R., & Dsurney, J. (2002). Licensure requirements for interjurisdictional forensic evaluations. *Professional Psychology: Research and Practice, 33,* 377–383.

United States v. Davis, 835 F.2d 274, 276 (11th Cir. 1988).

United States v. Kristiansen, 901 F.2d 1463, 1466 (8th Cir. 1990).

United States v. Salamanca, 990 F.2d 629, 636 (D.C. Cir. 1993).

Weiner, I., & Hess, A. (Eds.). (2005). *The handbook of forensic psychology* (3rd ed.). New York: Wiley.

Weissman, H., & DeBow, D. (2003). Ethical principles and professional competencies. In A. M. Goldstein (Ed.), *Forensic psychology.* Vol. 11 of *Handbook of psychology* (pp. 33–54). Hoboken, NJ: Wiley.

Wettstein, R. (2005). Quality and quality improvement in forensic mental health evaluations. *Journal of the American Academy of Psychiatry and the Law, 33,* 158–175.

Yantz, C., Bauer, L., & McCaffrey, R. (2006). Regulations governing out-of-state practice of psychology: Implications for forensic neuropsychologists. *Applied Neuropsychology, 13,* 19–27.

PART I

Criminal

2

Evaluation of Competence to Stand Trial in Adults

PATRICIA A. ZAPF AND RONALD ROESCH

This chapter provides a review of the legal context for competency evaluations and the relevant forensic mental health concepts, a discussion of the empirical foundations and limitations of competency evaluation, and information about the evaluation process, report writing, and testimony for legal professionals involved in cases where the competency issue is raised (see Zapf & Roesch, 2009, for a more detailed review).

LEGAL CONTEXT

The legal context for competency to stand trial in the United States can be traced back to English common law dating from at least the 14th century. The competency doctrine evolved at a time when defendants were not provided with the right to assistance of counsel and, in many cases, were expected to present their defense alone and unaided.

Various legal commentators have delineated several principles underlying the rationale for the competency doctrine. The Group for the Advancement of Psychiatry (1974) summarized four underlying principles: (1) to safeguard the accuracy of any criminal adjudication; (2) to guarantee a fair trial; (3) to preserve the dignity and integrity of the legal process; and (4) to be certain that the defendant, if found guilty, knows why he is being punished (p. 889). Bonnie (1992) explained that allowing only those who are competent to proceed protects the dignity, reliability, and autonomy of the proceedings. The underlying rationale, then, concerns both the protection of the defendant as well as the protection of the state's interest in fair and reliable proceedings.

Although the term *competency to stand trial* has been used for centuries, there has begun a recent shift in terminology to reflect the fact that the vast majority of cases are plead out before getting to trial and that the issue of "trial" competency can be raised at any stage of the proceedings—from arrest to verdict to sentencing. Bonnie (1992), Poythress and colleagues (1999, 2002), and others have suggested the use of terms such as *adjudicative competence* or *competence to proceed* to better reflect the reality of this doctrine. Throughout this chapter the terms *competency to stand trial*, *adjudicative competence*, and *competency to proceed* are used interchangeably.

Legal Standards for Competency

Legal standards for adjudicative competence clearly define competency as an issue of a defendant's present mental status and functional abilities as they relate to participation in the trial process. This distinguishes competency from *criminal responsibility*, which refers to a defendant's mental state at the time of the offense. In an extremely brief decision, the U.S. Supreme Court established the modern-day standard for competency to stand trial in *Dusky v. United States* (1960). Citing a recommendation of the Solicitor General, the Court held that "the test must be whether he has sufficient present ability to consult with his lawyer with a reasonable degree of rational understanding—and whether he has a rational as well as factual understanding of the proceedings against him" (p. 402).

Fifteen years after *Dusky*, the United States Supreme Court in *Drope v. Missouri* (1975) appeared to elaborate slightly on the competency standard by including the notion that the defendant must be able to "assist in preparing his defense" (p.171). Legal scholars, such as Bonnie (1993), as well as the *American Bar Association Criminal Justice Mental Health Standards* (1989), indicated that *Drope* added another prong to *Dusky* by requiring that defendant be able to "otherwise assist with his defense" (ABA, 1989, p. 170). Similarly, the addition of this "otherwise assist" prong to the *Dusky* standard has been affirmed in cases such as *United States v. Duhon* (2000).

The federal standard for competency and each of the states' competency standards mirror *Dusky*, either verbatim or with minor revision, but at least five states (Alaska, Florida, Illinois, New Jersey, Utah) have also expanded or articulated the *Dusky* standard to include specific functional abilities. Since the definition of competency varies by state, it is necessary for an evaluator to consult the relevant competency statutes and definitions before proceeding with the evaluation of a defendant's competency. Legal professionals who retain competency evaluators may wish to confirm that the evaluator is familiar with the relevant jurisdictional standards and procedures.

Case Law Subsequent to *Dusky*

Case law subsequent to *Dusky* serves to offer some elaboration and interpretation of that competency standard. In *Wieter v. Settle* (1961), the United States District Court for the Western District of Missouri determined that it was improper to further detain a defendant who had been charged with a misdemeanor offense and held for 18 months for *competency restoration* since prosecution was no longer probable. In delivering the court's opinion, Chief Judge Ridge delineated a series of eight functional abilities related to *Dusky* that a defendant must possess to be competent (see p. 320).

The U.S. Court of Appeals considered the relevance of amnesia to adequate participation in legal proceedings in *Wilson v. United States* (1968). The court, in *Wilson*, delineated six factors that need to be considered (see pp. 463–464). The *Wilson* factors clearly specify a functional approach to evaluating competency, in which the specific deficits of a defendant would be related to the legal context.

All defendants are provided the Constitutional right to assistance of counsel; however, defendants may choose to waive this right and represent themselves (to appear *pro se*). This raises the question of whether competence to waive counsel should be evaluated separately from competency to stand trial. The U.S. Supreme Court considered the issue of whether a higher standard should apply for waiving counsel or pleading guilty in *Godinez v. Moran* (1993). The U.S. Supreme Court rejected the argument that although the defendant was found competent to stand trial, he was not competent to waive his right to counsel and represent himself, and held

that "while the decision to plead guilty is undeniably a profound one, it is no more complicated than the sum total of decisions that a defendant may be called upon to make during the course of a trial…Nor do we think that a defendant who waives his right to the assistance of counsel must be more competent than a defendant who does not, since there is no reason to believe that the decision to waive counsel requires an appreciably higher level of mental functioning than the decision to waive other constitutional rights" (p. 2686). Thus, the Court in *Godinez* indicated that the *Dusky* standard is the Constitutional minimum to be applied, regardless of the specific legal context, and that a defendant's decision-making abilities appear to be encompassed within this standard.

The Supreme Court revisited the issue of competency to represent oneself (proceed *pro se*) in *Indiana v. Edwards* (2008), where it considered the issue of whether a State, in the case of a criminal defendant who meets the *Dusky* standard for competence to stand trial, can limit a defendant's right to self-representation by requiring that the defendant be represented by counsel at trial. The Court answered in the affirmative, thereby establishing that competence to proceed *pro se* requires a higher level of competence than competence to stand trial, but was silent on the issue of how this should be determined. The Court was clear to make the differentiation between their decision in *Edwards* and that in *Godinez* by stating that the issue in *Godinez* was whether the defendant was competent to waive counsel, not represent himself.

Competency Procedures

Legal procedures are well established to ensure that defendants are competent to proceed. In *Pate v. Robinson* (1966), the Supreme Court held that the competency issue must be raised by any officer of the court (defense, prosecution, or judge) if there is a *bona fide* doubt as to a defendant's competence. The threshold for establishing a *bona fide* doubt is low, and most courts will order an evaluation of competence once the issue has been raised. Commenting on its decision in *Pate*, the Supreme Court in *Drope v. Missouri* (1975) noted that "evidence of a defendant's irrational behavior, his demeanor at trial, and any prior medical opinion on competence to stand trial are all relevant in determining whether further inquiry is required, but that even one of these factors standing alone may, in some circumstances, be sufficient" (p. 180). The *Drope* Court added that even when a defendant is competent at the outset of trial, the trial court should be aware of any changes in a defendant's condition that might raise question about his competency to stand trial. Thus, the issue of competency can be raised at any time prior to or during a trial.

Mental health professionals are called upon to evaluate defendants with respect to their competency and once the evaluation has been completed and a report submitted to the court, a hearing is scheduled to adjudicate the issue of competence (these hearings usually take place in front of a judge but a few jurisdictions allow for a jury to hear the issue of competency in certain circumstances). *Cooper v. Oklahoma* (1996) established that incompetency must be proved by a preponderance of evidence, and not the higher standard of clear and convincing evidence. The evaluator's report is highly influential in the court's decisions. Often, the opinion of a clinician is not disputed, and the court may simply accept the recommendations made in the report. Indeed, research has shown that the courts agree with report recommendations upwards of 90% of the time (Hart & Hare, 1992; Zapf, Hubbard, Cooper, Wheeles, & Ronan, 2004). Thus, this appears to be the norm in those jurisdictions in which the court orders only one evaluator to assess competency. Hearings on the issue of competency appear to occur more often, although still relatively infrequently, in those jurisdictions where two experts are asked to evaluate competency.

Defendants determined to be competent may then proceed with trial or with another disposition of their criminal case. The trial of defendants found incompetent is postponed until competency has been restored or, in a small percentage of cases, until a determination is made that the defendant is unlikely to regain competency.

Competency Restoration

Until the landmark case of *Jackson v. Indiana* (1972), most states allowed the automatic and indefinite confinement of incompetent defendants. This resulted in many defendants being held for lengthy periods of time, often beyond the sentence that might have been imposed had they been convicted. This practice was challenged in *Jackson*. The U.S. Supreme Court in *Jackson* held that defendants committed solely on the basis of incompetency "cannot be held more than the reasonable period

of time necessary to determine whether there is a substantial probability that he will attain that capacity in the foreseeable future" (p. 738). The Court did not specify limits to the length of time a defendant could reasonably be held, nor did it indicate how progress toward the goal of regaining competency could be assessed. Nevertheless, this decision resulted in changes to state laws regarding confinement of incompetent defendants.

Many states now place limits on the maximum length of time a defendant can be held and, if a defendant is determined to be unlikely to ever regain competency, the commitment based on incompetency must be terminated. However, in many states the actual impact of *Jackson* may be minimal (Morris, Haroun, & Naimark, 2004). State laws regarding treatment of incompetent defendants vary considerably, and Morris and colleagues found that many states ignore or circumvent *Jackson* by imposing lengthy commitment periods before a determination of unrestorability can be made, or tie the length of confinement to the sentence that could have been imposed had the individual been convicted of the original charge(s). Even after a period of confinement and a determination that competency is unlikely to be restored in the foreseeable future it is possible that such defendants could be civilly committed, but *United States v. Duhon* (2000) makes clear that defendants who are not dangerous must be released. Charges against defendants who are not restorable are typically dismissed, although sometimes with the provision that they can be reinstated if competency is regained.

Medication

Medication is the most common and arguably most effective means of treatment for incompetent defendants; however, defendants do have the right to refuse medication. There have been two major cases decided by the U.S. Supreme Court dealing with the issue of the involuntary medication of defendants who had been found incompetent to stand trial. In *Riggins v. Nevada* (1992), David Riggins had been prescribed Mellaril® and found competent to stand trial. He submitted a motion requesting that he be allowed to discontinue the use of this medication during trial, in order to show jurors his true mental state at the time of the offense since he was raising an insanity defense. His motion was denied and he was convicted of murder and sentenced to death. The U.S. Supreme Court reversed his conviction, holding that his rights were violated. Specifically, the Court found that the trial court failed to establish the need for and medical appropriateness of the medication. In addition, the Court also addressed the issue of whether the involuntary use of antipsychotic medications may affect the trial's outcome (see p. 127).

The U.S. Supreme Court further specified the criteria to determine whether forced medication is permissible in the case of *Sell v. United States* (2003). In *Sell* the Supreme Court held that antipsychotic drugs could be administered against the defendant's will for the purpose of restoring competency, but only in limited circumstances. Writing for the majority, Justice Breyer noted that involuntary medication of incompetent defendants should be rare, and identified several factors that a court must consider in determining whether a defendant can be forced to take medication, including whether important governmental interests are at stake; whether forced medication will significantly further those interests (i.e., the medication is substantially likely to render the defendant competent to stand trial and substantially unlikely to interfere significantly with the defendant's ability to assist counsel); whether involuntary medication is necessary to further those interests (i.e., alternative, less intrusive treatments are unlikely to achieve substantially the same results); and whether administering drugs is medically appropriate (see p. 167).

FORENSIC MENTAL HEALTH CONCEPTS

Evaluation of a defendant's psychological functioning is an essential component of the assessment of competency. Though not clearly specified in the *Dusky* decision, most state laws require that a finding of incompetence be based on the presence of a mental disorder. Once the presence of mental disease or defect has been established, the following must ensue: (1) evaluation of relevant functional abilities and deficits; (2) determination of a causal connection between any noted deficits and mental disorder; and (3) specification of how these deficits may have an impact upon functioning at trial.

Mental Illness as a Prerequisite for Incompetence

Determination of serious mental disorder, cognitive deficit, or mental retardation is merely the first step in finding a defendant incompetent to stand trial.

As Zapf, Skeem, and Golding (2005) noted, "the presence of cognitive disability or mental disorder is merely a threshold issue that must be established to 'get one's foot in the competency door'" (p. 433). Although evaluators a few decades ago appeared to base competency decisions largely on a finding of *psychosis* or mental retardation (see Roesch & Golding, 1980, for a review), it is now recognized that the presence of a diagnosis, even severe mental disorder, is not by itself sufficient to find a defendant incompetent. Psychosis is significantly correlated with a finding of incompetence; that is, a majority of incompetent defendants are diagnosed with some form of psychosis (mental retardation and organic brain disorders account for most of the remaining diagnoses). However, only about half of evaluated defendants with psychosis are found incompetent (Nicholson & Kugler, 1991), a clear indication that incompetence is not equated with psychosis. Rather, it is necessary for the evaluator to delineate a clear link (causal connection) between a defendant's mental impairments and his ability to participate in legal proceedings. This is referred to as a *functional assessment of competency.*

Before turning to a discussion of functional assessment, it is important to note that a defendant may have clearly demonstrable pathology, but the symptoms or observable features may be irrelevant to the issue of competency. Such features would include depersonalization, derealization, suicidal ideation, and poor insight. Even a person who meets civil commitment criteria may be considered competent to stand trial, although there does appear to be a strong relationship between incompetence and commitability. For the most part, evaluators will need to determine that the level of mental disorder is severe enough to affect a defendant's ability to proceed with trial. A diagnosis is useful in this regard, but more attention should be paid to symptoms rather than broad diagnostic categories. Many incompetent defendants have a diagnosis of schizophrenia, for example, but it is the specific symptoms that will be relevant to the competency evaluation.

It is most helpful to evaluators if legal counsel is able to provide information regarding the types of symptoms (behaviors, observations) that appear to impair or limit his or her discussions or interactions with the defendant. Any observations regarding the defendant and his or her demeanor, thoughts, actions, or behaviors should be passed along to the evaluator. Although relevant symptoms can vary widely, there are a few that tend to be more prevalent in incompetent defendants. These include formal thought disorder (as indicated by disorganized speech, loose associations, tangentiality, incoherence, or word salad); concentration deficits; rate of thinking (abrupt and rapid changes in speech or profound slowing of thought or speech); delusions (strongly held irrational beliefs that are not based in reality); hallucinations (sensory perceptions in the absence of a stimulus); memory deficits; and mental retardation or intellectual or developmental disability.

Psycholegal/Competence-Related Abilities

A review of competency case law (including *Dusky, Drope, Wieter, Godinez, Edwards,* and other relevant cases), legal commentary (such as Bonnie's reconceptualization of the construct of competence, 1992, 1993), and the available body of literature on competency evaluation and research indicates a number of psycholegal abilities relevant to the issue of competence. These include understanding, appreciation, reasoning, consulting with counsel, assisting in one's defense, and decision-making abilities. Each of these areas will be an important and relevant area of focus for an evaluation of competency.

Understanding

Within the context of competence to stand trial, factual understanding generally encompasses the ability to comprehend general information about the arrest process and courtroom proceedings. The defendant's factual understanding of the legal process includes a basic knowledge of legal strategies and options, although not necessarily as applied to the defendant's own particular case (case-specific understanding usually is encompassed by appreciation [rational understanding]; see next section). Thus, the competence-related ability to understand involves the defendant's ability to factually understand general, legally relevant information.

Appreciation

Appreciation generally refers to a defendant's rational understanding and encompasses specific knowledge regarding and accurate perception of information relevant to the role of the defendant in his or her own case. Within the context of competence to stand trial, appreciation encompasses the ability to comprehend and accurately perceive specific information regarding how the arrest and courtroom processes have affected or will affect the defendant. The defendant's appraisal of the situation must be reality-based, and any decisions that he or she makes about the case must be made on the basis of reality-based information. Thus, the competence-related ability to appreciate involves the application of information that the defendant factually understands to the specific case in a rational (i.e., reality-based) manner.

Reasoning

Reasoning generally refers to a defendant's ability to consider and weigh relevant pieces of information in a rational manner in arriving at a decision or a conclusion. To demonstrate appropriate reasoning ability the defendant must be able to communicate in a coherent manner and make decisions in a rational, reality-based manner undistorted by pathology. It is important to distinguish between the outcome of a decision and the process by which the decision is made. What is important is not the outcome of the decision but that the defendant be able to use appropriate reasoning processes—weighing, comparing, and evaluating information—in a rational manner. In the case of a defendant who is proceeding with the assistance of an attorney, reasoning encompasses the ability of the defendant to consult with counsel and to make rational decisions regarding various aspects of participation in his or her defense.

Consulting and Assisting

Although the *Dusky* standard indicates that the defendant must be able to "consult with his lawyer," the U.S. Supreme Court in *Drope v. Missouri* (1974) used the terminology "assist in preparing his defense" and the Federal standard (U.S. Code Annotated, Title 18, Part III, chapter 13, section 4241) indicates that the defendant must be able to "assist properly in his defense." Thus, the defendant's ability to consult with and assist counsel must be considered as part of the competency assessment. The defendant must be able to engage with counsel in a rational manner; thus, effectively assisting counsel requires that the defendant be able to communicate coherently and reason.

Decision Making

Closely tied to the abilities to appreciate, reason, and assist counsel is the ability to make decisions. The U.S. Supreme Court decision in *Cooper v. Oklahoma* (1996) appeared to equate a defendant's inability to communicate with counsel with incapacity to make fundamental decisions. In addition, the Supreme Court in *Godinez* incorporated decision-making abilities about the case into the standard for competence. Thus, a defendant's decision-making abilities with respect to specific, contextually relevant aspects of the case need be considered in the trial competency evaluation. It is important to note that research examining the content of competency evaluation reports has shown that certain abilities important and relevant to competence to stand trial, such as decision-making abilities, have rarely been addressed by evaluators in their reports (LaFortune & Nicholson, 1995; Skeem, Golding, Cohn, & Berge, 1998). Thus, legal counsel should ensure that competency evaluators are including this information in their evaluation reports.

Functional and Contextual Nature of Competency and its Evaluation

A functional assessment dictates that competency to stand trial cannot simply be assessed in the abstract, independent of contextual factors. Thus, an evaluation of contextual factors should always take place. This is the essence of a functional approach to assessing competence, which posits that the abilities required by the defendant in his or her specific case should be taken into account when assessing competence. The open-textured, context-dependent nature of the construct of competency to stand trial was summarized by Golding and Roesch (1988):

> Mere presence of severe disturbance (a psychopathological criterion) is only a threshold issue—it must be further demonstrated that such severe disturbance in *this* defendant, facing *these* charges, *in light of existing* evidence, anticipating the substantial effort of a *particular* attorney with a *relationship of known characteristics*, results in the defendant being unable to rationally assist the attorney or to comprehend the nature of the proceedings and their likely outcome. (p. 79)

The importance of a person–context interaction has also been highlighted by Grisso (2003), who defined a functional assessment in the following manner:

> A decision about legal competence is in part a statement about *congruency or incongruency between (a) the extent of a person's functional ability and (b) the degree of performance demand that is made by the specific instance of the context in that case.* Thus an interaction between individual ability and situational demand, not an absolute level of ability, is of special significance for competence decisions. (pp. 32–33)

Obviously, a functional assessment requires evaluators to learn about what may be required of a particular defendant. Some of this information may be provided by the defendant but other information will need to come from court documents and from the defendant's legal counsel. Some cases are more complex than others and may, as a result, require different types of psycholegal abilities. As Rogers and Mitchell (1991) note, the requisite level of understanding for a complex crime is higher than for a less complex one. Thus, it may be that the same defendant is competent for one type of legal proceeding but not for others. In cases in which a trial is likely, a defendant's demeanor in court and the ability to testify will certainly be of relevance. A defendant who is likely to withdraw into a catatonic-like state if required to testify, or one who may appear to jurors as not caring or not paying attention to the trial due to medication side effects, may not be capable of proceeding. But these same defendants may be able to proceed if the attorney intends to plea bargain.

Unfortunately, research has indicated that evaluators often fail to relate specific abilities and deficits to the particular case (Heilbrun & Collins, 1995) and that they often fail to provide a discussion of the link between symptomatology and legal abilities in their evaluation reports (Skeem et al., 1998). Legal counsel should expect an evaluator to ask for detailed information regarding those abilities that will be required of the particular defendant in the particular case so as to guide their competency-related inquiries. In addition, legal counsel should expect that evaluators might ask to observe their interactions with the defendant so as to truly perform a functional evaluation of the defendant's ability to relate to counsel, communicate with counsel, and participate in his or her own defense. If these requests do not occur, legal counsel should feel comfortable in raising these issues with the evaluator so as to ensure that a contextual and functional evaluation, in line with current best practices, is conducted.

EMPIRICAL FOUNDATIONS AND LIMITS

Prior to 1980, research on competency to stand trial was limited; however, the past few decades have witnessed a surge in research on this issue and there currently exists a robust literature in this area. In addition to research on various aspects of competency, structured and semi-structured instruments for assessing competency to stand trial have been developed. A review of this literature is well beyond the scope of this chapter, but this section will highlight those areas in which a literature base exists and attempt to provide a representative sample of the findings. More detailed information about all aspects of this section can be found in Zapf and Roesch (2009).

Research on Adjudicative Competence

The available research on adjudicative competence has mainly focused on procedural and assessment issues, the characteristics of referred and incompetent populations, the reliability and validity of competency evaluation, and the development and validation of instruments for the evaluation of competency. In addition, a limited but growing literature is developing on the restoration of competence. We will attempt to highlight representative findings in each of these areas.

Procedural Issues

Poythress and colleagues (2002) reported a series of studies of defense attorneys in several jurisdictions who responded to questions about their perceptions of the competence of their clients. These researchers found that the lawyers had concerns about the competency of their clients in 8% to 15% of the cases; however, competency evaluations were requested in less than half of these cases (in some of those cases where competency evaluations were not requested, the attorney tried to resolve the concerns through informal means, such as including a family member in the decision-making process). Poythress and colleagues noted that the attorneys indicated that their concerns were based on the functional abilities of the clients, such as communicating facts and decision-making capacity.

Reasons other than a concern about a defendant's competency may at least partially account for the consistent finding that only a small percentage of defendants referred for competency evaluations are found incompetent. Roesch and Golding (1980) reported on 10 studies conducted prior to 1980 and found an average incompetency rate of 30%. They also noted a considerable range of rates, with some jurisdictions finding almost no referred defendants to be incompetent while others reported rates as high as 77%. A recent meta-analysis of 68 studies found the rate of incompetence to be 27.5% (Pirelli, Gottdiener, & Zapf, 2011).

Characteristics of Referred and Incompetent Defendants

A vast amount of the competency research has examined the characteristics of both referred individuals as well as those found incompetent. Defendants *referred* for competency evaluations are often marginalized individuals with extensive criminal and mental health histories. Research has indicated that the majority of these defendants tend to be male, single, unemployed, with prior criminal histories, prior contact with mental health services, and past psychiatric hospitalizations. Viljoen and Zapf (2002) compared 80 defendants referred for competency evaluation with 80 defendants not referred and found that referred defendants were significantly more likely to meet diagnostic criteria for a current psychotic disorder, to be charged with a violent offense, and to demonstrate impaired legal abilities. In addition, referred defendants were less likely to have had previous criminal charges. Notably, approximately 25% of non-referred defendants demonstrated impairment on competence-related abilities. In addition, approximately 20% of referred defendants either did not meet criteria for a mental disorder or demonstrated no impairment of competence-related abilities.

With respect to the characteristics of defendants found incompetent, a recent meta-analysis found that unemployed defendants were twice as likely to be found incompetent as those who are employed and those diagnosed with a psychotic disorder were approximately eight times more likely to be found incompetent as those without such a diagnosis (Pirelli et al., 2011).

Reliability and Validity of the Evaluation Process

Since evaluators are assessing a defendant's present ability to perform a series of relatively clearly defined tasks, it seems reasonable to expect that competency evaluations would be highly reliable. In fact, this is precisely what the numerous studies on reliability have shown, with agreement about the ultimate opinion regarding competency being reported in the 90% range (Golding et al., 1984; Rosenfeld & Ritchie, 1998; Skeem et al., 1998). However, a reliable system of evaluation is not necessarily a valid one. For example, at one time it was the case that evaluators equated psychosis with incompetency (Roesch & Golding, 1980). Thus, if clinicians agreed that a defendant was psychotic they would also agree that the defendant was incompetent. As noted in this chapter, while psychosis is highly correlated with incompetency, it is also the case that a large percentage of competent defendants experience psychotic symptoms. The view that psychosis and incompetency are not inextricably entwined has changed as evaluators have become better trained and more research is available to guide decisions.

The problem of evaluating validity is that there is no gold standard for competence against which to compare evaluator decisions/opinions. Relying on court decisions is not particularly helpful since agreement rates between evaluator recommendations and court determinations have been shown to be well over 90% (Cox & Zapf, 2004; Cruise & Rogers, 1998; Hart & Hare, 1992). How, then, can the issue of construct validity be assessed? Golding and colleagues (1984) suggested the use of a panel of experts, referred to as a "blue ribbon panel," to serve as an independent criterion. In their study, they asked two experts to make judgments about competency based on a review of records, reports from hospital evaluators, and evaluations using the Interdisciplinary Fitness Interview (IFI). Golding and colleagues found that "for the 17 cases seen by the blue-ribbon panelists, they agreed with the IFI panelists 88% of the time, with the hospital staff 82% of the time, and with the courts 88% of the time" and they concluded that "on the basis of these data it would be hard to argue for one criterion definition over another" (p. 331).

The aforementioned study illustrates the methodological problems inherent in studies of competency evaluations, particularly in terms of the lack of a "correct" outcome against which to compare different methods of decision making. We are left with the reality that there can be no hard criterion against which to test the validity of competency evaluations because we do not have a test of how incompetent defendants would perform in the actual criterion situations. Since incompetent defendants are not allowed to go to trial until competency is restored, there is no test of whether a defendant found incompetent truly would have been unable to proceed with a trial or other judicial proceedings. Short of the provisional trial, the ultimate test of validity will never be possible.

Restoration of Competence

Empirical research on competency restoration indicates that most defendants are restorable: Nicholson and McNulty (1992) reported a restoration rate of 95% after an average of two months; Nicholson, Barnard, Robbins, and Hankins (1994) reported a rate of 90% after an average of 280 days; Cuneo and Brelje (1984) reported a restoration rate of 74% within one year; and Carbonell, Heilbrun, and Friedman (1992) reported a rate of about 62% after three months. Thus, regardless of the upper time limits on competency restoration allowed by state statute, it is now the case that most incompetent defendants are returned to court as competent within six months (Bennett & Kish, 1990; Nicholson & McNulty, 1992; Pinals, 2005; Poythress et al., 2002) and the vast majority of incompetent defendants are restored to competency within a year.

Research has also examined the issue of nonrestorability. Mossman (2007) found that individuals with a longstanding psychotic disorder with lengthy periods of prior psychiatric hospitalizations, or irremediable cognitive deficits such as mental retardation, were well below average in terms of their chances of restoration.

The most common form of treatment for the restoration of competence involves the administration of psychotropic medication. Some jurisdictions have also established educational treatment programs designed to increase a defendant's understanding of the legal process or individualized treatment programs that confront the problems that hinder a defendant's ability to participate in his or her defense (Bertman et al., 2003; Davis, 1985; Siegel & Elwork, 1990). In addition, some jurisdictions have implemented treatment programs specifically targeted towards those defendants with mental retardation who are found incompetent to proceed.

The success of treatment programs for the restoration of competence is variable and dependent upon the nature of the treatment program and the type of defendant targeted. Anderson and Hewitt (2002) examined treatment programs designed to restore competency in defendants with mental retardation and found that only 18% of their sample was restored. Treatment programs that target defendants with various other types of mental disorders have met with more success in that larger proportions of the defendants are restored to competency; however, it is not clear that individualized treatment programs that target specific underlying deficits for each defendant are any more effective than educational programs that teach defendants about their legal rights (Bertman et al., 2003). What appears to be accurate is that successful restoration is related to how well the defendant responds to psychotropic medications administered to alleviate those symptoms of the mental disorder that initially impaired those functional abilities associated with trial competency (Zapf & Roesch, 2011).

Competency Assessment Instruments

Prior to the 1960s no *forensic assessment instruments* (a term coined by Grisso in 1986) existed to assist experts in the evaluation of various legal issues. Trial competency was the first area for which forensic assessment instruments were developed. The evolution of forensic assessment instruments for the evaluation of competency has gone from early checklists (e.g., Robey, 1965) and sentence-completion tasks (e.g., Lipsitt, Lelos, & McGarry, 1971) to self-report questionnaires (e.g., Barnard et al., 1991) to interview-based instruments without, and then with, criterion-based scoring. Suffice it to say, this is a large area of research and the interested reader should consult the following resources for more information: Grisso (2003); Melton, Petrila, Poythress, and Slobogin (2007); Zapf and Roesch (2009); and Zapf and Viljoen (2003).

Three instruments show a great deal of promise in terms of their utility in the evaluation of competency to stand trial: the MacArthur Competence Assessment Tool—Criminal Adjudication (MacCAT-CA; Poythress, et al., 1999), the Evaluation of Competency to Stand Trial—Revised (ECST-R; Rogers, Tillbrook, & Sewell, 2004), and the Fitness Interview Test—Revised (FIT-R; Roesch, Zapf, & Eaves, 2006). Each of these instruments can be used to assist in the evaluation of a defendant's competency status and each has its strengths and weaknesses. All three of these instruments show evidence of sound psychometric properties.

The MacCAT-CA uses standardized administration and criterion-based scoring, which increases its reliability and provides scores on three competence-related abilities—understanding, reasoning, and appreciation—that can be compared to a normative group of defendants. The methodology used, however, involves a vignette format that limits the ability to extrapolate to a defendant's own particular case.

The ECST-R uses a hybrid interview approach, containing both semi-structured and structured components, designed to assess competency to stand trial generally as well as specific competencies such as competency to plead and competency to proceed *pro se*. The ECST-R yields scores in four different areas—rational understanding, factual understanding, consulting with counsel, and overall rational ability—and also includes scales that screen for feigned incompetency.

Like the MacCAT-CA, the ECST-R is a norm-referenced instrument, which means that the scores obtained by a particular defendant can be compared to a normative group of defendants to provide an indication of how this particular defendant compares to other defendants on the various abilities measured. The structured approach of these two instruments limits the types of questions that can be asked of a particular defendant (of course, the evaluator should ask about all relevant contextual issues in addition to administering either the MacCAT-CA or the ECST-R).

The FIT-R provides an interview guide for assessing the relevant competency-related issues in three different areas—factual understanding, rational understanding (appreciation), and consulting/decision making. Its semi-structured format allows for broad discretion in the types of inquiries made so all contextual elements can be evaluated for each defendant.

THE EVALUATION
Selecting an Evaluator

Legal counsel able to select and retain forensic evaluators of their choice (as opposed to having them court-ordered) will want to consider the potential evaluator's knowledge, training, and education as well as his or her skill set and experience. The evaluation will typically consist of three elements—an interview, testing, and collateral information review—and so legal counsel may wish to inquire with potential experts regarding the methods they use for conducting competency evaluations, the instruments that they typically use (if any), their experience with competency evaluation in general, as well as their experience in the relevant jurisdiction.

Defense Counsel's Role in the Evaluator's Preparation

There are four ways in which defense counsel will play a role in the competency evaluator's preparation and evaluation. First, defense counsel should expect the competency evaluator to clarify the referral question. This is one of the first tasks that an evaluator should complete and so it will require a conversation with the referring party (which we assume to be the defense counsel since this is the most common referral source) about the basis for the referral. The evaluator will want to know what defense counsel has observed about his or her interactions and conversations with the defendant, whether the defendant has displayed any odd or unusual behaviors or beliefs, whether the defendant has been communicative with counsel, whether the defendant holds any animosity or mistrust for defense counsel, and the extent of the defendant's understanding of his or her charges as displayed to defense counsel. In addition, defense counsel should be prepared to provide information regarding why the referral for competency evaluation was requested.

Aside from information needed to clarify the referral question, evaluators will also look to defense counsel for specific information regarding the defendant's current charges and allegations. Providing information to the evaluator about the formal charges as well as a police report or some other report regarding the allegations for those charges will be an important initial step in assisting the evaluator in his or her preparation. Along with this, the evaluator will require information about the nature of the dispositions that the defendant might face in light of any previous criminal history, the likelihood of the defendant begin acquitted or convicted, and the likelihood of a plea deal being offered. This information will assist the evaluator in determining whether the defendant is able to provide a realistic view of his or her case and the possible outcomes. In addition, current best practices for competency evaluation require that the evaluator be able to assess the degree of congruence or incongruence between the defendant's capacities and the abilities required of him or her at trial (or for his or her relevant adjudicative proceedings). Thus, in order to do so, the evaluator must collect information regarding what will be required of the defendant for his or her proceedings. Defense counsel should expect the evaluator to ask a series of questions or obtain information using a standardized questionnaire regarding whether the defendant will be expected to make a decision regarding a plea bargain; whether evidence against the defendant is such that mounting a defense will depend largely on the defendant's ability to provide information (or whether there are additional information sources, aside from the defendant, that can be used); whether the case will involve a number of adverse witnesses; whether the defendant will be required to testify; whether the adjudication process will be lengthy; whether the adjudication hearing will be lengthy; and whether the adjudication hearing will be complex (i.e., difficult to follow, complicated evidence). Any information that the defense counsel can provide to the evaluator regarding the abilities that will be required of the defendant will assist in guiding the evaluation process.

The third way in which defense counsel will play a role in the evaluation process is by assisting the evaluator in obtaining relevant collateral records and information. Every competency evaluation requires that the evaluator review collateral information and/or interview collateral information sources to determine the weight to be given to the defendant's self-report. Competency evaluators are expected to go through legal counsel to obtain this information so as to meet the relevant requirements for discovery and attorney work product. Even in those situations where records are to be released directly to a mental health professional (as is sometimes the case with psychological test results), the initial request for information should be funneled through the defense attorney (the mental health professional can provide a release-of-information form to be signed by the defendant and used by the attorney to obtain the relevant documents).

Finally, the evaluator may request that he or she be allowed the opportunity to observe interactions between the defendant and defense counsel. This is to satisfy the functional component of competency evaluation whereby direct observation of the defendant and defense attorney engaging in discussion of the defendant's charges or defense strategy allows for a direct assessment of the defendant's abilities in this regard. Defense counsel can, of course, decide whether he or she will grant this request, but direct observation of these interactions will assist the evaluator in extrapolating to the trial context. Of note here is that information about the specific *content* of these discussions would be left out of the evaluation report; rather, observations regarding the *process* is the focus of these interactions.

The Goal of the Evaluation

The goal of the evaluation is for the evaluator to assess the degree of congruence or incongruence between the defendant's capacities and the abilities required of the defendant at trial (or his or her proceedings). To do this, the evaluator will assess the defendant's current mental status and his or her competence-related capacities (i.e., understanding, appreciation, reasoning, assisting/consulting, and decision making) within the specific context of the defendant's case (thus including any relevant abilities that will be required of the defendant for his or her proceedings); determine whether the cause of any noted deficits is a result of mental illness or cognitive impairment; and specify how the defendant's mental illness or cognitive symptoms may interact or interfere with his or her competence-related abilities by describing how this may present at trial. In addition, the evaluator should delineate the ways in which the court or defense counsel can assist the defendant in his or her functioning at trial (i.e., providing prescriptive remediation such as instruction regarding how best to work with the client to improve his or her functioning). Finally, many jurisdictions require the evaluator to include information regarding the likelihood and length of restoration and treatment recommendations for those defendants who appear to be incompetent.

The evaluator will use the data gathered through the evaluation process (interview, testing, and collateral information review) to arrive at a conclusion regarding the defendant's competency status; however, many evaluators believe that it is beyond their role to explicitly state their opinion regarding the defendant's competency status. That is, many evaluators are hesitant to speak to the ultimate legal issue, believing instead that this is for the court to determine. While the ultimate legal issue (competency status) is certainly a legal issue for the court to decide, counsel who desire the evaluator to provide an ultimate opinion should feel comfortable in making this request of the evaluator. Many evaluators will not provide such opinions unless explicitly asked or statutorily required to do so.

REPORT WRITING AND TESTIMONY

Court-ordered evaluators are required to complete a written report of their evaluation along with their opinions regarding the defendant's mental status and competence-related abilities. In most jurisdictions these written reports will be distributed to the prosecution and the defense as well as the court. In situations where the evaluator has been privately retained, however, there is no requirement for a written report and so the determination of whether a written report is to be provided is left with defense counsel. In these situations, the evaluator is expected to provide an oral report of his or her findings and opinions to defense counsel and await further instruction from counsel as to whether a written report is desired. Regardless of whether the evaluator was court-ordered or privately retained, the expectation is that the evaluator is an objective, neutral party who will include all relevant information in the written report. If the privately retained evaluator uncovers information that could be damaging or detrimental to the defense, he or she should provide this information to counsel in an oral report. If a written report is requested, it would be unethical for the evaluator to leave out relevant information not favorable to the defense.

Report Contents

Although there are numerous different ways to organize a forensic evaluation report, any competency evaluation report should contain the following types of information: relevant case and referral information; a description of the notification of rights provided to the defendant; a summary of the alleged offense (this should be from official documents and not the defendant's self-report); the data sources that were used or reviewed for the purposes of the evaluation (including any collateral interviews and the dates on which they occurred); background information on the defendant (typically a social history); a clinical assessment of the defendant (typically this will include a mental status exam as well as any relevant information or observations about the defendant's mental health and functioning); a forensic assessment of the defendant (with all relevant information regarding the defendant's competence-related abilities and/or deficits); and a summary and recommendations section (including any prescriptive remediation or information regarding treatment recommendations).

Forensic Evaluation

The forensic evaluation component of the written report is perhaps the most relevant and important to legal counsel and the court. This section of the report should include a description of the defendant's competence-related abilities and deficits; the cause for any noted deficits; the impact of symptoms on the defendant's performance or participation in the case; possible prescriptive remediation; conclusions or opinions regarding each of the jurisdictional criteria; and the prognosis for restorability.

The best forensic evaluation reports are those that explicitly delineate the linkage between the defendant's mental illness or cognitive impairment and any noted competence-related deficits *as well as* describe how these deficits might affect the defendant's functioning at trial. For example, it would not be enough to simply state that the defendant has delusional disorder and therefore is unable to rationally understand (appreciate) his or her role as a defendant. Instead, the evaluator should clearly delineate the necessary linkages for the court and describe how these might affect the defendant's functioning at trial. For example, the defendant displays a fixed delusional belief system whereby he believes that his father "owns" all of the judges in the State and therefore no judge in the State would ever convict him. This delusion compromises the defendant's ability to make rational decisions regarding his defense.

In addition to a clear delineation of the linkage between any mental illness or cognitive deficit and any noted deficits in competence-related abilities and a description of how these could affect the defendant's functioning at trial or in various relevant proceedings, the report should also include some form of prescriptive remediation for any noted deficits. For example, the evaluator might indicate that the defendant demonstrates lower cognitive functioning, which might affect his ability to fully understand and engage in his defense strategy, and then indicate that the defendant's understanding might be improved by using concrete, as opposed to abstract, examples and by using shorter sentences with smaller words.

Most jurisdictions require that the evaluator include additional information in the report for those defendants opined incompetent. This additional information typically includes the cause of the incompetence, the probability and estimated length of restoration, and treatment recommendations for restoration. Evaluators are expected to understand and abide by the various jurisdictional requirements for competency evaluation reports; however, legal professionals should be aware that

some research has indicated that not all evaluation reports include these statutorily required elements (Zapf et al., 2004). Legal consumers should not hesitate to bring any missing elements to the attention of the evaluator.

Inappropriate Report Contents

Two types of content are not appropriate for inclusion in a competency evaluation report. The first is the defendant's version of the circumstances surrounding the offense. A functional evaluation of competency requires that the evaluator inquire about the charges and allegations; however, evaluators are expected to exercise caution when writing the evaluation report so as not to include potentially incriminating information provided by the defendant. General statements regarding whether the defendant's account of events differs substantially from official accounts and whether this reflects an incapacity or deficit on the part of the defendant should be used instead of a summary of the defendant's account or the defendant's verbatim answers. Similarly, the *content* of observed interactions and/or discussions between defense counsel and the defendant is not appropriate for inclusion in the written report; rather, a description of the *process* of these interactions is what should be highlighted.

The second type of inappropriate report content involves the inclusion of information or opinions related to other legal issues. Evaluators should be careful to address only those referral questions that have been asked and to refrain from offering unsolicited information about other, possibly relevant, legal issues in the competency evaluation report. Opinions or conclusions regarding a defendant's future risk for violent behavior, or any other legal or psychological issue, have no place in a competency evaluation report. In many jurisdictions, competency evaluations and assessments of mental state at the time of the offense are often ordered simultaneously. In this situation, the evaluator may choose to prepare a separate report for each referral question or to address both referral questions within the same report. Legal consumers desiring two separate reports in this instance should make this clear to the evaluator.

Importance of Providing the Bases for the Opinion/Conclusions

The importance of delineating the linkages between mental illness, competence-related deficits, and functional abilities at trial (or for the purposes of the defendant's proceedings) has been highlighted throughout this chapter but with good reason. In a survey of forensic diplomates of the American Board of Forensic Psychology (ABPP), Borum and Grisso (1996) found that 90% of respondents agreed that detailing the link between mental illness and competence-related deficits in competency reports was either recommended or essential. However, an examination of competency-to-stand-trial reports from two states indicated that only 27% of the reports provided an explanation regarding how the defendant's mental illness influenced his or her competence-related abilities (Robbins, Waters, & Herbert, 1997). Further, in another study, only 10% of competency-evaluation reports reviewed provided an explanation regarding how the defendant's psychopathology compromised required competence-related abilities (Skeem et al., 1998). In addition to the issue of the linkage between mental illness and competence-related deficits, the extant research also indicates that examiners rarely (Skeem et al.) or never (Robbins et al.) assess the congruence between a defendant's abilities and the specific case context. Thus, legal consumers should be aware of the necessity for evaluators to provide the bases for their opinions and conclusions through clear indication of these linkages in the written report.

Testimony

In the majority of cases where the issue of competency is raised, a legal determination is made without a competency hearing (both parties typically stipulate to the evaluator's report). When a competency hearing is necessary, the forensic evaluator(s) will be called to testify about the evaluation. If the evaluator was privately retained, as opposed to court-ordered, it is helpful for the defense attorney to conduct a pretrial conference to inform the evaluator about relevant issues, such as the theory of the case, how the attorney would like the evaluator's testimony presented, and any relevant information about what the opposing side may try to prove. During this conference (if not before), the evaluator should inform the retaining attorney about any possible weaknesses in his or her evaluation methods, opinions, or conclusions as well as any possible weaknesses with the opposing side's opinion (if known). It is helpful to the evaluator if defense counsel also share issues that may be subject to scrutiny or become the focus of

cross-examination. In complex or high-profile cases the legal defense team may wish to ask the evaluator practice questions (both direct and cross-examination) to assist in preparing the evaluator for his or her testimony.

The evaluator should have provided a copy of his or her curriculum vitae to defense counsel (when privately retained) or the court (for court-ordered evaluations) prior to the day of the competency hearing, but he or she should also come prepared to testify with multiple copies of his or her CV. In cases where the evaluator was privately retained, the defense team may wish to go over the evaluator's CV with the evaluator ahead of time so the evaluator can highlight relevant experiences and qualifications to smooth the process of becoming qualified as an expert.

Regardless of whether the expert was court-ordered or privately retained, he or she is required to remain objective and neutral and to answer all questions in a straightforward manner. The evaluator should be well prepared to take the stand, having reviewed all relevant materials to the competency evaluation in addition to his or her written report.

SUMMARY

The purpose of this chapter was to present material relevant to legal consumers regarding the evaluation of competency to stand trial (adjudicative competence). The interested reader is directed to additional resources for further discussion of the information contained within this short chapter, including Grisso (2003); Melton, Petrila, Poythress, and Slobogin (2007); Pirelli, Gottdiener, and Zapf (2011); and Zapf and Roesch (2009).

REFERENCES

American Bar Association (1989). *ABA criminal justice mental health standards*. Washington, DC: Author.

Anderson, S. D., & Hewitt, J. (2002). The effect of competency restoration training on defendants with mental retardation found not competent to proceed. *Law and Human Behavior, 26,* 343–351.

Barnard, G. W., Thompson, J. W., Freeman, W. C., Robbins, L., Gies, D., & Hankins, G.(1991). Competency to stand trial: Description and initial evaluation of a new computer-assisted assessment tool (CADCOMP). *Bulletin of the American Academy of Psychiatry and the Law, 19,* 367–381.

Bennett, G., & Kish, G. (1990). Incompetency to stand trial: Treatment unaffected by demographic variables. *Journal of Forensic Sciences, 35,* 403–412.

Bertman, L. J., Thompson, J. W., Jr., Waters, W. F., Estupinan-Kane, L., Martin, J. A., & Russell, L. (2003). Effect of an individualized treatment protocol on restoration of competency in pretrial forensic inpatients. *Journal of the American Academy of Psychiatry and Law, 31,* 27–35.

Bonnie, R. J. (1992). The competence of criminal defendants: A theoretical reformulation. *Behavioral Sciences and the Law, 10,* 291–316.

Bonnie, R. J. (1993). The competence of criminal defendants: beyond *Dusky* and *Drope. Miami Law Review, 47,* 539–601.

Borum, R., & Grisso, T. (1996). Establishing standards for criminal forensic reports: An empirical analysis. *Bulletin of the American Academy of Psychiatry and the Law, 24,* 297–317.

Carbonell, J., Heilbrun, K., & Friedman, F. (1992). Predicting who will regain trial competence: Initial promise unfulfilled. *Forensic Reports, 5,* 67–76.

Cooper v. Oklahoma, 116 S. Ct. 1373 (1996).

Cox, M. L., & Zapf, P. A. (2004). An investigation of discrepancies between mental health professionals and the courts in decisions about competency. *Law and Psychology Review, 28,* 109–132.

Cruise, K. R., & Rogers, R. (1998). An analysis of competency to stand trial: An integration of case law and clinical knowledge. *Behavioral Sciences and the Law, 16,* 35–50.

Cuneo, D., & Brelje, T. (1984). Predicting probability of attaining fitness to stand trial. *Psychological Reports, 55,* 35–39.

Davis, D. L. (1985). Treatment planning for the patient who is incompetent to stand trial. *Hospital and Community Psychiatry, 36,* 268–271.

Drope v. Missouri, 420 U. S. 162 (1975).

Dusky v. United States, 362 U.S. 402 (1960).

Godinez v. Moran, 113 S. Ct. 2680 (1993).

Golding, S. L., & Roesch, R. (1988). Competency for adjudication: An international analysis. In D. N. Weisstub (Ed.), *Law and mental health: International perspectives* (Vol. 4, pp. 73–109). Elmsford, NY: Pergamon Press.

Golding, S. L., Roesch, R., & Schreiber, J. (1984). Assessment and conceptualization of competency to stand trial: Preliminary data on the Interdisciplinary Fitness Interview. *Law and Human Behavior, 8,* 321–334.

Grisso, T. (2003). *Evaluating competencies: Forensic assessment and instruments* (2nd ed.). New York: Kluwer Academic/Plenum Publishers.

Group for the Advancement of Psychiatry. (1974). *Misuse of psychiatry in the criminal courts: Competency to stand trial.* New York: Mental Health Materials Center.

Hart, S. D., & Hare, R. D. (1992). Predicting fitness for trial: The relative power of demographic, criminal and clinical variables. *Forensic Reports, 5,* 53–54.

Heilbrun, K., & Collins, S. (1995). Evaluations of trial competency and mental state at time of offense: Report characteristics. *Professional Psychology: Research and Practice, 26,* 61–67.

Indiana v. Edwards, 554 U.S. 164 (2008).

Jackson v. Indiana, 406 U. S. 715 (1972).

LaFortune, K., & Nicholson, R. (1995). How adequate are Oklahoma's mental health evaluations for determining competency in criminal proceedings? The bench and bar respond. *Journal of Psychiatry and Law, 23,* 231–262.

Lipsitt, P., Lelos, D., & McGarry, A. L. (1971). Competency for trial: A screening instrument. *American Journal of Psychiatry, 128,* 105–109.

Melton, G. B., Petrila, J., Poythress, N. G., & Slobogin, C. (2007). *Psychological evaluations for the courts: A handbook for mental health professionals and lawyers* (3rd ed.). New York: Guilford.

Morris, G. H., Haroun, A. M., & Naimark, D. (2004). Assessing competency competently: Toward a rational standard for competency-to-stand-trial assessments. *Journal of the American Academy of Psychiatry and Law, 32,* 231–45.

Mossman, D. (2007). Predicting restorability of incompetent criminal defendants. *Journal of the American Academy of Psychiatry and the Law, 35,* 34–43.

Nicholson, R., Barnard, G., Robbins, L., & Hankins, G. (1994). Predicting treatment outcome for incompetent defendants. *Bulletin of the American Academy of Psychiatry and the Law, 22,* 367–377.

Nicholson, R., & McNulty, J. (1992). Outcome of hospitalization for defendants found incompetent to stand trial. *Behavioral Sciences and the Law, 10,* 371–383.

Nicholson, R. A., & Kugler, K. E. (1991). Competent and incompetent criminal defendants: A quantitative review of comparative research. *Psychological Bulletin, 109,* 355–370.

Pate v. Robinson, 383 U. S. 375 (1966).

Pinals, D. (2005). Where two roads met: Restoration of competence to stand trial from a clinical perspective. *New England Journal of Civil and Criminal Confinement, 31,* 81–108.

Pirelli, G., Gottdiener, W. H., & Zapf, P. A. (2011). A meta-analytic review of competency to stand trial research. *Psychology, Public Policy, and Law, 17,* 1–53.

Poythress, N. G., Bonnie, R. J., Monahan, J., Otto, R. K., & Hoge, S. K. (2002). *Adjudicative competence: The MacArthur studies.* New York: Kluwer Academic/Plenum.

Poythress, N. G., Nicholson, R. A., Otto, R. K., Edens, J. F., Bonnie, R. J., Monahan, J., & Hoge, S. K. (1999). *The MacArthur Competence Assessment Tool—Criminal Adjudication.* Odessa, FL: Psychological Assessment Resources.

Riggins v. Nevada, 504 U. S. 127 (1992).

Robbins, E., Waters, J., & Herbert, P. (1997). Competency to stand trial evaluations: A study of actual practice in two states. *Journal of the American Academy of Psychiatry and Law, 25,* 469–483.

Robey, A. (1965). Criteria for competency to stand trial: A checklist for psychiatrists. *American Journal of Psychiatry, 122,* 616–623.

Roesch, R., & Golding, S. L. (1980). *Competency to stand trial.* Chicago, IL: University of Illinois Press.

Roesch, R. Zapf, P. A., & Eaves, D. (2006). *Fitness Interview Test—Revised: A structured interview for assessing competency to stand trial.* Sarasota, FL: Professional Resource Press.

Rogers, R., & Mitchell, C. N. (1991). *Mental health experts and the criminal courts: A handbook for lawyers and clinicians.* Scarborough, ON: Thompson.

Rogers, R., Tillbrook, C. E., & Sewell, K. W. (2004). *Evaluation of Competency to Stand Trial—Revised professional manual.* Lutz, FL: Psychological Assessment Resources.

Rosenfeld, B., & Ritchie, K. (1998). Competence to stand trial: Clinical reliability and the role of offense severity. *Journal of Forensic Sciences, 43,* 151–157.

Sell v. United States, 539 U. S 166 (2003).

Siegel, A.M., & Elwork, A. (1990). Treating incompetence to stand trial. *Law and Human Behavior, 14,* 57–65.

Skeem, J., Golding, S. L., Cohn, N., & Berge, G. (1998). Logic and reliability of evaluations of competence to stand trial. *Law and Human Behavior, 22,* 519–547.

United States v. Duhon, 104 F. Supp. 2d. 663 (2000).

Viljoen, J. L., & Zapf, P. A. (2002). Fitness to stand trial evaluations: A comparison of referred and non-referred defendants. *International Journal of Forensic Mental Health, 1,* 127–138.

Wieter v. Settle, 193 F. Supp. 318 (W.D. Mo. 1961).

Wilson v. United States, 391 F. 2d. 460 (1968).

Zapf, P. A., Hubbard, K. L., Cooper, V. G., Wheeles, M. C., & Ronan, K. A. (2004). Have the courts abdicated their responsibility for determination of competency to stand trial to clinicians? *Journal of Forensic Psychology Practice, 4,* 27–44.

Zapf, P. A., & Roesch, R. (2009). *Best practices in forensic mental health assessment: Evaluation of competence to stand trial.* New York: Oxford.

Zapf, P. A., & Roesch, R. (2011). Future directions in the restoration of competency to stand trial. *Current Directions in Psychological Science, 20,* 43–47.

Zapf, P. A., Skeem, J. L., & Golding, S. L. (2005). Factor structure and validity of the MacArthur Competence Assessment Tool—Criminal Adjudication. *Psychological Assessment, 17,* 433–445.

Zapf, P. A., & Viljoen, J. L. (2003). Issues and considerations regarding the use of assessment instruments in the evaluation of competency to stand trial. *Behavioral Sciences and the Law, 21,* 351–367.

3

Evaluation of Criminal Responsibility

IRA K. PACKER

In criminal cases, when a mental-state defense is considered, it is almost always necessary for attorneys to obtain an evaluation of the defendant by a forensic mental health professional. Professional standards have been developed to guide evaluators in conducting such evaluations (e.g., Packer, 2009). This chapter summarizes for attorneys the essential elements of those standards, to provide a basis for consulting with retained experts and preparing for cross-examination of opposing witnesses. The chapter begins with a brief overview of the historical development of the insanity defense, proceeds with an analysis of current legal criteria, and then focuses on standards that should guide mental health experts in conducting evaluations of mental states affecting criminal responsibility (insanity and diminished capacity). It concludes with guidelines that attorneys can use to assess the quality of forensic reports related to issues of criminal responsibility.

THE LEGAL CONTEXT

The insanity defense is based on the legal concept that culpability for criminal acts requires both an *actus reus* (bad act) and a *mens rea* (guilty mind). This is not a modern concept, and dates back to at least the Hebrew *Mishna* (almost two thousand years ago). The modern underpinning for the insanity defense standards prevalent in most U.S. jurisdictions stems from the case of Daniel M'Naghten in England in 1843. (For a detailed discussion of the M'Naghten case, see Moran, 1981.) M'Naghten was acquitted by reason of insanity of killing the secretary of the leader of the Tory Party, Sir Robert Peel (who was the target of the assassination). Public outrage at the verdict resulted in new criteria for the insanity defense being established in England

(known as the *"M'Naghten" standard*). This standard included the following criteria:

> to establish a defense on the ground of insanity, it must be proved that, at the time of the committing of the act, the party accused was laboring under such a defect of reason, from disease of the mind, as not to know the nature and quality of the act he was doing or if he did know it, that he did not know he was doing what was wrong (*M'Naghten case,* 1843).

Although this standard, or a variant of it, continues to be used in a majority of states, it has been criticized for its focus only on the "cognitive" aspect and ignoring the impact of various emotional states on impairing volitional control (e.g., American Law Institute, 1985). An early attempt to address this issue involved the inclusion of the "irresistible impulse" test—that is, a defendant could also be found insane if he or she acted in response to an impulse that was irresistible. However, this term was not amenable to careful definition and measurement. Specifically, how could mental health professionals and the legal system distinguish between an impulse that *could* not be resisted and an impulse that *was* not resisted? This dilemma was articulated succinctly by the American Psychiatric Association (1983): "[T]he line between an irresistible impulse and one not resisted is probably no sharper than that between twilight and dusk."

The next major advance regarding insanity jurisprudence was included in the model penal code proposed by the American Law Institute (ALI) in 1962. The ALI language indicated that a defendant would be found not guilty by reason of insanity (NGRI) if "as a result of mental illness or mental defect he lacked substantial capacity either to appreciate the wrongfulness of his conduct or to conform his conduct to the requirements of the law" (American Law Institute, 1985). The most significant differences from M'Naghten involve (1) use of the word "appreciate" versus "know"; (2) the meaning of the term "wrongfulness"; (3) the addition of the volitional prong ("conform conduct"), which represented a modification of the concept of "irresistible impulse"; and (4) use of the term "lacked *substantial* capacity."

The concept of appreciation was meant to broaden the conceptualization beyond intellectual knowledge to incorporate the need for an awareness of the significance of the act. The commentary that accompanied the development of the standard noted that the M'Naghten standard "does not readily lend itself to application of emotional abnormalities" (American Law Institute, 1985, p. 166). The term "wrongfulness" connotes that the focus should be on the defendant's appreciation of the moral wrongfulness of the behavior, not simply that it is legally prohibited, or criminal (e.g., Fingarette, 1972). The language of the volitional component also represented a departure from the term "irresistible impulse," as it changed the focus from an assessment of the strength of the impulse to the defendant's capacity to exercise control over impulses once they arose. In addition, the terminology "substantial capacity" recognized degrees of impairment, rather than requiring total incapacity.

However, even with this change in language, the volitional prong continued to be more controversial than the cognitive prong. Following John Hinckley's acquittal by reason of insanity in 1983 of the attempted assassination of President Ronald Reagan (and the serious wounding of his press secretary, James Brady) under the ALI standard, there was a public perception that the jury acquitted based on the volitional prong (although there is no clear evidence that they would have convicted under a standard that included only the cognitive prong). The Federal standard (followed suit by a number of states as well) was amended to eliminate the volitional prong from the insanity defense (Insanity Defense Reform Act, 1984). The abolition of the volitional prong was endorsed by both the American Psychiatric Association (1983) and the American Bar Association (1983). The American Psychological Association (1984), however, noting the lack of empirical data, argued that more research was needed before any changes could be recommended. At present, only 16 states continue to include the volitional prong in their definition of insanity.

One jurisdiction, New Hampshire, uses a totally different approach to the insanity defense, focusing on whether the criminal behavior was a "product" of mental disease or mental defect. Although no other jurisdictions currently use this standard, it is noted that one Federal Circuit adopted this standard for a brief period of time (*Durham v. U.S.,* 1954). Judge David Bazelon authored that opinion, based on concerns that (1) the M'Naghten standard was too narrow, and (2) mental health professionals were being forced to focus on the legal criteria, rather than on clinical assessments and analyses, which were their sources of expertise. This change was well intentioned, but in practice it did not result in clearer, more appropriate testimony, and it did not provide adequate guidance about how to determine whether a particular criminal behavior was indeed the "product" of the symptoms of a mental illness, as opposed to co-occurring personality or contextual variables. Thus, even if it were established that a defendant was suffering from a mental illness at the time of the offense, this did not necessarily imply that the particular criminal behavior was the result of the mental illness. In recognition of these difficulties, the same Circuit court reversed itself, rescinded the *Durham* standard, and adopted the ALI's standard for its jurisdiction (*U.S. v. Brawner,* 1972).

The Supreme Court has avoided addressing the issue of whether states are constitutionally required to adopt an insanity defense (certiorari denied in *Cowan v. Montana,* 1994). Indeed, as of 2011, four states have abolished the insanity defense (Idaho, Kansas, Montana, and Utah). However, in the case of *Clark v. Arizona* (2006), the Supreme Court did address a claim that Arizona's statute was unconstitutional because it eliminated one aspect of the M'Naghten standard (the first prong, "nature and quality of the act"). The Court rejected Clark's claim, and ruled that no specific language or standard is constitutionally required. In addition, the court addressed the meaning of the phrase "nature and quality" of the act, articulating the position that this prong did not add anything substantive beyond the wrongfulness prong. In their opinion they cited the language of the Arizona Court of Appeals: "It is difficult to imagine that a defendant who did not appreciate the 'nature and quality' of the act he committed would reasonably be able to perceive that the act was 'wrong'" (p. 350).

Legal Process

The insanity defense is an affirmative defense, requiring the defendant to raise the issue; however, there are differences across jurisdictions both in terms of who has the burden of proof once the insanity defense has been raised, and the standard of proof employed. The most stringent standard applied when the burden is placed on the defendant is "clear and convincing evidence," although in states where the burden is on the prosecution, the standard can vary from "preponderance of the evidence" through "beyond a reasonable doubt." It is noted, though, that these are the legal standards for the trier of fact to use; it is not within the purview of the forensic evaluator to opine on whether the particular standard of proof has been met. Rather, the evaluator may comment on the strength of the data forming the basis of the opinion and the degree of confidence in the opinion proffered.

Forensic clinicians either may be appointed as the court's expert, or may be retained by one of the attorneys. Many jurisdictions have provisions for the court to directly obtain evaluations either from state (or federal) employees, or from individuals or agencies that contract with the state. For this type of evaluation, there are a variety of models used, ranging from hospital-based to community-based (at the court, at a correctional facility, or in the evaluator's office). Most jurisdictions require either doctoral-level psychologists or psychiatrists to conduct these evaluations (Frost et al., 2006), and studies have found no substantial differences in the quality of reports produced by psychologists as compared to psychiatrists (Petrella & Poythress, 1983; Warren et al., 2004). There are also differences in legal procedures regarding dissemination of the report. In some jurisdictions, the report will be sent directly to the court and to both attorneys, whereas some states provide more safeguards before the report or specific data about the defendant's statements are provided to the prosecution. The relevant issue is that, as will be discussed below, criminal responsibility (CR) evaluations typically require a thorough inquiry into the defendant's account of the alleged offense, which may contain incriminating information.

This concern about incriminating statements made by a defendant relates not only to evaluations by the court's expert, but also to those provided by forensic evaluators retained by the prosecution. The American Bar Association's Criminal Justice Standards (Standard 7-3.4) specifically recommend that forensic evaluators not be permitted to share statements made by the defendant about the alleged offense with the prosecution prior to the defense providing notice of proceeding with an insanity defense, which will rely on testimony of a mental health expert. This issue was addressed, for example, in the Massachusetts case of *Commonwealth v. Stroyny* (2002). In that case, a psychiatrist retained by the prosecution revealed the defendant's account of the alleged offense to the prosecutor prior to the defendant affirmatively asserting that he would proceed with a defense of not guilty by reason of insanity. The court noted that if the psychiatrist was not aware of the legal privilege issue involved, "the prosecutor should immediately have terminated any conversation [with the psychiatrist] when it became clear that he was divulging communications by the defendant" (p. 1210). Although this ruling was specific to Massachusetts, the relevant point is that the prosecuting attorney should instruct the retained expert as to the rules in the particular jurisdiction.

A different set of issues arises when forensic evaluators are retained by the defense. In many jurisdictions, in such instances attorney–client privilege protects the information obtained during the CR evaluation. Under these circumstances, the information is provided only to the defense attorney, and it will be up to the attorney to release the report or call the expert to testify (*U.S. v. Alvarez*, 1975). However, other jurisdictions exempt these evaluations from the privilege. In the case of *U.S. ex rel. Edney v. Smith* (1976) an Appellate Court upheld the constitutionality of the defense expert being subpoenaed to testify by the prosecution. That court concluded, "any possible prejudice may be balanced, within limits not exceeded in this case, by the strong counterbalancing interest of the State in accurate fact-finding by its courts" (p. 1054). The *Edney* court ruled that the interests of the state in obtaining a just outcome superseded the defendant's rights. Although in the *Edney* case there was no requirement that the defense-retained evaluator's report or opinion be released to the prosecution once it was discovered, the prosecution was permitted to call the expert as a rebuttal witness. These different approaches to the issue (as exemplified by the opposing rulings by the *Alvarez* and *Edney* courts) have yet to be resolved by the Supreme Court. Thus, defense attorneys should clarify the rules in their particular jurisdiction with their retained expert.

FORENSIC MENTAL HEALTH CONCEPTS

In the context of the legal definitions of insanity discussed above, forensic mental health clinicians are retained to obtain, and provide to the legal system, clinical data and analysis concerning the defendant's functioning, mental status, and capacities at the time of the alleged offense. The evaluator will always need to perform a thorough clinical evaluation, although the impairments that the evaluation reveals might differ in their legal effect in different jurisdictions. The clinician's task is to integrate all the data into a forensic formulation, consistent with local laws, regarding the functioning and mental status of the defendant at the time of the alleged offense.

Diagnostic Categories

Regardless of their specific definitions of insanity, all jurisdictions require that a defendant asserting an insanity defense must show that he or she suffered from a severe mental impairment at the time of the alleged offense. Psychotic disorders (e.g., schizophrenia) and major affective disorders (e.g., major depression, bipolar disorder) are typically considered to meet this required level of severity. Although most successful insanity defenses involve one of these disorders (discussed below), this does not mean that other disorders will not qualify an individual for consideration for the insanity defense. Rather, in such instances, it is necessary to demonstrate how the disorder was of such severity as to impair the defendant's ability to rationally perceive or understand the circumstances surrounding the alleged offense or to make rational choices (e.g., Packer, 1983).

Although there is some disagreement about the value of a formal diagnosis, the dominant position in the field of forensic mental health is that inclusion of a diagnosis is often helpful. Specifically, diagnostic categories are useful in gathering, evaluating, and organizing data, and increase the credibility of the assessment (e.g., Melton et al., 2007; Packer, 2009). Nevertheless, it is important to recognize that the presence of a serious mental disorder does not provide a sufficient basis to draw conclusions about insanity. Thus, for example, one cannot assert that simply because a defendant suffered from paranoid schizophrenia his ability to control his behavior or appreciate wrongfulness was substantially impaired. Many people with these disorders are able to control their behaviors and appreciate wrongfulness much of the time. Rather, inclusion of the diagnosis provides a foundation for further discussion of whether the symptoms impaired the legally relevant *functional* capacities, related to the specific alleged offense, at the specific point in time at which the offense occurred.

Exclusionary Criteria

A caveat included in the ALI insanity standard, and also incorporated in many other jurisdictions, is that the terms "mental disease" or "defect" "do not include an abnormality manifested only by repeated criminal or otherwise antisocial conduct." This language is usually understood to exclude from the insanity defense individuals diagnosed with antisocial personality disorder, in the absence of other severe disorders. It is noted that more recently there has been a significant amount of research and theory around the concept of "psychopathy"—a term used to refer to individuals with core features of callousness, lack of remorse, and behavioral impulsivity, which often results in criminal behavior. This is a narrower concept than antisocial personality disorder, and Morse (2008), for example, has argued theoretically that these individuals should be considered to be mentally ill due to these impairments; however, he acknowledges that this is not the current legal interpretation. It is also noted that there was similar controversy over an earlier term—"sociopathy." The *Brawner* court (1972) disparagingly referred to the "week-end flip flop case" (*U.S. v. Brawner*, 1972, p. 978), in which a psychiatrist from St. Elizabeth's hospital testified on a Friday that a defendant with a sociopathic personality was not suffering from a mental disease, but then on Monday stated that the hospital had changed its policy and now considered sociopathy to constitute a mental disease for the purpose of the insanity defense. In addition to the legal system's reluctance to accept this argument, as Morse noted, most forensic evaluators do not accept it either. For instance, in a study of over 5,000 evaluations by Warren et al. (2004), identification of a primary diagnosis of personality disorder was negatively associated with a recommendation of insanity.

Defining the Cognitive Prong

All jurisdictions in the United States (except for New Hampshire, which uses the "product test") define the incapacities that mental disease or defect must have created at the time of the alleged offense in order to qualify for an insanity defense. These incapacities are categorized as the "cognitive" and "volitional" prongs of the definition of insanity. This section reviews the cognitive prong and how it has been conceptualized for purposes of guiding the forensic evaluation; the next section reviews the volitional prong.

The exact wording of the cognitive prong differs across states and the federal system, but the common element involves an assessment of the defendant's capacity to recognize that the alleged behavior was wrong. There has been much discussion, in the literature and case law, regarding the meaning of the term "wrongfulness," in terms of whether it refers to impairment of appreciation of legal wrongfulness (that is, did the defendant know it was against the law) or to moral wrongfulness (that is, contrary to society's moral standards). The discussion accompanying the development of the ALI standard indicate that wrongfulness was meant in the broader sense of including impairment in ability to appreciate that the act was morally wrong. This interpretation has been upheld in a number of cases (e.g., *Wade v. U.S.* (1970)). Even within M'Naghten jurisdictions, most courts have interpreted the standard to include impairment in appreciation of moral wrongfulness. For instance, in the case of *New York v. Schmidt* (1915), Judge Benjamin Cardozo eloquently argued that using the narrow definition of legal wrongfulness would "rob the rule of all relation to the mental health and true capacity of the criminal" (p. 949). Using a hypothetical example of a mother who kills her child based on the delusional belief that she has been so ordered by God ("deific decree"), he wrote that it would be "a mockery to say that, within the meaning of the statute, she knows that the act is wrong" (p. 949). An opposing point of view was adopted by the Supreme Court of Iowa in *State v. Hamann* (1979), which interpreted wrongfulness to refer to understanding that the act was legally wrong; however, the Iowa court recognized that it was in the minority, as most other jurisdictions had chosen to use the standard of moral wrongfulness.

In most cases, this distinction is not likely to be relevant; that is, most defendants will be able either to appreciate both the legal and moral wrongfulness of their behavior or will be impaired relative to both definitions. However, there will be some cases in which there is a distinction (e.g., the case of Andrea Yates, a woman who killed her children, in the context of delusional beliefs, and then called the police to inform them of what she had done; *Yates v. Texas*, 2005). Forensic evaluators, in such cases, should clearly articulate the defendant's particular symptoms and how they may have influenced reality testing and capacity to reason regarding both legal and moral wrongfulness.

Defining the Volitional Prong

As noted above, significant controversy has surrounded the volitional prong: that is, the criteria related to impairment in ability to control one's criminal behavior. Morse (1994) has articulated his opposition to the volitional prong on philosophical and conceptual grounds, arguing that self-described "compulsions" represent difficult choices between conflicting forces (that is, the pressure from the impulse to commit the wrongful act and the competing pressure to avoid the negative consequences of the act). The disorder that is often cited as best fitting the volitional prong is severe mania (Giorgi-Guarnieri et al., 2002; Vitacco & Packer, 2004). Some individuals with mania report phenomenological experiences of racing thoughts, and demonstrate accelerated speech, often with abrupt changes from one idea to another (*DSM-IV-TR*, American Psychiatric Association, 2000). Although manic states may also involve impairment in reality testing (e.g., grandiose thinking, such as believing that he or she has special abilities or distorted beliefs that he or she is extremely wealthy) that can impair the cognitive prong, in some cases there are few data to suggest such impairment. Rather, the most salient impairments relate to the individual's ability to reflect on his or her behavior and choose how to respond in a given situation, relevant to the volitional prong. However, manic conditions differ in degree of severity, and it is often difficult to assess retrospectively how manic the defendant was at the time of the alleged offense.

It is thus not surprising that the volitional prong is much less commonly used than the cognitive prong as the basis for an insanity defense. For instance, Warren et al. (2004), reviewing insanity evaluations in Virginia over a 10-year period, found that of all defendants recommended as meeting insanity criteria, only 9% were deemed to meet the volitional prong only (compared to 44% who met cognitive criteria only and 47% deemed to meet both the cognitive and volitional prongs). As noted above, only 16 states still maintain this element as part of their standard for the insanity defense. In those jurisdictions, the "representative criteria" outlined by Rogers (1987) represent the best attempt to date to operationalize the concept of volitional capacity. Rogers identified the following factors as relevant to such an assessment: (1) capacity to make choices, (2) capacity for delay, (3) regard for apprehension, (4) foreseeability and avoidability, and (5) result of a mental disorder.

The last criterion is not specific to the volitional prong but is incorporated into the threshold criterion of whether the individual suffered from a "diagnosable disorder of sufficient severity as to potentially impair volitional capacity" (Rogers, 1987, p. 848). If this question is answered affirmatively, then more detailed exploration of the other four criteria may be helpful in analyzing the data regarding the impact of the disorder on the defendant's volitional capacity, related to the specific alleged offense. Packer (2009), however, has cautioned against clinicians offering opinions that rely on the fourth criterion (foreseeability and avoidability) because this involves a judgment about the legal relevance of the loss of control. This criterion comes into play when a determination is made that the defendant did exhibit significant impairments in volitional control related to the specific acts that constitute the alleged offense, but could have taken steps earlier to minimize the risk of this occurring (e.g., by avoiding the situation). Such a determination goes considerably beyond the psychological and behavioral analysis of the defendant's functioning at the time of the alleged offense and, thus, the evaluator could provide some relevant information to the court but would not be in a position to opine whether this constituted a legally relevant volitional impairment.

The other three criteria are not necessarily independent of each other but, rather, represent different facets of behavior that can be attended to in the context of assessing the volitional prong. These are not meant to be quantified but, rather, are representative criteria, which direct inquiry and analysis.

Capacity to Make Choices

This factor focuses on the defendant's ability to have made a choice to engage in the alleged behavior. Did the defendant consider alternatives to the criminal behavior? What was the nature of the defendant's thought process regarding such alternatives? If no alternatives were considered, was there evidence that the defendant's ability to deliberate was impaired? Did the defendant make any attempts to resist acting on the impulse? Was the criminal act aimed at achieving a particular outcome?

Capacity for Delay

This factor focuses on the defendant's capacity or opportunity to stop the process of the alleged offense as it approached or occurred. Why did the defendant engage in the behavior at that specific time? Is there evidence that the defendant chose the circumstances and place for the offense? Was there evidence of planfulness or preparation?

Regard for Apprehension

This factor focuses on whether the defendant tried to avoid apprehension. The idea is that the defendant's efforts to avoid being caught would usually be inconsistent with the notion that the defendant was unable to regulate his or her behavior at the time of the alleged offense. (This dimension is also relevant to the cognitive prong, because it implies appreciation that the behavior was at least unlawful.) For instance, did the defendant engage in behaviors either prior to or subsequent to the act to avoid detection or apprehension?

These three factors are useful as guidelines for capacity to conform conduct at the time of the alleged offense. In different circumstances, any one of these factors may be more or less salient and relevant to the specific facts of the case. It is also important to note that these factors must be assessed in context. For example, a delusional defendant may attempt to avoid apprehension by the police because she believes that the police are allied with her "enemies" and are intent on killing her. Thus, just because she attempted to avoid apprehension does not indicate that her ability to control her behavior was unimpaired. Such a determination will require consideration of the totality of the circumstances of the particular case. As with all of the elements of the insanity defense, it is also important to assess these factors not only through the defendant's self-report but also through use of collateral information, such as witnesses' descriptions of the defendant's behavior and demeanor.

The Role of Intoxication

Voluntary intoxication due to alcohol or drugs is not considered a basis for an insanity defense in U.S. jurisdictions, based on statutes and case law. The rationale for this exclusion, as expressed in *Kane v. U.S.* (1968), is that the mental disorder that impairs the legally relevant abilities "must have been brought about by circumstances beyond the control of the actor" (p. 735). Thus, even if a defendant's mental state was so impaired that he or she would otherwise meet the cognitive or volitional prong, if this mental condition was a function of voluntary intoxication then it will not qualify for the insanity defense.

The situation becomes more complex when the impairment is not due to acute intoxication but rather to the cumulative effects of intoxication or a disorder initiated by substance use, but continuing past the period of intoxication. Most courts have recognized the concepts of *fixed insanity* (i.e., an individual who has developed long-term and permanent disabilities, such as dementia, as a result of a history of intoxication; e.g., *State v. Hartfield*, 1990) and *settled insanity* (a psychosis that was triggered by substance use but continues well beyond the point of intoxication, even if it is not permanent; e.g., *People v. Kelly*, 1973). The Colorado Supreme Court articulated a counter-argument in the case of *Bieber v. People* (1993). That court wrote that individuals are held accountable for all of the consequences, short term and long term, of ingesting substances that are known to cause impairment in reasoning, judgment, or behavior. The *Bieber* court is in the minority on this issue, as other courts have distinguished between acute intoxication and the long-term sequelae of substance use (e.g., *People v. Conrad*, 1986; *Porreca v. State*, 1981).

Based on these considerations, in combination with the high rate of substance abuse among individuals with mental illness, forensic evaluators need to pay careful attention to the issues of substance use among evaluees. The issues to be addressed include (1) whether there is evidence that the defendant was intoxicated at the time of the alleged offense; (2) data regarding the pattern of substance use around the time of the alleged offense; (3) data regarding the relationship between defendant's use of substances and experiences of symptoms of mental illness; (4) whether the alleged criminal behavior can be attributed primarily to the effects of acute intoxication; (5) whether the behavior can be attributed primarily to a preexisting psychotic disorder that was exacerbated by substance abuse; (6) whether the behavior can be attributed to a disorder that was induced by substance use but continued beyond the period of intoxication; (7) whether the impaired mental state was an atypical reaction to the use of alcohol or drugs (known as "idiosyncratic intoxication") or a reaction to the cessation of use (e.g., delirium tremens); and (8) if the defendant did have such a reaction, whether there were previous instances of impairment related to the alcohol or substance use. This last point is relevant because some courts have ruled that defendants' knowledge of their likely reaction to substance use can negate the insanity defense (e.g., *Commonwealth v. Berry*, 2010; *Kane v. U.S.*, 1968).

EMPIRICAL FOUNDATIONS AND LIMITS

Characteristics of Insanity Acquittees

Research on CR has been relatively limited; however, a number of studies have examined characteristics associated with a successful insanity defense. Melton et al. (2007) summarized the results of studies conducted between 1967 and 1985 in Michigan, New York, California, and Georgia. In those studies, the percentage of insanity acquittees with a diagnosis of a psychotic disorder ranged from 68% to 97%. These studies, however, did not compare insanity acquittees to defendants who were convicted. Boehnert (1989) compared 30 male defendants in Florida who were found not guilty by reason of insanity with 30 men, matched on crime, who were unsuccessful in the use of the insanity defense, having been found guilty and imprisoned. The insanity acquittees were more likely to have been previously found incompetent to stand trial (80% vs. 30%). Although formal diagnoses were not reported, Boehnert noted that 28 of the 30 insanity acquittees had a severe Axis I disorder, while 23 of the 30 convicted men appeared "less psychotic" (p. 38).

Packer (1987) compared 50 homicide defendants in Michigan (1980–1983) who were acquitted by reason of insanity (NGRI) with a randomly selected (within gender) group of homicide defendants evaluated for insanity but convicted. Consistent with Boehnert's data, the NGRI group was significantly more likely to have been found incompetent to stand trial (68%) than the guilty group (14%). Significant differences were also found with respect to previous conviction for a felony (NGRI 16% vs. 50% for the guilty group), prior psychiatric hospitalization (62% vs. 22%), and diagnosis of a psychotic disorder (82% vs. 14%).

Callahan et al. (1991) collected data across eight states and found that 84% of those acquitted by reason of insanity had received a diagnosis of "schizophrenia or another major mental illness (other psychotic or affective disorder)" (p. 336). Cochrane et al. (2001), using a large database of defendants (1,710 individuals) referred for evaluations of competency to stand trial and criminal responsibility in Federal courts, likewise found that those with a diagnosis of psychosis had the highest likelihood of being adjudicated NGRI. Reviewing a sample of defendants evaluated over a 10-year period in Virginia, Warren et al. (2004) found that 65% of defendants recommended as NGRI had received a diagnosis of psychosis (vs. only 26% of those recommended as sane). In that study, prior psychiatric hospitalization and *not* being under the influence of substances at the time of the offense were also significantly related to the recommendation for a finding of NGRI.

Although these studies do not represent a systematically thorough inquiry into the insanity defense in the United States, taken in aggregate they suggest that individuals who are found insane are likely to be diagnosed with a psychotic disorder. This does not mean that such a diagnosis is required for an insanity defense; however, it belies the public perception that the insanity defense is used capriciously.

Standards of Practice

In the most comprehensive study of forensic clinicians' opinions about standards of practice for CR evaluations, Borum and Grisso (1996) surveyed a group of forensic psychologists (53) and psychiatrists (43) who were either board certified or who had at least five years of forensic experience. Respondents were asked to rate the importance of a number of components in CR reports as essential, recommended, optional, or contraindicated. The authors considered 70% endorsement to be an indicator of consensus among forensic clinicians about the importance (or lack of importance) of various elements of CR reports. Table 3.1 shows those pieces of data considered to be essential.

Several other data elements were at least "recommended" by over 70% of each group but did not achieve the level of consensus required to be considered "essential." For instance, over 90% of each group recommended that a collateral description of the alleged offense (obtaining information from witnesses or others who encountered the defendant around the time of the alleged offense) be included. Given the significant emphasis in the literature on this element of forensic evaluations (e.g., Heilbrun et al., 2003), it is not clear why this component was

TABLE 3.1 ESSENTIAL TYPES OF DATA IN A CR REPORT

- Psychiatric history: information about the defendant's history of mental illness or mental retardation
- Mental health records: an indication that records were reviewed or at least attempts were made to procure such records
- Current mental status: this includes both a description of the defendant's mental state at the time of the interview (e.g., thought process, thought content, level of intellectual functioning) as well as a formal mental status exam
- Information obtained from the police report about the defendant's behavior at the time of arrest
- Statement about the defendant's use (presence or absence) of psychotropic medications at the time of the evaluation and in the period since the arrest
- Information about alcohol and/or substance abuse prior to the time of the alleged offense
- Defendant's disclosure: information obtained from the defendant about his or her behavior at the time of the alleged offense (or a statement that the examiner attempted to obtain the information but the defendant was unable or unwilling to provide such an account)

Reprinted by permission of Oxford University Press, Inc., Table 3.2 in Packer & Grisso (2011). Specialty Competencies in Forensic Psychology (source of data: Borum & Grisso, 1996).

not rated as essential by a higher percentage. Nevertheless, it is noteworthy that almost all respondents identified it as at least "recommended."

The Use of Structured Tools in CR Evaluations

Limited research has examined the use of standardized, structured assessment methods in CR evaluations. Some have focused on general psychological tests and others on "forensic assessment instruments," which collect data specific to the forensic questions involved in CR evaluations. In a survey by Borum and Grisso (1995), two thirds of forensic psychologists and psychiatrists deemed psychological testing as "recommended" or "essential" in CR evaluations (but only a small minority considered it essential). Respondents who reported using tests at least occasionally were also asked to identify specific instruments. Among the 50 psychologists who identified specific tests, 94% reported using the Minnesota Multiphasic Personality Inventory (MMPI-2) but only 32% reported use of the Rorschach. Borum and Grisso concluded that the results do not support a standard requiring psychological testing in every CR case, but do suggest that testing is the norm, rather than the exception, and that "psychologists ought to be held accountable to explain why they have *not* used psychological testing" (p. 471) in a CR case in which testing was not employed.

In a more recent study, Lally (2003) surveyed all psychologists who were listed as diplomates in Forensic Psychology by the American Board of Professional Psychology (ABPP). Sixty-four psychologists responded to the survey, which inquired about their opinion as to whether particular psychological tests and instruments were "unacceptable," "acceptable," or "recommended" for CR evaluations. The only two tests that more than half of the respondents "recommended" for CR evaluations were the MMPI-2 (Butcher et al., 2001) and the WAIS-III (Wechsler, 1997; this test was updated in 2008 to the WAIS-IV). Projective drawings, Thematic Apperception Test (TAT; Murray, 1943), and sentence completion were categorized as unacceptable (meaning that at least half the respondents rated it so), and the Rorschach was deemed to be equivocal.

Archer et al. (2006) surveyed a broader group of psychologists, including not only those board certified in Forensic Psychology by ABPP, but also members of the American Psychology-Law Society/ Division 41 of the American Psychological Association. They obtained 152 responses to a Web-based survey regarding the psychologists' use of a variety of instruments. This study did not focus on specific forensic issues (such as CR evaluations), but on the use of tests in adult forensic evaluations in general. They found that the MMPI-2 and the Personality Assessment Inventory (PAI; Morey, 1991) were the most commonly cited multi-scale inventories and the WAIS-III was the most commonly cited intelligence test. Among specialized tools related to malingering, the Structured Interview of Reported Symptoms (SIRS; now updated to SIRS-2; Rogers et al., 2010) and the Test of Memory Malingering (TOMM; Tombaugh, 1996) were the most frequently cited, followed by the Validity Indicator Profile (VIP; Frederick, 1997).

The results of these more recent surveys are similar to the results reported by Borum and Grisso in 1995. One interesting difference is the rate of acceptance and use of the PAI. This is likely attributable to the PAI being newer than the MMPI-2 and most of the respondents in the earlier study were likely trained prior to the development of the PAI (the average age in that study was 50 years old, with 17 years of forensic experience). Furthermore, only recently has there been more of a focus in the literature on the application of the PAI to forensic settings (Morey, 2007).

The only instrument that directly assesses criminal responsibility mentioned by respondents in any of these studies was the Rogers Criminal Responsibility Assessment Scales (RCRAS; Rogers, 1984). Nevertheless, in the Borum and Grisso survey, only 34% of respondents reported that they had used the RCRAS for CR evaluations. Lally (2003) found that 94% of the forensic diplomates in his survey rated the RCRAS as "acceptable" for CR evaluations. Thus, experienced forensic evaluators recognize use of this instrument as acceptable practice, but do not report using it frequently. It is important to note that the RCRAS comprises 30 data variables, which the examiner rates on 5- or 6-point scale. The variables in the RCRAS require clinical judgment in performing the rating, but there are no objective scoring criteria. The RCRAS then provides a decision-tree model for the ALI standard as well as the M'Naghten standard (there is also a model for "guilty but mentally ill"). The model for both insanity standards first requires a judgment on three variables: malingering, presence of an organic disorder, and presence of a major psychiatric disorder. If the defendant is deemed not to be malingering but to have either an organic or psychiatric disorder, the examiner is then directed to consider additional factors, dependent on the legal standard used in the relevant jurisdiction. It should be noted that the RCRAS does not produce a quantitative number, nor can it be used as a standalone measure of insanity (e.g., Melton et al., 2007; Packer, 2009); however, it can be used to guide an evaluator regarding which issues to address and provides a framework for integrating the data into an analysis relevant to the legal criteria.

THE EVALUATION
Data Collection

The main principle guiding data collection for CR evaluations is for forensic evaluators to obtain data that will allow them to develop a clinical formulation that can be applied to the relevant insanity standard. The primary issue is whether the defendant was suffering from a mental disorder severe enough to have affected reality testing or, depending on the jurisdiction, ability to exercise control over behavior specifically at the time of the alleged offense. Most of the elements of the history taking required for CR evaluations are similar to those used in standard clinical assessments, although with particular attention to evidence of patterns of substance use (especially close in time to the alleged offense) and criminal history, as these may be particularly relevant to the CR evaluation. As described in more detail by Packer (2009), the following elements are typically included in an insanity evaluation: family and developmental history, educational history, social history, employment history, mental health history, medical history (if relevant), religious history (in some cases, if relevant), substance use history, and criminal history.

Mental Status Examination

In addition to the history, a comprehensive and thorough mental status examination should be performed to assess the defendant's mental condition at the time of the evaluation. Observations of current symptoms often can provide information that will assist in developing hypotheses and eliciting data relevant to the reconstruction of the defendant's mental state at the time of the offense. It is important to keep in mind, however, that the defendant's

mental status at the time of the interview may differ from his or her condition at the time of the alleged offense, and care should be taken in extrapolating from one timeframe to the other.

Data Related to the Alleged Offense

The unique aspect of an insanity evaluation involves detailed information and inquiry regarding the specific alleged offense. As with all forensic evaluations, it is important for the evaluator to obtain information not only directly from the evaluee, but from third-party sources as well. Relevant information typically begins with the police report, although it may also be helpful to obtain copies of subsequent police investigations, including witness' statements, confessions made by the defendant to police, and grand jury minutes. Additional information is often necessary and can be obtained by interviewing individuals who have first-hand knowledge of the defendant's behavior and functioning during the time period relevant to the alleged offense, such as police officers, victims, witnesses, family, coworkers, and friends.

In obtaining the defendant's account, evaluators should ask very specific, probing questions about the defendant's thoughts, feelings, motivations, and behaviors. For instance, if a defendant reports having felt "paranoid" at the time, it is important for the evaluator to inquire more closely about what the defendant meant by that term, and to ask detailed questions regarding whom the defendant was afraid of or concerned about, whether particular individuals or a class of people were the focus of the concerns, what (specifically) the defendant thought this person or persons intended, how long the defendant maintained these beliefs, etc.

When asking about the defendant's reaction to the police, many examiners employ the "policeman at the elbow test." Often it is phrased as, "Would you have [committed the act] if a policeman had been nearby observing you?" The rationale behind this question is that it is believed to shed light on whether the individual had the ability to control or delay the behavior. Moreover, if the defendant responds in the negative, it suggests that he or she understood the illegal nature of the behavior. Despite the widespread use of this question, several caveats are in order. This is an abstract, hypothetical question requiring the defendant to consider what he or she *might* or *might not* have done at some earlier time. Even when responding honestly, defendants may not be able to accurately "postdict" what they would have done. In addition, as noted above, defendants are often in a different mental state at the time of the evaluation, thus making it even more difficult for them to evaluate how they *would have* reacted when their mental status was quite different. This type of question is more likely to be helpful if it elicits specific statements from the defendant about what he or she was thinking *at the time,* so evaluators should probe and inquire as necessary to elicit specific descriptions from the defendant of his or her thoughts and emotions. For instance, it is relevant to the analysis when a defendant reports that at the time he robbed a convenience store he noticed a police cruiser in the parking lot, was fearful of being noticed, and decided to delay robbing the store until he saw the officer drive away. This is a specific statement by the defendant of the content of his thought processes at the time, as opposed to a hypothetical extrapolation. This principle applies to other questions as well that may be posed to the defendant. More relevant than the defendant's current characterization of his or her motivation is the description provided of thoughts and emotions at the time of the alleged offense.

Response Style

In conjunction with attempting to corroborate the defendant's account with third-party information, forensic evaluators also assess the validity of the defendant's report. Criminal defendants may be motivated to engage in either positive impression management (attempting to minimize psychopathology because they do not want to be seen as mentally ill) or negative impression management (malingering or exaggerating symptoms in order to be found NGRI). It should be noted that the validity of clinical interviewing techniques alone for detecting malingering has not been established (e.g., Melton et al., 2007; Ogloff, 1990). Therefore, when there is reason to suspect that the defendant may be malingering, the standard of practice for forensic evaluators is to consider employing instruments specifically designed for this purpose. In cases in which there is a question of malingering of psychiatric (as opposed to cognitive) symptoms, the most widely used and accepted instrument is the SIRS (recently updated to SIRS-2; Rogers et al., 2010), although other screening measures are available. In addition, some standardized psychological tests

(such as the MMPI-2 and the PAI) also include validity scales, which provide an indication of the consistency and accuracy of the responses provided. Results from such instruments should *not* be considered the ultimate arbiter of malingering; rather, test results should be carefully weighed with the other available data in arriving at a conclusion about the likelihood that a defendant's presentation is exaggerated or feigned. Furthermore, it is important to understand that individuals who are genuinely mentally ill may nonetheless exaggerate; thus, evidence of exaggeration should not be used to categorically dismiss valid symptoms.

Among the most widely used and accepted tools for assessment of cognitive malingering (i.e., presentation of intellectual deficits or memory deficits) are the VIP (Frederick, 1997) and the TOMM (Tombaugh, 1996). Again, these instruments provide useful data but are not to be used and interpreted outside the context of a thorough clinical evaluation. Furthermore, the research literature has identified limitations for each of these instruments with particular populations. For instance, the recommended cutoff score for the TOMM appears to overestimate the rate of malingering in defendants with mental retardation/developmental disability (e.g., Hurley & Deal, 2006; Shandera et al., 2010) and elderly individuals with dementia (e.g., Teichner & Wagner, 2004), and the VIP is not recommended for individuals who are known to have mental retardation.

REPORT WRITING AND TESTIMONY

The most significant guiding principle in evaluating the quality of a CR report is that the reader should be able to fully understand the conclusions offered and the bases for those conclusions. Furthermore, standards of practice (e.g., Specialty Guidelines for Forensic Psychology, 2011) explicitly caution forensic evaluators not to omit data that are contrary to their own positions. Most importantly, the relationship between the data and conclusions should be explicitly articulated, including attributing all data used to the sources of that information. The reader should be able to follow the logic of the analysis tying the conclusions to the data. A useful schema for evaluating whether the bases for conclusions are adequately articulated was developed for competence to stand trial reports by Skeem and Golding (1998), and adapted to CR reports by Packer

(2009) (the schema characterizes the relationship between symptoms and impairment as either *none*, *implied*, *asserted*, or *articulated*). The standard of practice is that the report should clearly articulate the relationship between the data obtained (e.g., the clinical symptoms noted, the behaviors engaged in by the defendant at the time of the offense) and the specific functional impairment relevant to the legal standard for insanity. An example of an asserted relationship would be: "The defendant's ability to appreciate that her behavior was wrong was impaired by her delusional beliefs about her neighbor." This statement does not provide an adequate basis for the reader of the report to assess the validity of the examiner's conclusions regarding the specific insanity defense standard. By contrast, an articulated relationship between data and conclusions would be: "The defendant reported a delusional belief that her neighbor was part of a conspiracy to kill her. When he waved to her, she understood this gesture as a signal that he was about to shoot her, and she stabbed him in order to protect herself. Her ability to appreciate the wrongfulness of her conduct was substantially impaired by her paranoid thinking, which led her to believe that the stabbing was legally justified because she was acting in self-defense."

In addition, the report should identify the particular sources of information that were relied upon when citing specific data (e.g., "the arresting officer reported that the defendant was mumbling incoherently and could not understand what he was trying to tell him"). The evaluator should clearly convey whether his or her opinion relied heavily on the defendant's account, on collateral information, and/or on the results of testing. If the basis for an opinion is not adequately articulated in a report, it is advisable for the retaining attorney to contact the evaluator and request clarification.

"Ultimate Issue" Opinions

One of the most controversial questions in forensic mental health assessment is whether the evaluator should (in his or her report and/or testimony) offer an opinion on the ultimate legal issue being decided by the trier of fact. There are differences of opinion in the literature regarding the appropriateness and desirability of mental health experts offering such opinions (e.g., Rogers & Ewing, 2003; Tillbrook et al., 2003). In CR cases, this refers to addressing whether the defendant is sane or insane. Some commentators have distinguished ultimate opinions in CR ("the defendant was legally insane") from penultimate opinions ("the defendant was substantially impaired in his ability to appreciate the wrongfulness of his conduct"), noting that the latter are more firmly within the domain of mental health professionals (e.g., Slobogin, 2006). However, others have raised objections even to the penultimate form of opinion by mental health experts (e.g., Morse, 1978).

This controversy has not been settled and, in the previously cited study by Borum and Grisso (1996), no consensus was found among the psychiatrists and psychologists surveyed. In that study, only 20% of the respondents stated that ultimate issue opinions were contraindicated in criminal forensic reports (with 60% of the psychiatrists and 40% of the psychologists endorsing inclusion of such opinions). The Specialty Guidelines for Forensic Psychology (2011) neither endorse nor prohibit such opinions; the American Academy of Psychiatry and the Law (AAPL) *Ethics Guidelines for the Practice of Forensic Psychiatry* (American Academy of Psychiatry and the Law, 2005) is silent on the issue; and the AAPL Practice Guidelines for the insanity defense (Giorgi-Guarnieri et al., 2002) specifically state that "there is nothing to prevent its inclusion in a report" (p. S30). Furthermore, some jurisdictions require the forensic mental health evaluator to address the ultimate issue in CR cases, whereas others prohibit these types of conclusions (e.g., Federal Rules of Evidence, 704).

However, even in circumstances in which ultimate issue opinions are offered, such opinions should not exceed the data provided. Thus, if the data are not adequate to answer the question, the evaluator should refrain from offering an opinion on the ultimate legal issue of criminal responsibility, on the grounds of insufficient data. In such circumstances, the evaluator should explain in the report the basis for the inability to offer an opinion. This type of situation can occur, for example, when conflicting factual data cannot be resolved by a clinician, when the defendant is not able to provide a comprehensive account, or when the legal issues are unresolved (for example, when there is lack of clarity in the jurisdiction regarding the relevance of "settled" insanity).

Diminished Capacity

This chapter has focused on evaluations relative to the insanity defense; however, forensic evaluators may also be retained to conduct evaluations relative to the defense of *diminished capacity*. This defense applies only in cases of *specific intent* (e.g., assault and battery with intent to murder, first-degree murder) and focuses only on evidence of mental impairment related to the defendant's ability to form the required intent that is an element of the crime charged. Unlike the insanity defense, which is an affirmative defense, the prosecution has the burden of proving that the defendant had the requisite intent in order to convict. Furthermore, while insanity is a complete defense (that is, if found insane, the defendant is not guilty), diminished capacity is typically a partial defense, leading to conviction on a lesser included offense. In addition, most jurisdictions allow evidence of intoxication to be considered in assessing intent. The rationale is that since intent is an element of the crime, the prosecution must prove that the defendant had the requisite intent (see *U.S. v. Frisbee* (1985) and *U.S. v. Cameron* (1990) for a discussion of this issue; however, see also *Montana v. Egelhoff* (1996) for a case that upheld the exclusion of intoxication to negate intent).

The *diminished capacity* defense has been plagued by conceptual problems, as discussed by Morse (1979) and Clark (1999). Although it has sometimes been considered a "mini-insanity defense," this is not an accurate characterization. The distortions in reality testing that may impair a defendant's ability to appreciate the wrongfulness of his or her behavior can nevertheless leave intact the ability to form the requisite intent. For example, a defendant who believed that he was engaging in lawful self-defense when he shot a stranger because he thought this man was part of a conspiracy to kill him would nevertheless be considered to have formed the intent to kill (i.e., the defendant intended to kill the victim), albeit for irrational motives. As Clark (1999) and Morse (1979) have articulated, there are very few circumstances that would result in an inability or incapacity to form intent. Clark (1999) provided rare examples, including a defendant suffering from a seizure or a profoundly retarded individual who could not comprehend the concept of stealing; however, for the vast majority of cases, the presence of psychopathology or even severe intoxication is not likely to result in loss of *capacity* to engage in intentional behavior. The phenomenon of alcoholic "blackout," in which an individual has no memory for any events or behaviors that occurred during a period of extreme intoxication, represents a good example of this last point. Individuals who experience a blackout are not necessarily impaired in their ability to engage in intentional behavior during this period; indeed, one of the hallmarks of blackouts is that the individual does not remember engaging in behaviors that appeared quite organized and purposeful.

In other cases, the defendant may not assert *incapacity* to form intent, but rather claim that he or she *did not* form the requisite intent. California is one jurisdiction that has adopted this distinction formally (referred to as *diminished actuality*). California Penal Code Section 28 (2010) explicitly allows the admission of evidence about a defendant's mental state "solely on the issue of whether or not the accused *actually formed* a required specific intent, premeditated, deliberated, or harbored malice aforethought, when a specific intent crime is charged." When such a defense is raised, a forensic evaluator can describe the defendant's symptoms, mental status, and behaviors, and explain how these may or may not be consistent with a claim of failure to form the requisite intent. However, the evaluator would be overstepping professional boundaries by offering an opinion as to whether the defendant indeed formed the requisite intent (as this is a factual issue for the trier of fact to decide).

SUMMARY

The decision about which types of individuals to exclude from CR is a moral and legal decision, not a clinical one; however, forensic evaluators can play a crucial role by conducting a thorough and accurate examination of the defendant, focusing on those functional abilities relevant to the legal standard in the particular jurisdiction. When assessing the quality of a CR evaluation, the attorney should look for evidence that the evaluator conducted a comprehensive evaluation (see Packer, 2009); reviewed relevant records, including official accounts of the alleged offense; obtained, or attempted to obtain, information from third-party sources about the defendant; considered the defendant's response style; attempted to obtain a detailed account from the defendant of his or her thoughts, behaviors, and emotions at the time of the alleged offense; focused the inquiry on factors relevant to the specific legal standard in the jurisdiction (for instance, focused on the cognitive prong, rather than on ability to control behavior, in a M'Naghten jurisdiction); could provide a rationale for employment of particular tests or instruments; clearly articulated the relationship between the data obtained and conclusions offered, acknowledging the limitations of the data, when appropriate; and explained (when relevant) why alternative explanations were not deemed as credible.

REFERENCES

American Academy of Psychiatry and the Law. (2005). Ethics guidelines for the practice of forensic psychiatry. Retrieved January 6, 2011, from http://www.aapl.org/ethics.htm

American Bar Association. (1983). The insanity defense. *Mental Disability Law Reporter, 7,* 136–141.

American Bar Association. (1989). *Criminal justice mental health standards.* Washington, DC: Author.

American Law Institute. (1985). *Model penal code and annotations.* Washington, DC: Author.

American Psychiatric Association. (1983). APA statement on the insanity defense. *American Journal of Psychiatry, 140,* 681–688.

American Psychiatric Association. (2000). *Diagnostic and statistical manual of mental disorders* (4th ed., text rev.). Washington, DC: Author.

American Psychological Association. (1984). Text of position on insanity defense. *APA Monitor, 15,* 11.

Archer, R. P., Buffington-Vollum, J., Stredny R. V., & Handel, R. W. (2006). A survey of psychological test use patterns among forensic psychologists. *Journal of Personality Assessment, 87,* 85–95.

Bieber v. People, 856 P. 2d 811 (1993).

Boehnert, C. E. (1989). Characteristics of successful and unsuccessful insanity pleas. *Law and Human Behavior, 13,* 31–39.

Borum, R., & Grisso, T. (1995). Psychological test use in criminal forensic evaluations. *Professional Psychology: Research and Practice, 26,* 465–473.

Borum, R., & Grisso T. (1996). Establishing standards for criminal forensic reports: An empirical analysis. *Bulletin of the American Academy of Psychiatry and the Law, 24,* 297–317.

Butcher, J. N., Graham, J. R., Ben-Porath, Y. S., Tellegen, A., Dahlstrom, W. G., & Kaemmer, B. (2001). *Minnesota Multiphasic Personality Inventory–2 (MMPI-2): Manual for administration and scoring* (Rev. ed.). Minneapolis: University of Minnesota Press

California Penal Code, Section 28 (2010).

Callahan, L. A., Steadman, H. J., McGreevy, M. A., & Robbins, P. C. (1991). The volume and characteristics of insanity defense pleas: An eight-state study. *Bulletin of the American Academy of Psychiatry & the Law, 19,* 331–338.

Clark v. Arizona, 126 S. Ct. 2709 (2006).

Clark, C. R. (1999). Specific intent and diminished capacity. In A. K. Hess & I. B. Weiner (Eds.), *The handbook of forensic psychology* (2nd ed.). Hoboken, NJ: Wiley.

Cochrane, R. E., Grisso, T., & Frederick, R. I. (2001). The relationship between criminal charges, diagnoses, and psycholegal opinions among federal pretrial defendants. *Behavioral Sciences and the Law, 19,* 565–582.

Committee on the Revision of the Specialty Guidelines for Forensic Psychology (2011). Specialty guidelines for forensic psychology. Retrieved March 29, 2012, from http://www.ap-ls.org/aboutpsychlaw/SGFP_Final_Approved_2011.pdf Commonwealth v. Berry, 457 Mass. 602 (2010).

Commonwealth v. Stroyny, 760 N. E. 2d 1201 (2002).

Cowan v. Montana, 511 U. S. 1005 (1994).

Durham v. U. S., 214 F. 2d 862 (1954).

Fingarette, H. (1972). *The meaning of criminal insanity.* Los Angeles: University of California Press.

Frederick, R. (1997). *The Validity Indicator Profile.* Minneapolis, MN: National Computer Systems.

Frost, L. E., de Camara, R. L., & Earl, T. R. (2006). Training, certification, and regulation of forensic evaluators. *Journal of Forensic Psychology Practice, 6,* 77–91.

Giorgi-Guarnieri, D., Janofsky, J., Keram, E., Lawsky, S., Merideth, P., Mossman, D., Schwartz-Watts, D., Scott, C., Thompson, J., & Zonana, H. V. (2002). Practice guideline: Forensic psychiatric evaluation of defendants raising the insanity defense. *Journal of the American Academy of Psychiatry and the Law, 30,* S3–S40.

Heilbrun, K., Warren, J., & Picarello, K. (2003). Use of third party information in forensic assessment. In A. M. Goldstein (Ed.), *Forensic psychology: Emerging topics and expanding roles.* Hoboken, NJ: Wiley.

Hurley, K. E., & Deal, W. P. (2006). Assessment instruments measuring malingering used with individuals who have mental retardation: Potential problems and issues. *Mental Retardation, 44,* 112–119.

Insanity Defense Reform Act of 1984, 18 U.S.C. §17.

Kane v. U. S., 399 F.2d 730 (1968).

Lally, S. J. (2003). What tests are acceptable for use in forensic evaluations: A study of experts. *Professional Psychology; Research and Practice, 34,* 491–498.

Melton, G. B., Petrila, J., Poythress, N. G., & Slobogin, C. (2007). *Psychological evaluations for the courts: A handbook for mental health professionals and lawyers* (3rd ed.). New York: Guilford.

M'Naghten case, 8 English Reporter 718 (1843).

Montana v. Egelhoff, 518 U.S. 37 (1996).

Moran, R. (1981). *Knowing right from wrong: The insanity defense of Daniel McNaughten.* New York: The Free Press.

Morey, L. C. (1991). *Personality Assessment Inventory: Professional manual.* Odessa, FL: Psychological Assessment Resources.

Morey, L. C., Warner, M. B., & Hopwood, C. J. (2007). The Personality Assessment Inventory: Issues in legal and forensic settings. In A. M. Goldstein (Ed.), *Forensic psychology: Emerging topics and expanding roles.* Hoboken, NJ: Wiley.

Morse, S. J. (1978). Crazy behavior, morals, and science: An analysis of mental health law. *Southern California Law Review, 51,* 527–564.

Morse, S. J. (1979). Diminished capacity: A moral and legal conundrum. *International Journal of Law and Psychiatry, 2,* 271–298.

Morse, S. J. (1994). Causation, compulsion, and involuntariness. *Bulletin of the American Academy of Psychiatry and Law, 22,* 159–180.

Morse, S. J. (2008). Psychopathy and criminal responsibility. *Neuroethics, 1,* 205–212. DOI 10.1007/s12152-008-9021-9

Murray, H. A. (1943). *Thematic Apperception Test manual.* Cambridge, MA: Harvard University Press.

New York v. Schmidt, 110 N. E. 945 (1915).

Ogloff, J. R. P. (1990). The admissibility of expert testimony regarding malingering and deception. *Behavioral Sciences and the Law, 8,* 27–43.

Packer, I. K. (1983). Post-traumatic stress disorder and the insanity defense: A critical analysis. *Journal of Psychiatry & Law, 11,* 125–136.

Packer, I. K. (1987). Homicide and the insanity defense: A comparison of sane and insane murderers. *Behavioral Sciences and the Law, 5,* 25–35.

Packer, I. K. (2009). *Evaluation of criminal responsibility.* New York: Oxford University Press.

Packer, I. K., & Grisso, T. (2011). *Specialty competencies in forensic psychology.* New York: Oxford University Press.

People v. Conrad, 385 N. W. 2d 277 (1986).

People v. Kelly, 516 P. 2d 875 (1973).

Petrella, R. C., & Poythress, N. G. (1983). The quality of forensic evaluations: An interdisciplinary study. *Journal of Consulting and Clinical Psychology, 51,* 76–85.

Porreca v. State, 433 A 2d 1204 (1981).

Rogers, R. (1984). *Rogers Criminal Responsibility Assessment Scales (RCRAS) and test manual.* Odessa, FL: Psychological Assessment Resources.

Rogers, R. (1987). The APA position on the insanity defense: Empiricism vs. emotionalism. *American Psychologist, 42,* 840–848.

Rogers, R., & Ewing, C. P. (2003). The prohibition of ultimate opinions: A misguided enterprise. *Journal of Forensic Psychology Practice, 3,* 65–75.

Rogers, R., Sewell, K. W., & Gillard, N. D. (2010). *Structured Interview of Reported Symptoms* (2nd ed.). Lutz, FL: Psychological Assessment Resources.

Shandera, A. L., Berry, D. T. R., Clark, J. A., Schipper, L. J., Graue, L. O., & Harp, J. P. (2010). Detection of malingered mental retardation. *Psychological Assessment, 22,* 50–56.

Skeem, J., & Golding, S. (1998). Community examiners' evaluations of competence to stand trial: Common problems and suggestions for improvement. *Professional Psychology: Research and Practice, 29,* 357–367.

Slobogin, C. (2006). *Proving the unprovable: The role of law, science, and speculation in adjudicating culpability and dangerousness.* New York: Oxford.

State v. Hamann, 285 N. W. 2d 180 (1979).

State v. Hartfield, 388 S. E. 2d 802 (1990).

Teichner, G., & Wagner, M. T. (2004). The Test of Memory Malingering (TOMM): Normative data from cognitively intact, cognitively impaired, and elderly patients with dementia. *Archives of Clinical Neuropsychology, 19,* 455–464.

Tillbrook, C., Mumley, D., & Grisso, T. (2003). Avoiding expert opinions on the ultimate legal question: The case for integrity. *Journal of Forensic Psychology Practice, 3,* 77–87.

Tombaugh, T. N. (1996). *TOMM: The Test of Memory Malingering.* North Tonawanda, NY: Multi-Health Systems.

U. S. ex rel. Edney v. Smith, 425 F. Supp. 1038 (1976)

U. S. v. Alvarez, 519 F. 2d 1036 (1975)

U. S. v. Brawner, 471 F. 2d 969 (1972).

U. S. v. Cameron, 907 F. 2d 1051 (1990).

U. S. v. Frisbee, 623 F. supp. 1217 (1985).

Vitacco, M. J., & Packer, I. K. (2004). Mania and insanity: An analysis of legal standards and recommendations for clinical practice. *Journal of Forensic Psychology Practice, 4,* 83–95.

Wade v. U. S., 426 F. 2d 64 (1970).

Warren, J. I., Murrie, D. C., Chauhan, P., & Morris, J. (2004). Opinion formation in evaluating sanity at the time of the offense: An examination of 5175 pretrial evaluations. *Behavioral Sciences and the Law, 22,* 171–186.

Wechsler, D. (1997). *Wechsler Adult Intelligence Scale* (3rd ed.). San Antonio, TX: Psychological Corporation.

Yates v. Texas, 171 S. W. 3d 215 (2005).

4

Evaluation of Capacity to Waive Miranda Rights

ALAN M. GOLDSTEIN, NAOMI E. SEVIN GOLDSTEIN, AND HEATHER ZELLE

This chapter provides an overview of several topics related to a forensic mental health professional's evaluation of a defendant's capacity to have waived *Miranda* rights. The following information is intended to provide guidance for attorneys in their work with forensic mental health experts on this issue. The chapter begins with a brief review of the legal context in which the *Miranda* rights and waivers are situated and covers important case law related to the development of the *Miranda* rights. The legal requirements for making valid waivers are described, and the corresponding psycholegal terms are discussed. Empirical research is reviewed that is relevant to determining which factors may be related to *Miranda* comprehension deficits. The final portion of the chapter describes the steps involved in an evaluation of the capacity to waive *Miranda* rights, as well as key aspects of report writing and testimony by forensic mental health experts. Suggestions are provided for how attorneys may work effectively with experts in the context of a *Miranda* waiver evaluation.

LEGAL CONTEXT

The sociolegal purpose and history of the *Miranda* rights stem from the importance of confessions to police. Confessions have been shown to be critical for criminal prosecutions and are often considered to be the most persuasive form of evidence (Goldstein & Goldstein, 2010; Oberlander, Goldstein, & Goldstein, 2003). Because of the potential impact of confessions on the outcomes of cases, defense attorneys may, in some cases, challenge the admissibility of incriminating statements. They may question whether their clients had the requisite capacities to have validly waived *Miranda* rights during police questioning. Prosecuting attorneys may request an evaluation in order to obtain a rebuttal opinion.

There are few data to suggest how often attorneys challenge the admissibility of confessions based on *Miranda* waiver arguments. However, there is evidence that about 80% of suspects waive the rights to silence and counsel (Cassell & Hayman, 1996; Kassin et al., 2007; Leo, 1996) and that the majority of suspects offer self-incriminating statements when questioned by police (Pearse & Gudjonsson, 1997). Juveniles waive their rights even more frequently than adults (e.g., Ferguson & Douglas, 1970; Grisso & Pomicter, 1977; Viljoen, Klaver, & Roesch, 2005), and high rates are also estimated for individuals with mental retardation (e.g., Rogers & Shuman, 2005) and mental illness (e.g., Rogers, Harrison, Hazelwood, & Sewell, 2007).

The U.S. Supreme Court expressed concern about the inherently coercive nature of custodial interrogations in its *Miranda v. Arizona* (1966) opinion, in which the Court widened its focus beyond questions of voluntariness to issues of fairness. It reviewed a text commonly used to train police interrogators, *Criminal Interrogations and Confessions* (Inbau & Reid, 1962). The Court noted that many of the techniques used by trained interrogators put suspects at a disadvantage and might lead them to disregard their constitutionally guaranteed rights to silence and counsel. Ultimately, the Court determined that a balance could be struck between the need for interrogation and the protection of suspects' rights by implementing warnings that would remind and inform suspects of their rights.

In most jurisdictions, if a suspect is placed under arrest or made to believe that he or she is not free to leave police custody, the *Miranda* warnings must be read. Based upon precedent surrounding the waiver of Constitutional rights, a suspect must knowingly, intelligently, and voluntarily waive the rights in order for that waiver to be considered legally valid. Several factors have been identified by the courts that may raise questions about whether a waiver was knowing, intelligent, and voluntary and, therefore, whether it was valid. Many of the factors, such as intellectual impairment, neurological dysfunction, and developmental immaturity, can be assessed by forensic mental health professionals; therefore, attorneys may ask forensic mental health experts to evaluate clients' capacities to have waived their *Miranda* rights and, if needed, to provide written reports and testimony based on their findings.

Voluntariness presents specific considerations because it relates to the validity of the waiver of *Miranda* rights and the truthfulness of the confession itself. In *Crane v. Kentucky* (1986), the U.S. Supreme Court ruled that a defendant may challenge the credibility of a confession even if the waiver of rights and associated statement were ruled to be voluntary. As a result, forensic mental health professionals may evaluate voluntariness in three distinct forensic contexts: (1) evaluation of factors that may have affected the validity of a *Miranda* waiver, (2) evaluation of factors that may have contributed to a coerced confession, and (3) evaluation of the truthfulness of a confession (DeClue, 2005; Oberlander et al., 2003). This chapter focuses on the first context, the evaluation of a defendant's capacities to have provided a knowing, intelligent, and voluntary waiver of rights. The second context involves a legitimate area of psycholegal evaluation, but one for which no "best practice" standards have been established (Goldstein & Goldstein, 2010). The third context is an area in which no expert can legitimately offer an ultimate opinion (DeClue, 2005). At this time, there is no established standard of practice for evaluating the veracity of confessions.

Development of the Miranda Rights

Leading up to *Miranda v. Arizona*, several cases contributed to the development of limits of acceptable police practices during interrogations (*Brown v. Mississippi*, 1936; *Escobedo v. Illinois*, 1964; *Spano v. New York*, 1959). The decisions typically focused on the voluntariness of confessions and the impact of police practices on increasing the likelihood of false confessions. In *Escobedo*

v. Illinois (1964), a case decided the year before *Miranda v. Arizona*, the Court noted that no one informed Escobedo of his rights and stated, "No system of criminal justice can, or should, survive if it comes to depend for its continued effectiveness on the citizens' abdication through unawareness of their constitutional rights" (p. 490).

The Court's decision in *Miranda v. Arizona* (1966) reflected its growing concern about purposeful or inadvertent denials of suspects' constitutional rights to silence and legal counsel. The *Miranda* opinion addressed four separate cases with similar fact patterns in which the defendants were in police custody, interrogated, cut off from the outside world, in a police-dominated atmosphere, interrogated for several hours, and eventually confessed after initially denying involvement in the crimes. In its opinion, the Court did not attribute any misconduct to the interrogations, but stated, "The very fact of custodial interrogation exacts a heavy toll on individual liberty and trades on the weakness of individuals" (p. 455). The Court determined that safeguards were needed at the beginning of interrogations in order to ensure that suspects' statements were the product of free choice. The Court made it clear that the rights to silence and counsel can only be waived knowingly, intelligently, and voluntarily: "This Court has always set high standards of proof for the waiver of constitutional rights...and we reassert these standards as applied to in-custody interrogation" (*Miranda v. Arizona*, p. 475).

After the *Miranda* decision, several legal questions arose about the administration of the rights. The rights were further refined through hundreds of appeal court decisions and several U.S. Supreme Court opinions, some of which are reviewed here (see DeClue, 2005; Goldstein & Goldstein, 2010; and Melton, Petrila, Poythress, & Slobogin, 2007, for coverage of additional cases). The *Miranda* rights were applied to juveniles a year later (*In re Gault*, 1967). Ultimately, *Gault* extended all rights (except the right to trial by a jury of peers) afforded to adults in criminal courts to juveniles; therefore, the requirement that the *Miranda* warnings be administered prior to custodial interrogation also applied to youth.

In *Coyote v. United States* (1967), the Court held that the role of the court in *Miranda* waiver validity determinations involves "objectively determining whether in the circumstances of the case the words used were sufficient to convey the required warnings" (p. 308). In other words, the Court required that determinations be made based on consideration of the *totality of circumstances* related to the presentation of the rights, the interrogation process, and defendant-specific characteristics. A list of factors to be considered within the totality of circumstances approach is provided by *Coyote*, along with *Fare v. Michael C.* (which extended the approach to juveniles, 1979), *Johnson v. Zerbst* (1938), and *West v. United States* (1968). The list is illustrative rather than exhaustive and includes a suspect's age, intelligence, education, literacy and language ability, prior experience with the police and courts, mental health, conduct, maturity, and vulnerability, as well as the physical conditions of the interrogation, and whether the suspect was held incommunicado prior to interrogation (DeClue, 2005; Frumkin, 2000; Grisso, 1998a, 2003; Oberlander et al., 2003).

In 2000, the *Miranda* warnings were reaffirmed in *Dickerson v. United States*. The U.S. Congress attempted to supersede the *Miranda* decision through legislation in 1968 (18 U.S.C. 3501). The law instructed judges to consider the totality of circumstances to determine the voluntariness of confessions on a case-by-case basis. The law was upheld in federal court but largely ignored in federal cases because no successful challenges to *Miranda v. Arizona* had been made. In *Dickerson*, the U.S. Supreme Court clarified that *Miranda* was a constitutional decision of the Court and could not be superseded by an act of Congress. Nevertheless, some recent cases have narrowed the purview of *Miranda*.

In *Maryland v. Shatzer* (2010), the Court revisited the rule it created in *Edwards v. Arizona* (1981), which automatically extended a suspect's invocation of his *Miranda* right to counsel to subsequent interrogations. In *Shatzer*, the Court limited *Edwards'* reach so that the automatic extension of the right to counsel lasts for only 14 days after a suspect is released from custody. In *Berghuis v. Thompkins* (2010), the Court increased the threshold for invoking rights, requiring a suspect to make an unambiguous statement invoking the rights, while reducing the threshold for waiving rights, accepting implicit waivers demonstrated through a course of conduct indicating a waiver (e.g., replying "yes" or "no" to a few questions).

In contrast, the Court clarified the appropriate use of the *Miranda* warnings in a 2004 case. In *Missouri v. Seibert*, police interrogated the suspect without administering the warnings. After the suspect confessed and a brief time period had elapsed, the suspect was informed of his rights. He then waived his rights and confessed a second time. The Court made clear that the "question-first" method of interrogation was contrary to the purpose of *Miranda* and that warnings withheld until after interrogation and confession "will be ineffective in preparing the suspect for successive interrogation, close in time and similar in content" (p. 613).

Knowing

The Court indicated that *Miranda* waivers must be "knowing" and "intelligent" if they are to be considered valid; however, the Court did not define these terms, instead leaving individual states to develop their own definitions of these legal concepts. "Knowing" was defined by Melton and colleagues (2007) with a question: "did the defendant understand that he or she was waiving rights?" (p. 171).

Review of cases involving *Miranda* waivers led Grisso (2003) to conclude, "legal standards usually construe 'knowing' as a sum of the suspects' abilities to understand plus the manner in which they are informed [of their rights]" (p. 151). Other courts have noted the vulnerabilities of special populations, such as juveniles, individuals with mental illness, and individuals with neurological impairment, to misunderstanding the meaning of the warnings (e.g., *Fare v. Michael C.*, 1979; *People v. Lara*, 1967; *West v. United States*, 1968). Ultimately, regardless of how "knowing" is defined by a court, it is important to note, "no particular degree of capacity to understand these rights and entitlements necessarily satisfies the 'knowing' component" (Grisso, 2003, p. 151).

Intelligent

"Intelligent" has been distinguished from "knowing" by looking beyond a basic understanding of the meaning of the rights to whether a defendant was able to grasp the significance of the rights and potential consequences of waiving them (Goldstein & Goldstein, 2010; Grisso, 2003). Melton and colleagues (2007) defined "intelligent" in the form of a question: "was the waiver of rights the product of a rational reasoning process?" (p. 171).

Case law reveals variation in the depth of comprehension required. For example, in *People v. Williams* (1984) and *People v. Bernasco* (1990), the courts did not require understanding of the legal reasons underlying each right. The courts did not require suspects to understand the pros and cons of waiving the rights or the legal and strategic effects of waiving them. In contrast, other cases (e.g., *Coyote v. United States*, 1967; *People v. Baker*, 1973; *People v. Lara*, 1967) required more than basic, linguistic comprehension. These cases required a suspect to grasp the protected nature of a "right" and to recognize the advantages of obtaining legal representation before interrogation. The U.S. Supreme Court held in *Moran v. Burbine* (1986) that "the waiver must have been made with a full awareness of both the nature of the right being abandoned and the consequences of the decision to abandon it" (p. 421).

Voluntary

Drawing on its precedent concerning voluntary waivers, the Court in *Miranda* noted that courts need to consider factors surrounding the interrogation that may have "finally forced" a suspect to confess. In addition, evidence "that the accused was threatened, tricked, or cajoled into a waiver, will, of course, show that the defendant did not voluntarily waive his privilege" (p. 476). For forensic mental health professionals, the assessment of voluntariness focuses on the defendant's susceptibility to coercive police behaviors (DeClue, 2005; Goldstein & Goldstein, 2010; Oberlander et al., 2003). The focus on police behavior is demonstrated by *Colorado v. Connelly* (1986), a case in which the defendant argued that his confession was coerced by his command auditory hallucinations. The Court held that an individual is not deprived of his due process rights when there is no evidence of coercive police behavior causally related to a confession.

Typically, defendants are presumed to be capable of waiving their *Miranda* rights. Challenging the validity of a *Miranda* waiver requires that the defense file a pretrial motion requesting a suppression hearing, at which the prosecution bears the burden of proof to establish that the waiver was valid. In *Lego v. Twomey* (1972), the U.S. Supreme Court held that, to prove voluntariness, "the prosecution must prove at least by a preponderance of the evidence that the confession was voluntary. Of course, the States are free, pursuant to their own law, to adopt a higher standard" (p. 489). The burden of proof required varies across jurisdictions, with states like Colorado, Maine, Michigan, New York, Oklahoma, and Tennessee requiring a preponderance of evidence, whereas Massachusetts requires proof beyond a reasonable doubt.

If a waiver is ruled valid and a confession is entered into evidence, most jurisdictions allow the defense to challenge the veracity of the confession at trial (*Coyote v. United States*, 1967; *Jackson v. Denno*, 1964). As detailed in *Coyote v. United States*, "the jury should surely be told that if they find the defendant did not fully understand the meaning of the warning and advice given to him as stated in a confession, they may take that fact into consideration along with all the other facts and circumstances in determining the factual voluntariness of the statement" (p. 310) (see also *United States v. Inman*, 1965).

FORENSIC MENTAL HEALTH CONCEPTS

As with other areas of forensic mental health assessment, the legal requirements for waiving *Miranda* rights must be translated into psychological concepts (Grisso, 2003; Heilbrun, Grisso, & Goldstein, 2009). The legal standards of "knowing" and "intelligent" have been developed into psycholegal constructs that allow evaluators to better identify, operationalize, and assess these capacities. This section describes how "knowing" and "intelligent" are conceptualized, the difficulties of translating "voluntariness" into a psycholegal construct, and the courts' applications of the totality of circumstances approach.

The legal term "knowing" is translated into the forensic mental health field as "understanding." It has been defined as requiring a basic comprehension of the rights. This conceptualization frames several questions for the forensic mental health evaluator: If police delivered the rights in English, did the defendant understand English? If the police showed the defendant a written warning, could the defendant read? Did the defendant understand the vocabulary in the warning? Does the defendant understand the basic meaning of each of the warnings provided by police?

"Intelligent," on the other hand, is translated into "appreciation" in the forensic mental health field. Appreciation captures the core idea that more than simple comprehension is required for capacity to validly waive rights. Appreciation requires a defendant's abilities to apply the *Miranda* rights to his or her own interrogation, to weigh the pros and cons of waiving the rights, and to grasp the consequences of a waiver. A frequently used example that demonstrates the distinction between understanding and appreciation is the defendant who understands that he can have a lawyer, but does not appreciate why he would want a lawyer or the potential consequences of not having one (Frumkin & Garcia, 2003; Grisso, 1998b).

In contrast, voluntariness is not easily translated into a single psycholegal construct. As described above, waivers are not considered involuntary unless they were influenced by police coercion. The presence of physical or psychological coercion tends to be a factual matter for which there may or may not be supporting evidence, such as a DVD of the interrogation. Evaluators can, however, address issues related to an individual's susceptibility to police coercion based on characteristics like age, IQ level of suggestibility, arrest history, and education.

The totality of circumstances approach to considering factors relevant to *Miranda* waiver validity provides several relevant constructs that can be assessed by forensic mental health professionals during evaluations. The wide range of factors that fall within the totality of circumstances approach can be divided into those that relate to characteristics of the defendant and those that relate to the situational conditions of the interrogation (Grisso, 1998a).

Characteristics related to the defendant include age, intelligence, education, amount of prior contact with police officers, conduct, language ability, literacy, mental illness, and maturity (Frumkin, 2000; Goldstein et al., 2003; Grisso, 1998a; Oberlander & Goldstein, 2001). Relevant empirical research about such factors is reviewed in the next section of this chapter.

Situational conditions of interrogation include such information as whether the defendant was advised of the *Miranda* rights, number of times the warning was given, method of warning delivery, methods used to assess the suspect's comprehension of the warning, whether an interested adult was present during a juvenile's interrogation, length of the interrogation, timing of the confession, the physical arrangements of the interrogation, and police strategies used during interrogation (Grisso, 1981; Oberlander & Goldstein, 2001; Oberlander et al., 2003).

An evaluator must evaluate the degree to which a defendant understood the rights, appreciated the consequences of the waiver, and might have been susceptible to coercion (if coercion occurred). To determine a waiver invalid, no evidence of mental disease or defect is required, and the defense is not *required* to provide an explanation for deficits in understanding and appreciation of rights or

of susceptibility to police coercion. Nevertheless, the court usually wants an explanation of why the defendant would have had the identified deficits in these areas. Evaluators, therefore, should evaluate how defendant or situational characteristics contributed to the defendant's deficits in understanding and appreciation of rights and/or susceptibility to coercion.

Finally, it is important that evaluators distinguish between comprehension and susceptibility at the time of the interrogation rather than at the time of the evaluation. Typically, suppression hearings occur weeks, months, or years after the rights were waived and the confession was provided. Therefore, evaluators must consider intervening factors that may have improved comprehension and made a defendant less susceptible to coercion. Factors like cognitive-developmental maturation, increased knowledge of the nature and content of the warnings based on discussions with an attorney and fellow inmates, and improvement in mental health symptoms through the use of psychotropic medication can alleviate deficits that were present during the initial interrogation, at the time of the waiver. Alternatively, such factors as an intervening head injury or exacerbation of mental health symptoms from stress could intensify deficits, rendering them more extreme at the time of evaluation than at the time of interrogation.

EMPIRICAL FOUNDATIONS AND LIMITS

This section reviews the empirical literature that guides forensic evaluations of capacity to waive *Miranda* rights. First, research about the frequency of rights waivers is briefly reviewed. Then, we review research on the various factors that may play a role in a defendant's *Miranda* comprehension and susceptibility to police coercion; this information should inform what forensic mental health professionals choose to evaluate, what tools they use in their evaluations, and how they link totality of circumstances factors with deficits in *Miranda* comprehension. Available assessment tools for evaluating *Miranda* comprehension are also reviewed, including research on their frequency of use and acceptability in the field.

Frequency of Waivers

Research indicated that approximately 80% of suspects waive their rights (Cassell & Hayman, 1996; Leo,

1996) and that more than half of suspects in the United States and England offer self-incriminating statements (Pearse & Gudjonsson, 1997). Rates are higher, however, for vulnerable groups. Research has consistently demonstrated that juveniles waive their rights at particularly high rates. For example, two studies in the 1970s indicated that over 90% of juveniles waived their rights (Ferguson & Douglas, 1970; Grisso & Pomicter, 1977), and a recent study found similar results (Viljoen et al., 2005); of those youth who reported having been questioned by police, only 13% said that they asserted their right to silence, 10% said that they asked for a lawyer, and only one youth out of the 114 in the study reported having had a lawyer present during questioning.

There is little research about the prevalence of *Miranda* waivers by individuals with mental retardation, but a conservative estimate by Rogers and Shuman (2005) suggested that over 400,000 suspects per year waive their rights due to cognitive deficits. Research also reveals that suspects with mental retardation have greater difficulty comprehending *Miranda* rights (e.g., Clare & Gudjonsson, 1991; Everington & Fulero, 1999; O'Connell, Garmoe, & Goldstein, 2005), tend to produce socially desirable responses (Ellis & Luckasson, 1985), have heightened suggestibility (e.g., Everington & Fulero, 1999), and tend to comply with authority figures (Shaw & Budd, 1982).

Similarly, little research has examined waiver rates among individuals with mental illness, but a conservative estimate suggested that, each year, 695,000 defendants suffer from severe mental illness when making waiver decisions (Rogers, Harrison, Hazelwood, & Sewell, 2007). Moreover, research has indicated that such individuals have difficulty understanding the *Miranda* rights (Cooper & Zapf, 2008) and appreciating the reasons for exercising their rights (Rogers, Harrison, Hazelwood, et al., 2007).

Totality of Circumstances Factors

Research has demonstrated links between *Miranda* understanding and appreciation and several suspect-related and situation-related totality of circumstances factors. Age appears to be a critical factor in judges' decision making about rights waivers. It seems to be a primary factor in whether an individual chooses to invoke the rights, as youth waive their *Miranda* rights and offer confessions more often

than adults (e.g., Abramovitch, Peterson-Badali, & Rohan, 1995; Grisso & Pomicter, 1977; Viljoen et al., 2005). With regard to totality of circumstances and the ability to provide a valid waiver, research has demonstrated age to be one of the two most strongly and consistently linked factors (along with IQ; e.g., Abramovitch et al., 1995; Goldstein et al., 2003; Grisso, 1981).

Factors such as cognitive, psychosocial, and neurological development may also play a role in a defendant's ability to comprehend the *Miranda* rights. Waiving the *Miranda* rights requires abilities that involve abstract thought (e.g., understanding the concept of a right), interpreting the implications of waiving rights, and considering the benefits and costs of asserting or waiving rights. Research demonstrates that these abilities develop throughout adolescence (e.g., Baird & Fugelsang, 2004; Davies & Rose, 1999). In addition, the role of psychosocial maturity in judgments about legal decisions has been supported by research (e.g., Colwell et al., 2005; Grisso et al., 2003).

The second of the two primary totality of circumstances factors considered by judges is IQ; research has consistently demonstrated a strong relationship between IQ, particularly verbal IQ, and *Miranda* comprehension (e.g., Colwell et al., 2005; Goldstein et al., 2003; Grisso, 1981; Viljoen et al., 2005). Moreover, research suggests that age and IQ interact (e.g., Grisso, 1981; Viljoen & Roesch, 2005); therefore, the impact of both of these defendant characteristics should be examined when evaluating a defendant's *Miranda* comprehension (Frumkin & Garcia, 2003; Grisso, 1981).

Conflicting results have been found with regard to special education history (e.g., Grisso, 1981; Riggs Romaine, Zelle, Wolbransky, Zelechoski, & Goldstein, 2008), suggesting that special education history may be too general a variable (i.e., a variety of conditions and characteristics can result in placement in special education classes) to be considered a reliable factor. Instead, individual academic skills, such as reading and listening comprehension, may be better indicators of *Miranda* comprehension. Recent research suggested that academic achievement is a strong predictor of *Miranda* comprehension, in addition to age and IQ (Zelle et al., 2008).

Defendant background characteristics, such as gender, race/ethnicity, and socioeconomic status (SES), have also been studied. The majority of studies have found no gender differences in comprehension (e.g., Everington & Fulero, 1999; Goldstein et al., 2003; Grisso, 1981). No simple relationship has been demonstrated between race/ethnicity and *Miranda* comprehension, but some studies have found complex relationships when race/ethnicity is considered along with IQ, arrest history, and/or SES (e.g., Goldstein et al., 2003; Grisso, 1981). Some studies have examined SES independent of race/ethnicity, and although earlier research did not find a relationship between *Miranda* comprehension and SES (Grisso, 1981), a recent study found that youth from low-SES backgrounds were less likely to assert their rights (Viljoen et al., 2005).

Individuals with mental illness are more likely to come in contact with police than are those without mental illness (e.g., Schellenberg, Wasylenki, Webster, & Goering, 1992; Teplin, 2000). *Miranda* experts recommend considering the presence of mental illness at the time of interrogation when evaluating a defendant's capacity to have waived rights (Frumkin, 2000; Goldstein & Goldstein, 2010; Grisso, 2003), and U.S. courts have expressed concerns about waivers by individuals with mental illness (Viljoen & Roesch, 2005). *Miranda*-related comprehension errors made by adult inpatients are similar to those made by youth and individuals with cognitive deficits (e.g., Cooper & Zapf, 2008). Many studies have revealed relationships between psychosis and difficulty with *Miranda* comprehension (e.g., Cooper & Zapf, 2008; Viljoen, Roesch, & Zapf, 2002), although one study did not find a relationship (Rogers, Harrison, Hazelwood, et al., 2007). Fewer studies have examined the relationships between *Miranda* comprehension and depression, anxiety, attention-deficit/hyperactivity disorder, substance abuse, or personality disorders. The reader is referred to Goldstein and Goldstein (2010) for additional details about these relationships and other empirical research results.

Courts generally assume that prior experience with police provides exposure to the *Miranda* warnings, opportunities to learn the meaning of the warnings, and direct experiences about the consequences of a rights waiver (Grisso, 1981). Research, however, has suggested that a history of arrest does not have a direct relationship with *Miranda* comprehension (Cooper & Zapf, 2008; Goldstein et al., 2003; Grisso, 1981; Viljoen & Roesch, 2005).

Situational characteristics of an interrogation can also influence a suspect's ability to comprehend the rights or influence decisions about whether to assert or waive rights. Research has not examined a specific relationship between many of these characteristics and *Miranda* comprehension. Nonetheless, a well-informed evaluation should consider interrogation-related characteristics, as many of these have demonstrated effects on functioning and skills that are used to understand and appreciate *Miranda* rights and make an informed waiver decision. For example, the length of interrogation and sleep loss should be considered because research demonstrates that sleep loss decreases thinking and processing speeds (Dinges & Kribbs, 1991; McCarthy & Waters, 1997); reduces concentration (Williams, Lubin, & Goodnow, 1959); increases impulsivity in complex decision making (Harrison & Horne, 1996); and makes people less cautious (Hartley & Shirley, 1977).

Research has also suggested that parental presence may be detrimental in some cases, with many parents encouraging youth to waive their rights and comply with police requests (Grisso & Ring, 1979; Viljoen et al., 2005). In addition, wording of the *Miranda* warning may be taken into account, as the content of the warnings varies widely in length, complexity, and reading level across jurisdictions (Rogers, Hazelwood, Sewell, Shuman, et al., 2008). Nevertheless, there is little research on the effect of warning complexity on *Miranda* comprehension, with initial research showing mixed results (Cooper & Zapf, 2008; Messenheimer et al., 2009; Rogers, Harrison, Hazelwood, et al., 2007).

Miranda Comprehension and Decision Making

The relationship between *Miranda* comprehension and decision making about asserting or waiving rights also has empirical support. In a study with juveniles, the majority of youth (90%) who understood a waiver form said that they would not sign it, whereas 65% of youth who did not understand the form said that they would sign it (Abramovitch, Higgins-Biss, & Biss, 1993). In a vignette-based study of juvenile offenders, poorer *Miranda* comprehension was associated with a greater likelihood of a youth saying that he would falsely confess to police, although this effect diminished when age and IQ were taken into account (Goldstein et al., 2003). Viljoen and colleagues (2005) studied juvenile defendants' decisions during real interrogations and found that those youth who waived the right to counsel demonstrated poorer understanding and appreciation of the rights than did those who asserted their right. In fact, the abilities to understand and appreciate *Miranda* were better predictors of waiver decisions than were more general cognitive abilities.

Research on Assessment Methods

Several of the characteristics discussed above can be measured using established tools, such as intelligence tests, symptom inventories, and review of relevant written materials (e.g., school or police records). Assessment of *Miranda* waiver capacities is aided by the use of tools specifically developed to measure relevant psycholegal abilities. Grisso created one such set of instruments in the 1970s, the "Instruments for Assessing Understanding and Appreciation of *Miranda* Rights," a standardized research tool later adopted and published as a set of forensic assessment measures (Grisso, 1998b). The psychometric properties (i.e., reliability and validity) of the instruments were based on data collected in an extensive study that was completed in 1980 (Grisso, 1981). A revised version of the instruments was recently completed and published (Goldstein, Zelle, & Grisso, 2012). The instruments were updated for several reasons, consistent with instrument development recommendations (AERA/APA/NCME, 1999): (1) to simplify the language of the warnings to make them more applicable across jurisdictions; (2) to include a fifth statement, now common in most jurisdictions, that suspects may assert their rights at any time; (3) to update the instruments' norms; and (4) to update the psychometric properties and include additional psychometric analyses.

A second set of measures is currently under development by Rogers and colleagues. Their instruments consist of several scales created to assess *Miranda* comprehension and reasoning about waiver decisions. At the time this chapter was written, the scales were not yet published; for further details, see Rogers and colleagues (2009).

Grisso's instruments have gained widespread use and acceptance, as demonstrated by surveys of forensic evaluators. Lally (2003) surveyed American Board of Professional Psychology (ABPP) board-certified forensic psychologists about their use of different tools for forensic assessments of this issue and their opinions about those tools. With regard to *Miranda* evaluations, Grisso's instruments and the Wechsler Adult Intelligence Scale-III (Wechsler, 1997) were the only tools recommended by the majority of diplomates. Of American Psychological Association (APA)-member forensic psychologists who conduct *Miranda* evaluations, about 44% reported that they use Grisso's instruments in their evaluations (Ryba, Brodsky, & Shlosberg, 2007).

Research about relevant factors and assessment tools should inform evaluations by aiding experts in identifying and measuring relevant totality of circumstances factors. Such research and data can also help identify inappropriate interpretations that exceed the limits of the instruments or misuse research. They can inform evaluators about the conclusions that they may reach based on the limits of established knowledge in the field. It is important, for example, that an evaluator assess all relevant characteristics that may have affected an individual, based upon information about that person and informed by research. Similarly, a forensic mental health expert should use multiple instruments during an assessment, but the exact battery of instruments will depend on the specific questions and characteristics raised by each evaluation.

THE EVALUATION

This section briefly reviews the evaluation process. Full details on conducting assessments of the capacity to waive *Miranda* rights can be found in Goldstein and Goldstein (2010).

Thorough forensic evaluations require time and access to multiple sources of information (Heilbrun, Grisso, & Goldstein, 2009). Therefore, it is advisable that attorneys allow time to identify an appropriate expert, make fee arrangements, obtain relevant records, and schedule evaluation sessions. Experts also require time to interview third parties and prepare written reports. Scheduling evaluation sessions likely will involve the attorney, as he or she will inform facilities about the evaluation (if the defendant is in custody) and confirm the session with the client and the expert.

An evaluator should consider whether he or she has the background, experience, skills, training, and knowledge to accept a case. An expert should discuss the precise reasons for referral with the referring attorney, including the elements that led the attorney to seek the assessment (e.g., characteristics of the defendant's background and history, something about the defendant's presentation, and/ or something that the defendant said). An attorney also will have a role in the evaluation by answering questions about his or her interactions with the defendant, such as whether and to what extent the attorney has "educated" the client about the *Miranda* rights.

Sometimes, an attorney may wish to be present during an assessment. There is no consensus among forensic mental health experts about whether an attorney's presence is appropriate, and the issue has not been addressed by the U.S. Supreme Court (Shealy, Cramer, & Pirelli, 2008). If the attorney will be present during assessment, an evaluator should establish ground rules. An attorney may be asked (1) to refrain from participating in the evaluation and only observe the process; (2) to refrain from advising, interrupting, or speaking once the evaluation has begun; and (3) to sit behind the defendant to avoid distracting or unintentionally providing cues. Regardless of whether the attorney will be present during the assessment, it is recommended that the defense attorney be present at the start of the initial interview. If there is a question regarding the capacity of a defendant to have validly waived *Miranda* rights, the defendant may not be capable of providing informed consent for the evaluation, so the referring attorney should be present at the start of the first assessment session to provide authorization for the evaluation to continue if the defendant is unable to consent.

The difference between an attorney's role to defend the client and an evaluator's role to educate the trier of fact by providing a thorough, balanced, data-supported opinion can raise issues about the exchange of information. If specific information or records are required as an integral part of the evaluation, an expert should clearly inform an attorney about the reasons for needing the information. If an attorney feels that such information cannot be shared, an evaluator may be faced with deciding between proceeding with the assessment and withdrawing.

Best practice in forensic mental health assessment involves identifying, obtaining, and relying on third-party information because information obtained from a defendant must be corroborated (Goldstein, 2003, 2007; Grisso, 2003; Heilbrun, Warren, & Picarello, 2003; Melton, Petrila, Poythress, & Slobogin, 2007). Information to be obtained can be organized into several categories: the *Miranda* waiver form, school records, medical records, military records, mental health records,

arrest and jail records, and employment records. Evaluators should collect data to inform their opinions through defendant interviews, administration of traditional tests (e.g., IQ tests), administration of forensic assessment instruments, and administration of other forensically relevant instruments (e.g., tests of malingering and symptom exaggeration). Interviews of defendants typically take multiple sessions because of the amount of information to be obtained and the time needed to administer instruments. It is critical to note that a forensic opinion is only as good as the data upon which it is based. To reach a valid conclusion, an evaluator must have administered a battery of relevant, reliable, and valid tests; scored and rescored the tests to check for errors; obtained sufficient information from the defendant to form an opinion; reviewed relevant records; and interviewed relevant third parties. Consistency of reliable information within and across data is a cornerstone of forensic opinion (Heilbrun, Grisso, & Goldstein, 2009; Shapiro, 1991). Typically, some information will be inconsistent with the vast majority of data obtained. When atypical data are found but are considered insufficient to contradict the expert's conclusion, direct examination should allow the expert to explain why the information was treated as insufficient.

REPORT WRITING AND TESTIMONY

Whether an expert writes a report detailing the evaluation and the conclusions depends, in part, on whether the evaluator was appointed by the court or independently retained by counsel. If an expert was appointed by the court, the expert will typically submit a report to the judge, and the judge will make the report available to the defense and prosecution. On the other hand, if the expert was retained by counsel, the data collected and opinions reached are work product if and until the attorney requests a written report. Some jurisdictions allow an attorney to choose whether to submit a written report into evidence. Experts are ethically bound to report all relevant data if a report is requested, so an attorney's decision to request a written report should be based on the overall information and not just a selected portion of information. Beyond the primary purpose of providing information about a defendant's capacities to have provided a valid waiver, reports about *Miranda* capacities serve several other purposes. They can help (1) an expert to organize a large quantity of data into a logical summary, 2) structure direct examination and help attorneys provide for expert testimony, (3) serve as an outline for experts during direct examination and cross-examination to assist them with recalling details of their evaluation and reasoning, (4) provide a written report that can be reviewed by a judge after testimony has ended, and (5) fulfill some jurisdictions' requirements for a work product.

It is critical to recognize that several experts in the field hold that evaluators should not include ultimate-issue opinions in their reports or testimony because such opinions address legal questions and fall within the purview of the trier of fact (Grisso, 2003; Heilbrun, 2001; Heilbrun et al., 2008; Lipsitt, 2007; Melton et al., 2007; Weissman & DeBow, 2003). On the other hand, other respected authorities have argued that not providing an ultimate opinion deprives the trier of fact of valuable information and may confuse the issue (Braswell, 1987; Rogers & Ewing, 1989; Rogers & Shuman, 2005).

As with expert testimony on other issues, experts testifying about information relevant to the validity of Miranda waivers must be qualified as experts by the presiding judge, as outlined in the Federal Rules of Evidence (2001). Similarly, the subject matter to which experts can testify is limited to only those subjects that meet evidentiary standards. Judges may order Frye or Daubert hearings for experts testifying about the validity of Miranda waivers if new methodology is used in an assessment or unusual aspects of testimony will be offered.

In preparing for testimony, an attorney should carefully review the expert's curriculum vitae. Questions about the forensic mental health professional's specific expertise in evaluating Miranda waiver validity should be asked during voir dire. No one set of qualifications defines expertise in Miranda capacity, so there is no pro forma list of questions that can be used to qualify an expert. Nevertheless, the attorney should focus questions during voir dire on the expert's research, publications, teaching, professional continuing education presentations, forensic practice experience, and prior recognition as an expert in this specific area to establish the expert's credibility as an expert witness. In cases that involve a juvenile defendant, it may be helpful to highlight items on the expert's CV that involve assessing, treating, or conducting research on juveniles.

Direct examination testimony should cover the reason for referral, the methodology used to evaluate the defendant's capacity to waive Miranda rights, relevant research on the topic, and the opinions formed. Testimony also may address the reliability, validity, and relevance of the tests the expert used during the evaluation. Direct examination testimony also should address findings that are inconsistent with the final opinion. As such, the attorney and expert should prepare, in advance of cross-examination, questions that allow the expert to explain those data and findings. Cross-examination questions should not be problematic if the expert is familiar with the data, rescored all tests, reviewed the relevant research, and presented findings objectively during direct examination.

SUMMARY

Evaluations of Miranda waiver capacities, like other psycholegal evaluations, involve specialized knowledge of relevant legal and psychological concepts. This chapter provided a brief overview of important topics and described what are considered to be best practices for conducting evaluations of a defendant's capacity to have waived Miranda rights. The foregoing information is intended to help attorneys in working with forensic mental health experts by explaining the relevant steps in such evaluations, outlining what attorneys should expect to obtain from evaluations, and describing how evaluations and reports can help structure testimony when required. There is no one prescribed method for evaluations of the capacity to waive Miranda rights because each case presents a unique set of circumstances. Nonetheless, accepted practices in the field provide standards that should be applied in each case.

REFERENCES

Abramovitch, R., Higgins-Biss, K. L., & Biss, S. R. (1993). Young persons' comprehension of waivers in criminal proceedings. Canadian Journal of Criminology, 35, 309–322.

Abramovitch, R., Peterson-Badali, M., & Rohan, M. (1995). Young people's understanding and assertion of their rights to silence and legal counsel. Canadian Journal of Criminology, 37, 1–18.

American Educational Research Association, American Psychological Association, National Council on Measurement in Education (AERA/APA/NCME). (1999). Standards for educational and psychological *testing.* Washington, DC: American Educational Research Association.

Baird, A., & Fugelsang, J. (2004). The emergence of consequential thought: Evidence from neuroscience. *Philosophical Transactions of the Royal Society of London: Series B, 359,* 1797–1804.

Berghuis v. Thompkins, 130 S.Ct. 2250 (2010).

Braswell, A. L. (1987). Resurrection of the ultimate issue rule. *Cornell Law Review, 72,* 620–640.

Brown v. Mississippi, 297 U.S. 278 (1936).

Cassell, P. G., & Hayman, S. B. (1996). Police interrogation in the 1990s: An empirical study of the effects of *Miranda. UCLA Law Review, 43,* 840–931.

Clare, I., & Gudjonsson, G. H. (1991). Recall and understanding of the caution and rights in police detention among persons of average intellectual ability and persons with a mild mental handicap. *Issues in Criminological & Legal Psychology, 1,* 34–42.

Colorado v. Connelly, 479 U.S. 157 (1986).

Colwell, L. H., Cruise, K. R., Guy, L. S., McCoy, W. K., Fernandez, K., & Ross, H. H. (2005). The influence of psychosocial maturity on male juvenile offenders' comprehension and understanding of the *Miranda* warning. *Journal of the American Academy of Psychiatry and the Law, 33,* 444–454.

Cooper, V. G., & Zapf, P. A. (2008). Psychiatric patients' comprehension of *Miranda* rights. *Law and Human Behavior, 32,* 390–405.

Coyote v. United States, 380 F.2d 305 (10th Cir. 1967).

Crane v. Kentucky, 476 U.S. 683 (1986).

Davies, P. L., & Rose, J. D. (1999). Assessment of cognitive development in adolescents by means of neuropsychological tasks. *Developmental Neuropsychology, 15,* 227–248.

DeClue, G. (2005). *Interrogations and disputed confessions: A manual for forensic psychological practice.* Sarasota, FL: Professional Resource Press.

Dickerson v. United States, 530 U.S. 428 (2000).

Dinges, D. F., & Kribbs, N. B. (1991). Performing while sleepy: Effects of experimentally-induced sleepiness. In T. H. Monk (Ed.), *Sleep, sleepiness and performance* (pp. 97–128). Chichester, U.K.: Wiley.

Edwards v. Arizona, 451 U.S. 477 (1981).

Ellis, J., & Luckasson, R. A. (1985). Mentally retarded criminal defendants. *George Washington Law Review, 53,* 414–493.

Escobedo v. Illinois, 378 U.S. 478 (1964).

Everington, C., & Fulero, S. M. (1999). Competence to confess: Measuring understanding and suggestibility of defendants with mental retardation. *Mental Retardation, 37,* 212–220.

Fare v. Michael C., 442 U.S. 707 (1979).

Federal Rules of Evidence (2001). Washington, DC, U.S. Government Printing Office.

Ferguson, A. B., & Douglas, A. C. (1970). A study of juvenile waiver. *San Diego Law Review, 7,* 39–54.

Frumkin, I. B. (2000). Competency to waive *Miranda* rights: Clinical and legal issues. *Mental and Physical Disabilities Law Reporter, 24,* 326–331.

Frumkin, I. B., & Garcia, A. (2003). Psychological evaluations and competency to waive *Miranda* rights. *The Champion, 27,* 12–23.

Goldstein, A. M. (2003). Overview of forensic psychology. In I. B. Weiner (Series Ed.) & A. M. Goldstein (Vol. Ed.), *Handbook of Psychology: Vol. 11, Forensic psychology* (pp. 3–21). New York: Wiley.

Goldstein, A. M. (2007). Forensic psychology: Toward a standard of care. In A. M. Goldstein (Ed.), *Forensic psychology: Emerging topics and expanding roles* (pp. 3–44). Hoboken, NJ: Wiley.

Goldstein, A. M., & Goldstein, N. E. S. (2010). *Evaluating capacity to waive Miranda rights.* New York: Oxford University Press.

Goldstein, N. E., Condie, L. O., Kalbeitzer, R., Osman, D., & Geier, J. (2003). Juvenile offenders' *Miranda* rights comprehension and self-reported likelihood of offering false confessions. *Assessment, 10,* 359–369.

Goldstein, N. E. S., Zelle, H., & Grisso, T. (2012). *Miranda Rights Comprehension Instruments.* Sarasota, FL: Professional Resource Press.

Grisso, T. (1981). *Juveniles' waiver of rights: Legal and psychological competence* (Vol. 3). New York: Plenum.

Grisso, T. (1998a). *Forensic evaluation of juveniles.* Sarasota, FL: Professional Resource Press.

Grisso, T. (1998b). *Instruments for Assessing Understanding and Appreciation of Miranda Rights.* Sarasota, FL: Professional Resource Press.

Grisso, T. (2003). *Evaluating competencies: Forensic assessments and instruments* (2nd ed.). New York: Kluwer/Plenum.

Grisso, T., & Pomicter, C. (1977). Interrogation of juveniles: An empirical study of procedures, safeguards, and rights waivers. *Law and Human Behavior, 1,* 321–342.

Grisso, T., & Ring, M. (1979). Parents' attitudes toward juveniles' rights in interrogation. *Criminal Justice and Behavior, 6,* 211–226.

Grisso, T., Steinberg, L., Woolard, J., Cauffman, E., Scott, E., Graham, S., Lexcen, F., Reppucci, N. D., & Schwartz, R. (2003). Juveniles' competence to stand trial: A comparison of adolescents' and adults' capacities as trial defendants. *Law & Human Behavior, 27,* 333–363.

Harrison, Y., & Horne, J. A. (1996). Performance on a complex frontal lobe oriented task with "real-world" significance is impaired following sleep loss. *Journal of Sleep Research, 5,* 87.

Hartley, L., & Shirley, E. (1977). Sleep-loss, noise and decisions. *Ergonomics, 20,* 481–489.

Heilbrun, K. (2001). *Principles of forensic mental health assessment.* New York: Kluwer/Plenum.

Heilbrun, K., DeMatteo, D., Marczyk, G., & Goldstein, A. M. (2008). Standards of practice and care in forensic mental health assessment: Legal, professional, and principles-based considerations. *Psychology, Public Policy, and Law, 14*, 1–26.

Heilbrun, K., Grisso, T., & Goldstein, A. M. (2009). *Foundations of forensic mental health assessment.* New York: Oxford University Press.

Heilbrun, K., Warren, J., & Picarello, K. (2003). Third party information in forensic assessment. In I. B. Weiner (Series Ed.) & A. M. Goldstein (Vol. Ed.), *Handbook of Psychology: Vol. 11, Forensic psychology* (pp. 69–86). New York: Wiley.

In re Gault, 387 U.S. 1 (1967).

Inbau, F. E., & Reid, J. E. (1962). *Criminological investigations and confessions.* Baltimore: Williams & Wilkins.

Jackson v. Denno, 378 U.S. 368 (1964).

Johnson v. Zerbst, 304 U.S. 458 (1938).

Kassin, S. M., Leo, R. A., Meissner, C. A., Richman, K. D., Colwell, L. H., Leach, A. M., et al. (2007). Police interviewing and interrogation: A self-report survey of police practices and beliefs. *Law and Human Behavior, 31*, 381–400.

Lally, S. J. (2003). What tests are acceptable for use in forensic evaluations?: A survey of experts. *Professional Psychology—Research & Practice, 34*, 491–498.

Lego v. Twomey, 404 U.S. 477 (1972).

Leo, R. A. (1996). Inside the interrogation room. *Journal of Criminal Law and Criminology, 86*, 266–276.

Lipsitt, P. D. (2007). Ethics and forensic psychological practice. In A. M. Goldstein (Ed.), *Forensic psychology: Emerging topics and expanding roles* (pp. 171–189). Hoboken, NJ: Wiley.

Maryland v. Shatzer, 130 S.Ct. 1213 (2010).

McCarthy, M. E., & Waters, W. F. (1997). Decreased attentional responsivity during sleep deprivation: Orienting response latency, amplitude, and habituation. *Sleep: Journal of Sleep Research & Sleep Medicine, 20*, 115–123.

Melton, G. B., Petrila, J., Poythress, N. G., & Slobogin, C. (2007). *Psychological evaluations for the courts: A handbook for mental health professionals and lawyers* (3rd ed.). New York: Guilford.

Messenheimer, S., Riggs Romaine, C. L., Wolbransky, M., Zelle, H., Serico, J. M., Wrazien, L., & Goldstein, N. E. S. (2009, March). Readability and comprehension: A comparison of the two versions of the *Miranda* rights assessment instruments. Presented at the annual conference of the American Psychology-Law Society, San Antonio, TX.

Miranda v. Arizona, 384 U.S. 436 (1966).

Missouri v. Seibert, 542 U.S. 600 (2004).

Moran v. Burbine, 475 U.S. 412 (1986).

Oberlander, L. B., & Goldstein, N. E. (2001). A review and update in the practice of evaluating *Miranda* comprehension. *Behavioral Sciences and the Law, 19*, 453–471.

Oberlander, L. B., Goldstein, N. E., & Goldstein, A. M. (2003). Competence to confess. In I. B. Weiner (Series Ed.) & A. M. Goldstein (Vol. Ed.), *Handbook of Psychology: Vol. 11, Forensic psychology* (pp. 335–357). New York: Wiley.

O'Connell, M. J., Garmoe, W., & Goldstein, N. E. (2005). *Miranda* comprehension in adults with mental retardation and the effects of feedback style on suggestibility. *Law and Human Behavior, 29*, 359–369.

Pearse, J., & Gudjonsson, G. (1997). Police interviewing and legal representation: A field study. *Journal of Forensic Psychiatry & Psychology, 8*, 200–208.

People v. Baker, 440 N.E.2d 856 (Ill. 1973).

People v. Bernasco, 562 N.E.2d 958 (Ill. 1990).

People v. Lara, 432 P.2d 202 (Cal. 1967).

People v. Williams, 465 N.E.2d 327 (NY, 1984).

Riggs Romaine, C. L., Zelle, H., Wolbransky, M., Zelechoski, A. D., & Goldstein, N. E. S. (2008, August). Juveniles' *Miranda* rights comprehension: Comparing understanding in two states. Poster presented at the annual convention of the American Psychological Association, Boston, MA.

Rogers, R., & Ewing, C. P. (1989). Ultimate opinion proscriptions: A cosmetic fix and a plea for empiricism. *Law and Human Behavior, 13*, 357–374.

Rogers, R., Harrison, K. S., Hazelwood, L. L., & Sewell, K. W. (2007). Knowing and intelligent: A study of *Miranda* warnings in mentally disordered defendants. *Law and Human Behavior, 31*, 401–418.

Rogers, R., Harrison, K. S., Shuman, D. W., Sewell, K. W., & Hazelwood, L. L. (2007). An analysis of *Miranda* warnings and waivers: Comprehension and coverage. *Law and Human Behavior, 31*, 177–192.

Rogers, R., Hazelwood, L. L., Sewell, K. W., Blackwood, H. L., Rogstad, J. E., & Harrison, K. S. (2009). Development and initial validation of the Miranda Vocabulary Scale. *Law and Human Behavior, 33*, 381–392.

Rogers, R., Hazelwood, L. L., Sewell, K. W., Shuman, D. W., & Blackwood, H. L. (2008). The comprehensibility and content of juvenile *Miranda* warnings. *Psychology, Public Policy, and Law, 14*, 63–87.

Rogers, R., & Shuman, D. (2005). *Fundamentals of forensic practice: Mental health and criminal law.* New York: Springer.

Ryba, N. L., Brodsky, S. L., & Shlosberg A. (2007). Evaluations of capacity to waive *Miranda* rights: A survey of practitioners' use of the Grisso instruments. *Assessment, 14*, 300–309.

Schellenberg, E., Wasylenki, D., Webster, C. D., & Goering, P. (1992). A review of arrests among psychiatric patients. *International Journal of Law and Psychiatry, 15*, 251–264.

Shapiro, D. L. (1991). *Forensic psychological assessment: An integrative approach.* Needham Heights, MA: Allyn and Bacon.

Shaw, J. A., & Budd, E. C. (1982). Determinants of acquiescence and naysaying of mentally retarded persons. *American Journal of Mental Deficiency, 87*, 108–110.

Shealy, C., Cramer, R. J., & Pirielli, G. (2008). Third party presence during criminal forensic evaluations: Psychologists' opinions, attitudes, and practices. *Professional Psychology: Research and Practice, 39*, 561–569.

Spano v. New York, 360 U.S. 315 (1959).

Teplin, L. A. (2000). *Keeping the peace: Police discretion and mentally ill persons.* NIJ Journal. Washington, DC: National Institute of Justice.

United States v. Inman, 352 F.2d 954 (4th Cir. 1965).

Viljoen, J. L., Klaver, J., & Roesch, R. (2005). Legal decisions of preadolescent and adolescent defendants: Predictors of confessions, pleas, communication with attorneys, and appeals. *Law and Human Behavior, 29*, 253–277.

Viljoen, J. L., & Roesch, R. (2005). Competence to waive interrogation rights and adjudicative competence in adolescent defendants: Cognitive development, attorney contact, and psychological symptoms. *Law and Human Behavior, 29*, 723–742.

Viljoen, J. L., Roesch, R., & Zapf, P. A. (2002). An examination of the relationship between competency to stand trial, competency to waiver interrogation rights, and psychopathology. *Law and Human Behavior, 26*, 481–506.

Wechsler, D. (1997). *Manual for the Wechsler Adult Intelligence Scale—Third Edition.* San Antonio, TX: Psychological Corporation.

Weissman, H., & DeBow, D. (2003). Ethical principles and professional competencies. In I. B. Weiner (Series Ed.) & A. M. Goldstein (Vol. Ed.), *Handbook of psychology: Vol. 11, Forensic psychology* (pp. 33–53). New York: Wiley.

West v. United States, 399 F.2d 467 (5th Cir. 1968).

Williams, H. L., Lubin, A., & Goodnow, J. J. (1959). Impaired performance with acute sleep loss. *Psychological Monographs: General and Applied, 73*, 1–26.

Zelle, H., Riggs Romaine, C. L., Serico, J. M., Wolbransky, M., Osman, D. A., Taormina, S., Wrazien, L., & Goldstein, N. E. S. (2008, August). Adolescents' *Miranda* rights comprehension: The impact of verbal expressive abilities. Presented at the annual conference of the American Psychological Association, Boston, MA.

5

Evaluation of Sex Offenders

PHILIP H. WITT AND MARY ALICE CONROY

This chapter is designed to provide an introduction for judges and attorneys who are handling sex-offense cases. The chapter will provide an overview of the different legal contexts in which psychological evaluations of sex offenders are relevant or typically requested by attorneys or the court. Each different legal context makes different demands on the evaluator, focusing on varying legal issues. The chapter will review the best practices in conducting psychological evaluations in these various legal contexts, with the goal of allowing legal professionals to make informed use of these evaluations (see Witt & Conroy, 2009, for a more detailed review).

Sex offenses arouse strong emotions—disgust, anger, fear. For decades, these emotions have motivated specialized laws to manage sex offenders, with the goal of reducing sex-offense rates. Some laws are designed to monitor sex offenders closely, such as community-notification laws or parole supervision for life. Other laws aim to mandate treatment for sex offenders, such as statutorily enabled specialized treatment programs. Other laws have mixed purposes, such as sexually violent predator (SVP) civil commitment statutes, which are designed both to provide treatment and to remove from the community those offenders considered to be highest risk to the community.

The 1930s saw the first laws specifically targeted at sex offenders. These early laws, referred to as sexual psychopath laws (Melton, Petrila, Poythress, & Slobogin, 2007), were based on the assumption that sex offenders both were different than other criminals and were treatable. As Conroy summarizes (2003, p. 264):

> The first of the sexual psychopath laws, allowing for the commitment of sexual offenders to treatment facilities, was passed in Michigan

in 1937. Although that particular Michigan law was ultimately ruled unconstitutional by the Michigan Supreme Court, it was followed quickly by similar legislation in Illinois in 1938, and both California and Minnesota in 1939. The Minnesota statute soon reached the United States Supreme Court where it was deemed constitutional. The Justices ruled the Minnesota law sufficiently narrowed the class of persons to whom it could be applied to those who demonstrated "an utter lack of power to control their sexual impulses and.... are likely to attack or otherwise inflict injury, loss, pain, or other evil on the objects of their uncontrolled or uncontrollable desires." (*Minnesota ex rel Pearson*, 1940, p. 273)

By the 1960s, 26 states had enacted such laws (Lieb, Quinsey, & Berliner, 1998), which typically mandated some form of specialized treatment for all or a subset of convicted sex offenders. Although there was variability, many statutes allowed early release from incarceration or probation if the sex offender progressed well in treatment.

By the 1970s, however, the tide had turned. In many states, rehabilitation of sex offenders had been scrapped in favor of a punishment/just deserts model. Many of the early sexual psychopath laws were repealed during that period. Partially in the wake of Martinson's widely publicized criminology rehabilitation survey (Lipton, Martinson, & Wilks, 1975), the pithy conclusion of which was "nothing works," the pendulum swung away from correctional rehabilitation programs, including those for sex offenders. Only five states (Massachusetts, Nebraska, New Jersey, Oregon, and Washington) were applying these laws with any regularity in 1985 (Conroy, 2003).

The 1990s saw a return of sex offense-specific statutes. A series of heinous sex crimes—such as the rape and sexual mutilation of a young boy by Earl Shriner in Washington State in 1989 and the rape and murder of a young girl by Jesse Timmendequas in New Jersey in 1994—spurred a variety of sex-offender statutes, ranging from community notification to civil commitment to residency restrictions. Many of these laws remain in effect today and, if anything, are expanding in scope.

LEGAL CONTEXT

Attorneys commonly request psychological evaluations of sex offenders in five legal contexts (Fig. 5.1).

Pre-adjudication

Defense attorneys frequently send a sex-offender client for a psychological evaluation shortly after the client's arrest (or, in the case of individuals charged with possession of child pornography, after the execution of a search warrant). Both the defense attorney and the prosecution at this stage have an interest in the defendant's risk to the community—for bail consideration immediately and for plea negotiations eventually. Because these pre-adjudication evaluations frequently occur early in the legal process, often before indictment, discovery materials relating to the current offense may not yet be available to the psychologist if, as is typically the case in this context, the psychologist is retained by

the defense. Nonetheless, collateral information in regard to the defendant's history of behavior and mental health difficulties is important to any assessment of future behavior or risk (Conroy & Murrie, 2007; Witt & Conroy, 2009).

One question that no mental health expert can ever address is: Did the defendant commit the alleged sex offense (assuming that he denies having done so)? Despite popular belief to the contrary, no reliable profile exists that would allow an evaluator to determine whether an individual is or is not a sex offender. As we have noted elsewhere (Witt & Conroy, 2009):

> It is not uncommon for courts to ask if a particular defendant fits the test profile (e.g., the Minnesota Multiphasic Personality Inventory-2, or MMPI-2) of a sex offender. However, no MMPI-2 profile has been found to differentiate sex offenders from other offenders or from non-offenders. Taxonomies of sex offenders have been developed, as noted, but these taxonomies classify known sex offenders. They are not useful in determining whether an alleged sex offender has committed an offense. [citations omitted] (p. 43)

Moreover, the practice standards for the Association for the Treatment of Sexual Abusers (ATSA) are quite specific in this regard (ATSA, 2005, p. 11): "Evaluators do not offer conclusions

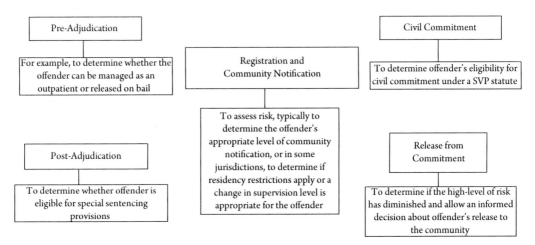

FIGURE 5.1 Legal contexts for sex offender evaluations. (Reprinted by permission of Oxford University Press, Inc., Figure 1 in Witt & Conroy (2009), Evaluation of Sexually Violent Predators.)

regarding whether an individual has or has not committed a specific act of sexual abuse."

Post-adjudication

There are three situations in which a post-adjudication (but pre-sentencing) evaluation is requested: voluntarily by the defense (usually with regard to mitigation at sentencing); by the defense as a condition of the plea agreement; and by the defense or prosecution in compliance with a specialized sentencing statute in the jurisdiction. The first two situations bear similarities, the focus in both typically being a risk assessment and treatment/management plan. The defendant's risk and a credible plan to manage this risk may have a bearing on the severity and circumstances of the sentence.

The third situation in which a post-adjudication (but pre-sentencing) psychological evaluation may be needed is in conformance with any special sentencing statutes in the jurisdiction. Although these statutes are jurisdiction-specific, so it is difficult to generalize regarding the specific psycholegal criteria to be addressed, many involve some form of mandated treatment. By way of example, in New Jersey the relevant statute (NJSA 2C:47-1) requires an assessment of four criteria regarding the defendant and his illegal sexual behavior: (a) repetitive; (b) compulsive; (c) amenable for treatment; and (d) willing to undergo treatment. Defendants found to meet all four criteria in New Jersey can be sentenced to a specialized treatment center to serve their sentence and will be subject to different parole procedures than in the general prison system.

Community-Notification Laws

In 1989, Jacob Wetterling, an 11-year-old boy, was kidnapped at gunpoint in Minnesota. Although Jacob was never found and no one was ever arrested, the assumption was that the kidnapper had sexual motives. In response, in 1994 Congress passed the Jacob Wetterling Act (42 U.S.C. §14071 (1994)), which required all states to develop sex-offender registries by 1997. Then, in 1994 in Hamilton, New Jersey, a convicted sex offender, Jesse Timmendequas, raped and murdered Megan Kanka, a seven-year-old girl. This offense spurred New Jersey to enact what would be referred to as Megan's Law, a sex-offender registration and notification law (NJSA § 2C:7-2). Over the following decade, all 50 states and the District of Columbia

have enacted some form of sex-offender registration and community-notification law.

These registration and community-notification laws have proved controversial. Due to the public perception that sex-offender recidivism rates are extremely high, these laws tend to be popular among the general public and, as a consequence, among legislators, who understandably respond to their constituents. However, the empirical evidence supporting these laws is quite weak. Relatively few studies have been conducted on the effectiveness of these laws, and those studies to date have so far been inconclusive. One study found at least some positive effect of community notification in Minnesota (e.g., Barnoski, 2005; Duwe & Donnay, 2008). However, studies in New York State (Sandler, Freeman, & Socia, 2008) and New Jersey (Zgoba et al., 2008) found no effect of that state's community-notification law in decreasing sex-offense rates. One study (Freeman, 2009) found that community-notification laws actually increased sex-offense rates.

In many states, the extent of community notification is risk-based. That is, some form of risk assessment of the sex offender takes place and those offenders seen as higher risk receive a broader extent of community notification. Many jurisdictions allow hearings at which the sex offender can challenge the proposed level of notification; typical grounds for such a challenge are that the risk assigned to the offender by the state is erroneously high. In other states, registration and community notification are statute-based; all offenders adjudicated of specific enumerated sex offenses must register and be subject to community notification of some form.

SVP Commitments

Beginning in the early 1990s, a number of states began to put into effect what have been termed SVP civil commitment statutes. Conroy (2003) provides a summary of the origins of these laws:

> In 1989, a particularly horrendous sex crime in the state of Washington breathed new life into the idea of committing violent sex offenders to treatment programs. Earl Shriner, a repeat violent sex offender who had failed to qualify for commitment under Washington's sexual psychopath law, raped a 7-year-old boy, cut off his penis, and left him to die. Although the child amazingly survived,

broad publicity regarding the brutality of the crime incensed the community and motivated legislators to immediate action. The next year, the state of Washington enacted the first of a second generation of sex offender civil commitment statutes. Known as Sexually Violent Predator (SVP) statutes [Washington Laws § 71.09.020, 1990], these laws differed from the earlier version in that commitment was generally applied *after* a term of incarceration was completed rather than in lieu of imprisonment. They also differed from more traditional civil commitment statutes in that neither a serious mental illness nor a recent dangerous act was a prerequisite. (p. 465)

As of 2008, 20 states had enacted SVP civil commitment statutes and as of 2006, the total number of persons being held in the United States as SVP commitments was roughly 2,600, with another 1,000 being detained pending commitment hearings (Deming, 2008). Witt and Conroy (2009, pp. 9–10) note four differences between SVP commitments and traditional civil commitments:

- SVP commitments do not require a recent overt act; traditional civil commitments usually do.
- SVP commitments occur after an offender has served his term of incarceration, whereas traditional civil commitments typically occur instead of incarceration.
- SVP commitments do not usually involve diagnoses of psychosis, whereas traditional civil commitments frequently involve such diagnoses.
- SVP civil commitments require assessment of *volitional impairment*, whereas traditional civil commitments do not.

Although there is some variability among jurisdictions, most SVP commitment statutes share similarities. A typical statute is that of Kansas, first enacted in 1994 and later revised in 2003 (*Kansas Stat. Ann.* § 59-29a02, 2003), which defines an SVP as "any person who has been convicted of or charged with a sexually violent offense and he suffers from a mental abnormality or personality disorder which makes the person likely to engage in the predatory acts of sexual violence." Some states allow as a foundation for SVP commitment

a finding of juvenile delinquency, incompetency, or not guilty by reason of insanity.

The Kansas statute is one of the better known given that two major court decisions have focused on that statute, and after the Kansas statute was upheld in the U.S. Supreme Court, a number of other states have adopted the wording of the Kansas statute, or some similar wording. The first major court challenge to the Kansas statute was *Kansas v. Hendricks* (1997). Kansas had filed its first SVP petition against Hendricks, who had previously molested 10 children, and at the conclusion of his 10 years in prison, Kansas applied to civilly commit him under its SVP statute. Hendricks challenged the law, and his challenge eventually reached the U.S. Supreme Court, which upheld the constitutionality of the Kansas SVP statute in a 5–4 decision. The Court concluded that use of the term "mental abnormality" did not violate due-process requirements and that in Hendricks's case, his diagnosis of pedophilia was sufficient to qualify him as SVP, given that it impaired his volitional control and made him likely to commit future sex offenses (p. 360). The Court also concluded that SVP commitments did not constitute double jeopardy.

A further challenge to the Kansas statute occurred in *Kansas v. Crane* (2002), which addressed perhaps the most controversial of all aspect of SVP commitments: the requirement that volitional impairment be found. There is considerable debate in both the psychological and legal community as to whether volitional impairment can be reliably assessed. In any case, the U.S. Supreme Court in *Crane* interpreted its previous holding in *Hendricks* and found "no requirement of complete or total lack of control," but only that "serious" impairment of control be present (p. 413).

The eventual result of this line of cases is that currently, an SVP civil commitment requires three interrelated elements (once an individual has committed any qualifying sex offense): mental abnormality, volitional impairment, and risk of future sex offense.

Release from Commitment

SVP commitments are performed upon those sex offenders who are seen as highest risk to re-offend, based upon the presence of a mental disorder (discussed in more detail below). As of 2006, there were 2,600 persons committed under SVP statutes in the U.S. (Deming, 2008). The figures regarding conditional release of SVP commitment cases are difficult to interpret, because different states have different language defining release and the circumstances of release vary among the states. For example, some states release SVP-committed persons only to supervised halfway houses, not full release. However, most studies indicate that the percentage of individuals granted release—other than for legal reasons—is small, with some states reporting no releases at all (Deming, 2008).

Determining when to release from commitment an individual who presumably was previously found to be at high risk is a difficult challenge. The individual's static risk factors (generally elements from the person's history, such as number of prior offenses or violations of release conditions) are unlikely to change. Therefore, the individual's release is likely to hinge on changes in dynamic risk factors (those that do change over time and may potentially be affected by interventions—for example, antisocial attitudes or response to mental health treatment). However, it is these dynamic risk factors that are the least researched. Those instruments that have been developed to assess dynamic risk variables, such as the Acute-2007 and the Stable-2007 (Hanson, Harris, Scott, & Helmus, 2007), have been developed on a community-dwelling population. Moreover, relatively few civilly committed sex offenders have been conditionally released to the community, so this issue remains mostly a hypothetical one (Arkowitz, Shale, & Carabello, 2008). One final difficulty is the lack of recidivism research to date on those relatively few sex offenders who have been released from civil commitment (Arkowitz et al., 2008). Jackson (2008) recommends that evaluators performing pre-release evaluations on SVP commitment cases first have an understanding of the offender's historical background, obtained from reviewing the file, and then examine the offender's chronological functioning while both incarcerated and committed (Jackson, 2008).

FORENSIC MENTAL HEALTH CONCEPTS

Pre-adjudication and post-adjudication evaluations vary greatly among the various jurisdictions. Although the relevant issues are similar—including risk assessment, risk management, treatment planning, and assessment of any specialized psycholegal issues within that jurisdiction—no cross-jurisdictional literature exists on definitions for

these constructs. This is not surprising since there is such variability among jurisdictions.

By way of example, in New Jersey, after a finding of guilty for any of a number of enumerated sex offenses, either by plea or trial, an individual is evaluated at a specialized facility to determine whether his illegal sexual behavior was part of a *repetitive* and *compulsive* course of conduct (N.J.S.A. 2C:47-1). Over time, case law has articulated jurisdiction-specific definitions of these two psycholegal constructs: repetitive and compulsive. Compulsive, perhaps the more ambiguous of the two constructs, has been defined in New Jersey as simply its common dictionary definition: an irresistible urge to perform some irrational act (*NJ v. Howard*, 1986). Although one can see an underlying concern here with volitional impairment, the definition is specific to both this jurisdiction and this statute.

One area in which broad, cross-jurisdictional definitions have been developed for psycholegal constructs is in SVP civil commitments. U.S. Supreme Court decisions have led to relative uniformity of statutes across jurisdictions, and common definitions have emerged regarding the three constructs of mental abnormality, volitional impairment, and risk. Nonetheless, case law may further define these concepts specific to a particular jurisdiction.

Mental Abnormality

All jurisdictions require some finding of mental abnormality as a foundation for an SVP civil commitment. The majority of the states use the following wording: "A congenital or acquired condition affecting the emotional or volitional capacity that predisposes the person to the commission of criminal sexual acts to a degree constituting the person a menace to the health and safety of others" (Sreenivasan, Weinberger, & Garrick, 2003, p. 473). As we have noted elsewhere (Witt & Conroy, 2009), mental disorders are broadly defined. There is no language requiring a specific diagnosis from the primary text used for diagnoses of mental illness, the *Diagnostic and Statistical Manual* (DSM) and, in fact, no requirement that a DSM diagnosis be given at all. In practice, however, DSM diagnoses are routinely given, and considerable testimony (and cross-examination) in SVP cases can focus on whether the offender meets specific criteria for a given diagnosis and whether that diagnosis qualifies him for an SVP commitment.

Ambiguity here results from the fact that mental health professionals and legal professionals use the term "mental disorder" in different ways. Witt and Conroy (2009) summarize these distinctions:

> For decades, forensic mental health experts have struggled with the gap between mental health constructs and legal constructs. Although the two types of constructs may sound similar, there is frequently not a direct correspondence between them. The two families of constructs have different roots and traditions. Legal constructs are the result of legislative statutes and interpreted case law. Mental health constructs flow from medical and behavioral science theory and validating research. (p. 19)

In traditional civil commitment cases, the individual being committed invariably has some serious Axis I diagnosis, such as psychosis. In fact, some traditional civil commitment statutes require that the individual's mental disorder be such that it damages the individual's perception of reality, thus implying a psychotic diagnosis. In SVP civil commitment cases, a psychotic diagnosis is the exception rather than the rule. Perhaps one of the more hotly debated aspects of SVP civil commitments is the fact that Axis II diagnoses (i.e., personality disorders) qualify in most jurisdictions as sufficient mental disorder for an SVP commitment.

One personality disorder meriting special mention is psychopathy. This is not a construct formally included in the DSM but is often an issue of considerable importance in sex-offender evaluations. Individuals said to have many psychopathic traits are generally described as significantly antisocial in lifestyle, interpersonally manipulative, lacking in empathy for others, failing to take responsibility for their behavior, and often devoid of remorse/guilt for their actions. Psychopathy is not equivalent to the DSM diagnosis of Antisocial Personality Disorder; rather, it is a much more aberrant constellation of personality traits, demonstrated by less than 25% of the incarcerated male population (Cunningham & Reidy, 1998). High scores on psychopathic traits have been linked to high risk for sexual and violent re-offending (Witt & Conroy, 2009); however, a low score on psychopathic traits (commonly seen among exclusive child molesters) simply indicates this is one high-risk factor the individual does not have and does not by itself establish low risk.

A few studies have examined what actually occurs in practice. That is, what are the diagnoses of individuals already committed under SVP statutes? Janus and Walbek (2000) examined the characteristics of 116 civil commitment sex-offender cases in Minnesota. They found that the most frequent diagnoses were substance abuse (52%); paraphilia (46%); personality disorder (18%); and both paraphilia and personality disorder (18%). Becker, Stinson, Tromp, and Messer (2003) examined an SVP sample in Arizona and found as the most common diagnoses paraphilia (56%) and personality disorder (77%). Looking more closely, Becker et al. found that 42% had a diagnosis of personality disorder not otherwise specified and 40% a diagnosis of antisocial personality disorder. Jackson and Richards (2007) examined SVP civil commitment cases in Washington State and found paraphilia (98%), personality disorder and paraphilia (86%), substance abuse (56%), and personality disorder but no paraphilia (50%). The most common personality disorder in the Washington State sample was antisocial personality disorder (41%). Similarly, Levenson (2004) found that, in Florida, about half of those referred for SVP commitment had a diagnosis of antisocial personality disorder, and Miller, Amenta, and Conroy (2005) reported that, in Texas, antisocial personality disorder was among the most common diagnoses in an SVP population. One can see that in practice evaluators include combinations of Axis I diagnoses, especially paraphilias, and Axis II diagnoses, particularly antisocial personality disorder.

One final caveat regarding the use of DSM diagnoses should be made. The DSM was never developed to be statutorily binding, but rather as a guide to assist clinical judgment. The volume itself specially states its listed criteria are meant:

> to serve as guidelines to be informed by clinical judgment and not meant to be used in cookbook fashion. For example, the exercise of clinical judgment may justify giving a certain diagnosis to an individual even if the clinical presentation falls short of meeting the full criteria for the diagnosis as long as the symptoms that are present are persistent and severe. On the other hand, lack of familiarity with DSM-IV or excessive flexibility and idiosyncratic application of DSM-IV criteria or conventions substantially reduces its utility

as a common language for communication. (APA, 2000, p. xxxii)

In addition, it should be noted that with the coming advent of the DSM-V, some diagnostic formulations and criteria might change significantly.

Volitional Impairment

As we have noted (Witt & Conroy, 2009, p. 29): "It is not sufficient for a sex offender to suffer a mental abnormality; to be eligible for an SVP commitment, the mental abnormality must cause volitional impairment as well." In *Kansas v. Hendricks* (1997), the U.S. Supreme Court noted 17 times that the mental abnormality must be directly linked to the offender's difficulty controlling dangerous sexual behavior (Miller et al., 2005). However, considerable debate exists among mental health and legal professionals as to whether there is any reliable way to assess and reach an opinion on volitional impairment. The argument can be best captured by a widely quoted statement from the American Psychiatric Association: "The line between an irresistible impulse and an impulse not resisted is probably no sharper than that between twilight and dusk" (1983, p. 685).

Court decisions on this issue vary to some extent among jurisdictions; however, a recent survey by Mercado, Schopp, and Bornstein (2005) of court decisions regarding volitional impairment from Minnesota illustrates how the courts are beginning to articulate the issues. Mercado and colleagues found Minnesota courts to reach the following conclusions regarding volitional impairment (summarized from Witt & Conroy, 2009, p. 32):

- There is no requirement that the impairment be caused by an extreme cognitive deficit resulting from conditions such as severe mental retardation, dementia, or organic brain damage, or psychosis, sleepwalking, or seizures.
- Planning or grooming behavior does not necessarily preclude a finding of volitional impairment, although such planning may be one factor potentially inconsistent with such a finding.
- Lack of insight into one's behavior may indicate volitional impairment.
- Loss of control may be situational, may result from removal of external controls, and need not be present all the time.

- Repeated illegal conduct despite consequences or fear of capture is relevant.
- Loss of control may be present even when the offender has entrenched beliefs that justify sexual contact with minors.

Mercado, Bornstein, and Schopp (2006) reviewed both case law and a relatively limited sample of empirical studies and concluded that four broad factors were considered by either legal or mental health professionals as relevant in determining volitional impairment: (a) verbalized lack of control, (b) history of sex crimes, (c) lack of offense planning, and (d) substance use.

Rogers and Shuman (2005) suggested four areas of consideration:

- *Lack of capacity for meaningful choice:* Does the behavior have a driven quality? In contrast, was there evidence of rational consideration of choices?
- *Disregard for personal consequences:* Does the behavior occur or continue despite negative personal consequences for the individual? In contrast, is there evidence of attempts to minimize the consequences of the actions, such as avoiding detection?
- *Incapacity for delay:* Was the individual unable to delay sexual gratification for lengthy periods? Is there evidence of opportunity-seeking behavior by the individual?
- *Chronicity:* Is the behavior enduring? Does the behavior consist of more than a few isolated instances?

Risk

The widely-relied-on Kansas statute defines risk as "likely to engage in repeated acts of sexual violence" (*Kansas Stat. Ann.* § 59-29a01, 2003). The words "likely to engage" immediately suggest a forward-looking, future-oriented assessment. Sreenivasan and colleagues (2003, pp. 477–478) review and discuss the various definitions of "likely" used in different jurisdictions, noting that some jurisdictions used more specific phrases, such as "highly likely," "probable," and "highly probable." Whether these supposedly clarifying phrases truly clarify anything is another question entirely. Missouri is perhaps the exception in this regard, given that case law in that jurisdiction uses the term "more likely than not," perhaps the clearest articulation of what is meant in any jurisdiction by the term "likely." A review of relevant case law and practice in a specific jurisdiction can shed light on what standard is being used for likelihood or propensity.

Risk assessment with regard to sexual violence has undergone considerable development in recent years. A few decades ago, most evaluators relied on unstructured clinical judgment to assess risk of future violence, sexual or otherwise. However, as Witt and Conroy note (2009, p. 38): "Decades of research on risk assessment accuracy have found that such unstructured clinical judgments are poor predictors of future dangerousness. In a widely cited work, Monahan (1981) reviewed early research on this area and found that, using unstructured clinical judgment, mental health professionals were wrong more often than right in predicting future violence in institutionalized mental patients."

Over the past decade, risk assessments have relied heavily on structured, empirically supported methods, using some structured instruments that have an empirical relationship to future sex offending (Miller et al., 2005). There are at present three variants of this approach (Doren, 2002; Witt & Conroy, 2009):

- Research-guided/structured professional judgment: This approach uses risk and protective factors gathered from the empirical literature to create a coherent structured guide. The guide developers conduct a rational analysis of the professional literature to select these various factors for inclusion in the instrument. Factors are included that have empirical support in the literature; however, no mathematical formula is used to weight them. An example of such a structured, empirically guided tool would be the Sexual Violence Risk-20 (SVR-20) (Boer, Hart, Kropp, & Webster, 1997).
- Actuarial: Actuarial instruments are those whose risk and (rarely) protective factors are selected on the basis of each of the criteria being empirically associated with future sex-offense recidivism. These factors are frequently a result of pooling a number of studies together in what is referred to as a meta-analysis. In addition, each item is given a weight and assigned a specific number of points. The rules for scoring and combining the criteria are mechanical, involving adding up points without deviation from the scoring manual. A prime example of an actuarial scale is the Static-99 (Hanson & Thornton, 1999, 2000).
- Clinically adjusted actuarial: This approach involves using an actuarial instrument as the foundation, but then considering other factors that may be unique to the individual. Witt and Conroy (2009) note that anecdotal evidence indicates that this approach is widely used by SVP evaluators.

Much debate currently exists in the field between those who believe that pure actuarial assessment should be preserved with no adjustments (Quinsey, Harris, Rice, & Cormier, 2006) and those who see advantages to considering more dynamic factors and issues specific to an individual (Knight & Thornton, 2007; Olver, Wong, Nicholaichuk, & Gordon, 2007; Wong, Olver, & Stockdale, 2009). However, there appears to be general agreement that factors simply based on an examiner's intuition that are not supported in research (e.g., denial of an offense, meeting the goals of a treatment program) should not be applied (e.g., Hanson & Morton-Bourgon, 2009).

EMPIRICAL FOUNDATIONS AND LIMITS
Adult Males

To date, the vast majority of the empirical research regarding sex offenders has been conducted on adult male offenders, beginning in the 1970s and 1980s (e.g., Abel et al., 1987; Groth, Burgess, & Holstrom, 1977). Witt and Conroy (2009) and Conroy and Witt (in press) provide an extensive review of research regarding risk factors and instruments available.

It may be appropriate to dispel misconceptions regarding the base rate of sexual-offending recidivism. Although the general public may believe that the recidivism rate among sex offenders is 100%, or very close to that figure, the reality is quite different. U.S. Bureau of Justice statistics from 1992, 1993, and 1995 indicate no higher rate of parole violations than among other offenders (Heilbrun, Nezu, Keeney, Chung, & Wasserman, 1998). Estimates based on reconvictions over a five-year period—admittedly, a conservative figure—indicate an overall recidivism rate for sex offenders of 13.4%, with an 18.9% rate for rapists and 12.7% for child molesters (Hanson & Bussiere, 1998).

Juvenile Males

Juvenile male offenders constitute a significant proportion of sex offenders, with some estimates indicating that 20% of sex offenses are committed by juveniles (Snyder, 2006). Although there are similarities between juvenile male offenders and adult male offenders, there are differences as well. Some research indicates that juvenile sex offenses are a better predictor of general criminal recidivism than of sex-offense recidivism (McCann & Lussier, 2008) and that, similarly, the primary factor associated with many juvenile sex offenses is a broadly delinquent, antisocial attitude, as opposed to specific sexual deviance (Hiscox, Witt, & Haran, 2007; Rasmussen, 1999). Recent years have seen the development of risk-assessment scales specific to juvenile sex offenders, such as two actuarial scales, the JSOAP-II (Prentky & Righthand, 2003) and the Juvenile Risk Assessment Scale (JRAS; Hiscox et al., 2007), and one structured professional judgment scale, the Estimate of Risk of Adolescent Sex Offender Recidivism (ERASOR; Worling, & Curwen, 2001). Although there is some moderate support in the literature for these scales, they lack the broad research base of the adult instruments.

Juvenile sex-offense recidivism rates vary widely, depending upon the criteria used for recidivism and the length of follow-up time, but generally studies find that juvenile male sex-offense recidivism rates are lower than those of adult male offenders. In one meta-analysis of over 1,000 juveniles, Alexander (1999) found that sex-offense recidivism ranged from roughly 5% to 21%, with follow-up periods of between one and more than five years. The recidivism rates varied by offense type: 5.8% for "rapists," 2.1% for "child molesters," and 7.5% for an "unspecified group." However, particularly in the sex-offender arena, there is always the real probability of underreporting of offenses. Therefore, it is impossible to provide a verifiable base rate for this population.

Adult Females

Relatively little research has been done on adult female offenders for two reasons. First, relative to adult male offenders, adult female offenders are relatively rare, constituting at most 2% of the sex-offender population. Therefore, it is difficult to obtain a large enough sample of female offenders to study. Second, recidivism rates among those groups of female offenders that have been studied are quite low, resulting in an even smaller population of recidivists, typically not enough to allow broad distinctions to be made between recidivists and non-recidivists among this population (Sandler & Freeman, 2007, 2009; Vandiver & Walker, 2002). In a recent study with perhaps the largest sample of adult female sex offenders, Sandler and Freeman (2009) found that only 1.8% of the sample was arrested on a new sex offense charge after five years, much lower than comparable studies of male sex offenders.

Child Pornography

In recent years, an increasing number of men have been arrested and prosecuted for downloading or trading child pornography over the Internet. This group of sex offenders has been studied over only perhaps the past five years. One study found that men arrested for child pornography actually had more deviant sexual-interest patterns (as measured by penile plethysmography) than men who had molested children (Seto, Cantor, & Blanchard, 2006)—a finding that understandably raises concerns regarding the potential risk of this population. Moreover, two studies within the Federal Bureau of Prisons raise the possibility that child pornography offenders have many previously undisclosed contact victims (Bourke & Hernandez, 2009; Hernandez, 2000).

The key question is: How likely is it that such an individual will commit a future sex offense, either contact or child pornography-related? To answer this question, one needs forward-looking studies, and given the relative newness of this offense type, such studies have begun to be conducted only within the past few years. However, results so far suggest that those individuals whose only criminal offense has been viewing or trading child pornography over the Internet have extremely low rates of recidivism for either further child pornography offenses or for contact sex offenses; those child pornography offenders with the highest recidivism rates are those with significant prior criminal histories (Eke & Seto, 2008; Endrass et al., 2009; Seto & Eke, 2005). Consistent with these results is a recent study by Li, Lee, and Prentky (2010), which found that among child pornography offenders, there was a linear positive relationship between likelihood of an actual contact sex offense and degree of generally conduct-disordered/antisocial behavior.

THE EVALUATION

Almost all sex-offender evaluations start with a file review. In SVP commitment cases, such files are typically voluminous, given that the individual presumably has a long, documented history to reach consideration for an SVP commitment. Consequently, it is important that the evaluator review collateral information—such as witness and victim accounts and other investigation materials. However, in pre-adjudication cases, the file may be thinner. Nonetheless, evaluators need to review as much historical record as can be assembled, as well as interview other collateral sources, such as individuals who might provide information about the offender's functioning—possibly including treatment providers, spouse, or work and housing supervisors (if incarcerated or committed).

The evaluation itself should be clearly related to the issue at hand. The evaluation should avoid speculation. The court is most likely not interested in tenuous hypotheses about the possible causes of an individual's sex offending, unless those hypotheses can be tied to supported evidence and related logically to the issue at hand. Moreover, the evaluation should keep in mind the psycholegal question that needs to be addressed; this psycholegal question should guide the entire evaluation process. For example, an SVP evaluation should clearly focus on the elements of mental disorder, volitional impairment, and risk. An evaluation for a state's community-notification statute should focus on whatever criteria are relevant in that jurisdiction (e.g., risk as defined in that jurisdiction).

REPORT WRITING AND TESTIMONY

The best reports do not contain extraneous and irrelevant information, but rather focus upon what information is germane to the psycholegal question being addressed. The report should document the sources of information, the observations drawn from those sources of information, and the inferences and conclusions that result, drawing clear, logical connections between the underlying observations and resulting conclusions (Conroy, 2006; Grisso, 2010; Melton et al., 2007; Witt & Conroy, 2009). There should be a separation between the observations and inferences, and then a clear

articulation of the reasoning that led to the conclusions. The report should be tailored to any jurisdictional requirements. Each jurisdiction conducts matters differently, and the report should be written with these jurisdictional considerations in mind. The retaining attorney or agency is frequently the best source of information about any jurisdictional requirements or expectations.

In an effort to determine empirically what constitutes a well-written (or poorly written) forensic report, Grisso (2010) recently conducted a study of 62 forensic reports that had been rejected after being submitted as practice samples by candidates for forensic diplomate status by the American Board of Forensic Psychology. Grisso examined the reasons why these forensic reports were found unacceptable, and he classified these reasons into five broad areas in which deficiencies were found: introductory materials, organization and style, data reporting, psychological test reporting, and interpretations and opinions. Witt (2010) then took the 10 most common reasons that Grisso found as grounds for failure and constructed a checklist for writing acceptable forensic reports. These 10 checklist elements are:

1. Forensic referral question stated clearly
2. Report organized coherently
3. Jargon eliminated
4. Only data relevant to forensic opinion included
5. Observations separated from inferences
6. Multiple sources of data considered, if possible
7. Psychological tests used appropriately
8. Alternate hypotheses considered
9. Opinions supported by data
10. Connections between data and opinions made clear

Although not all inclusive, Grisso's study and the checklist elements derived from that study can give the legal professional an overview of what constitutes a good forensic psychological report.

In particular, information in the report should be relevant to the legal issue at hand. Including extraneous information in the report can serve to distract the reader from the primary issue. As Conroy and Murrie (2007) note, evaluators should avoid including "red herring" information—that is, data that have no demonstrable relationship to the psycholegal referral question, but that simply serve as distracters. Legal professionals should keep these elements in mind when reviewing a forensic report concerning a sex offender.

When testifying, the evaluator serves as a teacher. Many of the constructs used by the evaluator are foreign to the lay public. Even relatively sophisticated legal audiences, such as judges and attorneys, may need a clear explanation of what the evaluator means if using terms of art, including "mental disorder," "risk," "volitional impairment," and the like.

In addition, the evaluator should make clear what facts are being assumed. In many sex-offender cases, and in all the legal contexts we discussed, facts are frequently in dispute, even post-adjudication. It is not the evaluator's role to act as a finder of fact. Rather, the evaluator has to make reasonable choices (Witt & Conroy, 2009):

- Provide a range of conclusions, depending upon what facts are assumed
- Provide a clear conclusion, indicating what factual assumptions are being made to reach that conclusion, but acknowledging that these are only assumptions, not findings of fact

There is considerable debate in the field concerning whether a mental health professional when testifying should offer an opinion on the ultimate legal issue (Melton et al, 2007)—for instance, whether a sex offender meets a specific criterion, such as appropriateness for SVP commitment. One school of thought believes that offering such ultimate-issue opinions is inappropriate for two reasons. First, mental health professionals have no special training or ability to give opinions on ultimate legal issues. Second, offering such ultimate-issue opinions invades the purview of the judge, the individual whom society has determined should be making such ultimate determinations. The opposing school of thought believes that legal professionals, including judges, want mental health professionals to offer ultimate-issue opinions, knowing that these opinions are only advisory. Ultimate issues are particularly controversial in the arena of SVP commitments because, as written, most statutes specify elements that are not clearly clinical in nature. For example, it is unclear whether "mental abnormality" or "behavioral abnormality" was intended to equate to any clinical diagnosis that mental health

professionals are trained to make. Turning to the element of behavioral control, mental health professionals lack specific methods for differentiating volitional impairment from conscious choice. If the psychologist determines either of these factors is not within his or her expertise, it becomes impossible to reach an ultimate conclusion regarding whether the person meets the criteria outlined in the statute for civil commitment. The issue is far from resolved, and may depend upon the opinions of each individual evaluator and practices within the specific jurisdiction of the evaluation.

SUMMARY

This chapter reviews five typical legal contexts in which psychological evaluations of sex offenders are requested: (1) pre-adjudication, (2) post-adjudication, (3) registration and community notification, (4) SVP commitment, and (5) release from commitment. The chapter discusses the issues specific to each context. In all contexts, an assessment of risk is relevant, given that virtually all psycholegal issues involve some consideration of the individual's propensity for future sex offending. However, beyond that, each legal context may have issues specific to only itself. For example, SVP commitment evaluations focus on three interrelated issues: (1) mental abnormality, (2) volitional impairment, and (3) risk. Each of these constructs may have a definition that is specific to that jurisdiction, and both legal and forensic mental health professionals need to be aware of jurisdiction-specific considerations.

The chapter reviewed the empirical foundations and limits, with particular consideration of special populations, such as juveniles, female sex offenders, and child pornography possession offenders. Although to date the bulk of the research has been performed on adult male sex offenders, data have been slowly accumulating on these special populations, allowing credible assessment of risk with them.

The chapter also reviewed the evaluation process itself, beginning with the pre-evaluation file review. The extent of a file review frequently depends on the context of the evaluation. Pre-adjudication evaluations, frequently being pre-indictment, may have relatively little documentation to review, whereas SVP evaluations, typically dealing with sex offenders with well-documented criminal histories, may have extensive files.

Finally, the chapter concluded with consideration of how the results of the evaluation are communicated: the report and testimony. Both report and testimony should be focused on the psycholegal issue at hand. Irrelevant information should be excluded from report or testimony. Additionally, no forensic psychological evaluation of an alleged sex offender should offer an opinion on the guilt or innocence of that alleged offender. There is no scientifically supported profile that one could use to determine guilt, and such statements of an alleged offender's guilt are specifically prohibited by the practice standards of the Association for the Treatment of Sexual Abusers.

REFERENCES

Abel, G. G., Becker, J. V., Mittelman, M. S., Cunningham-Rathner, J., Rouleau, J. L., & Murphy, W. D. (1987). Self-reported sex crimes of nonincarcerated paraphiliacs. *Journal of Interpersonal Violence, 2,* 3–25.

Alexander, M. (1999). Sexual offender treatment efficacy revisited. *Sexual Abuse: A Journal of Research and Treatment, 11,* 101–116.

American Psychiatric Association. (1983). Statement on the insanity defense. *American Journal of Psychiatry, 140,* 681–688.

American Psychiatric Association (2000). *Diagnostic and statistical manual of mental disorders (4th edition).* Washington, DC: American Psychiatric Association.

Arkowitz, S., Shale, J., & Carabello, K. (2008). Conditional release programs for civilly committed sex offenders. *Journal of Psychiatry and Law, 36,* 485–511.

Association for the Treatment of Sexual Abusers (2005). *Practice standards and guidelines.* Beaverton, OR: Author.

Barnoski, R. (2005). *Sex offender sentencing in Washington State: Has community notification reduced recidivism?* Olympia, WA: State Institute for Public Policy, Document No. 05-12-1202.

Becker, J. V., Stinson, J., Tromp, S., & Messer, G. (2003). Characteristics of individuals petitioned for civil commitment. *International Journal of Offender Therapy and Comparative Criminology, 47,* 185–195.

Boer, D., Hart, S., Kropp, R., & Webster, C. (1997). *Manual for the Sexual Violence Risk–20.* Burnaby, BC: Mental Health, Law, and Policy Institute, Simon Fraser University.

Bourke, M. L., & Hernandez, A. E. (2009). The 'Butner Study' redux: A report of the incidence of hands-on child victimization by child pornography offenders. *Journal of Family Violence, 24,* 183–191.

Conroy, M. A. (2003). Evaluation of sexual predators. In A. M. Goldstein (Ed.), *Handbook of psychology: Forensic psychology* (Vol. 11, pp. 463–484). New York: Wiley.

Conroy, M. A. (2006). Report writing and testimony. *Applied Psychology in Criminal Justice, 2,* 237–260.

Conroy, M. A., & Murrie, D. C. (2007). *Forensic assessment of violence risk: A guide for risk assessment and risk management.* New York: Wiley.

Conroy, M. A., & Witt, P. H. (in press). Evaluation of sexual predators. In R. K. Otto (Ed.), *Handbook of psychology* (2nd ed.): *Forensic psychology* (Vol. 11). New York: Wiley.

Cunningham, M. D., & Reidy, T. J. (1998). Antisocial Personality Disorder and psychopathy: Diagnostic dilemmas in classifying patterns of antisocial behavior in sentencing evaluations. *Behavioral Sciences and the Law, 16,* 331–351.

Deming, A. (2008). Sex offender civil commitment programs: Current practices, characteristics, and resident demographics. *Journal of Psychiatry and Law, 36,* 439–461.

Doren, D. M. (2002). *Evaluating sex offenders: A manual for civil commitment and beyond.* Thousand Oaks, CA: Sage.

Duwe, G., & Donnay, W. (2008). The impact of Megan's Law on sex offender recidivism: The Minnesota experience. *Criminology, 46,* 411–446.

Eke, A. W., & Seto, M. C. (2008, October). *Examining the criminal history and recidivism of registered child pornography offenders.* Paper presented at the Association for the Treatment of Sexual Offenders Convention, Atlanta, Georgia.

Endrass, J., Urbaniok, F., Hammermeister, L. C., Benz, C., Elbert, T., Laubacher, A., & Rossegger, A. (2009). The consumption of Internet child pornography and violent and sex offending. *BMC Psychiatry, 9,* 43–67. Retrieved from http://www.biomedcentral.com/content/pdf/1471-244x-9-43.pdf.

Freeman, N.J. (2009, May 18). The public safety impact of community notification laws: Rearrest of convicted sex offenders. *Crime & Delinquency Online,* Published as doi: 10.1177/0011128708330852.

Grisso, T. (2010). Guidance for improving forensic reports: A review of common errors. *Open Access Journal of Forensic Psychology, 2,* 102–115.

Groth, A. N., Burgess, A. W., & Holmstrom, L. L. (1977). Rape: Power, anger, and sexuality. *American Journal of Psychiatry, 134,* 1239–1243.

Hanson, R. K., & Bussiere, M. T. (1998). Predicting relapse: A meta-analysis of sex offender recidivism studies. *Journal of Consulting and Clinical Psychology, 66,* 348–362.

Hanson, R. K., Harris, A. H., Scott, T., & Helmus, L. (2007). *Assessing the risk of sexual offenders on community supervision.* Ottawa, ON: Department of the Solicitor General of Canada. Retrieved from http://www.publicsafety.gc.ca/res/cor/rep/_fl/crp2007-05-en.pdf.

Hanson, R. K., & Morton-Bourgon, K. E. (2009). The accuracy of recidivism risk assessments for sexual offenders: A meta-analysis of 118 prediction studies. *Psychological Assessment, 21,* 1–21.

Hanson, R. K., & Thornton, D. (1999). *Static-99: Improving actuarial risk assessments for sex offenders* (User Report 99-02). Ottawa, ON: Department of the Solicitor General of Canada.

Hanson, R. K., & Thornton, D. (2000). Improving risk assessments for sex offenders: A comparison of three actuarial scales. *Law and Human Behavior, 24,* 119–136.

Heilbrun, K., Nezu, C. M., Keeney, M., Chung, S., & Wasserman, A. L. (1998). Sexual offending: Linking assessment, intervention, and decision making. *Psychology, Public Policy, and Law, 4,* 138–174.

Hernandez, A. E. (2000). *Self-reported contact sex offenses by participants in the Federal Bureau of Prisons' sex offender treatment program: Implications for Internet sex offenders.* Poster session presented at the 19th annual Research and Treatment Conference of the Association for the Treatment of Sexual Abusers, San Diego, CA.

Hiscox, S. P., Witt, P. H., & Haran, S. J. (2007). Juvenile Risk Assessment Scale (JRAS): A predictive validity study. *Journal of Psychiatry and Law, 35,* 503–539.

Jackson, R. L. (2008). Sex offender civil commitment: Recommendations for empirically guided evaluations. *Journal of Psychiatry and Law, 36,* 389–431.

Jackson, R. L., & Richards, H. J. (2007). Diagnostic and risk profiles in a sample of sexually violent predators. *International Journal of Offender Therapy and Comparative Criminology, 51,* 313–323.

Janus, E. S., & Walbek, N. H. (2000). Sex offender commitments in Minnesota: A descriptive study of second-generation commitments. *Behavioral Sciences and the Law, 18,* 343–374.

Kansas v. Crane, 534 U.S. 407 (2002).

Kansas v. Hendricks, 521 U.S. 346 (1997).

Knight, R. A, & Thornton, D. (2007). *Evaluating and improving risk assessment schemes for sexual recidivism: A long-term follow up of convicted sexual offenders.* Washington, DC: U.S. Dept. of Justice, Document No. 217618.

Levenson, J. S. (2004). Sexual predator civil commitment: A comparison of selected and released offenders. *International Journal of Offender Therapy and Comparative Criminology, 48,* 638–648.

Li, N., Lee, A. F., & Prentky, R. (2010). *The role of antisociality in differentiating among child molesters with, and without, an Internet sexual offense.* Paper presented at AP-LS Convention, February 2010, Vancouver, B.C.

Lieb, R., Quinsey, V. L., & Berliner, L. (1998). Sexual predators and social policy. In M. Tonry (Ed.), *Crime and justice: A review of research* (vol. 23, pp. 42–114). Chicago: University of Chicago Press.

Lipton, D., Martinson, R., & Wilks, J. (1975). *The effectiveness of correctional treatment: A survey of treatment evaluation studies.* New York: Praeger.

McCann, K., & Lussier, P. (2008). Anti-sociality, sexual deviance, and sexual reoffending in juvenile sex offenders: a meta-analytic investigation. *Youth Violence and Juvenile Justice, 6,* 363–385.

Melton, G. B., Petrila, P., Poythress, N. G., & Slobogin, C. (2007). *Psychological evaluations for the courts: A handbook for mental health professionals and lawyers* (3rd ed.). New York: Guilford.

Mercado, C. C., Bornstein, B. H., & Schopp, R. F. (2006). Decision-making about volitional impairment in sexually violent predators. *Law and Human Behavior, 30,* 587–602.

Mercado, C. C., Schopp, R. F., & Bornstein, B. H. (2005). Evaluating sex offenders under sexually violent predator laws: How might mental health professionals conceptualize the notion of volitional impairment? *Aggression and Violent Behavior, 10,* 289–309.

Miller, H. A., Amenta, A. E., & Conroy, M. A. (2005). Sexually violent predator evaluations: Empirical limitations, strategies for professionals, and research directions. *Law and Human Behavior, 29,* 29–54.

Minnesota ex rel. Pearson v. Probate Court, 309 U. S. 270, 60 S. Ct. 523, 84 L. Ed. 744 (1940).

Monahan, J. (1981). *Predicting violent behavior: An assessment of clinical techniques.* Beverly Hills, CA: Sage.

N.J. v. Howard, 213 NJ Super. 587 (1986).

Olver, M. E., Wong, S. C. P., Nicholaichuk, T., & Gordon, A. (2007). The validity and reliability of the Violence Risk Scale-Sexual Offender version: Assessing sex offender risk and evaluating therapeutic change. *Psychological Assessment, 19,* 318–329.

Prentky, R. A., & Righthand, S. (2003). *Juvenile Sex Offender Assessment Protocol-II (JSOAP-II) manual.* Rockville, MD: U.S. Department of Justice, Office of Justice Programs, Office of Juvenile Justice and Delinquency Prevention.

Quinsey, V. L., Harris, G. T., Rice, M. E., & Cormier, C. A. (2006). *Violent offenders: Appraising and managing risk* (2nd ed.). Washington, DC: APA.

Rasmussen, L. A. (1999). Factors related to recidivism among juvenile sexual offenders. *Sexual Abuse: A Journal of Research and Treatment, 11,* 69–86.

Rogers, R., & Shuman, D. W. (2005). *Fundamentals of forensic practice: Mental health and criminal law.* New York: Springer Science and Business Media.

Sandler, J. C., & Freeman, N. J. (2007). Typology of female sex offenders: A test of Vandiver and Kercher. *Sexual Abuse: A Journal of Research and Treatment, 19,* 73–89.

Sandler, J. C., & Freeman, N. J. (2009). Female sex offender recidivism: A large-scale empirical analysis. *Sexual Abuse: A Journal of Research and Treatment, 21,* 455–473.

Sandler, J. C., Freeman, N. J., & Socia, K. M. (2008). Does a watched pot boil? A time-series analysis of New York state's sex offender registration and notification law. *Psychology, Public Policy, and Law, 14,* 284–302.

Seto, M. C, Cantor, J. M., & Blanchard, R. (2006). Child pornography offenses are a valid diagnostic indicator of pedophilia. *Journal of Abnormal Psychology, 115,* 610–615.

Seto, M. C., & Eke, A. (2005). The criminal histories and later offending of child pornography offenders. *Sexual Abuse: A Journal of Research and Treatment, 17,* 201–210.

Snyder, H. (2006). *Youth arrests 2004.* Washington, DC: Office of Juvenile Justice and Delinquency Prevention.

Sreenivasan, S., Weinberger, L.E., & Garrick, T. (2003). Expert testimony in sexually violent predator commitments: Conceptualizing legal standards of "mental disorder" and "likely to reoffend." *Journal of the American Academy of Psychiatry and the Law, 31,* 471–485.

Vandiver, D. M., & Walker, J. T. (2002). Female sex offenders: An overview and analysis of 40 cases. *Criminal Justice Review, 27,* 284–300.

Witt, P. H. (2010). Forensic report checklist. *Open Access Journal of Forensic Psychology, 2,* 233–240.

Witt, P. H., & Conroy, M.A. (2009). *Evaluation of sexually violent predators.* New York: Oxford University Press.

Wong, S. C. P., Olver, M. E., & Stockdale, K. C. (2009). The utility of static and dynamic factors in risk assessment, prediction, and treatment. In J. Andrade (Ed.), *Handbook of violence risk assessment and treatment* (pp. 83–120). New York: Springer.

Worling, J. R., & Curwen, T. (2001). *The Estimate of Risk of Adolescent Sex Offense Recidivism (Version 2).* Toronto, ON: Ontario Ministry of Community and Social Services.

Zgoba, K., Witt, P. H., Dalessandro, M., & Veysey, B. (2008). *Megan's Law: Assessing the practical and monetary efficacy.* U.S. Department of Justice report 225370, retrieved from https://www.ncjrs.gov/pdffiles1/nij/grants/225370.pdf.

6

Evaluation of Violence Risk in Adults

KIRK HEILBRUN, STEPHANIE BROOKS HOLLIDAY,
AND CHRISTOPHER KING

Violence is a significant problem in our society. It is directly related to public safety and the perception of safety, one of the most fundamental priorities for a legal system; however, unlike most of the other issues addressed in this book, the risk of violence is not an ultimate legal question. Appraising the risk of future violent behavior, and sometimes the need for interventions that would reduce that risk, are part of forensic mental health assessment (FMHA) that encompasses a range of legal questions (Heilbrun, 2009). Accordingly, this chapter will examine the process of violence risk assessment, including the legal background, the role of specialized risk-assessment tools, and the integration of risk assessment into the forensic evaluation. This has been adapted to make the material described in the best-practice series book (Heilbrun, 2009) of particular interest to legal professionals. For attorneys and judges involved in litigation in which violence risk assessment is conducted, the chapter will provide a framework that will facilitate a judgment about whether such risk assessment is consistent (whenever possible) with best practice—and whether it is reasonably comprehensive and consistent with broad risk-assessment principles.

LEGAL CONTEXT

Sociolegal Purpose and History
The risk of violence is an important aspect of a number of sociolegal contexts. For instance, danger to self or others is a cornerstone of U.S. civil commitment statutes. Risk of harm to others is also evaluated in a number of criminal contexts, including diversion, sentencing, and release decision making. Thus, risk assessment is an area in which the law has frequently sought expert opinions from mental health professionals.

Since the 1990s, there has also been a transition from the use of the term "dangerousness" to describe the focus of this type of forensic assessment. This term continues to be used in legal language, but researchers and scholars have become more precise when describing their target behaviors. Dangerousness has at least three components: *risk factors* (variables empirically associated with the probability that aggression will occur), *harm* (the amount and type of aggression being predicted), and *risk level* (the probability that harm will occur; National Research Council, 1989). To increase specificity and decrease reliance on personal values, researchers (e.g., Monahan et al., 1994) and forensic clinicians have substituted "risk assessment" for "dangerousness" in FMHA. Risk assessment immediately raises three questions: Risk of what outcome? How high is the risk? What influences contribute to the risk?

In addition, Andrews and Bonta (1990) outlined three distinct concepts: risk, needs, and responsivity (RNR). *Risk* refers to the principle that those with the highest likelihood of future criminal activity should receive more intensive levels of intervention. *Needs*, or *criminogenic needs*, are deficits related to the probability of future offending. *Responsivity* refers to the individual's likelihood of responding to intervention(s) designed to reduce the risk of criminal re-offending. A subsequent distinction between violence prediction and risk management (Heilbrun, 1997) emphasized the legal context of different decisions, with some focused on prediction and others on both risk appraisal and risk reduction. Prediction tends to focus on *static* risk factors (without the potential to change through planned intervention), while risk assessments focused on both risk appraisal and risk reduction also include *dynamic* risk factors, which have the potential to change through planned intervention. This distinction is important, as prediction-only approaches are appropriate for some legal questions, whereas both prediction and management are indicated for others.

Finally, researchers have provided a systematic description of risk-factor domains. Four classes of risk factors were described: *individual, contextual, historical,* and *clinical* (Steadman et al., 1994). These domains were used by investigators who were developing specialized risk-needs tools, and there is a fairly substantial consensus within the field regarding broadly applicable areas of risk factors for violent behavior and criminal offending.

Violence Risk Assessment: Legal Contexts
Violence risk assessment is not associated with a single legal question. The issue of violence risk is part of the evaluation of criminal responsibility, capital sentencing, civil commitment, and disposition and transfer of juvenile offenders. It may also be addressed when determining whether an individual found incompetent to stand trial meets the "dangerous to self or others" criterion of commitment. Risk-needs assessment may be used as a measure of treatment progress for individuals receiving treatment under the jurisdiction of a court or correctional system.

Legal Standards
Because legal standards for risk assessment vary according to legal question, it is not meaningful to describe those standards broadly. Instead, it is important to discuss the legal standards associated with particular considerations that combine to distinguish a particular type of FMHA risk assessment. The five considerations that commonly apply are (a) *nature of risk factors or indicators of risk,* (b) *level of risk,* (c) *severity of the harm* (physical aggression only? threats of harm? any illegal behavior?), (d) *length of the outcome period,* and (e) *context in which harm may occur* (Heilbrun, 2009). Legal standards, however, typically remain less specific and continue to use the terms "dangerous" and "dangerousness."

Because the law speaks of dangerousness, while forensic psychology and psychiatry focus on risk assessment, evaluators may address these five considerations to gather information that informs a decision maker's determination of an individual's dangerousness. However, the legal term "dangerous" may encompass behavior beyond violence to others, such as any criminal offending (e.g., evaluations for criminal responsibility; *Jones v. U.S.,* 1983). This is why it is essential for evaluators to review relevant statutes, case law, and administrative code to clarify the target behaviors. Several important standards for specific legal questions will now be discussed.

Correctional Transfers
In *Vitek v. Jones* (1980), the Supreme Court addressed the Fourteenth Amendment due-process considerations involved in the transfer of convicted offenders to a state mental hospital for treatment of mental disease or defect. The U.S. Supreme Court held that in such a situation, both notice and an adversarial hearing were necessary, but counsel was not (*Vitek v. Jones,* 1980). The standard for correctional transfers involves the presence of mental illness and serious threat of harm to self or others. However, the nature of the risk factors, severity of possible harm, and length of the period under consideration are not specified.

Criminal Responsibility Hospitalization and Release
In *Jones v. United States* (1983), the U.S. Supreme Court addressed the *nature* of dangerousness as it applies to individuals committed as not guilty by reason of insanity (NGRI). The majority opinion held that dangerousness is implied by the risk of *any* criminal offending, not just the risk of violent behavior.

Foucha v. Louisiana (1992) elaborated on the source of dangerousness in the context of an individual acquitted by reason of insanity who appeared to have regained sanity but continued to be dangerous due to his antisocial personality disorder. The Court held that, to justify involuntary commitment following acquittal by reason of insanity, both the mental illness *and* dangerousness prongs of the commitment criteria must be met. A determination of dangerousness absent a mental illness was deemed insufficient.

Capital Sentencing
Since the U.S. Supreme Court determined that capital sentencing is constitutional (*Gregg v. Georgia,* 1976; *Jurek v. Texas,* 1976; *Profitt v. Florida,* 1976),

courts have also required individualized sentencing. This involves the consideration of aggravating and mitigating circumstances. Texas, however, is unusual in explicitly citing risk of harm to others as a "special issue" to be weighed in the capital sentencing process (Cunningham, 2010).

In *Estelle v. Smith* (1981), the Court held that a defendant must be notified prior to an evaluation if the results of a pretrial evaluation could be used at capital sentencing. This decision, though, focused on the procedural aspects of admitting testimony and how the expert reached his opinions. In *Barefoot v. Estelle* (1983), the U.S. Supreme Court considered the process for evaluating future risk. The Court held that psychiatrists had some expertise in the area of predicting violent behavior, and that any limitations to this expertise could be exposed through cross-examination. This decision also allowed testimony in response to hypothetical questions.

Two other U.S. Supreme Court cases are relevant. In *Satterwhite v. Texas* (1988), the Court held that the admission of expert psychiatric evidence on future dangerousness at capital sentencing without adequate notice to the defense that the evaluation was being conducted went beyond harmless error, and was not permissible. The Court further held, in *Abdul-Kabir v. Quarterman* (2007), that the trial court's instruction to the jury at sentencing to focus only on the two special issues (the deliberateness of the crime, and whether the defendant would constitute a continuing threat to society) prevented jurors from meaningfully considering any mitigating evidence presented.

It is important to note that all four of these cases are from Texas, and that the impact of violence risk assessment in capital cases may be less compelling in other jurisdictions. Also, although the influence of where the defendant will live is hardly mentioned in these decisions, an individual convicted of capital murder will likely spend life in prison if not executed. Hence, the appropriate context for the evaluation is to appraise the risk of harm to others in a highly structured and secure prison, not the community.

Civil Commitment

The component of civil commitment criteria specifying that an individual must be "dangerous to self or others" has become far more influential since the 1970s. In *Lessard v. Schmidt* (1973), the degree of dangerousness constitutionally required for involuntary commitment was not specified. However, this case influenced the incorporation of a "recent overt act" in the dangerousness component required for involuntary civil commitment in many jurisdictions. In 1975, the Supreme Court addressed the potential impact of living situation on civil commitment decisions in *O'Connor v. Donaldson* (1975). The Court held that a non-dangerous individual who can survive safely in freedom by himself or with the help of willing and responsible family members or friends cannot be involuntarily committed.

Commitment of Sexually Violent Predators

In *Kansas v. Hendricks* (1997) the U.S. Supreme Court held that the definition of the term "mental abnormality" in Kansas's Sexually Violent Predator Act satisfies substantive due-process requirements for individuals who have completed serving a criminal sentence for a sexual offense. The Act allows the post-sentence commitment of sexually violent predators based on a finding of dangerousness to self or others resulting from a mental abnormality or personality disorder. Note that the *Hendricks* decision seemed to imply that sexual-offending risk was a distinct outcome for which special considerations were appropriate. However, if jurisdictions were to begin applying the Court's reasoning to other forms of violence, the result could be problematic: it would permit authorities to civilly commit offenders at risk for any type of violence upon correctional release based solely on the presence of a personality disorder.

Child Custody

The use of violence risk assessments in child-custody cases is just beginning to occur. In *Sandella v. Trischetti* (2008), for instance, the Court of Appeals in Arizona considered the expert testimony of a psychologist in deciding a custody dispute. Based on the results of an actuarial risk-assessment measure, the psychologist concluded that the father had a low risk of future violent behavior. Sole legal custody was ultimately awarded to the father. There does not appear to be any U.S. Supreme Court case law on violence risk assessment in the areas of child custody or child protection. Case law applicable to juvenile commitment/transfer evaluations is discussed elsewhere (see Andrews & Hoge, 2010).

Legal Procedures

There are two considerations relevant to the procedures involved in any violence risk assessment conducted by a forensic mental health professional. The first involves the need to tailor the evaluation specifically to the target question(s) (Heilbrun, 2009). The information gathered for a risk assessment may be extensive, but it is important to avoid information that is not relevant to the referral question (Heilbrun, DeMatteo, Marczyk, & Goldstein, 2008; Melton et al., 2007) because of its sensitive and potentially prejudicial nature. If the evaluation of violence risk is not formally requested, the evaluator should avoid comments on risk and risk-relevant needs.

The second major consideration involves disclosing information concerning the defendant's functioning that was not the subject of the evaluation, such as areas in which there is legal authority for breaking therapeutic privilege. Guidance in these instances is provided by the American Bar Association's *Criminal Justice Mental Health Standards*:

> If in the course of any evaluation, the mental health or mental retardation professional concludes that defendant may be mentally incompetent to stand trial, presents an imminent risk of serious danger to another person, is imminently suicidal, or otherwise needs emergency intervention, the evaluator should notify the defendant's attorney. If the evaluation was initiated by the court or prosecution, the evaluator should also notify the court. (1989, p. 73)

Ethical Considerations in FMHA Risk Assessment

When conducting a FMHA risk assessment, forensic evaluators must be careful to follow relevant ethical guidance. Such guidance includes the *Ethical Principles of Psychologists and Code of Conduct* (American Psychological Association, 2010), the *Principles of Medical Ethics with Annotations Especially Applicable to Psychiatry* (American Psychiatric Association, 2009), the *Specialty Guidelines for Forensic Psychologists* (Committee on Ethical Guidelines for Forensic Psychologists, 1991), and the *Ethics Guidelines for the Practice of Forensic Psychiatry* (AAPL, 2005). One important ethical issue cited by all four is confidentiality and the limits of

confidentiality. Because the issue of confidentiality differs in a forensic context from a therapeutic context, forensic clinicians should discuss limitations to confidentiality and the foreseeable uses of their reports (American Psychological Association, 2010; American Psychiatric Association, 2009; International Association for Correctional and Forensic Psychology Practice Standards Committee, 2010). These limits may vary with the type of evaluation.

FORENSIC MENTAL HEALTH CONCEPTS

Forensic mental health concepts, which also have been termed "functional legal capacities," are at the heart of FMHA. Because FMHA risk assessment is a part of a number of legal questions, the description of forensic mental health concepts must be sufficiently broad. The role of specialized risk-assessment tools, which have been instrumental in advancing the accuracy and forensic utility of various types of risk assessment, will play a prominent part in this discussion.

Identification of Forensic Mental Health Concepts

To identify the relevant forensic mental health concepts, it is important to consider context, purpose, population, parameters, and approach (Heilbrun, Yasuhara, & Shah, 2009).

Context

There are four contexts in which a risk assessment may be conducted: legal, clinical, school/workplace, and threats to protectees. This chapter focuses on legal contexts, in which a legal decision maker renders a decision in the course of litigation. This may include initial commitment or sentencing, release from incarceration or secure hospitalization, or steps associated with a planned release.

Purpose

The focus on risk assessment instead of dangerousness has allowed for greater precision in describing risk-factor domains (Kraemer, Kazdin, Offord, Kessler, Jensen, & Kupfer, 1997; Monahan & Steadman, 1994). In this context, "risk" refers to the probability that the examinee will engage in violence, offending, or the specified target behavior (Andrews & Bonta, 2006; Andrews, Bonta, & Hoge, 1990; Andrews, Bonta, & Wormith, 2006). Heilbrun (1997) distinguished between *prediction* and *risk management* components of risk assessment. Certain legal questions focus on *predicting* the likelihood of a target behavior, such as post-sentence *Hendricks* commitment for sexual offenders (see Witt & Conroy, 2009, for a fuller discussion). These evaluations may use *prediction-oriented* tools, which tend to focus on static risk factors. *Dynamic* risk factors and/or protective factors are also addressed when legal questions focus on *risk management*. Such dynamic risk factors have the potential to change through planned intervention (Andrews & Bonta, 2006; Andrews et al., 1990, 2006). An example of an evaluation with a risk-management focus would involve determining if a defendant is appropriate for diversion to a mental health court.

Populations

It is important to consider the population or subpopulation to which the individual being assessed belongs. Different groups may have distinctive (a) base rates of violence or offending, (b) risk factors and protective factors, and (c) risk-relevant interventions and management strategies. To define populations, evaluators may consider age, gender, mental health status, and location (e.g., correctional facility, secure hospital). This information informs the evaluator's decision about whether a given individual is sufficiently similar to the population on which a given specialized risk-assessment tool was validated. Racial/ethnic group is also important. Although it is not a primary determinant for selecting a given risk-assessment tool, empirical evidence regarding the limits of applicability of a risk-assessment tool with certain racial/ethnic groups should be considered (e.g., Snowden, Gray, & Taylor, 2010).

Parameters

In addition, it is important to define the target behavior, frequency, probability/risk category, setting(s), outcome period, and risk and protective factors. Specification of the target behavior being predicted is quite important, as it is relevant to the base rate and the concordance with the legal question. The target behavior can be defined by type of behavior (e.g., violent offending, any offending) and frequency (e.g., a single act vs. multiple acts). Also, the target outcome may be measured in a number of ways, including self-report, collateral observer report, and official records. The outcome

period may vary across legal questions, ranging from 24 hours to a number of years. The location of the individual (e.g., secure facility vs. community) should be considered as well.

Approach

Finally, evaluators should describe the basis for their conclusions regarding risk level and needs. If the evaluator uses a structured professional judgment tool, the tool may identify the specific risk and protective factors that are present. This may be more difficult with actuarial risk-assessment tools, which select predictors for their empirical relationship to outcome rather than their theoretical or commonsense relationship. Evaluators should also consider the congruence between the specialized tool selected and the nature of the evaluation (which may be gauged by clarifying context, purpose, populations, and parameters).

Strategy for Addressing FMHA Legal Standards that are General and Unelaborated

In many cases, the previously described parameters will not be clearly addressed. The vagueness associated with terms such as "dangerous" and "dangerousness" was one reason why medical and behavioral science moved to the use of the term "risk assessment." Whereas dangerousness is not easily elaborated, risk assessment raises questions concerning risk level, nature of the outcome, and contributing risk factors and protective factors (National Research Council, 1989). One useful strategy that has been employed in FMHA in the face of legal standards that are insufficiently specific is as follows: (a) focus on functional legal capacities (rather than the ultimate legal question), (b) clarify assumptions and definitions used in the evaluation, and (c) provide contingent conclusions varied by differing levels of outcome (Heilbrun, 2001). Although dangerousness is often treated as dichotomous in legal contexts, evaluators should communicate risk level using probabilities or multiple risk levels whenever possible.

Principles of Risk Assessment

It can be useful for legal professionals to consider risk assessment in its broadest terms. Although risk assessment can be a part of a range of evaluations on various different legal questions, there are some common principles that apply to this process (Table 6.1).

TABLE 6.1 PRINCIPLES OF RISK ASSESSMENT AND IMPLICATIONS
FOR BEST PRACTICE

PRINCIPLES OF RISK ASSESSMENT	IMPLICATIONS FOR BEST PRACTICE
1) Identification of the task	Identify whether assessment of risk-relevant needs is required as well as prediction.
2) Specification of the context	Specify the setting in which the risk of the target behavior is being appraised (e.g., residential vs. community).
3) Specification of outcome	Clarify the outcome(s) for which risk is being assessed and consider outcome specification at every stage of the evaluation.
4) Identification of population	Match the use of specialized risk assessment tool(s) with the population to which the evaluee belongs.
5) Estimate of base rate	Consider base rates of the specific outcome(s) for the population to which the evaluee belongs.
6) Identification of risk factors and protective factors	Describe the factors that contribute to future risk of the target behavior.
7) Individualization of assessment	Use both nomothetic and idiographic approaches.
8) Communication of risk in probability, frequency, or relative terms	Express risk with probability- or frequencies-based statements when using actuarial tools, but only with terms of relative risk when using structured professional judgment.
9) Description of risk-relevant needs	When indicated by the referral question, assess risk-relevant needs through the use of a specialized tool or other means.
10) Impact of values if the ultimate legal question is answered	If answering the ultimate legal question, acknowledge the role of personal values in determining "dangerousness."

EMPIRICAL FOUNDATIONS AND LIMITS

Approaches to Risk Assessment

This section will address the empirical foundations and limitations of several different approaches to risk assessment. There are two well-supported approaches to risk assessment: actuarial assessment and structured professional judgment.

Actuarial Assessment

Actuarial assessment is "a formal method" that "uses an equation, a formula, a graph, or an actuarial table to arrive at a probability, or expected value, of some outcome" (Grove & Meehl, 1996, p. 294). It uses quantified predictor variables, which are validated through empirical research, focusing on the outcome of interest (which must also be quantified). The predictors are commonly identified using a single dataset, or multiple datasets combined through meta-analytic techniques.

Structured Professional Judgment

Structured professional judgment (SPJ) uses specified risk factors that are not necessarily obtained from a particular dataset, although they are commonly identified through a review of the literature. Once selected, these items must be carefully operationalized so their presence can be reliably coded. Evaluators consider various sources of information (interviews, records, and other sources of information) in rating the presence of the specified items. Following this, evaluators weigh the presence of the risk factors and the anticipated intensity of management, treatment, or supervision needs, and use their professional judgment in drawing a conclusion about the individual's risk. Items are not scored to yield a total score, and in this way SPJ is more flexible but less precise than actuarial assessment.

There are a number of similarities between actuarial and SPJ approaches. Both rely on empirically derived risk and protective factors, and specify the variables to be considered. However, actuarial approaches yield a total score that is associated with an identified frequency of occurrence of the target outcome, while SPJ measures leave the final judgment to the evaluator.

Anamnestic Assessment

Anamnestic assessment (Melton et al., 2007) might better be characterized as a process than a specialized tool, and can be used along with a specialized tool as a way to individualize the assessment. The evaluator seeks information about past behavior that is similar to the target behavior, including preceding and subsequent thoughts, feelings, and behaviors; the act itself; those involved; and other relevant details (e.g., details regarding substance use, weapons, and victims). The evaluator then seeks to identify risk or protective factors based on patterns that are observed across different acts. This approach does not provide a good basis for prediction of future behavior, although it does allow the evaluator to gauge individual patterns.

Actuarial and SPJ Approaches to Risk Assessment: Empirical Foundations

There have been a number of meta-analyses examining actuarial approaches to risk assessment. In 1998, Bonta, Law, and Hanson reviewed studies of mentally disordered offenders, using the outcomes of general offending and violent re-offending. They identified a number of predictors that could potentially be incorporated into an actuarial assessment measure (Table 6.2).

Psychopathy and Risk-Assessment Tools

The variable of psychopathy has been consistently associated with violent offending in the community over a number of studies. The Psychopathy Checklist-Revised (PCL-R; Hare, 2003) is commonly used as a risk-assessment measure, although it was developed as a measure of a particular personality disorder. Meta-analyses have demonstrated the effectiveness of the PCL-R in prediction of general recidivism (Leistico, Salekin, DeCoster, & Rogers, 2008; Walters, 2003) and violent recidivism (Walters, 2003), and suggested that it is a stronger predictor of re-offending in the community than antisocial conduct in a structured setting (Leistico et al., 2008). A third meta-analysis (Gendreau, Goggin, & Smith, 2002) compared the predictive performance of the PCL-R to the Level of Service Inventory-Revised (LSI-R; Andrews & Bonta, 1995) with respect to both general and violent recidivism. There was a small difference in favor of the LSI-R for strength of association with violent recidivism, and the authors suggested the LSI-R may be the more appropriate tool for appraising the risk of violent re-offending in a population of general offenders.

The MacArthur Risk Assessment Study

The MacArthur Risk Assessment Study (Monahan et al., 2001; Steadman et al., 1998) was a large-scale, multisite single study designed to assess the risk of violent behavior in the community by those discharged from inpatient mental health treatment facilities. This study demonstrated that self-report and collateral report were both more sensitive to the risk of violence. It also found that psychiatric inpatients were no more likely to be violent or aggressive in the community than controls, that substance abuse greatly increased the risk of violent and aggressive behavior for both psychiatric inpatients and controls, and that psychiatric inpatients were more likely to have substance-abuse problems.

TABLE 6.2 PREDICTORS OF VIOLENT RECIDIVISM

Positive Predictors

- Objective assessment of risk (with the largest recidivism effect size = .30)
- Adult criminal history
- Juvenile delinquency
- Antisocial personality disorder
- Nonviolent criminal history
- Institutional adjustment

- Hospital admissions
- Substance abuse
- Family problems
- Violent history
- Single marital status

Negative Predictors

- Mentally disordered offender status
- Age

- Not guilty by reason of insanity
- Psychosis

(Bonta, Law, & Hanson, 1998)

In addition, it demonstrated that a number of neighborhood influences (e.g., concentrated poverty, single-parent families with children) contributed to increased violence risk (Silver, Mulvey, & Monahan, 1999).

The original MacArthur data were validated using another dataset (Monahan, Steadman, Robbins et al., 2005) to develop an actuarial tool for violence risk assessment of mentally disordered individuals in the community, the Classification of Violence Risk (COVR; Monahan, Steadman, Appelbaum, et al., 2005). This tool is demonstrably effective in predicting serious acts of violence in the community committed by individuals with serious mental illness who are not involved with the criminal-justice system.

Debate over the Use of Actuarial Measures

There has been recent debate concerning actuarial measures and their application to individual cases. Researchers have suggested that measures with overlapping categories of risk classification limit the accuracy of actuarial prediction in a single case (Cooke & Michie, 2010; Hanson & Howard, 2010; Hart, Michie, & Cooke, 2007). Actuarial tools should be derived and validated on large samples, both to ensure that confidence intervals are narrow and the risk categories do not overlap, and to enhance generalizability. However, the suggestion that actuarial tools are not useful when applied to individual cases has not been adopted in the field. This is discussed in detail elsewhere (see Harris, Rice, & Quinsey, 2008; Heilbrun, Douglas, & Yasuhara, 2009).

There has also been some debate about the appropriateness of an evaluator adjusting the weights of actuarial predictors, or overriding the conclusion of the actuarial measure. A recent study (Gore, 2007) concluded that clinical adjustment in the use of an actuarial tool (the Minnesota Sex Offender Screening Tool-Revised; Epperson et al., 2003) did not make a statistically significant difference in increasing or decreasing accuracy. Another study (Grann & Långström, 2007) found that four different weighting approaches did not increase accuracy over an unweighted approach, and that increased complexity reduced predictive accuracy on cross-validation. This suggests that use of multiple predictors or complex weighting has limited impact on predictive accuracy (Dawes, 1979; McGrath, 2008).

Related to this point, one study (Kroner, Mills, & Reddon, 2005) compared the predictive accuracy of (a) the PCL-R, LSI-R, and VRAG (three widely accepted actuarial tools), (b) another approach that used generally recognized risk factors for recidivism, and (c) four additional instruments that were constructed by randomly extracting risk factors from the first four instruments. None of the first four tools was more accurate in predicting post-release failure than the four instruments using randomly selected risk factors from among the entire pool, suggesting limits to the actuarial approach and perhaps a "ceiling" to overall predictive accuracy (see Heilbrun, Yasuhara, & Shah, 2009).

SPJ Tools

SPJ tools use the consideration of specified risk factors and protective factors to yield a final judgment (typically low, moderate, or high risk) that is not quantified. The SPJ approach makes the assumption of a positive relationship between the number of risk factors present and the level of risk (Douglas & Kropp, 2002). The elements of SPJ tools *can* be quantified for research purposes, to demonstrate that these elements are related to outcome as they are intended. But it is also important to describe the research that uses SPJ tools as they are intended to be used.

Comparing Actuarial and SPJ Approaches

Two recent chapters (Heilbrun, Douglas, & Yasuhara, 2009; Heilbrun, Yasuhara, & Shah, 2009) have described 12 published studies and one dissertation that investigate the link between final risk judgments that are made in the course of the SPJ assessment process and subsequent violence. Eleven of these studies suggested that such final judgments are significantly predictive of violent recidivism (Catchpole & Gretton, 2003; de Vogel & de Ruiter, 2005, 2006; de Vogel, de Ruiter, van Beek, & Mead, 2004; Douglas, Ogloff, & Hart, 2003; Douglas, Yeomans, & Boer, 2005; Enebrink et al., 2006; Kropp & Hart, 2000; McGowan, 2007; Meyers & Schmidt, 2008; Welsh, Schmidt, McKinnon, Chattha, & Meyers, 2008). Two of the 13 studies (Sjösted & Långström, 2002; Viljoen et al., 2008), by contrast, did not support a significant relationship between final judgments and target outcomes. Five studies addressed the additional question of whether the final judgment adds incremental predictive validity to the actuarial combination of the tool elements. Incremental validity was observed in all five of these studies (de Vogel et al., 2006; Douglas et al., 2003, 2005; Enebrink et al., 2006; Kropp & Hart, 2000).

The research base for SPJ approaches to risk assessment is more limited than that of actuarial approaches, as the development of SPJ tools has occurred more recently. But there is still a question of how it might compare generally with actuarial approaches. The approaches are similar in their approaches to data selection and coding, but differ in data combination.

Several studies have compared SPJ measures—combining their elements in actuarial fashion to yield a final score related to risk—with actuarial tools that are also used in this way. One study (Douglas, Yeomans, & Boer, 2005) compared an SPJ instrument used in this fashion with three actuarial tools and found effectiveness for all four measures. This supports several aspects of the actuarial approach to risk assessment as well as the final risk judgment of the SPJ instrument. Similar results were observed in a study in Germany comparing the HCR-20 (an SPJ tool), PCL-R (an actuarial tool), and LSI-R (an actuarial tool) (Dahle, 2006). The differences in predictive accuracy among these three measures were small and statistically nonsignificant, with both PCL-R total score and HCR-20 final risk judgment strong predictors of violence. A third study (de Vogel et al., 2004) yielded a conclusion more favorable to the SJP approach (the SVR-20; Boer, Hart, Kropp & Webster, 1997) than the actuarial approach (the Static-99; Hanson & Thornton, 1999) for assessing risk of sexual reoffense. Levels of predictive validity were good for both measures, but significantly better for the SPJ instrument. A fourth study (Catchpole & Gretton, 2003) compared two actuarial approaches and an SPJ approach with adolescents referred by juvenile judges, with an average follow-up period of 35.8 months (outcome periods ranged from 7–61 months). The SPJ tool (the SAVRY) was the most accurate.

These studies make it clear that the enhanced structure associated with either actuarial or SPJ approaches increases assessment accuracy (Monahan, 2008). Although two studies suggested some advantage in predictive accuracy using an SPJ approach, further research is needed before this conclusion can be made with confidence. Until then,

the evidence suggests that these two approaches are empirically supported at comparable levels.

Scientifically Supported, Unsupported, and Controversial Uses of Risk Assessment

In a recent chapter, Heilbrun and colleagues (2009) discussed existing scientific evidence and controversies in risk assessment. *Scientifically supported* uses of risk assessment include:

- Conclusions that persons scoring higher on validated actuarial risk-assessment instruments or rated as higher risk on validated SPJ instruments are at greater risk for violence than those scoring lower on these instruments
- Actuarial prediction strategies for group-based predictions, with large derivation and validation samples, using mean probability and including margin of error
- Use of extreme risk categories as more informative and less subject to limits of overlapping confidence intervals
- Indication that application of group-based data to an individual case or small number of cases will result in wider confidence intervals than application to a large number of cases

Scientifically unsupported uses include actuarial prediction strategies without large derivation and validation samples, or applying these predictions to populations not studied with derivation and validation samples. The evaluator should also avoid conclusions that a given individual has "X" probability of violence in the future, without providing the context of confidence intervals or cautions about less certainty in the individual case.

Scientifically controversial and/or largely untested uses include the assumption that there are reliable, known probability estimates that are robust across samples, even at the group level. The evaluator should also be cautious about using actuarial prediction strategies without citing the margin of error or uncertainty when the prediction is applied to single cases.

THE EVALUATION
Steps in Risk Assessment

There are several broad steps associated with FMHA risk assessment. These are steps that are part of any FMHA, but have particular features for risk assessment. For a more complete discussion of the steps involved in violence risk assessment, see Heilbrun (2009).

Referral and Identification of Violence Risk as an Element

The most fundamental question to consider is what legal issue(s) will be used to frame the evaluation. Because there is not a specific legal issue that provides the basis for FMHA risk assessment, it is important to determine whether the risk assessment is a contingent aspect of the evaluation (e.g., competence to stand trial), is simply a part of what is evaluated (e.g., civil commitment), or addresses the primary legal issue (e.g., post-sentence *Hendricks* commitment.)

Selection of Data Sources

Second, the evaluator should select data sources that inform the functional legal capacities. The functional legal capacities in FMHA risk assessment are the target behaviors (sometimes violence, other times criminal offending more broadly) and their associated risk and protective factors. Because violence risk is frequently one of many issues being evaluated in a given FMHA, the data sources selected will need to be appropriate for all the forensic issues at hand. The evaluator will typically conduct interviews, administer measures, and review records.

Communication of Findings

The evaluator should provide the sources of information, the resulting data and their interpretation, and the opinions linked to these interpreted data through explicitly described reasoning (Heilbrun, Grisso, & Goldstein, 2009; Lander & Heilbrun, 2009; Melton et al., 2007). It is important for the evaluator to provide data relevant to the evaluee's functional legal capacities, and link these capacities to the legal question before the court. Expert testimony, when provided, offers a distilled version of the results documented in the report, as well as support for these opinions in the course of cross-examination.

Judicial Finding

The culmination of the process involving FMHA is the finding made by the legal decision maker. Expert evidence on FMHA risk assessment is only part of the evidence that may be provided.

REPORT WRITING AND TESTIMONY

In addition, there are considerations regarding report writing and expert testimony on risk assessment for which evaluators should be prepared. These include:

1. Evaluators should distinguish risk assessment performed for treatment purposes from that conducted for forensic purposes (see Heilbrun, 2001), such as the limited opportunity to gather additional information in a forensic context.

2 All sources of information should be described and consistency across sources noted. Evaluators should attempt to find sources whose weaknesses are complemented by the strengths of others (Kraemer et al., 2003).

3. Evaluators should select psychological tests for relevance and reliability and be prepared to describe the derivation and validation research and any limitations of the test (or the present use of the test).

4. Evaluators should select specialized risk-assessment measures for relevance and reliability and be prepared to describe the fit with the legal question, derivation and validation research, and limitations.

5. Conclusions and opinions about risk assessment should be contextually relevant and take into account that legal outcomes (e.g., "dangerousness") are typically much broader than violence or violent offending and may include any criminal offending (*Jones v. United States*, 1983).

6. Evaluators should identify the prediction and risk-reduction elements of the legal question. If a prediction tool is used, then information should be gathered about dynamic risk factors/criminogenic needs from other sources if a risk-reduction opinion is needed.

7. The final scores obtained when administering an actuarial tool should not be altered. If the evaluator's final conclusion regarding risk differs from the category yielded by the actuarial tool, cite the obtained category and describe the reasoning for deviating.

8. Evaluators should consider source credibility.
9. Evaluators should be prepared to explain the science underlying the development of a given specialized tool. A lay version of the derivation/validation process, and statistical techniques such as logistic regression and tree-based analysis, should be provided upon request.
10. Risk communication language and concepts that are appropriate to the appraisal and conclusions should be used, including consideration of nomothetic and idiographic influences.

Answering the "Ultimate Legal Question"
Whether the evaluating clinician should directly answer the ultimate legal question has been debated extensively within the field of forensic mental health. The arguments for (Rogers & Ewing, 1989, 2003) and against (Melton et al., 2007; Morse, 2008; Tillbrook, Mumley & Grisso, 2003) answering the ultimate legal question have been expressed vigorously over the years, and the debate has not yielded a widely accepted intermediate position.

Initially, one argument against ultimate-issue conclusions was that reports offered a limited description of data and reasoning. However, there is now a greater emphasis on including data and reasoning in reports (AAPL, 2005; APA, in press), and there have been numerous advances in other relevant FMHA domains (Heilbrun et al., 2008). These advances have reframed the ultimate issue debate.

This ultimate-issue debate applies in various ways to risk assessment. FMHA risk assessment is conducted to address a variety of legal questions, and one consideration is how closely the violence risk assessment and ultimate legal question resemble one another. When the two are similar (e.g., sexually violent predator evaluations), it is easier for the legal decision maker to proceed from risk assessment to legal conclusion. For other evaluations, the risk of future violence is one of several considerations (e.g., civil commitment). However close the risk appraisal might be to the ultimate legal question, the forensic clinician is still not able to answer the "how much is enough?" question (Tillbrook et al., 2003) without going beyond the bounds of scientific and forensic expertise.

There may be times when the evaluator is required by statute or ordered by the court to respond to the ultimate legal question. In these instances, the evaluator should draw a clear distinction between the opinion as a forensic evaluator and the legal decision to be made by the court. For instance, the evaluator may designate a subsection of the report specifically for the ultimate legal opinion, noting that it is his or her "clinical opinion."

SUMMARY
Although risk assessment is conducted in a variety of contexts, this chapter has focused on evaluations performed in legal settings. FMHA risk assessment is similar in many respects to other kinds of forensic assessments. "Best practice" in this kind of risk assessment incorporates the considerations discussed in detail elsewhere (Heilbrun, 2009). Ultimately, however, it also requires attention to the influences specific to particular kinds of risk-assessment evaluations conducted in legal contexts.

REFERENCES
Abdul-Kabir v. Quarterman, 127 S. Ct. 1654 (2007).
American Academy of Psychiatry and the Law (2005). *Ethics guidelines for the practice of forensic psychiatry.* Bloomfield, CT: Author.
American Bar Association (1989). *Criminal justice mental health standards.* Washington, DC: Author.
American Psychiatric Association (2009). *Principles of medical ethics with annotations especially applicable to psychiatry.* Washington, DC: Author.
American Psychological Association (2010). *Ethical principles of psychologists and code of conduct: 2010 amendments.* Washington, DC: Author.
American Psychological Association (in press). Specialty guidelines for forensic psychologists. *American Psychologist.* Retrieved 4-3-12 from http://www.ap-ls.org/aboutpsychlaw/SpecialtyGuidelines.php
Andrews, D., & Bonta, J. (1995). *The Level of Service Inventory-Revised: User's manual.* North Tonawanda, NY: Multi-Health Systems.
Andrews, D., & Bonta. J. (2006). *The psychology of criminal conduct* (4th ed.). Newark, NJ: Lexis Nexis/ Matthew Bender.
Andrews, D., Bonta, J., & Hoge, R. (1990). Classification for effective rehabilitation: Rediscovering psychology. *Criminal Justice and Behavior, 17,* 19–52.
Andrews, D., Bonta, J., & Wormith, J. (2006). Recent past and near future of risk/need assessment. *Crime and Delinquency, 52,* 7–27.
Andrews, D., & Hoge, R. (2010). *Evaluation for risk of violence in juveniles.* New York, NY: Oxford.
Barefoot v. Estelle, 463 U. S. 880 (1983).

Boer, D., Hart, S., Kropp, R., & Webster, C. (1997). *Manual for the Sexual Violence Risk—20*. Burnaby, British Columbia, Canada: Mental Health, Law, and Policy Institute, Simon Fraser University.

Bonta, J., Law, M., & Hanson, K. (1998). The prediction of criminal and violent recidivism among mentally disordered offenders: A meta-analysis. *Psychological Bulletin, 123*, 123–142.

Catchpole, R., & Gretton, H. (2003). The predictive validity of risk assessment with violent young offenders: A 1-year examination of criminal outcome. *Criminal Justice and Behavior, 30*, 688–708.

Cooke, D. J., & Michie, C. (2010). Limitations of diagnostic precision and predictive utility in the individual case: A challenge for forensic practice. *Law and Human Behavior, 34*, 259–274.

Cunningham, M. (2010). *Evaluation for capital sentencing*. New York, NY: Oxford.

Dahle, K. P. (2006). Strengths and limitations of actuarial prediction of criminal reoffence in a German prison sample: A comparative study of LSI-R, HCR-20 and PCL-R. *International Journal of Law and Psychiatry, 29*, 431–442.

Dawes, R. M. (1979). The robust beauty of improper linear models in decision making. *American Psychologist, 34*, 571–582.

de Vogel, V., & de Ruiter, C. (2005). The HCR-20 in personality disordered female offenders: A comparison with a matched sample of males. *Clinical Psychology & Psychotherapy, 12*, 226–240.

de Vogel, V., & de Ruiter, C. (2006). Structured professional judgment of violence risk in forensic clinical practice: A prospective study into the predictive validity of the Dutch HCR-20. *Psychology, Crime & Law, 12*, 321–336.

de Vogel, V., de Ruiter, C., van Beek, D., & Mead, G. (2004). Predictive validity of the SVR-20 and Static-99 in a Dutch sample of treated sex offenders. *Law and Human Behavior, 28*, 235–251.

Douglas, K., & Kropp, P. R. (2002). A prevention-based paradigm for violence risk assessment: Clinical and research applications. *Criminal Justice and Behavior, 29*, 617–658.

Douglas, K., Ogloff, J., & Hart, S. (2003). Evaluation of a model of violence risk assessment among forensic psychiatric patients. *Psychiatric Services, 54*, 1372–1379.

Douglas, K., Yeomans, M., & Boer, D. (2005). Comparative validity analysis of multiple measures of violence risk in a general population sample of criminal offenders. *Criminal Justice and Behavior, 32*, 479–510.

Enebrink, P., Långström, & Gumpert, C. H. (2006). Predicting aggressive and disruptive behavior in referred 6- to 12-year-old boys: Prospective validation of the EARL-20B risk/needs checklist. *Assessment, 13*, 356–367.

Epperson, D. L., Kaul, J. D., Huot, S. J., Hesselton, D., Alexander, W., & Goldman, G. (2003). *Minnesota Sex Offender Screening Tool—Revised technical paper: Development, validation, and recommended risk level cut scores*. St. Paul, MN: Minnesota Department of Corrections.

Estelle v. Smith, 451 U. S. 454 (1981).

Foucha v. Louisiana, 504 U. S. 71 (1992).

Gendreau, P., Goggin, C., & Smith, P. (2002). Is the PCL-R really the "unparalleled" measure of offender risk? A lesson in knowledge cumulation. *Criminal Justice and Behavior, 29*, 397–426.

Gore, K. S. (2007). *Adjusted actuarial assessment of sex offenders: The impact of clinical overrides on predictive accuracy* (Doctoral dissertation). Available from ProQuest Dissertations and Theses database. (3274898)

Grann, M., & Långström, N. (2007). Actuarial assessment of violence risk: To weigh or not to weigh? *Criminal Justice and Behavior, 34*, 22–36.

Gregg v. Georgia, 428 U. S. 153 (1976).

Grove, W., & Meehl, P. (1996). Comparative efficiency of informal (subjective, impressionistic) and formal (mechanical, algorithmic) prediction procedures: The clinical-statistical controversy. *Psychology, Public Policy, and Law, 2*, 293–323.

Hanson, R., & Thornton, D. (1999). *Static 99: Improving actuarial risk assessments for sex offenders*. Ottawa, Ontario, Canada: Ministry of the Solicitor General of Canada.

Hanson, R. K., & Howard, P. D. (2010). Individual confidence intervals do not inform decision-makers about the accuracy of risk assessment evaluations. *Law and Human Behavior, 34*, 275–281.

Hare, R. (2003). *Manual for the Revised Psychopathy Checklist* (2nd ed.). Toronto, Ontario, Canada: Multi-Health Systems.

Harris, G. T., Rice, M. E., & Quinsey, V. L. (2008). Shall evidence-based risk assessment be abandoned? *British Journal of Psychiatry, 192*, 154.

Hart, S., Michie, C., & Cooke, D. (2007). The precision of actuarial risk assessment instruments: Evaluating the "margins of error" of group versus individual predictions of violence. *British Journal of Psychiatry, 190*, s60–s65.

Heilbrun, K. (1997). Prediction vs. management models relevant to risk assessment: The importance of legal context. *Law and Human Behavior, 21*, 347–359.

Heilbrun, K. (2001). *Principles of forensic mental health assessment*. New York, NY: Kluwer Academic/Plenum.

Heilbrun, K. (2009). *Evaluation for risk of violence in adults*. New York, NY: Oxford.

Heilbrun, K., DeMatteo, D., Marczyk, G., & Goldstein, A. M. (2008). Standards of practice and care in forensic mental health assessment: Legal, professional, and principles-based consideration. *Psychology, Public Policy, and Law, 14,* 1–26.

Heilbrun, K., Douglas, K., & Yasuhara, K. (2009). Violence risk assessment: Core controversies. In J. Skeem, K. Douglas, & S. Lilienfeld (Eds.), *Psychological science in the courtroom: Controversies and consensus* (pp. 333–357). New York, NY: Guilford.

Heilbrun, K., Grisso, T., & Goldstein, A. (2009). *Foundations of forensic mental health assessment.* New York, NY: Oxford.

Heilbrun, K., Yasuhara, K., & Shah, S. (2009). Violence risk assessment tools: Overview and critical analysis. In R. Otto & K. Douglas (Eds.), *Handbook of violence risk assessment tools* (pp. 1–17). New York, NY: Routledge.

International Association of Correctional and Forensic Psychology Practice Standards Committee. (2010). Standards for psychology services in jails, prisons, correctional facilities, and agencies. *Criminal Justice and Behavior, 37,* 749–808.

Jones v. United States, 463 U. S. 354 (1983).

Jurek v. Texas, 428 U. S. 263 (1976).

Kansas v. Hendricks, 521 U. S. 346 (1997).

Kraemer, H., Kazdin, A., Offord, D., Kessler, R., Jensen, P., & Kupfer, D. (1997). Coming to terms with the terms of risk. *Archives of General Psychiatry, 54,* 337–343.

Kraemer, H., Measelle, J., Ablow, J., Essex, M., Boyce, W., & Kupfer, D. (2003). A new approach to multiple informants: Mixing and matching context and perspectives. *American Journal of Psychiatry, 160,* 1566–1577.

Kroner, D., Mills, J., & Reddon, J. (2005). A coffee can, factor analysis, and prediction of antisocial behavior: The structure of criminal risk. *International Journal of Law and Psychiatry, 28,* 360–374.

Kropp, P. R., & Hart, S. (2000). The Spousal Assault Risk Assessment (SARA) guide: Reliability and validity in adult male offenders. *Law and Human Behavior, 24,* 101–118.

Lander, T. D., & Heilbrun, K. (2009). The content and quality of forensic mental health assessment: Validation of a principles-based approach. *International Journal of Forensic Mental Health, 8,* 115–121.

Leistico, A. R., Salekin, R. T., DeCoster, J., & Rogers, R. (2008). A large-scale meta-analysis relating the Hare measures to psychopathy and antisocial conduct. *Law and Human Behavior, 32,* 28–45.

Lessard v. Schmidt, 349 F. Supp. 1078 (1973).

McGowan, M. R. (2007). *The predictive validity of violence risk assessment within educational settings* (Doctoral dissertation). Available from ProQuest Dissertations and Theses database. (3257736)

McGrath, R. (2008). Predictor combination in binary decision-making situations. *Psychological Assessment, 20,* 195–205.

Melton, G., Petrila, J., Poythress, N., & Slobogin, C. (2007). *Psychological evaluations for the courts: A handbook for mental health professionals and lawyers* (3rd ed.). New York, NY: Guilford.

Meyers, J., & Schmidt, F. (2008). Predictive validity of the Structured Assessment for Violence Risk in Youth (SAVRY) with juvenile offenders. *Criminal Justice and Behavior, 35,* 344–355.

Monahan, J. (2008). Structured risk assessment of violence. In R. Simon & K. Tardiff (Eds.), *Textbook of violence assessment and management* (pp. 17–33). Washington, DC: American Psychiatric.

Monahan, J., & Steadman, H. (Eds.). (1994). *Violence and mental disorder: Developments in risk assessment.* Chicago: University of Chicago.

Monahan, J., Steadman, H., Appelbaum, P., Grisso, T., Mulvey, E., Roth, L., Robbins, P. C., Banks, S., & Silver, E. (2005). *Classification of Violence Risk: Professional manual.* Lutz, FL: PAR.

Monahan, J., Steadman, H., Robbins, P. C., Appelbaum, P., Banks, S., Grisso, T., Heilbrun, K., Mulvey, E., Roth, L., & Silver, E. (2005). Prospective validation of the multiple iterative classification tree model of violence risk assessment. *Psychiatric Services, 56,* 810–815.

Monahan, J., Steadman, H., Silver, E., Appelbaum, P., Robbins, P. C., Mulvey, E., Roth, L., Grisso, T., & Banks, S. (2001). *Rethinking risk assessment: The MacArthur Study of Mental Disorder and Violence.* New York, NY: Oxford.

Morse, S. (2008). The ethics of forensic practice: Reclaiming the wasteland. *Journal of the American Academy of Psychiatry and the Law, 36,* 206–217.

National Research Council. (1989). *Improving risk communication.* Washington, DC: National Academy.

O'Connor v. Donaldson, 422 U. S. 563 (1975).

Profitt v. Florida, 428 U. S. 242 (1976).

Rogers, R., & Ewing, C. (1989). Ultimate opinion proscriptions: A cosmetic fix and a plea for empiricism. *Law and Human Behavior, 13,* 357–374.

Rogers, R., & Ewing, C. (2003). The prohibition of ultimate opinions: A misguided enterprise. *Journal of Forensic Psychology Practice, 3,* 65–76.

Sandella v. Trischetti (In re Marriage of Trischetti), No. 1 CA-CV 07-0125, 2008 WL 4107989, at 2 (Ariz. Ct. App. Feb. 26, 2008).

Satterwhite v. Texas, 486 U. S. 249 (1988).

Silver, E., Mulvey, E. P., & Monahan, J. (1999). Assessing violence risk among discharged psychiatric patients: Toward an ecological approach. *Law and Human Behavior, 23,* 235–253.

Sjösted, G., & Långström, N. (2002). Assessment of risk for criminal recidivism among rapists: A comparison of four different measures. *Psychology, Crime, & Law, 8*, 25–40.

Snowden, R. J., Gray, N. S., & Taylor, J. (2010). Risk assessment for future violence in individuals from an ethnic minority group. *International Journal of Forensic Mental Health, 9*, 118–123.

Steadman, H., Monahan, J., Appelbaum, P., Grisso, T., Mulvey, E., Roth, L., Robbins, P. C., & Klassen, D. (1994). Designing a new generation of risk assessment research. In J. Monahan & H. Steadman (Eds.), *Violence and mental disorder: Developments in risk assessment* (pp. 297–318). Chicago: University of Chicago.

Steadman, H., Mulvey, E., Monahan, J., Robbins, P., Appelbaum, P., Grisso, T., Roth, L., & Silver, E. (1998). Violence by people discharged from acute psychiatric inpatient facilities and by others in the same neighborhoods. *Archives of General Psychiatry, 55*, 1–9.

Tillbrook, C., Mumley, D., & Grisso, T. (2003). Avoiding expert opinions on the ultimate legal question: The case for integrity. *Journal of Forensic Psychology Practice, 3*, 77–87.

Viljoen, J. L., Scalora, M., Cuadra, L., Bader, S., Chávez, V., Ullman, D., & Lawrence, L. (2008). Assessing risk for violence in adolescents who have sexually offended: A comparison of the J-SOAP-II, J-SORRAT-II, and SAVRY. *Criminal Justice and Behavior, 35*, 5–23.

Vitek v. Jones, 445 U. S. 480 (1980).

Walters, G. D. (2003). Predicting criminal justice outcomes with the Psychopathy Checklist and Lifestyle Criminality Screening Form: A meta-analytic comparison. *Behavioral Sciences and the Law, 21*, 89–102.

Welsh, J., Schmidt, F., McKinnon, L., Chattha, H., & Meyers, J. (2008). A comparative study of adolescent risk assessment instruments: Predictive and incremental validity. *Assessment, 15*, 104–115.

Witt, P. H., & Conroy, M. A. (2009). *Evaluation of sexually violent predators.* New York, NY: Oxford.

7

Evaluation for Jury Selection

MARGARET BULL KOVERA AND BRIAN L. CUTLER

The purpose of this chapter is to introduce practicing attorneys to the scientific psychological literature on jury selection. Beginning with an overview of the legal procedures and case law governing jury selection, we review the research on individual predictors of juror bias (demographics, personality, attitudes) and research on the effectiveness of traditional and scientific jury selection. We review the community survey—a tool commonly used by psychologists involved in scientific jury selection—and investigations of the need for change of venue due to prejudicial pretrial publicity. Our goal is to provide attorneys with insight into the value of psychology in jury selection and prepare them to work effectively with psychologists when the need arises.

Trial by jury is an important right in the United States. Before a trial can begin, a jury must be selected to hear the evidence, consider the attorneys' arguments, apply the law, and render a verdict. Although it is difficult to determine in actual cases whether the selection of particular jurors—as opposed to the strength of the evidence or the relative skill of the attorneys—resulted in a win or a loss, there is anecdotal evidence that jury selection can sway the outcome of a trial. For example, jury selection may have played a role in the acquittal of O. J. Simpson, who was charged with the brutal murders of his ex-wife and her friend. In this very high-profile case, both the prosecution and the defense hired trial consultants to assist them with jury selection. Both consultants had conducted research showing that African-Americans would be more likely than members of other racial or ethnic groups to believe the defense arguments that police misconduct produced the evidence against Mr. Simpson (Davis & Loftus, 2006; Toobin, 1996). This research contradicted Prosecutor Marcia Clark's intuition about who would make good prosecution jurors. She fired her jury consultant and worked to seat a jury

dominated by African-American women, whom she believed would be prosecution-prone, a jury that instead acquitted Simpson of the crimes with which he had been charged (Toobin, 1996).

Although it is impossible to know whether jury-selection strategies or some other feature of the trial (e.g., the evidence, attorney skill) produced the defendant's acquittal, Clark and her trial consultant used different approaches to develop a profile of a pro-prosecution juror. Clark used traditional jury-selection strategies that rely on attorneys' experience and implicit theories of juror behavior to make selection decisions. In contrast, the trial consultant used social-science methods to identify juror characteristics that are related to verdict preferences.

LEGAL CONTEXT

In the United States, jury selection is rooted in a defendant's Constitutional right to an impartial jury. Jury selection is a procedure designed to remove citizens who are unfit to serve on a jury because they hold biases that would prevent them from being impartial decision makers.

Voir dire is the pretrial hearing in which attorneys and/or the judge question prospective jurors in an attempt to uncover any bias that may threaten their impartiality. The primary goal of *voir dire* is to determine whether venirepersons are eligible to serve as jurors (e.g., that they are U.S. citizens, that they understand English) and that they are free from bias or can set aside any bias so that they can evaluate the evidence impartially and follow the law. Different courts allow greater or lesser latitude in the types of questions that may be asked of venirepersons. Under the most limited or minimal *voir dire* conditions, the judge alone asks questions of prospective jurors. The questions asked of venirepersons are typically few in number, are narrow in scope, and require only yes/no responses or a show of hands. The judge generally questions venirepersons in a group, even if the questions are sensitive in nature. Although few sensitive questions are typically asked under these conditions, it is possible that the judge will inquire about previous crime victimization, and it may be difficult for a juror to report that he or she has been the target of a violent or sexual crime in open court. Federal courts practice limited *voir dire*, as do most states, with judge-conducted *voir dire* practiced in California, Delaware, Illinois, Massachusetts, New Hampshire, and New Jersey (Rottman et al., 2000).

In contrast, other courts allow attorneys much more leeway in gathering information about venirepersons during *voir dire*. Four states have attorney-conducted *voir dire*: Connecticut, North Carolina, Texas, and Wyoming (Rottman et al., 2000). In other states, both judges and attorneys participate in *voir dire* questioning. Under expanded *voir dire* conditions, the attorneys are permitted to question the venirepersons; they ask more questions that are broader in scope and that allow for open-ended responses from the potential jurors. Although questioning is still typically done in open court, there are times when individual, sequestered *voir dire* may be allowed if the responses to questions may be sensitive or may taint other venirepersons. Finally, courts practicing extended *voir dire* procedures may be receptive to attorneys' motions to implement a juror questionnaire to collect information from venirepersons before *voir dire* begins. Venirepersons are more likely to admit to undesirable beliefs when responding to questions on surveys than in open court (Chrzanowski, 2005). In addition, collecting information using a survey may allow attorneys to restrict intensive questioning to a smaller number of venirepersons who exhibited bias on the questionnaire, saving the court time.

Laws and Procedures Governing Jury Selection

After observing venirepersons during *voir dire* and evaluating their answers to questions, attorneys may challenge the impartiality of venirepersons and request that they be removed from the pool of potential jurors. Attorneys may challenge a venireperson for cause if they believe that person, during the course of the *voir dire* questioning, has exhibited that he or she holds some bias or prejudice that would prevent a fair evaluation of the evidence. A bias that would lead to the dismissal of a potential juror could come from many sources, including personal experience, exposure to pretrial publicity, or prejudicial attitudes. For a challenge for cause to be successful, the attorney must persuade the judge that the venireperson revealed evidence of this bias during *voir dire* and that the venireperson is unwilling or unable to put that bias aside when evaluating trial evidence.

Theoretically, an unlimited number of potential jurors may be removed through challenges for cause. In practice, the number of challenges for cause is limited by an attorney's ability to convince a judge that a venireperson holds a bias that would interfere with his or her ability to evaluate the evidence fairly. Judges may deny the attorneys' requests to excuse a potential juror for cause because (1) they are not persuaded that the venireperson is biased in a way that would influence the evaluation of the case evidence or (2) they believe that the juror can set aside the bias when considering the evidence and be impartial. Judges' decisions about whether a venireperson can successfully set aside bias depend upon the confidence with which venirepersons assert their ability to be fair (Rose & Diamond, 2008).

Juror Rehabilitation as an Alternative to Excusing Venirepersons for Cause

Sometimes, when a venireperson appears biased, either the judge or one of the attorneys attempts to rehabilitate apparently biased jurors by educating them about the law or extracting promises from the venirepersons that they will ignore their prejudices and make their decisions based on the evidence presented at trial and the law (Cosper, 2003). Venirepersons who promise to set aside their biases and prevent them from affecting their judgments are deemed rehabilitated and may serve on the jury (Studebaker & Penrod, 2005). Some scholars have criticized this practice, believing that jurors agree to judges' requests to ignore their biases and follow law because of the social pressures inherent in the situation (e.g., Cosper, 2003). Studies of jury-selection practice suggest that it is a commonly used procedure (e.g., Giewat, 2001).

Two methods that judges use to rehabilitate potential jurors are to instruct jurors on the law—in an attempt to eliminate bias—or extract a public commitment to ignore the bias when deciding the case. In the first study to directly test whether juror rehabilitation effectively reduces juror bias, Crocker and Kovera (2010) found that although biased jurors remained more likely to find the defendant guilty than were unbiased jurors, instructing jurors on the related law and requesting that they ignore biases (the rehabilitation procedure) affected both biased and unbiased jurors similarly in that it reduced both the likelihood that they would render a guilty verdict and attitudinal bias toward the insanity defense equally for both groups. Crocker (2010) found that rehabilitation consisting of instruction on the relevant law and obtaining public commitment to set aside bias caused both biased and unbiased jurors to render fewer guilty verdicts but did not increase their sensitivity to variations in the strength of the evidence supporting a finding that the defendant was insane. Crocker (2010) also found that rehabilitation aimed at curing the effects of pretrial publicity exposure (a traditional suppression instruction to ignore pretrial publicity and a novel concentration instruction that urged the jurors to concentrate on the evidence) failed to mitigate the prejudicial effect of pretrial publicity.

Change of Venue as an Alternative Method of Alleviating Juror Bias

There are times when juror bias may be so virulent in a venue that juror rehabilitation is not a credible option and so prevalent that excusing all of the biased jurors will make it too difficult to seat a jury. The U.S. Supreme Court has recognized that there are times when prejudicial pretrial publicity can interfere with the defendant's right to a fair trial. Courts are to consider whether the substance, quality, and distribution of pretrial publicity created a prejudicial atmosphere in the venue and if so, the trial should be held in a different venue that was not subject to the biasing media (*Rideau v. Louisiana*, 1963). However, the Court has also suggested several other remedies for the effects of pretrial publicity, including continuances, extended *voir dire* questioning, rehabilitation, sequestered juries, and judicial instructions (*Sheppard v. Maxwell*, 1966).

Attorneys can support a motion for a change of venue with an affidavit from a jury consultant that describes evidence from a survey that compares the opinions held by community members in the current venue and at least one other venue in which the media coverage of the case was less extensive (Nietzel & Dillehay, 1983). Consultants may also present evidence from a content analysis of media

coverage of the case, comparing the extent and nature of the pretrial publicity in the different venues (Studebaker, Robbennolt, Pathak-Sharma, & Penrod, 2000). Judges may be more willing to grant a change of venue, rather than rely on one of the other available remedies for pretrial publicity, if the consultant can show that prejudicial media coverage is more extensive or that public opinion about the defendant is more negative in the current venue than in an alternative venue.

Peremptory Challenges

Attorneys also receive a prescribed number of peremptory challenges, which they can use to excuse potential jurors without providing reasons for their decisions. Peremptory challenges allow attorneys to strike potential jurors whom they believe will be biased against their side. The number of peremptory challenges that each attorney has varies by jurisdiction (e.g., state, circuit, or district courts), trial type (criminal vs. civil), crime seriousness (e.g., capital, felony, misdemeanor), and other factors, including size of the jury (Rottman & Strickland, 2006).

In federal criminal court, each side has 20 peremptory challenges in capital cases and 3 peremptory challenges in trials for misdemeanors. For felony charges tried in federal court, the prosecution has 6 peremptory challenges and the defense has 10 (Rule 24 of the Federal Rules of Criminal Procedure, 2010). Other factors may induce a judge to grant additional peremptory challenges if the judge believes that it is necessary to ensure an impartial jury, with extensive pretrial media coverage being one common reason for increasing the challenges granted to the defense.

Case Law Restricting the Use of Peremptory Challenges

Once an attorney has indicated that he or she wants to use a peremptory challenge to eliminate a potential juror, the judge will then excuse the challenged venireperson unless the opposing attorney claims that the attorney is challenging venirepersons because they belong to a protected group. In *Batson v. Kentucky* (1986), the Supreme Court described three steps that must be followed when the defense raises an objection to the prosecutor's use of peremptory challenges. First, the defense must make a case that the prosecutor's challenges were discriminatory by establishing that the defendant is a member of a cognizable group and that the prosecutor used peremptory challenges to excuse venirepersons who shared racial-group membership with the defendant. Once the defense has shown that the prosecutor's use of peremptory challenges was discriminatory, the burden of proof shifts to the prosecutors to provide neutral reasons—that is, reasons other than race—for excluding the venirepersons that they challenged. Finally, the judge must evaluate the evidence provided by both the defense and the prosecution and make a determination of whether the prosecution's peremptory challenges were racially biased.

In two recent cases, the Supreme Court upheld and clarified its ruling in *Batson*. In *Miller-El v. Dretke* (2005), the Court ruled that the prosecution's stated justifications for removing a black venireperson were equally applicable to white venirepersons who were not challenged. Moreover, the court ruled that the prosecution improperly provided a graphic description of the imposition of the death penalty to a majority of the black venire members but to only 6% of white venirepersons before inquiring about their feelings about the death penalty. The Court concluded that the differential manner in which the prosecution posed its questions about the death penalty could have contributed to any differences in the responses given by black and non-black venirepersons. Based on these findings, the Supreme Court overturned Miller-El's death sentence. In *Snyder v. Louisiana* (2008), the Supreme Court ruled that the prosecution had discriminated in its use of striking a black venireperson because the reasons that the prosecution provided for the strike were not supported by any evidence in the record.

Since *Batson,* the Supreme Court has decided cases that have extended the prohibition of race-based challenges to include situations in which the prosecutor excused all the black venirepersons even though the defendant was white (*Powers v. Ohio*, 1991). Similarly, the Supreme Court has also extended *Batson* to preclude defense attorneys from striking members of a specific racial group (*Georgia v. McCollum*, 1992) and to civil trials (*Edmonson v. Leesville Concrete Company*, 1991). Other cases have extended *Batson*'s protections to other cognizable groups, including gender (*J.E.B. v. Alabama*, 1994), religion (*State v. Fulton*, 1992), and sexual orientation (*People v. Garcia*, 2000).

Discrimination in the Use of Peremptory Challenges

Archival studies of jury selection in actual cases find that when black venirepersons are struck from the venire, it is more likely that the prosecution struck them than the defense (Baldus, Woodworth, Zuckerman, Weiner, & Broffitt, 2001). Moreover, when verdicts were appealed on the grounds that venirepersons were improperly excluded, the appeals usually were unsuccessful (Gabbidon, Kowal, Jordan, Roberts, & Vincenzi, 2008). The failure of *Batson* appeals is not surprising given that attorneys are proficient at generating race-neutral justifications for their challenges even when the evidence suggests that race played a role in their strike decisions (Sommers & Norton, 2008).

In an empirical test of whether venireperson race influences attorneys' peremptory challenge decisions, prosecutors read venireperson profiles across which venireperson race varied (Sommers & Norton, 2007). Regardless of the other characteristics of the venireperson, prosecutors were more likely to excuse the black venireperson than the white venireperson. Uniformly, the attorneys provided race-neutral explanations for their strike decisions. Thus, even if a court scrutinized the explanations provided by the attorneys, the attorneys provided credible race-neutral explanations for their race-based decisions.

Similarly, knowledge of the prohibition against gender discrimination in the use of peremptory challenges (*J.E.B. v. Alabama*, 1994) does not prevent gender from affecting which jurors are excused. In one study of jury selection in a simulated case of a woman charged with murdering her abusive husband (Norton, Sommers, & Brauner, 2007), more participants struck the woman than the man, even when they had received a reminder that the law prohibits removing potential jurors because of their gender. When justifying their strike decisions, participants cited the venireperson's role as the reason for the strike, even though the role was not predictive of strikes. Moreover, the reminder to be gender neutral, although it did not reduce gender bias in the strikes, increased participants' abilities to provide gender-neutral justifications.

FORENSIC CONSTRUCTS: MEASURING POTENTIAL PREDICTORS OF VERDICT

The practice of scientific jury selection involves the identification of juror characteristics that predict verdict inclinations in specific trials and that attorneys can assess to inform their use of challenges for cause and peremptory challenges. Some demographic characteristics—race, gender, age, socioeconomic status—may be reasonably easy to assess based on simple observation of the assembled venirepersons. Attorneys can collect information about other demographic characteristics of potential jurors—education, religious affiliation and practice, occupation, political affiliation—with simple inquiries, and it is likely that information is reliable. Other venireperson traits, including individual differences in personality, general juror bias, and case-specific attitudes, may be more difficult to assess reliably with single off-the-cuff questions.

The process of constructing psychometrically sound tools to assess personality and attitudes is fairly standard across content areas. First, researchers gather or create a large number of items that are designed to tap the constructs they are interested in measuring and present them to relevant populations who provide responses to the items. Next, researchers subject those responses to statistical analyses (e.g., factor analysis) to determine which of the items measure the same latent constructs. This process may be repeated, with the researchers dropping some items that do not co-vary with others from the scale and adding new items. Once the researchers have a set of items that appear to measure what the researchers intended to measure (a characteristic known as face validity) and are internally consistent (i.e., the items correlate with one another), they may also establish whether the scale possesses other forms of reliability and validity. For example, they may test to ensure that the new scale correlates with other scales that tap overlapping constructs (convergent validity) but does not correlate with other measures that are designed to test different constructs (divergent validity).

One advantage of using scales constructed using psychometric methods is that they have known reliability and validity (Lecci, Snowden, & Morris, 2004). Although it would be desirable to ask venirepersons to answer all items on a scale because the research on a scale's validity and reliability is established using the full scale (Brodsky, 2009), the judge may rule that only some subset of the questions may be asked. Some items may be more appropriate for use by the prosecution or plaintiff than by the defense, so each item should be evaluated to determine whether the item assesses information that will help in exercising challenges (Brodsky, 2009).

Personality Traits Thought to Be Related to Trial Judgments

The term "personality" refers to a pattern of thoughts, feelings, and behavior that manifests across situations and can be used to differentiate people from one another. There are a few personality traits that relate to people's perceptions of wrongdoing and punishment. Because these traits are related to concepts like determinations of wrongdoing and punishment for transgressions, it is likely that knowledge of whether venirepersons possess these traits may allow for the prediction of their trial judgments.

Belief in a Just World

People who believe in a just world have a tendency to believe that if something bad happens to others, it happened because they did something to deserve the harm (Hafer & Bègue, 2005; Lerner, 1980). Just-world beliefs represent an individual difference variable that describes one's conceptualization of the world as a just place and that can be assessed using self-report inventories. Although there have been attempts to create a more psychometrically sound measure of just-world beliefs, most studies use the 20-item Just World Scale (JWS) developed by Rubin and Peplau (1973).

Locus of Control

Locus of control refers to the extent to which people believe that they have control over the contingencies associated with their behavior. People with an internal locus of control believe that the consequences that they will receive are based on their behavior—which is under their control—or are due to some personal characteristic they possess. People with an external locus of control are more likely to believe that their outcomes are random, due to luck or chance, or under the control of someone else, and that nothing they can do will change the consequences they receive (Rotter, 1990). It is possible that people with an internal locus of control will be more likely than people with an external locus of control to find defendants responsible for the crimes with which they have been charged. One measure of locus of control is the Internal-External (I-E) Scale (Rotter, 1966), a 23-item scale that forces respondents to choose between two alternative options: an external locus item and an internal locus item.

Authoritarianism

Those who are high in authoritarianism are highly traditional, adhere to conservative social norms, and believe in punishing people who violate those norms (Adorno, Frenkel-Brunskwik, Levinson, & Sanford, 1950). In addition to supporting adherence to rules and punishing those who break them, those low in legal authoritarianism are more likely than their high-scoring counterparts to support civil liberties and defendants' rights under the Constitution (Narby, Cutler, & Moran, 1993). The Revised Legal Authoritarianism Questionnaire (Kravitz, Cutler, & Brock, 1993) is the measure of legal authoritarianism with the best reliability and validity.

Measures of General Juror Bias

Based on the assumption that jurors' decisions in criminal trials are a function of their evaluation of the probability that the defendant committed the crime with which he is charged and their criterion for how certain they must be about the defendant's guilt to find him guilty, Kassin and Wrightsman (1983) developed the Juror Bias Scale (JBS), which contains items designed to measure jurors' pretrial beliefs about the probability of commission (PC) and reasonable doubt (RD). In another attempt to create a measure of general juror bias, Lecci and Myers (2008) created the Pretrial Juror Attitudes Questionnaire (PJAQ). The PJAQ has six subscales: conviction proneness (which is conceptually similar to the RD scale from the JBS), system confidence, cynicism toward the defense (both of which overlap with the PC scale from the JBS), social justice, racial bias, and innate criminality.

Measures of Case-Specific Attitudes

Although there is merit in developing measures of general juror bias, there are ways in which these measures are limited. First, the measures that have been developed have concentrated on bias relevant to decision making in criminal trials, ignoring general juror bias in civil trials. Second, there

is a significant body of research on the social psychology of the attitude–behavior relationship, and a meta-analysis of that literature shows that attitudes toward specific objects or issues better predict specific behaviors—like rendering a verdict in a specific case—than do general attitudes (Kraus, 1995). Consistent with these findings, scholars have constructed measures of attitudes toward case-specific legal issues.

For example, several measures of attitudes toward insanity have been developed. The Insanity Defense Attitudes-Revised scale (Skeem, Louden, & Evans, 2004), which has the best reliability and validity, has two factors: a *strict liability* factor that taps whether people believe that mental health is related to capacity for quality decision making and that capacity is important for determining legal responsibility; and an *injustice and danger* factor that taps the extent to which people believe that the insanity defense is unfair and releases dangerous criminals into society. The scale is both reliable and valid.

Researchers have met with mixed success in developing reliable and valid measures of case-specific attitudes. One successful effort resulted in the Attitudes toward the Death Penalty Scale, which consists of 15 items representing five factors: General Support, Retribution and Revenge, Death Penalty is a Deterrent, Death Penalty is Cheaper, and Life Without Possibility of Parole Allows Parole (O'Neil, Patry, & Penrod, 2004). The Attitudes Toward Eyewitnesses Scale, which contains nine items and has good internal reliability, did not predict verdicts in one trial simulation in which the eyewitness identification was the crucial evidence (Narby & Cutler, 1994). Finally, there is at least one reasonably reliable measure of attitudes toward the civil-litigation crisis that taps respondents' agreement with statements that society has become too litigious and that civil jury awards are too large (Hans & Lofquist, 1994), but there appears to be no empirical evidence of its predictive validity.

EMPIRICAL FOUNDATIONS AND LIMITS

Attorneys tasked with exercising challenges under minimal *voir dire* conditions face a difficult task that is made more difficult by restricting the information available to them. Under minimal *voir dire* procedures, attorneys may not be able to ask any questions of the venire pool, with only the judge asking questions of the venirepersons. Minimal *voir dire* is unlikely to uncover more than basic demographic information from the venirepersons, including race, gender, marital and parental status, occupation, and whether one has been a victim of a crime.

Demographic Predictors of Verdict

Most available empirical evidence shows relatively weak relationships between demographic characteristics and verdict that are often moderated by other variables. For example, juror race does not have a reliable main effect on juror judgments but interacts with defendant race to influence verdict in criminal cases, with jurors rendering more guilty verdicts and longer sentences when the defendant is a member of a racial outgroup (Mitchell, Haw, Pfeifer, & Meissner, 2006). However, when racial issues are salient in a trial, the salience minimizes white juror bias against black defendants; that is, white jurors are more likely to convict a black defendant than a white defendant, but not when race is salient (Sommers & Ellsworth, 2001). Race is not reliably associated with damage awards or liability judgments in civil cases (Vinson et al., 2008).

Like race and ethnicity, juror gender is—at best—a weak and unreliable predictor of trial judgments, with inconsistent effects on damage awards (Diamond, Saks, & Landsman, 1998) and liability judgments (Vinson et al., 2008). Gender does reliably predict verdict in trials that involve allegations of child sexual abuse (e.g., Kovera, Gresham, Borgida, Gray, & Regan, 1997), rape (Brekke & Borgida, 1988), hostile work environment (Kovera, McAuliff, & Hebert, 1999), and murder of batterers by the women they battered (Schuller & Hastings, 1996). In these cases, mock jurors are more likely to vote for conviction when the defendant is of the opposite sex. In one study, this outgroup bias was mediated by attitudinal differences between men and women (Bottoms et al., 2011).

Finally, one study demonstrated a relationship between involvement with the legal system and verdict (Culhane, Hosch, & Weaver, 2004). Crime victimization in general did not predict verdicts in the simulated burglary case. However, those jurors who had been, or knew someone who had been, a victim of a property crime were more likely to convict than were jurors who had no such experience with this kind of victimization.

Personality Predictors of Verdict

Most personality traits have also proven to be an unreliable predictor of trial judgments. For example, some studies show a positive correlation between just-world beliefs and punitive attitudes toward offenders (e.g., Butler & Moran, 2007), but the relationship between just-world beliefs and verdict is often moderated by other variables such as gender (Ford, Liwag-McLamb, & Foley, 1998) and the socioeconomic status of the defendant (Freeman, 2006). The findings for the predictive validity of locus of control are similar inconsistent. In some jury-simulation studies, people with an internal locus of control suggested more severe punishments for a defendant (Sosis, 1974) and were more likely to find a defendant guilty (Álvarez, De la Fuente, & De la Fuente, 2009) than were people with an external locus of control. Other studies showed the opposite relationship between locus of control and verdict: mock jurors with an external locus of control were more likely to convict (Butler, 2010) and more likely to evaluate statutory mitigators of capital murder favorably (Butler & Moran, 2007) than were those with an internal locus, but these results are not universally obtained (e.g., Beckham, Spray, & Pietz, 2007).

In contrast, a meta-analysis of 20 studies that examined the relationship between authoritarianism and verdicts in a criminal case demonstrated that authoritarianism is a reliable predictor of verdict (Narby et al., 1993). The strength of the authoritarianism–verdict relationship varied as a function of crime type, with the smallest correlation between authoritarianism and verdict found in rape cases, a larger correlation found in murder cases, and the largest found in other felony cases. The correlation also was stronger when studies used measures of legal authoritarianism than when they used traditional measures of authoritarianism. Given these findings, attorneys will want to consider asking some *voir dire* questions that are designed to tap legal authoritarianism in criminal cases. They may be able to convince the judge to allow legal-authoritarianism questions by arguing that they provide information about whether venirepersons should be excused for cause because they hold attitudes that could lead them to deny defendants their civil liberties.

Attitudinal Predictors of Verdict

Although some scholars have raised concerns about the predictive validity of the original JBS (e.g., Myers & Lecci, 1998), there are a number of studies demonstrating its ability to predict verdicts in a variety of cases. For example, mock jurors who scored high on the JBS (i.e., showed pro-prosecution bias) were more likely to convict a juvenile who was being tried in adult court (Tang & Nunez, 2003) and judged a juvenile defendant to be a more dangerous offender (Tang, Nunez, & Bourgeois, 2009) than did mock jurors who had lower JBS scores (i.e., showed pro-defense bias). These findings are not specific to the United States. Mock jurors in Spain completed a Spanish translation of the JBS; pro-prosecution jurors were more likely to convict a defendant of murder than were pro-defense jurors (De la Fuente, De la Fuente, & García, 2003). Similarly, the majority of the Pretrial Juror Attitudes Questionnaire (PJAQ) subscales predict verdicts in expected ways across a variety of trial types, with the exception of a rape trial (Lecci & Myers, 2008). JBS scores also failed to predict mock jurors' verdicts in a rape trial simulation (Kassin & Wrightsman, 1983).

In almost all studies, case-specific attitudes were excellent predictors of verdict. In a jury-simulation study with undergraduates, negative attitudes toward psychiatrists—as measured by the Attitudes Toward Psychiatrists Scale—were associated with convicting the defendant as opposed to acquitting him because of insanity (Cutler, Moran, & Narby, 1992). Similarly, attitudes toward the insanity defense were negatively associated with conviction rates, with lower (less favorable) scores on the Attitudes toward the Insanity Defense scale leading to higher conviction rates (Cutler et al., 1992). The total score from the combined scales had an even stronger association with verdict. The Insanity Defense Attitudes-Revised (IDA-R) scale also predicted verdicts in a number of studies (Crocker & Kovera, 2010; Skeem et al., 2004).

Attitudes toward the death penalty also predict legal decisions. In a meta-analysis conducted before there was a validated measure of death-penalty attitudes, death-penalty attitudes predicted verdicts in capital murder cases and had an even stronger association with capital sentencing (Nietzel,

McCarthy, & Kern, 1999). Other studies find that death-penalty attitudes influence how people evaluate aggravating and mitigating circumstances in the penalty phase, with supporters evaluating aggravating factors more favorably and opponents evaluating mitigating factors more favorably (Butler & Moran, 2002). Several subscales of the validated measure of death-penalty attitudes were reliably associated with mock jurors' sentencing judgments in simulated capital trials, with the scale measuring general support for the death penalty providing the best prediction (O'Neil et al., 2004).

Unlike other attitudes tapping case-specific attitudes in criminal trials, the Attitudes Toward Eyewitnesses Scale (ATES) did not reliably predict verdicts in two trial-simulation studies (Narby & Cutler, 1994). It is unclear whether the scale, which lacks data on its validity, is a poor measure of eyewitness attitudes or whether eyewitness attitudes simply fail to affect verdicts, even in cases that hinge on eyewitness evidence.

Although case-specific attitudes are more successful predictors of verdict than are demographic characteristics, most personality traits, and measures of general juror bias, even the correlations between case-specific attitudes and verdict, are relatively modest. Despite relatively small correlations, attitudes may still play a critical role in trial outcomes. In one study, the use of data that could be collected under minimal *voir dire* conditions allowed for only chance accuracy (50%) when predicting jurors' verdicts, but the addition of data that could be collected only with extended *voir dire* increased predictive accuracy to 78% (Moran, Cutler, & Loftus, 1990). When the trial evidence is ambiguous, even the relatively small contribution of case-specific attitudes may mean the difference between a conviction and an acquittal (Moran, Cutler, & De Lisa, 1994).

The Effectiveness of Traditional and Scientific Jury-Selection Methods

Trial techniques manuals are replete with recommendations about how to conduct *voir dire* and what types of juror profiles are desirable for which types of cases. Litigation consultants are selling their services to attorneys who believe that scientific jury selection can help them select a more favorable jury. What does the available empirical evidence tell us about whether these assumptions are correct? Can attorneys eliminate biased venirepersons from the panel, or would they have better success if they hired a consultant who used social science methods to assist them with jury selection?

Effectiveness of Traditional Jury Selection

In one effort to evaluate attorneys' jury-selection performance, researchers conducted a series of studies to examine attorneys' lay strategies for judging jurors (Olczak, Kaplan, & Penrod, 1991). In the first of these studies, attorneys read various juror profiles and reported which characteristics and information they typically would seek during *voir dire*. Attorneys generally relied on a very small number of demographic and personality dimensions when making inferences about prospective jurors, suggesting that attorneys use rather unsophisticated stereotypes and strategies in making their decisions. These researchers also compared the performance of college students relative to that of attorneys and found that both groups engaged in similar, unsophisticated strategies in judging prospective jurors. Finally, they had law students and attorneys read a description of a manslaughter prosecution and subsequently rate the desirability of mock jurors who had previously rendered a verdict in the case. Both groups inaccurately judged mock jurors who had previously voted for conviction as more desirable from a defense perspective.

In a study of the *voir dire* process in four felony trials, potential jurors completed a measure of legal authoritarianism before and after the trial and researchers compared the attitudes of venirepersons who were seated on the jury, venirepersons who were challenged by the prosecution, and venirepersons who were challenged by the defense (Johnson & Haney, 1994). They also compared the attitudes of the seated jurors with the attitudes of two other potential juries that could have been seated if other methods of jury selection were used: a jury consisting of the first 12 venirepersons called into the courtroom and a jury consisting of 12 venirepersons randomly chosen from the venire pool. Although prosecutors used their challenges to eliminate venirepersons who were more pro-defense and defense attorneys used their challenges to eliminate venirepersons who were more pro-prosecution, the juries who were seated had attitudes that were similar to the attitudes of a randomly chosen set of 12 venirepersons and of the first 12 venirepersons called to serve.

Effectiveness of Scientific Jury Selection

There are relatively few empirical tests of whether scientific jury selection improves the abilities of attorneys to select a favorable jury. In the first test of the relative efficacy of traditional and scientific jury selection, law students received training in traditional or scientific jury selection methods (Horowitz, 1980). After training, the law students watched *voir dires* of close to one hundred community members and rated their desirability as jurors for four simulated trials. Law students who used scientific jury-selection methods were better able to predict the verdicts of the venirepersons than were the students who used traditional methods, but this result obtained in only two of the four trials.

In a study of the effects of consultants in actual capital trials (Nietzel & Dillehay, 1986), there was a relationship between the use of scientific jury selection and the likelihood that the jury sentenced the defendant to death. When there was no trial consultant, almost two thirds of the juries voted for death. When the defense hired a consultant to conduct scientific jury selection, only about one third of the juries recommended the death penalty. Perhaps the use of a jury consultant enabled the attorneys to better capitalize on the strong relationship between death-penalty attitudes and verdicts. However, because the use of scientific jury selection was not randomly assigned to trials, it is unknown whether there were other differences between the trials that used consultants and those that did not. Perhaps trials with consultants also had better attorneys with greater financial resources than did the trials without consultants.

CONDUCTING COMMUNITY SURVEYS

The purpose of a community survey is to gather information about juror characteristics or attitudes that predict venirepersons' predispositions toward the person hiring the consultant (typically the defendant or a plaintiff) and the case. Community surveys allow the consultant to collect demographic and case-relevant attitudinal information from the respondents that can then be explored for any relationships with respondents' verdict inclinations. In addition, surveys may provide respondents with information about the case and ask them to evaluate that information. Finally, community surveys—when conducted in multiple venues—can provide insight into the extent to which a venire has been biased by exposure to pretrial publicity.

Community Surveys for Jury Selection

There are several stages in the development, implementation, and analysis of a community survey conducted to support jury-selection efforts. The process will begin with an attorney contacting a jury consultant to inquire about his or her expertise and availability to assist with jury selection or a change-of-venue motion. Attorneys should contact a consultant as soon as they identify a need for one because the consultant will need enough lead time to gather information about the case, design the community survey, identify a survey research firm to administer the survey to a random sample of community members in relevant jurisdictions, analyze the data, and write a report. Each of these steps requires some time to complete.

To support jury selection, the consultant's work will involve the development and administration of a community survey, with data analysis designed to guide the development of profiles of jurors who will be favorably disposed to the hiring attorney's case. To aid in survey design, attorneys will need to provide the consultant with case materials, including any police reports, transcripts of depositions, and media accounts about the events related to the trial, including videos of local television news broadcasts when they are available. The consultant will want to meet with the hiring attorneys to learn their litigation strategy. After the attorneys have outlined their case strategy, the consultant should ask the attorney to speculate on the litigation strategy of the opposing attorney. The next step in the process is to develop and refine the survey instrument based on the information obtained from the conversation with the hiring attorney. Ultimately, the survey will contain questions that ensure that the respondents are qualified to serve as jurors in the relevant jurisdiction, a summary of the evidence and arguments for both sides and questions that assess respondents' verdict inclinations after hearing each major piece of evidence or argument, and questions assessing personality, attitudinal, or demographic characteristics that may predict verdict inclinations. More detail on the construction of community surveys can be found in Chapter 4

of Kovera and Cutler (2013). Once the survey is finalized the consultant will arrange with a survey research firm to collect the data from jury-eligible community members using random-digit dialing.

The report provided by the consultant should contain a description of how the sample of respondents was obtained, the demographic characteristics of the sample, and whether the characteristics of the sample are similar to the characteristics of residents of the venues from which the samples were drawn. It should also contain a detailed description of the survey, including information about the questions asked of the respondents and the options they had for responding. The report should provide a summary of the distribution of responses on the initial verdict-preference question so that the attorney has data on respondents' verdict inclinations based on the uncontested facts of the case, before exposure to arguments or evidence from either side. Then the report should provide descriptions of analyses that test whether verdict preferences change significantly with the introduction of new information. These analyses provide the attorney with information about which types of evidence or legal arguments are likely to have a significant effect on jurors' judgments.

The final section of the report should summarize the relationships between any personality, attitudinal, or demographic items and the final verdict inclination (i.e., the verdict inclination reported after all arguments and evidence from each side have been presented). This section should highlight the item that is the single best predictor of verdicts. Some consultants will provide the results of a decision-tree analysis, which identifies the single best predictor of a favorable verdict inclination. Among the respondents who have the most-predictive characteristic, the analysis identifies the next-best predictor of a favorable verdict inclination and so on until there are no more significant predictors of verdict inclination. The result is a set of characteristics representing the profile of a favorable juror.

Community Surveys to Support Change-of-Venue Motions

Although there are many similarities between community surveys designed to support motions for a change of venue and those designed to assist attorneys with their jury-selection decisions, there are some important differences and some unique issues that need to be considered when designing and conducting the survey. The attorney should discuss with the consultant which venues would be possible alternatives to the current venue so that community members in those venues can be sampled. In addition, the attorney should provide the consultant with the trial-relevant media reports that have appeared in the venue and alternate venues, or at a minimum provide the consultant with the primary media outlets in the venues so that the consultant can review the pretrial publicity in preparation for drafting the survey.

The survey should begin with questions that determine that the respondent is jury-eligible and lives within one of the venues to be surveyed. The next section of the change-of-venue survey should assess the respondents' media exposure. The section should begin with an item that assesses the respondents' self-report of how closely they follow the news and follow with questions that probe for exposure to case-relevant media using increasingly specific prompts. For those respondents who either recognized the case or recognized the defendant, the caller then probes for the favorability of their impressions of the defendant as well as the probable guilt of the defendant (in criminal cases). Many change-of-venue surveys contain items that assess respondents' self-reported ability to be fair and impartial jurors in the case that has been described. Although responses to these items assessing impartiality are typically uncorrelated with venirepersons' prejudgments of the defendant's guilt (Moran & Cutler, 1991), judges typically want to see how venirepersons respond to them (Posey & Dahl, 2002). The change-of-venue survey, like a jury-selection survey, may assess respondents' views on a variety of outcome-related issues, such as their opinions about whether the defendant is insane or the sentence that the defendant should receive if the defendant is facing the death penalty. The final section of the survey should collect demographic information from the respondent.

An affidavit to support a change-of-venue motion should begin with a description of the professional background of the person who will be swearing to its contents. The affidavit should contain a description of the survey instrument and the methods used to obtain the sample of respondents. The next section of the survey contains a description of the obtained results, starting with a description of the type of information the respondents knew about the case, any differences in negative impressions of the defendant, and pretrial judgments of the defendant's guilt as a function of venue. Sometimes the prejudice in the current venue is so great that there will be significant venue differences in whether respondents believe that they can put aside their opinions and decide the case only on the evidence. If this is the case, then that evidence should be presented in this section on differential prejudice. This section should present data on venue differences in how closely respondents in the different venues followed the case and whether self-reported exposure to pretrial publicity is correlated with negative impressions of the defendant and pretrial verdict inclinations. Finally, the affidavit should review the empirical literature on the effects of pretrial publicity on juror judgments and the relative ineffectiveness of the different safeguards intended to eliminate the prejudicial effects of pretrial publicity.

Consultation During Voir Dire

It is quite common for the consultant's contribution to jury selection to end with the delivery of his or her report. Some attorneys, however, prefer to have the jury consultant by their side during *voir dire* to assist with jury selection. Indeed, some attorneys would rather forgo a community survey and instead rely solely on consultants' observations about the venirepersons during *voir dire* and their recommendations based on those observations. Consultants who perform this task without the underlying data from a community survey are often relying on the same naïve intuitions and hunches on which attorneys rely in traditional jury selection. There may be some cases for which the consultant can glean some recommendations for jury-selection decisions based on empirical data on the predictive value of attitudes or demographic characteristics in similar cases. However, it is very difficult to make accurate *a priori* predictions about what types of characteristics will predict verdicts across cases, even if the cases share similar characteristics. Thus, in the absence of data from a community survey, consultants should limit their participation in *voir dire* to serving as an extra pair of eyes to observe venirepersons' behavior and communications for indications of bias, advising how to best construct supplemental juror questionnaires, or advising attorneys how to ask questions to elicit better information from jurors—as the consultant can make these recommendations based on existing empirical evidence.

Observation of Venireperson Behavior

One function that jury consultants can serve during *voir dire* is providing an extra set of eyes to observe venireperson behavior. Certainly the attorneys will be observing the venirepersons' actions as well, but the presence of a jury consultant as an extra observer has several advantages. First, although attorneys will be identified to the venirepersons as the attorneys in the case, unless the consultant sits at the attorney table, there is little reason for the venirepersons to identify the consultant as working for either side of the case. Because venirepersons sometimes break from managing their impressions when they leave the courtroom, it may be possible for the consultant to observe less-guarded behaviors outside of the courtroom (e.g., in the hallway while venirepersons are waiting to enter the courtroom). Consultants must not have direct interactions with venirepersons to avoid allegations of jury tampering.

Second, the consultant can serve as an important addition to the litigation team by observing juror behavior during the actual questioning. Understandably, attorneys who are questioning venirepersons will be distracted by deciding what question to ask next. They are also likely to focus on the person who is responding to their last question. However, venirepersons may convey their attitudes through facial movements or subtle behaviors while other venirepersons are responding because they might relax their impression management when they feel they are not the direct targets of evaluation. Because consultants are not engaged directly in the conversation between attorney and venireperson, it frees them to observe the behavior of other venirepersons at a time when they may be less likely to monitor their behavior.

Supplemental Juror Questionnaires

Consultants can also assist attorneys to prepare for *voir dire* by helping to develop supplemental juror questionnaires. The first role the consultant may play is to examine the results of the community survey for evidence that might support the need for supplemental questionnaires. If there is evidence that a large proportion of the venire holds an attitude or opinion that suggests they could not follow the law or weigh the evidence fairly, then an argument could be made that time could be saved in *voir dire* by using supplemental juror questionnaires

to identify those who might hold these problematic attitudes.

The second role that consultants might play is to help design the supplemental questionnaire that venirepersons complete before the start of *voir dire*. The consultant will not have direct input into the questions on the questionnaire but can make recommendations through the hiring attorney. Again, data from the community survey should guide the types of questions that are placed on the questionnaire, with the most desirable questions being the very items from the survey that best predicted verdict inclinations. The consultant should recommend the questions with the exact wording that is used in the community survey to maximize the ability of the attorney to make predictions about the venirepersons' verdict inclinations.

Advising Attorneys on *Voir Dire* Techniques

Consultants may also assist during *voir dire* by educating attorneys about evidence-based practices for eliciting better information from people. An example of guidance that a consultant could convey to an attorney is that an interviewer's self-disclosure encourages self-disclosure in others. At least one study showed that attorneys who adopted a more personable interaction style—including limited self-disclosure—were more successful in eliciting honest answers from mock venirepersons than were those who adopted a more formal style (Jones, 1987). Similarly, the advantages of asking open-ended questions to elicit information is common wisdom among psychologists but appears to be less well known—or at least less effectively practiced—among attorneys. There is good evidence that using a nondirective *voir dire* style will elicit better information from attorneys than a directive style (Middendorf & Luginbuhl, 1995).

SUMMARY

Jury consultants can play an important role in litigation. The use of a trial consultant to develop measures that will allow attorneys to assess juror bias more reliably can improve the quality of justice dispensed in our legal system and decrease discriminatory challenges based on race or gender. Consultants can also document the prejudicial effects of pretrial publicity to support attorneys' attempts to move trials to venues where a defendant is more likely to receive a fair trial. To achieve these goals, consultants should be familiar with the research on the construction of psychometrically reliable and valid assessments of attitudes and traits; should be well versed in survey administration, sampling procedures, and statistical analysis; and should remain up to date on the most recent empirical findings on jury behavior.

REFERENCES

Adorno, T. W., Frenkel-Brunswik, E., Levinson, D. J., & Sanford, N. (1950). *The authoritarian personality.* New York: Harper.

Álvarez, P., De la Fuente, E. I., Garcia, J., & De la Fuente, L. (2009). Psychosocial variables in the determination of the verdict object in trials for environmental crimes in Spain. *Environment and Behavior, 41,* 509–525.

Baldus, D. C., Woodworth, G. G., Zuckerman, D., Weiner, N. A., & Broffitt, B. (2001). The use of peremptory challenges in capital murder trials: A legal and empirical analysis. *University of Pennsylvania Journal of Constitutional Law, 3,* 3–169.

Batson v. Kentucky, 476 U.S. 79 (1986).

Beckham, C. M., Spray, B. J., & Pietz, C. A. (2007). Jurors' locus of control and defendants' attractiveness in death penalty sentencing. *Journal of Social Psychology, 147,* 285–298.

Bottoms, B. L., Kalder, A. K., Stevenson, M. C., Oudekerk, B. A., Wiley, T. R., & Perona, A. (2011). Gender differences in jurors' perceptions of infanticide involving disabled and non-disabled infant victims. *Child Abuse & Neglect, 35,* 127–141.

Brekke, N., & Borgida, E. (1988). Expert psychological testimony in rape trials: A social-cognitive analysis. *Journal of Personality and Social Psychology, 55,* 372–386.

Brodsky, S. L. (2009). *Principles and practice of trial consultation.* New York: Guilford Press.

Butler, B. (2010). My client is guilty of 'this,' but not guilty of 'that:' The impact of defense-attorney concessions on juror decisions. *American Journal of Forensic Psychology, 28,* 5–19.

Butler, B., & Moran, G. (2007). The impact of death qualification, belief in a just world, legal authoritarianism, and locus of control on venirepersons' evaluations of aggravating and mitigating circumstances in capital trials. *Behavioral Sciences & the Law, 25,* 57–68.

Butler, B. M., & Moran, G. (2002). The role of death qualification in venirepersons' evaluations of aggravating and mitigating circumstances in capital trials. *Law and Human Behavior, 26,* 175–184.

Chrzanowski, L. M. (2005). *Rape? Truth? And the media: Laboratory and field assessments of pretrial publicity in a real case.* Unpublished doctoral dissertation, City University of New York.

Cosper, C. A. (2003). Rehabilitation of the juror rehabilitation doctrine. *Georgia Law Review, 37,* 1471–1508.

Crocker, C. B. (2010). *An investigation of the psychological processes involved in juror rehabilitation.* Unpublished doctoral dissertation, The Graduate Center, City University of New York.

Crocker, C. B., & Kovera, M. B. (2010). The effects of rehabilitative *voir dire* on juror bias and decision making. *Law and Human Behavior, 34,* 212–226.

Culhane, S. E., Hosch, H. M., & Weaver, G. (2004). Crime victims serving as jurors: Is there bias present? *Law and Human Behavior, 28,* 649–659.

Cutler, B. L., Moran, G. P., & Narby, D. J. (1992). Jury selection in insanity defense cases. *Journal of Research in Personality, 26,* 165–182.

Davis, D., & Loftus, E. F. (2006). Psychologists in the forensic world. In S. I. Donaldson, D. E. Berger, & K. Pezdek (Eds.), *Applied psychology* (pp. 171–200). Mahwah, NJ: Erlbaum.

De La Fuente, L., De La Fuente, E. I., & García, J. (2003). Effects of pretrial juror bias, strength of evidence and deliberation process on juror decisions: New validity evidence of the Juror Bias Scale scores. *Psychology, Crime & Law, 9,* 197–209.

Diamond, S., Saks, M. J., & Landsman, S. (1998). Juror judgments about liability and damages: Sources of variability and ways to increase consistency. *DePaul Law Review, 48,* 301–325.

Edmonson v. Leesville Concrete Company, 500 U.S. 614 (1991).

Federal Rules of Criminal Procedure (2010).

Ford, T. M., Liwag-McLamb, M. G., & Foley, L. A. (1998). Perceptions of rape based on sex and sexual orientation of victim. *Journal of Social Behavior & Personality, 13,* 253–262.

Freeman, N. J. (2006). Socioeconomic status and belief in a just world: Sentencing of criminal defendants. *Journal of Applied Social Psychology, 36,* 2379–2394.

Gabbidon, S. L., Kowal, L. K., Jordan, K. L., Roberts, J. L., & Vincenzi, N. (2008). Race-based peremptory challenges: An empirical analysis of litigation from the U.S. Court of Appeals, 2002–2006. *American Journal of Criminal Justice, 33,* 59–68.

Georgia v. McCollum, 505 U.S. 42 (1992).

Giewat, G. R. (2001). Juror honesty and candor during *voir dire* questioning: The influence of impression management. *Dissertation Abstracts International: Section B: The Sciences and Engineering, 62.*

Hafer, C. L., & Bègue, L. (2005). Experimental research on just-world theory: Problems developments, and future challenges. *Psychological Bulletin, 131,* 128–167.

Hans, V. P., & Lofquist, W. S. (1994). Perceptions of civil justice: The litigation crisis attitudes of civil jurors. *Behavioral Sciences & the Law, 12,* 181–196.

Horowitz, I. A. (1980). Juror selection: A comparison of two methods in several criminal case. *Journal of Applied Social Psychology, 10,* 86–99.

J.E.B. v. Alabama ex rel. T. B., 114 S.Ct. 1419 (1994).

Johnson, C., & Haney, C. (1994). Felony *voir dire*: An exploratory study of its content and effect. *Law and Human Behavior, 18,* 487–506.

Jones, S. E. (1987). Judge- versus attorney-conducted *voir dire*: An empirical investigation of juror candor. *Law and Human Behavior, 11,* 131–146.

Kassin, S. M., & Wrightsman, L. S. (1983). The construction and validation of a juror bias scale. *Journal of Research in Personality, 17,* 423–442.

Kovera, M. B., & Cutler, B. L. (2013). *Jury selection.* New York: Oxford University Press.

Kovera, M. B., Gresham, A. W., Borgida, E., Gray, E., & Regan, P. C. (1997). Does expert testimony inform or influence juror decision-making? A social cognitive analysis. *Journal of Applied Psychology, 82,* 178–191.

Kovera, M. B., McAuliff, B. D., & Hebert, K. S. (1999). Reasoning about scientific evidence: Effects of juror gender and evidence quality on juror decisions in a hostile work environment case. *Journal of Applied Psychology, 84,* 362–375.

Kraus, S. J. (1995). Attitudes and the prediction of behavior: A meta-analysis of the empirical literature. *Personality and Social Psychology Bulletin, 21,* 58–75.

Kravitz, D. A., Cutler, B. L., & Brock, P. (1993). Reliability and validity of the original and revised Legal Attitudes Questionnaire. *Law and Human Behavior, 17,* 661–667.

Lecci, L., & Myers, B. (2008). Individual differences in attitudes relevant to juror decision making: Development and validation of the Pretrial Juror Attitude Questionnaire (PJAQ). *Journal of Applied Social Psychology, 38,* 2010–2038.

Lecci, L., Snowden, J., & Morris, D. (2004). Using social science research to inform and evaluate the contributions of trial consultants in the *voir dire. Journal of Forensic Psychology Practice, 4,* 67–78.

Lerner, M. J. (1980). *The belief in a just world: A fundamental delusion.* New York: Plenum.

Middendorf, K., & Luginbuhl, J. (1995). The value of a nondirective *voir dire* style in jury selection. *Criminal Justice and Behavior, 22,* 129–151.

Miller-El v. Dretke, 125 S.Ct. 2317 (2005).

Mitchell, T. L., Haw, R. M., Pfeifer, J. E., & Meissner, C. A. (2006). Racial bias in mock juror decision-making: A meta-analytic review of defendant treatment. *Law and Human Behavior, 29,* 621–637.

Moran, G., & Cutler, B. L. (1991). The prejudicial impact of pretrial publicity. *Journal of Applied Social Psychology, 21,* 345–367.

Moran, G., Cutler, B. L., & De Lisa, A. (1994). Attitudes toward tort reform, scientific jury selection, and juror bias: Verdict inclination in criminal and civil trials. *Law & Psychology Review, 18,* 309–328.

Moran, G., Cutler, B. L., & Loftus, E. F. (1990). Jury selection in major controlled substance trials: The need for extended *voir dire. Forensic Reports, 3,* 331–348.

Myers, B., & Lecci, L. (1998). Revising the factor structure of the Juror Bias Scale: A method for the empirical validation of theoretical constructs. *Law and Human Behavior, 22,* 239–256.

Narby, D. J., & Cutler, B. L. (1994). Effectiveness of *voir dire* as a safeguard in eyewitness cases. *Journal of Applied Psychology, 79,* 724–729.

Narby, D. J., Cutler, B. L., & Moran, G. (1993). A meta-analysis of the association between authoritarianism and jurors' perceptions of defendant culpability. *Journal of Applied Psychology, 78,* 34–42.

Nietzel, M. T., & Dillehay, R. C. (1983). Psychologists as consultants for changes in venue. *Law and Human Behavior, 7,* 309–355.

Nietzel, M. T., & Dillehay, R. C. (1986). *Psychological consultation in the courtroom.* New York: Pergamon Press.

Nietzel, M. T., McCarthy, D. M., & Kern, M. J. (1999). Juries: The current state of the empirical literature. In R. Roesch, S. D. Hart, & J. R. P. Ogloff (Eds.), *Psychology and law: The state of the discipline* (pp. 23–52). Dordrecht, Netherlands: Kluwer Academic.

Norton, M. I., Sommers, S. R., & Brauner, S. (2007). Bias in jury selection: Justifying prohibited peremptory challenges. *Journal of Behavioral Decision Making, 20,* 467–479.

O'Neil, K. M., Patry, M. W., & Penrod, S. D. (2004). Exploring the effects of attitudes toward the death penalty on capital sentencing verdicts. *Psychology, Public Policy, and Law, 10,* 443–470.

Olczak, P. V., Kaplan, M. F., & Penrod, S. (1991). Attorney's lay psychology and its effectiveness in selecting jurors: Three empirical studies. *Journal of Social Behavior and Personality, 6,* 431–452.

People v. Garcia, 77 Cal. App. 4th 1269, 92 Cal. Rptr. 2d 339 (2000).

Posey, A. J., & Dahl, L. M. (2002). Beyond pretrial publicity: Legal and ethical issues associated with change of venue surveys. *Law and Human Behavior, 26,* 107–125.

Powers v. Ohio, 499 U.S. 400 (1991).

Rideau v. Louisiana, 373 U.S. 723 (1963).

Rose, M. R., & Diamond, S. S. (2008). Judging bias: Juror confidence and judicial rulings on challenges for cause. *Law and Society Review, 42,* 513–549.

Rotter, J. B. (1966). Generalized expectancies for internal versus external control of reinforcement. *Psychological Monographs: General & Applied, 80,* 1–28.

Rotter, J. B. (1990). Internal versus external control of reinforcement: A case history of a variable. *American Psychologist, 45,* 489–493.

Rottman, D., Cantrell, M., Flango, C., Hansen, R., Moninger, C., & LaFountain, N. (2000). *State court organization: 1998.* Washington, DC: U.S. Government Printing Office.

Rottman, D. B., & Strickland, S. M. (2006). *State court organization: 2004.* Washington, DC: Bureau of Justice Statistics.

Rubin, Z., & Peplau, A. (1973). Belief in a just world and reactions to another's lot: A study of participants in the national draft lottery. *Journal of Social Issues, 29,* 73–93.

Schuller, R. A., & Hastings, P. A. (1996). Trials of battered women who kill: The impact of alternative forms of expert evidence. *Law and Human Behavior, 20, 167–187.*

Sheppard v. Maxwell, 384 U.S. 333, 362 (1966).

Skeem, J. L., Louden, J. E., & Evans, J. (2004). Venirepersons' attitudes toward the insanity defense: Developing, refining, and validating a scale. *Law and Human Behavior, 28,* 623–648. doi:10.1007/s10979-004-0487-7

Snyder v. Louisiana, 128 S. Ct. 1203 (2008).

Sommers, S. R., & Ellsworth, P. C. (2001). White jurors' bias: An investigation of prejudice against Black defendants in the American courtroom. *Psychology, Public Policy, and Law, 7,* 201–229.

Sommers, S. R., & Norton, M. I. (2007). Race-based judgments, race-neutral justifications: Experimental examination of peremptory use and the *Batson* challenge procedure. *Law and Human Behavior, 31,* 261–273.

Sommers, S. R., & Norton, M. I. (2008). Race and jury selection: Psychological perspectives on the peremptory challenge debate. *American Psychologist, 63,* 527–539.

Sosis, R. J. (1974). Internal-external control and the perception of responsibility of another for an accident. *Journal of Personality and Social Psychology, 30,* 393–399.

State v. Fulton, 57 Ohio St. 3d 120, 566 N.E.2d 1195 (1992).

Studebaker, C. A., & Penrod, S. D. (2005). Pretrial publicity and its influence on juror decision making. In N. Brewer & K. D. Williams, *Psychology and law: An empirical perspective.* New York: Guilford.

Studebaker, C. A., Robbennolt, J. K., Pathak-Sharma, M. K., and Penrod, S. D. (2000). Assessing pretrial publicity effects: Integrating content analytic results. *Law and Human Behavior, 24,* 317–337.

Tang, C., & Nunez, N. (2003). Effects of defendant age and juror bias on judgment of culpability: What happens when a juvenile is tried as an adult? *American Journal of Criminal Justice, 28,* 37–52.

Tang, C. M., Nunez, N., & Bourgeois, M. (2009). Effects of trial venue and pretrial bias on the evaluation of juvenile defendants. *Criminal Justice Review, 34,* 210–225.

Toobin, J. (1996, September 9). The Marcia Clark verdict. *The New Yorker, 72,* 58–71.

Vinson, K. V., Costanzo, M. A., & Berger, D. E. (2008). Predictors of verdict and punitive damages in high-stakes civil litigation. *Behavioral Sciences and the Law, 26,* 167–186.

8

Evaluation for Capital Sentencing

MARK D. CUNNINGHAM

Capital sentencing involves a determination of ultimate gravity: life and death quite literally hang in the balance. The irrevocable finality of this punishment is unique among sanctions in criminal law. This is both a challenging and sobering responsibility. The Supreme Court's recurrent predicate that "death is different" (see *Woodson v. North Carolina*, 1976) arguably extends to the mental health evaluations and testimony that are offered in these capital proceedings. Quite simply, the standards for an assessment correspond to the gravity of the determination. In recognition of the gravity of the issues at stake and to facilitate the most effective use of mental health experts and their findings at capital sentencing, this chapter provides an orientation for legal professionals of the legal and conceptual context of these evaluations, as well as how these assessments may inform critical considerations in the application of the death penalty.

LEGAL CONTEXT

The death penalty has a lengthy tenure in the criminal justice experience of the United States, having roots in English common law and dating from our colonial period. Though the death penalty *per se* has been a relatively static fixture in the United States, its application has been dynamic and evolving.

Primary Trends in Capital Jurisprudence

Three trends are evident in capital jurisprudence across the associated four centuries on this continent: (1) progressively restricted death-eligibility criteria; (2) increasing emphasis on individualized capital sentencing; and (3) emphasis on heightened reliability (as used in the legal and not behavioral science sense). These trends took on *constitutional* proportions as capital-sentencing statutes and procedures were revised following *Furman v. Georgia*

(1972), the Supreme Court decision that found the death penalty, as it was then being practiced, to be unconstitutional. The participation of forensic mental health experts at capital sentencing is both derived from these trends and framed by them.

Progressively Restricted Death-Eligibility Criteria

In the post-*Furman* "modern" capital-sentencing era, the death penalty in most jurisdictions was limited to intentional murders with specified characteristics (e.g., murder in the course of another felony). There are, however, exceptions. Many of the federal capital crimes, for example, omit from the definition of the offense the requirement that the killing be intentional (e.g., a carjacking in which "a death results"), and some jurisdictions make every intentional murder a potential capital crime. Death eligibility is further restricted by a requirement that the jury unanimously find at least a second-tier, statutorily defined aggravating factor (or "special issue" in Texas and Oregon), and, if the underlying murder offense did not include an "intent" requirement, that element as well.

Aggravating factors fall into two categories: statutory and nonstatutory. To differentiate, the jury must unanimously find at least one aggravating factor defined by statute for the defendant to be death-*eligible*, while nonstatutory aggravating factors, in those jurisdictions that allow them, inform the ultimate sentencing decision but do not establish eligibility for the death penalty. Death-penalty schemes are divided between those in which the jury or judge "weighs" aggravating factors and mitigating circumstances in determining the actual sentence, and those in which aggravating factors merely serve to define death eligibility. In the latter schemes, aggravating information, beyond the scope of the statutory aggravating factors, and mitigating information are considered by the jury in determining whether to impose the death penalty.

A series of Supreme Court decisions during the past 25 years have further narrowed the range of offenders who may be considered for the death penalty. Unlike earlier reforms of the death penalty that narrowed the class of death-eligible *offenses*, these modern-era exclusions of classes of defendants from death-penalty jeopardy have been based on cognitive, psychological, and/or moral-development limitations associated with the respective status or disorder of the *offender*, such as being less than 18 years old at the time of the capital murder (*Roper v. Simmons*, 2005) or being a person with mental retardation (*Atkins v. Virginia*, 2002).

Two additional U.S. Supreme Court decisions have expressed this trend toward progressively restricting the application of the death penalty, although these have focused on the point of execution rather than bars to death prosecution. In *Ford v. Wainwright* (1986), the Court ruled that it is unconstitutional to execute an offender who is "insane." The definition of such insanity (i.e., not competent to be executed) varies by jurisdiction but, at a minimum, requires that the condemned does not understand that an execution is imminent and/or the reason for that execution. The criteria for a death-sentenced offender to be incompetent for execution was arguably expanded (further restricting the application of the death penalty) by the Court in *Panetti v. Quarterman* (2007) with a holding that the requisite understanding must be rational as well as factual.

Increasing Emphasis on Individualized Capital Sentencing

The second trend in the history of the American death penalty is toward an individualized determination of death-worthiness or "culpability," rather than death being the mandatory punishment for certain crimes (summarized in *Woodson v. North Carolina*, 1976). A series of landmark Supreme Court decisions (e.g., *Lockett v. Ohio*, 1978; *Woodson v. North Carolina*, 1976) made an individualized consideration of any aspect of the character and background of the defendant and the circumstances of the offense "constitutionally indispensable" (p. 304) in death-sentencing proceedings.

Standards for defense mitigation investigations of the character and background of a capital defendant were more recently articulated in two Supreme Court decisions: *Wiggins v. Smith* (2003) and *Rompilla v. Beard* (2005). These decisions clarify for capital cases what constitutes effective assistance of counsel under the Sixth Amendment (see *Strickland v. Washington*, 1984). In *Wiggins*, the Court cited the *American Bar Association Guidelines for the Appointment and Performance of Defense Counsel in Capital Cases* (ABA, 1989; subsequently revised, ABA, 2003; for commentary see Santeramo, 2003) in holding that there must be a thorough investigation of all possible mitigating factors (i.e., any aspect of the character and background of the defendant or circumstances of the offense). The Court additionally found that a thorough investigation was fundamental to any strategic decision the defense might make regarding how or whether to utilize this information on the background and character of the defendant at trial. In *Rompilla*, the Court held that defense counsel has a continuing obligation to make reasonable efforts to obtain and review background information "even when a capital defendant's family members and the defendant himself have suggested that no mitigating evidence is available" (p. 374). The parameters and requirements of capital mitigation investigation are detailed in the *Supplementary Guidelines for the Mitigation Function of Defense Teams in Death Penalty Cases* (American Bar Association, 2008).

Another consideration for individualizing the application of the death penalty originated in a post-*Furman* capital-sentencing statute passed by the Texas legislature in 1973 and subsequently affirmed by the U.S. Supreme Court in *Jurek v. Texas* (1976). This "special issue" posed the question of "whether there is a probability the defendant would commit criminal acts of violence that would constitute a continuing threat to society." A determination of a capital defendant's probable future violent acts became an essential capital-sentencing factor or "special issue" in Texas and Oregon, and subsequently has been adopted as a statutory or nonstatutory aggravating factor in many jurisdictions. The prospect of the defendant's future violent conduct is not limited to a role as an aggravating factor; rather, evidence that the defendant is likely to have a *nonviolent* adjustment to prison may be offered by the defense as a mitigating factor known as "*Skipper* evidence" (see *Skipper v. South Carolina*, 1986).

Mental health experts are likely to make contributions in four primary, potentially overlapping, ways to individualized sentencing in a capital case. First, forensic mental health practitioners may identify adverse developmental factors and psychological vulnerabilities for the jury's consideration that would otherwise be missed. Second, mental health experts are uniquely capable of bringing science to bear on the nexus between adverse developmental experiences or psychological vulnerabilities and criminal outcome. Third, several statutory mitigating factors (discussed subsequently) involve impairments associated with psychological disorders or interpersonal vulnerabilities, which mental health experts are uniquely equipped to assess. Fourth, specialized knowledge of assessment methodology and interpretation, as well as normative, base rate, and other statistical data, is critical to illuminating the intellectual and neuropsychological capabilities of the defendant, context-specific risk assessments, and many other issues.

Emphasis on Heightened Reliability

A progressive evolution in procedures for heightened reliability constitutes a third trend in American capital jurisprudence. Some heightening of reliability was a byproduct of the previously identified restrictions in death-eligible offenses and classes of offenders, as well as in individualized sentencing procedures. Other reliability-heightening procedures in the post-*Furman* era have been more structural in nature. For example, to increase the likelihood that death-worthiness is differentiated from simple guilt, there are multiple, separate trials in front of the same jury. Depending on the jurisdiction, the capital trial may be bifurcated (i.e., a guilt phase followed by a sentencing phase, each with its own jury determination) or trifurcated, consisting of a guilt phase, an eligibility phase where special issues and/or aggravating factors are considered, and a selection phase. In 2002, the U.S. Supreme Court in *Ring v. Arizona* (2002) established that a capital defendant has a right to a jury determination at *each* phase of a death-determination trial, extending the holding from *Apprendi v. New Jersey* (2000) to capital sentencing. Capital defendants are typically afforded representation by at least two attorneys. This provision recognizes the complexity and breadth of death-penalty cases. Similarly, substantially greater fiscal resources are made available for defending death-penalty cases, as opposed to non-capital cases, including larger allocations for attorneys, investigators, and experts.

Appellate procedures are also more extensive in capital cases. This review is in two stages, direct appeal and post-conviction proceedings—both of which are reviewed at a state and federal level (except in federal capital cases, where only federal review occurs). The involvement of mental health experts in these appellate procedures is almost always associated with post-conviction claims of "ineffective assistance of counsel" (often referred to as IAC). Here the mental health professional may be asked to identify what could have been investigated and presented regarding mitigation and violence risk assessment at the sentencing phase but was not.

The ruling of the U.S. Supreme Court in *Estelle v. Smith* (1981) can also be viewed as part of a reliability-enhancing progression of decisions. This opinion has particular implications for State-retained mental health experts. In *Estelle*, the Court ruled that a meaningful exercise of Fifth Amendment rights against self-incrimination requires that the State-retained expert advise the defendant of the purposes and potential uses of the evaluation. Further, the Court held that a meaningful Sixth Amendment right to counsel required that defense counsel be informed prior to the evaluation.

The trend toward heightened reliability in the application of the death penalty, however, has had detours. As a result of the federal Antiterrorism and Effective Death Penalty Act (1996), as well as a series of U.S. Supreme Court decisions (e.g., *Herrera v. Collins*, 1993; *Keeney v. Tamayo-Reyes*, 1992; *Lockhart v. Fretwell*, 1993; *Sawyer v. Whitney*, 1992), appellate access has been limited and standards of review have been made more stringent. These can be viewed as counterbalancing reliability with timely implementation of sentencing. To simplify a complex area of the law, the defendant basically gets "one bite at the apple" in terms of raising issues at a State and federal level. Any issues not properly raised at the trial level (consistent with the jurisdiction's own procedures) or not brought to the attention of the appellate court (i.e., "exhausted") at the State level of direct appeal or post-conviction review may be forfeited at the federal level. Further, as to the vast majority of constitution violations, an error must be sufficiently grave that in its absence, it is reasonably probable that the jury would have come to a different verdict.

Also apparently inconsistent with enhanced reliability, there have been notable instances where the holdings of the Supreme Court were at odds with the scientific community. Despite an *amicus curiae* brief filed by the American Psychiatric Association (1982) describing the unreliability of expert assertions of future violence risk, in *Barefoot v. Estelle* (1983) the Court held that mental health experts could make such predictions at capital sentencing, even based on a hypothetical. Rather than establishing a standard of reliability for such testimony, the Court held that the reliability of these predictions could be adequately tested by cross-examination. After having established in *Jurek* that a probability of future violence was a valid consideration in individualizing the death penalty and that a lay jury could reliably make such a determination (for an analysis of capital jury predictive performance regarding prison violence, see Cunningham, Sorensen, & Reidy, 2009; Cunningham, Sorensen, Vigen, & Woods, 2011b), the Court reasoned that to identify psychiatrists as uniquely unqualified to render an opinion on the issue of violence risk at capital sentencing was akin to a request to "disinvent the wheel" (p. 896; for an analysis of the predictive performance and techniques of mental health experts to identify capital offenders who will commit violence in prison, see Cunningham & Sorensen, 2010; Edens, Buffington–Vollum, Keilin, Roskamp, & Anthony, 2005). Two briefs in *amicus curiae*, filed by the American Psychological Association (2005) and the Texas Psychological Association (2007), have called upon appellate courts to revisit the issue of what scientific standards should be required for expert testimony at capital sentencing regarding this issue.

Legal Procedures

As a broad overview, with variations and exceptions depending on the jurisdiction, a criminal case moves into the death-penalty category with the filing of a death-penalty notice by the prosecution. This notice specifies the aggravating factors upon which the prosecution will rely. Among these, depending on the jurisdiction, "future dangerousness" may be asserted as a statutory or nonstatutory aggravating factor. A second defense counsel may be appointed, if this has not already occurred. In some jurisdictions, at least one defense attorney must be "capital qualified" (i.e., has had experience in trying major felonies and capital cases in the past, and has participated in continuing legal education specific to capital litigation).

A sentencing-phase investigator (mitigation investigator, mitigation specialist), typically having an academic background in a mental health discipline or law, coordinates the retrieval of records and performs preliminary interviews of the defendant, family members, teachers, and other third parties (see ABA, 2008, for an expanded discussion of the activities and duties of the mitigation investigator). As defense counsel and the mitigation specialist begin to identify the nature of adverse developmental factors or psychological disorders in a defendant's background, forensic mental health experts, whose respective expertise will illuminate these hypotheses, may be retained.

Testimony by mental health experts almost never informs other aggravating factors, as these are either factual matters (e.g., created a grave risk of death to more than one person) or social values (e.g., the offense was especially heinous, atrocious, or cruel). As described previously in relation to *Estelle v. Smith* (1981), it is necessary that defense counsel be advised prior to a State-retained expert having any direct evaluative contact with a capital defendant.

Whether retained by the defense or the State, it is critically important that the mental health expert clarify whether a consultant (i.e., advocacy promoting) or expert witness (neutral, objective) function is anticipated, as these roles are mutually exclusive.

On a procedural level, the prosecution seeks to establish aggravating factors and the defense asserts mitigating factors. A more fundamental contest regarding attribution or the nature of choice, the influences on moral values, and the origins of behavior, however, rages behind these considerations of aggravating and mitigating factors. It is against this backdrop at capital sentencing that the testimony of mental health experts occurs.

Dueling Theories at Capital Sentencing: Free Will vs. Determinism

At capital sentencing the State invariably emphasizes *free will* in the extreme. If reduced to a single sentence, the State's position would sound something like the following: the capital offense is the result of the wholly volitional, unfettered choice of the defendant's malignantly evil heart (see Haney, 1995, 2005). This theory is typically advanced by detailing the incremental decisions (i.e., choices) surrounding the capital conduct and in the defendant's past misdeeds, as well as indicators that the defendant was able to exercise reflection and judgment in criminal and noncriminal activities contemporaneous to the capital offense. Because the focus of the State is on the offense and "choice-points" that are self-evident, forensic mental health experts are much less likely to be called to testify by the State at capital sentencing. Such testimony, when it does appear relative to this "evil choice" theory, is likely to include a diagnosis of antisocial personality disorder, in what may be offered as a clinical personification of an "evil heart." (for discussion of the etiology and sentencing implications of antisocial personality disorder, see Cunningham & Reidy, 1998a; Edens et al., 2005).

Experts may also be called by the State in rebuttal to address statutory mitigating factors that may have been asserted in testimony by defense mental health experts; provide alternative diagnostic formulations; point out errors or establish alternative findings regarding cognitive, neuropsychological, or other assessments; or clarify defense testimony that was overreaching. Even this testimony, though, is offered with the intention of diminishing the role of encumbrances on the defendant's volitional choice.

The explanation of the defense at capital sentencing, by contrast, is highly *deterministic*. The typical defense theory can also be simply expressed: the defendant's capital conduct, as with all behavior, is the result of the cumulative formative influences and complex interaction of bio-psycho-social factors. Distilled to its ultimate simplicity, the defense at capital sentencing asserts that childhood matters (and/or brain functioning matters, mental illness matters, etc.). This bio-psycho-social explanation for behavior is broadly consistent with the science of psychology, and thus it is understandable why the defense is more likely to retain mental health experts to evaluate adverse developmental factors and to testify regarding the impact of these on life trajectory and capital-offense etiology.

Interestingly, the Supreme Court appears to favor a deterministic theory, or at least finds a comprehensive investigation of potential adverse developmental factors to be essential. Recall that cases such as *Lockett* and *Woodson* made admissible "any aspect of the defendant's character and background," while *Wiggins* and *Rompilla* found that such information was essential for the defense to seek as it could fundamentally alter a capital jury's sentencing determination.

FORENSIC MENTAL HEALTH CONCEPTS
Mitigation

A capital juror is never required to impose the death penalty. Any given juror's rationale for determining that a capital life sentence is the most appropriate punishment may be deeply personal. Accordingly, what constitutes mitigation or a lessening of death-worthiness may be anything that a given juror determines is mitigating. The scope of evidence and argument that the defense may assert in mitigation is thus exceedingly broad.

The mitigation considerations of a capital jury are structured in many jurisdictions with statutory mitigating factors. These statutes were typically influenced by mitigating factors articulated in 1962 in the American Law Institute Model Penal Code §210.6.(4) Mitigating Circumstances. Among these are several that may be illuminated by mental health experts, including (1) the murder was committed while the defendant was under the influence of extreme mental or emotional disturbance; (2) the defendant acted under duress or under the domination of another person; (3) at the time of the murder, the capacity of the defendant to appreciate the criminality (wrongfulness) of his conduct or to conform his conduct to the requirements of law was impaired as a result of mental disease or defect or intoxication; and (4) the youth of the defendant at the time of the crime.

Additionally, Section 210.6 specified a broader category of mitigating factors: "including but not limited to the nature and circumstances of the crime, the defendant's character, background, history, mental and physical condition" (§ 210.6. Subsection 2). Capital-sentencing mitigation investigations and defenses typically focus on this catch-all category. The factors that may be offered as part of this general category may range from adverse formative factors, to psychological vulnerabilities and disorders, to past good deeds, to continuing relationships with others, to potential for a positive adjustment to prison, to remorse, to youthfulness, to offense-specific features, to other considerations.

Moral Culpability

Although the factors that may be considered to lessen death-worthiness are quite broad, at the core of capital mitigation is the concept of *moral culpability* (see *Burger v. Kemp*, 1987; citing *Woodson v. North Carolina*, 1976). Moral culpability is central to the rationale of *Wiggins v. Smith, Atkins v. Virginia,* and *Roper v. Simmons.* Moral culpability acknowledges the reality that we do not all come to our choices with equivalent psychological resources. Although two individuals might be found guilty of identical capital offenses and thus be equally *criminally responsible* (i.e., subject to punishment), the appropriate punishment could vary depending on what each brought, psychologically, to that offense. This is the essence of individualized capital sentencing under the constitution.

Moral culpability, as addressed by mental health evaluations at capital sentencing, can be conceptualized as a continuum of blameworthiness based on the developmental adversity, cognitive limitations, psychological disorders, and/or offense circumstances that increased the risk of deviant values, deficient self-control, and tragic choices. An appraisal of moral culpability involves the extent to which the background and circumstances of the defendant influenced, predisposed, or diminished the defendant's moral sensibilities and the exercise of volition or free will. Persons with no or minimal damaging or impairing factors have high moral culpability for their capital offenses as their choices are relatively unencumbered, while persons with many damaging and impairing factors have much lower moral culpability because their choices and/or their perception of these choices were more limited or pathologically channeled. The behavioral sciences are particularly well suited to illuminating formative adverse developmental factors, as well as psychological deficits and disturbances, which increase the risk of a criminal lifestyle and undermine the quality of choice that a capital defendant has exercised.

Criminal Responsibility vs. Moral Culpability

Criminal responsibility is a dichotomous guilt-phase issue relating to whether the defendant will suffer punishment for the offending conduct or is "not guilty by reason of insanity." Criminal responsibility also reflects that the defendant possessed the requisite *mens rea* (i.e., guilty mind) for the offense. The corollary questions associated with criminal responsibility are listed in the left column of Table 8.1.

The criminal responsibility questions are dichotomously answered (or assumed to be in the affirmative) in the guilt phase. Because the answer to each of these questions is always "yes" in every capital

TABLE 8.1 CONTRASTING PSYCHOLEGAL ISSUES

Criminal Responsibility	Moral Culpability
Guilt phase	Sentencing phase
Could he control himself?	What diminished his control?
Did he have a choice?	What shaped the choice?
Did he know right from wrong?	What shaped his morality and value system?

case resulting in a guilty verdict, these questions do not distinguish between capital offenders and thus are of no benefit to individualized sentencing. The questions of moral culpability in the right column in Table 8.1 represent gradations, as opposed to the dichotomous questions, of criminal responsibility. Moral culpability reflects the continuum of resources or impairing factors that extends *beyond* the bright line of criminal responsibility. Accordingly, it does not inform *whether* punishment will occur, rather *which* of the most severe punishments will be inflicted.

Importantly, evaluations of statutory mitigating factors emanating from the 1962 Model Penal Code and described above are *not* questions of criminal responsibility. Rather, those that may be illuminated by mental health expertise call for specific considerations of how the psychological or interpersonal capabilities of the defendant were *diminished* or *impaired* in relation to offense conduct—in an offender who has *already been found* to be criminally responsible as reflected in a guilty verdict. In other words, these statutory mitigating factors simply reflect structured or unstructured perspectives on the capital offender's moral culpability.

A capital jury is tasked with determining two issues: (1) where the offender falls on this continuum of moral culpability and (2) what level of moral culpability, in light of the capital offense and aggravating factors, renders the ultimate sanction appropriate. The role of the mental health expert is to illuminate the first of these issues, the damage-culpability continuum. It is the exclusive province of the jury to determine what level of moral culpability renders the offender appropriate or inappropriate for the death penalty.

In differentiating the continuum of moral culpability from the dichotomous standards of criminal responsibility, it is notable that an adverse factor(s) need not irresistibly "cause" the offending conduct in every instance of exposure in order for there to be a relevant nexus. Rather, criminally violent outcomes, as with many health and psychological disorders, typically stem from a complex interaction of vulnerability, risk, and protective factors. Commonsense analogies abound. For example, not all heavy smokers develop lung cancer. Similarly, a history of adverse developmental experiences does not invariably result in a criminally violent or markedly impaired adult outcome—only a much-increased likelihood of it (Cunningham, 2006).

Statutory Mitigating Factors Relating to Mental State at Time of Offense

As described previously, statutory mitigating factors involving mental state at time of offense reference a continuum extending beyond the bright-line criminal responsibility assessments of the guilt phase. There are two broad and not necessarily mutually exclusive ways of conceptualizing these structured inquiries of moral culpability. The first perspective would treat these in a diagnostic fashion, examining whether a severe mental disorder or disability was present that, while not *depriving* the defendant of wrongful awareness, had a materially destabilizing or significantly impairing effect at the time of the offense on the ability to *appreciate* the nature and wrongfulness of conduct, exercise rational judgment, modulate mood, and/or exercise self-control and autonomy (see American Bar Association, American Psychological Association, American Psychiatric Association, 2005).

A second perspective involves a broader and less diagnostic interpretation of these statutory mitigating factors. This approach is based on the lack of diagnostic requirement in the language of these statutory mitigating factors, as well as a capital jury's prerogative to find mitigating whatever the jury members determine to be mitigating. An analogy to health-related conditions may be useful in understanding this broader approach to mental state mitigating factors. Physical capability may be as impaired by chronic malnutrition as by acute disease. Similarly, the behavioral and social maladjustments stemming from chronic trauma exposure or pervasive corruptive socialization may functionally constitute as severe a "mental or emotional disturbance" and/or impact on moral sensibilities as gravely as an acute Axis I disorder (DSM-IV-TR).

Positive Relationship and Character Evidence

Another type of mitigation falling under the catch-all or unstructured category is evidence reflective of pro-social behaviors; positive relationships with community members, family, and children; and potential for further development or demonstrations of strengths. This type of evidence is quite commonly introduced at capital sentencing through lay witnesses.

Violence Risk Assessment

A consideration of a capital offender's likelihood of future serious violence became an individualizing capital-sentencing consideration in *Jurek v. Texas* (1976). This *individualizing* function is critical to an understanding of the task and related operational definitions, whether this probability is considered as an essential special issue (Texas, Oregon), alleged as an aggravating factor, or asserted as a mitigating factor. The parameters of this individualizing function are framed by the capital special issue affirmed by the U.S. Supreme Court in *Jurek*: "whether there is a probability the defendant would commit criminal acts of violence that would constitute a continuing threat to society." Most fundamentally, the special issue calls for an assessment of the *probability* of *acts* of a requisite *severity*, not a static state of *dangerousness*. Though "future dangerousness" is common shorthand for the unwieldy terminology of the *Jurek*-affirmed issue, this shorthand is both imprecise and potentially misleading. All capital offenders and, more broadly, all violent felons are dangerous. This is one of the primary rationales for their long-term prison incapacitation. Thus, if the question is whether a capital offender is dangerous, the answer is always "yes" and no individualizing function is served. Other differentials in the operational definition are also important. More specifically, if "probability" means "any possibility," no individualizing function is achieved. There is always some "possibility" for violence from any person. Consideration of severity of the contemplated act is important in serving both an individualizing function and proportionality. Proportionality acknowledges that the intervention bear some reasonable relationship to the harm that it is intended to prevent (see Cunningham, Reidy, & Sorensen, 2008, Cunningham, Sorensen, & Reidy, 2009; Slobogin, 2009). Regarding "society," prison is the primary, if not exclusive, context for a capital violence risk assessment. All jurisdictions allowing the death penalty now pro-vide an alternative sentence of life without parole (see Cunningham et al., 2009).

There is evidence from capital-jury research that the potential for future violence from a capital defendant has substantial impact on the sentenc-ing decision, whether or not future violence was overtly addressed at sentencing (for an expanded discussion, see Cunningham et al., 2009; Sandys, Pruss, & Walsh, 2009). Accordingly, the defense may assert a low probability of engaging in seri-ous violence in prison as a mitigating factor (see *Skipper v. South Carolina*), independent of whether future violence is asserted by the prosecution as an aggravating factor.

Mental Retardation (Developmental Disability)

In the aftermath of *Atkins*, determination of whether a capital defendant is a person with mental retarda-tion has become a third psycholegal issue for capital sentencing (see Macvaugh & Cunningham, 2009). Of relevance to mental health professionals, the operational definition of mental retardation as con-templated by *Atkins* varies widely from jurisdiction to jurisdiction (see DeMatteo, Marczyk, & Pich, 2007). Procedures for determining mental retarda-tion are also not uniform across jurisdictions. Of particular relevance to the retrospective nature of *Atkins* determinations, and a continuing topic of scholarly discussion, is how to report and interpret historically obtained IQ scores in light of progres-sive score inflation associated with aging norms (i.e., the Flynn Effect; see Cunningham & Tassé, 2010).

EMPIRICAL FOUNDATIONS AND LIMITS

Mental health evaluations conducted for capital-sentencing purposes require a foundation of spe-cialized knowledge that is augmented by targeted literature and data searches in any particular case. The specialized knowledge can be broadly sepa-rated into two broad arenas: (1) adverse factors and (2) violence risk assessment for prison.

Adverse Factors

A review of the literature of all conceivable adverse factors (including developmental, clinical, and envi-ronmental influences) is well beyond the scope of this chapter. Instead, this section will identify important sources and types of empirical data that

are relevant to evaluations and testimony regarding developmental adversity and psychological vulner-ability, and the nexus between these factors and criminally violent outcomes. These sources/types include clinical studies of death-row inmates, U.S. Department of Justice (DOJ)-sponsored studies and summaries, studies appearing in the profes-sional literature, and sociological data.

Clinical Studies of Death-Sentenced Inmates

One aspect of specialized knowledge entails famil-iarity with commonly encountered aspects of the developmental histories and clinical vulnerabilities of capital offenders, as these identify potentially important arenas of inquiry and assessment in any given case (see Cunningham & Vigen, 1999, 2002; Cunningham, in press). Associated research dem-onstrates that a substantial proportion of death-sentenced offenders have deficient intellectual capability, limited literacy, histories of neurologi-cal insults, evidence of neuropsychological impair-ments, psychological disorders, and histories of substance abuse/dependence, and are products of dysfunctional family systems.

DOJ-Sponsored Studies and Summaries

Central to a moral culpability analysis is the relation-ship between developmental factors or psychologi-cal vulnerabilities and criminal offending. A steadily expanding literature over the past three decades has illuminated this nexus by identifying *risk* and *protec-tive* factors for delinquency, criminality, and violence. DOJ, in an effort to provide an empirical foundation for preventative interventions, has become a major sponsor and clearinghouse of research regarding these risk and protective factors. Although these papers are specifically focused on a criminal trajec-tory beginning with chronic delinquency and youth violence, the underlying research often included adult samples. Both detailed research reports and summaries of this scholarship can be accessed online through the Office of Juvenile Justice and Delinquency Prevention, a sub-agency of DOJ (see particularly Hawkins et al., 2000; U.S. Department of Justice, 1995; Wasserman et al., 2003).

Studies in the Professional Literature

An extensive literature is available regarding how various developmental factors singly or collectively interact to increase the risk of substance abuse/

dependence, deviant life trajectory, and criminality. Similarly, an expanding literature describes the community violence risk implications of various psychological disorders, as well as substance abuse/dependence, intoxication, and toxicity. While DOJ has focused primarily on risk factors, other organizations have sponsored and published research on protective factors or developmental "assets." For example, Scales and Leffert (2004) synthesized research on developmental assets, demonstrating a significant cumulative effect from the 40 identified asset factors on both positive (increasing with asset concentration) and negative (inverse to asset concentration) adolescent outcomes. Because the range of relevant developmental factors and the associated factor-specific literature is so broad and constantly updating, any space-limited review would be incomplete and soon outdated. Instead it is recommended that literature searches regarding case-specific factors be undertaken as part of the evaluation interpretation process.

Sociological Data

Community adversity encountered by a capital defendant may also be illuminated by neighborhood and school-based data. Such data include comparative crime rates, school achievement scores, lead exposure levels, poverty and unemployment rates, etc., from one sector of a metropolitan area to another. An emerging discipline of Geographic Information Systems (GIS) mapping can provide assistance in retrieving, analyzing, and graphically depicting these sociological data, both in charts and map overlays.

Violence Risk Assessment for Prison

As described previously, violence risk assessments at capital sentencing by mental health professionals have often been controversial and sometimes notorious. This unfortunate legacy has resulted from intuitive applications of factors erroneously thought to be predictive (i.e., illusory correlations), an ignorance or disregard of relevant group data, and other recurrently observed errors (Cunningham & Reidy, 1999). The ultimate stakes at capital sentencing simply give no place for risk speculation masquerading as science.

Role of Group Statistical Data in Risk Assessments

Group statistical data is the foundation or implied basis of *all* violence risk-assessment techniques.

The various violence risk-assessment techniques, whether based on clinical history and interview, personality testing, violence risk-assessment instruments, analysis of past patterns of behavior (anamnestic), or direct application of base rates and correlates, all rely or purport to rely on group data (see Cunningham & Reidy, 2002). All are simply different ways of grouping individuals that are potentially meaningful in terms of comparative rates of violence in the context of interest (e.g., prison). This is the crux of whether a capital violence risk-assessment testimony is armchair speculation or scientifically sound: Are there prison violence data to support the grouping (e.g., characteristic, diagnosis, score) that is purported to be predictive?

Base rates (i.e., the rate of the behavior or characteristic of interest in the group) are the anchoring points of any individualized capital risk assessment and are fundamental to projecting meaningful probabilities. To illustrate from the extreme end of the prison base rate continuum, the rate of homicide of a correctional officer by an inmate is approximately 1 per 1,000,000 inmates per year. In many correctional departments, it has been decades since such a tragedy has occurred. To project that a specific offender has a capital-relevant risk of such a homicide in the face of this extreme infrequency would require an extraordinarily compelling basis. Stated more formally, the most accurate probability is the base rate of violence in the corresponding group to which the individual belongs. Departures from this base rate are likely to introduce increasing error unless based on empirically derived correlates (which most simply represent relevant subgroups; for prison-relevant risk correlates see Cunningham, Sorensen, Vigen, & Woods, 2011a). Failure to anchor the risk estimate to the base rate is a fundamental and unfortunately common error in violence risk assessments.

Group Data Informing Capital Risk Assessments

Group data providing base rates and most reliably informing violence risk assessments at capital sentencing include studies of the prison behavior of capital offenders sentenced to life terms (e.g., Cunningham, Reidy, & Sorensen, 2008), former death-sentenced inmates (e.g., Cunningham, Sorensen, Vigen, & Woods, 2011a), mainstreamed death-sentenced inmates (Cunningham, Reidy, & Sorensen, 2005), convicted murderers (e.g., Sorensen &

Cunningham, 2010), prison-wide data (e.g., Texas Department of Criminal Justice, 2011), offenders with personality disorders (see Edens et al., 2005), and offenders with various characteristics (see Cunningham et al., 2011a). Reliance on these data and an understanding of super-maximum risk-reduction interventions that can be brought to bear will almost invariably result in risk determinations of varying degrees of *improbability*. More specifically, these data illustrate several points:

1. Context is key. The convergence of factors resulting in serious violence in the community is rarely replicated in prison.

2. A continuing trajectory of violence from community to prison cannot be assumed. Neither inevitability nor even likelihood of serious violence in prison can be reliably inferred from a community violent offense of conviction.

3. Knowledge of the conviction-offense demographics of a prison population and the base rate of violence in the prison context of assessment is critically important to any scientifically informed projection of risk.

4. Because of the very high prevalence of antisocial personality disorder and associated personality traits among prison inmates, these features fail to predict serious prison violence.

5. The majority of capital inmates will not engage in serious violence during life terms in prison, whether death- or life-sentenced, and whether confined in the general prison population or under segregated, super-maximum security. Capital inmates are not disproportionately likely to commit serious violence in prison.

6. Given recurrently demonstrated base rates, predictions of serious violence in prison will invariably have high rates of false positives. Conversely, specifying a low probability of serious violence (marked improbability) will yield an extraordinarily high rate of overall accuracy (see Cunningham & Sorensen, 2010). Evaluators should consider these rates and resist the temptation to make any violence-*positive* predictions—except VERY rarely, and then only if super-maximum security measures have been defeated by this offender.

7. Prison works to inhibit and limit the occurrence of the most serious violence in prison. Even for the very rare offender who would be at markedly elevated risk of violence, institutional capabilities such as super-maximum confinement almost entirely negate any opportunity for serious violence.

THE EVALUATION

The designation of a forensic mental health evaluator as a witness, the specific questions addressed by that expert, and the methodology employed to assess these questions all have significant implications for the defendant's Constitutional rights and potentially for the sentencing determination (see Cunningham, 2006, 2010). These realities place a special burden on experts to provide notification to defendants and obtain informed consent from defense counsel regarding their participation, the options for that participation, and the associated implications.

Many of the decisions regarding the mental health expert's role and focus must be made in advance of evaluative contact with the defendant. These include:

1. *The focus and scope of the evaluation:* unstructured mitigation (e.g., adverse developmental factors, psychological disorders); structured mitigation regarding mental state at time of offense (i.e., statutory mitigating factors); structured mitigation regarding a specific factor (e.g., neuropsychological functioning, traumatic sexual exposures); and/or violence risk assessment as a mitigating factor or to illuminate its assertion as an aggravating factor. The same mental health expert may ethically and competently provide evaluations of multiple issues related to capital sentencing, such as assessing both mitigation factors and violence risk for prison. Much more problematic, however, are evaluations by the same expert that address *different stages* of the trial process in the same case (see Cunningham, 2006, 2010). The complications and hazards of such "bundled evaluations" may not be obvious to the defense counsel who naively requests, "Go see this guy and tell me what you think."

2. *Expert-witness role:* Forensic mental health professionals may perform varying expert-witness roles at capital sentencing. These can be broadly categorized as evaluation with direct assessment contact with the defendant, evaluation without direct assessment contact with the defendant, and teaching witness (see Cunningham, 2006, 2010; Lacourseiere, Weissenberger, & Stephani, 2002). Which of these roles the expert will occupy is one of the most important and far-reaching determinations defense counsel will make in retaining the expert. Accordingly, it is a fundamental aspect of informed-consent discussions.

3. *Parameters of evaluation:* Several considerations are critical to establish before the evaluation is initiated, including whether the defendant will be questioned regarding the capital offense and/or unadjudicated criminal conduct in the community, whether personality testing will be performed, and whether the focus of the evaluation will be diagnostic, as well as historical/developmental.

REPORT WRITING AND TESTIMONY

The written report of a capital-sentencing evaluation may serve varying purposes depending on the requirements of the jurisdiction, the request of retaining counsel, and the practice custom of the mental health expert. These include (1) to meet discovery requirements, (2) to utilize as an outline for testimony, (3) to utilize as part of a packet requesting that the prosecution not authorize or withdraw authorization for the death penalty, and/or (4) as a matter of personal practice or as a mechanism to organize and systematize findings and conclusions regarding the case. The expert should discuss any standard conventions regarding the preparation of a report with retaining counsel prior to undertaking the consultation. Regardless of the purpose, the report must fairly and accurately reflect the evaluation procedures, findings, reasoning, and conclusions of the expert.

Content of the Written Report

The content of the written report should reflect an expert integration of the defendant-specific data and research perspectives identified in the course of the evaluation. It should have no other agenda than to accurately and impartially distill the findings and implications of the evaluation procedures, and communicate these effectively.

Report Style

All reports should reflect the evaluation procedures, findings, reasoning, and conclusions of the mental health expert. That said, the style or organization of the report may vary, with respective benefits and costs to the consumer of the report.

Source-Driven Reports

Three primary models can be utilized in preparing the report of the capital-sentencing evaluation. The first type is organized by *sources* of data (i.e., history from interview, history from third-party sources, mental status, psychological testing, relevant research, and conclusions). The drawback of this type of report (or testimony) is that it requires that the "consumer" of the report hold a great deal of information in memory so that linkages can be made between the information provided by various data sources. As a result, report consumers who are not mental health professionals may have difficulty drawing a nexus between the data provided in the report and the life trajectory and criminal conduct of the defendant. This style of report is also more difficult to condense.

Narrative-Driven Reports

A second report model is organized as a chronology or *narrative* of the defendant's background, beginning with the grandparents and ending with the defendant's adulthood or the capital offense. The advantage of the narrative-driven report is in describing the generational reverberation of dysfunctional family processes and the sequential interplay of developmental deficits, traumatic experiences, and corruptive influences. The utility of the narrative-driven report is restricted to discussion of adverse developmental factors, and is not particularly suitable for reports of violence risk assessment for prison. As with the source-driven report, narrative-driven reports require the report consumer to recall events or symptoms and assign these to categories in giving meaning to the findings. The integration of research findings regarding the implications of the described events is also more challenging in the narrative-driven report.

Findings-Driven Reports

An alternative report model is organized by the *findings* derived from the data, rather than sources or sequence of data. In a findings-driven report, each adverse factor is specified. In a shorter report, these would be unelaborated. In an exhaustive report, each factor would be illustrated in anecdotal detail from various sources, followed by a research-based discussion of the implications of that factor for adolescent and adult outcome. Similarly, the findings-driven risk-assessment report would specify and describe the bases of factors associated with an increased or decreased risk of violence in prison. Findings-driven reports are easier for the consumer of the report to recall and understand, as categories for the data are provided. The findings-driven model is also quite flexible in expanding or condensing the detail and associated length of the report, and facilitates providing information on a single point across multiple sources and identifying the consistency (or lack thereof) across sources.

Length, Breadth, and Detail of Testimony

The testifying mental health expert can only answer the questions posed, and thus has only an advisory role in the nature and detail of the resultant testimony. In some cases, albeit infrequently at capital sentencing, only summary or conclusion-based testimony may be elicited from the expert. More often, the expert is asked to prepare for testimony that is data-intensive as opposed to conclusion-based. In preparing for this data-intensive testimony, the expert typically assists the attorney in understanding and outlining his or her findings. This assistance is a function of the expert having greater familiarity with the nature of the findings and bases of the opinions than the attorney. Often these testimony-preparation conferences are lengthy. Sharing the same pros and cons as the report models, the organization of the testimony of the expert at capital sentencing may be source-based, narrative-based, or findings-based.

Adverse Developmental Factors

Four elements are most important in testimony about adverse developmental experience and/or impairing factors, regardless of the testimony style: extensive anecdotal detail; aggregating negative events or features into categories of adverse factors; identification and discussion of the adverse factors; and research support for the nexus between these categories and negative outcomes.

Violence Risk Assessment

Testimony regarding violence risk assessment for prison most essentially specifies base rates of various severities of prison violence and factors that have a demonstrated relationship to prison violence, as well as preventative interventions that can be brought to bear. This testimony should also dispel common misconceptions that a conviction for murder or capital murder, or aberrant personality diagnosis or feature, is associated with a high probability of violence in prison. Because these conclusions are counterintuitive, it can be useful to provide the jury with summaries of the research studies reporting comparative rates of violence for convicted murderers (e.g., Sorensen & Cunningham, 2010), convicted capital murderers (e.g., Cunningham, Reidy, & Sorensen, 2008; Cunningham et al., 2011b), and offenders sentenced to life without parole (e.g., Cunningham, Sorensen, & Reidy, 2005; Cunningham & Sorensen, 2006). Scientifically grounded capital risk-assessment testimony will almost always identify varying degrees of *improbability* of serious violence in prison (see Cunningham & Sorensen, 2010; Cunningham, Sorensen, & Reidy, 2009). This testimony will also conclude that available super-maximum confinement options would negate almost any opportunity for the defendant to perpetrate serious violence (see Cunningham et al., 2009).

A particularly notorious legacy of mental health expert testimony regarding future violence prompts a specific caution. An assertion that future serious prison violence can be predicted by the presence of antisocial personality disorder or related characterizations of "psychopath" or "sociopath" is refuted by available data. Experts should not suggest such a nexus in their testimony, whether by direct assertion or by innuendo in introducing these characterizations. Given the intuitively obvious inflammatory impact of these personality characterizations on a capital-sentencing jury, as well as research demonstrating this impact (see Edens et al., 2005; Sandys et al., 2009), mental health professionals utilizing these terms in capital-sentencing testimony should carefully consider whether they have succumbed to undue influence and are no longer presenting their findings and conclusions in a fair manner or with the requisite objectivity.

Communicating Extensive Information and Complex Research

Challenges in Comprehensive Testimony

The number of adverse developmental factors in any given case, volume of supporting anecdotal data, and complexity of research findings demonstrating a nexus with delinquency, criminality, and violence result in challenges for both the expert and defense counsel as testimony is prepared. These issues will require careful consideration, extended discussion with defense counsel, and extensive preparation for testimony.

Demonstrative Exhibits

One response to the above challenges is to utilize digital demonstrative exhibits (i.e., PowerPoint slides) to accompany and illustrate some or most of the anticipated testimony. This option provides jurors with visual as well as auditory input, and a more overt organizational structure. Complex research findings are more understandable when the primary points are bulleted and accompanied by simple charts. Such demonstrative exhibits may further serve as an outline for the direct examination. Demonstrative exhibits also make possible the use of graphic models that simplify abstract conceptualizations.

Transparency of Bases of Opinion

The mental health expert should be prepared to illustrate from case-specific data any asserted adverse developmental or violence risk-assessment factors. All interview notes, as well as critical records, should accompany the expert to the witness stand so that these can be referred to, as well as scrutinized by opposing counsel. The expert should be prepared to detail the scientific support for interpretation of the data. Whenever possible, the specific research studies and statistical sources should be referenced or available for review or retrieval by opposing counsel. This transparency is most consistent with the role of the forensic psychologist in advocating for the data rather than a trial outcome.

SUMMARY

Effective utilization of mental health evaluations at capital sentencing is both conceptually complex and research-findings intensive. For an expanded discussion of these issues and findings, the reader is directed to following essential reading: ABA (2003, 2008), Cunningham (2006, 2010), Cunningham et al. (2009, 2011a), and Santeramo (2003).

REFERENCES

American Bar Association. (1989). *ABA guidelines for the appointment and performance of defense counsel in death penalty cases*. Retrieved October 13, 2009, from http://www.abanet.org/deathpenalty/resources/docs/1989Guidelines.pdf

American Bar Association. (February 10, 2003). *ABA guidelines for the appointment and performance of defense counsel in death penalty cases: Revised edition*. Retrieved October 13, 2009, from http://www.abanet.org/deathpenalty/resources/docs/2003Guidelines.pdf

American Bar Association. (2008). Supplementary guidelines for the mitigation function of defense teams in death penalty cases. *Hofstra Law Review, 36,* 639–1093. Retrieved on October 13, 2009, from http://law.hofstra.edu/Academics/Journals/LawReview/lrv_issues_v36n03.html

American Bar Association, American Psychological Association, American Psychiatric Association (2005). Report of the task force on mental disability and the death penalty. Retrieved December 24, 2009, from http://www.apa.org/pubs/info/reports/mental-disability-and-death-penalty.pdf

American Law Institute. (1962). *Model Penal Code §210.6.(4) Sentence of death for murder; further proceedings to determine sentence: Mitigating circumstances.* Philadelphia, PA: Author.

American Psychiatric Association. (1982). *Brief for the American Psychiatric Association as amicus curiae in Barefoot v. Estelle, in the United States Supreme Court.* Retrieved October 24, 2009, from http://archive.psych.org/edu/other_res/lib_archives/archives/amicus/82-6080.pdf

American Psychological Association. (2005). *Brief for the American Psychological Association as amicus curiae in support of Defendant-Appellant in U.S. v. Sherman Lamont Fields, in the United States Court of Appeals for the Fifth Circuit.* Washington: Author.

Antiterrorism and Effective Death Penalty Act of 1996, Pub. L. No. 104-132, 110 Stat. 1214. Retrieved October 13, 2009, from http://frwebgate.access.gpo.gov/cgi-bin/getdoc.cgi?dbname=104_cong_public_laws&docid=f:publ132.104.pdf

Apprendi v. New Jersey, 530 U. S. 466 (2000).

Atkins v. Virginia, 536 U. S. 304 (2002).

Barefoot v. Estelle, 463 U. S. 880 (1983).

Burger v. Kemp, 483 U. S. 776 (1987).

Cunningham, M. D. (2006). Informed consent in capital sentencing evaluations: Targets and content. *Professional Psychology: Research and Practice, 37,* 452–459.

Cunningham, M. D. (2010). *Evaluation for capital sentencing.* A volume in the *Oxford best practices in forensic mental health assessment series,* Series Editors: A. Goldstein, T. Grisso, and K. Heilbrun. New York: Oxford University Press.

Cunningham, M. D. (in press). Death-sentenced inmates. In L. Gideon (Ed.), *Special needs offenders in correctional institutions.* Thousand Oaks, CA: Sage Publications.

Cunningham, M. D., & Reidy, T. J. (1998a). Antisocial personality disorder and psychopathy: Diagnostic dilemmas in classifying patterns of antisocial behavior in sentencing evaluations. *Behavioral Sciences & the Law, 16*, 333–351.

Cunningham, M. D., & Reidy, T. J. (1999). Don't confuse me with the facts: Common errors in violence risk assessment at capital sentencing. *Criminal Justice and Behavior, 26*, 20–43.

Cunningham, M. D., & Reidy, T. J. (2002). Violence risk assessment at federal capital sentencing: Individualization, generalization, relevance, and scientific standards. *Criminal Justice and Behavior, 29*, 512–537.

Cunningham, M. D., Reidy, T. J., & Sorensen, J. R. (2005). Is death row obsolete? A decade of mainstreaming death-sentenced inmates in Missouri. *Behavioral Sciences & the Law, 23*, 307–320.

Cunningham, M. D., Reidy, T. J., & Sorensen, J. R. (2008). Assertions of "future dangerousness" at federal capital sentencing: Rates and correlates of subsequent prison misconduct and violence. *Law and Human Behavior, 32*, 46–63.

Cunningham, M. D., & Sorensen, J. R. (2006). Nothing to lose? A comparative examination of prison misconduct rates among life-without-parole and other long-term high security inmates. *Criminal Justice and Behavior, 33*(6), 683–705. doi: 10.1177/0093854806288273

Cunningham, M. D., & Sorensen, J. R. (2010). Improbable predictions at capital sentencing: Contrasting prison violence outcomes. *Journal of the American Academy of Psychiatry and the Law, 38*, 61–72.

Cunningham, M. D., Sorensen, J. R., & Reidy, T. J. (2009). Capital jury decision-making: The limitations of predictions of future violence. *Psychology, Public Policy, and Law, 15*, 223–256.

Cunningham, M. D., Sorensen, J. R., Vigen, M. P., & Woods, S. O. (2011a). Correlates and actuarial models of assaultive prison misconduct among violence-predicted capital offenders. *Criminal Justice and Behavior, 38*, 5–25.

Cunningham, M. D., Sorensen, J. R., Vigen, M. P., & Woods, S. O. (2011b). Life and death in the Lone Star State: Three decades of violence predictions by capital juries. *Behavioral Sciences & the Law, 29*, 1–22.

Cunningham, M. D., & Tassé, M. (2010). Looking to science rather than convention in adjusting IQ scores when death is at issue. *Professional Psychology: Research and Practice, 41*(5), 413–419. doi: 10.1037/a0020226

Cunningham, M. D., & Vigen, M. P. (1999). Without appointed counsel in capital postconviction proceedings: The self-representation competency of Mississippi death row inmates. *Criminal Justice and Behavior, 26*, 293–321.

Cunningham, M. D., & Vigen, M. P. (2002). Death row inmate characteristics, adjustment, and confinement: A critical review of the literature. *Behavioral Sciences & the Law, 20*, 191–210.

DeMatteo, D., Marczyk, G., & Pich, M. (2007). A national survey of state legislation defining mental retardation: Implications for policy and practice after *Atkins*. *Behavioral Sciences & the Law, 25*, 781–802.

Edens, J., Buffington–Vollum, J., Keilin, A., Roskamp, P., & Anthony, C. (2005). Predictions of future dangerousness in capital murder trials: Is it time to "disinvent the wheel"? *Law & Human Behavior, 26*, 59–87.

Estelle v. Smith, 451 U. S. 454 (1981).

Ford v. Wainwright, 477 U. S. 399 (1986).

Furman v. Georgia, 408 U. S. 238 (1972).

Haney, C. (1995). Symposium: The social context of capital murder: Social histories and the logic of mitigation. *Santa Clara Law Review, 35*, 547–609.

Haney, C. (2005). *Death by design: Capital punishment as social psychological system*. New York: Oxford University Press.

Hawkins, J. D., Herrenkohl, T. I., Farrington, D. P., Brewer, D., Catalano, R. F., Harachi, T. W., & Cothern, L. (2000, April). Predictors of youth violence. *Juvenile Justice Bulletin*. Washington: U.S. Department of Justice, Office of Justice Programs, Office of Juvenile Justice and Delinquency Prevention.

Herrera v. Collins, 506 U. S. 390 (1993).

Jurek v. Texas, 428 U. S. 262 (1976).

Keeney v. Tamayo-Reyes, 504 U.S. 1 (1992).

Lacourseiere, R. B., Weissenberger, G., & Stephani, A. J. (2002). Evaluating mental states without the benefit of a direct examination: Basic concepts and ethical and legal implications. In R. I. Simon & D. W. Shuman (Eds.), *Retrospective assessment of mental states in litigation: Predicting the past* (pp. 209–285). Washington, DC: American Psychiatric Publishing.

Lockett v. Ohio, 438 U. S. 586, 57 L Ed 2d 973 (1978).

Lockhart v. Fretwell, 506 U. S. 364 (1993).

Macvaugh, G., & Cunningham, M. D. (2009). *Atkins v. Virginia*: Implications and recommendations for forensic practice. *Journal of Psychiatry and Law, 37*, 131–187.

Panetti v. Quarterman, 551 U. S. 930 (2007).

Ring v. Arizona, 536 U. S. 584 (2002).

Rompilla v. Beard, 545 U. S. 374 (2005).

Roper v. Simmons, 543 U. S. 551 (2005).

Sandys, M., Pruss, H. C., & Walsh, S. M. (2009). Aggravation and mitigation: Findings and implications. *Journal of Psychiatry and Law, 37*, 189–236.

Santeramo, J. L. (Ed.) (2003). 'The guiding hand of counsel': ABA guidelines for the appointment and performance of counsel in death penalty cases. *Hofstra Law Review, 31*, 903–1345. Retrieved October 13, 2009, from http://www.abanet.org/deathpenalty/resources/docs/HofstraLawReview.pdf

Sawyer v. Whitley, 505 U. S. 333 (1992).

Scales, P. C., & Leffert, N. (2004). *Developmental assets: A synthesis of the scientific research on adolescent development*. Minneapolis, MN: Search Institute.

Skipper v. South Carolina, 476 U. S. 1 (1986).

Slobogin, C. (2009). Capital punishment and dangerousness. In R. F. Schopp, R. L. Wiener, B. H. Bornstein, & S. L. Willborn (Eds.), *Mental disorder and criminal law: Responsibility, punishment, and competence* (pp. 119–134). New York: Springer.

Sorensen, J. R., & Cunningham, M. D. (2010). Conviction offense and prison violence: A comparative study of murderers and other offenders. *Crime & Delinquency, 56,* 103–125.

Strickland v. Washington, 466 U. S. 668 (1984).

Texas Department of Criminal Justice. (2011). *Emergency Action Center select statistics: April, 2011.* Huntsville, TX: Author.

Texas Psychological Association (2007). Brief of the *amici curiae* Texas Psychological Association and Texas Appleseed in Support of Appellant, *Noah Espada vs. The State of Texas,* in the Court of Criminal Appeals of Austin, Texas.

U.S. Department of Justice (1995, June). Guide for implementing the comprehensive strategy for serious, violent, and chronic juvenile offenders. Juvenile Justice Bulletin: OJJDP Update on Programs. NCJ 153571. Office of Juvenile Justice and Delinquency Prevention.

Wasserman, G. A., Keenan, K., Tremblay, R. E., Coie, J. D., Herrenkohl, T. I., Loeber, R., & Petechuk, D. (April, 2003). Risk and protective factors of child delinquency. *Child Delinquency Bulletin Series.* U.S. Department of Justice, NCJ 193409.

Wiggins v. Smith, 539 U. S. 510 (2003).

Woodson v. North Carolina, 428 U. S. 280 (1976).

9

Evaluation for Eyewitness Identification

BRIAN L. CUTLER AND MARGARET BULL KOVERA

Our book (Cutler & Kovera, 2010) was designed to provide guidance to psychologists who give or are considering giving expert testimony on the psychology of eyewitness identification. Toward this end, we review the legal context in which eyewitness expert testimony is proffered and delivered, key psychological concepts in eyewitness identification, and the relevant psychological research on eyewitness identification to date. The latter chapters in the book are devoted to the mechanics of consultation and expert testimony on eyewitness identification. These topics include how to prepare for an evaluation, gather the information needed for evaluation, interpret the information about the eyewitnessing conditions and identification tests, and how to report one's evaluation in writing and in in-court testimony.

Attorneys who retain experts must become knowledgeable about the topic about which their experts will testify. In this regard, the attorney who reads our book will become knowledgeable about eyewitness science and the approach typically taken by eyewitness experts to their consultation and expert testimony. The informed attorney will be in a better position than the uninformed to decide whether expert testimony is needed in a given case and to engage the expert efficiently and effectively. In this chapter we summarize the more critical highlights of the eyewitness science and the expert's activity in the service of informing practicing attorneys about its content and format.

LEGAL CONTEXT

Eyewitnesses play a prominent role in many criminal cases. By providing descriptions of crimes and perpetrators, they may aid police investigators in the apprehension of criminal suspects. As criminal investigations proceed, detectives conduct subsequent interviews with eyewitnesses and eyewitnesses may identify crime perpetrators from lineups or photoarrays. If a case goes to trial, eyewitnesses may be called upon to recount the crime details and identify the crime perpetrator in court. *Eyewitness testimony* has proven to be highly influential with juries (Cutler & Penrod, 1995), and in some types of cases (e.g., robberies), it is often the only evidence linking the defendant with the crime.

Does the involvement of eyewitnesses in the criminal-justice system improve the quality of justice dispensed by our legal system? Crimes often take place under circumstances that facilitate memory errors. The nature of the crime itself can directly affect memory. Exposure to the crime perpetrator might be very brief and usually takes place under stressful conditions. The perpetrator may be from a racial group that is different from that of the witness and with which the witness has little personal experience. Perpetrators may threaten witnesses with a weapon, causing them to fear for their personal safety, even fearing that the perpetrator may intend to fatally harm them. It may take the police many months to locate a suspect to present to a witness in a lineup or photoarray. Such conditions may challenge the eyewitness's ability to recognize a crime perpetrator who is a complete stranger to him or her. Because of the unique and difficult circumstances in which crimes occur, eyewitnesses sometimes make mistakes.

How do we know that eyewitnesses make mistakes? Several sources of evidence can be brought to bear on this question. First, there is a substantial body of literature on *erroneous conviction*. There are a growing number of verified cases in which citizens have been convicted of serious crimes, imprisoned—sometimes for many years—and later found to be innocent of the crimes for which they were convicted and sentenced. In many such cases, eyewitness identification is the only evidence linking the defendant to the crime. Among the more recent and compelling studies of erroneous conviction is the ongoing work of the Innocence Project. Thus far their efforts have led to the exoneration of over 270 such individuals throughout the United States (www.innocenceproject.org). The Innocence Project and others have examined the factors leading to erroneous conviction (e.g., Borchard, 1932; Cutler, 2011; Frank & Frank, 1957; Garrett, 2008; Huff, 1987). Consistently, authors of these studies found *mistaken identification* to be the most common feature of erroneous conviction cases.

That mistaken eyewitness identifications occur should not *necessarily* be a problem for the criminal-justice system. False identifications may on occasion lead to false arrests, false indictments, or trials with innocent defendants, but other procedural safeguards exist to protect defendants from erroneous conviction resulting from mistaken eyewitness identification. These safeguards include the representation of the defendant by an attorney at lineups; the pretrial motions to have identification testimony based on the use of unduly suggestive procedures suppressed; the opportunity to question prospective jurors during jury-selection procedures (i.e., *voir dire*) about their willingness to scrutinize eyewitness identification testimony and to exclude from jury service those who express an unwillingness or inability to perform this function; the opportunity to cross-examine eyewitnesses thoroughly at trial; and instructions to the jury from the judge that provide guidance about how to evaluate the reliability of eyewitness testimony.

Each of these safeguards, however, has been found lacking for both conceptual and empirical reasons (Cutler, 2009; Van Wallendael et al., 2007). Defense attorneys are rarely present at pre-indictment identification procedures, and empirical evidence suggests that they may miss some forms of procedural bias like biased instructions even if they were present (Stinson, Devenport, Cutler, & Kravitz, 1996). If attorneys have difficulty identifying procedural bias then it is unlikely that they will be able to effectively argue about this bias in pretrial motions to suppress

the identification evidence. It appears as if judges are somewhat better at identifying procedural biases than are attorneys, but they misunderstand which method of lineup presentation produces more reliable identifications (Stinson, Devenport, Cutler, & Kravitz, 1997). Trial procedures such as *cross-examination* that are intended to educate jurors about the potential unreliability of evidence appear to have limited effectiveness (Devenport, Stinson, Cutler, & Kravitz, 2002). The limited effectiveness of cross-examination is due to the insensitivity of attorneys (who ask the questions) and jurors (who evaluate the testimony) to the factors known from scientific research to influence identification accuracy.

Expert testimony on eyewitness memory is among the more recently developed safeguards against wrongful conviction. Expert testimony on eyewitness memory differs in significant ways from expert testimony commonly provided by psychologists. Frequently, when psychologists testify as expert witnesses, their testimony is based on the evaluation of a defendant or litigant. For example, experts may offer opinions as to whether a defendant is competent to stand trial or to waive rights (see Chapters 2 and 16). The expert's testimony is based on an evaluation of the individual, typically a formal forensic mental health assessment. The expert may have interviewed the individual, studied the individual's medical history, and performed psychological tests on the individual. The expert then reports the results of the assessment and may provide a recommendation to the court during expert testimony. Monahan and Walker (1986) refer to this form of expert testimony as "social fact" evidence. The expert's testimony bears directly on a fact to be adjudicated, such as whether a defendant is competent to stand trial.

The eyewitness expert, however, does not perform an evaluation of the witness or offer any opinion or recommendation about the witness. Rather, the eyewitness expert testifies in general terms about the psychological processes underlying human memory and about the factors associated with the crime and identification that have been shown by the research to influence the likelihood of a false identification. In Monahan and Walker's (1986) scheme, expert testimony is an example of "social framework" testimony. The issue in dispute—the accuracy of the identification—is an instance to which a general theory or research finding applies. The expert, therefore, provides the framework, based on the current research on eyewitness memory, for evaluating the identification. The expert, for example, might testify that cross-race recognitions and identifications made by witnesses who were traumatized by a violent crime are less likely to be correct than same-race identifications and identifications made after witnessing less stressful events. The expert might also testify about how certain lineup procedures increase the likelihood of false identification. The expert does not, however, offer an opinion, actual or hypothetical, about the accuracy of eyewitness testimony in the case. Determining the accuracy of eyewitness testimony is clearly the province of the jury. Expert testimony is typically proffered by the defense in criminal cases in which eyewitness identification (or eyewitness recall) is being challenged.

The Experts

Who are the experts who offer testimony about eyewitness identification? Kassin, Tubb, Hosch, and Memon (2001) addressed this question via a survey of eyewitness experts. They identified 197 experts, of whom 65 provided survey responses. About half (52%) of the experts were cognitive psychologists, 26% were social or personality psychologists, 9% were developmental psychologists, 5% were clinical or counseling psychologists, and the remainder (6%) were from more than one sub-discipline of psychology. On average, the experts had written 2 books, 6.5 chapters, and 13 journal articles about eyewitness memory. The experts were much more likely to testify in criminal cases than in civil cases and were proffered far more often by the defense in criminal cases. The experts reported being asked to testify in 3,370 instances. They agreed to testify in 1,373 cases (i.e., in 41% of the cases in which they were asked to testify). They actually testified in 960 cases, representing 28% of the cases in which they were asked and 70% of the cases in which they agreed to testify. The percentage of cases in which experts actually testified is relatively small because many criminal cases are resolved through plea bargaining before the trial begins. Thus, an expert might agree to testify in a case but then is told that the defendant accepted a plea and the testimony is

no longer needed. In addition, an expert may agree to testify in a case before a judge rules that expert testimony on eyewitness topics is inadmissible in a particular case. In any case, the volume of testimony represents a significant increase over survey figures obtained an earlier study (Kassin, Ellsworth, & Smith, 1989).

Legal Standards for Expert Testimony

The legal standards governing admissibility of expert testimony on eyewitness memory are, of course, the same legal standards that govern expert testimony generally. The Federal Rules of Evidence (1975) consider an individual to be qualified as an expert if he or she is able to assist the trier of fact. The qualifications required to be admitted as an expert vary as a function of the demands of the testimony to be offered by the expert (Faigman, 2008). Many eyewitness experts possess doctoral degrees and have published extensively on the topic of eyewitness memory.

Several standards have governed the admissibility of expert testimony in U.S. courts, beginning with the *Frye* test (*Frye v. United States*, 1923), the Federal Rules of Evidence (1975), and a series of cases in the 1990s (*Daubert v. Merrell Dow Pharmaceuticals*, 1993; *General Electric Co. v. Joiner*, 1997; *Kumho Tire Company v. Carmichael*, 1999). The *Frye* rule required that the methods used by the expert must be generally accepted in the relevant scientific community. The *Frye* test governed admissibility decisions in federal and state courts for 50 years and continues to be the legal standard for admissibility in some states (e.g., California, Florida, New York). In the mid-1970s, the Federal Rules of Evidence (1975) were adopted and included a rule that specifically governed the admissibility of expert testimony (Rule 702). Rule 702 states that

> If scientific, technical, or other specialized knowledge will assist the trier of fact to understand the evidence or to determine a fact in issue, a witness qualified as an expert by knowledge, skill, experience, training, or education, may testify thereto in the form of an opinion or otherwise. (FRE, 1975, p. 14)

Although these new rules were binding only in federal courts, many state courts also adopted these evidentiary rules, either completely or with some modification, as well. This standard of admissibility appeared quite different from the earlier *Frye* test and arguments regarding which standard should prevail began appearing in the courts.

These arguments were finally resolved, at least for the federal courts, when the U.S. Supreme Court issued its decision in *Daubert v. Merrell Dow Pharmaceuticals, Inc.* (1993). In its decision, the Supreme Court developed a two-pronged test for admissibility. According to the first prong, expert testimony must be relevant to a debated issue in the case. According to the second prong, the evidence presented by the expert witness must be reliable by scientific standards. The Court further suggested several criteria for determining the reliability of the methodology underlying the evidence to be presented: whether the theory relied on by the expert and the hypotheses being tested in the research were falsifiable; whether the expert evidence had been subjected to peer review; whether there is a known error rate associated with the expert evidence; and whether the evidence is generally accepted in the relevant scientific community.

In the *Joiner* decision, the U.S. Supreme Court affirmed the trial court's role as the gatekeeper, requiring judges to evaluate the reliability of the expert's methods and not abdicate their responsibility by appealing to a liberal interpretation of the Federal Rules of Evidence (Copple, Torkildson, & Kovera, 2008). In the *Kumho* case, the U.S. Supreme Court ruled that the *Daubert* test, designed to determine the admissibility of scientific testimony, should apply to nonscientific expert testimony as well.

As applied to expert testimony on eyewitness memory, the defense attorney, if practicing in a *Frye* state, must establish that the methodology and/or the findings of the proffered research are generally accepted in the field. We typically take this to mean that the eyewitness research to be summarized by the expert must be generally accepted in the relevant psychological community. In federal courts and state courts that have adopted the federal *Daubert* test, the defense attorney proffering expert testimony must establish that eyewitness research is based on reliable scientific methods. General acceptance of eyewitness research is one of many factors that may be given consideration in the *Daubert* test.

As discussed above, the Kassin et al. survey studies demonstrate that expert testimony occurs with increasing frequency. This is particularly true in states with case law that is favorable to expert testimony on eyewitness memory. In other states, however, case law is less favorable to expert testimony, and getting expert testimony admitted is a significant challenge. Expert testimony may be denied on several grounds. Perhaps the most common reason for refusing to admit expert testimony is the belief that the expert's testimony is within the ken of the jury and therefore not helpful (Schmechel, O'Toole, Easterly, & Loftus, 2006). Other reasons for refusing to admit expert testimony include the belief that the research is not scientifically reliable and the belief that the expert testimony will prejudice the jury. The validity of these beliefs is questionable (Cutler & Kovera, 2010).

The legal procedures for expert testimony on eyewitness memory follow a familiar pattern. An expert's role in the case begins when an attorney with a case involving identification evidence makes initial contact with the eyewitness expert. This initial consultation usually consists of the attorney describing the facts of the case, an identification of topics, if any, about which the expert might testify, and a discussion of the expert's availability and fees. If an agreement is reached between the attorney and the expert, the attorney will provide the expert with any relevant discovery materials. After the expert reviews the discovery, there will likely be further consultation between the attorney and the expert. An expert retained early in the investigation may have a role in guiding discovery, suggesting documents that might be obtained from the other side or information that might be gathered that would be relevant to the expert's opinion. In cases that move forward to trial, the expert may be asked to prepare a report or affidavit for distribution to the opposing attorney and judge. In some cases, the opposing attorney may wish to depose the expert before the trial. The attorney and expert must then work together to prepare for an admissibility hearing (in some cases) and for testimony before the jury if the expert is allowed to testify at trial. This collaboration involves careful planning of the *direct examinations* and *redirect examinations*.

FORENSIC CONSTRUCTS

Eyewitness Identification Accuracy

When an eyewitness is asked to identify a perpetrator from a lineup, several outcomes are possible. Eyewitness scientists typically distinguish between correct identifications (the eyewitness correctly identifies the perpetrator), false identifications (the eyewitness identifies an innocent suspect as the perpetrator), correct rejections (the eyewitness correctly indicates that the perpetrator is not in the lineup), incorrect rejections (the eyewitness concludes that the perpetrator is not in the lineup when, in fact, the perpetrator is in the lineup), and filler identifications (the eyewitness identifies a filler, or a known-to-be-innocent person, as the perpetrator) as separate outcomes. The researchers are able to make this distinction because they rely heavily on crime-simulation methodology, whereby eyewitnesses are exposed to simulated crimes and are later shown photoarrays. Typically, the experimenter creates at least two types of lineups (or photoarrays): *perpetrator-present* and *perpetrator-absent lineups*. Perpetrator-present lineups contain the perpetrator and a set of fillers. These lineups represent the situation in which the suspect is guilty. Perpetrator-absent lineups contain a person who resembles but is not the perpetrator and a set of fillers. These lineups represent the situation in which the suspect is innocent.

General Impairment Factors

General impairment factors are factors associated with the conditions under which a crime was witnessed and that are known to affect the accuracy of eyewitness identification. Thus, they are called "general impairment factors" because their presence generally impairs the accuracy of eyewitness identification. Some of these factors are characteristics of the witness (e.g., the witness's race), some are characteristics of the perpetrators (e.g., whether the perpetrator was wearing a disguise), and some are situational factors (e.g., the stressfulness of the situation, whether there was a weapon present). These factors are also called *estimator variables* (Wells, 1978) because the presence of these factors allows for the estimation, in a very general manner, of the accuracy of an identification made by a witness under a particular set of witnessing conditions.

Identification Tests

Identification tests are the procedures used by the police that allow eyewitnesses to identify a suspect as the perpetrator of the crime that they witnessed. We call these procedures "tests" because they should be thought of as falling within the same category as other forensic identification tests. What is being tested in an identification test is the hypothesis that the suspect is the perpetrator. A positive identification of the suspect by the witness can be considered to be evidence supporting the hypothesis that the suspect is the perpetrator. A lineup rejection may be thought of as evidence against the hypothesis that the suspect is the perpetrator. In this context, a filler identification represents evidence against the hypothesis that the suspect is the perpetrator. The fundamental limitation of identification tests is that there are multiple reasons for which a witness might positively identify a suspect. One reason is the most obvious: witnesses might identify a suspect as the perpetrator because they recognize the suspect as the perpetrator based on their memory of the crime scene. Witnesses, however, might identify a suspect for a range of other reasons. Witnesses who are motivated to make a positive identification might guess who the suspect is, identify the suspect through the process of deduction, or base their identifications on influence by the investigator conducting the identification. The structure of the identification test can help rule out approaches such guessing, deduction, and influence and increase the likelihood that a positive identification is the product of the eyewitness' memory for the perpetrator.

There are several types of identification tests that crime investigators rely upon for collecting eyewitness identification evidence: mugshots, showups, photoarrays, and live lineups. Mugshot identifications involve providing the witnesses with books or stacks of photos of possible suspects. This is an exploratory procedure designed to generate leads rather than a confirmatory procedure designed to test whether a suspect is a perpetrator. As such, we do not focus on mugshot identifications in this chapter. Showups involve the presentation of a single suspect to a witness for identification. Showups typically take place very soon after a crime, and the suspect is physically present, although occasionally a witness is presented with a photo of a suspect for identification (i.e., without fillers). Photoarrays refer to identification tests in which the witness is shown a set of photos containing a suspect's photo. Live lineups involve having the witness view a set of physically present individuals including a suspect.

In most jurisdictions, showups and photoarrays are more common methods of identification than are live lineups. Research on eyewitness identification is most likely to use photoarrays as the identification task. The principles associated with the construction and presentation of photoarrays and live lineups are very similar. There has been no research documenting differences in how lineup construction and presentation methods differentially affect live lineups and photoarrays. Accordingly, we do not distinguish between these methods in our review of suspect bias factors or in expert testimony.

Suspect Bias Factors

Suspect bias factors refer to aspects of the identification test that bias the witness toward identifying the suspect regardless of whether the suspect is innocent or guilty. Suspect bias factors include the use of fillers in an identification test, the composition of the photoarray, and the procedures for conducting the photoarray.

Postdictors of Identification Accuracy

Postdictors of identification accuracy are variables that are sometimes used to evaluate the accuracy of eyewitness identification but do not fall under the categories of general impairment and suspect bias factors. Examples of postdictors include the confidence of the eyewitness and the accuracy or consistency of eyewitness recall of crime details. They are called "postdictors" because these factors are used to try to gauge the accuracy of eyewitness identification after it has been made.

EMPIRICAL FOUNDATIONS AND LIMITS

Studies of eyewitness identification include laboratory studies, field studies of simulated eyewitness events and of actual criminal investigations, and archival studies of actual criminal investigations. Most studies are conducted in laboratories. In most laboratory studies, university undergraduate students serve as eyewitnesses to simulated crimes. Sometimes, but not often, researchers use a sample of non-university students (e.g., community

members) as participants. The witnesses view a simulated crime enactment, such as an innocuous staged event in a classroom or laboratory or a videotaped simulation of a crime. Sometime later the witnesses are shown a photoarray and asked to identify the crime perpetrator. Studies typically rely on large sample sizes, usually dozens or hundreds of witnesses to the simulated crime. One of the main advantages of crime-simulation studies is that we know with certainty whether the identifications are correct or incorrect.

Three common features of laboratory studies are systematic manipulation of independent variables (e.g., the conditions under which the crime was viewed or the manner in which a lineup was conducted), random assignment of participants to conditions to control for individual differences that can affect identification performance and confound independent variables, and the use of perpetrator-absent and perpetrator-present lineups to examine the influence of the variables of interest on both correct and false identifications. These features enable us to draw causal conclusions about the effects of specific factors in identification performance.

Field studies are crime-simulation studies that are conducted in the community using ordinary citizens rather than in laboratories with university students as participants. Field studies have been conducted in convenience stores (e.g., Platz & Hosch, 1988) and in banks (Pigott, Brigham, & Bothwell, 1990). Field studies can have some of the main benefits of laboratory studies, including good control over conditions, the ability to manipulate factors of interest, random assignment, and the ability to assess the accuracy of identifications with certainty. Field studies more closely represent the conditions under which witnesses sometimes view perpetrators. Field studies do not simulate dangerous crimes but rather expose citizens to suspicious individuals.

A small but growing number of studies examine eyewitness identifications in actual crimes. Some of these studies are *archival* (e.g., Behrman & Richards, 2005), whereas others are *prospective* studies using actual crimes (e.g., Wright & Skagerberg, 2007). Some of these studies attempt to isolate the impact of specific factors on identification performance. Although high in realism, crime studies have other serious limitations. Because the researchers have little control over the crime and identification conditions, variables are often confounded with one another, making it very difficult to say with certainty whether a factor has a causal effect on identification performance. It is also very difficult to establish ground truth, so we often do not know whether identifications are correct or incorrect.

The development of a large and diverse literature on eyewitness identification has made meta-analytic techniques attractive and influential. *Meta-analysis* is a methodology for reviewing sets of studies to reach general conclusions about specific phenomena, examining trends across studies, and identifying variables that qualify the effects of certain factors on identification accuracy.

Each methodology contributes uniquely to our understanding of eyewitness identification and the psychological processes influencing it. Each method also has limitations. It behooves the expert, therefore, to be well schooled in the benefits and limitations of all methodologies relevant to eyewitness science.

Having reviewed the basic methodology of eyewitness research, we now turn to our review of the common conclusions in research on eyewitness identifications. These conclusions are often the subject of expert testimony. These summaries are very brief and general (see Cutler & Kovera, 2010, for more elaborate explanations and for explanations of more factors, including examples and qualifying conditions).

General Impairment Factors

Some general impairment factors are commonly relevant to cases in which eyewitness experts become involved. The own-race bias refers to the finding that witnesses are more accurate at recognizing same-race perpetrators than other-race perpetrators. Conversely, witnesses make more mistakes when attempting to identify other-race perpetrators than same-race perpetrators (Meissner & Brigham, 2001).

The level of stress associated with the crime influences identification accuracy. Witnesses who experience extreme stress are less likely to be accurate, but this effect is larger for correct identifications than for false identifications (Deffenbacher, Bornstein, Penrod, & McGorty, 2004).

The visual presence of a weapon tends to draw the attention of the witness. Consequently, when a weapon is visually present, we less effectively encode the perpetrator's characteristics and are less likely to accurately identify the perpetrator as compared to when there is no weapon visually (Steblay, 1992).

It is obvious that the wearing of a disguise that masks a perpetrator's facial and physical characteristics can impair identification accuracy, yet more subtle disguises can also impair identification accuracy. These subtle discuses include hats that cover the hair and hairline (Cutler, 2006) and changes in glasses, hairstyle, and facial hair and age-related changes (Read, 1995; Read, Tollestrup, Hammersley, McFadzen, & Christensen, 1990).

Exposure time refers to the amount of time that the witness is able to view the perpetrator's facial and physical characteristics. As exposure time increases, the likelihood of correct identification increases and the likelihood of false identification decreases (Shapiro & Penrod, 1986).

Occasionally, crimes take place in environments in which alcohol consumption occurs and one or more witnesses are under the influence of alcohol at the time of the crime. Considerable psychological research has demonstrated that alcohol intoxication impairs cognitive functioning and performance on a wide variety of tasks. The negative effects of alcohol intoxication on memory have been found to generalize to eyewitness identifications from showups and photoarrays (Dysart, 2008).

Retention interval refers to the amount of time that has passed between a crime and an eyewitness identification. The length of the retention interval is inversely related to identification accuracy (Shapiro & Penrod, 1986).

Sometimes witnesses mistakenly identify as a crime perpetrator a person who is familiar to them but was not the perpetrator of the crime; we refer to this type of error as *unconscious transference*. It is thought to be an "unconscious" error because the witness does not recall that the person is familiar because of exposure to that person from some context other than the witnessed crime. If witnesses are aware that they are familiar with the person from another context but nevertheless mistakenly identify the person as a crime perpetrator, this would be an example of conscious transference. Overall, the results for transference research are rather mixed but in their aggregate suggest small but reliable transference errors (Deffenbacher, Bornstein, & Penrod, 2006).

Suspect Bias Factors

Photoarray composition refers to the method of selecting fillers for the photoarray. Generally, there are two recognized approaches for selecting fillers. One method, labeled as *suspect-matched* (SM) fillers, is to select fillers based on their resemblance to the suspect. The other method, labeled *perpetrator-description-matched* (PDM), involves selecting fillers that match the witness's description of the perpetrator. Research comparing the two procedures shows that PDM photoarrays provide a better balance of increased correct identifications and decreased false identifications relative to SM photoarrays (e.g., Clark & Tunnicliff, 2001). The preferred method of choosing fillers is PDM.

The instructions given to the witness prior to showing the photoarray can influence the witness's tendency to make a positive identification. Instructions that suggest that the perpetrator is present increase the likelihood of a positive identification, regardless of whether the suspect is the perpetrator. Conversely, instructions that convey the fact that the perpetrator's photo might not be in the array or otherwise emphasize that it is important to avoid the mistaken identification decrease the likelihood of a positive identification (Clark, 2005; Steblay, 1997).

Traditionally, most investigators present a set of photos or lineup members to the witness simultaneously and ask the witness to identify the perpetrator from among the set of photos (Wogalter, Malpass, & McQuiston, 2004). Researchers have compared this simultaneous procedure with a procedure in which the presentation of photos or lineup members is done sequentially, wherein the witness is presented with each lineup member or photo individually and asked whether or not each person is the perpetrator. Crime-simulation research has reliably shown that the sequential presentation of photoarrays, as compared to simultaneous presentation, significantly reduces the likelihood of false identification from perpetrator-absent photoarrays. Simultaneous presentation produces a small but reliable increase in correct identifications from perpetrator-present photoarrays; however, the reduction in false identifications achieved through sequential presentation is much larger than the increase in correct identifications associated with simultaneous presentation (Steblay, Dysart, Fulero, & Lindsay, 2001; Steblay, Dysart, & Wells, 2011).

The lead investigator in the case typically conducts the photoarray or lineup procedure. Because the lead investigator knows which photo is the suspect's, the investigator has the opportunity to advertently or inadvertently influence the witness to select a specific photo from the photoarray. Blind administration, by contrast, requires that the photoarray be conducted by an investigator who does not know which photo is the suspect's and therefore is unable to advertently or inadvertently steer the witness toward selecting the suspect's photo—rather than a filler's photo—from the array. The belief that an investigator can convey the suspect's identity to the witness through the use of subtle or overt cues is substantiated by a well-accepted literature on research methods examining how experimenters' expectations influence their participants' behaviors (see Rosenthal, 1976) and by several laboratory studies of eyewitness identification (e.g., Greathouse & Kovera, 2009).

Postdictors of Identification Accuracy

The confidence expressed by the witness is frequently used to assess the accuracy of eyewitness identification. It is so common that it is specifically named as a factor in U.S. law that judges should consider when evaluating the suggestiveness of particular identification procedures (*Manson v. Braithwaite*, 1977) and in jury instructions regarding the factors to take into consideration when evaluating eyewitness identifications (*United States v. Telfaire*, 1978). Eyewitness confidence is probably the second-most-commonly studied variable in the eyewitness identification literature (the first being identification accuracy). A meta-analysis by Sporer, Penrod, Read, and Cutler (1995) found that the correlation between confidence and accuracy was modest in size overall and was significantly larger for witnesses who made a positive identification than for witnesses who rejected the lineup.

It is important to note that confidence correlates modestly with accuracy only under certain circumstances: when confidence is measured immediately after the identification and before the witness is provided with any information that validates or invalidates his identification. Considerable research has now shown that information that validates or invalidates a witness's identification, such as being told that a co-witness identified the same or a different person or receiving positive verbal reinforcement by the investigator, inflates confidence and attenuates the confidence–accuracy relation.

THE EVALUATION

At some point before the trial, experts will have all of the information they need (or will get) to formulate their opinions and, together with the defense attorney, plan their expert testimony. This information may include police reports, transcripts from prior hearings, and depositions with the eyewitness and police investigators, depending on the discovery rules of the jurisdiction. The point at which this occurs may vary as a function of the discovery issues discussed earlier. The interpretation process is relatively straightforward. The facts of the case should be compared against two data sources: the research literature concerning the factors that influence identification accuracy and best practices in identification tests. Once this interpretation is complete, the expert discusses this assessment with the attorney and discusses whether expert testimony should be offered in the case.

Proceeding sequentially through the case materials, the first question to ask is which well-established factors are relevant to this case. The set of discovery should be mined for the relevant general impairment factors, suspect bias factors, and postdictors. Cutler and Kovera (2010) provide more detailed suggestions, such as how to use a checklist for this purpose.

The second question can be addressed by comparing the identification procedure with existing sets of best practices. Whether the identification test was a showup, photoarray, or live lineup, the procedures vary, and written guidelines now exist for minimizing bias in each type of identification test. Several states (e.g., New Jersey, New York, North Carolina, and Wisconsin), have adopted new guidelines for collecting eyewitness identification evidence. Reform is in progress in other states as well.

Comparing the procedures used to best practices serves several purposes. First, the best practices provide useful benchmarks for the judge and jury. Second, the existence of guidelines and the

reform movement confirm that the psychological research and the opinions of the expert are relevant and accepted within some law-enforcement communities. Third, the guidelines mute the criticism that the research upon which the expert's opinion is based does not generalize to actual crimes, a point sometimes raised during cross-examination. The best-practice guidelines were based in large measure on the psychological research and are summarized as follows.

The best-practice literature on identification tests has evolved over time. The first government agency to produce a set of best practices was the U.S. Department of Justice (DOJ). A panel of attorneys, police officers, and psychologists convened by Attorney General Janet Reno produced the document entitled *Eyewitness Evidence: A Guide for Law Enforcement* (Technical Working Group, 1999). This guide addresses the collection and preservation of eyewitness evidence from police interviews with witnesses, field identification tests (showups), photoarrays, and lineups. Two additional points about the DOJ guide are noteworthy. First, the guide describes good procedures for conducting simultaneous and sequential lineups but expresses no preference for one or the other presentation method. Second, the guide does not emphasize blind identification procedures over nonblind procedures. The panel members from the judicial system (and presumably their constituents) had not yet warmed to the idea of blind procedures (for more about the development of the guidelines, see Wells et al., 2000).

In 1996 the American Psychology-Law Society's (AP-LS) Executive Committee convened a committee to develop a set of recommended practices for lineups and photoarrays. These recommendations were published in *Law and Human Behavior* (Wells et al., 1998). This document provides not only the recommendations but also the rationale behind these recommendations and is a must-read for any expert witness proposing to offer expert testimony about system variables, as well as for lawyers who regularly deal with eyewitness identification and may consider eyewitness expert testimony. The committee recommended four rules for identification tests: the lineup administrator should be blind to the suspect's identity, the administrator should warn the witness that the perpetrator may not appear in the lineup, the suspect should not stand out from the other lineup members, and the administrator should record witnesses' confidence immediately after an identification is made and before they receive any feedback about their identification decision.

Finally, the International Association of the Chiefs of Police (IACP, 2006) also developed guidelines for best practices in collecting eyewitness identification evidence. The extent to which these recommendations are evidence-based is unclear as the document describing the guidelines does not provide a discussion of the process by which these recommendations were created, nor does the document itself refer to specific research on which the recommendations are based. With that in mind, the IACP has promulgated guidelines for both showups and lineups (live and photo), with an expressed preference for conducting lineups whenever possible.

Since the publication of the DOJ guide and the AP-LS white paper, several states and jurisdictions have developed their own guidelines for identification procedures. These states include New Jersey, North Carolina, Wisconsin, and New York. There are differences among these guidelines. It is important to know whether the state and/or jurisdiction in which the evaluation is being conducted has current guidelines.

Although comparing procedures used in a specific case with best practices is a fruitful approach, the exercise clearly has limitations. It is typical for the prosecutor to argue that the best practices do not apply to the specific jurisdiction. The DOJ guide is just that—a guide. The procedures endorsed in the guide are not required of local police departments. Nevertheless, the exercise of comparing procedures in a case to established best practices can be useful for demonstrating the science behind identification tests, giving legitimacy to the research, and educating the judge and jury about how faulty procedures could result in earnest but mistaken identification by highly confident witnesses.

After comprehensive review and interpretation of the data, experts should discuss their findings with the attorney so that the attorney can decide whether to offer expert testimony in the case. The attorney may request a report from the expert at this stage or may prefer to discuss these matters without a report, as the report may be discoverable in some jurisdictions. Attorneys will want to know whether the expert testimony will help their case. The answer to this question will depend on the expert's findings concerning the levels and mix of general impairment factors, suspect bias factors, and postdictors.

When no suspect bias factors are present, expert testimony may be less useful to the defense. There is one less obvious scenario in which the usefulness of expert testimony is questionable, and that is when there are general impairment factors but no suspect bias factors. Expert testimony is most likely to be helpful in cases in which there are suspect bias factors.

REPORT WRITING AND TESTIMONY

The expert communicates his or her findings in several ways. First, after reviewing discovery and forming opinions, the expert reports these opinions to the attorney orally, in writing, or both orally and in writing. Second, assuming the case goes forward and the attorney chooses to proffer the expert testimony, the expert communicates those findings in court. Prior to testifying to the jury, however, the expert may first have to testify in an admissibility hearing so that the judge can determine whether the expert testimony will be admitted in court.

The expert's report can take one of several forms. Some attorneys request an affidavit. Others do not require a specific format and will even accept an e-mailed summary of the expert's findings.

The description of the expert's credentials should be brief. The attorney should have a copy of the expert's CV and submit it with the report and as an exhibit at an admissibility hearing or at a trial if the expert's testimony is admitted. The description of the discovery materials reviewed should be specific—the attorneys should be able to identify the specific document reviewed by its description in the report. The overview of the research on mistaken identification and erroneous conviction generally makes the point that mistaken identification is one of the leading precursors of erroneous conviction and helps support the need for expert testimony. The summary of each relevant factor serves as a preview of the expert testimony. In this section, the attorneys and the judges learn the substance of the expert testimony. The attorney should ensure that the expert explains that his or her opinions are based on published research. Citations and full references should be included in the report.

The attorney should request that the expert also summarize the research on general consensus and common sense (covered in detail in Cutler & Kovera, 2010). Our recommendation is based on the fact that prosecutors frequently challenge the admissibility of expert testimony by claiming that there is no general consensus about the research or that the research does not go beyond the common sense of the jury. Summarizing the research that demonstrates consensus and demonstrates that the research findings are sometimes at odds with common sense helps the defense attorney overcome these admissibility challenges. Further, the report provides the first opportunity to inform the judge that there is a corpus of empirical research addressing consensus among experts and common sense about eyewitness research.

As in all areas of expert testimony, preparation for testimony is paramount. Many attorneys are inexperienced with respect to eyewitness experts. An experienced expert may have much more experience testifying as an expert than the attorney has retaining and working with experts. An attorney who has little or no experience with eyewitness experts can learn much from an experienced expert about the preferred ebb and flow of expert testimony.

The attorney may request from the expert a list of sample questions for establishing the expert's qualifications—referred to by some attorneys as *voir dire* of the expert—and for direct testimony. These questions should pertain to the expert's qualifications and should be designed to elicit testimony about the relevant factors in the case (see below for more detail about the questions). In our experience, the attorney benefits from receiving these sample questions in two ways. First, the attorney learns from the experiences of the expert, and, second, the gesture saves the attorney a good deal of work. Note that we used the phrase "sample questions." The direct examination is the responsibility of the attorney. He or she may give the sample questions careful consideration and ultimately may use some or all of them, but the decision is that of the attorney, not that of the expert.

Prior to the trial, we recommend that the attorney confer with the expert for an hour or two about expert testimony. The attorney is in charge of the questions, and the expert is in charge of the answers. Attorneys may provide guidance to experts about how to answer questions, but the answers must be the expert's, not the attorney's. Reviewing the questions has several benefits. It is useful for the attorney to preview the expert's answers and take the opportunity to advise the expert about the use of certain language, identify aspects of the expert's testimony that are unclear, and recommend topics that deserve further elaboration. Reviewing all of the planned questions gives experts an opportunity to make sure that attorneys understand the expected answers to the questions they have written. This is an important step because many attorneys do not have a command over the eyewitness research and may have some unrealistic expectations about the expert's testimony. A second objective of the attorney–expert pretrial conference is to review the likely substance of cross-examination.

The pretrial conference gives the attorney the opportunity to socialize the expert about the particular court culture, prosecuting attorney, judge, and jury. Last, the attorney may use the pretrial conference to remind the expert of courtroom etiquette issues.

Direct and Cross-Examination During Admissibility Hearings and Trial

The purpose of the admissibility hearing is for the judge to decide whether the proffered expert testimony will be admitted at trial. The hearing provides the attorneys with the opportunity to present arguments in favor of or against expert testimony. There are some important differences in the examination and cross-examination of the expert in the admissibility hearing as compared to the jury trial. The questions asked of the expert may be somewhat different in the two types of proceedings. There is no jury present during an admissibility hearing; consequently, the expert does not speak to the jury but rather to the attorneys and the judge.

The admissibility hearing addresses the science behind expert testimony. Opponents of expert testimony may challenge its admissibility from a variety of perspectives. The opposing attorney may argue that the expert's testimony is merely a matter of common sense, and jurors possess the requisite knowledge to evaluate eyewitness memory (cf., Schmechel et al., 2006). They may further argue that the expert testimony will prejudice the jury—that it will generally create an unnecessary and unwarranted doubt in eyewitness testimony, causing jurors to discredit even reliable eyewitness testimony. The opposing attorney may argue that the person should not be considered an expert under the courts' rules and therefore should not be permitted to testify. Alternatively, the opposing attorney may argue that the eyewitness research upon which the expert testimony is based is not generally accepted in the scientific community and therefore does not meet the *Frye* standard.

A carefully designed direct examination will provide a compelling demonstration of the usefulness of the testimony while addressing the challenges described above. The examination should include a thorough review of the expert's credentials, discussion of the science of eyewitness testimony, general testimony about the stages and reconstructive nature of human memory, and discussion of specific general impairment factors, suspect bias factors, and postdictors identified by the expert as relevant in this case. The examination should also cover the fact that the research has been peer-reviewed, its level of general acceptance in the scientific community, and whether the factor is a matter of common sense. The examination may also compare the identification procedures with "best practices."

It is important to anticipate possible cross-examination strategies on each set of issues. The prosecutor may challenge the expert's credentials. He or she may challenge the validity of research methodology (e.g., the use of staged rather than real crimes). The prosecutor might also raise the fact that some vocal psychologists have challenged the generalizability of the eyewitness research to actual cases at conferences, in print, and in court. The prosecutor might be prepared to ask about studies of relevant factors that contradict the conclusion drawn by the expert. The prosecutor might expose the fact that the research cannot predict the amount of impairment or say anything about the accuracy of a specific eyewitness. The prosecutor may argue that the expert testimony is merely a matter of common sense. The prosecutor might expose all of the inconsistencies among the best-practice documents. The attorney and expert should be prepared to address such criticisms in redirect examination.

Many of the topics covered in the direct and cross-examination during the admissibility hearing may be replicated at trial, although there are some important differences. One difference is that the judge is the audience in an admissibility hearing, whereas the jury is the audience at a trial. With the jury as the audience, the expert should make extra efforts to use plain-language explanations, to elaborate on complex issues, to give concrete examples, to be a little repetitive, and to be a little animated so as to keep the jury's attention, as research shows that experts who are concrete and repetitive in their explanations are more influential (Kovera, Gresham, Borgida, Gray, & Regan, 1997).

Besides style, there are some differences in the substance of expert testimony between an admissibility hearing and a testimony before the jury. For example, having heard the qualifications of the expert during the admissibility hearing, the prosecutor may choose to stipulate to the expert's expertise and waive the *voir dire* questioning. This is a strategic decision in which the prosecuting attorney does not want the jury to hear a lot about the expert's qualifications. Defense attorneys differ widely in the level of research detail they desire in jury testimony. At one extreme, some defense attorneys will want the jury to hear all of the detail that was raised in the admissibility hearing. At another extreme, some defense attorneys will want to omit all of the detail about the research and have the experts merely summarize the conclusions of the research. Some of the issues raised during admissibility hearings are specific for the admissibility hearings, such as whether the testimony is within the common sense of the jury. The issue of whether eyewitness research is within the ken of the jury is relevant to arguments in favor of or opposed to the admissibility of expert testimony and does not speak to the issue that the jury must decide.

Attorneys who regularly retain eyewitness should have an interest in improving their experts' effectiveness. We recommend that attorneys provide feedback to the experts with whom they have worked. Sometime after the conclusion of the trial, the attorney should set up a time to speak with the expert by telephone. The purpose of the phone call is to provide constructive feedback on one's performance as an expert witness. Attorneys should be candid and constructive. The attorney might provide the expert with practical advice, such as make more eye contact with the jury, use more parochial language, and do not be so defensive—if there are limitations to the research, just acknowledge them. The attorney may simply say that it was a job well done, and this is always reinforcing to hear. The expert will undoubtedly learn about the trial outcome but should not take it as evidence of his or her skills. Trial outcomes are multiply determined. Further, there are some cases in which the defense attorney has little or no expectation of winning because the evidence is overwhelming, the prosecution has not offered an attractive plea, or the defendant insists on exercising his or her right to a trial. Thus, the attorney's feedback may be more important to the expert than the trial outcome.

Providing expert testimony about the reliability of eyewitness identification evidence can be an important service. Jurors appear unaware of many of the factors that influence the accuracy of eyewitness identifications, and expert testimony on the relevant research may help the jurors gauge the appropriate weight to give to an identification gained under a particular set of circumstances. Moreover, it is possible that jurisdictions will be moved to reform their identification procedures if they are frequently contested in court. To be effective, however, eyewitness experts need to be well versed in the current research on eyewitness reliability and to recognize the limitations of the research and the expertise that they provide.

SUMMARY

This chapter provided a summary of the more critical highlights of the eyewitness science and the expert's activity in the service of informing practicing attorneys about its content and format. Those who are interested in more detailed information on these topics are referred to our book (Cutler & Kovera, 2010) for a more in-depth examination of these critical topics.

REFERENCES

Behrman, B. W., & Richards, R. E. (2005). Suspect/ foil identification in actual crimes and in the laboratory: A reality monitoring analysis. *Law and Human Behavior, 29*, 279–301.

Borchard, E. M. (1932). *Convicting the innocent.* Garden City, NY: Garden City Publishing.

Clark, S. E. (2005). A re-examination of the effects of biased lineup instructions in eyewitness identification. *Law and Human Behavior, 29*, 395–424.

Clark, S. E., & Tunnicliff, J. L. (2001). Selecting lineup foils in eyewitness identification experiments: Experimental control and real-world simulation. *Law and Human Behavior, 25*, 199–216.

Copple, R. W., Torkildson J., & Kovera, M. B. (2008). Expert psychological testimony: Admissibility standards. In B. L. Cutler (Ed.), *Encyclopedia of psychology and law* (pp. 271–275). Thousand Oaks, CA: Sage.

Cutler, B. L. (2011). *Convicting the innocent: Lessons from psychological research.* Washington DC: American Psychological Association Press.

Cutler, B. L. (2006). A sample of witness, crime, and perpetrator characteristics affecting eyewitness identification accuracy. *Cardozo Public Law, Policy, and Ethics Journal, 4*, 327–340.

Cutler, B. L. (Ed.) (2009). *Expert testimony on the psychology of eyewitness identification.* New York: Oxford University Press (American Psychology-Law Society Series).

Cutler, B. L., & Kovera, M. B. (2010). *Evaluating eyewitness identification.* New York: Oxford University Press (Oxford Forensic Best Practices Series).

Cutler, B. L., & Penrod, S. D. (1995). *Mistaken identification: The eyewitness, psychology, & the law.* Cambridge: Cambridge University Press.

Daubert v. Merrell Dow Pharmaceuticals, 509 U.S. 579 (1993).

Deffenbacher, K. A., Bornstein, B. H., & Penrod, S. D. (2006). Mugshot exposure effects: Retroactive interference, mugshot commitment, source confusion, and unconscious transference. *Law and Human Behavior, 30*, 287–307.

Deffenbacher, K. A., Bornstein, B. H., Penrod, S. D., & McGorty, E. K. (2004). A meta-analytic review of the effects of high stress on eyewitness memory. *Law and Human Behavior, 28*, 687–706.

Devenport, J. L., Stinson, V., Cutler, B. L., & Kravitz, D. A. (2002). How effective are the expert testimony and cross-examination safeguards? Jurors' perceptions of the suggestiveness and fairness of biased lineup procedures. *Journal of Applied Psychology, 87*, 1042–1054.

Dysart, J. E. (2008). Alcohol intoxication, impact on eyewitness memory. In B. L. Cutler (Ed.), *Encyclopedia of psychology and law* (pp. 11–13). Thousand Oaks, CA: Sage.

Faigman, D. L. (2008). Expert testimony, qualifications of experts. In B. L. Cutler (Ed.), *Encyclopedia of psychology and law* (pp. 280–282). Thousand Oaks, CA: Sage.

Federal Rules of Evidence for United States Courts and Magistrates (1975). St. Paul, MN: West.

Frank, J., & Frank, B. (1957). *Not guilty.* London: Gallanez.

Frye v. United States, 293 F. 1013 (D.C. Cir. 1923).

Garrett, B. (2008). Judging innocence. *Columbia Law Review, 108,* 55–142.

General Electric Co., et al., v. Joiner et ux., 522 U.S. 136 (1997).

Greathouse, S. M., & Kovera, M. B. (2009). Instruction bias and lineup presentation moderate the effects of administrator knowledge on eyewitness identification. *Law and Human Behavior, 33,* 70–82.

Huff, C. R. (1987). Wrongful conviction: Societal tolerance of injustice. *Research in Social Problems and Public Policy, 4,* 99–115.

International Association of the Chiefs of Police (IACP). (2006). *Training key on eyewitness identification.* Alexandria, VA: International Association of the Chiefs of Police.

Kassin, S. M., Ellsworth, P. C., & Smith, V. L. (1989). The "general acceptance" of psychological research on eyewitness testimony: A survey of the experts. *American Psychologist, 44,* 1089–1098.

Kassin, S. M., Tubb, V. A., Hosch, H. M., & Memon, A. (2001). On the "general acceptance" of eyewitness testimony research. *American Psychologist, 56,* 405–416.

Kovera, M. B., Gresham, A. W., Borgida, E., Gray, E., & Regan, P. C. (1997). Does expert testimony inform or influence juror decision-making? A social cognitive analysis. *Journal of Applied Psychology, 82,* 178–191.

Kumho Tire Company v. Carmichael, 526 U.S. 137 (1999).

Manson v. Braithwaite, 432 U.S. 98, 1977.

Meissner, C. A., & Brigham, J. C. (2001). Thirty years of investigating the own-race bias in memory for faces: A meta-analytic review. *Psychology, Public Policy, and Law, 7,* 3–35.

Monahan, J., & Walker, L. (1986). Social authority: Obtaining, evaluating, and establishing social science in law. *University of Pennsylvania Law Review, 134,* 477–517.

Pigott, M. A., Brigham, J. C., & Bothwell, R. K. (1990). A field study of the relationship between quality of eyewitnesses' descriptions and identification accuracy. *Journal of Police Science and Administration, 17,* 84–88.

Platz, S. J., & Hosch, H. M. (1988). Cross-racial/ethnic eyewitness identification: A field study. *Journal of Applied Social Psychology, 18,* 972–984.

Read, J. D. (1995). The availability heuristic in person identification: The sometimes misleading consequences of enhanced contextual information. *Applied Cognitive Psychology, 9,* 91–122.

Read, J. D., Tollestrup, P., Hammersley, R., McFadzen, E., & Christensen, A. (1990). The unconscious transference effect: Are innocent bystanders ever misidentified? *Applied Cognitive Psychology, 4,* 3–31.

Rosenthal, R. (1976). *Experimenter effects in behavioral research.* New York: Irvington.

Schmechel, R. S., O'Toole, T. P., Easterly, C., & Loftus, E. F. (2006). Beyond the ken: Testing juror's understanding of eyewitness reliability evidence. *Jurimetrics, 46,* 177–214.

Shapiro, P., & Penrod, S. D. (1986). A meta-analysis of the facial identification literature. *Psychological Bulletin, 100,* 139–156.

Sporer, S. L., Penrod, S., Read, D., & Cutler, B. (1995). Choosing, confidence, and accuracy: A meta-analysis of the confidence–accuracy relation in eyewitness identification studies. *Psychological Bulletin, 118,* 315–327.

Steblay, N. M. (1992). A meta-analytic review of the weapon focus effect. *Law and Human Behavior, 16,* 413–424.

Steblay, N. M. (1997). Social influences in eyewitness recall: A meta-analytic review of lineup instruction effects. *Law & Human Behavior, 21,* 283–297.

Steblay, N. M., Dysart, J., Fulero, S., & Lindsay, R. C. L. (2001). Eyewitness accuracy rates in sequential and simultaneous line-up presentations: A meta-analytic comparison. *Law and Human Behavior, 25,* 459–474.

Steblay, N. M., Dysart, J., & Wells, G. L. (2011). Seventy-two tests of the sequential lineup superiority effect: A meta-analysis and policy discussion. *Psychology, Public Policy, and Law, 17,* 99–139.

Stinson, V., Devenport, J. L., Cutler, B. L., & Kravitz, D. S. (1997). How effective is the motion-to-suppress safeguard? Judges' perceptions of the suggestiveness and fairness of biased lineup procedures. *Journal of Applied Psychology, 82,* 211–220.

Technical Working Group on Eyewitness Evidence. (1999). *Eyewitness evidence: A guide for law enforcement.* Washington, DC: U.S. Department of Justice.

United States v. Telfaire, 1978 469 F.2d 552, 558-59.

Van Wallendael, L. R., Devenport, J. L., Cutler, B. L., & Penrod, S. D. (2007). Mistaken identification = erroneous convictions? Assessing and improving legal safeguards. In R. C. L. Lindsay, D. F. Ross, J. D. Read, & M. P. Toglia (Eds.), *Handbook of eyewitness testimony* (pp. 557–582). Mahwah, NJ: Erlbaum.

Wells, G. L. (1978). Applied eyewitness testimony research: System variables and estimator variables. *Journal of Personality and Social Psychology, 36,* 1546–1557.

Wells, G. L., Malpass, R. S., Lindsay, R.C.L., Fisher, R.P., Turtle, J. W., & Fulero, S. (2000). From the lab to the police station: A successful application of eyewitness research. *American Psychologist, 55,* 581–598.

Wells, G. L., Small, M., Penrod, S., Malpass, R. S., Fulero, S. M., & Brimacombe, C. A. E. (1998). Eyewitness identification procedures: Recommendations for lineups and photospreads. *Law and Human Behavior, 22,* 603–646.

Wogalter, M. S., Malpass, R. S., & McQuiston, D. E. (2004). A national survey of police on preparation and conduct of identification lineups. *Psychology, Crime and Law, 10,* 69–82.

Wright, D. B., & Skagerberg, E. M. (2007). Post-identification feedback affects real eyewitnesses. *Psychological Science, 18,* 172–178.

PART II

Civil

10

Evaluation for Guardianship

ERIC Y. DROGIN AND CURTIS L. BARRETT

Guardianship is a legal process designed to provide a substituted decision maker for persons who cannot manage their own personal or financial affairs. In this chapter, we focus on guardianship for adults, who are legally presumed competent unless proven otherwise. This is distinct from considerations in guardianship for children, who may have guardians appointed for them simply because of prolonged or even permanent absence of their natural parents or other prior caretakers. When we refer globally to "guardianship," we are addressing this notion in the prevailing modern context that considers personal and financial needs simultaneously, although we recognize that some statutes still provide for assigning a *guardian* to manage the former and a *conservator* to manage the latter. Our primary goal is to describe and contextualize the forensic evaluation process in a practical and accessible fashion, so that attorneys at any level of experience with guardianship matters can make the most effective use of the reports and testimony generated in these cases.

LEGAL CONTEXT
Functional Legal Constructs

In each case, guardianship evaluations require exploration of specific civil competencies. These are described in this section, with reference to specific state-law examples, as no comprehensive national standard has ever been implemented.

Testamentary Capacity

Testamentary capacity typically requires investigation of some combination of the following: whether the examinee (a) understands what it means to make a will; (b) is aware of the nature and extent of his property; (c) can describe a rational plan for distributing that property; and (d) can identify the "natural objects of one's bounty," characterized as "the persons one would normally expect to inherit the possessions in question" (Drogin, 2008, p. 633). New Hampshire's law on "Guardians and Conservators" (1994), for example, directs that "no person determined to be incapacitated thus requiring the appointment of a guardian...shall be deprived of any legal rights, including [the right] to make a will...except upon specific findings of the court" (§464-A:9). The Supreme Court of New Hampshire has confirmed in *In re Estate of Katherine F. Washburn* (1997) that the court must determine "(1) whether the testatrix possessed testamentary capacity to execute a will; and (2) if the testatrix had such capacity, whether the will is the offspring of a delusion or was executed during a lucid interval" (p. 662).

Voting

Although "the right to vote is perhaps the most basic privilege in a democratic society" (Parry & Drogin, 2007, p. 154), the National Voter Registration Act of 1993 provides that "the name of a registrant" may be "removed from the official list of eligible voters...by reason of criminal conviction or mental incapacity" (§1977). For example, Ohio statutes addressing "Cancellation of Registration" (2009) direct each political subdivision's probate judge to file "the names and residence addresses of all persons over eighteen years of age who have been adjudicated incompetent for the purpose of voting" (§3503.18), while statutes addressing "Civil Rights of Patients" (1989) identify voting as a "civil right" that would require a judicial proceeding beyond mere involuntary civil commitment (§5122.301), and statutes addressing the "Department of Developmental Disabilities" (2009) specifically identify "the right to participate in the political process" (§5123.62).

Marriage

As a general matter, "since possession of sufficient mental capacity is essential, statutes allow annulments on the grounds of mental incapacity at the time of the marriage, but marriages will not be annulled if entered into during a lucid interval" (Parry & Drogin, 2007, p. 153). In Illinois, for example, although statutory law does not address any competency-based impediments to *becoming* married, according to the Illinois Marriage and Dissolution of Marriage Act of 1977 it may subsequently be determined that "a party lacked capacity to consent to the marriage at the time the marriage was solemnized, either because of mental incapacity or infirmity" (§5/301). The Supreme Court of Illinois ruled in *Pape v. Byrd* (1991) that "the appointment of a guardian of a person is not sufficient, in and of itself, to show that the person was incompetent to have consented to a marriage" (p. 21), requiring instead that the probate court specifically address the person's competence to marry and make appropriate findings of fact and law before depriving a guardianship examinee of this particular right.

Automobile Driving

Distinct from other capacity-related options that are properly characterized as "rights," driving an automobile is more appropriately characterized as a privilege, tied to a license having been granted by a particular jurisdiction's Department of Motor Vehicles (DMV) or local equivalent. In Pennsylvania, for example, statutes addressing "Cancellation of Registration" (2009) make the state's Medical Advisory Board responsible for defining "disorders characterized by lapses of consciousness or other mental or physical disabilities affecting the ability of a person to drive safely" (§1518(a)). Probate courts seeking to determine whether a guardianship examinee should be deprived of a driver's license are likely to look to these criteria, as well as to those promulgated by the National Highway Traffic Safety Administration (NHTSA, 2007).

Financial Transactions

Often referred to as *conservatorship* or "guardianship of the estate," this legal construct addresses "the protected person's financial and property interests only" (Parry & Drogin, 2007, p. 139). In New Mexico, for example, the standard for guardianship-related disability concerning financial transactions, as described in statutes addressing "Protection of Persons Under Disability and Their Property" (1978), is one of "gross mismanagement, as evidenced by recent behavior, of one's income and resources, or medical inability to manage one's income and resources that has led or is likely in the near future to lead to financial vulnerability," and while neither "gross mismanagement" nor "medical inability" has ever been interpreted in this context by New Mexico appellate decisions, "functional impairment" is measured by a person's inability to manage his or her "financial affairs" (§45-5-101).

Independent Living and Medical Care

"Over time, disability rights advocates have had considerable success in modifying the prevailing societal belief that virtually all people with disabilities are vulnerable, exploitable, and incapable of making autonomous decisions that fundamentally affect their lives" (Batavia, 2003, p. 348). Such progress does not obscure the fact, however, that some persons with disabilities will continue to require the services of a guardian when independent living and self-directed medical care are no longer viable options. Delaware's statutory scheme for "Appointment of Guardians for Disabled Persons" (2008) defines a "disabled person" as an individual who "by reason of mental or physical incapacity is unable properly to manage or care for their own person," and who, as a consequence, is in danger of "substantially endangering" his own health or "becoming subject to abuse by other persons or of becoming the victim of designing persons" (§3901). *In re Last Will and Testament of Palecki* (2007) found the Delaware Court of Chancery underscoring the importance of allowing persons placed under this aspect of supervision "as much self-determination as possible" (p. 418).

Basic Legal Procedure in Guardianship Cases
Petition

If a person is alleged to be disabled and consequently incapable of managing his or her own personal or financial affairs, a formal mechanism is necessary for bringing this to the court's attention. Some states actually provide forms that an interested party—the *petitioner*—can download or obtain directly from the court. In other jurisdictions where no state-sanctioned form is available, the relevant guardianship statute may still prescribe a series of specific components that must be contained in the petition, such as the petitioner's name and address, the allegedly disabled person's name and address, the relationship (if any) between the petitioner and the allegedly disabled person, the nature of the alleged disability, the specific way in which the alleged disability affects the management of personal or financial affairs, and the names and addresses of any persons who could provide additional relevant information.

Hearing

If the local civil trial court—often a specially designated "probate court"—is convinced by the petition that there is "probable cause"—essentially, a "reasonable basis"—to believe that the allegedly disabled person may need a guardian, then it assigns the case to a prosecutor and may also appoint a defense attorney if the allegedly disabled person—often called the *respondent*—is not in a position to arrange for private counsel. State statutes typically designate the amount of time that a court-appointed evaluator (or evaluation team) has to examine the respondent, in anticipation of a hearing date. The hearing is conducted with both sides giving evidence before a judge and—in some states—a jury. The standard by which the case for guardianship must be made is *clear and convincing evidence*.

Adjudication

Bound by the specific standards provided by statutes and case law, the judge—or jury—will determine any need for guardianship on the basis of evidence presented during the hearing as well as whatever additional materials (such as expert reports) may be admitted for supplemental review. In some jurisdictions, there is an additional determination of whether a "full" or "partial" guardianship is more appropriate. In some jurisdictions, the guardianship may also be designated as "temporary" when instituted "to provide substituted consent for health care decisions" in the case of a "life-threatening situation" (Parry & Drogin, 2007, p. 139). As with any other legal proceeding, there is an opportunity for appeal if one side or the other concludes that the trial court has committed a significant error.

FORENSIC MENTAL HEALTH CONCEPTS

The core forensic mental health concept in guardianship is *disability* (labeled *incapacity* in some jurisdictions). Fundamentally, the guardianship evaluators whom counsel will be engaging—or cross-examining—must determine whether a person can actually do each of those things that make up the legal competency in question. Can examinees perform the tasks at issue, or can they not? Lawyers, judges, and mental health professionals alike are occasionally prone to view disability as a binary and universally applicable notion—"disabled" versus "not disabled"—without pausing to consider that this term has a different meaning for each of the jurisdictionally specific spheres of competency addressed by guardianship proceedings. In this section, we will review several types of competency (testamentary capacity, voting, etc.) and identify some key diagnostic formulations that may impair a respondent's functioning in each of these areas.

Testamentary Capacity

One diagnostic formulation suggested by the legal construct for testamentary capacity is delusional disorder, which according to the *Diagnostic and Statistical Manual of Mental Disorders* (DSM-IV-TR) is characterized by the presence of "nonbizarre delusions" (American Psychiatric Association, 2000, p. 329). Such delusions are different from the grossly psychotic notions one might associate with schizophrenia—instead, they are at least theoretically possible for persons other than the individual being subjected to a guardianship evaluation, such as having a special relationship with a powerful public figure or possessing far more property than one actually owns.

There are, or course, viable diagnostic alternatives for capacity-related delusional behavior, such as schizophrenia, substance abuse, or a host of physiologically based conditions that might permanently or even temporarily affect the examinee's ability to distinguish between fantasy and reality. Relevant to the advanced age of many guardianship examinees, Mueser (2000) has pointed out that "the onset of Delusional Disorder usually occurs in middle age, later than that of Schizophrenia" (p. 39).

Voting

A frequently cited diagnosis with respect to voting capacity is bipolar disorder, manifested in some cases by alternation between manic episodes and major depressive episodes. A manic episode is characterized by "a distinct period of abnormally and persistently elevated, expansive, or irritable mood"

(American Psychiatric Association, 2000, p. 362), while a major depressive episode involves components that may include "depressed mood," "loss of interest or pleasure," "fatigue or loss of energy," and "feelings of worthlessness or excessive or inappropriate guilt" (American Psychiatric Association, 2000, p. 356).

Guardianship examiners seeking clinical correlates of an apparent lack of understanding of the "nature and effect of voting" may find much relevant substance in the criteria for both manic episodes and major depressive episodes. During the former, guardianship examinees may be too distracted to process and articulate these notions, whereas during the latter, their degree of apathy may similarly render them incapable of the necessary focus. Counsel's expert witnesses should take care, of course, to accommodate the episodic nature of bipolar disorder, because some persons with even severe manifestations of this condition may enjoy prolonged, relatively symptom-free intervals that could coincide with scheduled election dates.

Marriage

Mental retardation is one clinical context in which the capacity to marry is likely to be addressed. According to the DSM-IV-TR, this diagnosis consists of the following three components: (1) Significantly sub-average intellectual functioning as manifested by an IQ of approximately 70 or below on an individually administered IQ test; (2) concurrent deficits or impairments in present adaptive functioning, involving such areas as communication, self-care, home living, or social/interpersonal skills; and (3) onset of these symptoms before the age of 18 years (American Psychiatric Association, 2000, p. 49).

As with any forensically relevant diagnostic finding, counsel must take care to discourage the court from tying marital capacity too closely to the binary notion of either presence or absence of mental retardation. For one thing, various ranges of mental retardation run from *profound* (an IQ level below 20 or 25) to *mild* (an IQ level of 50 or 55 to approximately 70), and it is not uncommon to see legally sanctioned marriages occurring within the latter range (Oliver, Anthony, Leimkuhl, & Skillman, 2002).

Such concerns having been acknowledged, it will be clear to any experienced attorney that a guardianship examinee with mental retardation may possess such pronounced intellectual limitations and face such adaptive barriers that the nature, effect, duties, and obligations of the marital relationship will remain beyond that examinee's grasp for the foreseeable future. Also, of course, mental retardation is not the only diagnostic formulation that may contribute to this result. A chronic and pervasive psychotic condition such as schizophrenia may also prevent a guardianship examinee from consistently recognizing legally relevant notions for establishing and maintaining a valid marriage (Hopper, Wanderling, & Narayanan, 2007).

Automobile Driving

In Pennsylvania, for example, the various disorders qualifying as mental disabilities are specified as those described in the DSM-IV-TR (or subsequent versions) that involve (1) inattentiveness to the task of driving because of, for example, preoccupation, hallucination, or delusion; (2) contemplation of suicide, as may be present in acute or chronic depression or in other disorders; or (3) excessive aggressiveness or disregard for the safety of self or others or both, presenting a clear and present danger, regardless of cause (67 Pa. Code §83.5(i)-(iii)).

This Pennsylvania regulation further notes that "while signs or symptoms of mental disorder may not appear during examination by the provider, evidence may be derived from the person's history as provided by self or others familiar with the person's behavior" (67 Pa. Code §83.5). This, of course, may raise issues as to the appropriateness of proffering a forensic finding when evidence of disability appears to rest entirely upon hearsay.

In addition, there are those who suggest that for liability containment as well as standard-of-practice reasons, this sort of assessment should be given a wide berth, even when the court would prefer to have the guardianship examiner's support in reaching its ultimate conclusion about driving capacity.

Appelbaum and Gutheil (2007) point out that "the availability of private, computerized assessments of driving skills constitutes another resource in cases in which it is difficult to determine whether a patient's driving is problematic" and that "patients or family members can be encouraged to make an appointment for this evaluation at an appropriate local facility," particularly for "patients with mild to moderate dementia, whose skills are declining but who are resisting the surrender of their car keys" (p. 154). The American Psychiatric Association

(1993) has gone so far as to state that "psychiatrists have no special expertise in assessing the ability of their patients to drive" and that "psychiatrists should not be expected to make such assessments in the usual course of clinical practice" (p. 1).

Financial Transactions

The complexity of stepwise processing in financial transactions means that clinical correlates are distributed across a broad span of potential diagnoses. According to the ABA/APA Assessment of Capacity in Older Adults Project Working Group (2008):

> Financial capacity is a multi-dimensional and highly cognitive mediated capacity. Accordingly, it is a capacity that is very sensitive to medical conditions that affect cognitive and behavioral functioning. Medical conditions that impair financial capacity include neurodegenerative disorders like Alzheimer's disease (AD) and Parkinson's disease, severe psychiatric disorders like schizophrenia and bipolar disorder, substance abuse disorders, and developmental disorders, such as mental retardation and autism. (p. 74)

In the currently contemplated forensic scheme, substance abuse—and its longer-term sequelae—may feature prominently in the legal construct and clinical correlates alike. Counsel should bear in mind that there are no such formal diagnoses as "addiction" or "alcoholism" in the DSM-IV-TR, which provides instead for distinctions between "substance abuse" and "substance dependence." Additional care should be taken to identify the presence of pathological gambling (American Psychiatric Association, 2000, pp. 671–674) or similar "addictions without substance" (Barrett & Limoges, 2011, p. 257).

Attorneys seeking to thwart efforts to impose guardianship will want to focus on the specifics of money management and to downplay any connection between intoxication, tolerance, or withdrawal symptoms and any financial difficulties the guardianship examinee might have experienced, because mere mismanagement, absent an appropriate clinical correlate, does not provide a legally supportable basis for the imposition of a substitute decision maker.

Independent Living and Medical Care

For those who once possessed the capacity for independent living and medical care but are now unable

to meet this standard, a common clinical correlate is the presence of dementia of the Alzheimer's type. According to the DSM-IV-TR, criteria for this disorder include a combination of such deficits as memory impairment, speech disturbance, and impaired coordination. Such problems are characterized by a gradual onset and a continuing decline in cognitive abilities (American Psychiatric Association, 2000, p. 157). Like other forms of dementia, this condition at the present time is irreversible and ultimately fatal.

Properly conducted guardianship evaluations in this area will rely in particular upon appropriate documentation and keen attention to differential diagnostic considerations. Persons who present with symptoms consistent with dementia of the Alzheimer's type may, in fact, be delirious due to an overdose or interaction of prescribed medications, may suffer from a vitamin deficiency due to malnutrition, or may simply be dehydrated. Unlike dementia of the Alzheimer's type, delirium is a reversible condition, and as such would not be an appropriate basis for depriving an individual of the right to determine his or her arrangements for independent living and medical care.

EMPIRICAL FOUNDATIONS AND LIMITS
Research on Characteristics of Guardianship Examinees
Age

Given that "it is by now axiomatic that the population of most North American and European countries is aging" (Petrila, 2007, p. 337), counsel should not be surprised to learn most of the scientific and legal scholarship in the guardianship arena over the past two decades has focused substantially on older adults (Drogin, 2007). Along these lines, Gavisk and Greene (2007) commented that "one consequence of longevity is an increase in the incidence of impairment in mental capacity...the collection of skills such as memory, reasoning, judgment, and decision making required to manage one's affairs and perform everyday tasks" (pp. 339–340).

Alzheimer's disease is the major cause of dementia for older persons (Evans, Funkenstein, & Albert, 1989). In addition, Macklin, Depp, Aréan, and Jeste (2006) noted that up to 80% to 90% of older persons with dementia would also manifest such psychiatric symptoms as agitation, anxiety, and depression. A certain degree of cognitive deterioration can be expected as a natural function of aging, separate from any identifiable disease process. On the basis of the results of a study of more than 1,100 respondents between the ages of 15 and 89, Foster, Cornwell, Kisley, and Davis (2007) determined that for verbal tasks, "individuals aged 15 to 19 and over 50 are impaired relative to participants in their 40s, and a linear decline is notable, beginning in the 40s," and "similarly, a linear decline is present in visuospatial memory, which beings in the 20s and becomes significant in the 40s" (p. 27).

Ethnicity

According to the American Psychological Association's *Guidelines for the Evaluation of Dementia and Age-Related Cognitive Change* (2012), "research to establish norms on commonly used clinical tests for specific ethical and racial populations is growing, but representative norms are still lacking in some cases" (p. 5). Karel (2007) emphasized the central importance of understanding "cultural attitudes, beliefs, and practices—related to racial, ethnic, religious, regional, and other influences" (p. 145), citing numerous examples of research that address such notions as a declining order of African Americans, Hispanic Americans, and non-Hispanic whites in preference for life-support intervention (Kwak & Haley, 2005), the greater preference of less as opposed to more acculturated Japanese Americans for consensus in reaching capacity-related decisions (Matsumura et al., 2002), and broad differences between various cultures regarding the value of informed consent (Kawaga-Singer & Blackhall, 2001).

Research on Characteristics of Guardianship Evaluators

Concerning the characteristics of psychologists serving as guardianship evaluators, Qualls, Segal, Norman, Niederehe, and Gallagher-Thompson (2002) queried 1,227 members of the American Psychological Association concerning their practices with the older adult population that constitutes the primary focus of guardianship evaluations, and concluded that:

> Although only a small percentage (3%) viewed geriatric patients as their primary professional target, 69% of respondents ($n = 845$) reported that they currently provided some type of psychological service to older adults…434

(51%) conducted assessments…the percentage of respondents offering services to older adults was highest among respondents working in long-term care (88%), independent practice (70%), or hospitals (57%). (p. 437)

According to the American Bar Association Commission on Law and Aging and the American Psychological Association (2005), "the most important criterion is the clinician's experience and knowledge in the assessment of older adults," with explicit recognition that "relevant medical boarded specialties include geriatric medicine, psychiatry, neurology, geriatric psychiatry, and forensic psychiatry," while for psychologists, "there is increasing specialization although the boarding process has not been as important as in medicine" (p. 32).

Research on Measures Employed in Guardianship Evaluations
Neuropsychological Testing

Not surprisingly, neuropsychological testing plays a prominent role in guardianship examinations. Gurrera, Moye, Karel, Azar, and Armesto (2006) administered a battery of 11 neuropsychological tests—including such frequently employed measures as the Trail Making Test, the Boston Naming Test, and components of the Wechsler Adult Intelligence Scale—to 88 individuals with an average age of approximately 75 years and diagnoses of mild to moderate dementia, to determine the effectiveness of these tests in predicting treatment decisional abilities. These authors reported that "performance on a neuropsychological test battery significantly predicted each treatment decisional ability," specifying that "the neuropsychological predictors examined in this study explained 78% of the common variance in understanding, 39.5% of the common variance in reasoning, and almost 25% of the common variance in appreciation" (p. 1370).

Computerized Assessment

Numerous paper-and-pencil tests and examiner-endorsed checklists continue to form the substantial basis of mental health assessment; however, it should be noted that computerized assessment is increasingly employed in the context of guardianship evaluations and will doubtless become a substantial factor in the decades to come. Fillit, Simon, Doniger, and Cummings (2008) have described how this modality is replacing often impractical neuropsychological testing with promising results, including positive ratings for ease of use by 73% of persons previously classified as non-computer users. Ease of use alone may not be sufficient to appease detractors of this approach, particularly in light of statistical anomalies with changed item orders in computerized personality testing (Ortner, 2008). Overall, the American Psychological Association has published *Guidelines for Psychological Practice with Older Adults* (2004), urging examiners to become "familiar with the theory, research, and practice of various methods of assessment with older adults, and knowledgeable of assessment instruments that are psychometrically suitable for use with them" (p. 237).

Research on Assessment Practice

Moye and colleagues (2007) conducted an intensive tri-state review (Massachusetts, Pennsylvania, and Colorado) of case files in 298 guardianship matters, and reported significant concerns—among others—in the following areas:

(1) *Format of Clinical Testimony Submitted to the Courts:* In Massachusetts, the mean length of the written reports was only 83 words, compared to 244 words in Pennsylvania and 781 words in Colorado. In Massachusetts, 75% of the reports were handwritten, and of these almost two-thirds contained illegible passages.

(2) *Evaluations of Clinical Status:* In Colorado, 18.6% of guardianship examinees were subjected to some form of cognitive screening, compared to only 5.3% in Pennsylvania and 5.2% in Massachusetts. Similar disparities were noted for neuropsychological testing (34.3% of Colorado cases, 1.8% of Pennsylvania cases, and 0.7% of Massachusetts cases) and for brain imaging (22.9% of Colorado cases, 1.8% of Pennsylvania cases, and 1.3% of Massachusetts cases). The overall incidence of interviews with family members ranged between 4.3% and 11.4% for these three jurisdictions.

(3) *Missing Prognoses:* Prognoses were offered in only approximately half of Colorado cases, and even less frequently in Pennsylvania and Massachusetts cases.

(4) *Conclusory Statements about Decision Making:* "Across states, 28.8% of the files included conclusory comments about decision making; that is they provided a general conclusion about decision making abilities but did not describe significant symptoms of mental impairment."

(5) *Conclusory Statements about Functioning:* "Across states, 64.1% of the files offered conclusory statements about functioning; that is, they included a statement about the ability to care for self with no description of specific functional symptoms."

(6) *Frequency of Limited Orders:* In Colorado, 34% of cases allowed for preservation of at least some rights for guardianship examinees; in Massachusetts and Pennsylvania, however, only one case in each state was characterized by a limited order of this nature. (pp. 608–609)

Concerning the last of these issues, Moye (2003) further observed that limited orders are applied in less than 15% of cases—a phenomenon typically traceable to the nature and contents of guardianship evaluations conducted by clinicians as opposed to any particular statutory requirement. Some jurisdictions are exceptional in this regard—for example, Millar and Renzaglia (2002) reviewed 221 cases in Michigan and found partial guardianships to have been applied in approximately 46% of adjudications in nine counties. The need for greater flexibility has been noted in foreign jurisdictions as well, including Israel (Melamed, Doron, & Shnitt, 2007) and Australia (Shaddock, Dowse, Richards, & Spinks, 1998).

THE EVALUATION

Thousands of careers and innumerable learned treatises have been devoted to the topic of forensic mental health assessment, such that the full scope of this process cannot possibly be contained within the current chapter. Counsel is referred to Drogin and Barrett (2010) for a comprehensive treatment of guardianship evaluations. Following is an overview of particularly salient considerations.

Data Collection: The Interview

It is not sufficient in any forensic context, including guardianship evaluations, simply to conduct a general clinical examination and then loosely apply those results to the various components of a properly crafted referral question. Drogin and Barrett (2003) identified the following general domains of inquiry for guardianship assessment that evaluators can combine with an age-appropriate clinical interview:

1. Identifying information
2. Orientation
3. Education
4. Finances
5. Self-care
6. Social contact and leisure pursuits
7. Testamentary capacity
8. Medical care
9. Automobile driving
10. Voting
11. Response to behavioral commands
12. Review of examination circumstances

By way of placing results from such inquiries in context, the following list of cognitive, emotional, and behavioral signs of incapacity was compiled by the American Bar Association Commission on Law and Aging and the American Psychological Association (2005, pp. 14–16):

1. Short-term memory loss
2. Communication problems
3. Comprehension problems
4. Lack of mental flexibility
5. Calculation problems
6. Disorientation
7. Significant emotional distress
8. Emotional inappropriateness
9. Delusions
10. Hallucinations
11. Poor grooming or hygiene

Data Collection: Obtaining Collateral Information

Heilbrun, Warren, and Picarello (2003) described a gratifyingly detailed scheme for obtaining, collecting, applying, and communicating collateral information. Their emphasis on "the importance of broadening the scope of the evaluation beyond the individual and his or her self-report" (p. 70) is particularly well placed in the context of guardianship evaluations, because examinees may be exceptionally poor historians, with an understandable tendency to minimize various manifestations of medical or psychological disability. According to Otto, Slobogin, and Greenberg (2007), collateral information is useful because "forensic examinees may be deliberately or inadvertently less than candid in their presentation," "even the candid examinee will usually not be aware of all legally relevant information," "information from third parties is necessary for administration of a number of forensically relevant instruments," and "information from collateral sources enhances the face validity of the examination and the competence of the expert in the eyes of the legal decision maker" (p. 191).

Data Collection: Psychological Testing

Evaluators may also employ psychological testing in guardianship cases. Whether to do so and, of course, which of the available tests to use with a given respondent are decisions to be made by the evaluator. The American Bar Association Commission on Law and Aging and the American Psychological Association (2005, pp. 62–67) have devised a list of more recently developed measures that may administered when capacity or competency is specifically in question. These include, among others, the following:

1. Community Competency Scale
2. Multidimensional Functional Assessment Questionnaire
3. Direct Assessment of Functional Status
4. Decision-Making Instrument for Guardianship
5. Adult Functional Adaptive Behavioral Scale
6. Functional Independence Measure
7. Hopemont Capacity Assessment Interview
8. MacArthur Competence Assessment Tool—Treatment

Data Interpretation

It is at this juncture that the guardianship evaluator steps to the fore as a clinician and mental health expert, providing an individualized, detailed, and professionally responsible perspective on the amassed data that form the basis of a forensic opinion. Heilbrun, Grisso, and Goldstein (2009; see also Chapter 1 in this handbook) identified a series of general considerations for forensic clinical interpretation that include the appropriate use of third-party information, objective and psychometrically sound testing, insight into the examinee's personal and subjective experience, and supportably sound scientific reasoning.

The ABA/APA Assessment of Capacity in Older Adults Project Working Group (2008) maintains that for older adults with allegedly diminished capacity, the properly constructed forensic interpretive framework calls for consideration of the relevant "legal standard," "functional elements," "diagnosis," "cognitive underpinnings," "psychiatric or emotional factors," "values," "risk considerations," "steps to enhance capacity," and "clinical judgment of capacity" (p. 23). Counsel will find that a correspondingly comprehensive approach enhances expert credibility and—most importantly—leads to more appropriate findings.

REPORT WRITING AND TESTIMONY

This section addresses a collection of issues common to most avenues of forensic mental health assessment and tailored to the specific context of guardianship. These include report organization, optimal levels of report detail, conveying interpretive logic, strategies for ensuring effective testimony, and addressing the ultimate legal issue.

Report Organization

The American Bar Association Commission on Law and Aging and the American Psychological Association (2005) identify the following "common elements of a clinical evaluation report" (p. 37) in the context of the assessment of older adults with diminished capacity:

1. Demographic information
2. Legal background and referral
3. History of present illness
4. Psychosocial history
5. Informed consent
6. Behavioral observations
7. Tests administered
8. Statement of validity
9. Summary of testing results
10. Impressions
11. Recommendations

Clearly, this is not the only valid approach to organizing the guardianship report. The order of these elements is not set in stone. Some could be combined, and some could be added—for example, those that describe the evaluator's credentials, the specified legal standard the report is designed to address, a separate list of documents reviewed (legal, medical, educational, and employment) and a separate list of attempted and achieved collateral contacts. More generally, Heilbrun and colleagues (2009) advised forensic mental health experts to "attribute information to sources," "use plain language," "avoid technical jargon," and, consistent with the preceding advice, to write reports "in sections, according to model and procedures" (p. 137).

Optimal Levels of Report Detail

In guardianship cases, as in other forensic matters, achieving the proper level of detail is a matter of carefully considered balance. On the one hand, providing too much information detracts from a report's narrative flow and may confuse or distract the reader with extraneous information. On the other hand, providing too little information may erode the reader's confidence in the guardianship report by creating the impression that the evaluator's conclusions and recommendations are poorly founded. This, in turn, could lead to a predictably but needlessly embarrassing cross-examination, and ultimately to the erosion of the expert witness' professional reputation. The most useful guardianship reports are those that convey enough detail to address all relevant and appropriate aspects of the referral question, while refraining at the same time from unproductive speculation and gratuitous literary flourishes.

Separate from issues of style and impression management are those details that should be excluded because they are, in and of themselves, inappropriate for a particular guardianship report. Specifically, some details may invoke the forensic clinician's ethical obligation, as described in the *Ethical Principles of Psychologists and Code of Conduct*, to "include in written and oral reports and consultations, only information germane to the purpose for which the communication is made" (American Psychological Association, 2002, p. 1066).

Examples of extraneous detail might include embarrassing historical information about an examinee that does not reflect disability and does not contribute to an understanding of current disability, compromising allegations concerning collateral contacts who clearly will not serve as a guardian or conservator for the examinee, and unfounded speculation about the status or motivations of other parties. Clearly, there are many kinds of data that will fall into a gray area in this regard.

Conveying Interpretive Logic

The guardianship report is more than simply a list of test results and interview statements, followed by the evaluator's isolated impressions and recommendations. Reports are given far greater credence when they describe *why* it is that the evaluator arrived at a certain forensic opinion. Key to this is the process of "confirming or disconfirming possible explanations for relevant capacities and behavior," described as "one of the important links that connects the sources of information and the raw data that they yield with the conclusions regarding relevant forensic capacities" (Heilbrun, 2001, p. 195).

Counsel's experts might assume, for example, that "everyone knows an IQ of 57 signals the presence of mental retardation." It would be more accurate, however, to observe that every *psychologist* knows this, and also that many laypersons do not realize that IQ is only one component of a properly ascribed mental retardation diagnosis. Nor does the examinee's failure to perform a particular task at a specific time automatically translate into a statutorily defined disability. For example, an inability to read directions on a bottle of pills may be the result of correctable poor vision, a lack of English language facility that has nothing to do with impairment, or a transitional delirium instead of a chronic and progressive dementia.

It would be a mistake for counsel's expert to rely on subsequent courtroom testimony to supply missing information and to flesh out what might appear to be interpretive "leaps of faith" in the guardianship report. Experienced witnesses know that they may or may not ever get a chance to tell "their side" of the story, due perhaps to inadequate direct examination, overly restrictive cross-examination, or their own unavailability to testify on a given date.

Strategies for Ensuring Effective Testimony

Reviewing various "maxims" developed by Brodsky (1991), Heilbrun (2001)—with forthright acknowledgement that there is "no place for deception" in forensic mental health assessment—highlighted several that constitute "stylistic approaches to enhancing the effectiveness of testimony," including the following:

1. "when challenged about insufficient experience, keep track of the true sources of your expertise"

2. "criticize your field as requested, but be poised and matter of fact and look for opportunities to gain control"
3. "explicitly relax or engage in productive work just before your court appearance"
4. "never accept the learned treatise as expertise unless you are master of it"
5. "when the time is right to disagree with cross-examination questions, do so with strength, clarity, and conviction." (pp. 274–279)

Counsel is best advised to prepare expert witnesses to confront personal shortcomings as well as alleged deficiencies in assessment methodologies and reports. For the expert witness engaged in such preparation, it is necessary to have proper access to counsel. Another of Brodsky's (1991) maxims is "meet with the attorney prior to the direct examination and be involved in preparing the questions" (p. 65). Witness testimony requires advance preparation, and Brodsky (2005) has indicated that it is appropriate to "pursue" attorneys who are "unavailable or reluctant to meet with their witnesses before trials" (p. 592).

Addressing the Ultimate Legal Issue

According to Ewing (2003), "until mid-twentieth century, courts generally proscribed expert opinions that went to what the courts called the ultimate issue: the specific question before the trier of fact... That reasoning has now been largely rejected and most jurisdictions allow ultimate opinion testimony" (p. 62). The primary reason for this change is the language in the Federal Rules of Evidence (1984) directing that in civil cases, "testimony in the form of an opinion or inference otherwise admissible is not objectionable because it embraces an ultimate issue to be decided by the trier of fact" (Rule 704, "Opinion on Ultimate Issue"). The adoption of this rule by a majority of states has enabled forensic clinicians in those jurisdictions to state plainly in their guardianship reports—and on the witness stand—that, for example, an examinee is "disabled" and "in need of the appointment of a guardian," without counsel having to fear an evidence-based objection.

Clearing evidentiary hurdles does not, of course, absolve counsel's expert witnesses of their own personal concerns regarding ethics and professionalism. The propriety of offering "ultimate issue" testimony, even when supported by law and local custom, is still briskly debated in the forensic mental health literature (e.g., Grisso, 2003; Heilbrun, 2001; Tippins & Wittman, 2005).

As Buchanan (2006) notes, "much of the harm that courts identify as stemming from evidence going to the ultimate issue could be avoided if evidence were given with greater transparency" (p. 20). In other words, encouraging one's witnesses to adhere to practices described in this chapter—particularly those involving the description of interpretive logic—will go a long way toward alleviating the court's concerns about experts being allowed to summarize the issues that their complex and detailed efforts are clearly designed to address.

SUMMARY

Attorneys who undertake to practice in the guardianship arena may find themselves challenged—and at first, virtually overwhelmed—by the unique mixture of specialized psychological information and jurisdiction-specific procedural requirements that these cases present. No unitary, all-embracing notion of "competency" exists in these matters; rather, counsel and evaluators alike must determine what legal and mental health standards apply to such distinct constructs as testamentary capacity, voting, marriage, automobile driving, and so forth. The psycholegal research that informs these notions can itself be rather sparse and even obscure, tempting one to conclude that social scientists and legal scholars have barely begun to develop a controlled, systematized means of investigation into practice-oriented guardianship topics. The psychological tests one sees employed in these cases are often minimally utilized, inadequately normed, or difficult for attorneys to obtain for their own review. Counsel may also find the case at hand to be complicated still further by what we have informally termed the "$25,000 rule," which refers to the tendency for intrafamilial tensions to escalate when guardianship estates are determined to be of moderate or greater financial value.

Within the space afforded by this chapter, we have tried to make your foray into guardianship practice as inviting and manageable as possible. Those seeking further guidance may wish to consult such additional resources as the fine trio of treatises resulting from a collaborative effort of the American Bar Association and the American Psychological Association (American Bar Association Commission on Law and Aging & American Psychological

Association, 2005; American Bar Association Commission on Law and Aging, American Psychological Association, & National College of Probate Judges (2006); American Bar Association/American Psychological Association Assessment of Capacity in Older Adults Project Working Group, 2008) and our own recent volume on guardianship evaluations in the "Best Practices" series published by Oxford University Press (Drogin & Barrett, 2010). We hope your legal practice in this area turns out to be every bit as stimulating and rewarding as we have found our own roles as researchers and evaluators.

REFERENCES

American Bar Association Commission on Law and Aging & American Psychological Association. (2005). *Assessment of older adults with diminished capacity: A handbook for lawyers.* Washington, DC: American Bar Association.

American Bar Association Commission on Law and Aging, American Psychological Association, & National College of Probate Judges (2006). *Judicial determination of capacity of older adults in guardianship proceedings.* Washington, DC: Authors.

American Bar Association/American Psychological Association Assessment of Capacity in Older Adults Project Working Group. (2008). *Assessment of older adults with diminished capacity: A handbook for psychologists.* Washington, DC: American Bar Association.

American Psychiatric Association. (1993). *The role of the psychiatrist in assessing driving ability.* Retrieved March 27, 2011, from American Psychiatric Association website, http://www.psych.org/Departments/EDU/Library/APAOfficialDocumentsandRelated/PositionStatements/199304.aspx.

American Psychiatric Association. (2000). *Diagnostic and statistical manual of mental disorders* (4th ed., text revision). Washington, DC: Author.

American Psychological Association. (2012). Guidelines for the evaluation of dementia and age-related cognitive change. *American Psychologist, 67,* 1–9.

American Psychological Association. (2002). Ethical principles of psychologists and code of conduct. *American Psychologist, 57,* 1060–1073.

American Psychological Association. (2004). Guidelines for psychological practice with older adults. *American Psychologist, 59,* 236–260.

Appelbaum, P. S., & Gutheil, T. G. (2007). *Clinical handbook of psychiatry and the law* (4th ed.). Philadelphia: Lippincott Williams & Wilkins.

Appointment of Guardians for Disabled Persons, Del. Code Ann. tit. 12 §3901 (2008).

Barrett, C. L., & Limoges, R. F. (2011). Addictions. In E. Y. Drogin, F. M. Dattilio, R. L. Sadoff, & T. G. Gutheil (Eds.), *Handbook of forensic assessment: Psychological and psychiatric perspectives* (pp. 255–274). Hoboken, NJ: Wiley.

Batavia, A. I. (2003). Disability rights in the third state of the independent living movement: Disability community consensus, dissent, and the future of disability policy. *Stanford Law and Policy Review, 14,* 347–350.

Brodsky, S. (1991). *Testifying in court: Guidelines and maxims for the expert witness.* Washington, DC: American Psychological Association.

Brodsky, S. L. (2005). Forensic evaluations and testimony. In G. P. Koocher, J. C. Norcross, & S. S. Hill (Eds.), *Psychologists' desk reference* (2nd ed., pp. 591–593). New York: Oxford University Press.

Buchanan, A. (2006). Psychiatric evidence on the ultimate issue. *Journal of the American Academy of Psychiatry and the Law, 34,* 14–21.

Cancellation of Registration, Ohio Rev. Code Ann. §3503.18 (2009).

Civil Rights of Patients, Ohio Rev. Code Ann. §5122.301 (1989).

Department of Developmental Disabilities, Ohio Rev. Code Ann. §5123.62 (2009).

Driver's License Examination, 75 Pa. Cons. Stat. §1518(a).

Drogin, E. Y. (2007). Guardianship for older adults: A jurisprudent science perspective. *Journal of Psychiatry and Law, 35,* 553–564.

Drogin, E. Y. (2008). Proxy decision making. In B. L. Cutler (Ed.), *Encyclopedia of psychology and law* (pp. 633–634). Thousand Oaks, CA: Sage.

Drogin, E. Y., & Barrett, C. L. (2003). Substituted judgment: Roles for the forensic psychologist. In I. B. Weiner (Series Ed.) & A. M. Goldstein (Vol. Ed.), *Comprehensive handbook of psychology: Vol. 11. Forensic psychology* (pp. 301–312). Hoboken, NJ: Wiley.

Drogin, E. Y., & Barrett, C. L. (2010). *Evaluation for guardianship.* New York: Oxford.

Evans, D. A., Funkenstein, H. H., & Albert, M. S. (1989). Prevalence of Alzheimer's disease in a community population of older persons. *Journal of the American Medical Association, 262,* 2551–2556.

Ewing, C. P. (2003). Expert testimony: Law and practice. In I. B. Weiner (Series Ed.) & A. M. Goldstein (Vol. Ed.), *Comprehensive handbook of psychology: Vol. 11. Forensic psychology* (pp. 55–66). Hoboken, NJ: Wiley.

Federal Rules of Evidence 704 ("Opinion on Ultimate Issue") (1984).

Fillit, H. M., Simon, E. S., Doniger, G. M., & Cummings, J. L. (2008). Practicality of a computerized system for cognitive assessment in the elderly. *Alzheimer's and Dementia, 4,* 14–21.

Foster, S. M., Cornwell, R. E., Kisley, M. A., & Davis, H. P. (2007). Cognitive changes across the life span. In S. H. Qualls & M. A. Smyer (Eds.), *Changes in decision-making capacity in older adults: Assessment and intervention* (pp. 25–60). Hoboken, NJ: Wiley.

Gavisk, M., & Greene, E. (2007). Guardianship determinations by judges, attorneys, and guardians. *Behavioral Sciences and the Law, 25,* 339–353.

Grisso, T. (2003). *Evaluating competencies: Forensic assessments and instruments* (2nd ed.). New York: Kluwer/Plenum.

Guardians and Conservators, N.H. Rev. Stat. Ann. §464-A:9 (1994).

Gurrera, R. J., Moye, J., Karel, M. J., Azar, A. R., & Armesto, J. C. (2006). Cognitive performance predicts treatment decisional abilities in mild to moderate dementia. *Neurology, 66,* 1367–1372.

Heilbrun, K. (2001). *Principles of forensic mental health assessment.* New York: Kluwer/Plenum.

Heilbrun, T., Grisso, T., & Goldstein, A. M. (2009). *Foundations of forensic mental health assessment.* New York: Oxford.

Heilbrun, T., Warren, J., & Picarello, K. (2003). Third party information in forensic assessment. In I. B. Weiner (Series Ed.) & A. M. Goldstein (Vol. Ed.), *Comprehensive handbook of psychology: Vol. 11. Forensic psychology* (pp. 69–86). Hoboken, NJ: Wiley.

Hopper, K., Wanderling, J., & Narayanan, P. (2007). To have and to hold: A cross-cultural inquiry into marital prospects after psychosis. *Global Public Health, 2,* 257–280.

Illinois Marriage and Dissolution of Marriage Act, 750 Ill. Comp. Stat. Ann. §5/301 (1977).

In re Estate of Katherine F. Washburn, 141 N.H. 658 (1997).

In re Last Will and Testament of Palecki, 920 A.2d 413 (Del. 2007).

Karel, M. J. (2007). Culture and medical decision making. In S. H. Qualls & M. A. Smyer (Eds.), *Changes in decision-making capacity in older adults: Assessment and intervention* (pp. 145–174). Hoboken, NJ: Wiley.

Kawaga-Singer, M., & Blackhall, L. J. (2001). Negotiating cross-cultural issues at the end of life. *Journal of the American Medical Association, 286,* 2993–3001.

Kwak, J., & Haley, W. E. (2005). Current research findings on end-of-life decision making among racially or ethnically diverse groups. *Gerontologist, 45,* 634–641.

Macklin, R. S., Depp, C., Aréan, P., & Jeste, D. (2006). Overview of psychiatric assessment with dementia patients. In G. Yeo & D. Gallagher-Thompson (Eds.), *Ethnicity and the dementias* (2nd ed., pp. 13–32). New York: Routledge/Taylor & Francis.

Matsumura, S., Bito, S., Liu, H., Kahn, K., Fukuhara, S., Kagawa-Singer, M., & Wenger, N. (2002). Acculturation of attitudes toward end-of-life care: A cross-cultural survey of Japanese Americans and Japanese. *Journal of General Internal Medicine, 17,* 531–539.

Melamed, Y., Doron, I., & Shnitt, D. (2007). Guardianship of people with mental disorders. *Social Science and Medicine, 65,* 1118–1123.

Millar, D. S., & Renzaglia, A. (2002). Factors affecting guardianship practices for young persons with disabilities. *Exceptional Children, 68,* 465–484.

Moye, J. (2003). Guardianship and conservatorship. In T. Grisso, *Evaluating competencies: Forensic assessments and instruments* (2nd ed., pp. 309–310). New York: Plenum Press.

Moye, J., Wood, S., Edelstein, B., Armesto, J.C., Bower, E. H., Harrison, J. A., & Wood, E. (2007). Clinical evidence in guardianship of older adults is inadequate: Findings from a tri-state study. *The Gerontologist, 47*, 604–612.

Mueser, K. T. (2000). Paranoia or delusional disorder. In A. E. Kazdin (Ed.), *Encyclopedia of psychology: Vol. 6* (pp. 35–39). Washington, DC: American Psychological Association.

National Highway Traffic Safety Administration (NHTSA). (2007). *Current screening and assessment practices.* Retrieved March 27, 2011, from National Highway Traffic Safety Administration website, http://www.nhtsa.dot.gov/people/injury/olddrive.

National Voter Registration Act, 42 U.S.C. §1977(gg) (1993).

Oliver, M. N., Anthony, A., Leimkuhl, T. T., & Skillman, G. D. (2002). Attitudes toward acceptable sociosexual behaviors for persons with mental retardation: Implications for normalization and community integration. *Education and Training in Mental Retardation and Developmental Disabilities, 37*, 193–201.

Ortner, T. M. (2008). Effects of changed item order: A cautionary note to practitioners on jumping to computerized adaptive testing for personality assessment. *International Journal of Selection and Assessment, 16*, 249–257.

Otto, R. K., Slobogin, C., & Greenberg, S. A. (2007). Legal and ethical issues in accessing and utilizing third-party information. In A. M. Goldstein (Ed.), *Forensic psychology: Emerging topics and expanding roles* (pp. 190–205). Hoboken, NJ: Wiley.

Pape v. Byrd, 582 N.E.2d 164 (Ill. 1991).

Parry, J. W., & Drogin, E. Y. (2007). *Mental disability law, evidence and testimony: A comprehensive reference manual for lawyers, judges and mental disability professionals.* Washington, DC: American Bar Association.

Petrila, J. (2007). Introduction to this issue: Elder issues. *Behavioral Sciences and the Law, 25*, 337.

Physical and Mental Criteria, Including Vision Standards Relating to the Licensing of Drivers, 67 Pa. Code §83.5(i)-(iii).

Protection of Persons Under Disability and Their Property, N.M. Code R. §45-5-101 (1978).

Qualls, S. H., Segal, D., Norman, S., Niederehe, G., & Gallagher-Thompson, D. (2002). Psychologists in practice with older adults: Current patterns sources of training, and the need for continuing education. *Professional Psychology: Research & Practice, 33*, 435–442.

Shaddock, A. J., Dowse, L., Richards, H., & Spinks, A. T. (1998). Communicating with people with an intellectual disability in guardianship board hearings. *Journal of Intellectual and Developmental Disability, 23*, 279–293.

Tippins, T. M., & Wittman, J. P. (2005). Empirical and ethical problems with custody recommendations: A call for clinical humility and judicial vigilance. *Family Court Review, 43*, 193–222.

11

Evaluation for Personal Injury Claims

ANDREW W. KANE, ERIN M. NELSON, JOEL A. DVOSKIN,
AND STEVEN E. PITT

In this chapter, the authors present attorneys with a best-practice model of expert mental health testimony in civil litigation alleging psychological injury so that lawyers can be informed consumers of forensic mental health experts.

LEGAL CONTEXT

Generally, tort law is designed to make the litigant whole or to restore the person to his or her condition prior to the commission of the tort. Thus, when the harms claimed are psychological—that is, when the litigant experiences emotional harm, cognitive impairment, or a loss of behavioral control—the courts turn to mental health professionals to advise them about the degree to which the litigant has been harmed, what can be done to restore functioning, and to compensate the litigant for his or her suffering, especially when the impairment or disability is or may be permanent.

When a plaintiff has been physically harmed, courts have traditionally had no difficulty allowing claims to be made; however, when the harm was solely psychological or emotional it has been difficult to get courts to accept these cases, until fairly recently. The concern was "that claims for psychological harm are easy to feign, difficult to verify, potentially limitless in frequency and amount, or somehow less deserving" than claims involving physical injuries (Shuman & Hardy, 2007, p. 529). Currently, however, all jurisdictions permit recovery of damages for emotional or mental injuries that are proximately associated with physical injuries (Shuman, 2005).

For many years, cases alleging psychological or emotional damages were generally allowed to proceed only if there was a physical impact (under the "impact rule," e.g., the plaintiff was hit by someone or something). This gradually gave way in the first part of the 20th century to a "zone of danger" test in which the plaintiff is alleged to have been placed in danger or fear of physical injury by virtue of the defendant's behavior. This was expanded to include a "bystander rule" under which an individual who wasn't in physical danger but who witnessed (and suffered significant psychological or emotional trauma from) a negligent action could sue for damages (Campbell & Montigny, 2004; Gabbay & Alonso, 2004; Shuman, 2005). Even so, courts still tend to question the validity of claims for psychological and emotional harm far more than those for physical harm (Shuman & Hardy, 2007). Courts may, however, welcome expert psychological and psychiatric testimony that helps the judge and jury understand mental disorders and psychological stress.

It was not until 1993, in *Harris v. Forklift Systems, Inc.*, that the Supreme Court indicated that evidence of psychological or emotional harm to an individual could be a substantial factor in determining whether an employer is responsible for sexual harassment. This was the first case in which the Supreme Court ruled that a psychological or emotional injury, in the absence of a physical injury, could be presented in the liability phase of a trial to demonstrate that a tort had occurred (Call, 2003).

Mental Health Experts

There are a number of legal issues for which an attorney may want to consider retaining a mental health professional (typically a psychiatrist or a psychologist) either as a consultant or testifying expert. For example, mental health concepts and/or opinion(s) are often relevant in cases including, but not limited to, psychiatric or psychological malpractice; impaired professionals; boundary violations; harassment; wrongful termination; discrimination;

negligent supervision and hiring; ADA claims; fitness for duty; civil rights violations; foreseeability of harm; and wrongful death. Any time a psychological or emotional issue is a salient feature of the litigation, an attorney may want to think about retaining a mental health expert.

Once counsel has identified a potential need for mental health expertise, it is important to identify whether specific credentials are required for the issue at hand. In tort litigation alleging psychological harms, three doctoral-level designations are most commonly needed: psychiatrist, psychologist, and neuropsychologist. All of these professionals complete graduate education in the study of human behavior and the assessment and treatment of emotional and mental disorders. However, despite this overlap, there are important differences with respect to education, training, and licensure. *Psychiatrist* is the term reserved for individuals who have completed medical school training and specialized in psychiatry. Psychiatrists are medical doctors who are identified as either M.D. or D.O. (Medical Doctor or Doctor of Osteopathy) and are able to prescribe medication. A *psychologist* is someone who has completed doctoral-level training in psychology. Psychologists are identified as either Ph.D. (Doctor of Philosophy in Psychology) or Psy.D. (Doctor of Psychology) and are primarily involved in assessment of psychopathology, personality and cognition, and psychotherapeutic interventions. A *neuropsychologist* is a psychologist with specialized training in the assessment of cognitive function, intellectual disability (formerly described as mental retardation), and brain injury.

In many cases, any of the aforementioned professionals will be qualified to address referral questions from counsel. That said, a great deal of time and energy can be saved by determining early on if a specific credential will be necessary. For example, in a standard-of-care matter, it may be necessary to retain an expert with analogous degree(s) to the party in question. Additionally, if the case involves a specific issue germane to one area of practice, the attorney may want to focus his or her search to a more narrow pool of experts. For example, if the case deals with psychotropic medication, the best choice would likely be a psychiatrist. If a case deals with a very specific issue, such as psychological consequences of a motor vehicle accident, the attorney may seek out a professional whose research and scholarship specifically addresses this issue.

Standards for Testimony: Frye and Daubert

Regardless of which type of mental health expert is retained, specific parameters are in place regarding the content of testimony. For many years, the dominant standard for admitting expert testimony in American courts was *Frye v. United States* (1923). *Frye* required that "the thing from which the deduction is made must be sufficiently established to have gained general acceptance in the particular field in which it belongs" (p. 1014).

The U.S. Supreme Court indicated that the Federal Rules of Evidence (2009) had superseded *Frye* in its ruling in *Daubert v. Merrell Dow Pharmaceuticals* (1993). The Supreme Court also specified a number of criteria that might be used by trial courts to assess the reliability (i.e., "trustworthiness," *Daubert*, 1993, footnote 9) of expert testimony. The Court emphasized that "all relevant evidence is admissible" (p. 587), specifically required that an "expert's testimony pertain to 'scientific knowledge'" (p. 590), and stated that expert testimony must "assist the trier of fact to understand or determine a fact in issue" (p. 592), among other possible requirements. In *Kumho Tire Co. v. Carmichael* (1999, p. 137), the Supreme Court "noted that *Daubert* discussed four factors— testing, peer review, error rates, and 'acceptability' in the relevant scientific community—which might prove helpful in determining the reliability of a particular scientific theory or technique." Specifically: (1) "whether it can be and has been tested…[and] can be falsified;" (2) whether the "theory or technique has been subjected to peer review and publication;" (3) that consideration be given to the "known or potential rate of error;" and (4) that there is "general acceptance of the particular technique within the scientific community" (*Daubert*, 1993, pp. 593–594).

The Supreme Court's ruling in *General Electric Co. v. Joiner* (1997) ensured that trial judges would have wide discretion in the application of the *Daubert* standard (Dvoskin & Guy, 2008). As a result of the combined influence of *Daubert*, *Joiner*, and *Kumho*, Rule 702 of the Federal Rules of Evidence was amended in 2000 to read Rule 702. Testimony by Experts:

> If scientific, technical, or other specialized knowledge will assist the trier of fact to understand the evidence or to determine a fact in issue, a witness qualified as an expert

by knowledge, skill, experience, training, or education, may testify thereto in the form of an opinion or otherwise, if *(1) the testimony is based upon sufficient facts or data, (2) the testimony is the product of reliable principles and methods, and (3) the witness has applied the principles and methods reliably to the facts of the case.* (Italicized portion was added to the old Rule 702.)

To the factors specified by the Supreme Court in *Daubert*, the Advisory Committee on the Federal Rules of Evidence (2000) added five additional suggested areas of consideration based on court rulings after *Daubert*:

(1) Whether experts are "proposing to testify about matters growing naturally and directly out of research they have conducted independent of the litigation, or whether they have developed their opinions expressly for purposes of testifying." (*Daubert v. Merrell Dow Pharmaceuticals, Inc.,* 1995, p. 1317). (2) Whether the expert has unjustifiably extrapolated from an accepted premise to an unfounded conclusion. (3) Whether the expert has adequately accounted for obvious alternative explanations. (4) Whether the expert "is being as careful as he would be in his regular professional work outside his paid litigation consulting." (*Sheehan v. Daily Racing Form, Inc.,* 1997, p. 942). (5) Whether the field of expertise claimed by the expert is known to reach reliable results for the type of opinion the expert would give.

The Supreme Court made it clear in *Daubert* and its two progeny (*General Electric Company v. Joiner* (1997) and *Kumho Tire Co. v. Carmichael* (1999)) that trial court judges are to exercise their gatekeeping functions. It should be noted, though, that trial judges are not required to question expert testimony.

Put simply, courts applying *Daubert* are encouraged to ask two questions of experts: (1) "Why should we believe you?" and (2) "Why should we care?" The first speaks to the credibility, reliability, and validity of experts' opinions and the facts and logic upon which they are based. The second addresses the need for the expert to identify the relevance of the opinions to be offered to the specific questions at bar. Consistent with long traditions of

Anglo-American law, this probative value must then be weighed against any prejudicial effects of the opinions to be offered (Dvoskin & Guy, 2008).

Forensic experts should base their testimony on both the prevailing standards of their jurisdictions[1] and on broader bases, such as research published in peer-reviewed journals. Experts should note, however, that the Supreme Court commented in *Kumho* on the potential for some of the best research to be found in non–peer-reviewed journals, so such journals should not be excluded from the expert's search of the professional literature. Experts should also be aware of evidence that peer review is a flawed assumption of trustworthiness, despite its prominent place in the Supreme Court decisions (Kane, 2007c). The "best practice" is to critically evaluate every source, not to uncritically assume that any source is trustworthy, even if formally peer reviewed, and regardless of how prestigious the journal. An expert whose work and testimony meets the standards of the Federal Rules is likely to do well in meeting the standards of his or her own jurisdiction(s).

Attorneys calling mental health experts as witnesses would be wise to ready themselves for challenges to the credentials of their expert. Before disclosing an expert witness, attorneys should carefully review such basic items as a *curriculum vitae*, a list of cases in which the expert has previously testified, a list of publications, licensure, and disciplinary history. This will help the attorney to ensure the expert meets any statutory criteria for expert testimony and anticipate any *Daubert* challenge of proffered experts.

Professional Negligence

If there is an allegation of negligence by a professional (e.g., psychologist, physician, engineer), the professional's conduct will be considered using two sets of standards: the standard of *practice* and the standard of *care*. According to Heilbrun, DeMatteo, Marczyk, and Goldstein (2008),

> Standards of care are judicial determinations that establish minimally acceptable standards

---

[1] The standard in Canada, for example, is based on *R. v. Mohan* (1994), in which the Supreme Court of Canada indicated that trial judges are to act as gatekeepers for expert evidence, that evidence be relevant, that experts are to assist the trier of fact in understanding the issues and evidence, and that experts must have specialized knowledge.

of professional conduct in the context of specific disputes (American Law Institute, 1965). By contrast, standards of practice are generally defined either as the customary way of doing things in a particular field (the "industry standard") or as "best practices" in a particular field (Caldwell & Seamone, 2007). Second, standards of practice are internally established by the field itself. This can occur informally, for instance, when a particular practice becomes "adopted" as the customary way of doing things. It can also occur more formally, for example, through development of practice guidelines applicable to practitioners in the specific field. (pp. 2–3)

Standards of care may have a basis in statute or administrative code, and adherence is mandatory. Standards of practice, in contrast, are generally aspirational rather than required. Failing to adhere to a standard of care is considered negligence, making the professional liable to malpractice claims. Failing to adhere to a standard of practice does not automatically open the professional to legal liability, but may cause the professional to be sanctioned by an ethics committee or a state licensing board (Heilbrun et al., 2008).

The Expert's Duties

With few if any exceptions, the expert's client is the attorney, and not the actual plaintiff or defendant.[2] Shuman and Greenberg (2003) suggest that experts often receive pressure from retaining attorneys to conclude, and to state in testimony, that the data accumulated by the expert and the conclusions based on that data support the attorney's theory of the case. The expert must resist this pressure, remaining impartial and advocating for his or her opinion, not for his or her retaining attorney, as required by professional ethics and the *Specialty Guidelines for Forensic Psychology* (2011). All witnesses, including experts, are to assist the fact finder, not any particular party (Saks & Lanyon, 2007).

However, forensic mental health experts may be retained by attorneys in one of two roles: (1) as a potential testifying expert or (2) as a consultant

who is part of the advocacy team, with the goal of winning the case, but without a plan for the expert to testify. Because mental health expert witnesses have an ethical duty to strive for objectivity, it is generally inappropriate to move from the second category (consultant/advocate) to a testifying role. Expert witnesses have a duty to accurately inform the trier of fact, whether this helps or hurts the attorney's chances to win at trial. Early on, a forensic mental health expert might be asked to consult with either attorney regarding the validity of the plaintiff's claim. In the case of the plaintiff's potential attorney, this consultation might occur even before the attorney accepts the plaintiff as a client. However, experts must always be very careful to maintain their objectivity unless and until it is decided that they will not testify.

Experts generally owe legal duties to the court, the retaining attorney, and third parties, with each involving a professional duty as well. The duty to the court is to offer testimony that is reliable, helpful, honest, and objective. The professional and ethical duty is to strive to provide assistance to the fact finder in a way that is consistent with the field's articulation of the components of good practice (see, e.g., *Specialty Guidelines for Forensic Psychology*, 2011).

The expert's duties to the retaining attorney include clear articulation of the referral questions (i.e., what the expert will likely be asked on direct examination at trial); accurate and careful review of relevant facts; formulation and clear articulation of opinions; clear articulation of the (especially evidentiary) foundation and limitations of each opinion; and performing his or her duties at the level of the standard of practice, while aiming for best practices.

While the retaining attorney has the right to decide which questions to ask of an expert, the expert's legal and ethical obligation is to present opinions fairly and with sufficient foundation, and to resist any attempt to distort, misrepresent, or leave out information that may be contrary to the position of the retaining attorney.

Of course, absolute objectivity is impossible to achieve, as every expert brings certain biases to each case. Instead of pretending to be free of bias, experts should take steps to correct for bias so as to maximize their objectivity. These steps include (a) transparency, or showing one's work; (b) humbly acknowledging the limitations of one's expertise; (c) inclusion of contrary findings or authorities; (d) seeking consultation; and

---

[2] Note, however, that in some cases, defense expert fees will be paid by an insurance company or the defendant organization. Identifying the client and how the fees are to be paid must be negotiated in advance.

(e) a willingness to admit when one does not know the answer to a question (Dvoskin, 2007).

A therapist may testify in the role of a "treating expert"; however, the treating expert should not be treated as an independent or objective witness, because he or she owes a duty to the patient as well as to the court and professional standards. In our view, the treating expert is ethically required to be primarily a fact witness.

Process of a Case

A personal injury claim may be filed whenever an individual (a plaintiff) has been injured, or feels injured, by the behavior (action or failure to act) of another individual or entity (the defendant), provided that the plaintiff can assert that the defendant owed a duty to the plaintiff, that the defendant breached that duty, that the plaintiff was injured as a result, that the defendant's action or behavior was the proximate cause of the plaintiff's injury, and that the plaintiff suffered as a result of the defendant's action or failure to act.

If there is an issue of psychological damages and/or professional negligence, the attorney(s) may retain a psychologist or other mental health professional as a consultant. Professionals retained as consultants typically work under attorney work-product privilege, meaning that all information is privileged unless the expert evidence is introduced as part of the claim, in which case the information ceases to be confidential and the consultant could be deposed, called to testify, or both. An additional exception in many jurisdictions is that psychologists are mandated reporters of specific acts such as child abuse, and a failure to report can lead to a licensing action against the psychologist. With the exception of mandated reports, consulting experts should be instructed to keep all work and communications related to the case confidential unless and until instructed otherwise by the retaining attorney or the court.

FORENSIC MENTAL HEALTH CONCEPTS

Heilbrun and his colleagues (2009) discuss, at length, principles of forensic mental health assessment (FMHA) that deal with causality, a central issue in personal injury evaluations. They note that human behavior is multidimensional and that numerous sources of information should be utilized to fully assess an individual. Similarly, Schultz (2003a) and Young, Kane, and Nicholson (2007)

emphasize the need for integration of a multifactorial process of determining causality.

Heilbrun and his co-authors emphasize the need to address functional abilities and to place them in the context of nomothetic (group) evidence—that is, evidence empirically derived from populations that are similar to that of the plaintiff. Methods utilized must be both valid and reliable, including use of psychological instruments appropriate for the population and the individual being assessed. Nomothetic data are scientifically and empirically based upon questionnaires and tests with forensic value, as well as on base rates and outcome data. They furnish normative data on the performance of groups in various areas, providing the basis for making assertions regarding the functioning and impairment, if any, of an individual. Further, population-level research addresses the prediction of outcomes, suggesting how specific interventions may assist with the management of the course of symptoms.

In contrast, idiographic evidence addresses information collected regarding a specific individual being assessed, usually the plaintiff. The assessment of the individual should resemble a scientific study, producing the simplest explanation for the data collected that accounts for all of the essential variables in the case. The evaluator then proceeds to address all reasonably likely explanations for the data assembled in order to arrive at conclusions that make scientific sense. This usually includes addressing the individual's personal and psychosocial history, functional capacities prior to and following the allegedly traumatic event or events, and response style, especially the possibility that the person may be exaggerating, feigning, or malingering. It is important to remember that the presence of malingering does not preclude the presence of real psychological distress or disability (Ackerman & Kane, 1998; Drob, Meehan, & Waxman, 2009; Kane, 2007a; Rogers, 2008).

More specifically, the FMHA in a personal injury context addresses (1) any mental disorders identified, (2) the legally relevant functional abilities affected by the allegedly traumatic incident(s), and (3) the nature and strength of any causal connection between the allegedly traumatic event(s) and the resultant functional abilities of the plaintiff (Heilbrun, 2001; Vore, 2007). One must also operationalize legal requirements into psychological terms, so that the professional literature can be searched and an appropriate evaluation conducted.

Schultz (2003) suggests that best practices include (1) applying a bio-psycho-social model, (2) use of standardized procedures, (3) using numerous information sources, including standardized tests and other instruments and collateral sources, (4) comparing the individual with relevant group data and base rates, (5) considering iatrogenic and litigation-related factors, and (6) comparison of current and premorbid levels of functioning.

The testifying expert should do a comprehensive, impartial evaluation using a bio-psycho-social approach (i.e., consideration of physical and biological factors, psychological factors, and social or environmental factors) that considers all of the pertinent evidence, uses valid and reliable methods of assessment and interpretation, considers the professional literature in coming to conclusions, and proffers testimony that is relevant, reliable, and helpful to the trier of fact (Kane, 2007b).

EMPIRICAL FOUNDATIONS AND LIMITS

The purpose of an evaluation in a personal injury case is to ascertain whether an individual has been psychologically injured by a traumatic event and, if so, to what extent. Broadly speaking, if there is evidence of a psychological injury, there are five possibilities: (1) the event is the sole cause of the psychological injury (rarely the case); (2) the event was the primary cause of the psychological injury (that is, the proximate cause), and *but for* the traumatic event the person would not have his or her present level of psychopathology or other psychological distress (e.g., grief; includes exacerbating a preexisting condition); (3) the traumatic event materially contributed to the assessed psychopathology or other psychological distress but was not the primary cause; (4) the traumatic event had little identifiable affect on the individual; (5) the traumatic event had no identifiable affect on the individual (i.e., all identifiable psychopathology was due to something other than the identified trauma) (Ackerman & Kane, 1998; Melton et al., 2007; Young, 2007).

Each evaluation must be designed to comprehensively address the issues identified by the referral question(s) in a given case.[3] The issue is not the

individual's current status, *per se*, but the degree to which, and ways in which, the individual differs from how he or she was before the traumatic event. To this end, the evaluator should consult multiple data sources, including records that address the individual's functioning prior to the trauma, to create a baseline against which post-trauma changes may be assessed (Heilbrun et al., 2009; Kane, 2007b; Melton et al., 2007; Young & Kane, 2007).

Contributing factors must also be considered. Social support, the individual's perception of support from his or her employer, and the individual's overall life satisfaction are likely to affect his or her level of adjustment (Koch, O'Neill, & Douglas, 2005). These and other factors may be assessed through testing and interviews of the individual, collateral interviews, diaries, and questionnaires.

Although there are no forensic assessment instruments specific to personal injury evaluations, there are a number of instruments that are forensically relevant (see Heilbrun et al., 2009). The most frequently used forensically relevant instrument is the Minnesota Multiphasic Personality Inventory, Second Edition (MMPI-2, Butcher et al., 2001), which has a substantial professional literature establishing patterns of responses associated with malingering, defensiveness, and numerous clinical factors that may be relevant to a specific personal injury evaluation (Butcher, 1995; Butcher & Miller, 2006; Goldstein, 2007; Pope, Butcher, & Seelen, 2006).

Clinical versus Actuarial Assessment

Psychologists have long debated the relative pros and cons of actuarial (statistical) versus clinical assessment. Actuarial assessments are those that are statistically based, involving the "use of data about prior instances, in order to estimate the likelihood or risk of a particular outcome" (American Psychological Association, 2009, p. 8), rather than such clinical methods as unstructured interviews and some projective methods. A third alternative, structured professional judgment (SPJ), utilizes standardized lists of questions, each of which refers to a variable that has been independently and empirically validated. The difference between actuarial and SPJ methods is that actuarial instruments require pre-assigned weights to each item, while SPJ instruments allow the evaluator to consider each item and weigh it according to the specifics of the instant case. Unfortunately, there exist no published SPJ instruments for personal injury evaluations at this

---

[3] There are, however, various models suggested by various authors (e.g., Greenberg, 2003; Grisso, 2003; Heilbrun, 2001; Melton et al., 2007; Wilson & Moran, 2004), any of which will provide a starting point for conducting an evaluation.

time. Research comparing actuarial and unstructured clinical assessments indicates that the actuarial method is better about half of the time, while there is no difference the other half of the time. When a valid and reliable actuarial or SPJ instrument is available and appropriate, it would be good practice to use it; however, the current state of the art also calls for clinical assessment methods to be used for a significant portion of a personal injury evaluation.

Every inferential opinion must be explicitly tied to the evidence and logic upon which it is based. In other words, experts should not ask triers of fact to "take their word" for any opinion. By spelling out the evidence and logic upon which opinion is based, experts allow triers of fact to scrutinize, weigh, and evaluate the strength of the opinion for themselves.

Base Rates

A "base rate [is] the naturally occurring frequency of a phenomenon in a population. This rate is often contrasted with the rate of the phenomenon under the influence of some changed condition in order to determine the degree to which the change influences the phenomenon" (American Psychological Association, 2009, p. 49). Both diagnosis and prognosis may be made in error if relevant base rates are not considered. In other words, before an expert can opine that a particular event caused a condition, it is important to know how often that condition occurs among the general population, thus accounting for the relative likelihood of simple coincidence. The probative value of the expert's testimony is limited if he or she is not aware of the base rate for each problem or symptom (Fleishman, Jackson, & Rothschild, 1999).

Error Rates

"Error rates" primarily refer to the likelihood of false-positive and false-negative errors, respectively, although other definitions exist (Krauss & Sales, 2003; Youngstrom & Busch, 2000). Evaluators should, therefore, use multiple sources with known error rates, if possible, to assess a given individual.

Experts must not rely exclusively on "cookbooks" or computerized interpretations, or interpretations suggested by single sources. Cookbooks offer lists of statements about people who have scale scores or test protocols similar to the evaluatee, but offer little or no information regarding how those statements were obtained. Computerized interpretations tend to focus on one or at most a few high scores of the evaluatee on a given test, leaving out potentially essential information regarding the evaluatee from other scales. Generally, no single test by itself will support a strong conclusion regarding most characteristics of the plaintiff.

THE EVALUATION

Obtaining Records

It will be difficult, if not impossible, for the expert to testify to a "reasonable degree of certainty" regarding changes in the plaintiff as a result of the allegedly traumatic incident if the expert has not conducted a review of records sufficient to support the expert's conclusions. A failure to review available, relevant records may be considered to be below the standard of practice (Ackerman & Kane, 1998; Heilbrun, 2001).

The expert's task in most cases is to advise the retaining attorney of the records that are needed for review (both records already in the attorney's possession and additional records not yet obtained). This will include records that describe the individual's functioning prior to the trauma, in order to create a baseline against which post-trauma functioning can be assessed.

Relevant records may include medical, psychotherapy, school, legal, employment, military, personnel, pharmacy, tax, and any other records that may identify the individual's ability to function prior to and after the traumatic event. Depositions and other legal documents may also provide independent information about the individual (Wilson & Moran, 2004).

Additionally, reports or interviews with credible collateral informants, such as former employers and neighbors, can also provide a good basis for comparison. The changes identified may not have been caused by the traumatic event but, rather, by other major life events. At a minimum, the records review should extend three to five years prior to the traumatic event. For many people, however, going back further will yield additional relevant information. Other information that may be of value includes evidence of lifestyle changes (e.g., through review of checkbook registers or credit-card statements [Greenberg, 2003] and personal diaries [Heilbrun, Warren, & Picarello, 2003]). Pharmacy records—both before and following the allegedly traumatic incident—will elucidate a physician's assessment of the plaintiff's status, as well as provide data on the direct and side effects of any prescribed medication. In addition, a review of the litigant's medications may assist in identifying pharmacological main or side effects that are part of the clinical picture.

Differential Diagnosis

The most common diagnostic system in North America is the *Diagnostic and Statistical Manual of Mental Disorders, Fourth Edition, Text Revision* (DSM-IV-TR; American Psychiatric Association, 2000). The strengths of DSM-IV-TR are its standardization and comprehensiveness, as well as its frequent usage in the United States and Canada. Its weakness is that diagnoses are explanatory constructs that are designed as "shorthand" to permit professionals to discuss characteristics of an individual's disorder(s). Further, each revision of the DSM was adopted by vote of a group of psychiatrists on the basis of their understanding of research, thereby representing a value judgment rather than a careful scientific analysis (Shuman, 2002; State Justice Institute, 1999). The authors of DSM-IV-TR also indicate that the inclusion of a diagnosis in the manual "does not imply that the condition meets legal or other non-medical criteria for what constitutes mental disease, mental disorder, or mental disability" (American Psychiatric Association, 2000, p. xxvii).

The most common diagnosis in personal injury cases is post-traumatic stress disorder (PTSD) (Ackerman & Kane, 1998; Koch, Douglass, Nicholls, & O'Neill, 2006). Unlike other conditions, a diagnosis of PTSD requires exposure to a traumatic event and, thus, a finding of fact that is usually beyond the scope of psychological or psychiatric expert testimony and is often at issue in the case. One can avoid this conundrum by focusing on symptoms, especially disabilities, instead of diagnostic labels.

Malingering

The DSM-IV-TR defines malingering as "the intentional production of false or grossly exaggerated physical or psychological symptoms, motivated by external incentives such as avoiding military duty, avoiding work, obtaining financial compensation, evading criminal prosecution, or obtaining drugs" (p. 739). Experts must show great caution in calling someone a malingerer, a stigmatizing label that may prevent an individual from getting appropriate care. It can also directly cause psychological trauma to the individual,

and could lead to the person losing disability income or employment benefits (Drob et al., 2009).

It must also be kept in mind that plaintiffs who exaggerate or show evidence of malingering may, in addition, have real, demonstrable psychological disorders. Malingering does not preclude the presence of real psychological distress or disability (Ackerman & Kane, 1998; Drob et al., 2009; Kane, 2007a; Rogers, 2008a).

One must also consider the psychological meaning of compensation. Some people seek money as compensation, but many people have additional or different motivations. Some people look for "justice" from the company or individual that caused an injury (Kane, 2007b; Resnick, 1997; Rogers, 2008b); other litigants wish to prevent similar injury to others. Yet others want to ensure that the evaluator understands the meaning and importance of the trauma and how terribly they have suffered (Resnick, 1997). In these instances, simply winning the case may be sufficient reward, whether there is money involved or not. In our experience, malingering is much more likely among those seeking only money than it is among those with other goals, for whom injunctive relief, simply winning the case, and especially the opportunity to be fairly heard (Tyler, 1984) may be ample reward.

Another factor to consider regarding the plaintiff's presentation is that plaintiffs' attorneys continually ask questions that encourage people with injuries to think about their injuries, potentially leading the plaintiff to see himself or herself as significantly—and possibly permanently—disabled. Family members, physicians, and other people may reinforce this attitude, particularly if they don't insist that the plaintiff function as well as he or she is able.

Timeline

One of the most valuable tools in a personal injury evaluation is a timeline of significant events in the plaintiff's life. The attorney should ensure that the mental health professional has records documenting all major events in the plaintiff's life, to permit the construction of a complete timeline. The timeline is most useful if it quotes sections of the records reviewed, making it a source of concrete information identified by the records that can be a reference for information in the report, in a deposition, and in court. All of the information in the timeline (and in the report) should be explicitly attributed to its source (Heilbrun, 2001).

Limits of the Evaluation Process

No assessment will answer all of the possible questions that may be relevant to a given personal injury case; therefore, the goal is to conduct a comprehensive assessment using a bio-psycho-social approach. The best assessment instruments available to address the referral question(s) should be utilized, to ensure that the results of the evaluation are as accurate as possible. When further assessment appears to have diminishing returns, it is appropriate to end the assessment process. This does not preclude additional follow-up if questions occur during report writing; however, one cannot count on having access to the plaintiff once the basic evaluation is completed, especially if one was retained by the defense in the case.

REPORT WRITING AND TESTIMONY

Having carefully considered the legal context, forensic mental health concepts, the empirical foundations and limits of an evaluation, and having conducted a comprehensive evaluation and interpreted the resulting data, the evaluator is ready to provide the retaining attorney with an oral report. If the oral report is not favorable to the attorney's case, the mental health professional may be asked to stop working on the case and not write a formal report (Melton et al., 2007). In most cases, however, the expert will be asked to write a report of his or her findings. If the expert is not identified as a testifying expert, he or she is a consultant to the attorney, and his or her work falls under the attorney work-product privilege (Weiner, 2006). With the possible exception of "duty to warn or protect" situations or mandated reports such as child abuse, the consultant is bound by the attorney work-product privilege.

In some cases the oral report will suggest that the psychologist's opinion on some questions might be helpful to the attorney's case, whereas in other cases it will not. It is acceptable for the attorney to narrow the scope of the psychologist's testimony by eliminating certain referral questions at this stage; however, the answer to each question that remains must be objective, impartial, and complete.

As a testifying expert, the mental health professional must remember that he or she is to be impartial, advocating for his or her opinion but not for either side in the case (Heilbrun, 2001; Melton et al., 2007). Although most evaluations will lead the

mental health professional to conclude that the data support one side more than the other, both sides should be presented and the expert's reasoning should be provided for each hypothesis evaluated and each conclusion drawn.

Most personal injury cases will involve one or more depositions well before a trial is scheduled to occur. The expert will typically issue a report prior to the scheduling of the deposition. The questioning, primarily by the opposing attorney(s), tests the ability of the expert to testify about the plaintiff and the specifics of the case, particularly focusing on the issue of causality. It is often an opportunity for the expert to learn of the theory of the case, as he or she will be asked to respond to questions regarding alternative interpretations of the data. Because the deposition is an opportunity for the opposing side to test the mettle of the expert, and because deposition testimony is part of the record, it is essential that the expert be as prepared as he or she would be for the trial. If the expert is permitted to review the transcript of the deposition for errors, this should always be done (Hess, 2006).

Structure of the Report

There are a number of models for writing reports (e.g., Heilbrun, 2001; Melton et al., 2007), but no specific model that must be followed; however, every report should contain a number of elements if it is to be valuable to the court.

We recommend that the report contain information in six domains:

1. The first section should include the identifying information, the referral question, the records reviewed, the tests and other instruments utilized, and an indication of who retained the expert and the purpose for which the expert was retained.

2. Next, we recommend a presentation and discussion of the information culled from the records reviewed. Medical, employment, school, and other records that address the functioning of the plaintiff prior to the accident or other tort provide a baseline against which the accident or other tort and its effect on the plaintiff can be assessed. This may include direct quotations or a summary of the most salient information. Pitt et al. (1999) strongly recommend that the interview

be video- and audio-recorded, which would allow the trier of fact to view the source material first hand. If the interview is recorded, it allows production of a transcript, which can be appended to the report. However, Kane points out that research on third-party observers and social facilitation strongly indicates that people respond differently to psychological testing and interviews when they know (or believe) they are being monitored or recorded, decreasing the validity and reliability of the evaluation (e.g., less openness, trying to avoid embarrassment) (American Academy of Clinical Neuropsychology, 2001; Barth, 2007; Committee on Psychological Tests and Assessment, 2007; McCaffrey, Lynch, & Yantz, 2005). Both the arguments for transparency and that for avoiding recording of interviews are valid positions; however, we believe that the pros of recording the interview often outweigh the cons and argue that the interview should be recorded whenever possible. Psychological testing, however, should not be recorded since test materials must be protected in an attempt to ensure they remain valid and reliable assessment tools.

3. The evaluator should describe the assessment process, the data obtained from the plaintiff and collaterals. It is important to describe the process of informed consent or notification used, so that it is clear that the plaintiff was appropriately informed about the considerations relevant to participating and understood the nature and purpose of the evaluation, the non-confidential nature of the evaluation, and that he or she had a right to consult with his or her attorney at any point in the evaluation. Each test or assessment instrument should be identified, and the relevant data obtained from its administration presented. Observations by the expert should be noted, plausible interpretations stated, and all information upon which conclusions are based included. Inferences should be distinguished from facts (Heilbrun, 2001; Heilbrun et al., 2009; Melton et al., 2007; Weiner, 2006) and speculation should be avoided.

4. Because allegations of malingering are usually part of the defense in a personal injury case, the evaluator should specify what was done to assess the possibility of malingering, and the conclusions formulated on the basis of that assessment.

5. Statements should be made regarding the conclusions drawn, relevant to the referral question(s), including:
   a. The pre-trauma psychological status of the individual
   b. Data from the evaluation (across all sources) that describe the current psychological status of the plaintiff
   c. Data relevant to whether the plaintiff was psychologically injured by the actions or failures to act of the defendant
   d. Evidence of proximate cause, if any
   e. If relevant, a discussion of "thin-skulled man" issues (i.e., did the plaintiff have a preexisting condition, physical or psychological, that may have increased the degree of harm)
   f. Data indicating what the plaintiff did to mitigate the damage from the accident
   g. Damages (including input, if indicated, from other experts)
   h. Prognosis, including the basis for statements made regarding the plaintiff's degree of recovery to date and expected recovery in the future
   i. Treatment needs, including (if possible) duration and projected costs of that treatment
   j. Limitations of the evaluator's opinions
6. A brief summary of the evaluation and the conclusions

If the case goes to trial, a well-structured report also contributes to the ability of the expert to prepare for deposition or trial testimony and to present the evaluation and its conclusions in a cogent manner (Heilbrun, 2001). A report that is sufficiently comprehensive and well written may facilitate a settlement of the case, eliminating the need for court testimony altogether (Melton et al., 2007).

Reasonable Degree of Psychological/ Medical Probability or Certainty

Since every evaluation has some limits, psychologists and psychiatrists should generally testify to a "reasonable degree of certainty, likelihood, or probability" regarding their statements and conclusions. Regarding "reasonable degree of...certainty," Heilbrun et al. (2009) note that there is no universally accepted definition of the term. If the expert merely states that the relationship is possible, rather than the relevant phrase required under the applicable law, the court may exclude the opinion (Shuman, 2005). Heilbrun et al. (2009) suggest that opinions be based on all of the sources of information utilized in the evaluation (interviews, tests, records, and so forth), in addition to a review of relevant, peer-reviewed professional literature, analysis of consistencies and inconsistencies, and consideration of alternative opinions. They also recommend that "opinions should incorporate sources with established reliability, and with validity for purposes consistent with the present evaluation" (p. 55).

Ultimate-Issue Testimony

The task of the expert is to provide the trier of fact with the information that will permit decisions regarding whether the defendant owed the plaintiff a duty, whether that duty was breached, whether the plaintiff was harmed as a direct result of that breach, whether, but for that breach, the defendant would not have sustained the psychological injury that was sustained, and the damages that the expert can identify that could be assessed to the defendant if responsible for the plaintiff's injury. The expert may reasonably state conclusions regarding his or her data and the conclusions drawn on the basis of those data, including hypotheses that were either accepted or rejected.

Mental health professionals debate whether to give an opinion on the ultimate legal issue(s). Often, the issues at bar are so clear and unambiguous that there is virtually no way to avoid exposing one's opinion about the ultimate issue. In other cases, an expert may feel quite strongly that legal questions are beyond his or her expertise, and simply refuse to provide an ultimate-issue opinion. As with so many issues, this question should be discussed in some detail with the retaining attorney prior to testimony being offered. In our experience, the best course in most cases is to answer any question that is not successfully objected to, unless doing so would violate the expert's oath or ethical obligations. Sometimes, however, the only correct answer will be, "I don't know."

Base Testimony on a Well-Conducted Assessment and Interpretation

The mental health professional who has performed an appropriate assessment, and who has accurately and fairly interpreted the data from the assessment, should have no difficulty testifying about what was done, the results of the assessment, and the meaning of the results. The thoroughness of the expert's work and the reliability of the expert's opinions will be evident from the quality of the information furnished in the report and testimony, and the accuracy of the interpretation will follow from the logic of the conclusions drawn.

SUMMARY

A thorough evaluation consisting of multiple methods of data gathering, including careful review of medical and other records, interviews of the plaintiff and collateral informants, questionnaires, and psychological testing, provides a best-practice basis for identifying what the plaintiff experienced, what the experience meant to him or her, the degree of feigning (if any), and the long-term consequences of the trauma. This information should prepare the expert well for testifying regarding the relevant aspects of the emotional trauma experienced by the plaintiff, whether proximate cause was present, and what damages, if any, are recommended.

REFERENCES

Ackerman, M. J., & Kane, A. W. (1998). *Psychological experts in personal injury actions.* New York: Aspen Law and Business.

Advisory Committee on the Federal Rules of Evidence. (2000). Notes of advisory committee on proposed rules. Washington, DC: Judicial Conference of the United States. Retrieved July 26, 2006 from http://www.law.cornell.edu/rules/fre/rule_702.

American Academy of Clinical Neuropsychology (2001). Policy statement on the presence of third party observers in neuropsychological assessments. *Clinical Neuropsychologist, 15,* 433–439.

American Law Institute, Restatement (Second) of Torts § 282 (1965).

American Psychiatric Association. (2000). *Diagnostic and statistical manual of mental disorders: Text revision* (4th ed.). Washington, DC: Author.

American Psychological Association (2009). *APA concise dictionary of psychology.* Washington, DC: Author.

American Psychological Association (2011). *Specialty guidelines for forensic psychology. American Psychologist,* in press.

Barth, R.J. (2007, July/August). observation compromises the credibility of an evaluation. *The Guides Newsletter*, 1–3, 8–9.

Butcher, J. N. (1995). Personality patterns of personal injury litigants: The role of computer-based MMPI-2 evaluations. In Y. S. Ben-Porath, J. R. Graham, G. C. N. Hall, R. D. Hirschman, & M. S. Zaragoza (Eds.), *Forensic applications of the MMPI-2* (pp. 179–201). Thousand Oaks, CA: Sage.

Butcher, J. N., Graham, J. R., Ben-Porath, Y. S., Tellegen, A., Dahlstrom, W. G., & Kaemmer, B. (2001). *MMPI-2 Manual for administration, scoring, and interpretation* (Rev. ed.). Minneapolis: University of Minnesota Press.

Butcher, J. N., & Miller, K. B. (2006). Personality assessment in personal injury litigation. In I. B. Weiner & A. K. Hess (Eds.), *The handbook of forensic psychology* (3rd ed., pp. 140–166). Hoboken, NJ: Wiley.

Caldwell, C., & Seamone, E. R. (2007). Excusable neglect in malpractice suits against radiologists: A proposed jury instruction to recognize the human condition. *Annals of Health Law*, 16, 43–77

Call, J. A. (2003). Liability for psychological injury: History of the concept. In I. Z. Schultz & D. O. Brady (Eds.), *Psychological injuries at trial* (pp. 40–64). Chicago, IL: American Bar Association.

Campbell, D. S., & Montigny, C. (2004). Psychological harm and tort law: Reassessing the legal test for liability. In T. Archibald & M. Cochrane (Eds.), *Annual review of civil litigation: 2003* (pp. 133–155). Toronto, ON: Thomson/Carswell.

Committee on Psychological Tests and Assessment (2007). *Statement on third party observers in psychological testing and assessment: A framework for decision making.* Washington DC: American Psychological Association.

Daubert v. Merrell Dow Pharmaceuticals, Inc., 43 F.3d 1311 (1995).

Daubert v. Merrell Dow Pharmaceuticals, Inc., 509 U.S. 579, 113 S.Ct. 2786 (1993).

Drob, S. L., Meehan, K. B., & Waxman, S. E. (2009). Clinical and conceptual problems in the attribution of malingering in forensic evaluations. *Journal of the American Academy of Psychiatry and the Law*, 37, 98–106.

Dvoskin, J. A. (2007). Presidential column. *AP-LS Newsletter*, 27, 2–3.

Dvoskin, J. A., & Guy, L. S. (2008). On being an expert witness: It's not about you. *Psychiatry, Psychology and Law*, 15, 202–212.

Fleishman, W., Jackson, J. R., & Rothschild, M. (1999). Defensive litigation strategy in scientific evidence cases. In J. J. Brown (Ed.), *Scientific evidence and experts handbook* (pp. 305–385). New York: Aspen Law and Business.

Frye v. United States, 293 F. 1013, 34 ALR 145 (D. C. Cir. 1923).

Gabbay, V., & Alonso, C. M. (2004). Legal aspects related to PTSD in children and adolescents. In R. R. Silva (Ed.), *Posttraumatic stress disorder in children and adolescents: Handbook* (pp. 60–82). New York: Norton.

General Electric Company v. Joiner, 118 S.Ct. 512, 522 U.S. 136 (1997).

Goldstein, A.M. (2007). Forensic psychology: Toward a standard of care. In A. M. Goldstein (Ed.), *Forensic psychology: Emerging topics and expanding roles* (pp. 3–41). Hoboken, NJ: Wiley.

Greenberg, S. A. (2003). Personal injury examinations in torts for emotional distress. In I. B. Weiner (Series Ed.) & A. M. Goldstein (Vol. Ed.), *Handbook of psychology: Vol. 11, Forensic psychology* (pp. 233–257). Hoboken, NJ: Wiley.

Grisso, T. (2003). *Evaluating competencies* (2nd ed.). New York: Kluwer/Plenum.

Heilbrun, K. (2001). *Principles of forensic mental health assessment.* New York: Kluwer/Plenum.

Heilbrun, K., DeMatteo, D., Marczyk, G., & Goldstein, A. (2008). Standards of practice and care in forensic mental health assessment: Legal, professional, and principles-based considerations. *Psychology, Public Policy and Law*, 14, 1–26.

Heilbrun, K., Grisso, T., & Goldstein, A. M. (2009). *Foundations of forensic mental health assessment.* New York: Oxford.

Heilbrun, K., Warren, J., & Picarello, K. (2003). Third party information in forensic assessment. In I. B. Weiner (Series Ed.) & A. M. Goldstein (Vol. Ed.), *Handbook of psychology, Volume 11, forensic psychology* (pp. 69–86). Hoboken NJ: Wiley.

Hess, A. K. (2006). Defining forensic psychology. In I. B. Weiner & A. K. Hess (Eds.), *The handbook of forensic psychology* (3rd ed., pp. 28–58). Hoboken, NJ: Wiley.

Kane, A. W. (2007a). Basic concepts in psychology and law. In G. Young, A. W. Kane, & K. Nicholson (Eds.), *Causality of psychological injury: Presenting evidence in court* (pp. 261–292). New York: Springer.

Kane, A. W. (2007b). Conducting a psychological assessment. In G. Young, A. W. Kane, & K. Nicholson (Eds.), *Causality of psychological injury: Presenting evidence in court* (pp. 293–323). New York: Springer.

Kane, A. W. (2007c). Other psycho-legal issues. In G. Young, A. W. Kane, & K. Nicholson (Eds.), *Causality of psychological injury: Presenting evidence in court* (pp. 325–367). New York: Springer.

Koch, W. J., Douglas, K. S., Nicholls, T. L., & O'Neill, M. L. (2006). *Psychological injuries: Forensic assessment, treatment, and law.* New York: Oxford.

Koch, W. J., O'Neill, M., & Douglas, K. S. (2005). Empirical limits for the forensic assessment of PTSD litigants. *Law and Human Behavior*, 29, 121–149.

Kraus, D. A., & Sales, B. D. (2003). Forensic psychology, public policy, and the law. In I. B. Weiner (Series

Ed.) & A. M. Goldstein (Vol. Ed.), *Handbook of psychology: Vol. 11, Forensic psychology* (pp. 543–560). Hoboken, NJ: Wiley.

Kumho Tire Co. v. Carmichael, 526 U. S. 137, 119 S. Ct. 1167 (1999).

McCaffrey, R., Lynch, J. K. & Yantz, C. L. (2005). Third party observers: Why all the fuss? *Journal of Forensic Neuropsychology, 4*, 1–15.

Melton, G. B., Petrila, J., Poythress, N. G., & Slobogin, C. (2007). *Psychological evaluations for the courts: A handbook for mental health professionals and lawyers* (3rd ed.). New York: Guilford.

Pitt, S. E., Spiers, E. M., Dietz, P. E., & Dvoskin, J. A. (1999). Preserving the integrity of the interview: The value of video tape. *Journal of Forensic Sciences, 44*, 1287–1291.

Pope, K. S., Butcher, J. N., & Seelen, J. (2006). *The MMPI, MMPI-2 & MMPI-A in court* (3rd ed.). Washington, DC: American Psychological Association.

R. v. Mohan, 2 S. C. R. 9 (1994).

Resnick, P. J. (1997). Malingering of posttraumatic disorders. In R. Rogers (Ed.), *Clinical assessment of malingering and deception* (2nd ed., pp. 130–152). New York: Guilford.

Rogers, R. (2008a). An introduction to response styles. In R. Rogers (Ed.), *Clinical assessment of malingering and deception* (2nd ed., pp. 3–13). New York: Guilford.

Rogers, R. (2008b). Current status of clinical methods. In R. Rogers (Ed.), *Clinical assessment of malingering and deception* (3rd ed., pp. 391–410). New York: Guilford.

Saks, M. J. & Lanyon, R. I. (2007). Pitfalls and ethics of expert testimony. In M. Costanzo, D. Krauss, & K. Pezdek (Eds.), *Expert psychological testimony for the courts* (pp. 277–295). Mahwah, NJ: Erlbaum.

Schultz, I. Z. (2003). Psychological causality determination in personal injury and workers' compensation contexts. In I. Z. Schultz & D. O. Brady (Eds.), *Psychological injuries at trial* (pp. 102–125). Chicago, IL: American Bar Association.

Schultz, I. Z., & Brady, D. O. (2003a). Preface: Definition and introduction to psychological injuries. In I. Z. Schultz & D. O. Brady (Eds.), *Psychological injuries at trial* (pp. 13–17). Chicago, IL: American Bar Association.

Sheehan v. Daily Racing Form, Inc., 104 F.3d 940 (7th Cir. 1997).

Shuman, D. W. (2002). Retrospective assessment of mental states and the law. In R. I. Simon & D. W. Shuman (Eds.), *Retrospective assessment of mental states in litigation* (pp. 21–45). Washington, DC: American Psychiatric Association.

Shuman, D. W. (2005). *Psychiatric and psychological evidence* (3rd ed.). Eagen, MN: West Publishing.

Shuman, D. W., & Greenberg, S. A. (2003). The expert witness, the adversary system, and the voice of reason: Reconciling impartiality and advocacy. *Professional Psychology: Research and Practice, 34*, 219–224.

Shuman, D. W., & Hardy, J. L. (2007). Causation, psychology and law. In G. Young, A. W. Kane, & K. Nicholson (Eds.), *Causality of psychological injury: Presenting evidence in court* (pp. 517–548). New York: Springer.

State Justice Institute. (1999). *The bench: Companion to a judge's deskbook on the basic philosophies and methods of science*. Retrieved November 6, 2004, from www.unr.edu/bench

Tyler, T.R. (1984). The role of perceived injustice in defendant's evaluations of their courtroom experience. *Law & Society Review, 18*, 51–74.

U.S. Supreme Court Federal Rules of Evidence (2009). Available at: http://judiciary.house.gov/hearings/printers/111th/evid2009.pdf

Vore, D.A. (2007). The disability psychological independent medical evaluation: Case law, ethical issues, and procedures. In A. M. Goldstein (Ed.), *Forensic psychology: Emerging topics and expanding roles* (pp. 489–510). Hoboken NJ: Wiley.

Weiner, I.B. (2006). Writing forensic reports. In I. B. Weiner & A. K. Hess (Eds.), *The handbook of forensic psychology* (3rd ed., pp. 631–651). Hoboken, NJ: Wiley.

Wilson, J. P., & Moran, T. A. (2004). Forensic/clinical assessment of psychological trauma and PTSD in legal settings. In J. P. Wilson & T. M. Keane (Eds.), *Assessing psychological trauma and PTSD* (2nd ed., pp. 603–636). New York: Guilford.

Young, G. (2007). Causality: Concepts, issues, and recommendations. In G. Young, A. W. Kane, & K. Nicholson (Eds.), *Causality of psychological injury: Presenting evidence in court* (pp. 49–86). New York: Springer.

Young, G., & Kane, A.W. (2007). Causality in psychology and law. In G. Young, A. W. Kane, & K. Nicholson (Eds.), *Causality of psychological injury: Presenting evidence in court* (pp. 13–47). New York: Springer.

Young, G., Kane, A.W., & Nicholson, K. (2007). Causality, psychological injuries, and court: Introduction. In G. Young, A. W. Kane, & K. Nicholson (Eds.), *Causality of psychological injury: Presenting evidence in court* (pp. 1–10). New York: Springer.

Youngstrom, E. A., & Busch, C. P. (2000) Expert testimony in psychology: Ramifications of Supreme Court decision in *Kumho Tire Co., Ltd. v. Carmichael. Ethics & Behavior, 10*, 185–193.

12

Evaluation for Civil Commitment

DOUGLAS MOSSMAN AND DEBRA A. PINALS

The Western world has long regarded persons with mental illness as individuals whose bizarre, pathetic, or violence-prone behavior often justifies their confinement, either for their own good or to safeguard others. U.S. law addresses these matters through civil commitment hearings, which, given their frequent occurrence, are the settings in which the legal system is most likely to receive and make decisions based upon the testimony of mental health professionals. This chapter summarizes our perspective on what constitute "best practices" in civil commitment assessments. We hope to help judges and attorneys understand how psychiatrists and psychologists should gather information and prepare to testify at hearings on involuntary psychiatric hospitalization.

LEGAL CONTEXT
Origins of Current Commitment Laws
U.S. proceedings for hospitalizing persons with mental illness differ greatly from civil commitment processes for sex offenders. Although early-19th-century laws focused on dangerousness, by the mid-20th century, commitment most often was imposed on persons who simply appeared to need treatment. When the American Bar Association surveyed U.S. commitment laws in the late 1950s (Lindman & McIntyre, 1961), just five states used dangerousness to self, others, or property as the sole reason for which courts could order involuntary hospitalization. Mid-20th-century state laws also skimped on procedural protections for persons facing civil commitment. Even the standard of proof by which courts needed to evaluate evidence was largely unspecified (Lindman& McIntyre, 1961).

Matters began changing substantially in the 1960s, a period when liberal political and legal reforms gave new meaning to longstanding American ideals of equal rights, freedom from government intrusion, and procedural protections for persons facing government attempts to deprive liberty. In 1967, California passed the Lanterman-Petris-Short (LPS) Act, which aimed "to end the inappropriate, indefinite, and involuntary commitment of mentally disordered persons" (§5001). Reflecting a "preference for liberty" in responding to mental illness (Karasch, 2003), the LPS made dangerousness to self or others the sole trigger for short-term (up to one month) initial commitments that required judicial review every 90 days. The LPS ultimately "shaped a generation of commitment statutes across the country" (Appelbaum, 2003, p. 26) that made it possible for institutionalized mental patients to enjoy previously denied civil rights protections. The LPS also coincided with the first of several major court decisions that elaborated the procedural and substantive rights of individuals facing possible commitment.

Major Decisions
Although actual civil commitment proceedings reflect local customs and patterns of operationalization, they must take place with broad constitutional limits on how legislatures fashion commitment laws and how courts implement those laws. Here, we offer short summaries of major civil commitment cases (see Pinals & Mossman, 2012, Ch. 1 for a more detailed review).

Lake v. Cameron (1966) was the D.C. Circuit Court of Appeals decision that first articulated the "least restrictive alternative" (LRA) doctrine, a notion now embodied in most states' statutes, which permits involuntary hospitalization only if no less restrictive treatment setting is appropriate. In *Lessard v. Schmidt* (1972), a federal court ruled that to order a person's commitment, the state must show beyond a reasonable doubt that the person was mentally ill and had committed some "overt act" proving he would harm himself or others immediately if not confined. *Lessard* also held that persons facing potential involuntary hospitalization deserved other constitutional protections afforded to individuals who face criminal charges, such as representation by counsel, a prohibition against hearsay evidence, and a privilege against self-incrimination.

In *O'Connor v. Donaldson* (1975, p. 575), the U.S. Supreme Court held unanimously that "there is still no constitutional basis for confining... persons involuntarily if they are dangerous to no one and can live safely in freedom." In a famously ambiguous sentence, the Court set this boundary on civil commitment: "a State cannot constitutionally confine without more [justification] a nondangerous individual who is capable of surviving safely in freedom by himself or with the help of willing and responsible family members or friends" (p. 576).

Parham v. J.R. (1979) tackled issues related to civil commitment of minors, holding that unless a parent has abused or neglected the child, the parent's belief that his child needs hospitalization, confirmed by a "neutral factfinder" who feels the child meets hospitalization criteria, adequately protects a minor's constitutional right to due process. The "neutral factfinder" need not be a court or judge: "an independent medical decisionmaking process" would suffice (*Parham*, p. 613).

In *Addington v. Texas* (1979), the U.S. Supreme Court considered whether the level of proof required for civil commitment should be "beyond a reasonable doubt," as in criminal cases. The *Addington* majority concluded that a "reasonable doubt" standard was too stringent, in part because the purpose of civil commitment is not punishment, but providing needed treatment. Also, the Court doubted whether one "could ever prove beyond a reasonable doubt that an individual is both mentally ill and likely to be dangerous." (p. 429) Setting the standard at proof by "clear and convincing" evidence would adequately protect individuals' liberty while letting states protect their mentally ill citizens.

The following year, however, the Supreme Court upheld a federal district court ruling that made a full civil commitment hearing a prerequisite for involuntarily hospitalizing prison inmates with mental illness in *Vitek v. Jones* (1980). A decade later, the Court decided that a psychiatric facility could face liability for false imprisonment if it allowed a patient of questionable competence to sign in "voluntarily" (*Zinermon v. Burch*, 1990).

In many jurisdictions, commitment standards for persons with developmental disabilities (the now-preferred term for "mental retardation") differ from the standards applicable to individuals with mental illness. A 1993 Supreme Court decision, *Heller v. Doe* (1993), upheld this practice as constitutional. Developmental disabilities are relatively static conditions with documentation extending back to childhood. The Court's majority therefore felt that a state might reasonably require proof of such conditions by just clear and convincing evidence, even if the state required proof beyond a reasonable doubt to authorize a commitment for mental illness.

General Legal Standards

Having a "mental disorder" or "mental illness" is a precondition of civil commitment. (We discuss this further below.) In most jurisdictions, statutes specify that commitment may occur when, because of a mental illness, a person is at risk for one or more of the following: coming to harm through self-neglect or "grave disability" to meet basic needs; physically injuring or killing himself or herself; or physically harming other persons. Statutes often contain additional provisions that allow consideration of a person's need for treatment, risk of physical deterioration without commitment, dangerousness to property, substance use, and the risk of relapse or mental deterioration. Statutes usually require courts to order placement in the least restrictive alternative setting available.

Legal Procedures

This chapter's authors work in Ohio and Massachusetts, and this section often highlights the procedures that lead to civil commitment hearings in these jurisdictions. Attorneys should supplement the following outline with detailed knowledge of laws and procedures where they practice. For simplicity of exposition, we focus here on involuntary psychiatric hospitalization, rather than involuntary outpatient treatment.

Initiating the Commitment Process

In some instances, civil commitment starts with the execution of a document (often an affidavit) describing the declarant's first-hand knowledge of recent behavior by the individual alleged to be mentally ill, including convincing evidence that the individual needs involuntary psychiatric treatment. States vary regarding who (besides mental health professionals) may initiate civil commitment proceedings, from any citizen (e.g., Ohio, see O.R.C. § 5122.10; New York, N.Y. Mental Hygiene Law § 9.27), to non-psychiatric professionals who encounter persons with mental illness in their work (such as police officers, guardians, or a prosecuting attorney; see, e.g., Ind. Code § 12-26-7-2), to parties (such as relatives, caregivers, guardians, and roommates) who have a reasonably expectable interest in the person alleged to be mentally ill. Some states require that the document be accompanied by a certificate completed by one or more examining clinicians.

The court of appropriate jurisdiction reviews the documentation for sufficiency and facts that create probable cause to believe the individual is mentally ill and subject to involuntary hospitalization. The court may then issue a "warrant" or "temporary order of detention" authorizing law-enforcement personnel (and sometimes, certain mental health personnel) to apprehend the person alleged to be mentally ill. The warrant or temporary order permits confinement only for a short period (typically three to five court days), after which the detained person must have a hearing concerning continued hospitalization.

Psychiatric Emergency

Circumstances often do not permit delaying intervention until an affidavit can be filed, so all U.S. jurisdictions have statutory provisions for emergency detention of persons with mental illness whose behavior or condition requires immediate action. Law-enforcement personnel (and in some locales, other officials with statutory authority to detain) may apprehend persons with mental illness and take them to hospital emergency departments or other appropriate locations for evaluation. Statutes often specify that the detention process should be as inconspicuous as possible.

Other Options

Many regions have screening agencies and "mobile crisis services" (Geller, Fisher, & McDermeit, 1995) staffed by mental health professionals, who try to direct persons needing mental health care to the right treatment sources. Of course, concerned family members, friends, school personnel, and employers may take individuals to hospital emergency rooms, and individuals with mental illness sometimes come on their own to hospitals for evaluation, only to find themselves involuntarily detained there.

Upon arrival at a health care facility, community responders (often the police) tell treatment professionals about circumstances that led to a person's detention and why the detainee represents a substantial risk of harm. Many jurisdictions have created specially colored forms ("pink slips" in Ohio and Massachusetts) that help clinicians record all legally required information about the detainee in case civil commitment is later pursued. A qualified clinician (typically, a psychiatrist or other physician) must examine the patient-detainee within a short time (typically 24 hours). If the clinician believes the detainee's condition and recent behavior do not satisfy commitment criteria, the facility must either release the detainee (unless a court has issued a temporary order of detention) or (if hospitalization would be appropriate) offer voluntary admission. Competent detainees who appear committable may and often do agree to undergo hospitalization voluntarily. But if they do not agree, their detention may continue only if hospital clinicians initiate further legal proceedings that will likely eventuate in a commitment hearing.

In most jurisdictions, clinicians have just two or three court days from the day a patient arrives to initiate legal paperwork required for a court hearing on involuntary hospitalization. Hospitals must give detained patients written information about their legal rights, such as the right to retain counsel, to have a hearing, and to be examined by an independent clinician (which may be at public expense for indigent respondents).

Commitment Hearings

Before the judicial commitment hearing, the patient-detainee—who has now become the "respondent" in a civil legal case—receives written notice of the hearing's time and location, the factual basis for the proposed commitment, potential witnesses, and (in most jurisdictions) the respondent's rights at the hearing.

Presentation of Evidence

The State is the legal proponent of any proposed civil commitment and carries the legal burden of showing that the respondent is mentally ill and subject to court-ordered hospitalization. The attorney presenting evidence favoring involuntary hospitalization calls witnesses—usually one or more clinicians; often family, friends, or other fact witnesses—and elicits testimony concerning what statements and actions by the respondent led to initiation of the commitment, evidence of mental illness, diagnosis and clinical prognosis, and the least restrictive treatment setting suitable for the respondent's care.

During cross-examination, the respondent (usually through counsel) may challenge clinicians' credentials, the adequacy of their database, and the soundness of their conclusions, or propose alternative settings for treatment. For example:

- "Isn't it possible he was acting in self-defense when he hit his mother?"
- "You said my client was hallucinating, but he also could have just been talking to himself, correct?"
- "Is it not true that my client could take the same medications as an outpatient?"

Privilege Issues

Treating clinicians often initiate civil commitment proceedings for their patients, and the clinicians who are providing care typically have the best information about respondents' mental conditions. Many states' rules of evidence include an exception to usual doctor–patient privilege standards that specifically permits testimony by treating clinicians in civil commitment hearings (see, e.g., Texas Evid. R. 509(e)(6)). Courts often hear additional testimony by non-treating, independent experts who are court-appointed or retained by one of the parties to the proceeding, and their testimony may not be barred by testimonial privilege if asserted by the respondent (see, e.g., Rev. Code Wash.§ 71.05.360(9)).

Commitment Outcomes

When courts order commitments, they usually must do so for limited, specific periods—typically three to six months. Hospitalizations of such length are rare these days, although they were common in the 1970s and 1980s, when most current civil commitment laws underwent major revisions. For that now-small fraction of persons who do not recover sufficiently after months of inpatient treatment, extensions of involuntary care require new court hearings that apply the same principles, rules, and criteria used in initial hearings. Commitment decisions may be appealed via legal procedures similar to those applicable to criminal convictions.

FORENSIC MENTAL HEALTH CONCEPTS

Earlier, we noted that courts may order civil commitment only upon a finding that the respondent (a) has a "substantial" mental disorder and (b) poses a "risk" of harm to him or herself or others because of that disorder. We now explore these concepts a bit further.

Substantial Mental Disorder

Statutes typically limit civil commitment to persons whose "substantial" mental disorders affect their "thought, mood, perception, orientation, or memory" *and* "significantly" or "grossly" impair their "judgment, behavior, capacity to recognize reality, or ability to meet the ordinary demands of life"— individuals, that is, who are experiencing obvious impairments in functioning. Several states' laws use official diagnostic terms to designate conditions that do *not* qualify a person for involuntary psychiatric hospitalization—common examples include mental retardation, other developmental disabilities, substance use disorders, and epilepsy. However, the types of psychiatric conditions that might qualify persons for civil commitment depend on how each jurisdiction construes the phrase "mental illness."

In most states, the words and phrases that designate commitment-justifying mental disorders need not fit formal or official diagnostic schemes. Often, state case law expressly tells courts to interpret wording in civil commitment statutes according to its ordinary usage, and not as professional diagnostic terminology (e.g., *People v. Doan*, 1985; *People v. Lang*, 1986). In a few states (e.g., Nevada and Utah), however, commitment laws expressly adopt psychiatric terminology to identify mental disorders that might justify involuntary hospitalization. Legal professionals should take note that at the time of this writing, diagnostic terminology was expected to undergo a major revision in 2013.

Risk or Danger

Commitment laws in most states direct courts and mental health professionals to focus primarily on recent and/or severe behavior when evaluating whether a respondent poses a risk to anyone. Statutes may require courts to draw additional conclusions about dangerousness beyond ascertaining that behavior or threats occurred, by requiring (for example) clear and convincing proof that the danger evidenced by overt behavior persists. Note, however, that *actual behavior* (which may include verbal behavior in the form of threats or actual neglect of self-care) is generally required for ordering involuntary hospitalization. In some cases, statutes require that the behavior have occurred within a certain time, such as the past month. Other states balance recentness with severity, so that past behavior that posed great potential harm might extend the period of relevance for civil commitment.

Danger to Self, Danger to Others, and "Grave Disability"

All states permit civil commitment of persons whose mental illness has rendered them physically dangerous to themselves (Brooks, 2007; Mossman, Schwartz, & Lucas, 2011). In this context, physical danger to oneself includes suicidal behavior (that is, threats of or attempts to take one's own life), non-life-threatening but physically harmful actions (e.g., self-mutilation that would cause permanent injury), and—in most states—"grave disability." This last notion refers to the condition of persons who have neither expressed wishes to harm themselves nor made direct attempts to do so, but have so neglected their basic needs (e.g., by not eating or dressing adequately) that they have put their bodies in peril. In most states where statutes do not explicitly mention grave disability as grounds for commitment, courts have interpreted statutes permitting commitment based on "danger to self" as allowing commitment for being "gravely disabled" (Brooks, 2007). All states also permit civil commitment of persons whose mental illness renders them physically dangerous to others. Most states require that individuals display behavioral evidence of violence towards others in the form of credible threats, threatening behavior, attempts to harm another, or actually harmful deeds (Mossman et al., 2011).

Although simply needing treatment cannot be the sole justification for involuntary hospitalization (*O'Connor v. Donaldson*, 1975) some jurisdictions (see, e.g., Ohio Rev. Code § 5122.01(B)(4); South Carolina Code 44-17-580(A)(1)) make need for treatment combined with other factors be a potential justification for civil commitment. Risk of serious physical deterioration is a variation on the "need for treatment" or "grave disability" justifications described above (see, e.g., Kansas Statute 59-2946(f)(3)). A few states (see, e.g., Alaska Statutes 47.30.915(10)(B)) explicitly include risk of property damage among their criteria for civil commitment.

In many jurisdictions, civil commitment statutes expressly state that a substance use disorder may not be the sole grounds for involuntary psychiatric hospitalization (e.g., Arizona Statutes 36-501(20)(a); Kansas Statutes Annotated 59-2946(f)(1); Revised Code of Washington 71.05.040). Several states, however, permit commitment for substance abuse (e.g., alcohol dependence), and a few jurisdictions (North Dakota, Oklahoma, South Dakota, and Wisconsin) permit civil commitment of pregnant women whose drinking poses a risk to their fetus. Finally, around one-third of U.S. states allow commitment for individuals who risk possible relapse of their illness or mental deterioration (see, e.g., Alabama Code § 22-52-10.49a).

The Practical Meaning of Dangerousness in Civil Commitment

In current everyday language, the word "danger" refers to "exposure to possible evil, injury, or harm" or "a source or instance of peril or risk." Similarly, "risk" refers to the "possibility of suffering harm or loss" or "a factor, course, or element involving uncertain danger" (Webster's II University Riverside Dictionary, 1988, pp. 346, 1013). In other words, "risk" and "danger" refer either to a probability of an adverse event or to the possible future adverse event itself.

In the civil commitment context, however, "risk" usually refers to actual past events, the relationship between these events and mental illness, and what these events say about the respondent's present "dangerousness" rather than to theoretically possible future events or probabilities. Terms like "risk," "danger," and "likelihood of harm" for purposes of civil commitment are often statutorily defined in terms of whether certain things—behavior or symptoms—have actually occurred (Mossman et al., 2011), just as in a criminal prosecution. Thus, in civil commitment cases, the trial court should ask, "Has the respondent *already done* something threatening or harmful?" Ordering a civil commitment involves a judgment about *future* behavior only if specific kinds of *past* behavior have occurred. More specifically, commitment statutes direct courts and clinicians to find out whether all the following are true:

- the respondent has a serious mental illness
- the respondent already did something that was threatening, potentially harmful, or actually harmful because of the illness

- the respondent still has the psychiatric problems that led to the threatening or actually harmful behavior
- the problems would continue or worsen without intervening hospitalization and treatment

Past deeds (including statements) and conditions that continue to be present constitute the primary legal bases for ordering someone's civil commitment. However, as we noted earlier, even when a respondent clearly poses a risk to self or others, almost all U.S. jurisdictions have statutory language that precludes involuntary hospitalization unless an inpatient placement would be the "least restrictive alternative" setting for appropriate care (Keilitz, Conn, & Giampetro, 1985).

EMPIRICAL FOUNDATIONS AND LIMITS

Research on Assessment Practices

The clinical data about which mental health professionals testify in commitment hearings are very similar to information clinicians gather for purposes of inpatient treatment. But how well do clinicians evaluate those data in light of statutory commitment criteria? One study looking at how well clinicians followed legal standards (Lidz et al., 1989) found that clinicians disagreed infrequently in applying commitment criteria to patients—a finding that implies consistency, if not accuracy.

Exploring patients' risk of suicide and violence are core features of clinical evaluation as well as evaluations related to commitment. Research shows that psychiatric illness is a major correlate of suicide, as are being male, being older, being white, and having disrupted marital status (American Psychiatric Association 2003). Knowledge of these risk factors has informed clinical interviewing for years.

Reliability of Psychiatric Diagnoses

Diagnoses provide the framework within which clinicians interpret patients' problems and plan their treatment. In statistical parlance, reliability refers to whether multiple evaluations of a patient are likely to yield the same diagnosis or to the likelihood that multiple independent evaluators will reach similar diagnoses. A related concept, "diagnostic stability," refers to the extent to which a patient's diagnosis remains unchanged over time (Whitty et al., 2005). Although no research (to our knowledge) looks

specifically at diagnostic reliability in civil commitment proceedings, a recent summary (Whitty et al., 2005) of research on the diagnostic stability of psychotic disorders suggests that, over follow-up periods ranging from one year to three-plus decades, schizophrenia is the most stable initial diagnosis, in that roughly 90% of initial schizophrenia diagnoses are retained at follow-up. Around 80% of diagnoses of affective psychosis persist, and approximately 70% of persons diagnosed with major depression remain so categorized later.

Studies examining diagnostic inter-rater reliability (i.e., a measure of whether more than one person will arrive at the same diagnosis of a person) have yielded mixed findings. In their comparison of patients' emergency room diagnoses with diagnoses rendered during subsequent hospitalizations, Lieberman and Baker (1985) found fairly good agreement in three broad categories that are relevant to civil commitment—psychotic disorders, major depression, and alcohol abuse. Although studies of diagnoses in pathology, neurology, and radiology reveal substantial disagreement, psychiatric diagnoses often have good diagnostic concordance. Pies (2007) therefore suggests that current psychiatric diagnoses are as reliable as diagnoses in "most other medical specialties" (p. 22).

Clinicians' Decisions to Initiate Commitment

Statutory criteria are key determinants in clinicians' decisions to seek commitment. Although nonstatutory clinical factors (e.g., having a place to live, support outside the hospital, and whether the patient was "crazy or sane") also influence decisions, these clinical factors are closely related to statutory criteria for commitment, which in many jurisdictions permit involuntary hospitalization if not doing so might lead to serious harm. Such statutory provisions invite mental health professionals to consider the clinical risks associated with allowing a patient to leave the hospital (Appelbaum & Hamm, 1982).

Looking at clinicians' judgments about dangerousness to others, inability to care for self, suicidality, and committability, Lidz and colleagues (1989) found generally high inter-rater reliability. Clinicians tended to disagree about whether to commit patients who want voluntary admission but also met the standard for involuntary hospitalization. In general, clinicians in the United States and Canada follow the intent of commitment statutes and do not try to get around dangerousness-based legal standards simply because they want to treat patients (Bagby, Thompson, Dickens, & Nohara, 1991). Clinicians differ in how frequently they decide to detain patients, and evaluation settings and the availability of hospital beds influence clinicians' judgments. But patient characteristics that are not directly relevant to dangerousness—including diagnosis, sex, age, and insurance status—do not predict detention decisions (Engleman, Jobes, Berman, & Langbein, 1998).

Alternatives to Hospitalization

In many locales, a dearth of community services often makes hospitalization the *only* "alternative" when severely ill psychiatric patients urgently need treatment. However, studies suggest that less restrictive treatments—for example, day hospitalization—are suitable for at least one-fourth of persons who currently undergo hospitalization (Marshall et al., 2001), and may help patients get better faster (Marshall et al., 2003) and feel more satisfied with care (Kallert et al., 2007). Other studies of patients who are willing to accept *voluntary* treatment suggest that residential care costs less and is just as effective as hospitalization (Fenton, Mosher, Herrell, & Blyler 1998; Hawthorne et al., 2005). These findings imply that when clinicians testify about the appropriateness of hospitalization, they need to understand what alternatives might be available for respondents.

When patients feel that they have received fair, respectful treatment, feel validated in their point of view, and feel they have a voice in the process, they are less apt to feel coerced, even if they are ultimately involuntarily committed (Lidz et al., 1995). Perceived coercion affects neither subsequent adherence to medication and attendance at outpatient treatment sessions (Bindman et al., 2005; Rain et al., 2003) nor treatment outcome (Steinert & Schmid, 2004; Wallsten, Kjellin, &Lindström, 2006). Patients may well view psychiatric care more positively, however, if they have more say in what happens to them.

Research on Outpatient Commitment

In an outpatient commitment (OPC), a court orders a person to get mental health care while living in the community (Group for the Advancement of Psychiatry [GAP], 1994). Consequences of not following the court order vary across jurisdictions, but most commonly they involve involuntary hospitalization. Most jurisdictions allow for OPC (Bazelon Center, 2004), although legal standards and implementation of this type of commitment vary greatly. Statutes often require that the subject be likely to do serious harm to others if not so committed or to stop treatment absent a court order, and/or to have a history of repeated hospitalizations. In some jurisdictions (e.g., New York), criteria for inpatient and outpatient civil commitment differ somewhat, while other jurisdictions (e.g., Kentucky, North Dakota, Rhode Island, and Pennsylvania) use the same or similar criteria but allow commitments to settings less restrictive than a hospital if clinically appropriate.

Mental health professionals have supported OPC as a way to help so-called "revolving-door" patients who, because they do not recognize that they have a mental illness, repeatedly and frequently undergo hospitalization, improve, get discharged, stop treatment, deteriorate mentally, and return to the hospital. Early before-and-after studies of OPC in revolving-door patients (e.g., Munetz, Grande, Kleist, & Peterson, 1996) reported reductions in emergency room visits, psychiatric hospital admissions, and inpatient lengths of stay.

Recent studies of OPC have employed randomized trials that permit comparison of groups, some of whom receive the intervention while others do not. Although some randomized studies (e.g., Swartz, Swanson, Hiday, Wagner, Burns, & Borum, 2001) suggest that OPC might reduce hospitalization and violence, the benefits appear modest. A recent assessment (Kisely, Campbell, & Preston, 2005) suggests that it takes 85 OPCs to avoid one hospital admission and 238 OPCs to prevent a single arrest. Studies evaluating New York state's Kendra's Law (New York State Office of Mental Health, 2005; Swartz, Swanson, Steadman, Robbins, & Monahan, 2009) suggest that OPC patients show increased use of case-management services, better adherence to psychiatric medication, better social functioning, and fewer harmful behaviors. Although these benefits may simply have resulted from providing better services to OPC patients (Geller, 2006), a comprehensive examination (Swartz et al., 2009) showed that in New York, OPC lowered rates of relapse, hospitalization and arrest. Sustained improvement was higher for patients under OPC orders for longer than six months, and the OPC order itself was an independent statistical factor in achieving better outcomes, and over and above the additional services that patients received.

THE EVALUATION

When performing the types of forensic evaluations described in other chapters of this book, mental health professionals typically confer beforehand with the retaining attorney, then spend lots of time examining records, conducting detailed interviews, and writing reports. Conducting civil commitment evaluations is very different. In the authors' experience, civil commitment hearings themselves are often quick and perfunctory, with little attention paid to the legal, clinical, and forensic issues at stake. Testifying at civil commitment hearings is part of treating clinicians' daily routine in some settings, and participation by independent experts is uncommon. Hearings often take just a few minutes, and prolonged adversarial proceedings may be discouraged and counterproductive because they would both delay treatment and extend a respondent's confinement.

Occasionally, however, civil commitment cases generate unusual controversy or are managed by particularly engaged legal representatives, and testifying witnesses encounter zealous legal advocacy and vigorous cross-examination. In this section, we summarize how clinicians conduct civil commitment evaluations when they anticipate that cross-examination and fact-finder decision-making will subject their findings and opinions to careful scrutiny.

We begin by noting the two possible relationships between evaluator and respondent: (1) the respondent is the evaluator's patient or (2) the evaluator is examining someone else's patient. We refer to the latter relationship as that of an "independent examiner." U.S. mental health professionals try not to serve as expert witnesses concerning their own patients because the ethical obligations of courtroom witnesses often conflict with the obligations of treating clinicians (Greenberg & Shuman, 2007; Strasburger, Gutheil, & Brodsky, 1997). In some circumstances, however, providing expert testimony about one's patient may be appropriate, expected, and accepted practice (American Academy of Psychiatry and the Law, 2005; Heltzel, 2007). Civil commitment hearings are one such circumstance, because giving expert testimony about a seriously ill patient fulfills the clinician's duty to get that patient treatment.

Civil commitment respondents may be too psychotic, thought-disordered, or cognitively impaired to give meaningful information about themselves or why they came to the hospital. Mental health professionals must therefore amplify their observations of patients with "collateral data"—our jargon for information obtained from sources other than patients, such as legal documents, medical records, and statements by acquaintances and relatives. In jurisdictions without hearsay exceptions, professionals who anticipate testifying at a commitment hearing must think about whether collateral data (and, perhaps, their entire opinion) might be excluded. For this reason, examining clinicians read pertinent background documents and others' allegations about the respondent's recent behavior so they can ask about these matters during the examination, and later testify about what the respondent told them.

Attorneys occasionally want to attend a client's examination. Some professionals demur for fear that attorneys will influence or taint the evaluation; other professionals actually *like* having an attorney present because this allows the attorney to experience directly the information on which the expert will base his or her opinion. When an attorney is present, the evaluator will usually plan to have the attorney sit outside the respondent's field of vision (e.g., behind the respondent) to prevent signaling.

When the evaluator is a treating clinician, access to relevant medical records usually poses little problem, as these generally accompany emergency department materials sent to the inpatient unit upon admission. For privately retained evaluators, however, the retaining attorney may need to get the respondent's authorization and provide records to the evaluator before the evaluation, or make advance arrangements for the evaluator to view records and examine the evaluee at the retaining facility. Potential collateral data sources that an evaluator might pursue include initial detention documents, ambulance records, police records, medical records from emergency room contact before hospitalization, medical records from current and past hospitalizations, family members, and neighbors.

The Interview

To the extent that a respondent's mental condition and level of cooperation will permit, an interview should elicit information sufficient to justify a well-founded opinion concerning whether the respondent meets the jurisdiction's commitment criteria. Gathering such information involves applying interviewing and observation skills that are part of mental health professionals' standard clinical repertoire.

Structured Diagnostic Interviews

A "structured diagnostic interview" is a set of inquiries developed to make sure evaluators systematically explore a patient's symptoms. Structured interviews standardize data collection and improve inter-rater reliability, which is why they are used in clinical drug trials, epidemiological studies, and academic research, though they are not commonly used in routine patient care. Some writers (Rogers & Shuman, 2000) have suggested that structured interviews would improve certain kinds of forensic evaluations. However, a large fraction of civil commitment respondents cannot participate in even brief interviews, let alone a detailed, systematic assessment of their symptoms. Although no research quantifies this problem, a review by Pinals, Tillbrook, and Mumley (2006) found that for various reasons, two-fifths of individuals hospitalized because of their possible incompetence to stand trial could not undergo evaluation with the MacArthur Competence Assessment Tool–Criminal Adjudication. Moreover, a civil commitment determination aims only to establish whether the respondent has a *substantial* disorder fitting one or more of several *broad* categories that causes *gross* impairment in functioning. The sorts of precise, detailed diagnoses obtained during structured interviews of cooperative subjects may have limited relevance to the legal needs of a trial court.

Other Assessment Instruments

Civil commitment evaluators may occasionally use rating scales or symptom checklists to help them identify or quantify psychopathology. These tools are not used routinely, however, because many respondents will not cooperate with a systematic evaluation. Also, severity of psychiatric symptoms correlates with needing treatment, but not necessarily with risks of harm to self or others. Finally, rating scales only summarize things numerically, whereas courts need detailed information about specific actions and clinical findings that support a respondent's needing hospitalization.

Other chapters in this book describe specially designed forensic assessment instruments (FAIs) for specific evaluation tasks. No one has designed FAIs for use in civil commitment evaluations, however, and no one is likely to do so, for three reasons:

- Legal standards differ significantly enough across U.S. jurisdictions to make development of a "national" instrument impractical.
- The chief tasks in a civil commitment evaluation are diagnosing mental illness and deciding where treatment should take place, which are fundamental clinical skills that all psychologists and psychiatrists who treat seriously ill patients should possess.
- Legal criteria for commitment focus the trial court's attention primarily on the respondent's actual, *past* events and actions, rather than functional capacity or probabilities of future acts, which is what FAIs typically assess.

However, mental health experts may occasionally adduce information gleaned from FAIs used to assess violence risk (e.g., Classification of Violence Risk™ [Monahan et al., 2005]; HCR-20 [Webster, Douglas, Eaves, & Hart, 1997]; Brøset Violence Checklist [Almvik, Woods, & Rasmussen, 2000]) to support their judgments about persistence of substantial risk relevant to violence (Mossman et al., 2011).

REPORT WRITING AND TESTIMONY

For most types of forensic assessments, independent evaluators prepare detailed reports but rarely get called to testify at hearings or trials. For civil commitment assessments, however, the reverse is true: evaluators usually do not prepare formal reports, but they can count on going to court to testify. In this section, we summarize elements of good report writing in those rare instances that require it. We then describe what we think our mental health colleagues should do when providing testimony.

In most civil commitment cases, an affidavit (or "petition" in some locales) is the principal legal document generated by mental health professionals. As we noted earlier, many jurisdictions have special, colored forms with checkbox sections that direct clinicians to designate what type of risk a patient poses and other information needed to satisfy legal requirements.

One feature of affidavit completion can be surprisingly difficult for clinicians: the provision of legal *facts* sufficient to show probable cause that the patient is potentially subject to hospitalization by court order. To mental health professionals, things like diagnoses ("schizophrenia") or symptoms ("hallucinations") are medical "facts" about patients that prove they need treatment. For this reason, mental health professionals often record their diagnostic conclusions about patients, not realizing that courts view such statements as *opinions* that do not suffice to establish probable cause. When this chapter's authors train post-residency psychiatrists on how to provide input to courts, we spend a great deal of time teaching them how to translate and apply clinical data to legal standards—skills in which most psychologists and psychiatrists receive no formal training. Attorneys who frequently represent hospitals might usefully help mental health professionals better understand the types of legal "facts" that courts prefer to see in commitment documents.

Some jurisdictions permit or accept written documents prepared by clinicians in lieu of in-person testimony, largely as a time- or money-saving measure. These courts sometimes provide guidelines, specific formats, or fill-in forms for submitting such information. Clinicians should complete these documents legibly, including (as with affidavits) the respondent's statements and behavior as evidence of mental illness or dangerousness.

In many cases, the crucial clinical data showing that a respondent poses a risk to others would also represent evidence of a crime (e.g., an assault) if introduced at a criminal trial. Some jurisdictions have statutory provisions that prohibit information introduced at a civil commitment hearing from being used for purposes of a subsequent criminal prosecution (e.g., Rev. Code Wash.§ 71.05.390(19)) or that make the contents of a hearing private and confidential, which may have the same practical effect. Nonetheless, we recommend that clinicians refer to possibly-illegal-but-not-yet-proven acts as "alleged" (e.g., "Mr. Smith's alleged assault on a bystander") in a report written for court (although not necessarily in medical records) and think carefully about how much information they should include in such a report if a respondent's action has given or may give rise to criminal charges. Notwithstanding these cautionary notes, if the clinician determines that the alleged facts include needed clinical details that may be critical to the civil commitment decision, the clinician would be remiss if he or she did not describe them.

When clinical reports are needed, they should formulate and express opinions that address the elements of the statute. Concerning a respondent who meets the criteria for civil commitment, the evaluator's opinion should explain how the respondent's actions meet the criteria for mental illness and how the "mental illness" creates "a likelihood of serious harm." Civil commitment is a *one-point-in-time decision*; courts have neither clinical responsibility for respondents nor the ability to act clinically to reduce their risk. Therefore, clinicians' written documents should ideally inform courts and attorneys about the risk immediately related to the upcoming decision on civil commitment. Statements about the magnitude, imminence, likelihood, and frequency of potentially harmful acts can be useful to courts, as can information (when available) about specific risk factors and why hospitalization should mitigate the risk (Heilbrun, O'Neill, Stevens, Strohman, Bowman, & Lo, 2004).

Many thoughtful forensic mental health professionals are uncomfortable expressing "ultimate opinions" in their reports or during testimony, believing only a court should make such pronouncements and not wanting to appear to usurp the court's role. For this reason, forensic mental health professionals are divided about whether they should include explicit opinions about the ultimate issue.

Judges and lawyers appear to prefer testimony on the ultimate issue (Redding, Floyd, & Hawk 2001), and forensic clinicians are often asked their opinions in questions that include ultimate-issue language. We suggest that evaluators do something equivalent to saying "2 + 2" without saying "4." Concerning a suicidal inpatient who appears to meet criteria for commitment, for example, the evaluator would describe the signs and symptoms of illness and state that these demonstrate the presence of a "substantial disorder" with "gross impairment"; the evaluator would also enumerate risk factors, recent behaviors, and other relevant findings. The evaluator might conclude with a statement (couched in the statutory phrasing from the local jurisdiction) that these findings support the presence of an immediate risk of serious harm or death if hospitalization does not continue. This approach conveys unambiguously to the court what the evaluator thinks without appropriating the court's prerogative to determine whether the respondent "meets the commitment criteria."

Testimony

Dedicated clinicians often have a hard time divorcing their evaluation findings and conclusions from considerations of what would be *best* for respondents. Needing treatment is not a sufficient condition for commitment, however, and clinicians' testimony should also address whether a mentally ill respondent meets statutory criteria for involuntary hospitalization.

Many jurisdictions have case law or statutes allowing hearsay exceptions for civil commitment hearings that permit professionals to testify about information related by family members to support an opinion about involuntary hospitalization (e.g., Iowa Code § 229.12(3); *In re Melton* (D.C. 1991)) or to quote medical records without prior testimony from the custodian of the record (e.g., Wash. Rev. Code § 71.05.360). Information from such collateral sources often is crucial. In states without such hearsay exceptions (e.g., Ohio), attorneys representing the proponent of commitment may need to speak to testifying professionals before hearings to learn whether the professionals' findings and direct observations will suffice to support commitment. If not, attorneys may need to arrange for testimony from family members or other persons who witnessed what the patient-respondent did that resulted in emergency hospitalization.

Most states' statutes on doctor–patient privilege contain an exception that allows treating clinicians to testify at civil commitment hearings. In states that do not have such an exception (e.g., Ohio, *In re Ratz*, 2003), independent experts must obtain and convey information to courts in forms that comport with evidentiary rules. Information about a patient's previous psychiatric treatment is often a critical part of a diagnostic and therapeutic evaluation. Despite this, not all states permit the introduction of such information in legal hearings (e.g., Ohio, *In re Miller*, 1992).

A pre-hearing conference between an attorney and the clinician who will be providing direct testimony can be invaluable. Describing findings and opinions aloud will often help the clinician recognize and then tell the attorney about the strengths and weaknesses of the case. Also, because commitment criteria are written in legal language, attorneys can help clinicians (especially those with less forensic training) articulate their clinical observations so that they are relevant to legal commitment criteria. In those uncommon cases where opposing counsel will vigorously challenge a testifying clinician's expertise, attorneys can prepare their witnesses for what to expect. Attorneys can help clinicians who are not experienced expert witnesses understand that challenges to their expertise are not personal—it's just part of how courts do business.

Experienced clinicians are not necessarily effective expert witnesses. Attorneys can help their own experts do well as witnesses by showing the experts direct-examination questions before the hearing. Doing this allows an expert to help the attorney make sure that direct-examination questions will get at key points about a respondent's condition or dangerousness.

Attorneys should not assume that psychiatrists and psychologists can answer any mental health questions off the top of their heads, including simple-sounding questions like "What is mental illness?" or "What is a delusion?" Actually, these two questions are *quite hard* to answer unless one has thought about them a lot or has previously learned some pithy, one-sentence responses. Experienced forensic mental health professionals develop a repertoire of "canned" answers for attorney questions like these. But most clinicians—including skilled, experienced clinicians—have trouble coming up with answers and definitions of concepts on the spot (even though they know perfectly well how to apply the concepts). Showing prospective experts questions in advance can let them prepare answers and avoid looking stupid or incompetent.

Attorney preparation usually helps inexperienced testifying experts avoid big gaffes during testimony. If, however, an attorney feels that an expert's testimony has not quite gotten at key points, here are some thoughts about getting information that is more relevant during direct examination. Concerning experts testifying on direct examination that the respondent meets commitment criteria:

- If an expert is giving conclusory statements (opinions) and providing too few observations ("facts"), the attorney might induce the witness to be a clinician-teacher—a comfortable role for many doctors—by asking (for example), "Doctor, would you give the court examples of the things Mr. Doe did and said that led you to conclude he has schizophrenia?"
- If an expert is describing symptoms but not explaining how those symptoms cause

impairment, an attorney might ask, "Doctor, you said Ms. Doe was grossly impaired. Would you describe the things you *saw* that led you to this conclusion?"

- The expert should explain how previous behavior that is evidence for risk arises from the respondent's mental illness. If this has not happened spontaneously, an attorney might ask, "Doctor, how was this behavior related to Mr. Roe's mental illness?"

Experts sometimes conclude that respondents do not meet commitment criteria despite their recent behavior or obvious mental problems. Here, we list some reasons why this can occur:

- Many persons (especially physicians) feel that a medical condition that compromises insight should occasion intervention to override foolish choices by patients. But simply having a mental disorder and needing treatment do not, by themselves, make an individual eligible for commitment.
- Risky behavior by someone with a mental illness sometimes stems from poor judgment, not from a psychiatric disorder. A person with a mental illness who hitchhikes at night could get assaulted or hit by a car—but so might a hitchhiker without mental illness.
- Criminal behavior is not necessarily dangerous behavior.
- Some people are taken to hospitals during personal crises, but they settle down quickly and would, if permitted, obtain outpatient treatment voluntarily and safely. If the urgent concerns that have led to their emergency detention abate after a few days of inpatient care, these persons might not qualify for civil commitment.
- Sometimes, an emergency detention gives concerned relatives an opportunity to mobilize resources to safeguard their loved ones and arrange treatment. When responsible persons will care for a non-dangerous mentally ill person, hospitalization might not be necessary.

SUMMARY

As we noted earlier, civil commitment hearings are often casual and perfunctory. Many times, this bothers mental health professionals. Even when we believe involuntary hospitalization is justified and absolutely necessary, we still care about our patients' rights. Most mental health professionals find courts and cross-examination unsettling and intimidating. Yet we urge attorneys and courts to do their best to give patients good representation and thoughtful hearings, even if not rigorously contested. Given the fundamental liberty rights that are at stake in civil commitment proceedings, legal and mental health professionals should share the same goal: enhancing patients' personhood and respecting their humanity.

REFERENCES

Addington v. Texas, 441 U.S. 418 (1979).

Alabama Code § 22-52-10.49a.

Alaska Statutes § 47.30.915(9).

Almvik, R., Woods, P., & Rasmussen K. (2000). The Brøset Violence Checklist (BVC): sensitivity, specificity and inter-rater reliability. *Journal of Interpersonal Violence, 12,* 1284–1296.

American Academy of Psychiatry and the Law. (2005). *Ethics guidelines for the practice of forensic psychiatry.* Accessed August 1, 2011, from http://www.aapl.org/ethics.htm

American Psychiatric Association. (2003). *Practice guideline for the assessment and treatment of patients with suicidal behaviors.* Accessed August 1, 2011, from http://www.psychiatryonline.com/pracGuide/pracGuideTopic_14.aspx

Appelbaum, P.S. (2003) Ambivalence codified: California's new outpatient commitment statute. *Psychiatric Services, 54,* 26–28.

Appelbaum, P. S., & Hamm, R. M. (1982). Decision to seek commitment: Psychiatric decision making in a legal context. *Archives of General Psychiatry, 39,* 3447–3451.

Arizona Statutes § 36-501(20)(a)

Bagby, R. M., Thompson, J. S., Dickens, S. E., & Nohara, M. (1991). Decision making in psychiatric civil commitment: an experimental analysis. *American Journal of Psychiatry, 148,* 28–33.

Bazelon Center. (June, 2004). *Involuntary outpatient commitment: Summary of state statutes.* Washington, DC: Author. Retrieved August 1, 2011, from http://www.bazelon.org/LinkClick.aspx?fileticket=CBmFgyA4i-w%3d&tabid=324.

Bindman, J., Reid, Y. Szmukler, G., Tiller, J. Thornicroft, G., & Leese, M. (2005). Perceived coercion at admission to psychiatric hospital and engagement with follow-up—a cohort study. *Social Psychiatry and Psychiatric Epidemiology, 40,* 160–166.

Brooks, R. A. (2007). Psychiatrists' opinions about involuntary civil commitment: Results of a national survey. *Journal of the AmericanAcademy of Psychiatry and the Law, 35,* 219–228.

Engleman, N. B., Jobes, D. A., Berman, A. L., & Langbein, L. I. (1998). Clinicians' decision making about involuntary commitment. *Psychiatric Services, 49,* 941–945.

Fenton, W. S., Mosher, L. R., Herrell, J. M., & Blyler, C. R. (1998). Randomized trial of general hospital and residential alternative care for patients with severe and persistent mental illness. *American Journal of Psychiatry, 155,* 516–522.

Geller, J. L. (2006). The evolution of outpatient commitment in the USA: From conundrum to quagmire. *International Journal of Law and Psychiatry, 29,* 234–248.

Geller, J. L., Fisher, W. H., & McDermeit, M. (1995). A national survey of mobile crisis services and their evaluation. *Psychiatric Services, 46,* 893–897.

Greenberg, S. A., & Shuman, D. W. (2007). When worlds collide: therapeutic and forensic roles. *Professional Psychology: Research and Practice, 38,* 129–132.

Group for the Advancement of Psychiatry, Committee on Government Policy. (1994). *Forced into treatment: The role of coercion in clinical practice,* Report no. 137. Washington, DC: American Psychiatric Press.

Hawthorne, W. B., Green, E. E., Gilmer, T., Garcia, P., Hough, R. L., Lee, M., Hammond, L., & Lohr, J. B. (2005). A randomized trial of short-term acute residential treatment for veterans. *Psychiatric Services, 56,* 1379–1386.

Heilbrun, K., O'Neill, M. L., Stevens, T. N., Strohman, L. K., Bowman, Q., & Lo, Y.-W. (2004). Assessing normative approaches to communicating violence risk: A national survey of psychologists. *Behavioral Sciences and the Law, 22,* 187–196.

Heller v. Doe, 509 U.S. 312 (1993).

Heltzel, T. (2007). Compatibility of therapeutic and forensic roles. *Professional Psychology: Research and Practice, 38,* 122–128.

In re Melton, 597 A.2d 892, 908 (D.C. 1991).

In re Miller, 63 Ohio St. 3d 99, 585 N.E. 2d 396, 404 (1992).

In re Ratz, 2003 Ohio 1569, 2003 Ohio App. LEXIS 1497 (Ohio Ct. App., Montgomery County Mar. 28, 2003).

Iowa Code § 229.12(3).

Kallert, T. W., Priebe, S., McCabe, R., Kiejna, A., Rymaszewska, J., Nawka, P., Ocvár, L., Raboch, J., Stárková-Kalisová, L., Koch, R., & Schützwohl, M. (2007). Are day hospitals effective for acutely ill psychiatric patients? A European multicenter randomized controlled trial. *Journal of Clinical Psychiatry, 68,* 278–87.

Kansas Statutes Annotated 59-2946(f)(1) & 59-2946(f)(3)

Karasch, M. (2003). Where involuntary commitment, civil liberties, and the right to mental health care collide: An overview of California's mental illness system. *Hastings Law Journal, 54,* 493–523.

Keilitz, I., Conn, D., & Giampetro, A. (1985). Least restrictive treatment of involuntary patients: Translating concepts into practice. *St. LouisUniversity Law Journal, 29,* 691–745.

Kisely, S., Campbell, L. A., & Preston, N. (2005). Compulsory community and involuntary outpatient treatment for people with severe mental disorders. *Cochrane Database of Systematic Reviews, 3,* Art. No.: CD004408. DOI: 10.1002/14651858.CD004408. pub2.

Lake v. Cameron, 364 F.2d 657 (D.C. Cir. 1966).

Lanterman-Petris-Short (LPS) Act, Cal. Welf & Inst. Code §5000 *et seq.*

Lessard v. Schmidt 349 F.Supp. 1078 (1972).

Lidz, C. W., Hoge, S. K., Gardner, W., Bennett, N. S., Monahan, J., Mulvey, E. P., & Roth, L. H. (1995). Perceived coercion in mental hospital admission. Pressures and process. *Archives of General Psychiatry, 52,* 1034–1039.

Lidz, C. W., Mulvey, E.P., & Appelbaum, P.S. (1989). Commitment: The consistency of clinicians and the use of legal standards. *American Journal of Psychiatry,146,* 176–181.

Lieberman, P. B., & Baker, F. M. (1985). The reliability of psychiatric diagnosis in the emergency room. *Hospital & Community Psychiatry, 36,* 291–293.

Lindman, F., & McIntyre Jr., D. (Eds.). (1961). *The mentally disabled and the law: The report of the American Bar Foundation on the rights of the mentally ill.* Chicago: University of Chicago Press.

Marshall, M., Crowther, R., Almaraz-Serrano, A., Creed, F., Sledge, W., Kluiter, H., Roberts, C., Hill, E., & Wiersma, D. (2003). Day hospital versus admission for acute psychiatric disorders. *Cochrane Database Systematic Reviews,* 2003(1), CD004026.

Marshall, M., Crowther, R., Almaraz-Serrano, A., Creed, F., Sledge, W., Kluiter, H., Roberts, C., Hill, E., Wiersma, D., Bond, G. R., Huxley, P., & Tyrer, P. (2001). Systematic reviews of the effectiveness of day care for people with severe mental disorders: (1) acute day hospital versus admission; (2) vocational rehabilitation;(3) day hospital versus outpatient care. *Health Technology Assessment, 5,* 1–75.

Monahan, J., Steadman, H. J., Appelbaum, P. S., Grisso, T., Mulvey, E. P., Roth, L. H., Robbins, P. C., Banks, S., & Silver, E. (2005). *Classification of Violence Risk (COVR).* Lutz, FL: Psychological Assessment Resources.

Mossman, D., Schwartz, A. H., & Lucas, E. (2011). Risky business versus overt acts: what relevance do "actuarial," probabilistic risk assessments have for judicial decisions on involuntary psychiatric hospitalization? *Houston Journal of Health Law and Policy, 11,* 365–453.

Munetz, M. R., Grande, T., Kleist, J., & Peterson, G.A. (1996). The effectiveness of outpatient civil commitment. *Psychiatric Services, 47,* 1251–1253.

New York Mental Hygiene Law § 9.27.

New York State Office of Mental Health. (2005). *Kendra's Law: Final report on the status of assisted outpatient treatment.* Retrieved from http://www.omh.ny.us/omhweb/Kendra_web/finalreport/summary.htm

O'Connor v. Donaldson, 422 U.S. 563 (1975).

Ohio Rev. Code §§ 5122.01 and 5122.10.

Parham v. J.R., 442 U.S. 584 (1979).

People v. Doan, 141 Mich. App. 209, 215 (Mich. Ct. App. 1985).

People v. Lang, 113 Ill. 2d 407, N.E.2d 1105 (1986).

Pies, R. (2007). How "objective" are psychiatric diagnoses? (Guess again.). *Psychiatry 4*(10), 18–22.

Pinals, D. A., & Mossman, D. (2012). *Evaluation for civil commitment.* New York: Oxford University Press.

Pinals, D. A., Tillbrook, C. E., & Mumley, D. (2009). Violence risk assessment. In F. M. Saleh, A. J. Grudzinskas, J. M. Bradford, & D. Brodsky (Eds.), *Sex offenders: Identification, risk assessment, treatment and legal issues.* New York: OxfordUniversity Press, pp. 49–69.

Pinals, D. A., Tillbrook, C. E., & Mumley, D. L. (2006). Practical application of the MacArthur Competence Assessment Tool-Criminal Adjudication (MacCAT-CA) in a public sector forensic setting. *Journal of the AmericanAcademy of Psychiatry and the Law, 34,* 179–188.

Rain, S. D., Williams, V. F., Robbins, P. C., Monahan, J., Steadman, H. J., & Vesselinov, R. (2003). Perceived coercion at hospital admission and adherence to mental health treatment after discharge. *Psychiatric Services 54,* 103–105.

Redding, R. E., Floyd, M. Y., & Hawk, G.L. (2001). What judges and lawyers think about the testimony of mental health experts: A survey of the courts and bar. *Behavioral Sciences and the Law, 19,* 583–594.

Rev. Code Wash. §§ 71.05.040, 71.05.360(9), 71.05.390(19), and 71.09.030.

Rogers, R., & Shuman, D.W. (2000). *Conducting insanity evaluations* (2nd ed.). New York: Guilford.

South Carolina Code 44-17-580(A)(1).

Steinert, T., & Schmid, P. (2004). Effect of voluntariness of participation in treatment on short-term outcome of inpatients with schizophrenia. *Psychiatric Services, 55,* 786–91.

Strasburger, L. H., Gutheil, T. G., & Brodsky, A. (1997). On wearing two hats: Role conflict in serving as both psychotherapist and expert witness. *American Journal of Psychiatry, 154,* 448–456.

Swartz, M. S., Swanson, J., Hiday, V. A., Wagner, H. R., Burns, B. J., & Borum, R. (2001). A Randomized controlled trial of outpatient commitment in North Carolina. *Psychiatric Services, 52,* 325–329.

Swartz, M. S., Swanson, J. W., Steadman, H. J., Robbins, P. C., & Monahan, J. (2009). *New York State assisted outpatient treatment program evaluation.* Durham, NC: Duke University School of Medicine. Retrieved from http://www.macarthur.virginia.edu/aot_final-report.pdf

Texas Evid. R. 509(e)(6).

Vitek v. Jones, 445 U.S. 480 (1980).

Wallsten, T., Kjellin, L., & Lindström, L. (2006). Short-term outcome of inpatient psychiatric care—impact of coercion and treatment characteristics. *Social Psychiatry and Psychiatric Epidemiology, 41,* 975–980.

Webster, C. D., Douglas, K. S., Eaves, D., & Hart, S. D. (1997). *HCR-20: Assessing Risk for Violence (Version 2).*Burnaby, BC, Canada: Mental Health, Law, and Policy Institute, Simon Fraser University.

Webster's II New Riverside University Dictionary. (1988). Boston, MA: Houghton Mifflin.

Whitty, P., Clarke, M., McTigue, O., Browne, S., Kamali, M., Larkin, C., & O'Callaghan, E. (2005). Diagnostic stability four years after a first episode of psychosis. *Psychiatric Services, 56,* 1084–1088.

Zinermon v. Burch, 494 U.S. 113 (1990).

13

Evaluation for Harassment and Discrimination Claims

JANE GOODMAN-DELAHUNTY AND WILLIAM E. FOOTE

Despite acknowledgment that noneconomic damages address "the primary elements of life" and that "it turns reality on its head to give transcendence to the pecuniary" (Komesar, 1990, p. 58), the importance of nonpecuniary losses has long been neglected (Abel, 2006). In cases of workplace discrimination where psychological injuries arise, the plaintiff can recover nonpecuniary or compensatory damages. Lawyers, forensic evaluators, and courts who must assess the eligibility of a plaintiff for compensatory damages may be guided by a five-stage model to assess the status of the plaintiff before the alleged harassment, during those events, and following harassment incidents. By examining the complainant's status at these points in time, legal causation can be assessed, and symptoms or problems compensable by the defendant can be distinguished from those that are a result of other life events. This chapter describes the types of mental and emotional injuries most commonly caused by workplace harassment and discrimination; distinguishes garden-variety emotional distress from claims that put a plaintiff's medical condition at issue; and outlines the role of a mental health practitioner in evaluating plaintiffs and testifying about these matters in court.

LEGAL CONTEXT

The Nature of Compensatory Damages in Workplace Discrimination Cases

Awards of monetary compensation to injured parties for noneconomic or general losses date back to Roman times (O'Connell & Bailey, 1972) but remain controversial, at least in part because there is no obvious external measure of the losses claimed, and vast variability in awards (Studdert, Kachalia, Salomon, & Mello, 2011). Debate over the term "hedonic damages" used in the law since the 1980s (*Sherrod v. Berry,* 1988) has centered on whether it encompasses all noneconomic damages, including pain and suffering. The more widely accepted usage of the term is confined to loss of enjoyment of life (i.e., loss of capabilities for enjoyment of life, not loss of happiness *per se*) (Swedloff & Huang, 2010). A useful tool in the form of a scale to assess these losses was developed by Andrews, Meyer, and Berla (1996). Nonetheless, the availability of hedonic damages and compensation for loss of consortium varies somewhat by jurisdiction. Litigation-induced stress is not ordinarily recoverable as an element of damages (*Zimmerman v. Direct Fed. Credit Union,* 2001).

Legal Framework

The principle that underlies an award of compensatory damages is *restitutio in intergum,* or "make-whole" relief, to attempt to restore the victim of discrimination to the position that he or she would have occupied but for the discrimination (*Albemarle Paper Co. v. Moody,* 1975). Legislation enabling the recovery by prevailing plaintiffs of monetary awards to compensate them for nonpecuniary losses sustained following intentional workplace discrimination under U.S. Federal antidiscrimination laws is relatively recent: the Civil Rights Acts of 1991 amended Title VII (Civil Rights Act of 1964) for this purpose.

Many state and local antidiscrimination statutes have a longer tradition of allowing these claims and impose fewer limitations and restrictions (Friedman, 2006). For instance, caps on the recoverable sum applicable in federal court ($50,000 to $300,000, depending on the size of the employer) may not apply in state or local court. Plaintiffs' lawyers often advise clients to avoid lodging claims in federal court (Clermont & Schwab, 2009). While legal counsel may prefer to litigate claims for workplace psychological injuries under state law, state courts look to federal case law for guidance, even in the absence of pendent federal claims. A precedential model of compensation is often applied to calibrate amounts awarded by judges (Gilbert, 2011), and on a motion for *remittitur*, jury awards that clearly exceed the maximum reasonable award may be reduced (Ritz, 2007).

Compensatory damages available under the Civil Rights Act of 1991 include (a) past and future pecuniary losses and (b) past and future nonpecuniary damages. Past pecuniary losses, also known as special damages, are out-of-pocket expenses incurred by the victim because of discrimination— for example, to pay for medical expenses or the costs of psychological counseling. Claims of future pecuniary losses may include the victim's lost earning potential or costs of future planned courses of medical treatment or psychological counseling to restore the plaintiff. Nonpecuniary or general damages, which are the focus of this chapter, include elements such as psychological and psychiatric injuries, emotional and physical pain and suffering, mental anguish, loss of enjoyment of life, loss of health, inconvenience, injury to one's character or reputation, and injury to one's professional standing. Nonpecuniary and future pecuniary damages are less certain and precise and in federal court are subject to a statutory cap or limit of $300,000, based on the size of the employer. Most compensatory damages claims are retrospective, for past injuries.

Compensatory damages may be claimed only in cases of intentional discrimination under Title VII of the Civil Rights Act of 1964. This encompasses a claim of a hostile and abusive workplace environment. Two types of discrimination are exempt from compensatory damages: they are not available in cases of age discrimination under the Age Discrimination in Employment Act (ADEA) (1967), or where an employer made a good-faith effort to accommodate a disabled employee under the Americans with Disabilities Act (1990, amended 2008). The Genetic Information Nondiscrimination Act (GINA) of 2008 includes compensatory damages. Compensation is available for acts of reprisal or retaliation, unless the underlying claim was for age discrimination under the ADEA. Causes of action

for discriminatory conduct that are based on tort claims do not uniformly encompass recovery for mental distress (Nates et al., 2007). Legal doctrines that require physical injuries before an accompanying claim for psychological injury is allowed have been steadily eroding.

Many types of workplace actions and inactions can result in liability for intentional discrimination. Statistics posted by the U.S. Equal Employment Opportunity Commission disclosed that in 2010, most claims filed were for retaliation (36%) and racially based charges (35%), followed by hostile workplace environment or harassment claims (30%), of which approximately one third were for sexual harassment (11%). A plaintiff may allege a cause of action based on disparate treatment as well as a hostile and abusive workplace environment, each of which has its own elements of proof. Many employees alleged discrimination on multiple bases and theories. More than one quarter of all claims were accompanied by a retaliation charge in addition to the underlying claim of discrimination based on sex, race, religion, or disability, etc. Since at trial a plaintiff may not prevail on all allegations, an evaluating expert may be needed to separate harm caused by a nonprevailing claim (e.g., racial harassment) from that caused by a prevailing cause of action (e.g., reprisal and retaliation) in order to assist a trier of fact to discern the compensable injuries.

Garden-Variety Damages vs. Diagnosable Injuries

Most damages following workplace discrimination are temporary in nature, are fairly short-lived, and do not result in diagnosable, enduring disorders that require ongoing treatment or therapy. These are known as garden-variety damages, and include consequences such as such as ordinary grief, frustration, humiliation, embarrassment, career disruption, anger, sadness, fear, sleeplessness, nervousness, etc., that are understandable to a trier of fact such as a reasonable layperson (*Ricks v. Abbott Labs*, 2001). Garden-variety damages are foreseeable forms of emotional distress that do not require medical attention (*Kankam v. Univ. of Kansas Hospital Authority*, 2008) rather than any specific diagnosable condition.

More serious reactions to workplace discrimination are often dependent upon the nature of the discrimination, the protagonist (coworkers vs.

immediate supervisor), and the vulnerabilities of the employee who is the target of the harassment or discrimination (Foote & Goodman-Delahunty, 2005). Subjective elements to mental distress and disorders arise because of individual differences. For example, a plaintiff's personality may influence the vulnerability of a worker to traumatic stress, and also the outcome of trauma exposure.

Work termination cases, where discrimination is established primarily by circumstantial evidence, do not usually involve injurious harassing conduct, and are often thought less likely to produce severe emotional injury than are claims of harassment by an incumbent employee who faces daily stressors on the job (Friedman, 2008b). However, victims of harassment and other forms of discrimination who constructively discharge or who are terminated may face unemployment. Meta-analyses have shown that mental health consequences for unemployed workers are more severe than those of incumbent workers: significant differences emerged on several indicators, including mixed symptoms of distress, depression, anxiety, psychosomatic symptoms, subjective well-being, and self-esteem (Paul & Moser, 2009). A plaintiff may be particularly vulnerable because of a preexisting experience of abuse or racism (Friedman, 2008a), or a personality disorder that makes him or her more prone or vulnerable to victimization (Drukteinis, 2011). Several meta-analyses have been conducted on the effects of past childhood sexual abuse as a predisposing vulnerability factor (Greeson, Bybee, & Raja, 2008; Jumper, 1995; Neumann, Houskamp, Pollack, & Briere, 1996; Paolucci, Genuis, & Violato, 2001).

Exposure to a hostile work environment or workplace harassment can give rise to a range of adverse health outcomes (Guthrie, Taplin & Oliver, 2009), often producing more profound and enduring injuries. As a general rule, the severity of reaction is directly related to the severity of the harassment. The duration of the harassment also determines the seriousness of the target's reactions, with more protracted episodes of harassment producing more debilitating outcomes. When harassment is more frequent, more profound negative psychological outcomes occur (Fitzgerald et al., 1997), although research has confirmed that even low-frequency sexual harassment can produce measurable negative consequences (Schneider, Swann, & Fitzgerald, 1997).

In a workplace discrimination case, the four most common types of nonpecuniary damages claimed (Friedman, 2006) are (1) emotional distress, supported by testimony by the victim or an expert about the nature, extent, and symptoms experienced; (2) physical pain and suffering, supported by medical evidence of a condition caused by the discrimination; (3) loss of enjoyment of life and loss of society or hedonic damages (e.g., withdrawal from normal social activities, changes in one's relationship with others and social activities; and ability to fulfill family obligations) and (4) loss of consortium (e.g., if the victim's ability to have sexual relations was diminished).

Proving Compensatory Damages

Research has confirmed that approximately one third of discrimination suits that proceed to trial in federal court are successful, and that the remedies obtained in that forum are modest, with only a select few plaintiffs securing more substantial compensatory damage awards (Nielsen, Nelson, & Lancaster, 2010). These findings pose a challenge to lawyers to avoid leaving their clients undercompensated. Proof of noneconomic injuries is often neglected by lawyers who focus on matters pertaining to liability and out-of-pocket losses. This can leave them underprepared to establish the nature and scope of psychological injuries to adequately compensate their clients.

Difficulties in proving damages for emotional distress have a number of sources: (a) psychological injuries are intangible and thus are more difficult to assess and measure than are physiological injuries; (b) acknowledged individual variability in coping with discrimination means that not all employees respond in the same fashion, limiting the value of individual comparisons; (c) many victims' self-reports of the impact of discrimination are poor, as they may be inarticulate when it comes to describing the nature and extent of the harm endured; (d) some victims fail to causally connect the consequences with the origin (e.g., bruxism or grinding of the teeth may not be an expected consequence of psychological distress); (e) some victims may experience a sense of shame that they were victimized and repress symptoms and avoid discussing the impact (e.g., many male victims are socialized to appear tough and resilient and are reluctant to admit psychological injuries); (f) retrospective assessment of compensatory damage claims is often complicated by memory deficits and attribution errors by victims (Drukteinis, 2011), and difficulties in teasing apart causation; (g) research findings on common reactions of victims of discrimination are scattered, hard to synthesize, and inaccessible to many legal professionals; (h) skepticism about the validity of claims for psychological distress exists on the part of the employers, coworkers, members of the general public, and courts (Goodman-Delahunty & Foote, 2011); "plaintiphobia" is widespread (Clermont & Schwab, 2009).

Courts have acknowledged that individual workers respond differently to discriminatory events at work. Thus, it is not a prerequisite in bringing a discrimination claim that the plaintiff alleges any psychological injuries (*Harris v. Forklift Systems, Inc.,* 1993). The U.S. Supreme Court emphasized that emotional distress injuries cannot be presumed to result from a violation of the plaintiff's rights; instead, there must be "proof that such injury actually was caused" (*Carey v. Piphus,* 1978). Proof of compensatory damages has two elements: (1) proof of actual harm or injury and (2) proof of causation (Kokenge, 2011). The plaintiff must establish *proximate* cause—that is, that it is more likely than not that discrimination by the employer was one of the causes of emotional distress. However, it is not necessary that the discrimination be the sole cause of any consequential emotional distress.

Experts on compensatory damages are not required in discrimination cases (Moss & Huang, 2009); testimony from the plaintiff, family members, coworkers, counselors, teachers, and treating medical or mental health professionals is often the basis of this proof. Medical evidence can "lend support to a claim for emotional distress," but "such evidence is neither required nor necessarily probative, though at some level of claimed distress, the absence of medical attention may be suggestive" (*Miner v. City of Glen Falls,* 1993, p. 663). Awards of sums in the range of $300,000 in the absence of expert or medical testimony have been upheld (Case, 2011; *Miller v. Alldata Corp,* 2001). Although psychological expert testimony is not required (*Howard v. Burns Bros., Inc.,* 1998), in the Second Circuit subjective testimony by the plaintiff alone was "generally insufficient to sustain an award of emotional distress damages" (*Patrolmen's Benevolent Ass'n. v. New York,* 2003, p. 50).

Where the victim's injuries are more extensive and serious than garden-variety damages, a treating physician's notes and records and an evaluating expert are recommended. However, lawyers are not always aware of the potential contribution of an evaluating mental health professional in proving compensatory damages. The expert evidence can support the credibility of the plaintiff and other witnesses to establish liability and damages. This can be accomplished by an evaluating expert who (a) identifies issues that typically arise when plaintiffs are exposed to discriminatory treatment at work (e.g., changes that victims of serious psychological injury undergo in their behavior and physical, psychological, and/or social functioning [general causation]); (b) specifies emotional distress that is less obvious (e.g., loss of enjoyment of work); (c) elaborates the functional impairment of the victim in various contexts (e.g., work, home, social circle); (d) includes a diagnosis of the victim's condition, if appropriate; (e) provides an account of how discrimination or harassment caused a psychological injury of the magnitude and duration experienced by the plaintiff, taking into consideration the particular vulnerabilities or special sensitivities of the victim (specific causation) (i.e., the "eggshell skull" rule applies, that you take the plaintiff as you find him or her); (f) estimates the future duration of harm (Friedman, 2008b).

Key Legal Procedures

Relatively few plaintiffs prevail, particularly in federal courts (Nielsen et al., 2010), and thus many legal proceedings are bifurcated on issues of liability and damages. If a defendant is found liable, settlement of compensatory damages claims may ensue without a formal hearing or trial on this topic. In these situations, and in employment cases formally referred for resolution by means of arbitration or settlement, damages for injuries are typically lower. Results of a recent study of outcomes in arbitration revealed that employees prevailed 21% of the time, a rate lower than that in employment litigation trials, and that the median award of $36,500 and the mean award of $109,858 were both substantially lower than award amounts reported in employment litigation (Colvin, 2011).

One helpful method of dealing with the challenge faced by a client in describing and specifying aspects of emotional distress is to prepare an affidavit describing the impact of the discrimination and the specific symptoms endured. This document can be provided in response to the disclosure required by Rule 26 (a) (1) (A) (iii) ("computation of each category of damages"), or in response to an interrogatory on damages (Friedman, 2008b). The document can assist in streamlining discovery and provides a point of focus and memory aid for the claimant and defense counsel in a deposition. Once a plaintiff asserts that his or her mental or physical condition is a basis for recovery, this operates as a waiver of any "psychotherapist" privilege otherwise available to the party regarding confidential statements to a treating mental health professional (Wright & Graham, 2007).

With respect to compensatory damages claims, the legal procedures implemented may vary depending on the severity of injuries alleged. Thus, it is important to establish whether the injuries sustained are garden variety, diagnosable, or disabling. Pursuant to Federal Rule of Civil Procedure 35, a plaintiff must submit to a physical or mental examination "on a motion for good cause" shown, when the mental or physical condition of the person is "in controversy" (*Schlagenhauf v. Holder*, 1964). When there is good cause, a defendant employer can seek a physical and/or mental examination of a plaintiff who intends to claim for emotional distress. Good cause exists when (a) the plaintiff has asserted a specific cause of action for intentional or negligent infliction of emotional distress; (b) the plaintiff has alleged a specific mental or psychiatric injury or disorder; (c) the plaintiff has claimed unusually severe emotional distress; (d) the plaintiff has offered expert testimony in support of his or her claim for emotional distress damages; and (e) the plaintiff concedes that his or her mental condition is "in controversy" within the meaning of Rule 35(a) (*Fox v. Gates Corp.*, 1998). The examiner is usually a certified or licensed psychiatrist or psychologist.

The consequence for a plaintiff of putting his or her emotional state at issue is that the defendant is entitled to enquire about anything that may have caused disruption, including prior illness, surgery, substance abuse treatment, a criminal record, bankruptcy, loss of loved ones, etc. "Any privacy interests in a patient's treatment for mental distress will be waived should the plaintiff put her psychological state in issue by seeking damages for such harm" (*Fisher v. SW. Bell Tel. Co.*, 2010). Generally, a plaintiff who does not intend to prove the extent of any injuries by introducing evidence of physical conditions or evidence of treatment or call any witness to testify about symptoms and treatment does not waive the privilege.

Several considerations affect the decision whether or not to place a client's mental state in controversy—for instance, whether the plaintiff has sought therapy, what other issues were occurring in the plaintiff's life around the time of the discrimination, prior trauma in the plaintiff's life, prior courses of psychotherapy, whether the plaintiff is amenable to being examined by the defendant's Rule 35 expert, and how comfortable the plaintiff is testifying about his or her situation and permitting his or her therapist to do the same (Ritz, 2007).

One question that arises is whether a Rule 35 examination is warranted if the plaintiff alleges only garden-variety damages, no expert testimony will be presented, no specific psychological or psychiatric disorder was diagnosed, and no treatment was prescribed (Caterine & Mullen, 2011). Specific emotional distress is distress that is supported by "a therapeutic professional's testimony, whether treating or forensic" (Ritz, 2007, p. 353). "Depression" and "anxiety" are examples of diagnosable conditions. In some jurisdictions, if a plaintiff claims garden-variety emotional distress, then counseling and medical records need not be produced (*Hucko v. City of Oak Forest*, 1999). Accordingly, some plaintiffs rely on the garden-variety doctrine to avoid a Rule 35 examination. For instance, in a case of sexual harassment and retaliation in which the plaintiff made no claim for psychological injury, the jury nonetheless awarded $11.7 million in punitive damages (Friedman, 2008a; Sandomir, 2007). But, in other jurisdictions, even if you claim garden-variety emotional distress, you have to produce medical records (Caterine & Mullen, 2011).

Although typically the doctrine that the plaintiff has a duty to mitigate losses does not apply to nonpecuniary damages, some exceptions exist. For example, Massachusetts courts allow failure to mitigate as a defense to emotional distress damages (Friedman, 2008b).

A forensic practitioner must bring to the task a thorough familiarity with the relevant research literature on consequences of discrimination. To be able to theorize appropriately about causation of harm, the evaluating psychologist needs to know quite a lot about the potential outcomes of exposure to workplace discrimination and harassment.

The *Daubert-Kumho* standard (*Daubert v. Merrell Dow Pharmaceuticals, Inc*, 1993; Goodman-Delahunty & Foote, 1995; *Kumho Tire Co. v. Carmichael*, 1999) and the systematic approach outlined below will allow practitioners who are familiar with the literature to integrate theories and case facts to reach an informed and evidence-based opinion on causation of harm.

FORENSIC MENTAL HEALTH CONCEPTS

Psychologists may provide information to the judge or jury about a number of aspects of compensatory damages in an employment discrimination case, including the presence, nature, and effect of emotional injuries experienced by plaintiffs and the cause of those harms. If both psychologists and lawyers could design the world, they would both choose one in which plaintiffs have uncomplicated lives. The absence of a history of prior trauma, preexisting disorders, and ongoing emotionally damaging relationships would provide a blank canvas upon which the psychological impact of job-related actions could be painted. Absent such an ideal world, both psychology and the legal system have developed ways of separating the effect of workplace events from the sometimes complicated pattern of events in the rest of the worker's life. To that end, the Five-Stage Model for assessment of damages in civil actions was developed (Foote & Lareau, in press; Goodman-Delahunty & Foote, 2009, 2011). This model tracks over a temporal path both the development and impact of psychological problems and the sources of causation of those problems. The model focuses on function rather than diagnosis. This emphasis is essential because psychiatric diagnosis only tells the court how a mental health professional categorizes the plaintiff's problems according to the *Diagnostic and Statistical Manual of Mental Disorders* (DSM-IV-TR; APA, 2000). The

diagnosis does not inform the court how the person has functioned over time in various arenas of life and how the person is engaging in essential life tasks at the time of trial.

Two people with the same diagnosis (e.g., posttraumatic stress disorder [PTSD]) may present very differently (Breslau et al., 1998; Breslau, Reboussin, Anthony, & Storr, 2005; Kessler et al., 1995). One person may be restricted to his home by fears of leaving the house, may have disrupted sleep from frequent nightmares, may be interrupted in daily tasks by unbidden and disturbing images and thoughts, and may be unrealistically fearful about future negative events (Roth et al., 2006). The other person may have mild intrusive thoughts, but push them aside and keep working; may have some fears associated with certain places, but is able to avoid those places; and may have disturbed sleep, but is able to manage sleep hygiene well enough to feel rested on most days. Thus, the Five-Stage Model focuses on four different areas of life functioning, and an array of symptoms, rather than a diagnosis.

Using a 4×4 matrix, the model examines four arenas of the plaintiff's life: activities of daily living (ADLs), interpersonal relationships, the workplace, and hedonics. Within these four domains, the model examines four types of symptoms: cognitive, affective, physiological, and interpersonal, as shown in Table 13.1.

Key Contexts
Activities of Daily Living (ADLs)

The essential tasks of ADLs are reviewed by health professionals to establish how well a person functions on a day-to-day basis (Vore, 2006). These include such tasks as personal hygiene; household chores; reading; use of electronic equipment; social activities; family responsibilities; community/religious activities; exercise regimen; sleep/wake

---

TABLE 13.1 MATRIX TO ASSESS COMPENSATORY DAMAGES

	Symptoms of Injury or Impairment			
Context	Cognitive	Affective	Physiological	Interpersonal
ADL	e.g., poor concentration,	e.g., anger, hostility,	e.g., fatigue, teeth-grinding,	e.g., avoidance,
Relationships	distraction, confusion,	aggression, distress,	weight change, sleep	withdrawal
Work	vigilance	depression	disturbance, headaches	
Hedonics				

cycle; eating habits, including any weight gain or loss; driving activities; financial management; doctor's visits; and academic pursuits. ADLs are so fundamental that if a person cannot perform these functions, then outside assistance, such as a home health care aide, is often necessary. Moreover, if ADLs are impaired, it is likely that other arenas of the person's life will be disrupted.

Relationships

People rarely exist in a social vacuum. In home, family, and job contexts, getting along with others is critical for day-to-day functioning. In addition, for most people, relationships provide quality of life based upon the richness of those connections.

Work

The ability to function in job settings is critical for not only the remuneration gained from work, but the inherent value of performing familiar tasks, and exercising skills and knowledge. If workplace discrimination renders a worker incapable of performing work functions, both monetary and non-monetary damages may result.

Hedonics

The ability to enjoy life or the quality of life is a significant basis for compensatory damages (Bagenstos & Schlanger, 2007). The evaluating psychologist focuses upon activities that most people see as sources of pleasure in life: recreational activities, such as sports or hunting; hobbies; and social activities with family and friends.

Key Symptoms or Problem Areas

Cognitive

Many emotional disorders, particularly those related to depression and anxiety, produce disrupted thinking processes (Kessler, Zhao, Blazer, & Swartz, 1997). Most sensitive are memory and concentration, but more serious disorders can impair problem solving and the ability to anticipate the consequences of one's actions. Impaired cognitive functions may interfere directly with job-related tasks.

Affective

How a worker feels emotionally can have serious consequences for day-to-day functioning. A very sad mood or an angry, confrontational attitude can disrupt family and workplace relationships

(e.g., with coworkers, supervisors, vendors, or customers).

Physiological

Sleep disorders, headaches, gastrointestinal disturbances, and many other physical problems may impair day-to-day functioning. In some cases, these are symptoms of underlying anxiety or depression, and may require medical intervention.

Interpersonal

In the contexts of home, family, and work environments, the ability to get along with others is critical. A worker with impaired interpersonal functioning may not be able to effectively collaborate with coworkers or to interact effectively with supervisors or other essential individuals in the workplace.

An Introduction to the Five-Stage Model to Evaluate Workplace Injuries

Stage 1

Evaluating experts begin by gaining a detailed picture of the plaintiff's life before the alleged discrimination began. This is referred to as the "day before" analysis. The evaluator is particularly concerned with preexisting conditions. These disorders can relate in three ways to emotional harms caused by the alleged discrimination. First, in some cases, they do not contribute at all, and the disorders that began before the alleged discrimination may continue without affecting the damages in the case. The psychologist must be careful to avoid mistaking preexisting disorders for the consequences of discrimination. Second, the preexisting condition may make the plaintiff more vulnerable to the impact of discrimination, producing an "eggshell skull" scenario. For instance, some individuals may have personality disorders or preexisting PTSD that make them more prone or vulnerable to victimization (Drukteinis, 2011). The existence of an ongoing or co-occurring event may serve as a vulnerability factor that would predicate reactions to alleged harassing events. Third, the preexisting condition may exacerbate the harm incurred.

Stage 2

This portion of the evaluation focuses on the period during which the alleged discrimination occurs. In most workplace discrimination cases, the duration of sexual harassment or a racially hostile work environment may encompass days, weeks, or months.

Emotional problems caused by discrimination often take time to develop and to affect other aspects of the plaintiff's life.

Stage 3

A protracted interval between the alleged discriminatory events and the psychological evaluation is not unusual in discrimination cases. During this interval, the plaintiff may experience a number of changes in functioning both related and unrelated to the alleged discrimination.

Stage 4

This is the interval during which the psychological evaluation takes place and all the information about the plaintiff is collated. During this stage, the evaluator assesses for exaggeration or minimization of symptoms, and attempts to identify symptoms or problems that are ongoing.

Stage 5

The evaluator takes the information consolidated in Stage 4 and attempts to project the plaintiff's status into the future. Future medical and mental health needs are described, costs of future treatment are estimated, and a description is provided of how the problems generated by the alleged discrimination may affect the plaintiff's ability to earn a living.

EMPIRICAL FOUNDATIONS AND LIMITS

Extensive research has been conducted on psychological injuries that follow exposure to workplace discrimination (see Foote & Goodman-Delahunty, 2005; Goodman-Delahunty & Foote, 2011). This body of research includes case studies of individual victims and members of class actions, experimental simulations, and multisite employee surveys using cross-sectional, correlation, or longitudinal measures in which mental health and other symptoms of workers who self-reported exposure to discrimination were compared with symptoms of workers who experienced no discrimination. These findings have been aggregated into several large-scale meta-analyses. A major outcome of the meta-analyses is confirmation that workplace discrimination and harassment is a stressor, and of links between exposure to perceived workplace discrimination and physical as well as psychological pain and suffering (Bowling & Beehr, 2006; Rospenda, Richman, & Shannon, 2009). For instance, a study using data from 134 studies in which worker exposure to racial, gender, and sexual-orientation discrimination as well as physical and psychological symptoms was measured showed that 90% of the victims exposed to higher levels of discrimination had lower mental health scores and 83% experienced physical health consequences (Pascoe & Richman, 2009). Social support was shown to be a buffer for mental health but not the physical health consequences of discrimination. Perceived discrimination was associated with heightened psychological and physical stress responses as well as increased participation in unhealthy behaviors. These relationships persisted even when important covariates were controlled. Moderating variables included social support and coping style. Comparisons of consequences of nondiscriminatory occupational stress (caused by an intense or increased workload) with consequences of general workplace harassment and/or sexual harassment (e.g., Shannon et al., 2009) yielded statistically significant consequences for the discriminatory conduct only.

Researchers have measured multiple and different symptoms experienced by victims of discrimination (Goodman-Delahunty & Foote, 2011). For example, some have focused on associations between exposure to perceived discrimination and increases in substance abuse (Shannon et al., 2009); others have examined a range of physical outcomes, including increased risks of adiposity and cardiovascular disease (Albert & Williams, 2011). Although researchers have not always used standard measures, results of the meta-analyses shed light on symptoms most commonly experienced by discrimination victims on the job to their mental and physical health, in their daily functioning and their enjoyment of life. Table 13.2 displays findings from longitudinal studies and meta-analyses where causation of harm assessed in each domain produced robust and reliable effects.

Specific details of the discrete symptoms of mental health changes and physical health changes that were included in these measures are itemized in the studies included in the meta-analyses. Notably, the effects of workplace harassment on job stress, mental health, and physical health persisted for more than one year, and enduring long-term mental health consequences overshadowed positive employment experiences (Hoobler et al., 2010).

TABLE 13.2 MAJOR FINDINGS ON THE CONSEQUENCES OF
WORKPLACE DISCRIMINATION

	Manifested Symptoms			
	Cognitive	**Affective**	**Interpersonal**	**Physiological**
ADLs	decreased psychological well-being[2,6]	anxiety[1]	cultural identity crisis[5]	alcohol consumption increase[7]
	coping strategies[5]	depression[1,3,4,6]		generic strain[1,6]
	personal strength[5]	distress[2,6,7]		health decline[6,8]
		emotional exhaustion[1,3]		physical symptoms[1,2,6]
		mental health decline[5,8]		
		PTSD[8]		
Work	burnout[1]	job stress[2]	coworker dissatisfaction[2,8]	
	counterproductive behavior[1]	frustration[1]	decreased workgroup productivity[8]	
	organizational deviance[4]	low satisfaction with supervisor[2,8]	interpersonal deviance[4]	
	poor performance[2]	negative emotion[1]	job withdrawal[2,8]	
	turnover intention[1,3,4]		low organizational commitment[1,2,8]	
	work withdrawal[2,4,8]		supervisor-directed deviance[4]	
Hedonics	poor overall well-being[1]	dissatisfied with life[1,8]		health dissatisfaction[2]
		dissatisfied with work[1,2,3,4,8]		
Relationships	low self-esteem[1]		decreased social support[5]	

Sources: [1]Bowling & Beehr, 2006; [2]Chan et al., 2008; [3]Herschovis & Barling, 2010; [4]LaPierre, Spector, & Leck, 2005; [5]Lee & Ahn, 2011; [6]Pascoe & Richman, 2009; [7]Shannon et al., 2009; [8]Willness, Steele, & Lee, 2007.

THE EVALUATION

The Five-Stage Model is a method of sequential data gathering and sorting to address legally relevant damages and causation, as illustrated in Table 13.3. By using each stage as an evaluation guide, expert assessors can ensure a thorough assessment of injuries.

Five-Stage Model to Evaluate Workplace Injuries
Stage 1

Medical, vocational, and other case-relevant documents are third-party sources of information essential to the evaluation (Heilbrun, Warren, & Picarello, 2004), and these are usually the first data to be analyzed. Forensic psychologists often request every scrap of paper generated in the life of the plaintiff, but must settle for particular records. Of critical importance are the plaintiff's medical records,

which allow a determination of the presence of pre-existing disorders attended to and treated by physicians. In some cases, a history of sleep disorder or gastrointestinal problems may signal emotional problems that a family practitioner may have failed to recognize as symptoms of preexisting anxiety or depressive disorders. Work records are of special importance in employment cases. How the plaintiff functioned in other work settings and in the workplace in issue prior to the alleged discrimination is critical in determining the existence of ongoing emotional disorders.

Employment records may provide a picture of how the worker got along with others in the work environment, and performance measures may reveal preexisting job problems.

Military records may disclose similar information and may provide a history of war-related trauma in veterans. Financial records indicate how

TABLE 13.3 FIVE-STAGE MODEL TO ASSESS CAUSATION OF HARM IN WORKPLACE DISCRIMINATION CLAIMS

Time Period	Causation Issue	Measures
Day before onset of alleged discrimination	**Preexisting conditions:** Continuous/for later exacerbation Vulnerability Assess past affective, cognitive, interpersonal, and physiological symptoms	**Functional analysis in:** Activities of daily living Relationships Workplace functioning Hedonic injuries
During discrimination	**Rule out:** Work stress, family problems, financial difficulties, and illness	**Injury onset:** Natural history of disorder from discrimination Comorbidity
After discrimination	**Rule out:** Financial change not caused by discrimination, family problems, and litigation stress	**Subsequent injuries:** Onset of injuries caused by reprisal Fallout from unemployment
Day of assessment	**Consequences of discrimination:** Assess current affective, cognitive, interpersonal, and physiological symptoms **Rule out** malingering/exaggeration, exacerbation of preexisting condition Remainder attributable to discrimination	**Functional analysis in:** ADLs Relationships Workplace functioning Hedonic injuries
Future		Future treatment needs Projected loss of work capacity

the plaintiff spent money, and may shine a clear light on quality-of-life issues. Documents produced in the course of litigation (e.g., civil complaint, answers to interrogatories, affidavits, depositions) are often rich sources of information concerning the plaintiff's status "the day before" the alleged discrimination.

The clinical interview with the plaintiff is a critical part of the Stage 1 procedures (Heilbrun, 2001). At best, this process employs both open-ended and pointed questions, and taps into the plaintiff's own perspective on life events. Psychologists take into account the common tendency on the part of plaintiffs to minimize preexisting problems and perhaps exaggerate post-discrimination difficulties. Good interviewers record the plaintiff's verbatim statements, as these often reflect the person's emotions related to the events described.

Collateral interviews (discussions with friends, coworkers, and family members) are sources of information that help validate the information gathered from plaintiff interviews and documentary sources (Heilbrun, Rosenfeld, Warren, & Collins, 1994). It is often helpful to ask the plaintiff for a list of names and numbers for individuals most familiar with the plaintiff's status before and after the alleged discrimination. In addition, the examiner may wish to speak to coworkers, supervisors, neighbors, and others who may provide additional information about the plaintiff's pre-discrimination status. As noted earlier, the plaintiff's functional status before the alleged discriminatory event is the major focus of the Stage 1 data gathering. A comprehensive listing of cognitive, physiological, affective, and interpersonal functioning should be developed. At the end of this phase of the evaluation, the examiner should have a clear picture of how the plaintiff was functioning in daily activities, work, relationships, and recreational activities on "the day before" the alleged discrimination.

Stage 2

Using the same sources of information as in Stage 1, the focus shifts to the dynamics of emotional reactions to workplace discrimination. Psychological research has shown that the status of the worker during workplace discrimination is rarely static, and often follows predictable patterns (e.g., Gruber &

Smith, 1995). For example, in sexual harassment cases, the targeted worker may at first fail to recognize the actions of the harasser (Pryor, 1987) or may attempt to view the objectionable behavior as a one-time or benign event. Over time, if the worker experiences ongoing stress because of the repeated inappropriate behavior, this may be reflected in changes in physiological functioning (Chan, Lam, Chow, & Cheung, 2008). The worker may begin to experience interpersonal problems such as impaired sexuality and increasing marital problems (Gruber & Smith, 1995). Recent research indicated that alcohol abuse may increase over time when workers are exposed to a hostile work environment (McGinley, Richman, & Rospenda, 2011). Temporally based patterns may develop—for instance, the worker comes to dread going back to work on Monday, and may feel as if holding on until Friday each week is almost impossible (Lapierre et al., 2005).

Some events, particularly sexual assaults or instances of public humiliation, may produce reactions similar to PTSD. Although it is a rare for workplace discrimination to produce frank PTSD, traumatic reactions are nevertheless observed and may produce significant impairments (Foote & Goodman-Delahunty, 2005). Symptoms related to discrimination often result in increased absenteeism and reduced functioning in the workplace and may generate employer discipline (Lapierre et al., 2005; Schneider et al., 1997). Workers experiencing reprisal for reporting the alleged discrimination may become alienated from coworkers and supervisors.

Stage 3

The dynamics of emotional reactions related to the alleged discrimination are a focus of this stage of the analysis. In many cases, the worker will have left the workplace because of an allegedly wrongful or constructive discharge (*Rupp v. Purolator Courier Corp.,* 1994). The emotional fallout from involuntary discharge can be significant, as are the financial changes that may occur following job loss. Emotional reactions that began in the workplace, particularly those related to traumatic incidents, may change over time. In some cases, traumatic reactions spontaneously improve over a period of weeks or months (Hickling & Blanchard, 2006; Kessler et al, 1997). In other cases, the person's functioning deteriorates because of the development of secondary or *comorbid* disorders. For example, the majority of individuals with diagnosable PTSD also have at least one comorbid disorder (Breslau et al., 1998). For men, these are usually externalizing problems like substance abuse (Baldwin, Marcus & DeSimone, 2010). Women, who tend to internalize, are more likely to develop depression and emotionally based medical illnesses (Kessler et al., 1995).

The plaintiff may have sought medical or psychological treatment during this interval. The psychologist would review records of that treatment, and perhaps speak with the treatment providers to gain a picture of not only the therapist's working diagnosis but also the progress made. At the end of the third stage, the examiner should have a picture of the course of the plaintiff's life in the post-discrimination period.

Stage 4

This evaluation interval brings together the data gathered in Stages 1 through 3 and introduces a focus on the plaintiff's current status. The interviews with the plaintiff and with collaterals include questions about how the plaintiff is currently functioning, with particular emphasis on current symptoms and problems.

The psychologist will select appropriate psychological assessment instruments. Commonly used in this context are cognitive measures, including the Wechsler Adult Intelligence Scale-IV (Psychological Corporation, 2008a), the Wechsler Memory Scale-IV (Psychological Corporation, 2008b), and the Wide Range Achievement Test-4 (Wilkinson & Robinson, 2006). These are designed to document impairments in functioning related to the impact of anxiety or depression on the plaintiff's attention, concentration, or energy level.

The psychologist also uses scales to assess the plaintiff's current emotional functioning, including the Minnesota Multiphasic Personality Inventory 2 (see Greene, 2011) or its rival, the Minnesota Multiphasic Personality Inventory 2-Revised Form (see Ben-Porath & Tellegen, 2008). Other commonly used measures are the Personality Assessment Inventory (Morey, 2007) and the Millon Clinical Multiaxial Inventory-III (Millon, 1994). These measures provide an opportunity for the evaluator to assess the plaintiff's emotional functioning in a setting in which emotional difficulties may be compared with those of defined populations of individuals. These measures also provide a picture of the plaintiff's strengths and weaknesses.

Both the cognitive and emotional disorder assessment should incorporate measures of response bias to determine if the plaintiff is attempting to portray problems as much more or less severe than they really are. Attempts to embellish the claim are often attributed to "secondary gain," a term used more by lawyers than psychologists.

Psychologists recognize that any plaintiff in a lawsuit has multiple reasons to exaggerate or feign emotional disorders, or to attribute disorders to the alleged discrimination that in fact arose from another source. The use of extensive malingering and exaggeration measures in the assessment and the cross-validation of symptoms through multiple sources help reduce the probability that these sources of error will result in inappropriate or excessive damages.

The Stage 4 analysis provides information essential in compensatory damages cases. First, the psychologist should have a well-defined view of the plaintiff's current symptoms or problems. Second, the data should indicate whether these difficulties are a result of the alleged discrimination or unrelated causes. Third, the analysis provides a description of the functional limitations resulting from problems or symptoms related to the discrimination. Fourth, a comparison of these limitations with the functional status of the plaintiff on "the day before" the alleged discrimination began yields the emotional harms that are attributable to the discrimination as opposed to alternative sources.

The Stage 4 analysis recognizes that because of the dynamic nature of discrimination-related psychological injuries, some emotional patterns may have developed as a result of the discrimination, but have either resolved spontaneously or been successfully treated. These should not be ignored, as they may constitute a basis for compensatory damages. These more transitory problems may also set the stage for the development of emotional disorders in the plaintiff's later life.

Stage 5

Providing evidence about the plaintiff's future damages is the focus of the final stage of analysis. Information on reduced job functioning may be passed on to a vocational expert or forensic economist who can translate the evaluator's findings and predictions into job-market figures for lost future income.

The assessment of emotional disorders and the review of the plaintiff's treatment history should provide a basis for determining future treatment needs. A thorough understanding of how the plaintiff's emotional disorders combine to produce the current symptoms can enable the examiner to develop a treatment plan best suited to return the plaintiff to the highest possible level of functioning. This treatment plan may include assistance in ADLs, individual or group psychotherapy and the use of psychotropic medication. Research indicates that for PTSD, depression, and other discrimination-related disorders, optimal treatment includes some combination of counseling and medication. If the plaintiff has been suicidal, provision should be made for inpatient treatment.

REPORT WRITING AND TESTIMONY
The Evaluation Report

Since most employment discrimination cases settle before trial, preparation of a comprehensive report that is understandable to laypeople is essential. Referring counsel can facilitate a high-quality report by explicitly specifying referral questions in a letter to the examining psychologist. Familiarity with the Five-Stage Model can assist in formulating these questions, because the model focuses on issues of causation and damages throughout the evaluation process. By Stages 4 and 5, the psychologist should have sufficient information to answer the most important referral questions: (1) Is there evidence of a mental disorder or other emotional problems for the plaintiff? (2) Which of these problems are, to a reasonable scientific (or psychological or medical) probability, caused by the action of the defendants? (3) For those psychological consequences of the actions of the defendant, what is the impact on the plaintiff's ability to function in the workplace? (4) For those psychological consequences of the actions of the plaintiff, what is the impact on the plaintiff's ability to function in daily activities, in intimate relationships, in social activities, in recreational activities, and in relation to his or her family? (5) In relation to identified emotional or psychological damages, what are the plaintiff's treatment needs? (6) How much, in current costs, is the amount that this treatment would require to fund? (7) What would be the duration of such treatment? (8) What improvement could be expected on the basis of that treatment? (9) Are there symptoms or problems that would be expected to persist in spite of state-of-the-art treatment? (10) Will the emotional damages experienced by the plaintiff lead to later dysfunction that is not currently evident?

To provide a foundation to answer these questions the psychologist's report should address the following elements. The report should begin with identifying information, including the birth date of the plaintiff. The referral source and a brief summary of the referral questions should be provided. The report should describe the informed-consent procedures used by the psychologist prior to the evaluation and should describe all sources of information used (documents reviewed, interviews, testing, etc.). In narrative form, the report should summarize the plaintiff's history, including the plaintiff's account of the alleged discrimination and the plaintiff's account of the impact of the discriminatory events. These should be followed by test data from the evaluation and a description of how those data relate to the referral questions. In a summary section, the psychologist should address each of the referral questions and competing theories for the causation of injuries. If, for example, there is evidence of serious financial problems experienced by the plaintiff's family that could account for the anxiety disorder observed in the evaluation, the psychologist should be able to explicate whether and to what extent those problems contributed to the disorder.

The cautious lawyer may wish to review the draft report before it is completed, since recent changes in Federal Rule of Civil Procedure 26 allow referring counsel to obtain and review drafts of expert reports without disclosing them. Care must be taken that such a review or revision does not cast an appearance of bias on the expert.

Although the length, content, and style of forensic reports submitted in workplace discrimination cases may vary greatly depending on the nature and complexity of the case, there are several key features to include. First, the evaluating expert must ensure that all of his or her case-relevant findings are presented in a "detailed manner that will facilitate later inquiry and testimony" (Goodman-Delahunty & Foote, 2011, p. 181). A high level of detail in reports is important because, in some cases, this may be the only opportunity that the expert has to fully itemize all of the key details of

the plaintiff's condition. In some jurisdictions, the judge may restrict the expert to opinions expressed in the written report. A wide breadth of detail ensures that the expert will not be restricted in regards to in-court testimony.

Second, although experts should err on the side of too much detail in their reports, it is important that the detail is "both relevant and non-prejudicial" (Goodman-Delahunty & Foote, p. 181), in line with the best-evidence rule for inclusion of information. To ensure that the most relevant information is collected in an objective manner, it is advisable that expert evaluators use the structured guide provided by the Five-Stage Model to assist them in the collection and interpretation of all case-relevant information.

Third, the report should be written in lay terms, keeping technical terms to a minimum. Through its detail and structure, the report can assist lawyers to guide experts through their deposition and trial testimony. The content of the report can serve as a key tool to assist triers of fact in making important decisions about the amount to award in compensation. Consequently, the expert's report and subsequent testimony should be viewed as an opportunity to integrate the information discovered in the assessment process and to convey this in an objective and easy-to-understand manner that will assist the triers of fact.

Testimony

Since trials rarely occur in employment discrimination cases, most expert testimony is presented in discovery depositions scheduled by opposing counsel. Because of the centrality of the deposition in these cases, referring counsel should take time to meet with the examining expert to plan for the deposition. These discussions may be the topic of deposition questions, so counsel should be cautious in what is said, lest they hear their own words repeated on the record by the expert. Even experienced expert witnesses find a session to discuss the expert testimony helpful in preparing for this critical work. If the expert is aware of opposing counsel's theory of the case, the expert can better anticipate questions. Possession and review of opposing experts' reports and test data are essential. A frank discussion of the strengths and weaknesses of the expert's data in relation to the case can assist the expert in explaining the data to the finder of fact.

All aspects of preparation for deposition testimony apply equally to trial. The Five-Stage Model may assist in explaining to the jury what the expert did and the nature of the expert's findings. The pretrial meeting should take place before the deadline for exhibits in the trial has passed so that the expert and retaining counsel can review exhibits that best explicate the expert's findings. The structure of testimony should anticipate cross-examination questions so that the expert can deal with difficult issues first in a friendly as opposed to an adversarial context.

SUMMARY

Employment discrimination cases often pose special problems for both lawyers and experts. In many cases, plaintiffs have experiences of prior trauma that may complicate the pattern of observed psychological injuries. Likewise, in the intervals during and following the alleged employment discrimination, the plaintiff may experiences stresses, traumas, and losses that produce emotional reactions similar to those observed in discrimination cases. Determining the impact of non-employment discrimination experiences is a major task of the expert. The Five-Stage Model to assess compensatory damages provides a systematic method to examine workplace discrimination compensatory damages claims and increases the comprehensiveness and accuracy of the forensic evaluation.

REFERENCES

Abel, R. (2006). General damages are incoherent, incalculable, incommensurable, and inegalitarian (but otherwise a great idea). *DePaul Law Review, 56*, 53–329.

Age Discrimination in Employment Act, 29 U.S.C. §201 (1967).

Albemarle Paper Co. v. Moody, 422 U.S. 405 (1975).

Albert, M. A., & Williams, D. R. (2011). Invited commentary: Discrimination—an emerging target for reducing risk of cardiovascular disease? *American Journal of Epidemiology, 1373*, 1240–1243.

American Psychiatric Association. (2000). *The diagnostic and statistical manual of mental disorders* (4th ed., text revision). Washington, DC: Author.

Americans with Disabilities Act of 1990, 42 U.S.C.A. §12101 *et seq.* (West 1993).

Americans with Disabilities Amendment Act of 2008, Pub. Law 110-325 (2009).

Andrews, P., Meyer, R. G., & Berla, E. P. (1996). Development of the lost pleasure of life scale. *Law and Human Behavior, 20*, 99–111.

Bagenstos, S. R., & Schlanger, M. (2007). Hedonic damages, hedonic adaptation, and disability. *Vanderbilt Law Review, 60*, 745–797.

Baldwin, M. L., Marcus, S. C., & De Simone, J. (2010). Job loss discrimination and former substance use disorders. *Drug and Alcohol Dependence, 110*, 1–7.

Ben-Porath, Y. S., & Tellegen, A. (2008). *MMPI-RF: Manual for administration, scoring and interpretation.* Minneapolis, MN: University of Minnesota Press.

Bowling, N.A., & Beehr, T. A. (2006). Workplace harassment from the victim's perspective: A theoretical model and meta-analysis. *Journal of Applied Psychology, 91*, 998–1012.

Breslau, N., Kessler, R. C., Chilcoat, H. D., Schultz, L. R., Davis, G. C., & Andreski, P. (1998). Trauma and posttraumatic stress disorder in the community: The 1996 Detroit Area Survey of Trauma. *Archives of General Psychiatry, 55*, 626–632.

Breslau, N., Reboussin, B. A., Anthony, J. C., & Storr, C. L. (2005). The structure of posttraumatic stress disorder. *Archives of General Psychiatry, 62*, 1343–1351.

Carey v. Piphus, 435 U.S. 247 (1978).

Case, K. (2011, March). *A plaintiffs' attorney's guide to maximizing emotional distress damages.* Paper presentation at the American Bar Association Employment Rights & Responsibilities Committee Midwinter Meeting, San Juan, Puerto Rico.

Caterine, M. J., & Mullen, S. (2011, March). *Availability of Rule 35 exams where plaintiff claims "garden variety" emotional distress.* Paper presentation at the American Bar Association Employment Rights & Responsibilities Committee Midwinter Meeting, San Juan, Puerto Rico.

Chan, D. K. S., Lam, C. B., Chow, S. Y., & Cheung, S. F. (2008). Examining the job-related, psychological, and physical outcomes of workplace sexual harassment: A meta-analytic review. *Psychology of Women Quarterly, 32*, 362–376.

Civil Rights Act of 1964, 42 U.S.C. §2000e et seq., as amended (1964).

Civil Rights Act of 1991, Pub. L. No. 102–106, §106 (1991).

Clermont, K. M., & Schwab, S. J. (2009). Employment discrimination plaintiffs in federal court: From bad to worse? *Harvard Law and Policy Review, 3*, 103–132.

Colvin, A. J. S. (2011). An empirical study of employment arbitration: Case outcomes and processes. *Journal of Empirical Legal Studies, 8*, 1–23.

Daubert v. Merrell Dow Pharmaceuticals, Inc., 509 U.S. 579 (1993).

Drukteinis, A. M. (2011, March). *Psychiatric opinions in employment stress claims.* Presentation at the American Bar Association Employment Rights & Responsibilities Committee Midwinter Meeting, San Juan, Puerto Rico.

Fisher v. S.W. Bell Tel. Co., 361 F. App. 974 (10th Cir. 2010).

Fitzgerald, L. F., Drasgow, F., Hulin, C. L., Gelfand, M., & Magley, V. J. (1997). Antecedents and consequences of sexual harassment in organizations: A test of an integrated model. *Journal of Applied Psychology, 82,* 578–589.

Foote, W. E., & Goodman-Delahunty, J. (2005). *Evaluating sexual harassment: Psychological, social, and legal considerations in forensic evaluations.* Washington, DC: American Psychological Association.

Foote, W. E., & Lareau, C. R. (in press). Psychological evaluation of emotional damages in tort cases. In I. B. Weiner & A. Goldstein (Eds.), *Handbook of psychology, Volume 11, Forensic psychology* (2nd ed.). New York: John Wiley & Sons, Ltd.

Fox v. Gates Corp., 179 F.R.D. 303, 307 (D. Colo. 1998).

Friedman, J. (2006, June). *Proof of emotional pain and suffering damages in employment discrimination cases.* Presentation at the National Employment Law Association Conference, Palm Springs, California.

Friedman, J. (2008a, March). *Compensatory damages, punitive damages and remittitur under federal, NY State and NY City Law.* Presentation at the National Employment Law Association Conference, New York, NY.

Friedman, J. (2008b, October). *Damages: Maximizing your client's recovery representing workers in harassment & retaliation claims.* Presentation at the National Employment Law Association Conference, Chicago, IL.

Genetic Information Nondiscrimination Act of 2008. Pub.L.110–233,122 Stat. 881 (2008).

Gilbert, G. M. (2011). *Compensatory damages and other remedies in federal sector employment discrimination cases* (4th ed.). Arlington, VA: Dewey Publications, Inc.

Goodman-Delahunty, J., & Foote, W. E. (1995). Compensation for pain, suffering and other psychological injuries: The impact of *Daubert* on employment discrimination claims. *Behavioral Sciences & the Law, 13,* 183–206.

Goodman-Delahunty, J., & Foote, W. E. (2009). Forensic evaluations advance scientific theory: Assessing causation of harm. *Pragmatic Case Studies in Psychotherapy,5,* 38–52.

Goodman-Delahunty, J., & Foote, W. E. (2011). *Evaluation for workplace discrimination and harassment.* New York: Oxford.

Greene, R. (2011) *The MMPI-2/MMPI-RF: An interpretive manual.* New York: Allyn & Bacon.

Greeson, M. R., Bybee, D., & Raja, S. (2008). The co-occurrence of childhood sexual abuse, adult sexual assault, intimate partner violence, and sexual harassment: A mediational model of posttraumatic stress disorder and physical health outcomes. *Journal of Consulting and Clinical Psychology, 76,* 194–207.

Gruber, J. E., & Smith, M. D. (1995). Women's responses to sexual harassment: A multivariate analysis. *Basic and Applied Social Psychology, 17,* 543–562.

Guthrie, R., Taplin, R., & Oliver, J. (2009). Workplace harassment—A health issue: Anti-discrimination cases and workers' compensation claims. *International Journal of Discrimination and the Law, 10,* 163–190.

Harris v. Forklift Systems, Inc., 510 U.S. 17 (1993).

Heilbrun, K. (2001) *Principles of forensic mental health assessment.* New York: Kluwer Academic

Heilbrun, K., Rosenfeld, B., Warren, J. I., & Collins, S. (1994). The use of third-party information in forensic assessments: A two state comparison. *Bulletin of the American Academy of Psychiatry & Law, 22,* 399–406.

Heilbrun, K., Warren, J., & Picarello, K. (2004). Third party information in forensic assessment. In A.M. Goldstein (Ed.), *Handbook of psychology: Forensic psychology* (pp. 69–86). Hoboken, NJ: John Wiley & Sons.

Hershcovis, M. S., & Barling, J. (2010). Comparing victim attributions and outcomes for workplace aggression and sexual harassment. *Journal of Applied Psychology, 95,* 874–888.

Hickling, E. J., & Blanchard, E. B. (2006). *Overcoming the trauma of your motor vehicle accident: A cognitive behavioral treatment program, Therapist guide.* New York, NY: Oxford University Press.

Hoobler, J. M., Rospenda, K. M., Lemmon, G., & Rosa, J. (2010). A within-subject longitudinal study of the effects of positive job experiences and generalized workplace harassment on well-being. *Journal of Occupational Health Psychology, 15,* 434–451.

Howard v. Burns Bros., Inc., 149 F.3d 835 (8th Cir. 1998).

Hucko v. City of Oak Forest, 185 F.R.D. 526, 529 (N.D. Ill. 1999).

Jumper, S. A. (1995). A meta-analysis of the relationship of child sexual abuse to adult psychological adjustment. *Child Abuse & Neglect, 19,* 715–728.

Kankam v. Univ. of Kansas Hospital Authority, US Dist. LEXIS 73318 (D. Kan. 2008).

Kessler, R. C., Sonnega, A., Bromet, E., Hughes, M., et al. (1995). Posttraumatic stress disorder in the National Comorbidity Survey. *Archives of General Psychiatry. 52,* 1048–1060.

Kessler, R. C., Zhao, S., Blazer, D. G., & Swartz, M. (1997). Prevalence, correlates, and course of minor depression and major depression in the National Comorbidity Survey. *Journal of Affective Disorders, 45,* 19–30.

Kokenge, P. (2011, August). *Compensatory damages.* Presentation at the EEOC Institute Excel Conference, Baltimore Maryland.

Komesar, N. K. (1990). Injuries and institutions: Tort reform, tort theory, and beyond. *New York University Law Review, 65,* 23–77.

Kumho Tire Co. v. Carmichael, 526 U.S. 137 (1999).

Lapierre, L., Spector, P., & Leck, J. (2005). Sexual vs. non-sexual workplace aggression and victims' overall job satisfaction: A meta-analysis. *Journal of Occupational Health Psychology, 10,* 155–169.

Lee, D. L., & Ahn, S. (2011). Racial discrimination and Asian mental health: A meta-analysis. *Counseling Psychologist, 39,* 463–489.

McGinley, M., Richman, J. A., & Rospenda, K. M. (2011). Duration of sexual harassment and generalized harassment in the workplace over ten years: Effects on deleterious drinking outcomes. *Journal of Addictive Diseases, 30,* 229–242.

Miller v. Alldata Corp, 14 Fed. Appx. 457 (6th Cir. 2001).

Millon, T. (1994). *Millon clinical multiaxial inventory manual* (3rd ed.). Minneapolis, MN: National Computer Systems.

Miner v. City of Glen Falls, 999 F.2d 655, 663 (2d Cir. 1993).

Morey, L. C. (2007). *Personality Assessment Inventory professional manual* (2nd ed.). Lutz, FL: Psychological Assessment Resources.

Moss, S. A., & Huang, P. H. (2009). How the new economics can improve discrimination law, and how economics can survive the demise of the "rational actor." *William and Mary Law Review, 51,* 183–259.

Nates, J. H., Kimball, C. D., Axelrod, D. T., Goldstein, R. P., & Conason, R. L. (2007). *Damages in tort actions.* Newark, NJ: MatthewBender.

Neumann, D. A., Houskamp, B. M., Pollock, V. E., & Briere, J. (1996). The long-term sequelae of childhood sexual abuse in women: A meta-analytic review. *Child Maltreatment: Journal of the American Professional Society on the Abuse of Children, 1,* 6–16.

Nielsen, L. B., Nelson, R. L., & Lancaster, R. (2010). Individual justice or collective legal mobilization? Employment discrimination in the post civil rights United States. *Journal of Employment Studies, 7,* 175–201.

O'Connell, J., & Bailey, T. M. (1972). The history of payment for pain and suffering. *University of Illinois Law F, 1,* 83–109.

Paolucci, E. O., Genuis, M. L., & Violato, C. (2001). A meta-analysis of the published research on the effects of child sexual abuse. *Journal of Psychology, 135,* 17–36.

Pascoe, E. A., & Richman, L. (2009). Perceived discrimination and health: a meta-analytic review. *Psychological Bulletin, 135,* 531–554.

Patrolmen's Benevolent Ass'n. v. New York, 310 F.3d 43 (2d Cir. 2002), cert. denied, 123 S. Ct. 2076 (2003).

Paul, K. I., & Moser, K. (2009). Unemployment impairs mental health: Meta-analyses. *Journal of Vocational Behavior, 74,* 264–282.

Pryor, J. B. (1987). Sexual harassment proclivities of men. *Sex Roles, 17,* 269–290.

Psychological Corporation (2008a). *Wechsler Adult Intelligence Scale-IV Technical Manual.* New York: Author.

Pychological Corporation (2008b). *Wechsler Memory Scale-IV Technical Manual.* New York: Author.

Ricks v. Abbott Labs, 198 F.R.D. 647 (D. Md. 2001).

Ritz, S. (2007). Damages in discrimination cases: How to get the most out of your case while re-injuring your client the least (and how to keep the verdict once it's been rendered). In: *Litigating employment discrimination claims* 759 (pp. 353–364). New York: Practicing Law Institute.

Rospenda, K. M., Richman, J. A., & Shannon, C. A. (2009). Prevalence and mental health correlates of harassment and discrimination in the workplace: Results from a national study. *Journal of Interpersonal Violence, 24,* 819–843.

Roth, T., Jaeger, S., Jin, R., Kalsekar, A., Stang, P. E., & Kessler, R. C. (2006). Sleep problems, comorbid mental disorders, and role functioning in the National Comorbidity Survey Replication. *Biological Psychiatry, 60,* 1364–1371.

Rupp v. Purolator Courier Corp., 790 F. Supp. 1069 (D.Kan.1992), aff'd, 45 F.3d 440 (10th Cir. 1994).

Sandomir, R. (2007, December 11). Garden settles harassment case for $11.5 million. *New York Times.* Retrieved from http:// topics.nytimes.com/top/reference/timestopics/people/t/isiah_thomas/index.html

Schlagenhauf v. Holder, 379 U.S. 104 (1964).

Schneider, K. T., Swan, S., & Fitzgerald, L. F. (1997). Job-related and psychological effects of sexual harassment in the workplace: Empirical evidence from two organizations. *Journal of Applied Psychology, 82,* 401–415.

Shannon, C. A., Rospenda, K. M., Richman, J. A., & Minich, L. M. (2009). Race, racial discrimination, and the risk of work-related illness, injury, or assault: findings from a national survey. *Journal of Occupational Environmental Medicine, 51,* 441–448.

Sherrod v. Berry, 629 F. Supp. 159 (N.D. Ill. 1985), aff'd, 827 F.2d 1985 (7th Cir. 1987), *vacated on other grounds and remanded,* 835 F.2d 1222 (7th Cir. 1988).

Studdert, D. M., Kachalia, A. B., Salomon, J. A., & Mello, M. M. (2011). Rationalizing noneconomic damages: A health utilities approach. *Law & Contemporary Problems, 54,* 47–77.

Swedloff, R., & Huang, P. H. (2010). Tort damages and the new science of happiness. *Indiana Law Journal, 85,* 553–595.

Vore, D. (2006). The disability psychological independent medical evaluation: Case law, ethical issues and procedures. In A. Goldstein (Ed.), *Forensic psychology: Emerging topics and expanding roles* (pp. 489–510). Hoboken, NJ: Wiley and Sons.

Wilkinson, G. S., & Robertson, G. J. (2006) *Wide Range Achievement Test 4 (WRAT4) professional manual.* Lutz, FL: Psychological Assessment Resources.

Willness, C. R., Steel, P., & Lee, K. (2007). A meta-analysis of the antecedents and consequences of workplace sexual harassment. *Personnel Psychology, 60,* 127–162.

Wright, C., & Graham, K. (2007). *Federal practice and procedure.* St. Paul, MN: West Publishing Co.

Zimmerman v. Direct Fed. Credit Union, 262 F.3d 70 (1st Cir. 2001).

14

Evaluation of Workplace Disability

LISA DRAGO PIECHOWSKI

The determination of an individual's eligibility for disability benefits based on a mental health condition is not always a straightforward process. Differences of opinion may arise between the claimant and the entity responsible for awarding benefits. The resolution of such disputes may require input from an independent evaluator, such as a forensic psychologist or psychiatrist, to help clarify the nature and validity of the claimant's condition and its effect on the claimant's work capacity. This chapter is directed toward lawyers who are involved in this process, either as advocates for the claimant or as advisors to the entity providing benefits, to assist them in better understanding best practices of psychological evaluations in this context. It is hoped that this information will assist attorneys in making the most effective use of these evaluations.

LEGAL CONTEXT

The term "disability" has a variety of meanings, both clinical and legal. Likewise, being designated as disabled has important implications for the individual in terms of entitlement to benefits, conferring legally protected rights, securing educational opportunities, or, conversely, in limiting the individual's access to certain activities or pursuits. Legal determinations of disability occur in the context of employment rights (e.g., Americans with Disabilities Act), educational access (e.g., Individuals with Disabilities Education Act), and entitlement to monetary compensation resulting from an inability to work. This chapter will focus on the evaluation of disability with respect to the latter context: the determination of an individual's eligibility to receive disability insurance benefits. Such benefits may be sought from a number of different sources, depending on the circumstances of the claimant. These sources include private disability insurance

policies, public- and private-sector employee benefits, federal entitlement programs, and worker's compensation. Each source of benefits is controlled by a different body of law, which delineates, to a greater or lesser extent, the definition of disability, the process of claims evaluation, and the avenues available for dispute resolution.

Individual Disability Insurance

A disability insurance policy is a contract between the policyholder and the insurance company. In exchange for premiums paid by the policyholder, the insurance company agrees to provide a monetary benefit in the event that the insured party becomes disabled as defined under the terms of the policy. Although policies differ, a common definition of disability includes the inability to perform the substantial and material duties of one's own occupation due to sickness or injury that occurs while the policy is in effect. Thus, a valid disability claim requires both the substantiation of the presence of a condition as well as proof that this condition creates impairment in the functional abilities of the claimant to perform his or her occupation.

Private disability insurance policies purchased by individuals must be distinguished from disability benefits provided by an employer as part of an employee's health benefits. Private disability insurance is regulated by state law. The state with jurisdiction is usually determined by the current residence of the claimant. With private disability insurance, a claimant who is denied benefits or whose claim has been terminated can request an appeal of the decision by the company. If this decision is unfavorable to the claimant, the claimant can initiate legal proceedings in the form of a civil action against the company. Such cases may be heard in state courts, or when the policyholder and the insurance company are from different states, and the amount in dispute exceeds $75,000, the matter may be removed to federal court.

Group Disability Insurance

Group disability coverage provided as part of an employee's health care benefits is governed by the Employee Retirement Income Security Act of 1974 (ERISA). Thus, in cases involving employer-paid benefits, ERISA preempts state laws (*Pilot Life Insurance Company v. Dedeaux*, 1987). ERISA establishes a set of administrative procedures that must be followed in the event of a dispute between the claimant and the company. These procedures include specific timelines and an internal appeals process. Only when this process has been exhausted does the claimant have the right to proceed to litigation. The only evidence that can be presented in an ERISA case is the administrative record that was assembled during the appeal process and relied upon by the claims reviewer. There are two standards under which this evidence can be reviewed. The *arbitrary and capricious standard* relates to whether the denial of the claim was rational and based on fact or if the denial was an "abuse of discretion." Alternatively, a *de novo standard* may be applied. When the latter standard is used, the court sets aside the original decision and makes its own decision based on a fresh review of the evidence.

The U.S. Supreme Court in *Firestone Tire & Rubber Company v. Bruch* (1989) ruled that the *de novo* standard must be used unless the benefit plan documents specifically granted the plan administrator discretion to interpret the plan eligibility for benefits. Subsequently, in *Metropolitan Life Insurance Company et al. v. Glenn* (2008), the Court affirmed the principles set out in *Firestone* in determining the appropriate standard of judicial review. The *Glenn* Court also addressed the conflict of interest that exists when the benefit administrator (i.e., the entity that decides the claim) also funds the plan's benefits. The Court ruled that this conflict of interest must be considered in the court's review of claim denials.

Social Security Disability

Social Security disability is regulated by a vast body of law comprising statutory law, regulatory law, rulings, and court decisions. As described in the Social Security Act (42 U.S.C. § 423) and the Code of Federal Regulations (20 C.F.R. §§ 404.1500-404.1599), and upheld by the U.S. Supreme Court

in decisions including *Heckler v. Campbell* (1983) and *Bowen v. Yuckert* (1987), determination of disability follows a prescribed evaluation process. The Social Security Act's definition of disability requires the claimant to show a medically determinable physical or mental impairment that must be expected to result in death or to last for at least 12 months. The burden of proof of disability rests with the claimant. Once a claimant is determined to be disabled, termination of benefits on the grounds that the person is no longer disabled must rest on affirmative evidence that the individual's condition has improved. The burden of proof for termination of benefits rests with the state agency.

In terms of mental disorders, the Social Security Administration (SSA) defines specific diagnostic categories and provides the criteria used to substantiate both the presence of the disorder and the associated functional limitations. Although substance addiction is listed in the diagnostic categories, Title II of the Social Security Act was amended in 1996 such that Social Security disability benefits were terminated to individuals disabled primarily by drug addiction and alcoholism. Thus, a person with substance addiction is eligible for benefits only if he or she is also disabled due to other medical or mental health problems.

Worker's Compensation

The purpose of worker's compensation is to provide for workers who become ill or are injured on the job. Worker's compensation is a "no fault" system intended to reduce the need for litigation. Benefits are fixed and limited by statute, and include medical treatment and compensation for lost wages. Worker's compensation benefits are handled differently in each state and are governed by statutes, case law, and administrative practices. Claims for worker's compensation benefits may be contested by the employer, and denial of benefits may be appealed by the employee. In most states, worker's compensation disputes are decided by special administrative agencies utilizing administrative law judges. Although these administrative decisions may be appealed to the state court system, the scope for possible litigation of worker's compensation disputes is limited.

Litigation of Disability Disputes

Legal remedies available to address disability disputes are determined by the source of benefits.

Litigation options are statutorily defined in worker's compensation, Social Security disability, and employer-paid benefit cases and are limited to the initiation of benefits, the reinstatement of terminated benefits, and/or the retroactive payment of past-due benefits. Broader alternatives are available in individual disability insurance cases, and may include claims for punitive damages as well as claims for past and future benefits. Given this diversity of laws that govern disability benefits, it is difficult to identify key cases applicable to all sources of benefits. Some of the core questions courts have addressed include establishing the existence of a factual disability, determination of occupation, and risk of disability/risk of relapse.

To meet the relevant definition of disability, the claimant must demonstrate that it is illness or injury that prevents him or her from working (a factual disability) as distinguished from social or legal disabilities, in which the inability to work is the result of circumstantial factors such as incarceration, the loss of a professional license, or adverse publicity. *Massachusetts Mutual Life Insurance Company v. Ouellette* (1992) provides an example of such a case. In this Vermont case, an optometrist was charged with lewd and lascivious conduct with a minor. He lost his license to practice optometry and was incarcerated. He then filed a claim for total disability benefits, asserting he suffered from the mental disorder pedophilia, which prevented him from performing the duties of his occupation. It was noted that Ouellette had suffered from this disorder for more than 10 years prior to his arrest, and that he had never sought treatment until after being arrested. Despite the disorder, he had continued to practice optometry until prevented from doing so by the loss of his license and incarceration. The court supported Mass Mutual's denial of Ouellette's claim for benefits.

The presence of legal or social impediments does not negate the possibility of a factual disability, however. Consider, for example, the Ninth Circuit's decision in *Damascus v. Provident Life and Accident Insurance Company* (1996). Damascus, a dentist, had his license to practice placed on probation and later revoked based on mental illness, inappropriate care of patients, negligence, and unprofessional conduct. Provident denied the claim, asserting that Damascus was legally disabled due to the actions of the State Dental Board. The trial court granted Provident's motion for summary judgment, but on appeal, the Ninth Circuit Court reversed and remanded, noting that there was a dispute of fact as to whether the loss of his license was due to Damascus's being mentally incompetent to practice.

Another issue that has been the focus of litigation is determining the occupation of the claimant. As noted previously, disability relates to the capacity to perform the duties of one's occupation. Thus, identifying the specific occupation and the associated duties is critical in determining eligibility for benefits. Most policies define "own occupation" as the occupation the claimant was performing at the onset of the disability claim. In *Emerson v. Fireman's Fund* (1982), the Eleventh Circuit court noted, "When an insured changes occupations, it is his occupation at the time of disability, not at the time the policy went into effect that controls" (p. 1267). Disputes may arise when the claimant's most recent work activities vary from the duties performed at the time the policy was purchased, when the claimant's occupational duties are atypical for the occupation, when the claimant is engaged in more than one occupation, or when the claimant has a particular specialty within an occupation.

Disputes may also arise when a claimant has recovered or his or her symptoms are in remission, but he or she remains out of work due to risk of relapse or risk of disability. This is often seen in disability cases related to cardiac conditions and in cases related to substance abuse. In the Third Circuit Court, *Lasser v. Reliance Standard Life Insurance Company* (2003), Lasser, an orthopedic surgeon, sought disability benefits due to a significant cardiac condition after his doctors warned him that the stress of performing surgery could aggravate his condition. The court found for Lasser, noting that, as long as there was a "medically unacceptable risk" of a future heart attack or death, Lasser was entitled to benefits.

In risk-of-relapse cases related to substance abuse, the direction of the court has been less clear (Vore, 2007). A number of risk-of-relapse cases have concerned anesthesiologists who became addicted to the opioid medications used in the operating room. In most of these cases, the claimant has successfully completed a course of treatment and has maintained abstinence for an extended period of time. The claimant seeks to extend disability benefits due to fears that relapse would occur if he or she were to return to the operating room and had access to the substances in question. The insurance company asserts that the claimant's condition is in remission and that there are no active symptoms that impair the claimant's functioning. Courts have tended to base rulings on what is judged to be the imminent risk of relapse of the claimant.

In *Laucks v. Provident Companies* (1997), an anesthesiologist who had maintained abstinence for a period of five years was denied disability benefits when he returned to work as a physician in another specialty. In finding for Provident, the court noted that Laucks evinced no continuing cognitive or motor impairments, and there was no evidence that Laucks was unable to control his addiction, given his five-year abstinence.

In *Holzer v. MBL Life Assurance Corporation* (1999), a different conclusion was reached. Holzer, an anesthesiologist, had a sustained recovery from opioid addiction. He had been advised by his treatment providers, however, not to return to work in anesthesiology, due to risk of relapse. His claim for disability benefits was denied. The court, in denying summary judgment, reasoned that factual issues existed regarding the problems and risks to patients in the operating room, as well as the potential harm to Holzer if he returned to work and relapsed.

FORENSIC MENTAL HEALTH CONCEPTS

Regardless of the source of disability benefits, decisions about whether a claimant is entitled to benefits are based on the definition of disability as articulated in the relevant policy language, statutes, regulations, and case law. A standard definition of disability refers to the inability to perform the substantial and material occupational duties due to sickness or injury. Therefore, the ultimate disability decision is based on an assessment of the claimant's work capacity in the context of the applicable legal framework. In some cases, the information obtained in the course of the claim evaluation process may yield insufficient or conflicting data. There may be questions about the nature of the claimant's condition or the extent to which this condition impairs the claimant's ability to perform his or her occupational duties. In the case of a disability claim related to a mental health diagnosis, an independent medical examination (IME) may be sought from a licensed psychologist or psychiatrist.

It is important to understand the role of the evaluator and the nature of the information the evaluation can yield. A forensic mental health evaluator is not able to answer the ultimate-issue question: Does the claimant meet the legal definition of disability? Although the evaluator may be able to assess the clinical aspects of the claimant's condition and functional capacity, disability determinations are ultimately legal ones, requiring an analysis of the relevant contract language, statutes, and/or regulations. Thus, the task for the forensic evaluator is to provide relevant psychological data that will assist the adjudicator in rendering a decision. To accomplish this, the evaluation data must be converted from psychological concepts into constructs related to the definition of disability. This linkage between the legal and the clinical aspects of forensic work has been termed "forensic mental health concepts" (Heilbrun, 2001). These concepts form the bridge between the legal definitions of disability and the mental health data that are within the purview of the forensic evaluator.

The process of disability evaluation flows from the legal definition of disability. The definition is composed of standards, each of which must be met in order for the claimant to be adjudicated as disabled. Most legal definitions of disability include three elements: the presence of a condition; the inability to perform work duties; and the causal connection between condition and work incapacity. When a forensic disability evaluation is sought, these legal standards must be translated into specific questions that can be addressed by the evaluator. These referral questions communicate to the forensic evaluator the specific issues that should be answered through the evaluation.

A key component of any forensic evaluation is an analysis of functional capacity. Grisso (2003) has defined functional capacity as that which an individual can do or accomplish, as well as the knowledge, understanding, or beliefs that may be necessary for that accomplishment. Functional capacity is distinct from psychiatric diagnosis and is shaped by the specific context (situational demands). In an evaluation of disability, the relevant functional capacities are those corresponding to the duties of the claimant's occupation.

Although the claimant must have a valid illness or injury to qualify for disability benefits, the claimant's diagnosis is not dispositive of his or her functioning. It cannot be assumed that the presence of a particular condition is necessarily related to a specific level of functioning. There is no mental disorder that precludes all types of functioning. In addition, two individuals with the same diagnosis might function quite differently. Thus it is more useful for the evaluator to directly observe functional abilities than to rely on inferences based on diagnosis or symptoms. However, functional impairments alone are insufficient to determine disability status: deficits in functioning must be causally related to the presence of a mental disorder.

Impairment has been defined as a "significant deviation, loss or loss of use of any body structure or body function in an individual with a health condition, disorder, or disease" (American Medical Association, 2008, p. 5). Impairment is both observable and measurable. It is causally related to a health condition, but it is distinct from symptoms. Leo and Del Regno (2001) noted that a common error made by clinicians is failing to distinguish between subjective symptom report and clinically observed data. Because impairment is defined in terms of a loss of function, the presence of a mental health disorder does not determine the existence or explain the nature of any impairment. Impairment also does not determine work incapacity, as the significance of any impairment in functioning can be determined only in relation to the occupational demands of the claimant.

Disability can be conceptualized as an interaction between the functional abilities of the claimant and the demands of the claimant's occupation. When the demands of the job exceed the claimant's functional abilities, the claimant's work capacity would be inadequate. On the other hand, the claimant's work capacity would be adequate if his or her functional abilities met or exceeded the demands of the job. Gold and Shuman (2009) proposed this as a function of "supply and demand," with "supply" referring to the claimant's functional ability and "demand" to the requirements of the job.

The claimant's occupational demands are determined by the specific duties of his or her job. Every job has a distinctive set of core and peripheral occupational duties. Core duties are typically listed in an employee's job description. These duties are so vital to the performance of the job that, if they are not performed, the very nature of the job would significantly change. Peripheral duties, on the other hand, are duties that may be performed in the course of the job, but are not essential. In other words, peripheral duties could be changed or eliminated without altering the meaning of the job itself.

Just as job duties form the basis of the occupation, functional abilities can be thought of as the building blocks of job duties. Functional abilities are observable and measurable. Identifying and assessing relevant functional abilities is a central component of a disability evaluation. For the purpose of a psychological disability evaluation, functional abilities can be divided into three broad domains: cognitive demands, interpersonal demands, and emotional demands. *Cognitive demands* include areas such as concentration, memory, comprehension, expression, processing, and problem solving. *Interpersonal demands* involve the ability to engage in appropriate interactions with coworkers, supervisors, and the public. *Emotional demands* focus on areas such as stress tolerance, emotional control, mood stability, and judgment. By examining the job description and related information, the forensic evaluator can determine the demands required to perform the core job duties in question and the level of ability needed to meet these demands. This allows the evaluator to decide how to measure the claimant's functional capacity in each area.

To summarize, in assessing disability, the forensic evaluator must begin by establishing the existence of a condition and identifying the symptoms and manifestations of this condition that are present in the claimant. The claimant's individual job duties must be determined and translated into measurable functional capacities. This allows the forensic evaluator to provide the claims adjudicator with data relevant to rendering a determination of disability by linking the psychological condition and symptoms to the claimant's capacity to perform his or her occupational duties. These links between condition, symptoms, functional capacity, and occupational duties must be clearly established and logically connected.

EMPIRICAL FOUNDATIONS AND LIMITS
Mental Health and Work Disability

Although most individuals with mental health disorders are able to work, emotional and cognitive impairments can interfere significantly with their vocational performance. According to the National Health Interview Survey, 16.2 million working-age people (i.e., 10.5% of the population between the ages of 18 and 64) have a work limitation (Stoddard, Jans, Ripple, & Kraus, 1998). The Current Population Survey estimated that 34% of work disabilities limit the kind or amount of work that can be done, while 66% of those with work disabilities are unable to work at all (Stoddard et al., 1998). Mental disorders account for 4.9% of these work disabilities (Stoddard et al., 1998). The National Institute of Mental Health (2001) estimated that 22.1% of Americans ages 18 and older (about 44.3 million people) suffer from a diagnosable mental disorder in a given year.

Major depression is the leading cause of disability in the United States for ages 15 to 44 (NIMH, 2001). It affects almost 10 million American adults each year, and about twice as many women as men. Depression can have a significant impact on work functioning. Specific impairments in occupational functioning related to depression have been identified. A longitudinal study comparing patients with depression to those with rheumatoid arthritis and to healthy individuals found depression-related impairments affected those individuals' performance of mental-interpersonal tasks, time management, output tasks, and physical tasks. These functional deficits persisted even after an improvement in clinical symptoms, such that clinical improvement did not result in full recovery of job performance (Adler et al., 2006). Mildly impaired executive functions were found in another study, including impaired verbal fluency, inhibition, working memory, set-maintenance, and set-shifting (Stordal et al., 2004). Depressed persons were found to spend more days in bed than people with chronic medical conditions such as hypertension, diabetes, and arthritis (Wells et al., 1989).

It has been estimated that as many as 80% of people with depression can be treated effectively, generally without missing much time from work or needing costly hospitalization (U.S. Department of Health & Human Services, 1999). Effective treatments for depression include medication, psychotherapy, or a combination of both. These treatments usually begin to relieve symptoms in a matter of weeks. Unfortunately, the use of antidepressant medications (specifically SSRIs) was found to be associated with impaired episodic memory and poorer recognition memory (Wadsworth, Moss, Simpson, & Smith, 2005).

Bipolar disorder has been described as a chronic, relapsing condition (Tse & Walsh, 2001). Less common than major depression, bipolar I disorder has a lifetime prevalence of 3.3% and bipolar II disorder has a lifetime prevalence of 1.1% (Hasin et al., 2005). Bipolar disorder affects about 1.2% of American adults each year, affecting both men and women equally (NIMH, 2001). The average age of onset for the first manic episode is in the twenties. According to one study, in addition to episodes of mania, 79.5% of those diagnosed with bipolar disorder had also experienced at least one clinically significant episode of depression. The most frequent symptoms reported for manic episodes were elevated or irritable mood (95.5%), excessive activity (93.7%), racing thoughts (91.1%), and reduced need for sleep (90.2%). The symptoms most frequently appearing in depressive episodes were dysphoria with anhedonia (79.5%), suicidal ideation (78.6%), loss of energy (68.7%), poor concentration (64.3%), initial insomnia (58.0%), and diminished libido (58.9%). Over 85.7% reported at least one episode of delusional thinking, with the majority of these episodes lasting less than a week (Morgan et al., 2005).

Hammen, Gitlin, and Altshuler (2000) observed that there is dramatic variability in the work functioning of bipolar patients. Tse and Walsh (2001) noted that employment rates tend to be low compared with that of the general population. They reviewed 10 studies examining employment rates of individuals with bipolar disorder, finding employment rates ranging from 27% to 72%. The effect of cognitive factors on the functioning of individuals with bipolar disorder has been explored in a number of studies. Assessing functioning across manic, hypomanic, depressed, and euthymic states, Martinez-Aran et al. (2004) found that patients with bipolar disorder tended to perform more poorly than normal controls on measures of verbal memory and executive functions. Comparing patients with bipolar disorder in depressed versus euthymic states, Martinez-Aran et al. (2004) found that the depressed group demonstrated poorer verbal fluency. Borkowska and Rybakowski (2001) compared the cognitive functioning of bipolar depressed patients and unipolar depressed patients. The bipolar patients had a higher degree of frontal lobe–related dysfunction than did the unipolar patients. This included poorer visual-spatial and visual-motor abilities. These findings were unrelated to the intensity of the depressive symptoms. MacQueen et al. (2007) found that bipolar patients who had undergone treatment with electroconvulsive therapy (ECT) had greater deficits in aspects of learning and memory than did bipolar patients who had no history of ECT.

Martinez-Aran et al. (2004) looked at how bipolar patients functioned in between active episodes: in others words, they explored the gap between clinical recovery and functional recovery. They found that low-functioning patients had higher levels of cognitive dysfunction, which was independent of illness severity. Lower-functioning patients were found to perform worse on measures of verbal memory and executive function. Thompson et al. (2007) explored the cognitive functioning of bipolar patients during periods of remission, finding deficits in the executive control of working memory—that is, the inability to monitor the contents of working memory. Malhi et al. (2007) found support for the persistence of cognitive deficits beyond the remission of symptoms, including changes in attention and memory that were correlated with psychosocial functioning.

Anxiety disorders include, among others, panic disorder, obsessive-compulsive disorder (OCD), posttraumatic stress disorder (PTSD), generalized anxiety disorder, and agoraphobia. Anxiety disorders affect about 13.3% of American adults between the ages of 18 and 54 each year (NIMH, 2001) and often accompany other mental disorders, including depression, eating disorders, and substance abuse. Women are more likely than men to suffer from anxiety disorders. Individuals with anxiety disorders, including panic disorder, generalized anxiety disorder, social phobia, and OCD, had significantly higher work disability than control subjects (Kennedy et al., 2002). Panic disorder with agoraphobia was associated with severely impaired work efficacy, primarily related to avoidant behavior (Latas et al., 2004). Untreated OCD has been associated with higher rates of unemployment and decreased work productivity (Fireman et al., 2001). Other studies have investigated cognitive dysfunction among patients with OCD, including deficits in executive functioning, information processing, visuospatial memory, and verbal fluency (Cohen, Lachenmeyer, & Springer, 2003; Greisberg & McKay, 2003).

PTSD has been studied extensively. According to the DSM-IV-TR, the diagnosis of PTSD requires exposure to a traumatic event in which the person experienced, witnessed, or was confronted with an event or events that involved actual or threatened death or serious injury, or threat to the physical integrity of the self or others; and that the person's response involved intense fear, helplessness, or horror. It has been estimated that one third of the population will be exposed to a trauma of this nature at some point in their lives (Brunello et al., 2001). Among those exposed to such events, most people will not develop PTSD. Brunello et al. noted that only 10% to 20% of people exposed to severe trauma develop PTSD. In situations involving compensation, however, rates of reported PTSD are significantly higher. Rosen (2004), for example, noted that rates of 86% had been reported in the context of a maritime accident. Koch, O'Neill, and Douglas (2005) reported that approximately 50% of those suffering from PTSD have a spontaneous remission of symptoms in the first year; however, as many as 10% of those with PTSD stay chronically distressed. Work impairment associated with PTSD includes high levels of depression, reduced time-management ability, over-concern or anxiety with physical injuries, impaired memory, decreased concentration, and reduced motivation (Taylor et al., 2006).

Substance abuse and dependence tend to have a negative effect on work functioning. Those with alcohol abuse disorders tend to have lower earnings than other workers. This may be attributed, at least in part, to the fact that those with alcohol use disorders tend to miss more work time (Mullahy & Sindelar, 1993). In addition, Lehman and Bennett (2002) noted that research had found that employee substance use was associated with an increased likelihood of job-related accidents, absenteeism, tardiness, negative work behaviors, and acts of workplace deviance such as vandalism and theft. In addition, alcohol abuse and dependence have been associated with significant cognitive impairments. Harper (2007), for example, found that even uncomplicated alcoholics showed signs of structural changes in the brain and cognitive dysfunction. Duka et al. (2003) found that repeated withdrawal from alcohol was associated with cognitive impairments related to frontal lobe function. Impaired performance on cognitive tasks sensitive to frontal lobe damage was found in those with relatively mild alcoholism compared to social drinkers.

Work issues become particularly difficult to sort out when the addiction is to a substance present in the claimant's work environment. Such is the case with anesthesiologists who become addicted to anesthetic drugs such as fentanyl, a highly potent opioid analgesic up to 800 times more potent than morphine (Gold et al., 2006). Gold et al. noted that while only 5.6% of the licensed physicians in Florida are anesthesiologists, nearly 25% of the physicians being followed for substance abuse or addictions practice this specialty. In addition, anesthesiologists account for 75% of the physicians addicted to fentanyl. As the work of an anesthesiologist requires access to and work with fentanyl and similar substances, this creates a heightened possibility of relapse. Gallegos et al. (1992) found that failure to complete or to continue to participate in a recovery program contributed to relapse. Among those who participate in and complete programs for impaired physicians, the recovery rate is generally high (Bohigian et al., 1996).

Methodology and Procedures of Disability Evaluation

Psychologists frequently utilize data from psychological or neuropsychological testing when evaluating disability claimants. However, there is no one protocol or approach recommended in the literature for evaluating disability. Heilbrun (1992) suggested selecting tests based on consideration of the following factors: (a) commercial availability and adequate documentation in two sources; (b) a reliability coefficient of .80 or greater; and (c) relevance to the legal issue or to the psychological issue underlying the legal issue. Marlowe (1995) suggested the following criteria for test selection in forensic evaluations: (a) support in the literature; (b) having items that address all relevant content domains; (c) standard administration procedures and justified norms; and (d) reasoning that validly links data to conclusions.

One way to address whether a given test should be used is by considering the frequency with which that test has been utilized in forensic evaluations according to published surveys (Kane, 2008). Boccaccini and Brodsky (1999) surveyed 80 psychologists regarding tests used in emotional injury cases. The Minnesota Multiphasic Personality Inventory (MMPI) was the most frequently used instrument (used in 89% of emotional injury cases), followed by the Wechsler Adult Intelligence Scale (WAIS) (50%), the Millon Clinical Multiaxial Inventory (MCMI) (39%), the Rorschach (28%), the Brief Symptom Inventory (18%), the Trauma Symptom Inventory (15%), the Symptom Checklist-90 (14%), the Structured Interview of Reported Symptoms (SIRS) (11%), the Personality Assessment Inventory (PAI) (11%), the Halstead-Reitan (7%),

and the Thematic Apperception Test (TAT) (3%). An average of 4.83 tests per evaluation was used.

Lally (2003) surveyed 64 psychologists about the frequency of their use of various tests and their opinions about the acceptability of test usage in six different areas of forensic practice (mental status at time of offense, risk for violence, risk for sexual violence, competence to stand trial, *Miranda* waiver, and malingering psychopathology). In terms of malingering psychopathology, the following tests were deemed "recommended": the MMPI-2 (64%) and SIRS (58%). "Acceptable" tests were the MMPI-2 (92%), SIRS (89%), WAIS-III (75%), Rey (68%), PAI (53%), Validity Indicator Profile (VIP) (53%), and Halstead-Reitan (51%). Tests considered "unacceptable" were projective drawings (89%), sentence completion (72%), TAT (72%), 16PF (66%), and the Rorschach (55%).

Archer, Buffington-Vollum, Stredney, and Handel (2006) surveyed 152 psychologists about test usage in forensic evaluations. The most frequently used tests, by category, were the MMPI (multiscale inventories), the Beck Depression Inventory (clinical scales), the Rorschach (unstructured personality tests), the WAIS (cognitive and achievement tests), and the Halstead-Reitan (neuropsychological tests). In terms of instruments used to assess malingering, the SIRS and the Test of Memory Malingering (TOMM) were used most frequently.

Disability evaluations, like other forensic evaluations, should include an assessment of the credibility of the claimant's presentation. Estimates of the base rate of dissimulation in disability evaluations vary widely. Mittenberg et al. (2002) examined the rate of probable malingering and symptom exaggeration through a survey of the American Board of Clinical Neuropsychology membership. Based on a review of 3,688 disability cases, the rate of malingering or symptom exaggeration was found to be 30%. In a review of the literature, Samuel and Mittenberg (2005) reported that estimates of the base rate for malingering ranged from 7.5% to 33% of disability claimants. They suggested that malingering in disability claims can be motivated by factors such as financial incentives, socioeconomic problems, antisocial acts or behavior, career dissatisfaction, or work conflict. It appears to be well established that a certain percentage of disability claimants exaggerate, embellish, or feign their degree of impairment.

Sumanti et al. (2006) investigated the presence of noncredible psychiatric and cognitive symptoms in 233 "stress claim" worker's compensation litigants. They found that between 9% and 29% of the sample were identified as endorsing noncredible psychiatric symptoms using the PAI validity indices. Between 8% and 15% of the sample were documented as displaying noncredible cognitive symptomatology on the Dot Counting Test and the Rey 15-Item Test. Their data also suggested that the occurrence of psychiatric malingering was independent of feigned cognitive symptoms. This supports the notion that multiple detection strategies may be more useful than a single strategy.

Various MMPI-2 validity scales have been identified as being useful in the detection of exaggerated symptomatology. In addition to the more familiar F (infrequency) scale, support has been found for the use of the Fake Bad Scale (FBS) (Larrabee, 2008), the Infrequency Psychopathology scale (Fp) (Arbisi & Ben-Porath, 1995), and the Response Bias Scale (RBS) (Gervais et al., 2007). Each of these scales was developed using a different methodology and for a different specific purpose. The FBS was developed by Lees-Haley et al. (1991) for use with personal injury cases to detect noncredible symptom presentations as expressed in litigation settings. The Fp was developed using items infrequently endorsed by psychiatric inpatients to provide a more accurate index of symptom overreporting (Arbisi, 1995). The RBS was developed by Gervais et al. by identifying MMPI-2 items that were differentially endorsed by individuals passing or failing a measure of cognitive effort, the Word Memory Test.

Specialized methods for the detection of feigned psychopathology include the SIRS, M-FAST, and SIMS. Alwes, Clark, Berry, and Granacher (2008) compared the effectiveness of the SIMS and M-FAST at screening for feigned psychiatric and neurocognitive symptoms in 308 individuals undergoing neuropsychiatric evaluation for worker's compensation or personal injury claims. Both tests showed statistically significant discrimination between probable feigning and honest groups. Both the M-FAST and SIMS had high sensitivity and negative predictive power when discriminating between probable psychiatric feigning versus honest groups, but neither of the procedures was as effective when applied to probable neurocognitive feigners versus honest groups. These results support the use of the M-FAST and SIMS in screening for feigned psychopathology, but not for feigned neurocognitive symptoms.

In terms of standalone measures of cognitive symptom validity, Lynch (2004) reviewed the literature regarding the determination of effort level in forensic neurocognitive assessment. Lynch concluded that there were several effort-level measures that withstood the scrutiny of cross-validation research. These included the Computerized Assessment of Response Bias (CARB), PDRT, TOMM, VIP, Victoria Symptom Validity Test (VSVT), and WMT. Moore and Donders (2004) found that the TOMM and the California Verbal Learning Test-Second Edition (CVLT-II) were useful in assessing invalid test performance in patients with traumatic brain injuries. The results indicated that 15% of the patients performed in the invalid range. Financial compensation seeking and psychiatric history both resulted in an almost fourfold increase in the likelihood of invalid performance on the TOMM or CVLT-II. Rosen and Powell (2003), using a case-study approach, found that forced-choice symptom validity tests such as the Portland Digit Recognition Test could be utilized to detect malingering in claims of PTSD in addition to claims of memory deficits due to brain injury. Flaro, Green, and Robertson (2007) compared performance on the WMT of adults with traumatic brain injury, tested as part of a worker's compensation, disability, or personal injury claim, with the performance of parents ordered by the court to undergo a parenting assessment. Only 60% of those in the first group, who stood to gain financially by appearing impaired on testing, performed credibly on the WMT, while 98% of those in the second group, who were motivated to do their best on testing in order to regain custody of their children, did so.

Support for aggregating results of multiple measures for the detection of dissimulation was demonstrated in a study by Larrabee (2008). The performance of litigants with definite malingering was contrasted with that of nonmalingering patients with moderate and severe traumatic brain injury on five procedures: the Visual Form Discrimination Test, the Finger Tapping Test, Reliable Digit Span, Wisconsin Card Sorting Test Failure to Maintain Set score, and the FBS of the MMPI-2. The data suggested that failures on these instruments provided strong evidence for diagnosis of probable malingering when two were failed, and very strong evidence for probable malingering, if not definite malingering, when three were failed.

THE EVALUATION

Evaluation of disability is a complex process requiring the collection and integration of a large amount of data. The use of multiple sources of data is essential for a comprehensive assessment. Thus, the first step in the IME process is to identify potential data sources and determine appropriate methods of data collection for each source. Typically, data sources include written documents and records, information obtained directly from the claimant, data from psychometric assessment, and information obtained from collateral sources. By utilizing a variety of sources, the evaluator can compare information obtained from each source to obtain a more complete and objective understanding of the claimant's condition and functional capacity.

Prior to meeting with the claimant, the evaluator should review written records pertaining to the disability claim. It is essential that the evaluator be provided with certain critical data, including a detailed job description and medical records relevant to the claimant's reported condition. Additional information, such as past treatment records, claim forms, financial data, investigative reports, and employment records, can assist the evaluator in developing an accurate understanding of the claimant's difficulties and his or her functioning before and after the onset of the claimed disability.

Once the evaluator has had the opportunity to thoroughly review the written documentation, the evaluator can proceed with the face-to-face examination of the claimant. It is essential that the evaluator obtains and documents the claimant's informed consent before beginning any aspect of the examination. The examination usually begins with an interview of the claimant. A thorough interview generally takes a minimum of two or three hours due to the breadth of information that should be covered. In addition to obtaining the claimant's point of view on his or her condition and impairments, this interview also provides the opportunity for the evaluator to observe the claimant's appearance, speech, affect, and behavior, as well as to make an informal assessment of his or her attention, concentration, and memory.

Psychological and/or neuropsychological tests are usually administered following the interview. Test selection should be based on the nature of the claimant's reported impairments, the nature of his or her occupational duties, and the validity and reliability of the test. In general, evaluators should avoid tests that are uncommon or obscure. Tests should never be used for other than their intended purposes, and standard administrative procedures must be followed. This means that all tests must be completed in the evaluator's office and under supervision.

If the claimant is reporting disability as a result of a psychiatric condition, testing should be utilized that provides information helpful in determining the nature and severity of the claimant's condition and the symptoms he or she experiences. Multiscale personality inventories, such as the MMPI-2 and PAI, are particularly useful. They include sophisticated validity scales for the detection of exaggerated or other distorted response sets, as well as facilitating an assessment of a broad range of psychopathology. There is a considerable research base supporting the use of these inventories in forensic settings.

The claimant's cognitive functioning may be at issue in a variety of circumstances. Although some elements of cognitive functioning can be appropriately assessed by clinical psychologists, full neuropsychological assessment batteries should not be undertaken by psychologists who have not had formal education, training, and experience in neuropsychology. Full batteries typically include assessments of intelligence, academic achievement, executive functions, attention and concentration, processing speed, language, visual-spatial skills, motor functioning, sensory functioning, learning, and memory. A full neuropsychological battery is usually called for when the claimant's primary complaints are related to cognitive dysfunction due to traumatic brain injury or an organic condition, such as dementia.

In other circumstances, such as when the claimant indicates he or she is experiencing memory problems related to depression, a full neuropsychological battery might not be necessary. Instead, the evaluator might perform a "cognitive screening" as part of the IME. Depending on the nature of the claimant's complaints, a targeted assessment of the claimant's intellectual functioning or memory or the use of a screening instrument designed to assess a range of cognitive functions might be appropriate. It should be understood that a cognitive screening is not equivalent to a comprehensive neuropsychological battery in terms of scope and detail.

A formal assessment of the claimant's effort and credibility should be included in every disability evaluation. Instruments should be selected on the basis of the claimant's reported impairments. The use of multiple measures is recommended. Psychometric approaches to assessing the authenticity of psychiatric symptoms typically compare the examinee's portrayal of the nature and severity of his or her symptoms to what is known about the course of valid psychiatric conditions. Approaches to detecting feigned cognitive deficits differ from the methods used to evaluate the validity of psychiatric symptoms. These instruments are designed to detect submaximal performance, as evidenced by the claimant deliberately giving incorrect answers, failing to give full attention to tasks, making careless or random responses, or intentionally working at a slower pace.

The next phase of the evaluation is obtaining collateral data from sources familiar with the claimant's condition and functioning. Potential collateral sources include treatment providers, family members, and professional associates of the claimant. The purpose of a collateral interview is not to obtain the collateral's opinion about the claimant's disability status, but to gather relevant observational data from the collateral's perspective. Collateral interviews can be performed in person or over the phone. The claimant's authorization must be obtained before the evaluator contacts any collateral source.

After data collection is completed, the evaluator must analyze and interpret these data prior to formulating his or her opinion. Data interpretation requires an orderly, methodical approach, consistent with the scientific method. Lawyers should expect that the report includes the identification and testing of alternative hypotheses regarding the claimant's condition, functional limitations, and work capacity. Because evaluation data may include conflicting or inconsistent information, there should be evidence that the evaluator gave consideration to the relative weight and validity of these data. Data inconsistencies should not be ignored or discarded, but should be incorporated into the process of hypothesis testing.

In light of the reported base rate of symptom exaggeration in disability evaluations, it is critical that the evaluator attempt to assess the credibility of the claimant's self-report. There appears to be a consensus in the literature that the best way to approach this is by comparing information from a variety of sources, including interviews with the claimant and collaterals, review of clinical records, and psychological test results. A determination of malingering should never be based on psychometric testing alone. It is important to note that the presence of symptom exaggeration does not preclude the simultaneous existence of a valid condition. Some claimants exaggerate the severity of their difficulties in order to ensure that they will be taken seriously. Even when claimants intentionally feign certain symptoms, there may be other (genuine) symptoms, either at a less severe level or of an entirely different nature, that are present.

REPORT WRITING AND TESTIMONY

Although the majority of disability claims do not end up in litigation, disability evaluations, almost without exception, require the creation of a written report. There is no set format for a disability evaluation report, so the evaluator is free to design whatever structure best facilitates the presentation of the relevant material. An ideal report organizes the material in a way that reflects the logical progression of the evaluation process, provides a coherent foundation for the evaluator's opinions, and uses language that is clear and comprehensible to a lay reader. Regardless of the format, the report should include identification of the claimant and the evaluator, a statement documenting that the claimant gave informed consent for the evaluation, and a listing of all the records reviewed, tests administered, and collateral sources interviewed.

Lawyers should expect the report to contain a clear separation of data and opinion. In general, the report should present the data that were collected in the course of the evaluation first, since these data provide the basis for the evaluator's opinion. The records reviewed should be summarized. The interview of the claimant should be described in detail and should include the evaluator's observations of the claimant's presentation and behavior. Psychological and neuropsychological test data should be communicated in a manner that will be easily understood and not misconstrued by the reader. The evaluator should identify individual instruments by name and with a description of what each instrument measures. Terms used to describe the test data, such as "impaired" or "borderline," should be operationally defined. Information obtained from collateral sources should be summarized and attributed to the source.

The formulation presents the evaluator's opinion as it was developed through considering and analyzing all the information collected over the course of the evaluation. Everything needed to understand the formulation should have already been presented in the body of the report. The formulation should be confined to information that is relevant to the purpose of the evaluation as defined by the referral questions. Evaluators should not offer opinions that go beyond the scope of their evaluations or the limits of their expertise. Each referral question should be clearly answered. The basis for each answer should be contained within the body of the report. The response to each question should refer to the report data supporting the answer.

As noted previously in this chapter, disability determinations are ultimately legal matters, requiring an analysis of the relevant contract language, statutes, and/or regulations that define the claimant's eligibility for benefits. The evaluator should not be asked to determine disability, as he or she lacks important information necessary to make this determination. The evaluator should remain focused on describing the claimant's condition, functional capacity, and impairments. It is important to remember that "inability to work" is not the same as "disability." The evaluator may have and express an opinion regarding the claimant's ability to return to work. Questions about work ability ask the evaluator to consider the nature of the claimant's condition and his or her impairments relative to the demands and requirements of the job rather than to make a legal determination of "disability" status or eligibility for disability benefits. Stating that the claimant is not able to return to work is not the same as stating that the claimant is disabled.

Relatively few disability cases require testimony in court. However, when the evaluator is required to testify in court or at an administrative hearing, a well-crafted written report can provide an effective outline for testimony. As described by Heilbrun (2001), testimony is based on the data obtained in the course of the evaluation. If the data collected are insufficient to support the evaluator's conclusions, this cannot lead to effective testimony. Effective testimony requires clear and persuasive communication. As with the written report, it is critical to employ everyday language to explain the findings and conclusions of the evaluation. In giving testimony, evaluators must be careful to not misrepresent the weight, nature, or certainty of the evaluation findings or allow any other party to do so. This, however, does not preclude the evaluator from testifying in a manner that is strong and persuasive.

SUMMARY

Best practices of mental health disability evaluation require an organized approach rooted in empirically supported methods and an understanding of the specific legal context in which the benefits are being sought. This context establishes the relevant definition of disability, which provides the basis for the determination of the claimant's eligibility for benefits. Regardless of context, all disability evaluations are based on an analysis of the claimant's functional capacity, which is related to, but distinct from, the claimant's diagnosis. It is hoped that by better understanding best practices of psychological evaluation in this area, lawyers will be able to make more effective use of these evaluations in their work. For a more detailed discussion of psychological disability evaluations the reader may wish to consult Piechowski (2011, 2012) and Gold and Shuman (2009).

REFERENCES

Adler, D., McLaughlin, T. J., Rogers, W. H., Chang, H., Lapitsky, L., & Lerner, D. (2006). Job performance deficits due to depression. *American Journal of Psychiatry, 163*, 1569–1576.

Alwes, Y. R., Clark, J. A., Berry, D. T. R., & Granacher, R. P. (2008). Screening for feigning in a civil forensic setting. *Journal of Clinical and Experimental Neuropsychology, 30*, 1–8.

American Medical Association (2008). *Guidelines to the evaluation of permanent impairment* (6th ed.). Chicago, IL: American Medical Association Press.

Arbisi, P. A., & Ben-Porath, Y. S. (1995). An MMPI-2 infrequent response scale for use with psychopathological populations: The infrequency psychopathology scale, F(p). *Psychological Assessment, 7*, 424–431.

Archer, R. P., Buffington-Vollum, J. K., Stredney, R. V., & Handel, R. W. (2006). A survey of psychological test use patterns among forensic psychologists. *Journal of Personality Assessment, 87*, 84–94.

Boccaccini, M. T., & Brodsky, S. L. (1999). Test use in emotional injury cases. *Professional Psychology: Research and Practice, 30*, 253–259.

Bohigian, G. M., et al. (1996). Substance abuse and dependence in physicians: The Missouri Physicians' Health Program. *Southern Medical Journal, 89*, 1078–1080

Borkowska, A., & Rybakowski, J. A. (2001). Neuropsychological frontal lobe tests indicate that bipolar depressed patients are more impaired than unipolar. *Bipolar Disorders, 3,* 88–94.

Bowen v. Yuckert, 482 U.S. 137 (1987).

Brunello, N., Davidson, J. R. T., Deahl, M., Kessler, R. C., Mendlewicz, J., Racagni, G., Shalev, A.Y ., & Zohar, J. (2001). Posttraumatic stress disorder: Diagnosis and epidemiology, comorbidity and social consequences, biology and treatment. *Neuropsychobiology, 43,* 150–162.

Code of Federal Regulations (20 C.F.R. §§ 404.1500-404.1599).

Cohen, Y., Lachenmeyer, J. R., & Springer, C. (2003). Anxiety and selective attention in obsessive-compulsive disorder. *Behavior Research and Therapy, 41,* 1311–1323.

Damascus v. Provident Life and Accident Insurance Company, 933 F. Supp. 885, (N.D. Cal. 1996).

Duka, T., Townshend, J. M., Collier, K. and Stephens, D. N. (2003). Impairment in cognitive functions after multiple detoxifications in alcoholic inpatients. *Alcoholism: Clinical and Experimental Research, 27*(10), 1563–1572.

Emerson v. Fireman's Fund, 691 F.2d 510, 1982.

Fireman, B., Koran, L. M., Leventhal, J. L., & Jacobson, A. (2001). The prevalence of clinically recognized obsessive-compulsive disorder in a large health maintenance organization. *American Journal of Psychiatry, 158,* 1904–1910.

Firestone Tire & Rubber Company V. Bruch, 489 U.S. 101 (1989).

Flaro, L., Green, P., & Robertson, E. (2007). Word Memory Test failure 23 times higher in mild brain injury than in parents seeking custody: The power of external incentives. *Brain Injury, 21,* 373–383.

Gallegos, K. V., Lubin, B. H., Bowers, C., Blevins, J. W., Talbott, G. D., & Wilson, P. O. (1992). Relapse and recovery: Five- to ten-year follow-up study of chemically dependent physicians—The Georgia experience. *Maryland Medical Journal, 41,* 315–319.

Gervais, R., Ben-Porath, Y., Wygant, D., & Green, P. (2007). Development and validation of a response bias scale (RBS) for the MMPI-2. *Assessment, 14,* 196–208.

Gold, L. H., & Shuman, D. W. (2009). *Evaluating mental health disability in the workplace.* New York: Springer.

Gold, M. S., Melker, R. J., Dennis, D. M., Morey, T., Bajpai, L. K., Pomm, R., & Frost-Pineda, K. (2006). Fentanyl abuse and dependence: Further evidence for second-hand exposure hypothesis. *Journal of Addictive Diseases, 25,* 15–21.

Greisberg, S., & McKay, D. (2003). Neuropsychology of obsessive-compulsive disorder: A review and treatment implications. *Clinical Psychology Review, 23,* 95–117.

Grisso, T. (2003). *Evaluating competencies: Forensic assessments and instruments* (2nd ed.). New York: Kluwer Academic/Plenum Press.

Hammen, C., Gitlin, M., & Altshuler, L. (2000). Predictors of work adjustment in bipolar I patients: A naturalistic longitudinal follow-up. *Journal of Consulting and Clinical Psychology, 68,* 220–225.

Harper, C. (2007). The neurotoxicity of alcohol. *Human & Experimental Toxicology, 26,* 251–257.

Hasin, D. S., Goodwin, R. D., Stinson, F. S., & Grant, B. F. (2005). Epidemiology of major depressive disorder: Results from the National Epidemiological Survey on Alcoholism and Related Conditions. *Archives of General Psychiatry, 62,* 1097–1106.

Heckler v. Campbell, 461 U.S. 458 (1983).

Heilbrun, K. (1992). The role of psychological testing in forensic assessment. *Law and Human Behavior, 16*(3), 257–272.

Heilbrun, K. (2001). *Principles of forensic mental health assessment.* New York: Kluwer.

Holzer v. MBL Life Assurance Corporation, U.S. Dist. LEXIS 13094, 1999 WL 649004 (1999).

Kane, A. (2008). Forensic psychology, psychological injuries, and the law. *Psychological Injury and Law, 1,* 36–58.

Kennedy, B. L., Lin, Y., & Schwab, J. (2002). Work, social, and family disabilities of subjects with anxiety and depression. *Southern Medical Journal, 95,* 1424–1427.

Koch, W. J., O'Neill, M., & Douglas, K. (2005). Empirical limits for the forensic assessment of PTSD litigants. *Law and Human Behavior, 29,* 121–149.

Lally, S. (2003). What tests are acceptable for use in forensic evaluation? A survey of experts. *Professional Psychology: Research & Practice, 34,* 491–498.

Larrabee, G. (2008). Aggregation across multiple indicators improves the detection of malingering: relationship to likelihood ratios. *Clinical Neuropsychologist, 22,* 666–679.

Lasser v. Reliance Standard Life Insurance Company, U. S. App. LEXIS 19345 (3d Cir. 2003).

Latas, M., Starcevic, V., & Vucinic, D. (2004). Predictors of work disabilities in patients with panic disorder with agoraphobia. *European Psychiatry, 19,* 280–284.

Laucks v. Provident Companies, et al., 97-CV-1507, M.D. PA, 1999 WL 33320463 (M.D. PA.).

Lees-Haley, P. R., English, L. T., & Glenn, W. J. (1991). A Fake Bad Scale on the MMPI-2 for personal injury claimants. *Psychological Reports, 68,* 208–210.

Lehman, W., & Bennett, J. (2002). Job risk and employee substance use: The influence of personal background and work environment factors. *American Journal of Drug and Alcohol Abuse, 28,* 263–286.

Leo, R. J., & Del Regno, P. (2001). Social Security claims of psychiatric disability: Elements of case adjudication and the role of primary care physicians. *Primary Care Companion Journal of Clinical Psychiatry, 3,* 255–262.

Lynch, W. J. (2004). Determination of effort level, exaggeration, and malingering in neurocognitive assessment. *Journal of Head Trauma Rehabilitation, 19,* 277–283.

MacQueen, G., Parkin, C., Marriott, M., & Hasey, G. (2007). The long-term impact of treatment with electroconvulsive therapy on discrete memory systems in patients with bipolar disorder. *Journal of Psychiatry and Neuroscience, 32,* 241–249.

Malhi, G., Ivanovski, B., Hadzi-Pavlovic, D., Mitchell, P. B., Vieta, E., & Sachdev, P. (2007). Neuropsychological deficits and functional impairment in bipolar depression, hypomania and euthymia. *Bipolar Disorders, 9,* 114–125.

Marlowe, D. (1995). A hybrid decision framework for evaluating psychometric evidence. *Behavioral Sciences and the Law, 13,* 207–228.

Martinez-Aran, A., Vieta, E., Reinares, M., Colom, F., Torrent, C., Sánchez-Moreno, J., Benabarre, A., Goikolea, J.M.,...& Salamero M. (2004). Cognitive function across manic or hypermanic, depressed and euthymic states in bipolar disorder. *American Journal of Psychiatry, 161,* 262–270.

Massachusetts Mutual Life Insurance Company v. Ouellette, 159 Vt. 187, 617 A. 2d 132 (1992).

Metropolitan Life Insurance Company et al. v. Glenn, 554 U.S.06-923(2008).

Mittenberg, W., Patton, C., Canyock, E. M., & Condit, D. C. (2002). Base rates of malingering and symptom exaggeration. *Journal of Clinical and Experimental Neuropsychology, 24,* 1094–1102.

Moore, B. A., & Donders, J. (2004). Predictors of invalid neuropsychological test performance after traumatic brain injury. *Brain Injury, 18,* 975–984.

Morgan, V., Mitchell, P. B., & Jablensky, A. V. (2005). The epidemiology of bipolar disorder: Sociodemographic, disability and service utilization data from the Australian national study of low prevalence (psychotic) disorders. *Bipolar Disorders, 7,* 326–337.

Mullahy, J., & Sindelar, J. (1993). Alcoholism, work, and income. *Journal of Labor Economics, 11,* 493–520.

National Institute of Mental Health (2001). *The numbers count: Mental disorders in America.* Washington, DC: NIMH Publication No. 01–4584.

Piechowski, L. D. (2012). Forensic evaluation of disability and worker's compensation. In R. Otto (Vol. Ed.), *Handbook of psychology: Vol. 11. Forensic psychology* (2nd ed). Hoboken, NJ: Wiley.

Piechowski, L. D. (2011). *Best practices in forensic mental health assessment: Evaluation of workplace disability.* New York: Oxford University Press.

Pilot Life Insurance Company v. Dedeaux, 481 U.S. 41 (1987).

Rosen, G. (2004). Litigation and reported rates of posttraumatic stress disorder. *Personality and Individual Differences, 36,* 1291–1294.Rosen, G., & Powell, J. (2003). Use of a symptom validity test in the forensic assessment of posttraumatic stress disorder. *Anxiety Disorders, 17,* 361–367.

Samuel, R., & Mittenberg, W. (2005). Determination of malingering in disability evaluations. *Primary Psychiatry, 12,* 60–68.

Social Security Act (42 U.S.C. § 423).

Stoddard, S., Jans, L., Ripple, J., & Kraus, L. (1998). *Chartbook on work and disability in the United States, 1998.* Washington, DC: U.S. National Institute on Disability and Rehabilitation Research.

Stordal, K. I., Lundervold, A. J., Egeland, J., Mykletun, A., Asbjørnsen, A., Landrø, N. I., Roness, A., Rund, B. R.,...& Lund, A. (2004). Impairment across executive functions in recurrent major depression. *Nordic Journal of Psychiatry, 58,* 41–47.

Sumanti, M., Boone, K., Savodnik, I., & Gorsuch, R. (2006). Noncredible psychiatric and cognitive symptoms in a workers' compensation "stress" claim sample. *Clinical Neuropsychologist, 20,* 754–765.

Taylor, S., Wald, J., & Asmundsom, G. (2006). Factors associated with occupational impairment in people seeking treatment for posttraumatic stress disorder. *Canadian Journal of Community Mental Health, 25,* 289–301.

The Employee Retirement Income Security Act of 1974 (ERISA).

Thompson, J. M., Gray, J. M., Hughes, J. H., Watson, S., Young, A. H., & Ferrier, I. N. (2007). Impaired working memory monitoring in euthymic bipolar patients. *Bipolar Disorders, 9,* 478–489.

Tse, S., & Walsh, A. (2001). How does work work for people with bipolar disorder? *Occupational Therapy International, 8,* 210–225.

U.S. Department of Health and Human Services (1999). *Mental health: A report of the Surgeon General.* Rockville, MD: Substance Abuse and Mental Health Services Administration.

Vore, D. A. (2007). The disability psychological independent medical evaluation. In A. Goldstein (Ed.), *Forensic psychology: Emerging topics and expanding roles* (pp. 489–510). Hoboken, NJ: Wiley.

Wadsworth, E. J. K., Moss, S. C., Simpson, S. A., & Smith, A. P. (2005). SSRIs and cognitive performance in a working sample. *Human Psychopharmacology: Clinical & Experimental, 20,* 561–572.

Wells, K. B., Stewart, A., Hays, R. D., Burnam, A., Rogers, W., Daniels, M., Berry, S., Greenfield, S., & Ware, J. (1989). The functioning and well-being of depressed patients. *Journal of the American Medical Association, 262,* 914–919.

PART III

Juvenile and Family

15

Evaluation for Child Custody

GERI FUHRMANN AND ROBERT A. ZIBBELL

Child custody evaluations are often considered to be the most complex of all forensic mental health assessments (FMHAs). They require examination of family members as individuals and in interaction with each other. The evaluation of child custody is a subspecialty area that requires training in both child and adult psychological assessment in addition to forensic mental health. Thus, most adult-trained forensic mental health professionals are not qualified to conduct these evaluations. The legal standard in child custody cases, the Best Interests of the Child Standard (BICS), is vague and gives minimal guidance for judicial decision making, contributing to the notion that child custody decisions are more art than science. The BICS eludes clear definition given the many ways that children can be adequately parented. The absence of a well-defined legal standard leads to a lack of clarity regarding what factors a forensic evaluator should be assessing. Insufficient empirical studies and few valid psychological tests to measure important aspects of functioning are additional challenges. Not surprisingly, the quality and format of child custody evaluations can vary greatly, given the multiple factors that contribute to familial functioning and the multiple methods of assessment and differences in training. This has resulted in a disproportionate number of ethics complaints against professionals who conduct child custody evaluations (Sparta & Stahl, 2006). In response, professional organizations, in particular the American Psychological Association (APA) and the Association of Family and Conciliation Courts (AFCC), have promulgated guidelines for child custody evaluations (APA, 2009; AFCC, 2007). Few types of FMHAs have similar guidelines. Since the development of professional directives, practice has become more uniform among evaluators (Bow & Quinnell, 2001; Zelechoski, 2009). Custody evaluations contribute important and valid information to inform legal decisions affecting children and families when completed by knowledgeable forensic mental health professionals.

This chapter provides attorneys with an overview of evaluations for child custody. After reviewing the legal context in which these FMHAs arise, the relevant mental health concepts and a brief review of the pertinent literature are provided. An overview of the evaluation process, report writing, and testimonial issues are included to inform attorneys what to expect and how to best understand these evaluations. Finally, some of the ethical challenges and controversies faced by mental health professionals and relevant for legal professionals are discussed.

LEGAL CONTEXT

Historically, child custody determinations have reflected the societal values of their time and culture. Until the 19th century, children were the responsibility of fathers and paternal rights dominated custody decisions. As agrarian life and the need for children to work on family farms diminished, consideration of children's interests slowly emerged in family law cases. The *parens patriae* responsibility of the courts and the widely held belief in women's innate superiority as parents resulted in maternal preference trumping paternal dominance in child custody decisions. The *tender years* presumption held that mothers were preferable custodians for young children. This idea remained largely unchallenged and dominated legal decisions until the second half of the 20th century, when social upheaval brought women's roles into the spotlight. In *Watts v. Watts*, 350 N.Y.S.2d 285 (1973), the New York court wrote, "The simple fact of being a mother does not, by itself, indicate a capacity or willingness to render a quality of care different from that which the father can provide." Current legal thinking favors custody decisions based on children's best interests. The term "child custody evaluation" is typically used to describe a mental health professional's assessment in family law cases involving parents disputing care of their children. Custody, however, is not the focus of many evaluations. A more accurate phrase would be "forensic evaluation in the context of a child custody case." The focus of an evaluation is often on appropriate parenting plans for children in light of the facts of cases. For example, concerns may center on whether a mentally ill parent's contact with her 5-year-old child should be supervised or the reasons behind a 12-year-old boy's refusal to have contact with his father. Factors contributing to a disrupted or potentially unsafe parent–child relationship (rather than disputed legal or physical custody) are primary issues in some "custody" assessments. Recently, some authors have called these types of assessments "parenting plans evaluations" (Kuehnle & Drozd, 2011) to more accurately reflect its focus. Most commonly, however, the term "child custody evaluation" is used and understood in reference to the assessment of a wide range of issues that may affect parental access to and care of children.

Legal Standard for Child Custody

The BICS has replaced maternal preference and the tender years presumption as the basis for deciding child custody in contested cases. What is actually in children's best interests, however, is ill defined and the subject of scholarly debate. The oft-cited opinion in *Painter v. Bannister* (1966) exemplifies the concern that personal values guide judicial decisions in the absence of clear criteria to determine best interests. In that case, the Iowa Court determined that 7-year-old boy's interests were better served in the custody of his grandparents, who offered a stable, conventional, and Midwestern lifestyle, rather than with his father, who offered a more stimulating, albeit bohemian, lifestyle in California. The Court opined that "security and stability in the home are more important than intellectual development in the proper development of a child" (p. 156). Critics of BICS note that its definitional vagueness likely results in increased reliance on judicial discretion. That discretion contributes to variability of outcome in family law cases (Kohm, 2008). Many states have attempted to define BICS by adopting the language of the Uniform Marriage and Divorce Act (1970). UMDA directs courts to consider rel-

evant factors when deciding child custody, including the wishes of the parents and the child, the relationship between the child and family members, the overall adjustment of the child, and each individual's psychological and mental health (§ 402).

While the UMDA is a start at defining components of BICS, it does not give guidance as to what weight to assign any one factor. The UMDA directive to consider "all relevant factors" suggests recognition that a child's best interests are unique to each child and cannot be adequately codified. Some states have provided additional direction for judges and evaluators by further defining BICS in their statutes. There is a wide range of statutory specificity among the states. Massachusetts is an example of a state that offers little statutory clarification of what is intended by "best interests": "the happiness and welfare of the children shall determine their custody. When considering the happiness and welfare of the child, the court shall consider whether or not the child's present or past living conditions adversely affect his physical, mental, moral or emotional health" (Massachusetts General Law, M.G.L. c. 208 §31). In contrast, Michigan has adopted a detailed definition of BICS (Michigan's Child Custody Act, M.C.L.A. §733.23, 1970, amended 1980, 1993). It includes twelve factors to be "considered, evaluated, and determined by the court," including the quality of the parent–child relationship; the parental capacity of each caregiver; and the stability of the home environment. Michigan's statute more specifically defines areas for the court to consider in determining best interests, including each parent's ability to encourage a relationship between the children and the other parent and the existence of domestic violence.

Critics contend that the ill-defined BICS contributes to an increase in disputed custody cases. In response, the American Law Institute (ALI) has proposed the *approximation rule* to be the standard in child custody cases (ALI, 2000). Briefly, that rule suggests that the proportion of parenting after separation should approximate the ratio of parenting during the relationship. Supporters argue that the rule provides a formula to determine parenting time after separation and increases predictability, thereby decreasing the number of cases that litigate, minimizing the role of judicial discretion, and addressing the concerns about the current BICS. Opponents express strong concern that any formula to assign parenting time is too simplistic and is a static solution that does not appreciate the unique dynamics of family growth and development. Only West Virginia has adopted the approximation rule as the standard for deciding child custody cases (WV Code §48-9-206). There is also case law that allows the consideration of the approximation rule as one factor in determining custodial responsibility (*In re Marriage of Hansen*, 2007).

Legal Process

Child custody evaluations can be requested by attorneys or ordered by the court at different times in the legal proceedings. During hearings on complaints for divorce or paternity, a motion may be filed or the court, *sua sponte*, may order an evaluation. This is most likely to occur when parties cannot resolve their differences through negotiation and/or there are special circumstances about the case that mental health expertise might clarify. Circumstances that may give rise to requests for FMHAs may include, but are not limited to, parental psychiatric illness or substance abuse; child psychiatric/medical illness or other special needs; disrupted parent–child relationship; and/or allegations of domestic violence or maltreatment. Another frequent juncture at which forensic mental health evaluations may be ordered is after the divorce or paternity action is finalized. In this situation, some change of circumstance, such as one party wishing to move out of state, impels a parent to seek a modification of the original order.

Mental health professionals may become involved in custody cases in different ways. Most often, evaluators are *court appointed* or hired by a court appointee (e.g., guardian *ad litem*). An evaluator can also be *hired by one attorney as an evaluator* to assess an issue germane to the attorney's client. It is clinically and ethically ill advised, however, to evaluate a child in a child custody evaluation without both parents' awareness and permission. Therefore, the evaluator is limited in what he or she can offer when hired by one party to the dispute. Mental health professionals are also *hired by one attorney as a science expert*. In this situation, the mental health professional is retained as an expert to provide information on what is known about a certain topic. For example, an expert may be engaged to describe the research findings related to disclosure of sexual abuse in young children or the issues regarding the care of children with autistic spectrum disorders. Mental health professionals hired by one attorney as science experts do not evaluate the child or family members involved in the litigation. Finally, a mental health professional may be *hired by one attorney as a consultant* and requested to help in trial preparation. All of the four roles mentioned above are valid for mental health professionals. However, for ethical reasons, mental health professionals must try to avoid serving in more than one of these roles in the same case.

Although the skills and knowledge base of child clinical and child forensic mental health professionals overlap, a mental health professional must be careful not to serve in both clinical and forensic capacities for a family. Taking on dual roles (e.g., providing a custody evaluation for a psychotherapy client) may constitute an ethical breach and may be grounds for a complaint to the mental health professional's licensing board (Table 15.1).

FORENSIC MENTAL HEALTH CONCEPTS

In the absence of legal definition of which factors should be assessed and the presence of judicial pressure to aid in contentious custody cases, forensic mental health evaluators historically provided evaluations that might have lacked consistency. The development of guidelines to direct forensic practice arose as a consequence of an increase in demand for psychological input in family court, the growth of forensic mental health as a specialty area of practice (Heilbrun, Grisso, & Goldstein, 2009), and an increase in complaints to psychology licensing boards. Some scholars have modified the widely accepted principles of forensic psychological assessment (Heilbrun, 2001) to the specific demands of child custody evaluations in order to promote better practice (Kirkpatrick, 2004). Influential professional organizations have summarized current consensus relevant to the interpretation of the BICS. In particular, APA (2009) and AFCC (2007) have promulgated guidelines for its members who conduct child custody evaluations. APA's *Guidelines for Child Custody Evaluations in Family Law Proceedings* have greater focus on what *categories of information* should be assessed by psychologists who conduct child custody evaluations. AFCC's *Model Standards of Practice for Child Custody Evaluations* have greater focus on the *process* of forensic assessment. Both of these guidelines are *aspirational*—that is, they suggest best practice rather than minimum standard of practice.

TABLE 15.1 DIFFERENCES BETWEEN CHILD CLINICAL AND CHILD CUSTODY EVALUATIONS

	Clinical	Child Custody
Purpose of evaluation	Diagnose, treat, advocate for client/patient	Inform judicial decision making
Who is the client?	Child and/or family	Court
Confidentiality?	Yes	Limited. Essential that limits of confidentiality are discussed with clients/collaterals and documented in report.
Sources of information	Patient/parents are viewed as reliable	Multiple sources of data gathering; validation of parental views is sought
Evaluator's demeanor	Helpful, empathic, rarely challenging	Impartial, neutral, skeptical, sometimes challenging
Documentation	Supports diagnoses and meets institutional and health insurance requirements	Details data obtained, impressions and bases for opinions
Access to report	Parents/guardian	Access controlled by court
Responsibility for fees	Health insurance/self-pay	Determined by court; often self-pay or funded court clinics

The challenge for the forensic evaluator is to translate the legal standard, BICS, into *psycholegal constructs* that can be assessed. Psycholegal constructs provide the conceptual link between legal standards and behavioral or psychological factors. They guide evaluators in selecting areas to address in their evaluations. Essentially, psycholegal concepts translate into the "things to be measured" in an FMHA.

As mentioned previously, the legal standard for child custody, BICS, does not state or even imply *what* should be measured. Other legal standards are more informative. For example, for civil commitment a person must be "in need of treatment and a danger to self or others," so a psychological assessment would focus on dangerousness and treatment needs. In lieu of a similarly informative standard in child custody, an amalgamation of statutory definitions, professional guidelines, factors derived from research, and consensus in the field have resulted in the following list of general areas to be assessed.

1. Parent Attributes: Functional Abilities and Deficits Especially as Relates to Parenting

In child custody disputes, parents are assumed to be competent and their strengths and weaknesses are compared to each other, not to a minimum standard of parenting as is the case in child protection cases (Budd, Clark, & Connell, 2011).

However, there is not a clear consensus about what capacities or activities constitute "parenting" or "good enough" parenting. This is understandable, given the wide diversity in parenting styles and the complexity of family dynamics. Functional abilities and capacities of parents, rather than personality, mental status, or morals, are parent attributes. Parental understanding of and ability to meet the child's specific developmental needs is an example of a parental attribute. Many authors have suggested essential realms of parenting abilities that should be considered in child custody evaluations, including the ability to create a positive parent–child relationship that provides safety and promotes growth; an understanding of a child's developmental and unique needs; the capacity to put a child's needs before one's own; and the appropriateness of parenting style (see Fuhrmann & Zibbell, 2012; Gould & Martindale, 2007).

2. Child Needs: Information about Psychological Functioning and Developmental Needs

A custody evaluation typically assesses a child's functioning, including developmental, physical, social, academic, behavioral, and psychological concerns. Particular attention is paid to special needs or special talents that may have ramifications for parenting. For example, a child with autism or a child who is musically gifted would benefit from parenting that is informed and attentive to those characteristics. Custody-specific concerns are also addressed when appropriate, such as the impact of parental separation, domestic violence, and/or the child's preference regarding the custody outcome.

3. Resulting Fit: Information about the Relationship between Each Parent and Each Child, Particularly the Congruence between Each Parent's Capacities and Each Child's Needs

The relationship between each parent and each child across the developmental lifespan is central to most custody evaluations. The "fit," often referred to as "goodness of fit," refers to the congruence or match between the parent's capacities and the child's needs. When considering "fit," the evaluator considers the quality of attachment and the role of development. For example, some people are at their best with dependent infants but are less capable with defiant teenagers.

4. Co-parenting Relationship: Information about the Relationship Between the Parents

Evaluating the nature of the post-separation relationship between adults is not emphasized in professional guidelines (AFCC, 2007; APA, 2009) but is typically highlighted in case law, statutes, and practice. The deleterious effects of high levels of interparental conflict on children are well documented in empirical and clinical literature (Johnston & Roseby, 1997; Melton, Petrila, Poythress, & Slobogin, 2007). High conflict in family law cases is a red flag and may prompt requests for mental health evaluations and targeted interventions. Assessments include evaluations of the type, level, and history of interparental conflict in addition to the involvement of the children in their parents' disputes. The impact of parental conflict on children is a critical focus of most evaluations for child custody. This information is often one of the most important factors on which evaluators base their opinions. For example, couples whose relationships were always marked by intense disagreement are unlikely to be able to cooperatively parent in the future, whereas couples who were able to effectively communicate and solve problems until their relationships deteriorated are more likely to be able to again cooperatively parent after the legal matters have resolved and healing has occurred. Baseline

behavior and situational behavior are assessed by evaluators. Baseline behavior refers to how someone functions in the absence of significant stressors. People typically return to their baseline behavior after crises, such as custody disputes, are resolved. In addition to interparental conflict, evaluators assess co-parenting skills, including the ability to negotiate and support the child's relationship with the other parent. Sometimes called the "friendly parent" clause, this is often one of the factors that statutes (e.g., Alabama, Kansas, Iowa, and Wyoming) require courts to consider under the BICS.

EMPIRICAL FOUNDATION AND LIMITS

There is a large literature relevant to evaluations of separating parents and children. The range of topics is as great as the variables that arise in any given case. Forensic mental health evaluations are informed by the research and clinical literature pertinent to the specifics of the case being evaluated. Highlights of research in some of the most common areas are briefly reviewed below and can be found in greater depth in other texts (e.g., Fuhrmann & Zibbell, 2012; Gould & Martindale, 2007; Rohrbaugh, 2008). The reader is cautioned, however, that all research has limitations and the results of group-based data do not apply uncritically to a single case. Research results *inform* but do not *dictate* evaluators' opinions of families.

Impact of Divorce on Children

Two seminal longitudinal studies, the California Children of Divorce Project (Wallerstein & Blakeslee, 1996) and the Virginia Longitudinal Study of Divorce (Hetherington & Kelly, 2002), provided an important base of knowledge and impetus for the subsequent increase in research on the effect of parental divorce on children. Current research findings indicate that divorce or parental separation has a significant but small impact on child adjustment, with the largest effect experienced just prior to or soon after the separation. While most children of divorce show resilience over time, they may exhibit stress-related behaviors that did not exist prior to the separation. Children whose parents separate are distinguished by the experience of painful struggles unfamiliar to their peers in nondivorced families. Some research suggests that children of separated parents manifested troublesome behaviors likely linked to familial stress even before the separation

(Block, Block, & Gjerde, 1988). Most children, however, return to their baseline level of adjustment as their parents adapt to the post-separation changes in their lives. In summary, children whose parents separate are likely to experience emotional distress but are no more likely to develop mental illness than their peers from nonseparated families.

Risk and Resilience

Research on the impact of parental separation on children has focused on factors that increase the likelihood of poor outcome (risk) and, conversely, enhance the likelihood of good outcome (resilience) (Kelly & Emery, 2003). Some of the factors that are associated with better outcomes for children include having a well-adjusted residential parent; consistent, good parenting; regular and meaningful contact with each parent; and adequate familial economic resources and residential stability. The converse of these factors contributes to children's risk of poor outcome after parental separation. High rates of conflict between parents significantly increase the risk of psychological difficulties in children (Fuhrmann & Zibbell, 2012).

Domestic Abuse

Domestic violence is the most frequent negative behavior alleged in custody disputes (Dutton, 2005). Children who witness parental domestic abuse may suffer emotional distress that can affect their mood, behavior, health, and cognitive/academic status (Kelly & Johnson, 2008). Some children experience symptoms consistent with posttraumatic stress disorder (PTSD; Chemtob & Carlson, 2004). In addition, exposure to psychological or mental abuse between parents can result in heightened anxiety, distractibility, and acting-out behaviors in children (Cummings, Schermerhorn, Davies, Goeke-Morey, & Cummings, 2006).

Domestic abuse is not homogenous and authors have categorized subtypes. One useful typology of domestic abuse (Kelly & Johnson, 2008) includes the following: (1) in *coercive-controlling abuse*, physical abuse is used to intimidate and to exert power and control in an intimate relationship; (2) in *conflict-oriented abuse*, physical violence is reactive and related to conflict between the partners; it consists of less severe forms of aggression (physical: slap, kick, push; verbal: insult/putdown, curse) and is very common; and (3) in *psychological aggression*, also called mental or emotional

abuse, conflict does not include physical violence. Differentiating types of abuse helps to inform the forensic evaluator about the dynamics of the family, the potential risks for a victimized partner, and the nature of the risk for children who are exposed to those behaviors.

Child Maltreatment

The incidence of reported allegations of child maltreatment in custody disputes is only around 1% to 2% (Bala & Schuman, 1999). When alleged, they often precipitate a request for a FMHA, so they are frequently addressed in evaluations for child custody (Horvath, Logan, & Walker, 2002). PTSD and acute stress disorder are common reactions to child maltreatment, affecting between 25% and 50% of child victims of physical abuse (Famularo, Fenton, Kinscherff, & Ayoub, 1994) and up to 70% of child victims of sexual abuse (Kendall-Tackett, Williams, & Finkelhor, 1993). The corollary of that finding is that not all children who were victims of sexual abuse will manifest symptoms. In addition, some sexualized behaviors are developmentally normative (Friedrich, 2005), so sexual abuse evaluators must consider the developmental status of the child. Some nonabused children's reactions to emotional distress can also include sexualized behaviors (Silovsky & Nice, 2002). In addition, family practices such as co-bathing and family nudity can result in sexualized behaviors in children (Friedrich, Fisher, Dittner, Acton, Berliner, Butler, et al., 2001). Of more concern are boundary violations, such as children who witness adult sexual relations or are otherwise exposed to adult sexuality (Johnson, 2005). These can also lead to children behaving in a sexual manner. In general, allegations of child maltreatment, especially sexual abuse, are often difficult to assess and require specialized expertise by an evaluator. There is substantial research on the reliability and credibility of children's reports of abuse, particularly sexual abuse. The findings indicate the need for a heightened level of skill and caution, the addition of recording technologies, and the use of a structured interview protocol (Kuehnle & Connell, 2009).

Parental Psychiatric Disorder

Parental psychiatric illness is frequently the impetus for an FMHA. The literature on parenting and adult psychiatric disorders underscores the importance of assessing the social and familial context of the disorder in addition to the psychiatric illness itself. Historically, mothers have been the primary caretakers of children, so studies have focused on psychiatrically ill mothers rather than fathers. In general, mothers with psychiatric disorders are not different from nondisordered parents in their level of concern about the welfare of their children. Psychiatric illness does, however, affect the likelihood of retaining custody of children. Mothers with major mental illnesses and multiple hospitalizations were the most at risk of losing custody of their children (Joseph, Joshi, Lewin, & Abrams, 1999). Not surprisingly, the quality of parenting declines with more severe mood disorders, such as major depressive and bipolar disorder (Kahng, Oyserman, Bybee, & Mowbray, 2008). The forensic evaluator should evaluate at a minimum the nexus between the demonstrable effects of the disorder on parenting in a particular family and "the impact of that illness on the child" (Jenuwine & Cohler, 1999, p. 303). Paramount considerations are the nature of the illness, the parent's understanding of the disorder, the availability and efficacy of treatment, compliance with treatment, and the presence of supportive adults who take over caretaking roles for the child and the parent in case of psychiatric deterioration (Fuhrmann & Zibbell, 2012).

Parental Substance Abuse

As with psychiatric disorders, parental substance abuse is often alleged in child custody disputes and is a frequent reason for an FMHA. Screening for substance abuse and, when present, assessing its effects on parental and family functioning is an affirmative responsibility of the forensic evaluator.

Maternal substance abuse can be missed as it is likely to be less public than for men. In addition, treatment or recovery can be more complicated in women than it is in men, due in part to the greater social stigma and disapproval associated with female substance abusers (DiClemente, 2006). Regardless of gender, even moderate substance use can be problematic, particularly when such use demonstrably compromises intimate relations and parenting (Douglas & Skeem, 2005). Other burdens, such as psychiatric disorder or economic struggle, can further stress a substance-abusing adult's capacity to parent effectively (Fuhrmann & Zibbell, 2012). There is no one set of emotional or behavioral responses by children to living with a substance-abusing parent, as research has found an increased

incidence of internalizing (anxiety/depression) as well as externalizing (acting-out) symptoms (McMahon & Giannini, 2003). The existence of parental substance abuse, *per se*, does not predict negative outcomes in children, because parental monitoring, adaptability, and family support and cohesiveness can mitigate the negative effects of the substance abuse (El-Sheikh & Buckhalt, 2003). As with parental psychiatric disorder, the task for the custody evaluator is to assess the type and severity of abuse and its link to diminished parenting and impact on the child.

Parental Alienation

One of the more controversial areas of interest in custodial disputes is the issue of alienation of a child from one parent. Parental alienation refers to the efforts of one parent to marginalize the other parent's relationship with the child. The child in this dynamic is typically aligned with the favored parent against the other parent in the absence of reasonable justification (e.g., abuse or neglect). Parental sabotage of a child's relationship with his or her other parent can be intentional and extreme (e.g., telling the child inappropriate, exaggerated, or untrue information about the parent) to subtle and unintentional (e.g., a parent who blatantly ignores or criticizes the other parent in the other child's presence). Alienating behaviors are common among divorcing parents and most often exhibited by the residential parent. A child's refusal to see one parent may occur in up to 20% of high-conflict divorces, while resistance to contact with one parent can happen in up to half of high-conflict cases (Johnston, Walters, & Oleson, 2005). In its more severe form, a child either resists or refuses contact with one parent and complains about that parent in terms disproportionate to the reality. Alternatively, in a moderate form of alienation, a child may complain to one parent about the time spent with the other parent but continue to go along with the parenting plan. If there is litigation, the disfavored or rejected parent may allege that the preferred or favored parent has initiated a campaign of sabotage of the former's relationship with the child. The evaluator has the task of determining whether the reported alienation is *irrational*, in that there is no apparent basis for it, or *rational*, in that there is a basis in problematic behavior by the rejected parent (Warshak, 2001). In analyzing the components that contribute to the poor parent–child relationship, the evaluator has to consider the child's temperament and developmental status that might contribute to the problems in parental contact (Johnston et al., 2005). This problem can be difficult to both evaluate and remedy and has been the source of heated debate in the field (Walker, Brantley, & Rigsbee, 2004). There is not yet long-term outcome research on the efficacy of different legal and psychological remedies for families in which alienation has been identified. Intensive, multimodal approaches (e.g., individual and family therapies) have shown promise (Friedlander & Walters, 2010), as have reports from residential programs geared toward improving parent–child relationships (Sullivan, Ward, & Deutsch, 2010; Warshak, 2010). Johnston and Goldman (2010) reported that almost all children who rejected contact with nonabusive parents reconnected after the age of majority. Current best practice suggests that evaluators consider the contributions of the child, favored parent, and rejected parent to gain appreciation of the impaired parent–child relationship (Friedlander & Walters, 2010).

Parenting Plans and Outcomes

Courts frequently ask evaluators to recommend a parenting plan, often in conjunction with a request for an opinion on the "type of custody." Despite a significant amount of divorce research, there is no empirical basis for recommending specific time arrangements or schedules. The research can provide broad indicators for offering advisory opinions on parenting schedules, although one must observe the caveat that each case is fact-specific and recommendations need to be based on the particulars of the individual family. Some states, such as Arizona, Oregon, and Massachusetts, have created model parenting plans for the courts and for separating parents that are available online.

One area of controversy is the issue of shared parenting or joint physical custody, which refers to a parenting plan in which a child spends significant amounts of time in the care of both parents. The lack of concise definitions of "shared parenting" or "joint physical custody" hinders investigations of its impact of children. Bauserman's (2002) oft-cited study synthesized data from many studies (i.e., a meta-analysis). Findings suggested that "joint custody" arrangements that included joint legal and/or joint physical custody were better for children. However, the research failed to measure interparental conflict as a variable that might influence the advisability of shared parenting arrangements. The existing surveys indicate that where there are low levels of conflict and high levels of cooperation, parents are more likely to self-select shared parenting plans to their children's advantage (McIntosh, Smyth, Kelaher, Wells, & Long, 2010). The current literature advises caution with respect to shared physical custody in the presence of high interparental conflict.

The advisability of overnights with the nonresidential parent for infants and toddlers is another area of dispute. This issue interacts with questions of how very young children develop and sustain secure bonds with each parent and whether they need the overnight presence of a primary caretaker to develop in a healthy manner and learn to regulate their emotions when distressed. One school of thought suggests that children develop secure attachments with both parents simultaneously (Lamb & Kelly, 2001) and so does not view time away from one parent as inherently harmful. Another line of thinking suggests that attachments develop sequentially rather than concurrently and therefore discourages overnights with young children due to concern that it will interrupt the formation of secure attachments (George, Solomon, & McIntosh, 2011). Research that compares children who have had regular overnight time with nonresidential parents to those who have had one primary base during their early years have found mixed results. Some studies support the conclusion that young children are unharmed and may benefit from overnights with both parents (Pruett, Ebling, & Insabella, 2004), while other studies suggest that nights away from the primary caretaker for young children may lead to less secure attachments, more stress, and decreased ability to develop self-regulation skills (McIntosh et al., 2010). This professional argument has been ongoing for many years and does not appear to be approaching resolution.

Psychological Assessment Instruments

Surveys of judges and attorneys indicate a high level of expectation that, if a psychologist is performing the forensic evaluation, he or she will employ psychological tests (Ackerman, Ackerman, Steffen, & Kelley-Poulos, 2004). Few psychological tests have been designed or standardized for a custody-disputing population, and they have not been demonstrated to correspond to parenting capacity (Melton et al., 2007). This concern has been partially addressed for the MMPI-2 by the development of databases for parents who are contesting custody (Bathurst, Gottfried, & Gottfried, 1997). In addition, there is debate about what added value (i.e., incremental validity) test results have for child custody evaluations. That noted, psychologists who do not administer psychological tests might have to explain the rationale for their decision.

The use of psychological testing as an additional data source for adults in child custody evaluations has increased over the past 20 years, according to multiple surveys. Many psychologists use a variety of personality tests (e.g., Minnesota Multiphasic Personality Inventory 2 [MMPI-2], Millon Clinical Multiaxial Inventory-III [MCMI-III], and the Rorschach Inkblot Test), although they do not use them in every case. The MMPI-2 is the most commonly administered instrument (Ackerman & Pritzl, 2011).

Custody-specific psychological instruments designed to administer to children—for instance, ASPECT (Ackerman & Schoendorf, 1992) and the Bricklin tests (Bricklin, 1995)—are used less than a quarter of the time (Ackerman & Pritzl, 2011). These instruments have been criticized for a lack of validity, inadequate standardization, and untested reliability over time (Otto, Buffington-Vollum, & Edens, 2003). The consensus is that evaluators should not rely on them in custody assessments because of the several psychometric challenges of these instruments, although they may have use as part of a clinical interview.

Some parenting inventories are used in custody evaluations. The Parent-Child Relationship Inventory (Gerard, 1994) and Parenting Stress Index (PSI; Abidin, 1995) are examples of measures with better psychometric foundations and whose use has been increasing in custody evaluations (Ackerman & Pritzl, 2011). In sum, psychological tests, particularly for adults, can provide additional information for an FMHA, although they should be used cautiously and interpreted conservatively when used for other than the purpose for which they were designed.

THE EVALUATION
Selecting an Evaluator

Attorneys' input into the selection of the forensic mental health evaluator varies across jurisdictions and may depend on the availability of resources. Some states maintain lists of court-approved evaluators and assign cases accordingly. Attorneys can often stipulate to a particular mental health professional, or alternatively the court may ask the attorneys for a short list of names from which to choose. In some jurisdictions, a guardian *ad litem* might decide on who is to do the evaluation.

When able to choose, attorneys should consider the qualifications of the evaluator. The prospective evaluator's curriculum vitae should reflect relevant training and experience across several areas. In particular, solid clinical and academic training in child and adolescent psychiatry or psychology is required, together with knowledge of relevant legal and forensic practice standards. Some areas require additional training and skills—for example, an assessment of an allegation of sexual abuse in a young child.

Attorneys' Role in the Evaluation

Attorneys have an active role prior to the start of an evaluation but are primarily uninvolved during the period of assessment. In preparation for the evaluation, the mental health professional is likely to ask the attorneys for assistance. Attorneys may be asked to clarify referral questions and, if relevant, fee agreements. Attorneys can provide legal history, pleadings, and other relevant documents (e.g., hospital records, police reports, child protection reports) to the evaluator. Any records provided should also be provided to the other counsel. If the attorneys do not already possess their clients' relevant medical/psychiatric records, it is often more efficient for mental health professionals to obtain them directly from medical facilities with appropriate signed releases. Evaluators cannot provide copies of protected records to the attorneys, but information that is relied upon in forming opinions should be summarized in the forensic report. The evaluator should clarify confusion or discrepancies about fees, timelines, qualifications, expectations, and process before any appointments with the clients. Typically, attorneys explain the role of mental health evaluators to their clients, emphasizing that they are neutral, evaluate issues related to best interests of the children, and do not make decisions but provide psychological knowledge that informs judicial decision making. Clarifying expectations for attorney–evaluator communication during the evaluation is helpful. It is preferable not to have case-related contact except for procedural issues and exceptional circumstances. Of course, *ex parte* communications between the evaluator and either attorney must be avoided so any correspondence or discussion that occurs includes both attorneys. Generally, the standard of practice is for mental health professionals to provide a Memorandum of Understanding to the parents prior to or at the beginning of the first interview. Attorneys can request a copy to review before the evaluation commences.

Process of Evaluation

FMHAs include multiple sources and methods of data collection. Evaluations for child custody typically consist of individual interviews with each parent, developmentally appropriate individual interviews with each child, observations of parent–child interactions, collateral contacts, and review of records. Home visits and psychological testing are used when they contribute to the issues being assessed. Informed consent is obtained at the start of interviews, including with children, for whom explanations are tailored consistent with age and verbal abilities. The developmental status and needs of the children determine the specific methods and logistics of the evaluation. Additional information on the content and process of evaluations can be found in several texts (e.g., Fuhrmann & Zibbell, 2012; Gould & Martindale, 2007; Rohrbaugh, 2008; Stahl, 2011).

Interpretation

The most difficult part of a child custody evaluation is organizing and interpreting the copious amounts of data obtained during the evaluation. Experienced evaluators have developed ways to organize the information. Frequently, the data can be organized as pertains to the four factors common to most custody evaluations (parent attributes, child needs and abilities, resulting fit, and parent–parent relationship), with particular attention to statutory requirements and specific referral questions. Evaluators' opinions are derived from and supported by the data. During assessments, forensic evaluators generate hypotheses about the issues of concern to the court and look for information that confirms or disconfirms those hypotheses. The strength of an opinion rests on its being corroborated by multiple sources. For example, if asked about the extent and impact of a parent's anger, an evaluator might confidently describe angry outbursts as a significant problem affecting parenting if collateral contacts, observation, interview, and records converge to support this opinion. In contrast, if the data gathered are not supportive of this opinion or are contradictory, then the evaluator should refrain from firm conclusions on the issue and provide the information with alternative explanations for the discrepancies in the data.

REPORT WRITING AND TESTIMONY

Child custody evaluations are typically longer than other types of forensic reports. Legal professionals have complained about and questioned the amount of detail contained in these reports. The report, however, must include a statement of what was done as part of the evaluation, including who was interviewed, when, and for how long; what tests were administered; what records were reviewed; and what collateral sources were contacted. Often there are multiple family members, and each one must be assessed individually and in relation to each other. The longest section of the report contains a summary of the data collected. The final section contains the evaluator's analysis of the data and opinions relevant to the legal matter. It should be clear to the reader that the expressed opinions are derived from the data gathered and documented in the body of the report. Forensic reports should be professional and detailed and should clearly reflect the evaluator's methods, opinions, and the data from which those opinions were derived. The reader should be able to follow the logic trail from data to conclusions to opinions.

Functions of the Forensic Report

There are both *intended* and *unintended* functions of a child custody report that influence how it is written. *Intended* functions include:

1. A documentary function. As noted previously, the report delineates what was done and what information was gathered.
2. An organizing function. A large, multi-problem family may provide boxes of records, interview notes, and collateral contacts. The report imposes conceptual order and a method of separating relevant from superfluous information.
3. An interpretive function. In language that is understandable to its several audiences, the report explains the meaning of the information obtained as relates to the reasons for referral.

4. An evidentiary function. In the event of a trial, the report will likely be an exhibit in the proceedings and the primary basis upon which attorneys will examine the forensic evaluator-witness.
5. An advisory function. Depending on the order of the court and the standard of practice in the jurisdiction, the report might recommend some actions to be taken.

In practice, the child custody report may also serve *unintended* functions:

1. A mediation function. There are few studies to quantify this, but it has been reported that 71% of cases settled after learning the results of their child custody evaluation (Ash & Guyer, 1986). In practice, child custody evaluations are used more frequently to mediate settlements than as evidence in trials (Bow, Gottlieb, & Gould-Saltman, 2011).
2. Third-party information function. This occurs when the court permits the report to be released to a therapist or parenting coordinator to inform care of the family.
3. A healing or restorative effect. The report can help parents emotionally get over the "impasse of divorce" (Johnston & Campbell, 1988) by facilitating understanding of the failed relationship and their children's needs.
4. A negative or hurtful effect. Conversely, parents may react with hurt and anger to the information and conclusions contained in the report. The intimate details of failed relationships and people's shortcomings, when reported, can incite strong negative reactions. This might inadvertently fuel the preexisting conflict.

Report Contents
Although formats may vary, child custody reports should generally contain the following information:

1. Orientation to the evaluation, including identifying information; reason for referral (what the court ordered); names and ages of family members evaluated; summary of activities performed, including dates and length of contacts, psychological tests administered, list of collateral contacts, list of reviewed records; brief synopsis of the current situation; and a description of the warning of limits of confidentiality given
2. Parent data, including individual history (including education, social, medical, psychological, legal, and occupational); history of the relationship (including conflict and domestic abuse); parenting and co-parenting history (including observation of parent–child interaction); psychological test data, if administered; concerns related to the other parent relevant to the evaluation; special circumstances (e.g., cultural/ethnic/geographic); and preferred outcome of the present dispute
3. Child data, including individual history (including developmental, medical, psychological, social, educational); special needs (including difficulties and exceptional abilities); child's understanding and experience of parental dispute; psychological test data, if administered; parental concerns regarding child; and the child's current concerns and wishes
4. Collateral and documentary data, including summary of collateral interviews and a summary of relevant documents
5. Conclusions, including interpretation of the data relevant to the court's referral questions (typically including opinions about parental attributes, child needs, parent–child relationship, and interparental relationship) and recommendations if allowed and if supported by the findings

What Every Family Law Attorney Should Know about Recommendations and Conclusions in Child Custody Evaluations
Whether forensic mental health evaluators should offer opinions on ultimate legal issues (e.g., which parent should have legal and physical custody) has been the subject of heated discussions at conferences and in the literature (Tippins & Wittman, 2005). Most forensic scholars strongly caution against making recommendations on legal issues, noting that they exceed psychological expertise. It is argued that custodial decisions rest on societal values, not psychological knowledge, and that there is neither sufficient empirical nor clinical

basis to support opinions about what is essentially a value-laden question (Melton et al., 2007; Tippins & Wittman, 2005). Advocates for such an advisory role note that mental health professionals have the greatest relevant knowledge of family dynamics, parenting, and children's needs and are trained to integrate clinical and empirical knowledge to inform opinions (Fridhandler, 2007). Furthermore, it has been suggested that if evaluators are precluded from making recommendations, then settlements are less likely to occur, to the detriment of children (Bala, 2005). Despite concerns, most evaluators, if not prohibited by the court, offer recommendations on legal questions (Bow et al., 2011), and most judges and attorneys prefer them (Bow & Quinnell, 2004). Professional organizations (APA, AFCC) do not take definitive stances on this issue, which at times polarizes its memberships. Professional directives (AFCC, 2007; APA, 2009) advise evaluators to be aware of this controversy. They recommend that if opinions are offered, they should derive from "sound psychological data" (APA, 2009, p. 18) and focus on the child's best interest. In the context of this debate, evaluators may choose to avoid opinions and recommendations on the ultimate legal issue. Rather, evaluators can give opinions on the likely impact of alternative parenting plans or the likely risks to a child of being in the care of each parent. Most importantly, the "rationale for the expressed opinion should be transparent so that the court can understand the bases for the opinion and make its own determination as befits the facts of the case" (Kruh & Grisso, 2009, p. 186).

Attorneys should expect forensic evaluators to articulate the nexus between concerns and parenting. It is insufficient for a parent to be described as depressed, financially irresponsible, or impulsive. It is important that the *link* between the concern and the issue before court (usually something about parenting) be articulated. The next step is to link that parenting deficit to specific impacts on the involved children. For example, Ms. Wilson's excessive fatigue, a symptom of her depression, diminishes her ability to provide adequate supervision for 5-year-old Jack. Recently, Jack was reportedly unable to wake his mother when he was feeling ill. Similarly, the best evaluators will provide linkage between a child's needs and parenting strengths. For example, Andy's need for routine and structure, a feature of Asperger's disorder, is understood and provided by his father, whose calm parenting style suits this aspect of Andy's special needs. A behavior that may sound like a significant problem may have little impact on parenting, while other behaviors that do not sound problematic may be harmful for the children involved. A parent's prescription drug abuse may not be so significant if it is limited to times when the children are with the other parent. Alternatively, concern about a parent's dating may seem inconsequential until one learns that the parent is dressing seductively and displaying inappropriate affection for the new partner in front of the adolescent children, who are distressed by these behaviors. It is reasonable for attorneys to expect evaluators to provide the bases for their opinions, including the linkages between concerns and parenting specific children.

Testimony

Evaluators testify in only a minority of their cases, since the majority of child custody cases settle before trial. It is customary for the forensic evaluator to be subpoenaed by the attorney wishing testimony. Fee arrangements vary, but common practice is for the evaluator's time for preparation and court to be paid by the side requesting testimony. One controversial issue is whether the evaluator-witness can be prepared for testimony by the attorney who requests his or her presence. Since the forensic evaluator is typically appointed by the court or hired by the court's designee, such as a guardian *ad litem* or law guardian, pretrial discussion can create the potential for bias. During testimony, the expert witness is required to remain neutral and to present data accurately and objectively without regard for who requested the testimony. Expert witnesses in the area of child custody must guard against giving opinions that exceed what the data or the state of psychological knowledge will support, working outside their areas of competence, and failing to provide information that contradicts or mitigates the strength of conclusions.

SUMMARY

This chapter provides a brief overview of the legal context, psycholegal constructs, and process of a forensic evaluation for child custody. For a more in-depth discussion, attorneys are directed to texts devoted to this topic, including Fuhrmann and Zibbell, 2012; Gould and Martindale, 2007; Rohrbaugh, 2008; and Stahl, 2011.

REFERENCES

Abidin, R. (1995). *Parenting stress index* (3rd ed.). Odessa, FL: Psychological Assessment Resources.

Ackerman, M., Ackerman, M., Steffen, L., & Kelley-Poulos, S. (2004). Psychologists' practices compared to the expectations of family law judges and attorneys in child custody cases. *Journal of Child Custody, 1,* 41–60.

Ackerman, M., & Pritzl, T. (2011). Child custody evaluation practices: A 20-year follow-up. *Family Court Review, 49,* 618–28.

Ackerman, M., & Schoendorf, K. (1992). *ASPECT: Ackerman-Schoendorf Scales for Parent Evaluation of Custody—Manual.* Los Angeles, CA: Western Psychological Services.

American Law Institute. (2000). *Principles of the law of family dissolution: Analysis and recommendations.* Washington, DC: Author.

American Psychological Association. (2009). *Guidelines for child custody evaluations in family law proceedings.* Washington, DC. Author. Retrieved on April 14, 2010, at: http://www.apa.org/practice/guidelines/child-custody.pdf

Ash, P., & Guyer, M. (1996). The functions of psychiatric evaluation in contested child custody and visitation cases. *Journal of the American Academy of Child Psychiatry, 25,* 554–561.

Association of Family and Conciliation Courts. (2007). Model standards of practice for child custody evaluation. *Family Court Review, 45,* 70–91.

Bala, N. (2005). Tippins and Wittmann asked the wrong question. *Family Court Review, 43,* 554–562.

Bala, N., & Schuman, J. (1999). Allegations of sexual abuse when parents have separated. *Canadian Family Law Quarterly, 17,* 191–243.

Bathhurst, K., Gottfried, A., & Gottfried, A. (1997). Normative data for the MMPI-2 in child custody litigation. *Psychological Assessment, 9,* 205–211.

Bauserman, R. (2002). Child adjustment in joint-custody versus sole-custody arrangements: A meta-analysis. *Journal of Family Psychology, 16,* 91–102.

Block, J., Block, J., & Gjerde, P. (1988). Parental functioning and the home environment of families of divorce: Prospective and concurrent analyses. *Journal of the American Academy of Child & Adolescent Psychiatry, 27,* 207–213.

Bow, J., Gottlieb, M., & Gould-Saltman, D. (2011). Attorneys' beliefs and opinions about child custody evaluations. *Family Court Review, 49,* 301–312.

Bow, J., & Quinnell, F. (2001). Psychologists current practices and procedures in child custody evaluations: Five years after American Psychological Association guidelines. *Professional Psychology: Research and Practice, 32,* 261–268.

Bow, J., & Quinnell, F. (2004). Critique of child custody evaluations by the legal profession. *Family Court Review, 40,* 164–176.

Bricklin, B. (1995). *The custody evaluation handbook: Research-based solutions and applications.* New York: Bruner-Mazel.

Budd, K., Clark, J., & Connell, M. (2011). *Best practices in forensic mental health assessment: Evaluation of parenting capacity in child protection.* New York: Oxford.

Chemtob, C., & Carlson, J. (2004). Psychological effects of domestic violence on children and their mothers. *International Journal of Stress Management, 11,* 209–226.

Cummings, E., Schermerhorn, A., Davies, P., Goeke-Morey, M., & Cummings, J. (2006). Interparental discord and child adjustment: Investigations of emotional security as an explanatory mechanism. *Child Development, 77,* 132–152.

DiClemente, C. (2006). Natural change and the troublesome use of substances. In W. Miller & K. Carroll (Eds.), *Rethinking substance abuse: What the science shows, and what we should do about it* (pp. 81–96). New York: Guilford.

Douglas, K., & Skeem, J. (2005). Violence risk assessment: Getting specific about being dynamic. *Psychology, Public Policy, and the Law, 11,* 347–383.

Dutton, D. (2005). Domestic abuse assessment in child custody disputes: Beware the domestic violence research paradigm. *Journal of Child Custody, 2,* 23–42.

El-Sheikh, M., & Buckhalt, J. (2003). Parental problem drinking and children's adjustment: Attachment and family functioning as moderators and mediators of risk. *Journal of Family Psychology, 17,* 510–520.

Famularo, R., Fenton, T., Kinscherff, R., & Ayoub, C. (1994). Maternal and child posttraumatic stress disorder in cases of child maltreatment. *Child Abuse & Neglect, 18,* 27–36.

Fridhandler, B. (2007). Science and child custody evaluations: What qualifies as "scientific?" *Journal of Child Custody, 5*(3/4), 256–275.

Friedlander, S., & Walters, M. (2010). When a child rejects a parent: Tailoring the intervention to fit the problem. *Family Court Review, 48,* 98–111.

Friedrich, W. (2005). Correlates of sexual behavior in young children. *Journal of Child Custody, 2,* 41–55.

Friedrich, W. N., Fisher, J., Dittner, C., Acton, R., Berliner, L., Butler, J., et al. (2001). Child Sexual Behavior Inventory: Normative, psychiatric and sexual abuse comparisons. *Child Maltreatment, 6,* 37–49.

Fuhrmann, G., & Zibbell, R. (2012). *Best practices in forensic mental health assessment: Evaluation for child custody.* New York: Oxford.

George, C., Solomon, J., & McIntosh, J. (2011). Divorce in the nursery: Infants and overnight care. *Family Court Review, 49*(3), 521–528.

Gerard, A. (1994). *Parent-Child Relationship Inventory.* Los Angeles: Western Psychological Services.

Gould, J., & Martindale, D. (2007). *The art and science of child custody evaluations.* New York: Guilford.

Heilbrun, K. (2001). *Principles of forensic mental health assessment.* New York: Kluwer.

Heilbrun, K., Grisso, T., & Goldstein, A. (2009). *Best practices in forensic mental health assessment: Foundations of forensic mental health assessment.* New York: Oxford.

Hetherington, E., & Kelly, J. (2002). *For better or worse: Divorce reconsidered.* New York: Norton.

Horvath, L., Logan, T., & Walker, R. (2002). Child custody cases: A content analysis of evaluations in practice. *Professional Psychology: Research and Practice, 33,* 557–565.

In re Marriage of Hansen, 733 N.W.2d 683 (Iowa 2007).

Jenuwine, M., & Cohler, B. (1999). Major parental psychopathology and child custody. In R. Galatzer-Levy & L. Kraus (Eds.), *The scientific basis of child custody decisions* (pp. 285–318). New York: Wiley.

Johnson, T. (2005). Young children's problematic sexual behaviors, unsubstantiated allegations of sexual abuse, and family boundaries in child custody disputes. *Journal of Child Custody, 2,* 111–126.

Johnston, J., & Campbell, L. (1988). *Impasses of divorce: The dynamics and resolution of family conflict.* New York: Simon & Schuster.

Johnston, J., & Goldman, J. (2010). Outcomes of family counseling intervention with children who resist visitation: An addendum to Friedlander and Walters (2010). *Family Court Review, 48,* 112–115.

Johnston, J., & Roseby, V. (1997). *In the name of the child: A developmental approach to understanding and helping children of conflicted and violent divorce.* New York: The Free Press.

Johnston, J., Walters, M., & Oleson, N. (2005). It is alienating parenting, role reversal, or child abuse? A study of children's rejection of a parent in child custody disputes. *Journal of Emotional Abuse, 4,* 191–218.

Joseph, J., Joshi, S., Lewin, A., & Abrams, M. (1999). Characteristics and perceived needs of mothers with serious mental illness. *Psychiatric Services, 50,* 1357–1359.

Kahng, S., Oyserman, D., Bybee, D., & Mowbray, C. (2008). Mothers with serious mental illness: When symptoms decline, does parenting improve? *Journal of Family Psychology, 22,* 162–166.

Kelly, J., & Emery, R. (2003). Children's adjustment following divorce: Risk and resilience perspectives. *Family Relations, 52,* 352–362.

Kelly, J., & Johnson, M. (2008). Differentiation among types of intimate partner violence: Research update and implications for interventions. *Family Court Review, 46,* 476–499.

Kendall-Tackett, K., Williams, L., & Finklehor, D. (1993). Impact of sexual abuse on children: A review and synthesis of recent empirical studies. *Psychological Bulletin, 113,* 164–180.

Kirkpatrick, H. D. (2004). A floor not a ceiling: Beyond guidelines—an argument for minimum standards of practice in conducting child custody and visitation evaluations. *Journal of Child Custody, 1,* 61–76.

Kruh, I., & Grisso, T. (2009). *Best practices in forensic mental health assessment: Evaluation of juveniles' competence to stand trial.* New York: Oxford.

Kohm, L. (2008). Tracing the foundations of the best interests of the child standard in American jurisprudence. *Journal of Law & Family Studies, 10,* 337–376.

Kuehnle, K., & Connell, M. (Eds.). (2009). *The evaluation of child sexual abuse allegations: A comprehensive guide to assessment and testimony.* New York: Wiley.

Kuehnle, K., & Drozd, L. (Eds.). (2011). *Parenting plan evaluations: Applied research for the family court.* New York: Oxford.

Lamb, M., & Kelly, J. (2001). Using the empirical literature to guide the development of parenting plans for young children: A rejoinder to Solomon and Biringen. *Family Court Review, 39,* 365–371.

Massachusetts General Law c. 208 §31.

McIntosh, J., Smyth, B., Kelaher, M., Wells, Y., & Long, C. (2010). *Three reports prepared for the Australian government* (pp. 85–152). Available at http://www.ag.gov.au/www/agd/agd.nsf/Page/Families_FamilyRelationshipServicesOverviewofPrograms_ResearchProjectsonSharedCareParentingandFamilyViolence

McMahon, T., & Giannini, F. (2003). Substance abusing fathers in family court: Moving from popular stereotypes to therapeutic jurisprudence. *Family Court Review, 41,* 337–353.

Melton, G., Petrila, J., Poythress, N., & Slobogin, C. (2007). *Psychological evaluations for the courts: A handbook for mental health professionals and lawyers* (3rd ed.). New York: Guilford.

Michigan's Child Custody Act, M.C.L.A. §733.23 (1970, amended 1980, 1993).

Otto, R., Buffington-Vollum, J., & Edens, J. (2003). Child custody evaluation. In I. Goldstein & I. Weiner (Eds.), *Handbook of psychology, Vol. 11. Forensic psychology* (pp. 179–207). New York: Wiley.

Painter v. Bannister, 140 N.W.2e 152 (Iowa 1966).

Pruett, M., Ebling, R., & Insabella, G. (2004). Critical aspects of parenting plans for young children. *Family Court Review, 42,* 39–59.

Rohrbaugh, J. (2008). *A comprehensive guide to child custody evaluations: Mental health and legal perspectives.* New York: Springer.

Silovsky, J., & Nice, L. (2002). Characteristics of young children with sexual behavior problems: A pilot study. *Child Maltreatment, 7,* 187–197.

Sparta, S., & Stahl, P. (2006). Psychological evaluation for child custody. In G. Koocher & Sparta, S. (Eds.), *Forensic mental health assessment of children and adolescents* (pp. 203–229). New York: Oxford.

Stahl, P. (2011) *Conducting child custody evaluations: From basic to complex issues.* Thousand Oaks, CA: Sage.

Sullivan, M., Ward, P., & Deutsch, R. (2010). Overcoming barriers family camp: A program for high-conflict divorced families where a child is resisting contact with a parent. *Family Court Review, 48,* 116–135.

Tippins, T., & Wittman, J. (2005). Empirical and ethical problems with custody recommendations: A call for clinical humility and judicial vigilance. *Family Court Review, 43,* 266–269.

Uniform Marriage and Divorce Act. (1970). National Conference of Commissioners on Uniform State Laws. Chicago, IL.

W. Va. Code §48-9-206 (2001).

Walker, J., Brantley, K., & Rigsbee, J. (2004). A critical analysis of parental alienation syndrome and its admissibility in family court. *Journal of Child Custody, 1,* 47–74.

Wallerstein, J., & Blakeslee, S. (1996). *Second chances: Men, women and children a decade after divorce.* New York: Houghton Mifflin.

Warshak, R. (2001). Current controversies regarding parental alienation syndrome. *American Journal of Forensic Psychology, 19,* 29–59.

Warshak, R. (2010). Family bridges: Using insights from social science to reconnect parents and alienated children. *Family Court Review, 48,* 48–80.

Watts v. Watts, 350 N.Y.S. 2d. 285 (1973)

Zelechoski, A. (2009). *The content of child custody evaluation reports: A forensic assessment principles-based analysis.* Unpublished Dissertation.

16

Evaluation of Competence to Stand Trial in Juveniles

IVAN KRUH AND THOMAS GRISSO

This chapter is intended to assist attorneys and judges involved in cases in which the competence to stand trial of a juvenile may be at issue. To most effectively utilize consultations with mental health professionals about this issue, attorneys and judges should appreciate current recommendations for best examination practices in the evaluation of juveniles for competence to stand trial (CST). This chapter is intended to foster that appreciation (see Kruh & Grisso, 2009, for more detailed guidance).

LEGAL CONTEXT

The authors of Chapter 2 explained that criminal defendants' ability to meaningfully participate in their trial, or CST, is considered "fundamental to an adversary system of justice (*Drope v. Missouri*, 1975)." Because of evolving ideas about juvenile offending, the application of this issue to juvenile defendants is a much more recent phenomenon.

Since the turn of the last century, juvenile defendants have typically been adjudicated in a separate legal system distinguished by its *parens patriae* philosophy and exclusively rehabilitative goals intended to serve the "best interests of the child." Proceedings tended to be informal and expeditious, with little regard for the youths' ability to meaningfully participate (Grisso, 1998). The few juveniles tried in criminal courts typically arrived there after case-specific judicial scrutiny. CST was rarely an explicit court consideration in making such *transfer* decisions, but this oversight limited concern about youth who were incompetent to stand trial (IST) being tried in criminal courts.

Concern about CST within juvenile court began to arise in the 1960s. Supreme Court decisions, such as *Kent v. United States* (1966) and *In re Gault* (1967), extended due-process protections to youth facing juvenile court trial, including rights to be represented by counsel, avoid self-incrimination,

and confront and cross-examine witnesses. In subsequent decades, responses to perceptions of increased juvenile violence lowered the age restrictions for juvenile court adjudication, increased the adjudication of misbehaviors traditionally managed out of court, increased the severity of potential sentences, and increased emphasis on punishment, accountability, and community protection. Taken together, these factors yielded a more "criminalized" juvenile court system within which CST concerns grew.

Changes to the mechanisms by which juveniles are transferred to criminal court trials have also increased concerns about juvenile CST. Since the 1990s, legislatures have allowed for the criminal court adjudication of younger juveniles, for a wider array of allegations, and without judicial determination. This has resulted in a massive increase in the number of juveniles tried as adults (Grisso, 2003b) and has likely increased the developmental and psychological heterogeneity of this group (Bonnie & Grisso, 2000). Still, few jurisdictions require that the CST of juveniles adjudicated in criminal court be established or screened, raising concern that greater numbers of IST youth may now face criminal trial.

Like all criminal defendants, juveniles tried in criminal court must be CST; however, not all states have visited the issue of whether *juvenile court* defendants must be CST and the U.S. Supreme Court has never ruled on the matter. Of state appellate courts that have addressed juvenile court CST, all but one (Oklahoma; *G.J.I. v. State of Oklahoma*, 1989) has concluded that it is a constitutional requirement (e.g., Louisiana: *In re Causey*, 1978) or is an extension of due-process protections (e.g., Georgia: *In the Interest of S.H., A Child*, 1996). It is now a "virtually inescapable conclusion" that CST is required of juvenile court defendants (Bonnie

& Grisso, 2000, p. 94), and CST is increasingly raised by defense counsel (Bonnie & Grisso, 2000; Grisso, 2003b).

Legal Procedures

The legal procedures for addressing the CST of juvenile defendants in criminal court are likely the same as those used with all criminal defendants (see Chapter 2). In juvenile court, procedural aspects of addressing CST are probably more variable. For example, laws regarding *competence restoration* services with juvenile defendants are usually minimally developed and there is great procedural variability across states (Grisso, 1998; Viljoen & Roesch, 2007).

As the authors of Chapter 2 explained, the case of *Dusky v. United States* (1960) established the modern standard for CST in its holding that the defendant must have sufficient present ability to consult with a lawyer, and a rational as well as factual understanding of the proceedings. Beyond the *Dusky* standard, the Court has required that defendants be able to assist in preparing a defense (*Drope v. Missouri*, 1975) and to participate in legal decisions required as the case unfolds (*Godinez v. Moran*, 1993). Traditionally, IST must be a result of mental disorder or cognitive defect, and many jurisdictions have added this predicate requirement through local statutes and/or case law.

It is clear that the *Dusky* standard and its progeny are generally applicable to juvenile defendants in criminal and juvenile courts, but the history of this use is limited. By 2004, 36 states had addressed juvenile court CST in statutes or case law, but they have generally provided only vague legal standards (Johnson, 2006). Important questions about juvenile CST remain either unanswered or inconsistently answered across jurisdictions, causing confusion for attorneys, judges, and juvenile CST examiners alike. The following questions are among the most important ones.

Does CST in Juvenile Court Require the Same Types and Degree of Capacities as CST in Criminal Court?

Despite the history discussed above, juvenile-justice systems still aim to serve as an agent of rehabilitative services for its young, often developmentally limited, participants to a greater extent than is typical in criminal-justice systems. As a result, there has been disagreement about whether the CST stan-

dard should be applied uniquely in juvenile court relative to criminal court.

Within the professional literature, some have suggested the use of a *lower bar* for CST in juvenile court compared to criminal court. This would require that juvenile court defendants possess the same types of abilities required of criminal court defendants, but those abilities would not need to be as well developed to be considered adequate (Grisso, 1997; Redding & Frost, 2001; Scott & Grisso, 2005). For example, the ability to meaningfully participate in court for juvenile defendants might need to be similar to those of typical adolescents (*adolescent norms standard*) or similar to typical youth of the same age (*age-peer norms standard*). Others have suggested an *adjusted bar* in which only a subset of criminal court CST requirements are of concern in juvenile court (Bonnie & Grisso, 2000). Specifically, typical juvenile court cases might require only a fundamental understanding of the purpose of the proceedings and an ability to communicate rationally with counsel without consideration of a rational understanding of the proceedings or decision-making abilities (*basic understanding and communication standard*).

Another suggestion has been the *flexible bar* in which the CST standard is matched to the level of needed protection in a given case (Bonnie & Grisso, 2000; Scott & Grisso, 2005). That is, a lower or adjusted bar could be used in cases involving possible sanctions that are less severe or more rehabilitative than would occur in criminal court, but the typical criminal court standard (*adult norms standard*) would be used in cases where the juvenile faces sanctions similar to those imposed by criminal courts. Still others have suggested that an adult norms standard should be used in all juvenile court cases because, in practice, the threshold for criminal court CST is already low (APRI, 2006; Kruh, Sullivan, Ellis, Lexcen, & McClellan, 2006).

Appellate courts have generally not addressed the issue of how to apply the CST standard in juvenile court, and cases that have addressed the issue have generally been unreported. Some of these courts have upheld an adult norms standard (e.g., Minnesota: *In the Matter of the Welfare of D.D.N.*, 1998), while others have supported some form of lowered requirements for juvenile court CST (e.g., Ohio: *In re Michael Roger Johnson*, 1983; Michigan: *People v. Carey*, 2000).

What Are the Legally Relevant Causes of Incompetence for Juvenile Defendants in Juvenile or Criminal Court?

Traditionally, a finding of IST either explicitly or implicitly requires that the relevant court-related deficits are due to a mental disorder (most commonly psychosis) or cognitive defect (most commonly mental retardation). Despite lacking any of these traditional *predicate requirements*, many juvenile defendants with less severe disorders (e.g., learning or attentional disorders) still exhibit incapacitating CST deficits because childhood disorders interact with developmental status (discussed below). Further, children's mental health problems are more difficult than are adults' to fit neatly into diagnostic categories, such that children with very real impairments may not meet criteria for any particular diagnosis. Finally, because youth are constantly developing, some may experience serious weaknesses in *Dusky*-related abilities simply because the requisite skills are not adequately mature and not due to any diagnosable mental condition.

The law has generally not addressed whether the legally relevant causes of IST differ for juvenile defendants in either criminal or juvenile court. A few states have explicitly added developmental immaturity as a possible source of juvenile court IST through statute (e.g., Florida: Rule of Juvenile Procedure 8.095(d)(2)(A) and Statutes 985.223(2)) or case law (e.g., California: *Timothy J. v. Sacramento County*, 2007). Where laws are unclear about such issues, the available evidence suggests that juvenile courts tend to recognize IST based on immaturity-related deficits (Borum & Grisso, 2007; Otto, Borum, & Epstein, 2006). In one unreported case, however, the court held that deficits associated with immaturity did not meet the legal requirement for a mental disorder and could not form the basis for a juvenile court IST finding (*Washington v. Swenson-Tucker*, 2006).

Do "Interested Adults" Play a Role in Juvenile CST?

In most legal contexts, adolescents are not viewed as autonomous agents and it is assumed that interested adults, such as caregivers, will act on the child's behalf using mature judgment and advocacy. In contrast, there are no commonly accepted procedures for the broad involvement of interested adults in the defense of juveniles, and the expectation is that juvenile defendants must possess CST autono-mously (Barnum, 2000; Grisso, 2005a). Nonetheless, adults can and often do play subtle or even overt roles in the functioning of young defendants. As occurred in the highly publicized case of *Tate v. Florida* (2003), for example, interested adults may pressure youth to handle their case in certain ways.

Should Juveniles Found IST Be Provided the Same Type of Restoration/Remediation Services as Adult Defendants?

When adult defendants are found IST, the underlying cause is usually a mental disorder and *competence restoration* typically entails time-limited treatment through medications targeting the impairment-causing symptoms. However, normal developmental immaturity will at least be a contributing factor in many juvenile IST cases. Immaturity is generally not responsive to medication, education, or other interventions and, instead, requires the passage of time for sufficient capacities to develop. In fact, because the term "competence restoration" implies the return of abilities that were once present, this term is not descriptive of the situation for many juvenile defendants. The term "competence remediation" is more accurate. Even for youth who are IST primarily due to a mental disorder, typical adult services are often inappropriate. Childhood disorders associated with CST deficits (e.g., attentional deficits; communication disorders) do not respond to medications as directly or as rapidly as do psychotic disorders.

Remediation procedures designed for incompetent adult defendants are often a poor fit for incompetent juvenile defendants. Remediation of juveniles may require less intensive psychiatric intervention but take longer than adult CST restoration. These unique aspects of juvenile CST remediation are rarely addressed in law. Some courts informally allow time to pass before trial so that the youth's skills can develop (Barnum, 2000; Grisso, 1998), but this approach may require longer trial delays than statutes allow. Virginia has implemented a model solution through a specialized intensive outpatient juvenile CST remediation program in which professionally trained counselors travel to IST youth. The counselors provide an average of three 90-minute sessions weekly that are multimodal and individualized to the needs of each youth and supplement these services (e.g., coordinate mental health services) as needed (see Warren et al., 2009).

FORENSIC MENTAL HEALTH CONCEPTS

Legal and forensic mental health professionals involved in juvenile CST cases depend upon forensic mental health concepts (also called *psycholegal* concepts) to gain clarity about the psychological factors that are most relevant to the legal questions being addressed and to facilitate communication across the disciplines. As a result, it is critical that attorneys using juvenile CST evaluation reports to make decisions and legal arguments have an understanding of these concepts.

The Four Capacities of Competence to Stand Trial

The two-pronged *Dusky* standard and subsequent court decisions discussed above leave ambiguity about the specific functional capacities required for CST. A number of psycholegal CST conceptualizations have been presented in recent years (see Kruh & Grisso, 2009, for a review), but no one model has gained dominance in the field. These CST models differ in important ways and the model used to conceptualize a given case can affect the opinion yielded. Nonetheless, the models do demonstrate relative consistency in the requisite CST abilities identified. Although they have not been identified empirically and they probably overlap with one another (Grisso, 2003a; Zapf & Roesch, 2005; Zapf, Viljoen, Whittemore, Poythress, & Roesch, 2002), four primary CST capacities emerge across these models.

Understanding refers to a basic factual understanding of the purpose and the process of the court proceedings the defendant is facing. This typically refers to abilities to recall and recognize the basic roles of courtroom personnel, the charges and possible penalties one is facing, the nature of available pleas, the overall trial process from arraignment to disposition, and one's rights as the case unfolds.

Appreciation involves the abstract manipulation of what is factually understood, the appropriate contemplation of the implications and significance of what is understood, and the application of that knowledge in actual case-related situations without distortion or irrationality. Although threats to appreciation in adult defendants are most commonly associated with psychotic delusions (e.g., a defendant believing that her defense attorney is a CIA agent plotting to kidnap her), threats in youth are more likely to stem from distorted beliefs rooted in concrete thinking and incomplete understanding that causes overgeneralizations, undergeneralizations, confusion, immature presumptions, and erroneous beliefs (e.g., a juvenile who does not believe that he can plead not guilty because it would be lying).

Assisting refers to the ability to participate with and meaningfully aid the defense attorney in developing and presenting the defense in consultations and in court. Assisting requires that defendants can adequately communicate with counsel about matters relevant to the case (Bonnie, 1992; Rogers & Shuman, 2005). It also requires that defendants be able to help identify potential sources of relevant information and witnesses, help identify reasons for confronting opposing witnesses, and provide information relevant to building a defense (Rogers & Shuman, 2005). In court, assisting requires the ability to follow and comprehend witness testimony so that counsel can be alerted to distortions, as well as the ability to provide testimony with relevance, coherence, and independence of judgment. Threats to assisting in youth are commonly associated with limitations in memory, attention, tracking, processing, verbal reception and expression, interpersonal perspective taking, ability to develop rapport with strangers, and time perception (Cauffman & Steinberg, 2000; Steinberg & Schwartz, 2000; Tobey, Grisso, & Schwartz, 2000).

Decision making refers to the ability to make autonomous, self-interested, and rational decisions about the case with input from counsel regarding common matters such as entering a plea, proceeding to trial, accepting a plea agreement offer, testifying, calling particular witnesses, or offering particular defenses (Bonnie & Grisso, 2000; Rogers & Shuman, 2005). Juvenile court defendants may also need to make unique decisions, such as strategic decisions about being adjudicated in juvenile versus criminal court. Youth may be at risk for decision-making limitations when their abstraction abilities are inadequate for imagining alternative courses of action, thinking of potential consequences of various actions, estimating the probability of various outcomes, weighing the desirability of various outcomes, and engaging in comparative deliberation (Grisso, 2000).

Notably, some CST models collapse *assisting* and *decision making* into a single concept. With juvenile defendants, however, it is uniquely helpful to keep these concepts distinct, especially since some proposals for how the CST standard should be applied in juvenile court reduce or eliminate the need for adequate decision-making skills but retain necessary assisting skills. In addition, there are unique developmental threats to decision making that are critical to consider in juvenile CST cases.

Predicate Requirements

Relevant deficits must be caused by underlying problems recognized by law to result in a finding of IST; however, the mere presence of these *predicate requirements* does not determine or create a presumption of incompetence. If an individual lacks adequate abilities in one or more of the four areas described above, the inquiry then turns to whether the deficits are related to a predicate condition. In criminal court, consideration has traditionally focused on severe psychological conditions, especially psychotic disorders or mental retardation. The application of CST to juveniles, however, requires consideration of nontraditional predicates.

Case-related functioning can be limited in serious ways by a wide array of mental health issues that either initially emerge or markedly increase in severity during late childhood or adolescence (Kazdin, 2000). For example, symptoms resulting from borderline intellectual functioning, learning disorders, behavior disorders, anxiety, depression, attentional disorders, pervasive developmental disorders, and prodromal psychoses may all yield relevant impairment (Grisso, 1997, 2005b; Viljoen & Roesch, 2005). Part of the issue is that these childhood mental disorders can occur within the context of normal development, and disorders and development interact in such complex ways that developmental psychopathologists find it difficult to draw clear distinctions.

Significant physical, cognitive, social, and emotional changes occur for normally developing youth between ages 11 and 18. As a result, some youth may lack the skills and abilities required of competent defendants because of *developmental immaturity* alone, even in the absence of mental illness. As a psycholegal concept, the term "immaturity" must be carefully defined. First, youth are never globally "immature." Rather, they may demonstrate immature development in a specific domain, such as cognitive immaturity or social immaturity. Development is always domain-specific:, for example, a child who is developing normally socially may demonstrate cognitive delays, or vice versa.

Immaturity must also always be understood relative to an identified comparison point, such as "typical adult functioning" or "typical age-peer functioning." For example, a normally developing 12-year-old will not be considered cognitively immature when she is compared to other 12-year-olds, but will be considered immature when compared to adults. The 12-year-old is evidencing *incomplete development* relative to typical adults. Another 12-year-old, however, may demonstrate cognitive abilities that are lagging behind those of most 12-year-olds, and might be said to evidence *delayed development.*

"Normal development" is often difficult to specify as most estimates have been based on white, middle-class children and may not generalize to the disproportionately minority, low-socioeconomic-status and developmentally delayed youth typical in juvenile courts. Development is also complicated by the fact that it is nonlinear and includes spurts, delays, and temporary regressions. Development can be highly sensitive to environmental influences and may differ between contexts, such as when a child evidences different abilities with his doting mother than with his demanding schoolteacher.

Two broad and interrelated domains of development are particularly relevant to juvenile CST determinations: cognitive and psychosocial (Grisso, 2005b). Delays in these domains are not uncommon among justice-involved youth and can clearly affect functioning in meetings with attorneys and in court. Cognitive development includes the improvement of attention, information processing, verbal fluency, deductive reasoning, problem solving, judgment, and abstract thinking, and the ability to apply these skills with consistency. Some of this cognitive development is related to biological changes, such as improved functioning in the prefrontal cortex (see Steinberg, 2007, for a review).

Adolescence is also a period of substantial psychosocial development as self-identity forms, assertiveness and independence grow in relationships with family members, and peer relationships expand, become more intimate, and take on more importance (Steinberg, 2007). Four aspects of psychosocial development have demonstrated particular relevance to decision-making capacities, which until fully developed can yield the proverbial "poor teenage judgment" (Cauffman, Woolard, & Reppucci, 1999; Scott, Reppucci, & Woolard, 1995; Steinberg & Cauffman, 1996). *Autonomy* refers to the abilities to think and behave in ways that are self-reliant, self-governing, and independent so that decisions can be based on appropriate consideration of the opinions of others, rather than reflect expanded or inadequate conformity or compliance. *Risk perceptions and attitudes* refer to the unique ways adolescents evaluate risk, including the tendency to foresee fewer possible outcomes of their risky behavior, underestimate the likelihood of negative outcomes, and overvalue having fun and gaining the approval of others. *Temperance* refers to the ability to maintain emotional and behavioral control by modulating impulsivity. *Perspective taking* includes the ability to take the perspective of other people, imaginatively shift perspectives, and think about issues multidimensionally (*interpersonal perspective*). Perspective taking also refers to the ability to consider both long-term and short-term implications of decisions and actions (*temporal perspective*).

Given the ongoing developmental process within these biological, cognitive, and psychosocial domains, one can imagine the potential for a myriad of CST-related deficits. Juvenile defendants may struggle with more complex legal concepts (like plea agreements), have difficulty remembering information offered by counsel, blindly agree to everything their attorney suggests, sabotage their relationship with counsel to gain peer acceptance, impulsively base decisions on anger or sadness, reject a good plea agreement in favor of the attention gained by going to trial, or accept a bad plea agreement due to an underestimate of the negative long-term consequences of having a juvenile offense history (to name just a few).

EMPIRICAL FOUNDATIONS AND LIMITS

To understand juvenile CST evaluators and their reports, attorneys should be familiar with the relevant research findings and limitations. Studies of juvenile CST have appeared in the literature only in the past 15 years or so and the currently available knowledge is minimal. However, it is almost certain that research in this area will continue to grow significantly and rapidly in the future.

Typical Practices in Juvenile CST Evaluations

Two studies have described examiners' practices in conducting juvenile CST evaluations. One study (Ryba, Cooper, & Zapf, 2003a, 2003b) was conducted nationally but was small in scale, and the other study (Christy, Douglas, Otto, & Petrila, 2004) was large but was limited to Florida; thus, neither study adequately portrays what is occurring nationally and cannot guide clinical practice. Notably, however, both studies found that examiners commonly provide ultimate juvenile CST opinions (an issue of controversy that is further discussed below).

Juvenile CST Evaluation Referrals

A number of studies have examined the characteristics of juvenile court defendants referred for CST evaluation (e.g., Baerger, Griffin, Lyons, & Simmons, 2003; Kruh, Sullivan, Ellis, Lexcen, & McClellan, 2006; McKee & Shea, 1999). Race and gender ratios were consistent with typical juvenile justice-involved youth, but CST examinees tended to be younger than general juvenile defendant samples. Juvenile CST examinees tend to have histories of special education and mental health services. Two of the studies examined specific mental health diagnoses of youth referred for CST evaluations but were discrepant in their findings; however, across the studies, as many as half of juvenile CST examinees exhibited an Intelligence Quotient (IQ) at or below 70.

Correlates of IST

Numerous studies have examined the factors correlated with overall CST functioning and/or the four factors of CST (understanding, appreciation, assisting, decision making) in juveniles (e.g., Baerger et al., 2003; Ficke, Hart, & Deardorff, 2006; Grisso, 1981; Grisso et al., 2003; Kruh et al., 2006; Poythress, Lexcen, Grisso, & Steinberg, 2006; Redlich, Silverman & Steiner, 2003; Viljoen, Odgers et al., 2007; Viljoen & Roesch, 2005; Viljoen, Zapf, & Roesch, 2007; Warren, Aaron, Ryan, Chauhan, & DuVal, 2003). Across these studies, four main factors are related to CST abilities among youth: age, intelligence, learning/academic problems, and mental health problems. Studies examining multiple-variable models and CST deficits have also supported the predictive utility of these four domains.

Nearly every study examining the relation between CST and age has found that younger age is associated with poorer overall CST functioning, as well as poorer functioning within each of the four capacities of understanding, appreciation, assisting, and decision making. Younger age is also associated with greater compliance with authority, reduced ability to imagine risky outcomes in legal decisions, and an overemphasis on short-term over long-term consequences of decisions.

Youth with lower intellectual abilities are also more likely to have CST deficits. Lower intelligence estimates and diagnoses of mental retardation are almost always associated with poorer performance on overall estimates of CST, as well as functioning within each of the four capacities. Verbal intelligence and attentional abilities may have particular relevance in the IQ–CST relationship, and age and intelligence interact such that young age and lower IQ yield particularly high risk for CST deficits. This interaction also has been found within appreciation, assisting, and decision making.

Learning or academic problems and mental health problems also appear to be associated with reduced CST skills among juveniles, but results have been less consistent than with age and intelligence.

Studies have found few CST differences based on gender, socioeconomic status, legal system experience, the nature of the instant offense, or whether trial is in juvenile or criminal court. Most studies have found no relation between race and broad measures of CST; however, minority youth have performed poorer than white youth on measures of understanding of the role of defense counsel and of the nature of legal rights, as well as trust in and willingness to disclose information to defense counsel.

CST Forensic Assessment Instruments with Juveniles

CST forensic assessment instruments (FAIs) are structured, quantitative interview tools designed for focused assessment of the functional legal abilities relevant to CST. Two of these instruments, both of which were originally designed for use with adult defendants, have been examined in research with juvenile populations. Burnett and colleagues (2004) found that juveniles performed more poorly than jailed adults on the MacArthur Competence Assessment Tool—Criminal Adjudication (MacCAT-CA; Poythress et al., 1999). In addition, MacCAT-CA scores are correlated with age and intelligence among youth (Burnett et al., 2004; Ficke et al., 2006; Grisso et al., 2003). These findings provide some preliminary evidence that the measure is *valid* (that it is assessing CST, as purported). However, assessments of *reliability* (the ability of the measure to yield consistent findings) have varied greatly

across studies (Burnett et al., 2004; Poythress et al., 2006; Warren et al., 2003), with particular weaknesses in sections of the MacCAT-CA designed to assess appreciation and decision making. Additionally, several items evidence age-related measurement bias and may underestimate an adolescent's legal capacities (Viljoen, Slaney, & Grisso, 2009).

Another instrument, the Fitness Interview Test—Revised (FIT-R; Roesch, Zapf, & Eaves, 2006) has demonstrated good to strong reliability with juveniles (Viljoen et al., 2005; Viljoen & Roesch, 2005; Viljoen, Vincent, & Roesch, 2006; Viljoen, Zapf, & Roesch, 2007). Scores on the FIT-R were correlated with age and intelligence, as well as several measures of mental health problems (Viljoen & Roesch, 2005). Again, this provides only preliminary evidence of validity.

Juvenile CST Standards

Several studies have examined juvenile CST standards. In response to juvenile case vignettes, judges, attorneys, and mental health professionals more often saw otherwise identical youth as IST when they were facing more serious charges, suggesting that these professionals tend to use a flexible bar approach and raise the CST bar when potential sanctions are more serious (Jones, 2004). Another study found that empirical approximations of different CST standards (adult norm standard; adolescent norm standard; and basic understanding and communication standard) yielded inconsistent classifications of youth as CST or IST (Viljoen et al., 2007), showing that the particular standard applied can influence juvenile CST determinations in individual cases.

Small-scale surveys examining the rates at which examiners base recommendations of juvenile IST on developmental factors have yielded widely inconsistent results (Grisso & Quinlan, 2005; Ryba et al., 2003a), thus illustrating examiner confusion likely related to the fact that few jurisdictions have offered legal guidance on the application of developmental immaturity to CST.

Examiner Opinions and Court Determinations

Of youth referred for CST evaluation, the percentage of those found IST varies greatly (from 3% to 41%) across studies (Kruh et al., 2006; Levitt & Trollinger, 2002; McGaha, McClaren, Otto, & Petrila, 2001). When examiners can offer an opinion of "questionable," this occurs at relatively high rates (13% to 15%; Cowden & McKee, 1995; Kruh et al., 2006), perhaps due to unresolved legal issues and/or clinical complexity. A study comparing examiner opinions and judicial determinations found extremely high rates of agreement, suggesting that judicial reliance on examiner opinions is high (Kruh et al., 2006).

Competence Remediation

Two studies have examined the mental health diagnoses of youth referred for competence remediation (Levitt & Trollinger, 2002; McGaha et al., 2001), but the results are so discrepant that a reliable perspective is not possible and generalizability of the findings to other jurisdictions is unclear. There also has been little research on the efficacy of juvenile CST remediation. A study of the Florida juvenile CST remediation program (McGaha et al., 2001) found that age did not predict the likelihood of successful remediation, but the presence of mental retardation was an important impediment to remediation. Studies have also found that brief remediation interventions, such as simple verbal instruction or an instructional video, do not adequately improve the functioning of juvenile defendants (Cooper, 1997; Viljoen, Odgers, et al., 2007).

THE EVALUATION

Attorneys must be able to properly digest evaluation reports, use them to develop case strategies, and effectively present evaluation findings in court. In doing so, attorneys must accurately gauge and identify the strengths and weaknesses of a given evaluation. At times, attorneys also may be called on to assist examiners as they conduct their evaluations. Therefore, attorneys should be knowledgeable about standard and best practices examiners use when conducting juvenile CST evaluations.

Preliminary Steps

Examiners conducting juvenile CST evaluations must possess specialized expertise in the practice standards that distinguish forensic assessment from general clinical practice, as well as expertise in child development, developmental psychopathology, and practice standards for conducting developmentally appropriate assessments. Lacking such expertise can lead to basic mistakes in practice and interpretation. Juvenile CST examiners must also learn about the procedures and processes of the justice systems, as well as the patterns of development, mental health problems, and patterns of offending typical of juvenile offenders. Juvenile CST examiners must also be able to maintain objectivity despite internal threats (such as beliefs about the functions of the juvenile-justice system) and external threats (such as the influence of the attorneys by whom they tend to be hired).

Examiners will need proper authorization, such as a court order or a formal request by an attorney, to conduct the evaluation and to clarify the appropriate flow of evaluation information. They will want to clarify that an evaluation of CST is, indeed, being appropriately sought, and assess the possibility that other psycholegal questions are also at hand. They are likely to ask for preliminary information about the clinical issues that have elicited CST concerns, as they may need to decline the referral if they do not possess the relevant knowledge or cannot consult with others possessing that expertise. Examiners will also seek to clarify relevant procedures (e.g., timeline for completing the evaluation), methods (e.g., number of sessions with the youth), and products (e.g., need for a written report).

Prior to the evaluation, examiners often contact the youth's defense attorney to confirm that the youth is appropriately represented, to alert defense counsel to the plans for the evaluation, to determine whether the defense attorney plans to be present for the defendant interview, and to obtain the defense attorney's perceptions of the child's problems, case, and reasons for the CST concerns. The examiner is also likely to contact the youth's caregivers, whether parents or others, to notify them of the evaluation, to clarify their expectations, and to discuss how the evaluation will be conducted.

Overview of Data Collection

Juvenile CST examiners should pursue only relevant data, or data that have a logical and/or empirically demonstrated connection with the issue of juvenile CST (Heilbrun, 2001). These data include historical information, such as features of the youth's cognitive, social, emotional, and behavioral development across stages and within different social contexts, the implications of any major life experiences, any medical, mental health, or other conditions, and the family context within which all of this development occurred. Because CST is a question of current mental state, the assessment of current developmental and clinical status is also relevant, by direct observation, focused mental status questioning, symptom interviewing, and/or psychological testing. Information from caregivers and third-party sources is also relevant. Finally, of most direct relevance is the assessment of current CST functioning in terms of the youth's understanding, appreciation, assisting, and decision-making abilities.

To reduce errors, data collection should be conducted in ways that enhance reliability (i.e., dependability and credibility), such as obtaining data from multiple sources and/or using standardized and objective data-collection methods (like standardized interview schedules and sound psychological tests; Grisso, 2005a; Rogers & Shuman, 2005). In juvenile CST evaluations, all methods of data collection, including the selection of standardized tools, the sources of information that are sought, and the manner in which interviews are conducted, must be developmentally sensitive and appropriate. Attorneys should not expect data collection to look identical across cases, as the process requires case-specific flexibility. Still, most evaluations will pursue information from caregivers, from third-party sources, and from interviewing, observing, and, sometimes, testing the youth.

Data Collection

A common obstacle examiners experience is difficulty obtaining critical third-party data sources, such as written records and/or interviews with collateral informants. It is important for attorneys to appreciate the need for this information and, when possible, to use the means at their disposal to help examiners gain access. Without this information, examiners may have difficulty assessing the veracity of other data they have accessed (Heilbrun et al., 2003), such as information obtained directly from the youth. To put current functioning in proper developmental context, examiners will commonly ask to obtain both older and newer information from mental health and medical providers, teachers and school officials, social service representatives, and probation officers. Because the evaluation is focused upon the youth's specific functioning within the legal context, best practices will also include questioning the defense attorney about what he or she knows and has seen in working with the youth to that point.

A particularly critical source of third-party information in juvenile CST evaluations is caregivers (Grisso, 2005b; Viljoen & Roesch, 2007),

including both family members and members of broad caretaking systems, like foster care or other case-management situations. Caregivers can provide examiners with historical information and information about the youth's typical functioning in CST-relevant domains, such as learning ability, decisional style, or attentional capacity (Grisso, 2005b). A caregiver interview also helps the examiner to assess the caregiver–youth relational style and the caregiver's attitudes toward the youth's legal predicament to consider whether the caregiver may influence the youth in problematic ways, such as threatening the autonomy of the youth's legal decisions (Grisso, 2005a; Viljoen, Klaver, & Roesch, 2005).

Of course, juvenile CST evaluation examiners will invariably ask to interview and directly assess the youth. The main goals in interviewing the youth are to obtain and integrate his or her social history, obtain lifelong diagnostic information, assess current developmental and clinical status, and assess current CST abilities (Grisso 1998, 2005b). To help examiners obtain useful information, attorneys should do what is possible to facilitate adequate environmental conditions (e.g., privacy, quiet, space, appropriate room temperature), physical conditions (e.g., unrestrained youth), and psychological conditions (e.g., appropriate medication levels, minimal acute stressors). Because examiners may want to vary aspects of the interview across cases, attorneys may want to question the examiner about his or her plans so that the best interview can be targeted.

Every interview of the youth (and of caregivers) ethically (and sometimes legally) must begin with a notification of rights and an explanation of the evaluation process. An issue of potential concern to attorneys may be the manner in which the examiner intends to manage self-incriminating statements made during the interview. Sometimes the use of such statements is clearly guided by law, but other times it is more ambiguous. Attorneys often want to discuss this with the examiner prior to the interview. Sometimes the notification process raises concerns or confusion in the youth. Examiners are expected to explain and further educate the youth, but never to coerce the youth into participating, nor should they allow other adults to coerce the youth. Attorneys should expect examiners to honor any persistent refusal to participate by the youth and to be contacted by the examiner if the youth declines to participate. Given these sensitive issues, many defense attorneys prefer, where it is legally permissible, to observe the notification, if not the entire interview, of the youth.

The examiner pursues two broad types of data in the interview and direct assessment of the youth: (a) clinical and developmental information and (b) information about abilities directly relevant to CST. Collecting clinical and developmental information typically involves an interview about the youth's history and questioning about past and present mental health symptoms. Data collection also includes observations and questions about the youth's current mental status, including the youth's mood, level of disorientation, fund of basic knowledge, memory abilities, abstraction abilities, social and practical judgment, and possible psychotic thinking. Attorneys should remember that examiners must meet local requirements for acting on risk of imminent harm to the youth or harm to others that may become evident during the mental status examination.

Evaluation of the youth's CST functioning includes observations throughout the interview process. For example, communication abilities, attentional skills, and behavioral controls are observed (Barnum, 2000; Grisso, 2005a) throughout the interview. Best practices may include observing the youth during attorney–client interactions and/or during actual court hearings; these contexts more closely approximate the realities the youth will encounter in the case and may provide the examiner with a more realistic picture of the youth's functioning. When such observations are not feasible, examiners may ask to review transcripts or recordings of recent hearings or they may reenact hearings through role-plays or the use of videotaped hearings.

The most common method for collecting functional data regarding CST capacities is with direct questioning in a *functional CST interview*. The primary goal is the systematic evaluation of the youth's abilities within each of the *Dusky* prongs using developmentally appropriate methods (see Kruh & Grisso, 2009). Functional CST interviews of juveniles differ from those with adults in that extra attention must be given to developmental threats to understanding, appreciation, assisting, and decision making. Extra attention will also be given to the youth's ability to learn relevant information that he or she did not previously possess.

Examiners using best practices for conducting the functional CST interview will integrate a flexible style of case-specific questioning targeting issues that are of greatest concern in the youth's own case with a predetermined set of questions commonly considered relevant to CST. Flexible interviewing allows examiners to interview youth with different issues, evaluate the youth's consideration of his or her own case, consider varied and complex contextual considerations common in juvenile cases, and consider various legal standards and definitions across jurisdictions. Structured interview content reduces the examiner's risk of missing important information, increases consistency across examiners, and helps examiners effectively communicate their findings to the court.

A number of standardized CST assessment tools are available for possible use in juvenile CST evaluations. Attorneys should appreciate that these tools are not interchangeable, as they vary in their structure, rigor of administration, detail and objectivity of scoring criteria, breadth of coverage of CST domains, empirical support, conceptual quality, and generalizability to real-word situations (Grisso, 2005a; Rogers & Shuman, 2005). Examiners may use the Juvenile Adjudicative Competence Interview (JACI; Grisso, 2005a), which was developed to be sensitive to developmental issues common with juveniles but lacks the quantitative rigor of a true FAI. Alternatively, examiners may use one of several measures designed as FAIs for use with adult defendants (e.g., FIT-R or MacCAT-CA, as discussed above). However, these measures lack adequate data with juveniles to be considered true FAIs when used with youth.

In certain cases, juvenile CST examiners will administer standardized psychological tests, which serve to reduce examiner-based errors in identifying the youth's cognitive skills, psychological traits, and/ or clinical conditions. However, testing is expensive, time-consuming, and taxing for the youth, and may not add to the evaluation when clear data are already available. Therefore, psychological testing is not needed in every case and attorneys should not assume that evaluations lacking test data are inferior to those that include it. In fact, the use of many diverse tests can sometimes signal a lack of clarity about the referral question by the examiner. When testing is conducted, it must be relevant to identifying CST deficits or the causes of those deficits, be standardized and adequately supported by research, comply with the professional and ethical standards applicable to testing, and be appropriate for the youth's age, ethnicity, and clinical issues. Common targets of psychological testing in juvenile CST cases include intelligence, learning abilities, developmental maturity, specific mental disorders, neuropsychological abilities, and response styles, such as exaggeration or denial of problems.

Data Interpretation

Once data have been collected, they must be interpreted by the examiner and used to form evaluation opinions that are of use to the attorneys and the court. The complexity of this process varies from case to case, but always involves a scientific analysis that includes generating hypotheses, considering alternative hypotheses, and an attempt (which may not always be possible) to identify the "best hypothesis"—the one that is most consistent with the data (Heilbrun, 2001). To allow the court to adequately consider the merits of the examiner's reasoning, attorneys will want to ensure that the examiner has made explicit and transparent how each evaluation opinion was reached, including the data that were relied upon and the basic underlying logic of the opinion (Grisso, 2003a; Viljoen & Roesch, 2007).

REPORT WRITING AND TESTIMONY

Written reports are standard practice when a juvenile CST evaluation has been court-ordered or conducted under statutory mandate, and they are requested in many cases in which an attorney has retained the examiner. Because relatively few juvenile CST cases proceed to a formal CST hearing requiring expert testimony, the written report is often the primary mode of communication between the expert and the parties or the court. Therefore, attorneys should carefully consider the quality of the reports they receive from juvenile CST examiners. Juvenile CST reports should use language that is comprehensible to a non-expert, include only probative and relevant information, be objective, differentiate between data and opinions, and be as brief as clarity allows. Attorneys should be aware, however, that the need to review a large number of data sources, to describe complex clinical and developmental characteristics of defendants, and to discuss the unresolved status of the law around key issues are significant challenges to brevity and clarity in juvenile CST reports.

Well-organized reports are easier for attorneys and judges to digest, yet there is no single way to organize juvenile CST reports. Preliminarily, all reports should include identifying information about the defendant and the case, as well as specifics of the evaluation (such as where and when the defendant was interviewed). The report should specify what rights the defendant was notified about before the evaluation, and it is a best practice to also explain how well that notification was comprehended. The report should ideally explain the reasons why CST was questioned and how the examiner conceptualized CST. Additionally, each data source relied upon by the examiner to reach his or her opinions must be identified, including the records reviewed, interviews conducted, and psychological tests performed. It is a best practice for examiners to also explain any concerns about the validity of their data and how these were managed, as well as to specify any data that were pursued but not obtained.

Report Content

There are several models for structuring the primary content of the report (see Kruh & Grisso, 2009, for a detailed discussion), but attorneys will want to ensure that three broad domains have been included. First, clinical and developmental data should be presented, including relevant details from the defendant's history, information about the defendant's current mental and developmental status, and the results of any psychological testing. Second, data specific to the issue of CST should also be presented, including a description of the youth's abilities and deficits in relation to his or her role as a defendant. Finally, the evaluation opinions should be offered. Based upon Grisso's (2003a) model for opining about legal competencies, Kruh and Grisso (2009) detailed a best-practices model for the assessment of juvenile CST addressing functional, causal, contextual, conclusory, and remediation questions. Attorneys must remember that, as will be highlighted below, answering these questions is often difficult due to both legal and clinical ambiguities. Examiners may regularly need to offer the available information, highlight the ambiguities, and allow the court to determine relevance (Christy, Douglas, Otto, & Petrila, 2004; Grisso, 2005a).

The functional opinion should tell the attorneys and the court what the youth is capable of knowing, understanding, believing, doing, and deciding within the role of defendant (Grisso, 1998, 2003a,

2005a; Otto, Borum, & Epstein, 2006). This discussion should tell the report readers what deficits, if any, were revealed by the evaluation. Attorneys should consider whether the interpretations are developmentally sensitive, take care to distinguish between understanding and appreciation, consider the underlying rationale for decisions rather than the decisions themselves, and consider whether the youth benefits from being taught information. The examiner should have conceptualized the pattern of deficits clearly and explained the extent to which available data corroborate this pattern.

In the causal opinion, examiners identify the source(s) of the functional deficits. Attorneys should be offered a plausible causal connection between the functional deficits and any mental illnesses, cognitive deficits, developmental problems, or "nonclinical" factors, like cultural expectations or malingering (Grisso, 2003a). Attorneys should be aware that multiple contributors may be interacting with one another, but there may be limited means with which to offer a fine-tuned analysis of those interactions. The causal opinion helps the court to determine whether any legal predicates (e.g., "mental disease or defect") have been met.

In evaluations that have used best practices, attorneys will notice that examiners have considered contextual issues, such as the fit between the types and degrees of the youth's deficits and the demands that the particular court situation will place upon the youth (Grisso, 1998; Viljoen & Roesch, 2007). To address these issues, the attorneys' input and expectations can be critical to help the examiner consider the nature of the proceedings, such as the likelihood that they will be complex or long or will involve sophisticated defenses or technical testimony. Examiners may sometimes need to consider whether the defense attorney's own style and characteristics and/or the characteristics of the courtroom are more likely to enhance the defendant's functioning or detract from it, so they may seek to get to know the defense attorney and to observe or ask about the judge's style. The contextual opinion may also help guide the attorneys and the court to make adjustments that can enhance the youth's functioning, such as when an examiner points out that a youth is likely to have difficulty understanding the spoken vocabulary typically used by the defense attorney unless it is simplified.

The conclusory opinion addresses the ultimate legal issue of whether the juvenile is CST or IST.

Although attorneys and judges often desire conclusory opinions, the appropriateness of this type of opinion has been hotly debated in the professional literature, with limited resolution (Otto, 2006). Attorneys should expect juvenile CST examiners to be particularly cautious about offering ultimate-issue opinions. First, the procedures and tools available for assessing juvenile CST are in an early stage of development relative to some other areas of forensic practice. Second, there remain fundamental definitional ambiguities in law about critical issues such as functions, standards, predicates, and contextual factors (Grisso, 1998; 2005b; Viljoen & Roesch, 2007). As a result, conclusory opinions are often impossible to draw without examiners making idiosyncratic assumptions. Well-formed functional, causal, contextual, and remediation opinions are often all that is needed to allow the court to reach its own informed determination. When examiners do offer conclusory opinions, they often will be phrased in conditional, "if/then" terms because of unresolved issues (e.g., "If developmental immaturity is a legal basis for a finding of incompetence in this court, then it would be my opinion that the youth is incompetent").

Finally, if there is a possibility that the defendant will be found IST, the examiner will opine about whether remediation efforts are warranted. The examiner will base this opinion on which, if any, of the deficits identified by the evaluation are likely to be successfully remediated and what interventions are most likely to work (Grisso, 1998; Mossman et al., 2007). Broad types of intervention include psychiatric medications and education. Compared to psychotic adult IST defendants, the mental health problems of juvenile IST defendants are often complex and medication interventions are less straightforward. Educational interventions tend also to be more complicated, and a number of jurisdictions have developed specialized curricula for teaching youth case-related "facts." The mere rote learning of facts, though, is inadequate for CST (see *United States v. Duhon,* 2000). More sophisticated educational interventions are just now beginning to be discussed in the juvenile CST literature (see Viljoen & Grisso, 2007). Examiners will explain where and how appropriate remediation services can be accessed and discuss the expected timeframe for successful remediation in light of local statutory timeframes. Attorneys should be aware that remediation opinions often will be based upon clinical judgment since there are few empirical data about this issue with youth.

Testimony

When juvenile CST cases do proceed to a hearing, attorneys are advised to meet with the examiner beforehand. Given the inherent clinical/developmental and legal complexities in juvenile CST cases, these meetings provide an educational opportunity for examiners and attorneys alike. They also provide an opportunity to discuss ways in which to educate the court about controversies and ambiguities. For example, specific questions regarding child mental health issues, juvenile CST evaluation procedures, and laws that are relevant to the case can be worked out prior to the court appearance. Discussion may address how the examiner's evaluation differed from that of an opposing expert; however, efforts to solicit consultation from the examiner about focused ways to impeach an opposing expert can compromise the examiner's objectivity and/or his or her appearance of neutrality. Examiners may also ask to meet with the defendant and/or caregivers prior to court to discuss potentially psychologically damaging testimony, such as misunderstandings of the term "incompetence," or the details of statements made by caregivers about the youth. Key questions that attorneys can consider for the examination of juvenile CST experts have been offered by Grisso (2005a) and Kruh and Grisso (2009).

SUMMARY

Juvenile CST is an area of forensic mental health practice that is still in a relatively early stage of development. This can create many challenges as legal concepts are translated into mental health terms and back again to legal standards. The better juvenile attorneys understand the challenges that face juvenile CST examiners and the current recommendations in the field for managing them, the better equipped they will be to use evaluations to provide relevant and probative information to the court.

REFERENCES

American Prosecutors Research Institute. (2006). *A prosecutor's guide to psychological evaluations and competency challenges in juvenile court.* Alexandria, VA: Author.

Baerger, D. R., Griffin, E. F., Lyons, J. S., & Simmons, R. (2003). Competency to stand trial in preadjudicated and petitioned juvenile defendants. *Journal of the American Academy of Psychiatry and the Law, 31,* 314–320.

Barnum, R. (2000). Clinical and forensic evaluation of competence to stand trial in juvenile defendants. In T. Grisso & R. G. Schwartz (Eds.), *Youth on trial: A developmental perspective on juvenile justice* (pp. 73–103). Chicago, IL: University of Chicago Press.

Bonnie, R. J. (1992). The competence of criminal defendants: A theoretical reformulation. *Behavioral Sciences and the Law, 10,* 291–316.

Bonnie, R. J., & Grisso, T. (2000). Adjudicative competence and youthful offenders. In T. Grisso & R. Schwartz (Eds.), *Youth on trial* (pp. 73–103). Chicago: University of Chicago Press.

Borum, R., & Grisso, T. (2007). Developmental considerations for forensic assessment in delinquency cases. In A. Goldstein (Ed.), *Forensic psychology: Emerging topics and expanding roles* (pp. 553–570). Hoboken, NJ: Wiley.

Burnett, D. M. R., Noblin, C. D., & Prosser, V. (2004). Adjudicative competence in a juvenile population. *Criminal Justice & Behavior, 31,* 438–462.

Cauffman, E., & Steinberg, L. (2000). (Im)maturity of judgment in adolescence: Why adolescents may be less culpable than adults. *Behavioral Sciences and the Law, 18,* 741–760.

Cauffman, E., Woolard, J., & Reppucci, N. D. (1999). Justice for juveniles: New perspectives on adolescents' competence and culpability. *Quinnipiac Law Review, 18,* 403–419.

Christy, A., Douglas, K. S., Otto, R. K., & Petrila, J. (2004). Juveniles evaluated incompetent to proceed: Characteristics and quality of mental health professionals' evaluations. *Professional Psychology: Research and Practice, 35,* 380–388.

Cooper, D. K. (1997). Juveniles' understanding of trial-related information: Are they competent defendants? *Behavioral Sciences and the Law, 15,* 167–180.

Cowden, V. L., & McKee, G. R. (1995). Competency to stand trial in juvenile delinquency proceedings: Cognitive maturity and the attorney-client relationship. *Journal of Family Law, 33,* 629–660.

Drope v. Missouri, 420 U.S. 162, 95 S. Ct. 896 (1975).

Dusky v. United States, 362 U.S. 402 (1960).

Ficke, S. L., Hart, K. J., & Deardorff, P. A. (2006). The performance of incarcerated juveniles on the MacArthur Competence Assessment Tool—Criminal Adjudication (Mac-CAT-CA). *Journal of the American Academy of Psychiatry and the Law, 34,* 360–373.

Florida Statutes, 985.223(2).

Florida Rule of Juvenile Procedure, 8.095(d)(1)(B).

G.J.I. v. State of Oklahoma, 778 P.2d 485 (Okla. Crim., 1989).

Godinez v. Moran, 509 U. S. 389 (1993).

Grisso, T. (1981). *Juveniles' waiver of rights: Legal and psychological competence.* New York: Plenum.

Grisso, T. (1997). The competence of adolescents as trial defendants. *Psychology, Public Policy, and Law, 3,* 3–32.

Grisso, T. (1998). *Forensic evaluation of juveniles.* Sarasota, FL: Professional Resource Press.

Grisso, T. (2000). What we know about youth's capacities as trial defendants. In T. Grisso & R. Schwartz (Eds.), *Youth on trial: A developmental perspective on juvenile justice* (pp. 9–31). Chicago: University of Chicago Press.

Grisso, T. (2003a). *Evaluating competencies: Forensic assessments and instruments* (2nd ed.) New York: Kluwer/Plenum.

Grisso, T. (2003b). Forensic evaluation in delinquency cases. In A. M. Goldstein (Ed.), *Handbook of psychology: Volume 11, Forensic psychology* (pp. 315–334). Hoboken, NJ: Wiley.

Grisso, T. (2005a). *Evaluating juveniles' adjudicative competence: A guide for clinical practice.* Sarasota, FL: Professional Resource Press.

Grisso, T. (2005b). *Clinical evaluations for juveniles' competence to stand trial: A guide for legal professionals.* Sarasota, FL: Professional Resource Press.

Grisso, T., & Quinlan, J. (2005). Juvenile court clinical services: A national description. *Juvenile and Family Court Journal, 56,* 9–20.

Grisso, T., Steinberg, L., Woolard, J., Cauffman, E., Scott, E., Graham, S., Lexcen, F., Reppucci, N. D., & Schwartz, R. (2003). Juveniles' competence to stand trial: A comparison of adolescents' and adults' capacities as trial defendants. *Law & Human Behavior, 27,* 333–363.

Heilbrun, K. (2001). *Principles of forensic mental health assessment.* New York: Kluwer Academic/Plenum.

Heilbrun, K., Warren, J., & Picarello, K. (2003). Third party information in forensic assessment. In A.M. Goldstein (Ed.), *Handbook of psychology: Vol. 11, Forensic psychology* (pp. 65–87). Hoboken, NJ: Wiley.

In re Causey, 363 So.2d 472 (La.1978).

In re Gault, 387 U.S. 1 (1967).

In re Michael Roger Johnson (Ohio 1983), unreported.

In the Interest of S.H., A Child, 469 S.E.2d. 810 (Ga. Ct. App., 1996).

In the Matter of the Welfare of D.D.N., 582 N.W.2d 278, 281 (Minn. Ct. App. 1998).

Johnson, K. M. (2006). Juvenile competency statutes: A model for state legislation. *Indiana Law Journal, 81,* 1067–1095.

Jones, M. (2004). The varying threshold of competence to proceed in juvenile court: Opinions of judges, attorneys, and forensic examiners. *Dissertation Abstracts International: Section B: The Sciences and Engineering, 64,* (3-B), 1498.

Kazdin, A. E. (2000). Adolescent development, mental disorders, and decision making of delinquent youths. In T. Grisso & R. Schwartz (Eds.), *Youth on trial: A developmental perspective on juvenile justice* (pp. 9–31). Chicago: University of Chicago Press.

Kent v. United States, 383 U.S. 541 (1966).

Kruh, I., & Grisso, T. (2009). *Evaluations of juveniles' competence to stand trial.* New York: Oxford University Press.

Kruh, I. P., Sullivan, L., Ellis, M., Lexcen, F., & McClellan, J. (2006). Juvenile competence to stand trial: A historical and empirical analysis of a juvenile forensic evaluation service. *International Journal of Forensic Mental Health, 5,* 109–123.

Levitt, G., & Trollinger, J. (2002). Juvenile competency to stand trial: Challenges, frustrations and rewards of restoration training. *American Journal of Forensic Psychiatry, 23,* 57–65.

McGaha, A., McClaren, M., Otto, R. K., & Petrila, J. (2001). Juveniles adjudicated incompetent to proceed: A descriptive study of Florida's competence restoration program. *Journal of the American Academy of Psychiatry and Law, 29,* 427–431.

McKee, G. R., & Shea, S. J. (1999). Competency to stand trial in family court: Characteristics of competent and incompetent juveniles. *Journal of the American Academy of Psychiatry and the Law, 27,* 65–73.

Mossman, D., Noffsinger, S. G., Ash, P., Frierson, R. L., Gerbasi, J., Hackett, M.,…& Zonana, H. V. (2007). AAPL Practice guideline for the forensic psychiatric evaluation of competence to stand trial. *Journal of the American Academy of Psychiatry and the Law, 35,* S3–S72.

Otto, R. K. (2006). Competency to stand trial. *Applied Psychology in Criminal Justice, 2,* 82–133.

Otto, R. K., Borum, R., & Epstein, M. (2006). Evaluation of children in the juvenile justice system. In D. Faust (Ed.), *Coping with psychiatric and psychological testimony* (6th ed.). New York: Oxford University Press.

People v. Carey, 615 N.W.2d 742, 748 (Mich. Ct. App, 2000).

Poythress, N., Lexcen, F. J., Grisso, T., & Steinberg, L. (2006). The competence-related abilities of adolescent defendants in criminal court. *Law and Human Behavior, 30,* 75–92.

Poythress, N. G., Nicholson, R, Otto, R. K., Edens, J. F, Bonnie, R. J, Monahan, J., & Hoge, S. K. (1999). *The MacArthur Competence Assessment Tool-Criminal Adjudication professional manual.* Odessa, FL: PAR.

Redding, R. E., & Frost, L. E. (2001). Adjudicative competence in the modern juvenile court. *Virginia Journal of Social Policy and the Law, 9,* 353–409.

Redlich, A. D., Silverman, M., & Steiner, H. (2003). Preadjudicative and adjudicative competence in juveniles and young adults. *Behavioral Sciences and the Law, 21,* 393–410.

Roesch, R., Zapf, P. A., & Eaves, D. (2006). *Fitness Interview Test—Revised: A structured interview for assessing competency to stand trial.* Sarasota, FL: Professional Resource Press.

Rogers, R., & Shuman, D. (2005). *Fundamentals of forensic practice: Mental health and criminal law.* New York: Springer.

Ryba, N. L., Cooper, V. G., & Zapf, P. A. (2003a). Assessment of maturity in juvenile competency to stand trial evaluations: A survey of practitioners. *Journal of Forensic Psychology Practice, 3,* 23–45.

Ryba, N. L., Cooper, V. G., & Zapf, P.A. (2003b). Juvenile competence to stand trial evaluations: A survey of current practices and test usage among psychologists. *Professional Psychology: Research and Practice, 34,* 499–507.

Scott, E., & Grisso, T. (2005). Developmental incompetence, due process, and juvenile justice policy. *North Carolina Law Review, 83,* 102–147.

Scott, E., Reppucci, N. D., & Woolard, J. (1995). Evaluating adolescent decision making in legal contexts. *Law and Human Behavior, 19,* 221–244.

Steinberg, L. (2007). *Adolescence* (8th ed.). New York: McGraw-Hill.

Steinberg, L., & Cauffman, E. (1996). Maturity of judgment in adolescence: Psychosocial factors in adolescent decision making. *Law and Human Behavior, 20,* 249–272.

Steinberg, L., & Schwartz, R. (2000). Developmental psychology goes to court. In T. Grisso & R. Schwartz (Eds.), *Youth on trial: A developmental perspective on juvenile justice* (pp. 9–31). Chicago: University of Chicago Press.

Tate v. State, 864 So.2d 44, Fla. 4th DCA (2003).

Timothy J. v. Sacramento County, 150 Cal. App. 847 (Cal. Ct. App., 2007)

Tobey, A., Grisso, T., & Schwartz, R. (2000). Youths' trial participation as seen by youths and their attorneys: An exploration of competence-based issues. In T. Grisso & R. Schwartz (Eds.), *Youth on trial: A developmental perspective on juvenile justice* (pp. 225–242). Chicago: University of Chicago Press.

United States v. Duhon, 104 F. Supp. 2d 663 (W. D. La. 2000).

Viljoen, J. L., & Grisso, T. (2007). Prospects for remediating juveniles' adjudicative competence. *Psychology, Public Policy, and Law, 13,* 87–114.

Viljoen, J. L., Klaver, J. & Roesch, R. (2005). Legal decisions of preadolescent and adolescent defendants: Predictors of confessions, pleas, communication with attorneys, and appeals. *Law and Human Behavior, 29,* 253–277.

Viljoen, J. L., Odgers, C., Grisso, T., & Tillbrook, C. (2007). Teaching adolescents and adults about legal proceedings: A comparison of pre- and post-teaching scores on the Mac-CAT-CA. *Law and Human Behavior, 31,* 419–432.

Viljoen, J. L., & Roesch, R. (2005). Competence to waive interrogation rights and adjudicative competence in adolescent defendants: Cognitive development, attorney contact, and psychological symptoms. *Law and Human Behavior, 29,* 723–742.

Viljoen, J. L., & Roesch, R. (2007). Assessing adolescents' adjudicative competence. In R. Jackson (Ed.), *Learning forensic assessment* (pp. 291–312). London: Lawrence Erlbaum Associates.

Viljoen, J. L., Slaney, K. L., & Grisso, T. (2009). The use of the MacCAT-CA with adolescents: An item response theory investigation of age-related measurement bias. *Law and Human Behavior, 33,* 283–297.

Viljoen, J. L., Vincent, G. M., & Roesch, R. (2006). Assessing adolescent defendant's adjudicative competence: Interrater reliability and factor structure of the Fitness Interview Test—Revised. *Criminal Justice and Behavior, 33,* 467–487.

Viljoen, J. L., Zapf, P. A., & Roesch, R. (2007). Adjudicative competence and comprehension of Miranda rights in adolescent defendants: A comparison of legal standards. *Behavioral Sciences and the Law, 24,* 1–19.

Warren, J. I., Aaron, J., Ryan, E., Chauhan, P., & DuVal, J. (2003). Correlates of adjudicative competence among psychiatrically impaired juveniles. *Journal of the American Academy of Psychiatry and the Law, 31,* 299–309.

Warren, J. I., DuVal, J., Komarovskaya, I., Chauhan, P. Buffington-Vollum, J., & Ryan, E. (2009). Developing a forensic service delivery system for juvenile adjudicated incompetent to stand trial. *International Journal of Forensic Mental Health, 8,* 245–262.

Washington v. Swenson-Tucker, 131 Wash. App. 1045, Unreported.

Zapf, P. A., & Roesch, R. (2005). An investigation of the construct of competence: A comparison of the FIT, the MacCAT-CA, and the MacCAT-T. *Law and Human Behavior, 29,* 229–252.

Zapf, P. A., Viljoen, J. L., Whittemore, K. E., Poythress, N. G., & Roesch, R. (2002). Competency: Past, present, and future. In J. R. P. Ogloff (Ed.), *Taking psychology and law into the 21st century* (pp. 171–198). New York: Kluwer Academic/Plenum.

17

Evaluation of Juveniles' Risks and Needs

ROBERT D. HOGE

This chapter focuses on the forensic assessments of risk for criminal activity in juveniles. These assessments may form the basis of an expert's testimony in court, but expert reports may also be used in plea negotiations and determining treatment needs for post-adjudication planning. This chapter is specifically directed at attorneys and judges involved in juvenile cases. It is designed to provide them with an understanding of best practices regarding forensic assessments and to assist them in making effective use of assessments within the legal context.

The terms "criminogenic risk" and "criminogenic needs" (referred to as risk and needs) are key to the following discussion. Risk factors are characteristics of the youth or his or her circumstances associated with criminal activity. Examples include a prior history of criminal activity, school failure, negative peer associations, and poor self-control. Circumstantial factors include factors such as family dysfunction and poor parenting practices. Need factors refer to risk factors that can be changed, and, if changed, reduce the level of risk. Criminal history is a static risk factor, which means that it cannot be changed. However, negative peer associations and poor parenting practices are risk factors that can be changed and, where changed, may reduce the level of risk.

The chapter begins with a discussion of the legal contexts in which risk and needs assessments are relevant. This is followed by discussions of mental health concepts and empirical research relevant to risk assessments. Procedures for describing and evaluating risk assessments are presented, followed by a review of the major standardized risk/needs assessment instruments. The chapter concludes with sections on conducting risk assessments, ethical and legal issues, and report writing and testimony.

LEGAL CONTEXT

Risk and risk/needs assessment are relevant within a variety of decision contexts in the juvenile-justice system. Note should be made that due-process and confidentiality issues discussed later may be relevant in all of these decision areas.

Pre-charge Diversion

Many systems provide for diverting youth from the police and judicial system before charges are laid. This provision is generally provided for youth without a serious criminal history who have committed relatively nonserious crimes. In some cases the diversion may simply be accompanied by a caution or warning, while in others specific community-based treatment programs may be offered. The latter would be designed to address personal or social needs of the young person.

Both risk and risk/needs assessments are relevant to pre-charge diversion decisions. Risk assessments may be important because diversion is normally reserved for youth at low or moderate risk of continued criminal activity, although well-resourced programs may accept higher-risk youth (Altschuler, 1998). If the diversion program will involve a rehabilitative component, then risk/needs assessments are required to identify the specific needs of the young person.

Post-charge Diversion

Provision is also made in some systems for diversion of the youth from the judicial system after a charge has been laid. This decision generally rests with the police or prosecution. The same requirements for risk and risk/needs assessment exist here as with pre-charge diversion programs. Eligibility for diversion, where pre- or post-charge, generally depends on the nature of the offense, the youth's acceptance of responsibility for his or her actions, and level of risk. Within formal diversion programs community-based services may be available to address the factors placing the youth at risk. Diversion decisions are often made by police or prosecutors in an informal manner; however, a number of diversion models exist where formal assessment procedures are used to assess risk and need factors and where a formal intervention program is designed.

Broad-based risk/needs assessment instruments are particularly useful to guide diversion decisions. They provide information about the level of risk for re-offending presented by the youth as well as specific need areas that should be addressed in the diversion program. Note that issues of due process and client confidentiality may arise in connection with pre- and post-charge diversion decisions. A risk/needs assessment may be conducted to assist in determining the appropriate intervention to provide the youth. However, if a charge is subsequently made, the use of this information in the subsequent proceedings may represent a violation of due process (Grisso, 1998).

Post-charge Detention

Three choices are normally available once a youth has been charged with a crime: release on own recognizance, release with bail or other conditions, or detention. This decision will depend in part on the nature of the offense, but it will also depend in some cases on judgments about the youth's mental status and risk for re-offending during the interval before trial. Where significant mental health issues are detected, a more thorough assessment will be appropriate. Legal counsel may be involved in this decision.

Detention in custody or remand may be ordered for youth who are charged with a serious crime or judged at high risk for re-offending. In this case a formal risk assessment may be appropriate. However, collecting information about need factors such as negative peer associations or substance abuse may not be appropriate in this context. First, under most circumstances pre-charge detention is of limited duration and little effort at rehabilitative efforts is made. Second, the youth has not yet been convicted of a crime, and the information collected in the needs assessment may prejudice subsequent proceedings.

Transfer to Criminal Court/ Waiver to Adult Court

Transferring the case of a juvenile to criminal court for adjudication is mandatory for certain crimes

in some jurisdictions; however, in other cases, the transfer decision depends on judicial discretion. A number of factors may enter into these decisions. First, transfers are generally reserved for more serious crimes. Second, the likelihood of a transfer is increased if the young person is perceived at high risk for re-offending, particularly violent re-offending. Amenability to treatment is a third consideration in some cases. Finally, the presence of a significant cognitive developmental delay or mental illness will often lead to the decision to retain the case in the juvenile court or refer the youth to the mental health system.

Risk assessments are relevant to cases in which a youth is being considered for waiver to adult court. *Kent v. United States* (1966) lists a number of considerations to guide the court in these decisions, including risk and protection of the public and the likelihood of rehabilitation of the youth. Thus, lawyers representing youth in these cases would benefit from a forensic assessment that focuses on risk and treatment amenability (see Chapter 18).

Disposition Decisions

The following dispositions are usually available to the juvenile court following a finding of guilt: dismissal with no further action, a custody sentence of some type and duration, or a sentence involving a period of probation. This decision is often guided by an assessment provided by a psychologist or a pre-disposition report prepared by a probation officer or other court official.

The role of risk and risk/needs assessments in these disposition decisions is complicated. It could be argued, for example, that allowing risk and risk/needs assessments to influence sentencing may distort the process and create an unfair situation for the youth. Providing one youth with a longer sentence than another who committed the same crime and with the same criminal history because the first youth exhibits more criminogenic needs can be considered unfair.

However, these assessments can be considered important within the sentence. Knowing the youth's criminogenic needs can, for example, be important in the context of a custody sentence. It can guide decisions about the kinds of services to provide the youth in that setting. Similarly, probation orders should be accompanied by information about the specific needs and responsivity characteristics of the young person to guide rehabilitative efforts within the disposition. It is in this context that pre-disposition reports guided by careful risk and risk/needs assessments can be very beneficial to the process (Hoge, 2001, 2008; Hoge & Andrews, 1996, 2010).

Juvenile judicial and correctional systems including rehabilitative goals will generally design the dispositions to reflect the needs of the youth and the services available within the system. For example, where the youth's criminal activity was associated with dysfunctional parenting within the home, substance abuse, and association with antisocial peers, the judge may direct that services to meet those specific needs should be provided within the probation disposition. Similarly, if significant mental health issues are exhibited by the youth, a referral to relevant psychological services might be indicated.

In cases where some indications of significant cognitive or emotional disabilities are present, a full psychological assessment conducted by a mental health professional may be indicated. This may be required in some jurisdictions or a matter of policy in others. These assessments will be based on appropriate standardized and clinical procedures.

A full mental health assessment is generally not required for most youth receiving a finding of guilt. Nevertheless, and again particularly where a rehabilitative ideal is present, some guidance is required to recommend the level of monitoring required within either probation or custody and appropriate services. This guidance will normally be provided by a probation officer through the pre-disposition reports. In many cases these reports are based on informal clinical procedures. However, standardized screening and assessment instruments are available to assist this process. This may involve using a risk screening instruments (described later) to provide some information about the youth's likelihood of engaging in another criminal act. A more satisfactory course is to use a standardized risk/needs instrument (also described below) to provide information about the youth's risk level and also areas of need to address to reduce the level of risk.

FORENSIC MENTAL HEALTH CONCEPTS

Risk assessment is considered in a broad context to include both risk prediction and risk management. Heilbrun (2001) made the important distinction between risk prediction and risk management, both of which are relevant to risk assessment. Risk prediction involves simply predicting the likelihood that the youth will engage in antisocial behavior of some sort. The concern in some cases is with the prediction of general criminal activity and in other cases with more specific forms of illegal actions such as violent or sex offenses. Risk management, on the other hand, involves identifying risk factors that can be addressed to reduce the risk of criminal activity. Legal professionals should expect that an evaluator will focus on both identifying the level of risk posed by a youth and also how that risk can be managed through a variety of intervention and monitoring techniques.

Risk for Re-offending

Estimates of the youth's risk for committing another offense is an important consideration in pretrial detention, transfer, and postsentence disposition decisions. Detention prior to trial is usually reserved for youth who have committed serious crimes and/or are judged at risk for committing a new offense. The same considerations generally apply to decisions about transfers to the criminal courts. Risk assessments may also be relevant to post-charge referrals to alternative measures programs and sentencing/disposition decisions. A judge, for example, may sentence a youth to custody based on information that the youth is at high risk for re-offending.

Assessments of risk for re-offending may focus on the commission of any new offense or a specific type of offense such as violent or sexual offending. The term "dangerousness" is sometimes used in connection with risk of violent offending. Research on factors associated with general, violent, and sexual re-offending among youth has a long history, and we now have considerable information about characteristics of the youth and his or her circumstances associated with persistence of criminal activity (Hoge & Andrews, 2010; Thornberry & Krohn, 2003).

Assessments of risk for criminal activity are commonly based on informal evaluations conducted by police, prosecutors, or others within the juvenile system. However, a number of well-validated measures of risk for re-offending have been developed for juveniles (Hoge & Andrews, 1996, 2010; Vincent, Terry, & Maney, 2009). These are generally in the form of checklists designed for completion by a mental health professional or others within the juvenile system (e.g., intake officers, probation officers). Some of these measures include only historical or static factors (e.g., age at first arrest, number of arrests, parole violations). These are treated as static variables because they are not subject to change. An example is the Colorado Security Placement Instrument, which is composed of seven items reflecting the youth's history of antisocial behavior and contacts with correctional and mental health institutions. Other risk instruments, also termed risk/need instruments, include both static and dynamic items. The latter are risk factors that are subject to change, and, if changed, reduce the probability of future offending.

The Risk/Need/Responsivity Model

A useful framework for ensuring that risk is considered in the context of risk management is the Risk/ Need/Responsivity (RNR) model (Andrews & Bonta, 2010a, b; Andrews, Bonta, & Hoge, 1990). Criminogenic risk factors represent variables associated with an increased likelihood that the youth will engage in antisocial behaviors. A history of criminal activity, dysfunctional parenting, and substance abuse are three commonly recognized risk factors. Some risk factors, such as history of criminal activity, are considered static risk factors; they are historical and not subject to change. Other risk factors, such as dysfunctional parenting and substance abuse, are considered dynamic risk factors. That is, they are subject to change, and, if changed, can reduce the probability of engaging in criminal activities. These are also referred to as criminogenic need factors or simply need factors. The identification of these factors is critical to risk management since they will serve as targets of intervention. As indicated below, some standardized assessment measures focus only on static risk factors, while others also provide for the assessment of dynamic risk or need factors. The former will be referred to as risk-assessment instruments and the latter as risk/needs instruments.

Responsivity factors represent the third construct within the RNR model. Two categories of responsivity factors are identified. General responsivity refers to the nature and context of the intervention. Interventions may, for example, involve punitive, psychodynamic, or behavioral strategies. Context also refers to the relationship established within the service delivery. The latter may, for example, reflect a positive or negative approach to the youth on the part of the clinician.

Specific responsivity factors refer to characteristics of the youth or his or her circumstances. These can be further divided into negative and positive factors. Negative responsivity factors represent problematic conditions that might affect the outcome of intervention efforts. Depression, anxiety, exposure to marital conflict, and cultural/ ethnic issues are examples of factors that, while not necessarily directly related to the criminal activity, should be taken into account in case planning. Positive responsivity factors are strengths or competencies the youth brings to the situation. Examples include emotional maturity, interest in sports, and the availability of a concerned and cooperative parent. The RNR model emphasizes the importance of strength-based case management, and it is in this context that the assessment of strengths or competencies becomes important (Andrews, Bonta, & Wormith, 2011).

The RNR model includes three principles that highlight the importance of carefully assessing risk and need factors in the youth (Andrews & Bonta, 2010a, b; Andrews et al., 1990). The Risk Principle states that intensive services should be reserved for high-risk youth, while lower-risk youth should receive less intensive services. The Need Principle states that services provided to the youth should focus on his or her specific needs—that is, those factors directly contributing to his or her risk of offending. Finally, the Responsivity Principle states that planning for interventions should recognize potential interactions between general and specific responsivity factors. In other words, the intervention selected should match positive and negative characteristics of the youth.

The RNR model, by focusing on the needs of the youth and the use of evidence-based practices, encourages a rehabilitative and strength-based approach to dealing with youth at risk for criminal activity. An increasing body of empirical evaluation research demonstrates the value of such an approach, particularly where compared with more punitive strategies (Andrews & Bonta, 2010a, b). Also important is research support for the position that rehabilitative strategies are more cost-effective than punitive strategies (Drake, Aos, & Miller, 2009).

EMPIRICAL FOUNDATIONS AND LIMITS

A growing body of empirical research is developing with respect to risk factors associated with youthful criminal activity. Somewhat less research is available on need and responsivity factors, but empirical work is beginning to appear.

Some of the research on risk factors derives from cross-sectional and longitudinal research on criminal activity in young people. The longitudinal research is particularly important because it provides direct information about the linkage between potential risk factors with future criminal activity. Reviews of this work have been provided by Farrington (2006), Loeber and Farrington (2000), and Rutter (2003). The other source of this information is from validation research conducted with existing risk/needs assessment instruments. This research has also provided us with important information about the factors associated with youth crime (Heilbrun, Lee, & Cottle, 2005; Hoge & Andrews, 2010; Lipsey & Derzon, 1998).

The major risk factors identified in this research include history of conduct disorders/criminal actions; dysfunctional parenting; poor school/vocational achievement; antisocial peer associations; substance abuse; poor use of leisure time; dysfunctional behavioral and personality traits; and antisocial attitudes, values, and beliefs. These are not the only factors that place youth at risk for criminal activity, but they consistently emerge in research as the strongest factors. Research also indicates that these risk factors generalize across gender and ethnic-group membership. The relative importance of the variables and the dynamics of their functioning may vary across those groups, but the basic set of risk factors appears universal.

As indicated above, a distinction is made between static risk factors and dynamic risk factors (need factors). In fact, all of the variables listed above except those referring to criminal history can be considered need factors. All are capable of being modified and reductions in the area of need should provide reductions in the likelihood of re-offending. While the status of these as need factors has received less empirical attention than as risk factors, research is beginning to appear supporting the view that changes in these factors are, in fact, associated with changes in re-offending rates (Andrews & Bonta, 2010a, b; Dowden & Andrews, 1999).

As we will see below, the identification of relevant risk and need factors is important from the point of view of effective case management but is also relevant to evaluating the validity of standardized instruments for assessing risk and needs. The validity of these measures will be limited by the extent to which relevant variables are included.

THE EVALUATION

A number of distinctions are relevant to the process of forming predictions of risk. These will be reviewed here and further illustrated with the subsequent discussions of specific instruments. One important distinction is among the general formats of assessment employed. Many assessments of risk in forensic contexts are based on unstructured clinical judgments. For example, the police or prosecutor may interview the youth and parent and, on the basis of his or her professional experience, make a judgment about the level of risk for continued criminal activity. This judgment in turn may influence a decision about pretrial detention, incarceration, etc.

The other two forms of assessment procedures involve more structure than purely clinical assessments, although the degree of structure may vary. Structured professional judgments incorporate structured procedures into the clinical process. In this case a checklist or interview guides the professional through the evaluation process and in forming judgments about the risk or need level of the youth. This permits the professional to form an estimate of the overall level of risk of the youth and to identify specific areas of risk and need. The items in the assessment instrument or guide are generally based on theoretical and empirical considerations.

The third procedure, actuarial assessment, introduces an additional element of structure. In this case, a checklist or interview guides the professional through the evaluation process but, in addition, a formula is provided to translate scores from the individual items into a composite index of risk. The composite may be formed from a simple summing of items or on the basis of a weighting formula. The composite may in turn be expressed in probabilistic terms (e.g., youth exhibits a 40% of re-offending within a 12-month period) or a range (e.g., low, moderate, high probability of risk). Actuarial instruments may focus only on risk factors or may include both risk and need items.

Considerable empirical research indicates that structured professional judgment and actuarial standardized procedures yield more valid estimates of risk than clinical procedures (Borum, 2006; Grisso & Tomkins, 1996; Grove & Meehl, 1996; Hoge, 2008). The value of standardized assessments is also supported through research on best practices that demonstrated that systems employing standardized procedures are more effective than those employing clinical procedures (Andrews & Bonta, 2010a; Andrews, Bonta, & Wormith, 2011; Dowden & Andrews, 1999). The value of specific standardized instruments, whether based on structured professional judgment or actuarial procedures, depends ultimately, of course, on the psychometric properties of the measures. This is discussed further below.

Some risk-assessment instruments have been developed as screening tools and others are considered comprehensive instruments. Screening instruments are designed to provide initial information about some aspect of the youth's functioning. They are generally short, easy to administer, and easy to interpret. They may contain only risk items or both risk and need items. The Massachusetts Youth Screening Instrument–Version 2 (MAYSI–2; Grisso & Barnum, 2003) is an example of the type of screening instrument sometimes used as youth enter pretrial detention. It provides preliminary information about the presence of a mental health issue. Where symptoms are identified, a more comprehensive assessment would be conducted. Screening instruments can often be employed by non-mental health providers with training in the procedure. These are generally used as an initial assessment tool to determine if more intensive assessments are appropriate.

Psychological assessments involving comprehensive instruments, on the other hand, involve the collection of more extensive information and a more in-depth assessment of the characteristics of the youth and his or her circumstances. Comprehensive assessment instruments focus on a broad range of risk factors and, in the case of some instruments, need and responsivity factors as well. Where need and responsivity factors are included, the comprehensive instrument can serve to both estimate the youth's risk for continued criminal activity and also assist in managing risk. These instruments usually involve training in administration and scoring. Examples will be presented below.

It is important to note a distinction between forensic assessments and therapeutic assessments. The former are conducted to inform forensic decisions and the latter to aid in formulating a therapeutic treatment program. These two types of assessments differ in some important respects, including freedom to refuse participation and confidentiality rules.

Several cautions should be noted regarding the conduct of forensic assessments, particularly those involving youth. First, it is important to recognize that youth are going through a developmental process, and that the functioning of the youth in many areas is less advanced than that of adults (Steinberg & Belsky, 1996). The limits exhibited by youth in reasoning abilities and in the capacity to interpret and regulate emotional states, function in social relations, and engage in the decision process have direct relevance to forensic decisions. The ability of youth to solve problems can be limited; therefore, an important consideration in forensic assessments of youth is the documentation of the cognitive and emotional limitations of the youth.

The situation with respect to development is further complicated by the fact that development does not proceed at the same pace. Not all 14-year-olds are at the same level of development or maturity. Further, different aspects of cognitive and emotional functioning may develop at different rates within the youth: the 14-year-old may be sexually mature but very limited in cognitive reasoning abilities. These developmental considerations must be taken into account in making forensic decisions, particularly those involving cognitive or emotional functioning.

A second complication is that legal and procedural guidelines for forensic decisions are sometimes ambiguous and may vary across jurisdictions (Grisso, 1998; Melton, Petrila, Poythress, & Slobogin, 2007). This often complicates the design of assessment batteries.

The third caution is that a clear and direct link does not always exist between an assessment and the forensic decision (Heilbrun, 2010). Often, a clinical judgment is required to make the connection with the ultimate forensic question. However, empirical research is beginning to appear in which the actual relevance of assessments for forensic decisions is being explored. Instead of asking how a given assessment outcome relates to the forensic decision, this research is asking what aspects of functioning are actually relevant to a decision. Once that is established, a more valid choice can be made among assessment alternatives.

The importance of intelligent decisions about how risk assessments inform a forensic decision cannot be overemphasized. The primary recommendation is that forensic assessments should be conducted by trained and certified professionals using the best standardized assessment tools available. Decisions made about youth at all stages of the judicial process are extremely important to the youth and to society, and thus it is imperative that those decisions be made in an optimal manner.

Evaluating Assessment Instruments

Reliability and validity are the two primary bases for evaluating any psychological measure (Sattler & Hoge, 2006). Reliability refers to the stability or consistency of a measure. More formally, it refers to the relative proportion of error and true variance within a measure. Risk/needs assessment instruments are normally evaluated through inter-rater agreement procedures. This involves establishing the extent to which two observers using the same information produce similar ratings independently.

Validity is a somewhat more difficult concept, although it is critical to the evaluation of any psychological measure. A number of different forms of validity are relevant to these evaluations, but predictive validity and dynamic validity are the most important forms in evaluating a risk-assessment instrument. In the case of *predictive validity* we are asking about the extent to which scores from the measure actually predict future criminal or other antisocial behavior. It is also important to establish predictive validity separately for each group being evaluated. *Dynamic validity* refers to the extent to which changes in risk/ need scores are associated with changes in behavior. If reductions in risk and needs are associated with reduced re-offending and increases are associated with increased re-offending, confidence in the validity of the instrument is increased.

Reliability and validity are characteristics of the instrument. However, the use of an instrument in a specific situation will be influenced by the way in which it is administered and interpreted. Research in a wide variety of areas has shown that decisions based on standardized measures supported by reliability and validity research are superior under most circumstances to those based on clinical assessments (e.g., Grove & Meehl, 1996). As well, as discussed below, court testimony based on standardized instruments will often carry more credibility than that based solely on clinical procedures.

Comprehensive Risk/Needs Instruments

A number of research-based comprehensive risk/ needs instruments have been developed. With the exception of the Estimate of Risk of Adolescent Sexual Offence Recidivism (ERASOR), all of the measures described in this section are designed as measures of general criminogenic factors. The instruments identified are in the form of checklists or rating scales, are accompanied by detailed manuals, and are supported by reliability and validity analyses. More detailed descriptions of the measures as well as information about their psychometric properties are available from Grisso, Vincent, and Seagrave (2005), Hoge, Vincent, & Guy, (in press), Otto and Douglas (2010), and Vincent, Terry, and Maney (2009). Screening instruments focusing only on risk factors such as the Arizona Juvenile Assessment Form or North Carolina Assessment of Risk are not reviewed here. A brief discussion of the comprehensive measures follows.

Estimate of Risk of Adolescent Sexual Offense Recidivism–2

The ERASOR (Worling & Curwen, 2001) is a structured clinical assessment tool focusing specifically on risk for continued sexual offending of youth aged 12 to 18 with a history of sexual offending. The instrument yields an overall estimate of risk based on the total number of items checked and the clinician's judgment about the observed pattern of risk. No actuarial formula determines the overall risk score. The pattern of items checked provides guidance to the clinician on the optimal intervention strategy.

The ERASOR is in the form of a 25-item checklist. Items refer to various attitudinal and behavioral factors relevant to sexual offending. Examples of items include "obsessive sexual interests/preoccupation with sexual thoughts," "diverse sexual assault behaviors," and "lack of intimate peer relationships." The items are divided into five scales: Sexual Interests, Attitudes, and Behaviors; History of Sexual Assaults; Psychosocial Functioning; Family Functioning; and Treatment Responses.

Limited psychometric information regarding the ERASOR is available at present (Worling & Curwen, 2001). Detailed guidelines for administering and scoring the instrument are available, as is a specialized training program. The measure can be used by a non-mental health professional with this specialized training. The authors of the instrument emphasize the importance of using multiple sources of information in completing the measure.

Risk-Sophistication-Treatment Inventory

The RSTI (Salekin, 2001, 2004) is a semi-structured interview and rating scale designed to help clinicians assess risk for dangerousness, sophistication-maturity, and treatment amenability as well as treatment needs for juvenile offenders aged 9 to 18 years. It was designed specifically for use in waiver to adult court cases, but it is also applicable to a broader range of cases in which risk and treatment issues are considered. The instrument is reviewed in detail in Chapter 18.

Structured Assessment of Violence Risk in Youth

The SAVRY (Borum, Bartel, & Forth, 2003) represents the structured professional judgment format and is specifically designed for evaluating risk for violent actions for youth between the ages of 12 and 18. Items are derived from the research literature.

The 24 items of the checklist are divided into three categories: Historical (e.g., "history of violence"); Individual (e.g., "negative attitudes"); and Social (e.g., "poor parental management"). Each item is scored in terms of level of severity (low, moderate, high). A total score is based on the assessor's judgment of the pattern and severity of risk factors. Also included are six strength or protective items: Prosocial Involvement, Strong Social Support, Strong Attachments and Bonds, Positive Attitude Toward Authority, Strong Commitment to School, and Resilient Personality Traits. These are scored present or absent. The intention is that the pattern of risk and protective factors can assist in case planning and management.

Psychometric support for the SAVRY has been provided (Borum, Bartel, & Forth, 2005; Borum, Lodewijks, Bartel, & Forth, 2010). The authors of the instrument indicate that no special training is required to use the measure, although a familiarity with the manual is important.

Washington State Juvenile Court Assessment

The WSJCA (Barnoski, 2004) comprises a two-part assessment process in which a brief screening instrument is first administered. Youth obtaining a moderate or high score on that measure are then administered the full WSJCA measure. Only the latter measure is described here. The WSJCA is an example of a structured professional judgment format, although scoring keys are provided in the manual for the different domains.

Scoring of the 132 items on the checklist reflects whether an item represents a static risk factor, a dynamic risk factor, or a protective factor. The items are divided into six domains: Criminal History, School, Employment, Family, Mental Health, and Aggression. While it is possible for the WSJCA to be administered by non-mental health professionals, an extensive training program is provided and recommended. Barnoski and Markhussen (2005) provide psychometric support for the measure. In addition, a slightly different version of the WSJCA, the Youth Assessment and Screening Instrument, has also been developed.

Youth Level of Service/Case Management Inventory

The YLS/CMI (Hoge & Andrews, 2011) is an example of an actuarial risk/needs measure that also incorporates responsivity factors. It is designed for ages 12 to 18. The measure also includes a professional override feature to allow the examiner some discretion in forming an overall level of risk and needs. This provides the examiner an opportunity to override the score if he or she thinks that is merited by special considerations. The YLS/CMI has six parts: Part I: Assessment of Risk and Needs; Part II: Summary of Risk/Needs Factors; Part III: Assessment of Other Needs/Special Considerations, Part IV: Professional Override; Part V: Contact Level; and Part VI: Case Management Plan.

Part I of the instrument includes 42 items reflecting characteristics of the offender (e.g., antisocial peer associates, chronic alcohol use) or his or her circumstances (e.g., inadequate parental supervision). The items are divided into eight domains: Prior and Current Offenses/Dispositions; Family Circumstances/Parenting; Education/Employment; Peer Relations; Substance Abuse; Leisure/Recreation; Personality/Behavior; and Attitudes/Orientation. An opportunity is also provided to indicate areas of strength in these domains. Subsequent sections of the YLS/CMI provide an opportunity to record responsivity factors, professional overrides, and case plans. The latter involve the identification of specific goals and means of achieving the goals.

The YLS/CMI–2 is a revised version of the earlier YLS/CMI. However, Part I has not been altered. Support for the reliability and validity of the risk/

needs assessment (Part I) has been presented by Hoge and Andrews (2011) and Hoge (2005).

Conducting the Risk/Needs Assessment

The selection of an assessment instrument with well-established reliability and validity is the first step in the assessment process. It is also important for the evaluator to ensure that the psychometric properties have been established for the individuals being assessed. In cases where the psychometric properties for the instrument have not been established on the relevant population of individuals, the measure may still be used but extra caution should be exercised in interpreting the scores.

The next consideration is the expertise and training of the individual conducting the assessment. All of the comprehensive instruments reviewed above can be administered and interpreted by mental health professionals or non-mental health professionals such as probation officers or counselors; however, in the latter case, some background in adolescent psychology is important. Each of the measures, with the exception of the SAVRY, requires specialized training in administration, scoring, and interpretation.

Other issues in the conduct of assessments include that the evaluator establish rapport with the youth, collect interview data from the youth and others, integrate information from a variety of sometimes conflicting sources, and prepare a final report based on scores from the risk/needs assessment instrument. Legal professionals who retain or work with evaluators in this context can assist the evaluation process by ensuring that all relevant sources of information have been made available to the evaluator, thus ensuring a comprehensive evaluation.

Additional psychological measures may be useful in compiling information to complete the comprehensive instruments. These may include attitude scales, tests of educational achievement and competencies, and personality tests. For example, a measure of antisocial attitudes such as the How I Think Questionnaire (HIT; Gibbs, Barriga, & Potter, 2001) can be useful in assessing the youth's attitudes and values regarding social issues. Mental health professionals completing the instruments might also employ standardized personality and pathology measures such as the Millon Adolescent Clinical Inventory (MACI; Millon, 1993) or the MAYSI–2 (Grisso & Barnum, 2003).

One other practical consideration deserves mention. The risk/needs assessment will constitute part of a larger information-gathering and decision-making process within the juvenile-justice agency. It is essential that clear rules be provided regarding the role of the assessment in the system. Among other things, this will help avoid the ethical and legal problems noted in the following section.

Ethical and Legal Considerations

A number of ethical issues may arise in connection with forensic assessments (Grisso, 2005; Heilbrun, 2001, 2010; Hoge & Andrews, 2010; Melton, Petrila, Poythress, & Slobogin, 2007). Especially relevant in the current context are issues relating to due process and confidentiality.

Due process is directed toward ensuring that youth be treated fairly within the juvenile-justice system:

> For youth who are charged with delinquencies, the juvenile justice system has a mandate to insure that the legal process judges their responsibility for their alleged delinquencies fairly, and that the system does not abuse its discretion deciding on penalties and rehabilitative measures when youths are found delinquent. (Grisso, 2005, p. 9)

Specific issues of due process arise in the case of risk and risk/needs assessment. As indicated earlier, while an assessment of risk for continued criminal activity may be relevant to a decision regarding pretrial detention, it is not relevant to adjudicative decisions or, normally, to dispositions such as length of sentence. Exceptions to the latter may occur where criminal history may be considered or where the judge considers likelihood of responding to treatment in determining sentence length. Identifying a range of criminogenic needs in the youth should not be used as the basis for either adjudicative or disposition decisions. However, once a disposition has been decided, whether institutional or community-based, the risk/needs assessment can be important in establishing a case plan.

Observing informed-consent rules is sometimes complicated in the case of risk/needs assessment. These inevitably involve collecting personal information about the youth and his or her family. This is generally viewed as justified where the assessment is court-ordered. Where this type of order does not exist, the youth should be fully informed about the purpose of the assessment and the uses to be made of the information collected.

Legal guidelines regarding the treatment of youth within the judicial system are sometimes available to guide these decisions. Mental health professionals such as psychologists, psychiatrists, and social workers will be bound by professional standards established by their professional organizations. Finally, judicial systems dealing with juvenile offenders should have explicit guidelines regarding ethical and legal issues (Grisso & Vincent, 2005; Mulvey & Islin, 2008).

REPORT WRITING AND TESTIMONY

The communication of the risk and needs assessments through reports and court testimony is an important part of the assessment process. The communication may be presented by written or oral means by a psychologist or other professional. In some cases the format of the report may follow structured guidelines and in other cases the professional will have latitude in forming the report. Similarly, expert testimony in court may follow statutory guidelines, while in other cases more latitude is available.

There will be occasions where a narrow focus on risk or risk/needs may be appropriate. This might be the case, for example, where an assessment of risk is required to assist in a post-charge detention decision. More often, though, risk assessments are embedded within a more comprehensive report. The preparation of a report will always depend on the purpose of the report and the audience and should always be written with regard to due-process guidelines. An important consideration in this respect is that information not directly related to the legal question at issue should not be included in a report since doing so may prejudice the process (Grisso & Appelbaum, 1992; Heilbrun, 2010). Another important consideration is with respect to clarity: it is important to ensure that in written reports and oral testimony in court the language is comprehensible to the intended audience, whether judges, lawyers, or other court officials.

Judges and lawyers will often want direct information about the level of risk presented by the youth. In many cases the index will be presented in qualitative terms (e.g., low, moderate, high, or very high risk). In other cases a more quantitative index will be used. This might involve, for example, a standardized score based on a sample of youth. For example, the index might indicate that the youth's level of risk is equal to the average of a sample of comparable youth or is higher than 80% of other youth in the sample. Risk indices of these types can be useful in assisting decisions about the youth, but they must be used with caution. They are designed to help guide decisions but not to dictate those decisions (Grisso, 2005; Hoge & Andrews, 2010; see Chapter 6).

Several cautions in the use of these risk assessments should be reemphasized. First, it must be kept in mind that, because emotions and behaviors can change in unexpected ways during adolescence, risk and need scores may fluctuate over time. This means that the estimates should be used for short- rather than long-term predictions. Lawyers should expect risk-assessment reports to be explicit about this limitation. Further, risks and needs should be reassessed at periodic intervals. A second caution relates to the importance of attending not only to risk factors but to need factors as well. A report should address the factors placing the youth at risk for continued criminal activity and what efforts can be taken to address the needs underlying that risk. This represents a risk-management approach, and it is not only morally defensible but, to the extent it encourages a rehabilitative approach, will also result in more positive effects on youth crime than a narrow punitive approach.

SUMMARY

Risk and risk/needs assessments are commonly conducted in juvenile-justice systems. Sometimes these are conducted informally and sometimes through the use of standardized procedures such as those outlined in this chapter. The assessments are linked to important decisions about the youth at all stages of processing. The argument provided in this chapter is that sound empirical evidence exists in favor of the use of standardized assessments rather than informal clinical procedures. The standardized instruments and procedures have been shown repeatedly to result in better assessments and better decisions. Further, the use of risk/need-assessment tools encourages the adoption of a positive and rehabilitative approach to the youth, which, in turn, has been shown to lead to better outcomes, particularly in comparison with punitive approaches.

REFERENCES

Altschuler, D. M. (1998). Intermediate sanctions and community treatment for serious and violent offenders. In R. Loeber & D. P. Farrington (Eds.), *Serious and violent juvenile offenders: Risk factors and successful interventions* (pp. 367–385). Thousand Oaks, CA: Sage.

Andrews, D. A., & Bonta, J. (2010a). *The psychology of criminal conduct* (5th ed.). Cincinnati, OH: Anderson.

Andrews, D. A., & Bonta, J. (2010b). Rehabilitating criminal justice policy and practice. *Psychology, Public Policy, and Law, 16,* 39–55.

Andrews, D. A., Bonta, J., & Hoge, R. D. (1990). Classification for effective rehabilitation: Rediscovering psychology. *Criminal Justice and Behavior, 17,* 19–52.

Andrews, D. A., Bonta, J., & Wormith, J.S. (2011). The Risk/Need/Responsivity (RNR) model: Does adding the Good Lives Model contribute to effective crime prevention? *Criminal Justice and Behavior, 38,* 735–755.

Barnoski, R. (2004). *Assessing risk for re-offense: Validating the Washington State Juvenile Court Assessment* (Report No. 04-03-1201. Olympia, WA: Washington State Institute for Public Policy.

Barnoski, R., & Markussen, S. (2005). Washington State Juvenile Court Assessment. In T. Grisso, T. Vincent, & D. Seagrave (Eds.), *Mental health screening and assessment in juvenile justice* (pp. 271–282). New York: Guilford.

Borum, R. (2006). Assessing risk for violence among juvenile offenders. In S. Sparta & G. Koocher (Eds.), *The forensic assessment of children and adolescents: Issues and applications* (pp. 190–202). New York: Oxford University Press.

Borum, R., Bartel, P. A., & Forth, A. E. (2003). *Manual for the Structured Assessment of Violence Risk in Youth (SAVRY).* Tampa, FL: University of South Florida.

Borum, R., Bartel, P. A., & Forth, A. E. (2005). Structured Assessment of Violence Risk in Youth. In T. Grisso, T. Vincent, & D. Seagrave (Eds.), *Mental health screening and assessment in juvenile justice* (pp. 311–323). New York: Guilford.

Borum, R., Lodewijks, H., H., Bartel, P. A., & Forth, A. E. (2010). Structured Assessment of Violence Risk in Youth (SAVRY). In R. K. Otto & K. S. Douglas (Eds.), *Handbook of violence risk assessment* (pp. 63–79). New York: Routledge.

Dowden, C., & Andrews, D. A. (1999). What works in young offender treatment: A meta-analysis. *Forum on Corrections Research, 11,* 21–24.

Drake, E. K., Aos, S., & Miller, M. G. (2009). Evidence-based public policy options to reduce crime and criminal justice costs: Implications in Washington State. *Victims & Offenders, 4,* 170–196.

Farrington, D. P. (2006). Key longitudinal-experimental studies in criminology. *Journal of Experimental Criminology, 2,* 121–141.

Gibbs, J. C., Barriga, A. Q., & Potter, G. B. (2001). *How I Think (HIT) questionnaire.* Champaign, IL: Research Press.

Grisso, T. (1998). *Forensic evaluation of juveniles.* Sarasota, FL: Professional Resource Press.

Grisso, T. (2005). Evaluating the properties of instruments for screening and assessment. In T. Grisso, T. Vincent, & D. Seagrave (Eds.), *Mental health screening and assessment in juvenile justice* (pp. 71–97). New York: Guilford.

Grisso, T., & Appelbaum, T. S. (1992). Is it unethical to offer predictions of future violence? *Law and Human Behavior, 16,* 621–633.

Grisso, T., & Barnum, R. (2003). *Massachusetts Youth Screening Instrument–Version 2: User's manual and technical report.* Sarasota, FL: Personal Resource Press.

Grisso, T., & Tomkins, A. J. (1996). Communicating violence risk assessments. *American Psychologist, 51,* 928–930.

Grisso, T., & Vincent, G. (2005). The context for mental health screening and assessment. In T. Grisso, T. Vincent, & D. Seagrave (Eds.), *Mental health screening and assessment in juvenile justice* (pp. 44–70). New York: Guilford.

Grisso, T., Vincent, G., & Seagrave, D. (Eds.). (2005). *Mental health screening and assessment in juvenile justice.* New York: Guilford.

Grove, W. M., & Meehl, P. E. (1996). Comparative efficiency of informal (subjective, impressionistic) and formal (mechanical, algorithmic) prediction procedures: The clinical-statistical controversy. *Psychology, Public Policy, and the Law, 2,* 293–323.

Heilbrun, K. (2001). *Principles of forensic mental health assessment.* New York: Kluwer Academic/Plenum.

Heilbrun, K. (2010). *Violence risk assessment in adults.* New York: Oxford University Press.

Heilbrun, K., Lee, R., & Cottle, C. (2005). Risk factors and intervention outcomes: Meta-analyses of juvenile offending. In K. Heilbrun, N. Goldstein, & R. Redding (Eds.), *Juvenile delinquency: Prevention, assessment and interventions* (pp. 111–133). New York: Oxford University Press.

Hoge, R. D. (2001). *The juvenile offender: Theory, research, and applications.* Norwell, MA: Kluwer.

Hoge, R. D. (2005). Youth Level of Service/Case Management Inventory. In T. Grisso, T. Vincent, & D. Seagrave (Eds.), *Mental health screening and assessment in juvenile justice* (pp. 283–294). New York: Guilford.

Hoge, R. D. (2008). Assessment in juvenile justice systems. In R. D. Hoge, N. G. Guerra, & P. Boxer (Eds.), *Treating the juvenile offender* (pp. 54–75). New York: Guilford.

Hoge, R. D., & Andrews, D. A. (1996). *Assessing the youthful offender: Issues and techniques.* New York: Plenum.

Hoge, R. D., & Andrews, D. A. (2010). *Evaluation of risk for violence in juveniles.* New York: Oxford.

Hoge, R. D., & Andrews, D. A. (2011). *Youth Level of Service/Case Management Inventory user's manual.* North Tonawanda, NY: Multi-Health Systems.

Hoge, R. D., Vincent, G. M, & Guy, L. S. (in press). Risk and needs assessment of early adult criminal activity. In R. Loeber & D. P. Farrington (Eds.), *Transitions from juvenile delinquency to adult crime: Criminal careers, justice policy and prevention.* New York: Oxford.

Kent vs. United States, 383 U.S. 541 (1966).

Lipsey, M. W., & Derzon, J. H. (1998). Predictors of violent or serious delinquency in adolescence and early adulthood: A synthesis of longitudinal research. In R. Loeber & D. P. Farrington (Eds.), *Serious and violent juvenile offenders: Risk factors and successful interventions* (pp. 86–105). Thousand Oaks, CA: Sage.

Loeber, R., & Farrington, D. P. (2000). Young children who commit crimes: Epidemiology, developmental origins, risk factors, early interventions, and policy implications. *Development and Psychopathology, 12,* 737–762.

Melton, G., Petrila, J., Poythress, N. G., & Slobogin, C. (2007). *Psychological evaluations for the courts: A handbook for mental health professionals and lawyers* (2nd ed.). New York: Guilford.

Millon, T. (1993). *Millon Adolescent Clinical Inventory.* Minneapolis, MN: National Computer Systems.

Mulvey, E. P., & Iselin, A. (2008). Improving professional judgments or risk and amenability in juvenile justice. *The Future of Children, 18,* 35–57.

Otto, R. K., & Douglas, K. S. (2010) (Eds.). *Handbook of violence risk assessment.* New York: Routledge.

Rutter, M. (2003). Crucial paths from risk indicator to causal mechanism. In B. B. Lahey, T. E. Moffitt, & A. Caspi (Eds.), *Causes of conduct disorder and juvenile delinquency* (pp. 3–24). New York: Guilford.

Salekin, R. T. (2001). Juvenile transfer to adult court: How can developmental and child psychology inform policy decision making? In B. L. Bottoms, M. B. Kovera, & B. D. McAuliff (Eds.), *Children, social science, and U.S. law* (pp. 203–232). New York: Cambridge University Press.

Salekin, R. T. (2004). *Risk-Sophistication Treatment Inventory (RST-i) professional manual.* Lutz, FL: Psychological Assessment Resources.

Sattler, J., & Hoge, R. D. (2006). *Assessment of children: Behavioral, social, and clinical foundations* (5th ed.). San Diego, CA: Sattler.

Steinberg, L., & Belsky, J. (1996). An evolutionary perspective on psychopathology in adolescence. In D. Ciddhetti & S. L. Toth (Eds.), *Rochester symposium on developmental psychopathology, adolescence: Opportunities and challenges* (pp. 93–124). Newbury Park, CA: Sage.

Thornberry, T. P., & Krohn, M. D. (2003). *Taking stock of delinquency: An overview of findings from contemporary longitudinal studies.* New York: Kluwer/Plenum.

Vincent, G. M., Terry, A., & Maney, S. (2009). Risk/needs tools for antisocial behavior and violence among youthful populations. In J. Andrade (Ed.), *Handbook of violence risk assessment and treatment for forensic mental health practitioners* (pp. 337–424). New York: Springer.

Worling, J. R., & Curwen, M. A. (2001). *Estimate of Risk of Adolescent Sexual Offense Recidivism (ERASOR).* Toronto, ON: Thistletown Regional Centre.

18

Evaluation for Disposition and Transfer of Juvenile Offenders

RANDALL T. SALEKIN, KIMBERLY M. PRICE, KATHRYN E. TANT,

ELIZABETH W. ADAMS, XINYING ANG, AND JILL ROSENBAUM

Attorneys working with youth who come into contact with the law may find themselves involved in disposition decision making cases. Such cases are typically handled within the juvenile-justice system where judges are charged with determining the best placement for youth. These cases are focused on rehabilitation. In other, more serious juvenile cases, attorneys may find themselves on cases where youth are being considered for transfer to adult court. With respect to transfer, some attorneys may be defending youth who are facing transfer to adult court while other attorneys may wish to seek charges for a given youth in adult, rather than juvenile, court. Still others may find themselves working toward achieving a reverse transfer when youth find themselves automatically in adult court. In each of these cases, the attorney may wish to hire a psychologist or other mental health professional to gather information on a given youth, write a report, and provide expert testimony to the courts.

The purpose of this chapter is to provide information to attorneys about the juvenile disposition process as well as the waiver process and the types of information they can expect to learn from psychological reports and testimony. Specifically, the goals of this chapter are six-fold. First, we provide information on the legal context of juvenile disposition and waiver evaluations. Second, we discuss chief forensic mental health concepts. It should be noted here that the forensic mental health concepts are relevant to both types of evaluations. These include the criteria originally outlined for transfer as well as two broad mental health concepts—personality and the honesty of reporting (veracity). Third, we provide information on the empirical

foundations and the limitations regarding forensic mental health concepts and their predictive merit. Fourth, we provide specific information on how forensic clinicians conduct the evaluation. Fifth, we provide specific information on report writing and testimony. In closing, we sketch out guidelines for how attorneys and clinicians can work together to avoid bias in psychological reporting of information and we examine how the clinical evaluation of youth might eventually help us shape policy for youth to create a more developmentally sensitive juvenile-justice system.

LEGAL CONTEXT

The juvenile courts were created in the United States in the 1890s to address the popular belief that children and adolescents are developmentally different than adults and therefore should be processed in developmentally sensitive courts. In the first quarter of the 20th century, critics of the juvenile-justice movement suggested that the juvenile court system was not appropriately punitive toward serious younger criminals nor did it appropriately control crime, especially for those who were violent and over the age of 16 years. Accordingly, by the mid-20th century juvenile laws were revised to include conditions for the transfer of youthful offenders to criminal court (Tanenhaus, 2000). These revisions were meant to serve as a safety valve to remove severe juvenile offenders from the less severe youthful offenders.

The revisions stemmed from a significant rise in violent youthful crime from the late 1980s to the late 1990s, with a 70% increase in the number of youthful offenders arrested for violent offenses during that decade (Jordan & Myers, 2007).

Consequently, there was an increased public perception of the dangerousness of youthful offenders, and society demanded greater crime control and more punitive treatment of violent young offenders. In reaction, it is believed that the juvenile-justice system became more focused on crime-control models, with various states adding additional provisions for the transfer of offenders to criminal court (Woolard, Odgers, Lanza-Kaduce, & Daglis, 2005). These changes are reflected in the significant increase in the number of youthful offenders held in prisons—from 1,600 in 1988 to 8,000 in 1998 (Austin, Johnson, & Gregoriou, 2000). As of mid-2008, approximately 3,500 youthful offenders were being held as adults in local jails and 6,400 youthful offenders were incarcerated in state prisons (West & Sabol, 2009).

Despite fluctuations in the rate of violent crime in U.S. society and the varying rate of youth being transferred to adult court, surges in violence over the past decades have left us with a number of mechanisms for transferring juveniles to adult court. At present, every state allows for the transfer of youthful offenders to adult court (Redding, 2010). Estimates of youth transfer indicate that as many as 200,000 youthful offenders are being processed as adults on a yearly basis (Woolard et al., 2005). However, of that sum, approximately 14,000 are processed by judicial waiver (Griffin, Addie, Adams, & Firestine, 2011), suggesting that the majority of these offenders are transferred by other mechanisms. It is difficult to know the exact estimates regarding transfer because, according to the Office of Juvenile Justice and Delinquency Prevention, the latest statistics on transfer are missing data from 29 states (Griffin et al., 2011). We briefly outline the mechanisms for transfer below.

Mechanisms for Transfer to (or from) Adult Court

There are currently four different mechanisms by which youthful offenders can be processed in adult court. The first mechanism is judicial waiver: after a hearing, a judge determines if the offender should be transferred. This procedure is currently available in 45 states (Griffin et al., 2011; Snyder & Sickmund, 2006). The second mechanism is statutory exclusion (automatic transfer), which indicates that the state's laws allow for the automatic transfer of offenders of a certain age who performed a specific crime (e.g., a 14-year-old who committed first-

degree murder). This is currently allowed in 29 states. The third mechanism is prosecutorial discretion, wherein attorneys have the right to prosecute a case in either juvenile or criminal court because both courts can claim jurisdiction for that case (this mechanism is currently allowed in 15 states). The minimum offender age range for transfer by judicial waiver, statutory exclusion, and prosecutorial discretion, across the 50 states, ranges from no specified age to 17 years (16 for prosecutorial discretion).

In general, there are several criteria that determine whether an offender will be transferred. The primary criteria include the offender's age and the severity of the offense. The minimum age at which an offender can be transferred is highly dependent upon the offense (e.g., if the crime was person-, property-, or drug-related). Depending on the state, the minimum age for transfer can depend on the nature of the crime, with laws allowing younger offenders (e.g., 12 years old) to be transferred if they are accused of more violent felonies against persons (e.g., murder) (see Griffin et al., 2011; Snyder & Sickmund, 2006).

The fourth mechanism by which juvenile offenders can be transferred to adult court is blended sentencing statutes, or extended jurisdiction statutes, which provide for a combination of juvenile and adult components. The adult components of these sentences are usually enforced only if the offender violates the juvenile component of his or her sentence or if he or she commits a new crime (Fagan, 2008).

However, there are compensating mechanisms that allow for the consideration of individual differences in the judicial process. The reverse waiver, or decertification, of young offenders from adult to juvenile court is one of such mechanisms, and it is provided in 24 states (Griffin et al., 2011). In these situations, if after a hearing, the judge in the criminal court determines that it is more appropriate to prosecute the case in juvenile court than adult court, the youth will be decertified, or returned, to the juvenile court for processing (this can occur in 14 states). Sometimes a youth can be tried and convicted in adult court but judges impose juvenile dispositions rather than criminal ones, returning the juvenile to the juvenile correctional system for treatment and rehabilitation (this can occur in 18 states).

Two cases were key in helping shape both disposition evaluations for youth as well as transfer cases: *Kent v. United States* (1966) and *In re Gault* (1967). Because of Judge Fortas's dissatisfaction with the handling of transfer cases, he delineated factors that should be considered before transferring youth to adult court. What is important about these cases is that they provided structure to the evaluation of youth and highlighted prime concepts to be considered in the process of transfer. As it turns out, the concepts are important in all juvenile evaluations. Below, we delineate how these cases led to the mental health concepts thought to be related to best practice in this area. In addition, two other pertinent constructs are outlined because of their importance in assessing juvenile offenders.

FORENSIC MENTAL HEALTH CONCEPTS

Several mental health concepts are primary to best practice in juvenile disposition decision making and transfer evaluations. These concepts include the assessment of (i) veracity, (ii) personality/pathology, (iii) risk, (iv) maturity, and (v) treatment amenability (Salekin, Salekin, Clement, & Lesitico, 2005). The latter three pertain directly to the transfer criteria. We discuss the origin and specify some defining details of each concept below.

Criteria for Transfer

In the landmark case *Kent v. United States* (1966), the U.S. Supreme Court established guidelines for the judicial waiver of youthful offenders to criminal court. The *Kent* case provided eight criteria upon which transfer determinations should be made:

1) the seriousness of the alleged offense to the community and whether the protection of the community requires waiver; 2) whether the alleged offense was committed in an aggressive, violent, premeditated or willful manner; 3) whether the alleged offense was against persons or against property, greater weight being given to offenses against persons especially if personal injury resulted; 4) the prosecutive merit of the complaint, i.e., whether there is evidence upon which a Grand Jury may be expected to return an indictment; 5) the desirability of trial and disposition of the entire offense in one court when the juvenile's associates in the alleged offense are adults who will be charged with a crime; 6) the sophistication and maturity of the

juvenile as determined by consideration of his home, environmental situation, emotional attitude and pattern of living; 7) the record and previous history of the juvenile, including previous contacts with juvenile service programs, other law enforcement agencies, juvenile courts and other jurisdictions, prior periods of probation, or prior commitments to juvenile institutions; and 8) the prospects for adequate protection of the public and the likelihood of reasonable rehabilitation of the juvenile (if he is found to have committed the alleged offense) by the use of procedures, services and facilities currently available to the Juvenile Court. (pp. 566–567)

Although these *Kent* criteria were established by the Supreme Court, states have been left to decide how these criteria should be incorporated into the transfer process. Heilbrun, Leheny, Thomas, and Huneycutt (1997) reviewed statutes of the 50 states and the District of Columbia and examined the statutes' provisions regarding the transfer of youthful offenders to criminal court. They found that the following criteria were repeatedly important to the decision to waive an offender: (1) the offender's treatment needs, (2) risk assessment, (3) characteristics of the offense, (4) sophistication-maturity, and (5) if the offender had a mental illness or intellectual disability. Support has been garnered to show that these five concepts can be further narrowed to include only three concepts: (1) potential dangerousness (risk), (2) sophistication-maturity, and (3) amenability to treatment (Kruh & Brodsky, 1997; Salekin, 2002; Salekin & Grimes, 2008). In juvenile court guidelines written by the National Council of Juvenile and Family Court Judges (NCJFCJ, 2005) and published by the Office of Juvenile Justice and Delinquency Prevention (OJJDP), the NCJFCJ echoed that these three concepts capture the necessary criteria in the decision to retain or waive jurisdiction of juvenile offenders. Although dangerousness has always been a factor to consider, maturity and amenability to treatment have more recently and increasingly across the states been explicitly listed as criteria to consider in transfer decisions.

Despite increasing consensus that maturity and treatment amenability are key concepts in understanding juvenile offenders, the defining features of each of these constructs have not been well understood. Thus, this is where attorneys may seek help from mental health professionals to provide information to the courts regarding the forensic mental health concepts. Because of the centrality of the constructs to disposition decision making and transfer, the empirical foundations and limitations of each will be discussed below. The information provided below is typically the type of information that psychologists would examine in order to assess each important construct, but the section also discusses the limitations of the science in this area.

Before discussing these specific forensic mental health concepts below, it should be mentioned that there are two other broad concepts that must be considered in juvenile evaluations: the veracity of reporting (for the youth and family members) and the personality/pathology of the youth. With respect to veracity, clinicians and attorneys will want to know if the information they obtain is accurate. In the evaluation section of this chapter, we will briefly discuss ways to determine this. In addition, evaluations should cover the personality/pathology of the youth. This information is usually gathered to determine if the youth meets a specific DSM-IV (soon to be DSM-V) diagnosis, but clinicians may also be interested in the youth's personality functioning, and this may be obtained through general personality measures. Although beyond the scope of this chapter, the links between personality and pathology are becoming much clearer, and it is likely that some clinicians may choose assessment tools that operate from one paradigm or measures that bridge the traditional nomenclature with modern personality theories (see Salekin, Jarrett, & Adams, in press).

EMPIRICAL FOUNDATIONS AND LIMITS

Best-practice evaluation of youth is based on clinical information that is gathered in a systematic way and that is based on an empirical foundation (see Salekin, in press). The empirical foundation strengthens what clinicians can say about a youth. Specifically, this information fortifies their ability to generate hypotheses, describe youth, and forecast behavior, thereby allowing for best practice in this area with the most accurate reports possible. Although there exists an empirical base for the forensic mental health concepts mentioned above, there are also limitations to the assessment of key concepts and thus limits to the science behind juvenile evaluations where these concepts are so frequently discussed.

Below we discuss the science and limitations for the three main psycholegal constructs.

Risk for Dangerousness

Numerous legal and mental health scholars have acknowledged that the potential for dangerousness is an important construct for juvenile court judges to consider in disposition decision making and their decision to waive a youthful offender to adult court (Brannen et al., 2006; Heilbrun et al., 1997; NCJFCJ, 2005). Despite its importance, psychological researchers and legal scholars have noted that there are challenges in assessing and using this concept. Specifically, three challenging issues arise with this concept: (1) what is dangerousness, (2) how do we tap it, and (3) to what extent does it have predictive merit? Below we discuss what "risk for dangerousness" is and three pertinent areas of research that may help attorneys and clinicians better understand the risk that youth potentially pose to the community: developmental pathways to offending, psychopathy-like features, and prototypical items (derived from psychologists and juvenile court judges) that are thought to be central to dangerousness. Many of the factors that make youth a potential risk overlap, and the science behind them is central to their use.

Before discussing the empirical foundations of the concept, it is important to consider the ways in which dangerousness can be defined. There are likely a variety of ways in which the term "risk for dangerousness" can be defined. For the purposes of juvenile evaluations, we intentionally leave the term broad, because narrowing it further (e.g., "risk for violence") may not accurately reflect the degree to which youth may be dangerous to the community due to their turbulent lifestyle (e.g., chronic offending, burglaries, and drug trade). We suggest that where possible, clinicians provide attorneys and juvenile court judges with information regarding general re-offending rates and more specific rates for violent re-offending. Although it may be the risk for violent re-offenses that is most pertinent to disposition decision making and transfer decisions, examining both types of information (general and violent re-offending) provides a more comprehensive assessment of the youth's potential dangerousness to self and the community; thus, this information may be deemed important by juvenile court judges (Chen & Salekin, 2012). Moreover, there is an empirical foundation for both. The factors considered important to dangerousness assessment and their empirical foundations are discussed further below.

Developmental Pathways to Offending

Psychologists often look to developmental pathways to antisocial behavior because they serve as one helpful model and informative source when examining a youth's potential for future offending. Moffitt's (1993, 2007) seminal antisocial taxonomy paper described two trajectories for youths presenting with antisocial behavior: adolescence-limited and life-course-persistent antisocial behavior. This model could be very informative to those conducting transfer evaluations. As her title implies, there is little continuity in the antisocial behavior of individuals on the adolescence-limited trajectory. These individuals demonstrate antisocial behavior during adolescence and tend to have adequate interpersonal skills, a stable mental health history, and average or better academic grades. In comparison, youth who fall in the life-course-persistent pattern exhibit antisocial behavior early, frequently, and throughout their lives (e.g., biting in preschool, petty crime during junior high, to felony crimes as adults). According to some research, these individuals' antisocial behavior presents itself across situations (e.g., home, work, school) and has been associated with negative life outcomes such as addiction, unpaid debt, violent abuse, unstable

relationships, and homelessness (Sampson & Laub, 1990). Over the past few decades, research has continued to show that the Moffitt (1993) taxonomy has validity (Bersani, Nieuwbeerta, & Laub, 2009; Moffitt, 2007; Piquero et al., 2001). There are a number of different developmental pathways to draw knowledge from, and Loeber's (1990) early supposition that there are different developmental trajectories children and adolescents can take in their delinquency/criminal careers is supported by this research. In essence, early, frequent, and severe antisocial behavior is predictive of more negative outcomes (Farrington et al., 2008; Kreuter & Muthen, 2008).

There are many risk-trajectory studies in the literature available to a clinician considering risk assessment and thus available to attorneys (e.g., Barker, Trentacosta, & Salekin, 2011). Different methods of analysis, such as growth modeling and latent class growth analysis, are now providing researchers with a varying number of descriptions of these trajectories. These studies examine desisters, moderate offenders, and severe offenders. In deciding to use crime trajectories to inform one's assessment, it is recommended that attorneys and clinicians providing the information to the courts be aware of the different pathways youth can take and what factors might moderate the progression along a pathway (Chen & Salekin, 2012). Table 18.1 provides information about antisocial pathways

TABLE 18.1 DEVELOPMENTAL MODEL AND OFFENSE RATES, MODEL PROGRESSION, AND STABILITY

Theorist	Model	Type of Offending	% Early	% Mid	% Late
Tatem Kelley et al. (1997)	Experimenters	Court nonviolent	—	15	15
	Persisters	Self-report violent	—	10	5
		Court nonviolent	—	75	70
		Self-report violent	—	75	80
	Persisters				
	Overt	Self-report violent	100	88	98
	Covert	Self-report violent	98	96	95
Moffitt (1993)	Adolescent Limited	Any	0	12	32
	Life Course Persistent	Any	5	4–5	5
Lynam et al. (2009)	Psychopathy stability		.74	.65	.73

Note: % equals the percentage of youth who would offend when fitting into a particular class (e.g., life course persistent). The second Persisters group in the table lists and the percentage of youth who passed through the Loeber pathways as predicted (e.g., for covert, minor covert behavior -> property damage -> moderate serious delinquency; for overt, minor aggression -> physical fighting -> violence). Moffitt numbers represent the percentage of youth who met criteria for life persistent versus adolescent limited boys out of a representative sample of boys. Lynam numbers for psychopathy stability estimates (double entry correlations).

and the empirical research to show the number of youth who progress through a given pathway or the degree of stability for a concept like psychopathy.

Psychopathic-like Features

Psychologists also typically consider personality in youth in their assessment of dangerousness. There are still questions as to whether this construct of callousness or psychopathy has merit in youth; however, at a descriptive level the traits appear to have some reliability and validity. The research base for adolescent psychopathy has grown substantially in the past two decades (Salekin & Lynam, 2010). In fact, there are now many more studies on this topic, and research appears to be growing exponentially each year. This larger research base has shown that psychopathy in youth is predictive of later offending and of violent offending, although the timeline here tends to be approximately two to three years (Leistico, Salekin, DeCoster, & Rogers, 2008). Clinicians and attorneys can look to meta-analytic studies in this area to gain information on the relation between youth psychopathy and anti-social behavior (Leistico et al., 2008).

Although research has shown that psychopathy may serve as part of a clinical evaluation for juvenile disposition decision making and transfer, we do not support the use of the term "psychopathy" without properly updating court personnel as to what it means in terms of its moderate stability, potential treatment amenability, and so forth (Salekin & Grimes, 2008). Although consideration of psychopathy and antisocial behaviors as predictors of future serious recidivism may provide useful information, it is critical for attorneys to know that there is considerable controversy as to whether it is, in fact, psychopathy that is being assessed. Clinicians are typically very cautious when using the term to avoid inappropriately limiting a youth's life chances. This is because there are limitations as to what we know in terms of the long-term life outcomes of youth with these characteristics (Salekin & Lynam, 2010). Research is expanding in this area, and in future decades more resolution on this topic will be reached. Until that time, we would contend that attorneys and clinicians should acknowledge the limitations regarding its assessment and predictive capabilities (see Vitacco, Salekin, & Rogers, 2010, for further details of using psychopathy in forensic cases). Moreover, this is not a formal DSM-IV diagnosis, although it is being considered for the DSM-V manual (Frick & Moffitt, 2010).

Prototypical Items

Salekin, Yff, Neumann, Leistico, and Zalot (2002) have attempted to better define the concept of "future dangerousness" through prototypical and factor analytic methods. Clinical psychologists, forensic diplomats, and juvenile-justice judges indicated that the following factors are related to potential dangerousness: (1) participating in serious and unprovoked violence; (2) demonstrating severe antisocial personality traits; (3) lacking in remorse, guilt, or empathy; (4) having histories including violence against other persons; and (5) demonstrating a leadership role in the crime (Salekin et al., 2002). Many of these items come from case law. Also, crime components (planning and premeditation) have been interpreted by judges to be indicative of the dangerousness of an offender (Sellers & Arrigo, 2009). There is evidence that elements of the crime can predict the transfer and decertification of youthful offenders (Burrow, 2008). Specifically, the degree of violence, type of crime committed (e.g., homicide, robbery, or assault), and presence of a weapon (especially a firearm) are all significantly associated with the probability of a juvenile being transferred and remaining in adult court (Burrow, 2008). Past crime components can be considered in conjunction with different criminal trajectories and potentially psychopathic features, as discussed above, and may help in the development of a broader conceptualization of the offender's potential dangerousness.

There is some evidence of convergence among the concepts mentioned above. Specifically, some research suggests that the majority of youthful offenders with psychopathic traits fall on the life-course-persistent trajectory (Moffitt, 1993). The occurrence of the life-course trajectory in individuals has a low base rate (Penney & Moretti, 2005), but the individuals that make up this group are thought to account for higher rates of offending. For example, in her review of the literature examining the differential association of life-course-persistent offenders with serious and violent offending, Moffitt (2007) concluded that although life-course-persistent offenders accounted for 10% of the offenders in one study, they accounted for 43% of the group's violent crime. The psychopathic youth are also more likely to offend violently, which would fit with the life-course-persistent group analyses. Moreover, the individual items from prototypical studies are also likely to overlap with the key items that identify more chronic offenders in pathway models as well as psychopathic features, thereby accounting for this overlap (see Salekin, 2004; Spice, Viljoen, Gretton, & Roesch, 2010). There is also research emerging on oppositional defiant disorder that may shed further light on the stepping stones that youth may take to progress toward a more volatile personality (Barker & Salekin, in press).

Sophistication-Maturity

Youthful offenders' levels of sophistication and maturity have also been shown to be an important consideration for juvenile judges in their determination of disposition or to transfer a youth, and this is also delineated in *Kent* (Brannen et al., 2006; NCJFCJ, 2005). Explanations for this construct's influence include beliefs that youthful offenders' sophistication-maturity can affect their criminal decision making and the likelihood for them to re-offend in the future (e.g., their future dangerousness) (Cauffman & Steinberg, 2000). Sophistication-maturity consists of three factors: autonomy (e.g., self-concept), cognitive abilities (decision-making skills), and emotional skills (delay of gratification) (see Salekin, Rogers, & Ustad, 2001; Salekin et al., 2002; Salekin & Grimes, 2008; Spice et al., 2010). From a legal perspective, the maturity construct relates to many other factors that attorneys should be aware of, such as the culpability and the ability to plan crimes, understanding of behavioral norms, and criminal sophistication (Harris, 2008; NCJFCJ, 2005; Salekin et al., 2002). Therefore, it is not surprising that legal professionals are interested in the maturity of youth.

However, developmental maturity is a complex construct. On the one hand it is likely linked to responsibility (culpability). It can also be tied to more sophisticated crimes because of cognitive skills and emotion-regulation skills that are put to use for antisocial means. Bringing further complexity to the construct, developmental maturity might well be linked to positive treatment outcomes. In fact, this was recently found in a study by Jordan (2008). When youth have better cognitive skills they are more likely to understand and participate in cognitive therapies with better success, should they be willing to marshal these cognitive skills toward pro-social ends. Despite the complexity of developmental maturity, attorneys should aim to seek information on this construct, keeping in mind that psychologists are well positioned to provide useful information. Specifically, we contend that clinicians can provide pertinent information on the maturity of youth, which should then help to inform, in context with other factors, legal decisions and treatment plans.

Salekin and Grimes (2008) provided a model that captures the multiple factors to be considered in such evaluations, and their model helps to deal with some of the complexity in the construct. Their model suggests that attorneys and clinicians consider the youth's environment, developmental status (e.g., age), level of psychopathology, and predicament to determine his or her level of maturity. The maturity construct is so important to the notion of the juvenile-justice system that it should be incorporated into the assessment of risk and amenability. In sum, determining the youth's level of maturity is important in risk assessment and in tailoring treatment to individual needs, given the juvenile-justice system's overarching philosophy to rehabilitate.

Treatment Amenability

Treatment amenability is a vital construct in disposition and transfer evaluations (NCJFCJ, 2005; Salekin et al., 2001). Although the law tends to view this construct in terms of the length of time juveniles have in the juvenile-justice system and whether their personality and conduct are amenable to treatment, further resolution of the construct has been sought. Because it is less frequently studied within the psychology or legal fields, researchers have used prototypical and factor analytic methodology to better define this concept. For instance, Salekin and colleagues (Salekin et al., 2001, 2002) found that similar factors loaded on the amenability-to-treatment concept: (1) responsibility and motivation to change; (2) consideration and tolerance of others (e.g., able to tolerate frustration, caring toward others); (3) family cooperation (e.g., stability of the offender's home); and (4) susceptibility to peer influence, pro-social behavior, and good court conduct (e.g., social competence). This suggests that core items may play a particularly important role in the decision to waive a juvenile to adult court. In addition, there is evidence that the results of previous treatment attempts constitute an important component of amenability to treatment (NCJFCJ, 2005).

Recent studies have shown that amenability can have a protective effect for adolescent offenders (see Leistico & Salekin, 2003). For instance, Salekin, Lee, Schrum-Dillard, and Kubak (2010) discovered that youth high in motivation to change on the Risk-Sophistication-Treatment-Inventory (RST-I) were less likely to offend three years after they were initially assessed for their amenability to treatment (i.e., motivation to change). Spice and colleagues (2010) showed that RST-I—amenability is inversely associated with violent conduct-disordered symptoms and also negatively associated with transfer to adult court. Jordan (2008) found that RST-I—developmental maturity (pro-social) was also indicative of positive treatment outcomes. These findings suggest that it may be important to inform court personnel how protective a variable amenability may be.

Considering that one of the *Kent* criteria includes whether the offender can be "reasonably rehabilitated" through the juvenile court's current capabilities and available services (*Kent v. United States*, 1966), courts determining transfer cases (e.g., *P.K.M. v. State*, 1989) have stressed the importance of considering only currently available resources in the decision to waive an offender. However, Melton, Petrila, Poythress, and Slobogin (2007) have suggested that clinician recommendations with respect to treatment amenability should include not only readily available interventions, but also available interventions that may be more difficult to establish, and a consideration of all treatments that may work but are not currently accessible (new treatment programs showing evidence in the social science literature). Regardless of the information provided by an evaluation, however, state laws provide for the transfer of a juvenile if there is reason to believe that the juvenile court is unable to rehabilitate an offender (Heilbrun et al., 1997). Therefore, there is reason to believe that recommendations unrealistically beyond services available to the juvenile court would be irrelevant to many juvenile court judges' decision to waive an offender (Grisso, 2000; NCJFCJ, 2005).

Moreover, the definition of treatment in this context is also essential to the consideration of offender rehabilitation. Mulvey (1984) suggested that a variety of interventions could fall under the category of treatment and that statutes imply that there is an assumed general definition of treatment. Mulvey added that a few states have defined added qualifiers regarding treatment such as "treatment is not limited to the psychotherapy or mental health interventions" in Virginia (p. 201). Grisso (2000) added that states' treatments include not only probation programs, rehabilitation facilities, and mental health facilities run by that state, but also other states' facilities as well. Research is needed on the interaction between amenability and the various treatment options.

Evaluation of amenability to treatment should include consideration of psychological disorders and the degree to which they are either amenable or resistant to change, and greater detail on the specific disorder should be provided (Salekin & Grimes, 2008). For example, psychopathy in adolescents may be linked with difficult and potentially disruptive behavior in treatment settings, but there is research to show that progress can also be made with this group, including reductions in offending (Salekin, 2010; Salekin, Worley, & Grimes, 2010). However, as mentioned earlier, specialized treatment may not be available in all juvenile-justice systems. Therefore, evaluations should carefully consider needed treatments and whether they are currently, or could be made, available to the offender. In addition, it can be helpful to consider the offender's motivation for change and the offender's family's expectations of treatment, as these factors have been shown to affect amenability to treatment (Salekin & Grimes, 2008; Salekin et al., 2010). There is also some evidence that the offender's age should be considered, since developmental research and the courts tend to find younger offenders to be more amenable to treatment than their older counterparts (Loving & Patapis, 2007). However, even late adolescence is considered to be a fairly malleable time in one's life.

THE EVALUATION
Hiring a Adolescent Forensic Expert

The aforementioned constructs are key to disposition decision making and to the transfer decision in upward judicial transfers and also in downward reverse waivers. Forensic evaluations of youth in direct file cases may also be pertinent as defense attorneys may argue that the case would be better handled in juvenile court, whereas prosecuting attorneys would argue that the youth should be processed in adult court. Regardless of the mechanism, attorneys may seek psychological information on these constructs to better understand the youth's psychological makeup and how his or her characteristics may map onto *Kent* criteria.

In seeking a forensic mental health professional who works on disposition or transfer cases, attorneys should look for a practitioner who has expertise in evaluating the constructs mentioned above. Preferably, this expert would have forensic knowledge about the juvenile-justice system, knowledge about child and adolescent clinical psychology, and knowledge of the developmental psychology literature. Presumably, if the expert is a child and adolescent forensic psychologist he or she should have knowledge of the aforementioned psychology subfields. However, very few psychology programs offer the combination of training in these three areas simultaneously, so attorneys who cannot determine the mental health professional's training by reviewing his or her curriculum vitae may wish to ask the expert if he or she has knowledge in these chief areas of psychology.

If it is determined that the forensic mental health professional is an expert in these areas, then the attorney or judge may wish to retain the mental health professional. The next step in the process is to clarify the referral question—what does the attorney want to be assessed, and what is the psychologist capable of assessing? After it is clear what the attorney or judge is expecting with respect to the referral question and the psychologist has deemed that this is an appropriate assessment for him or her, the psychologist starts the process of evaluating the youth. There are a couple of other points that attorneys should know, however, before the formal evaluation can begin.

First, forensic mental health professionals are trained to be impartial. That is, they do not work for one side (prosecution or defense), like a legal team might, to have a youth transferred or retained in one versus another court. Rather, the mental health professional evaluates the youth and provides the most accurate information, whether or not this information works for the attorney's case. This impartiality is an ethical obligation of the psychologist. Second, the forensic mental health professional has to disclose to the youth the limits of confidentiality. In the case of transfer evaluations, the mental health professional has to be clear with the youth and the youth's family that the information he or she gleans from the evaluation will not be confidential and that he or she will have to disclose the

findings to the attorney and juvenile court judge in the form of a psychological report and will provide testimony with regard to the evaluation. The mental health professional will also have to inform the youth and family that if questions should arise that go beyond the information contained in the report, the expert may also have to disclose further information if it is pertinent to the case.

The youth and family will then be asked if they would like to participate in the evaluation. Should they chose not to participate in the evaluation, such a decision would then also be included in a brief report. If the youth and family do agree to participate in the evaluation, the clinician would work toward establishing rapport, while ensuring that the youth understands the purpose of the evaluation, subsequent report, and potential testimony. The clinician would then start to gather information on the standard for disposition evaluations and/or transfer evaluations in the state where the evaluation is being conducted. It is likely that the standard will involve the assessment of the pertinent constructs of risk, maturity, and treatment amenability previously discussed, as well as the two other broad mental health concepts (veracity of reporting and personality/pathology).

Conducting the Psychological Evaluation

Once mental health professionals know the question being asked by the court (disposition), the standard being evaluated, the criteria that underlie the standard, the psychological concepts they will evaluate, as well as the research that accompanies those constructs, they will proceed to the next stage of the evaluation, which involves a comprehensive assessment of the youth. Attorneys should know that a strong evaluation takes time. Specifically, on beginning the evaluation, the forensic expert will allow adequate time to gather and assess the data required for this complex undertaking. The first step for the forensic examiner is to review the relevant documents, including police, medical, psychiatric, social, and school reports. Attorneys also have a vested interest in gathering and providing some of this information. A comprehensive developmental history including home, school, and neighborhood environment is essential. A broad perspective in gathering the information is important because context (the youth's legal situation and current environment) may be at least as relevant as personality and behavior. Thus, contacting numerous third-party sources (police, schools) is crucial to the evaluation.

Clinical and Structured Interviews

Clinical interviews will be conducted to collect data on the youth. As with any forensic evaluation, the clinical interview can be an invaluable tool for gathering information from juvenile offenders as well as their parents. Much of the information gleaned from the interviews will be used by clinicians to provide to attorneys in the form of psychological reports. Judges may also request and choose to examine this information when considering disposition or waiver to adult court. Interviews can provide clinicians with flexibility in exploring juvenile offenders' criminal and detention or incarceration history, treatment history, academic achievement and school attendance, family dynamics and supports, peer relationships and influences, and history of antisocial behavior—all of which can be central to the simultaneous assessment of risk (Wiebush, Baird, Krisberg, & Onek, 1995), maturity, and treatment amenability.

Structured interviews are also likely to be given, and these interviews typically examine *Diagnostic and Statistical Manual of Mental Disorders–Fourth Edition* (DSM-IV) psychopathology. There are many interviews available now, such as the Kiddie SADS, DISC, MAGIC, and DBD. These interviews are highly reliable and valid and offer an excellent source of information to clinicians and attorneys. They provide a way in which to glean information systematically that can lead to an accurate diagnosis, should some form of mental disorder be present. Even subclinical symptom information can be highly informative.

Self-Report Measures

Self-report behavioral and personality measures will also likely be administered. These measures allow the youth to rate himself or herself on characteristics and potential symptoms that can help shed light on potential diagnoses, and they have the benefit of providing the youth and/or parent perspective. Some measures also provide information not only on symptoms and problems but also on strengths, which can also be helpful information, Depending on the measure used different constructs can be indexed, so choosing measures can be important for clinicians to consider. Importantly, self-report measures provide one way to investigate response

styles (see Salekin, Kubak, & Lee, 2008). This, as mentioned in the introduction, is one of the important forensic mental health concepts to investigate.

Specialized Psychological Tests

Once a thorough developmental history has been completed and the broadband testing regarding personality and potential DSM symptoms has been completed, the transfer evaluation is likely to center on what has been culled and refined from the *Kent* criteria. Decision makers in the disposition decision-making process or transfer process (likely to be judges or prosecutors) are prone to consider all three psychological constructs simultaneously, as well as other factors. Some attention has been paid to the relative importance of each of these constructs on the decision to transfer an offender to adult court.

Brannen et al.'s (2006) survey of juvenile court judges found that of the three constructs, potential dangerousness had the greatest impact on juvenile judges' decisions in transfer cases. Yet assessment of risk for dangerousness is, as mentioned, an imprecise science (Sellers & Arrigo, 2009). The courts have also made statements referring to the necessity to protect society from the dangerous juvenile offender. For example, in *Otis v. State* (2004), the court stated that "it could be inferred from the serious and violent nature of the offense that the protection of society demands that *Otis* be tried as an adult" (p. 607). In addition, the courts have confirmed that they were not required to weigh all factors equally and that there were no specific equations used in reaching their conclusions. Despite the weighted importance of potential dangerousness, clinicians should consider all three constructs for their evaluations, and attorneys will likely want to know about the youth's placement on each of these dimensional constructs. Whether attorneys use the information in balance is a legal question, but it could be argued that each of the factors is important to present in psychological reports and testimony and for the courts to consider. The weighting of factors likely differs depending on the evaluation.

Traditionally, the *Kent* factors have been evaluated by clinical interview alone. Grisso (1998) also has provided a structure for the evaluation, which entails traditional interviewing. This system could also be coupled with appropriate psychological measures to augment traditional interviewing.

Specifically, the RST-I (Salekin, 2004) is one instrument that has been shown to be reliable and valid and centers on the three constructs salient in transfer cases (Jordan, 2008; Salekin, 2004; Spice et al. 2010). The RSTI, through a semi-structured interview and a clinician rating form, examines youthful offenders' presenting problems, family history, relationships with non-family members, education and employment history, criminal history, developmental maturity, treatment history, and perceived level of responsibility for the crime they are accused of committing. These items capture the characteristics discussed as central components of the potential risk, sophistication-maturity, and amenability-to-treatment concepts.

There are other actuarial and specialized scales that may also facilitate the assessment. With respect to dangerousness assessments, a number of instruments have been designed to examine the chances of future criminal behavior (Mulvey & Iselin, 2008). To measure youthful offenders' risk for violence, measures include the Structural Assessment of Violence Risk for Youth (SAVRY; Borum, Bartel, & Forth, 2005) and the Youth Level of Service/Case Management Inventory (YLS/CMI; Hoge, 2005). The YLS/CMI also assesses treatment needs, which overlap with the amenability concept somewhat. In addition, the SAVRY examines protective factors, which are also likely linked to amenability, but it does not fully tap the construct. As mentioned, only the RSTI taps maturity and specifically targets treatment amenability.

If the evaluation is focused on severe conduct disorders, clinicians may choose to use a measure of oppositional defiant disorder and conduct disorder symptomatology (as measured by one of the structured interviews) and also measures of psychopathy for its relevance to future dangerousness (see Salekin & Lynam, 2010). The Psychopathy Checklist: Youth Version (PCL:YV, Forth, Kosson, & Hare, 1996/2003) has been studied for over a decade in this field (Salekin & Lynam, 2010). In addition, it is not uncommon for juvenile-justice systems to administer risk-assessment tools to juvenile offenders upon processing, the results of which can be incorporated into clinical evaluations as collateral data (Krysik & LeCroy, 2002). However, the use of risk assessment in youthful offenders as predictors of future violence is only moderately predictive of later offending (Grisso & Appelbaum, 1992); a percentage of youth, even those at risk,

do not re-offend. The aforementioned interviewing and testing is one common way to provide data to the clinician regarding the youth's functioning. This information, when taken together, forms the foundational basis for the report.

REPORT WRITING AND TESTIMONY

A psychological report will likely be generated for the attorney or the juvenile court judge. Psychological reports should be concise and clearly written in a language that can be easily understood by legal professionals and laypersons. Any technical information will likely be placed in an appendix and can be explained by the mental health professional. The report itself may vary across clinicians, but several main sections should be included: (1) reason for referral, (2) interviews and tests administered, (3) background information, (4) behavioral observations, (5) findings, (6) interpretation of findings, (7) diagnoses, (8) psycholegal concepts assessed, and (9) summary and conclusions. There may be more or less in the way of sections, but most reports are written in a format somewhat like the one mentioned above. In terms of the summary and potential recommendations, it is not uncommon for mental health professionals to offer several possible outcomes, depending on what happens to the youth. For instance, an adolescent might be considered dangerous (i.e., a risk to the community) if nothing is changed in his environment when he returns home. However, if a series of interventions are implemented, he may be viewed as at a moderate or even low risk for re-offending. Psychologists will typically not offer information on the ultimate issue, as this is within the purview of the legal decision maker. However, they offer specific treatment options that they feel would help the youth improve his or her mental health and conduct.

Informing the Courts

Juvenile disposition and transfer evaluations present an opportunity for attorneys and clinicians to communicate on important issues. Clinicians can provide information to the court regarding the importance of the constructs of not only risk but also sophistication-maturity and amenability to treatment, especially if the two constructs are being underemphasized (Brannen et al., 2006). As previously discussed, the courts are often primarily concerned with offenders' risk for dangerousness, especially in transfer cases. However, given the emphasis of the juvenile-justice system and the interests of society more broadly, it is important for attorneys and clinicians to work together to better understand the best way to utilize information about a youth, which could be important for future policy in this area. An emphasis on the constructs of maturity and amenability to treatment may very well highlight a treatment model for the offender instead of a protection-from or potentially even punitive model. By providing a broader picture of youth, we believe that attorneys, clinicians, and the courts will become increasingly aware of the developing adolescents' need for continued growth. In the next section, we sketch out our concluding comments and also raise some issues that require further thought by both attorneys and clinicians as we continue to work toward a more developmentally sensitive model for handling youthful offenders.

SUMMARY

Although this chapter seeks to help attorneys better understand what types of reports they might expect from mental health professionals, we hope that both psychologists and attorneys will continue to work toward developing an improved legal system and rehabilitation system. There continues to be research to show inequities in the processing and handling of youth who are tried as adults (e.g., lengthier times in the system) (Steiner, 2009). In addition, the prison system has not yet developed programs that can provide the appropriate counseling and educational interventions for the youthful offenders for whom they are responsible (Austin et al., 2000). This might be highly critical for first-time offenders when they come into contact with the law. Precise reports that deal with youths' needs effectively may prevent a cascade of developmental problems. In transfer cases, if youth bypass the juvenile-justice system or briefly pass through, there are concerns about youthful offenders' interaction with adult offenders, which could have a negative impact on their pro-social development (Forst, Fagan, & Vivona, 1989), and that transfer may not serve as a deterrent for all youth (Gatti, Tremblay, & Vitaro, 2009; Steiner & Wright, 2006). Finally, it is important to be aware that although research regarding the assessment of juveniles is improving, the science with respect to prediction shows only modest success. It might be that after youthful offenders

are transferred to adult court, evaluations for future risk should be periodically performed since there is the possibility that the offenders would no longer fall in the high-risk category as they might have been at the time of their transfer. Similar arguments could be made for measures of maturity and amenability to treatment, as these scores may change over time. This underscores the importance of multiple assessments of the pertinent constructs across time for youth in correctional settings (this would be good practice whether youth are in juvenile or adult systems).

One example of a policy change in this regard might be to provide "blended" sentences for all youthful offenders, such that they will be evaluated at the beginning of the juvenile component of their sentence and at the end of the juvenile component. Having two (or more) assessments of potential risk, maturity, and amenability to treatment, before and after serving a juvenile sentence, may help inform whether imposing the adult component of the blended sentence is appropriate.

There is currently no optimal solution for how to handle difficult cases (disposition or transfer), but attorneys are likely to benefit from mental health professionals' evaluations of youth, which put them in a better position to understand the individual characteristics of the youth. Whether or not these policy changes take place, collaboration between psychologists and attorneys on disposition and transfer cases is likely to result in more accurate clinical assessments and better decision making. Ultimately, the goal is that the best practice in this area will lead to thoughtful and considerate treatment of youth, with the two aims of improving well-being and conduct and also acknowledging the parameter of public safety.

REFERENCES

Austin, J., Johnson, K. D., & Gregoriou, M. (2000). *Juveniles in adult prisons and jails: A national assessment.* Washington, DC: U.S. Department of Justice, Office of Justice Programs. Retrieved from http://www.ncjrs.gov/pdffiles1/bja/182503.pdf

Barker, E. D., & Salekin, R. T. (in press). Irritable oppositional defiance and callous unemotional traits: Is the association partially explained by peer victimization? *Journal of Child Psychology and Psychiatry.*

Barker, T. D., Trentacosta, C. J., & Salekin, R. T. (2011). Are impulsive adolescents differentially influenced by the good and bad of neighborhood and family? *Journal of Abnormal Psychology, 120,* 981–986.

Bersani, B. E., Nieuwbeerta, P., & Laub, J. H. (2009). Predicting trajectories of offending over the life course: Findings from a Dutch conviction cohort. *Journal of Research in Crime and Delinquency, 46,* 468–494.

Borum, R., Bartel, P., & Forth, A. (2005). Structured assessment of violence risk in youth. In T. Grisso, G. Vincent, & D. Seagrave (Eds.), *Mental health screening and assessment in juvenile justice* (pp. 311–323). New York: Guilford.

Brannen, D. N., Salekin, R. T., Zapf, P. A., Salekin, K. L., Kubak, F. A., & DeCoster, J. (2006). Transfer to adult court: A national study of how juvenile court judges weigh pertinent Kent criteria. *Psychology, Public Policy, and Law, 12,* 332–355.

Burrow, J. (2008). Reverse waiver and the effects of legal, statutory, and secondary legal factors on sentencing outcomes for juvenile offenders. *Crime and Delinquency, 54,* 34–64.

Cauffman, E., & Steinberg, L. (2000). (Im)maturity of judgment in adolescence: Why adolescents may be less culpable than adults. *Behavioral Sciences and the Law, 18,* 741–760.

Chen, D., & Salekin, R. T. (2012). Transfer to adult court: Enhancing clinical forensic evaluations and informing policy. In E. L. Grigorenko (Ed.), *Handbook of juvenile forensic psychology and psychiatry* (pp. 105–125). New York: Springer.

Fagan, J. (2008). Juvenile crime and criminal justice: Resolving border disputes. *The Future of Children, 18,* 81–118.

Farrington, D. P., Loeber, R., Jollife, D., & Pardini, D. A. (2008). Promotive and risk processes at different life stages. In R. Loeber, D. P. Farrington, M. Stouthamer-Loeber, & H. R. White (Eds.), *Violence and serious theft: Development and prediction from childhood to adulthood* (pp. 169–230). New York: Routledge.

Forst, M., Fagan, J., & Vivona, T. S. (1989). Youth in prisons and training schools: Perceptions and consequences of the treatment-custody dichotomy. *Juvenile and Family Court Journal, 40*(1), 1–14.

Forth, A. E., Kosson, D. S., & Hare, R. D. (1996/2003). *The Psychopathy Checklist: Youth Version manual (draft version and published version).* Toronto: Multi-Health Systems.

Frick, P. J., & Moffitt, T. E. (2010). *A proposal to the DSM-V Childhood Disorders and ADHD Disruptive Behavior Disorders Work Groups to include a specifier to the diagnosis of conduct disorder based on the presence of callous unemotional traits.* Washington, DC: American Psychiatric Association.

Gatti, U., Tremblay, R. E., & Vitaro, F. (2009). Iatrogenic effect of juvenile justice. *Journal of Child Psychology and Psychiatry, 50,* 991–998.

Griffin, P., Addie, S., Adams, B., & Firestine, K. (2011). *Trying juveniles as adults: An analysis of state transfer laws and reporting.* U.S. Department of Justice. Office of Juvenile Justice and Delinquency Prevention, 1–27.

Grisso, T. (1998). *Forensic evaluation of juveniles.* Sarasota, FL: Professional Resource Press.

Grisso, T. (2000). Forensic clinical evaluations related to waiver of jurisdiction. In J. Fagan & F. Zimring (Eds.), *The changing borders of juvenile justice* (pp. 13–43). Chicago: The University of Chicago Press.

Grisso, T., & Appelbaum, P. S. (1992). Is it unethical to offer predictions of future violence? *Law and Human Behavior, 16,* 621–633.

Harris, A. (2008). The social construction of "sophisticated" adolescents: How judges integrate juvenile and criminal justice decision-making models. *Journal of Contemporary Ethnography, 37,* 469–506.

Heilbrun, K., Leheny, C., Thomas, L., & Huneycutt, D. (1997). A national survey of U.S. statutes on juvenile transfer: Implications for policy and practice. *Behavioral Sciences & the Law, 15,* 125–149.

Hoge, R. (2005). Youth Level of Service/Case Management Inventory. In T. Grisso, G. Vincent, & D. Seagrave (Eds.), *Mental health screening and assessment in juvenile justice* (pp. 81–95). New York: Guilford.

In re Gault, 387 U.S. 1 (1967).

Jordan, M. J. (2008). *Readiness for change as a predictor of treatment effectiveness: An application of the transtheoretical model.* Doctoral dissertation. University of North Texas. Denton, Texas.

Jordan, K. L., & Myers, D. L. (2007). The decertification of transferred youth: Examining the determinants of reverse waiver. *Youth Violence and Juvenile Justice, 5,* 188–206.

Kent v. United States, 383 U.S. 541 (1966).

Kreuter, F., & Muthen, B. (2008). Analyzing criminal trajectory profile: Bridging multilevel and group-based approaches using growth mixture modeling. *Journal of Quantitative Criminology, 24,* 1–31.

Kruh, I. P., & Brodsky, S. (1997). Clinical evaluations for transfer of juveniles to criminal court: Current practices and future research. *Behavioral Sciences and the Law, 15,* 151–165.

Krysik, J., & LeCroy, C. W. (2002). The empirical validation of an instrument to predict risk of recidivism among juvenile offenders. *Research on Social Work Practice, 12,* 71–81.

Leistico, A. R., & Salekin, R. T. (2003). Testing the reliability and validity of the Risk, Sophistication-Maturity, and Treatment Amenability Instrument (RST-i): An assessment tool for juvenile offenders. *International Journal of Forensic Mental Health, 2,* 101–117.

Leistico, A. R., Salekin, R. T., DeCoster, J., & Rogers, R. (2008). A large-scale meta-analysis relating the Hare measures of psychopathy to antisocial conduct. *Law and Human Behavior, 32,* 28–45.

Loeber, R. (1990). Development and risk factors of juvenile antisocial behavior and delinquency. *Clinical Psychology Review, 10,* 1–41.

Loving, J. L., & Patapis, N. S. (2007). Evaluating juvenile amenability to treatment: Integrating statutes and case law into clinical practice. *Journal of Forensic Psychology Practice, 7,* 67–78.

Lynam, D. R., Charnigo, R., Moffitt, T. E., Raine, A., Loeber, R., & Stouthamer-Loeber, M. (2009). The stability of psychopathy across adolescence. *Development and Psychopathology, 21,* 1133–1153.

Melton, G. B., Petrila, J., Poythress, N. G., & Slobogin, C. (2007). *Psychological evaluations for the courts: A handbook for mental health professionals and lawyers.* New York: Guilford.

Moffitt, T. E. (1993). Adolescence-limited and life-course-persistent antisocial behavior: A developmental taxonomy. *Psychological Review, 4,* 674–701.

Moffitt, T. E. (2007). A review of the research on the taxonomy of life-course persistent versus adolescence-limited antisocial behavior. In D. J. Flannery, A. T. Vazsonyi, & I. D. Waldman (Eds.), *The Cambridge handbook of violent behavior and aggression* (pp. 49–74). Cambridge: Cambridge University Press.

Mulvey, E. (1984). Judging amenability to treatment in juvenile offenders: Theory and practice. In N. Reppucci, L. Weithorn, E. Mulvey, & J. Monahan (Eds.), *Children, mental health, and the law* (pp. 321–352). Beverly Hills, CA: Sage.

Mulvey, E. P., & Iselin, A. R. (2008). Improving professional judgments of risk and amenability in juvenile justice. *The Future of Children, 18,* 35–57.

National Council of Juvenile and Family Court Judges. (2005). *Juvenile delinquency guidelines: Improving court practice in juvenile delinquency cases.* Washington, DC: U.S. Department of Justice, Office of Juvenile Justice and Delinquency Prevention. Retrieved from http://www.ncjfcj.org/images/stories/dept/ppcd/pdf/JDG/juveniledelinquencyguidelinescompressed.pdf

Otis v. State, 142 S.W.3d 615 (Ark. 2004).

P.K.M. v. State, 780 P.2d 395 (1989).

Penney, S. R., & Moretti, M. M. (2005). The transfer of juveniles to adult court in Canada and the United States: Confused agendas and compromised assessment procedures. *International Journal of Forensic Mental Health, 4,* 19–37.

Piquero, A. R., Blumstein, A., Brame, R., Haapanen, R., Mulvey, E. P., & Nagin, D. S. (2001). Assessing the impact of exposure time and incapacitation on longitudinal trajectories of criminal offending. *Journal of Adolescent Research, 16,* 54–74.

Redding, R. E. (2010). *Juvenile transfer laws: An effective deterrent to delinquency?* Washington, DC: U.S. Department of Justice, Office of Juvenile Justice and Delinquency Prevention. Retrieved from http://www.ncjrs.gov/pdffiles1/ojjdp/220595.pdf

Salekin, R. T. (2002). Clinical evaluation of youth considered for transfer to adult criminal court: Refining practice and directions for science. *Journal of Forensic Psychology Practice, 2,* 55–72.

Salekin, R. T. (2004). *Risk-Sophistication-Treatment Inventory: Professional manual.* Lutz, FL: Psychological Assessment Resources.

Salekin, R. T. (2010). Treatment of child and adolescent psychopathy: Focusing on change. In R. T. Salekin & D. R. Lynam (Eds.), *Handbook of child and adolescent psychopathy* (pp. 343–373). New York: Guilford.

Salekin, R. T. (in progress). *Evaluation for disposition and transfer of juvenile offenders.* New York: Oxford University Press.

Salekin, R. T., & Grimes, R. (2008). Clinical forensic evaluations for juvenile transfer to adult criminal court. In R. Jackson (Ed.), *Learning forensic assessment* (pp. 313–346). New York: Routledge.

Salekin, R. T., Jarrett, M. A., Adams, E. W. (in press). Assessment and measurement of change considerations in psychotherapy research. In J. S. Comer & P. K. Kendall (Eds.), *The Oxford handbook of research strategies for clinical psychology.* New York: Oxford University Press.

Salekin, R. T., Kubak, F. A., & Lee, Z. (2008). Deception in children and adolescents. In R. Rogers (Ed.), *Clinical assessment of malingering and deception* (pp. 343–364). New York: Guilford.

Salekin, R. T., Lee, Z., Schrum-Dillard, C. L., & Kubak, F. A. (2010). Child psychopathy and protective factors: IQ and motivation-to-change. *Psychology, Public Policy and Law, 16,* 158–176.

Salekin, R. T., & Lynam, D. R. (2010). Child and adolescent psychopathy: The road ahead. *Handbook of child and adolescent psychopathy* (pp. 401–419). New York: Guilford Press.

Salekin, R. T., & Lynam, D. R. (2010). *Handbook of child and adolescent psychopathy.* New York: Guilford Press.

Salekin, R. T., Rogers, R., & Ustad, K. L. (2001). Juvenile waiver to adult criminal court: Prototypes for dangerousness, sophistication-maturity, and amenability to treatment. *Psychology, Public Policy, and Law, 7,* 381–408.

Salekin, R. T., Salekin, K. L. Clements, C. B., & Leistico, A. R. (2005). Risk-Sophistication-Treatment Inventory. In T. Grisso, G. Vincent, & D. Seagrave (Eds.), *Mental health screening and assessment in juvenile justice* (pp. 341–356). New York: Guilford.

Salekin, R. T., Worley, C. B., & Grimes, R. D. (2010). Treatment of psychopathy: A review and brief introduction to the mental model approach for psychopathy. *Behavioral Sciences and the Law, 28,* 235–266.

Salekin, R. T., Yff, R. M., Neumann, C. S., Leistico, A. R., & Zalot, A. A. (2002). Juvenile transfer to adult courts: A look at the prototypes for dangerousness, sophistication-maturity, and amenability to treatment through a legal lens. *Psychology, Public Policy, and Law, 8,* 373–410.

Sampson, R. J., & Laub, J. H. (1990). Crime and deviance over the life course: the salience of adult social bonds. *American Sociological Review, 55*, 609–627.

Sellers, B. G., & Arrigo, B. A. (2009). Criminology: Adolescent transfer, developmental maturity, and adjudicative competence: An ethical and justice policy inquiry. *Journal of Criminal Law and Criminology, 99*, 435–487.

Slobogin, C. (2007). Treating kids right: Deconstructing and reconstructing the amenability to treatment concept. *Journal of Contemporary Legal Issues, 10*, 299–333.

Snyder, H. N., & Sickmund, M. (2006). *Juvenile offenders and victims: 2006 national report*. Washington, DC: U.S. Department of Justice, Office of Juvenile Justice and Delinquency Prevention.

Spice, A., Viljoen, J. L., Gretton, H. M., & Roesch, R. (2010). Psychological assessment for adult sentencing of juvenile offenders: An evaluation of the RSTI and the SAVRY. *International Journal of Forensic Mental Health, 9*, 124–137.

Steiner, B. (2009). The effects of juvenile transfer to criminal court on incarceration decisions. *Justice Quarterly, 26*, 77–106.

Steiner, B., & Wright, E. (2006). Assessing the relative effects of state direct file waiver laws on violent juvenile crime: Deterrence or irrelevance?. *Journal of Criminal Law & Criminology, 96*, 1451–1478.

Tanenhaus, D. S. (2000). The evolution of transfer out of the juvenile court. In J. Fagan & F. Zimring (Eds.), *The changing borders of juvenile justice* (pp. 13–43). Chicago: University of Chicago Press.

Tatem Kelley, B., Loeber, R., Keenan, K., & DeLamatre, M. (1997). *Developmental pathways in boys' disruptive and delinquent behavior*. U.S. Department of Justice: Office of Juvenile Justice and Delinquency Prevention.

Vitacco, M. J., Salekin, R. T., & Rogers, R. (2010). Forensic issues for child and adolescent psychopathy. In R. T. Salekin & D. R. Lynam (Eds.), *Handbook of child and adolescent psychopathy* (pp. 374–397). New York: Guilford Press.

West, H. C., & Sabol, W. J. (2009). *Prison inmates at mid-year—2008—Statistical tables*. Washington, DC: U.S. Department of Justice, Office of Justice Programs, Bureau of Justice Statistics. Retrieved from http://bjs.ojp.usdoj.gov/content/pub/pdf/pim08st.pdf

Wiebush, R. G., Baird, C., Krisberg, B., & Onek, D. (1995). Risk assessment and classification for serious, violent, and chronic juvenile offenders. In J. C. Howell, B. Krisberg, J. D. Hawkins, & J. J. Wilson (Eds.), *Serious, violent, & chronic juvenile offenders* (pp. 171–212). Thousand Oaks, CA: Sage.

Woolard, J. L., Odgers, C., Lanza-Kaduce, L., & Daglis, H. (2005). Juveniles within adult correctional settings: Legal pathways and developmental considerations. *International Journal of Forensic Mental Health, 4*, 1–18.

19

Evaluation of Parenting Capacity in Child Protection Matters

JENNIFER R. CLARK, MARY CONNELL, AND KAREN S. BUDD

Legal professionals working in child protection matters, whether judges or lawyers representing the state, a parent, or a minor, often seek expert guidance from mental health professionals. Mental health evaluations may be requested at various points and may serve different functions. Evaluations may be sought for information regarding a parent's caregiving capacities, risk and protective factors associated with placement or visitation, a child's emotional or psychological needs, or intervention strategies that may assist parenting or child development. The following case examples illustrate some challenges legal professionals may face when deciding on the direction of a case.

Case Example 1. *A mother with a history of chronic schizophrenia and psychiatric hospitalizations has been compliant with treatment and medication for the past 6 months. In that time she has demonstrated improved ability to function independently and has displayed notably improved parenting skills when interacting with her 3-year-old daughter. The mother's lawyer has requested that the mother be granted unsupervised visits with her daughter.*

Case Example 2. *A 2-year-old boy was removed from his mother's care at birth because he tested positive for heroin. He has resided in the same foster home since leaving the hospital, has developed a strong attachment to the foster parents, and, according to the caseworker, has "thrived" in their care. For the past 9 months, his mother has been substance-free, has attended all recommended services, and has participated in regular visits with her son. The court seeks information to determine whether it is in the child's*

best interest to continue to work toward his reunification with his mother or to move toward permanency in his foster home.

Case Example 3. *A boy was removed from his mother because of her incapacity to parent. At the time of removal, his father's identity was unknown. As the case progressed toward termination of the mother's parental rights, the father was identified and notified of his paternity and of the child's placement in substitute care. He is pursuing custody of his son, but the Child Protective Services caseworker is concerned about the father's history of arrests for minor crimes, his insistence that his son's significant emotional and behavioral difficulties would resolve if he were no longer in foster care, and his reluctance to participate in services due to his belief that he "did nothing wrong" and should not be subject to scrutiny.*

Mental health evaluations can have a substantial impact on court decisions in child protection cases (Budd, 2005) and thus on the lives of children and families. At their best, they can provide an informed, objective perspective that enhances the fairness of child welfare decisions (American Psychological Association [APA] Committee on Professional Practice and Standards, 2011). "At their worst, they can contribute inaccurate, biased, and/or irrelevant information that violates examinees' rights and/or impairs the decision-making process" (Budd, 2005, p. 430). It is paramount that legal professionals are educated consumers of the mental health information upon which they rely to inform legal decisions. This chapter aims to equip legal professionals with the information necessary to answer the following questions:

- When do I need mental health information?
- How do I find a qualified expert?
- How do I ensure that the mental health information will be useful for its intended purpose?
- How do I determine if the mental health information is reliable?
- How do I interpret the mental health information?
- How do I address the mental health information during testimony?

This chapter provides a summary of legal standards and procedures relevant to child protection matters, a description of forensic mental health concepts, and a review of relevant empirical research. Although the primary focus of the chapter is on assessment of parenting capacity, assessment of the child is addressed when relevant in the context of assessing parental caregiving capabilities. More detailed discussion of the issues covered in this chapter may be found in *Evaluation of Parenting Capacity in Child Protection* (Budd, Connell, & Clark, 2011).

LEGAL CONTEXT
The Court's View of Parents' Rights and Society's Responsibility to Protect Children

Society and the courts have evolved in their appreciation for who is responsible for protecting children. On the one hand is the constitutional right to parent one's children, and on the other hand is the state's obligation to look after the welfare of children when parents cannot or do not do so. Several early Supreme Court decisions held that the Fourteenth Amendment protects the fundamental liberty of parents to make decisions regarding their children (e.g., *Griswold v. Connecticut*, 1965; *Meyer v. Nebraska*, 1923; *Pierce v. Society of Sisters,*1925). Since these early decisions, the Supreme Court has dealt with numerous petitions to interpret state laws restricting the rights of parents to unfettered access, care, and control of their children.

Set against this backdrop of the right to parent one's children is another value, a generally recognized responsibility of society to protect its children. The doctrine of *parens patriae*, or "country [nation] as parent," recognizes that government has a strong interest in the care and nurturing of children and others who cannot function independently (Otto

& Melton, 1990). Laws pertaining to the custody of children and termination of parental rights have arisen because society assumes the responsibility to protect children when families are disrupted or seriously dysfunctional. In *Prince v. Massachusetts* (1944), the Supreme Court held that the government has broad authority to regulate the actions and treatment of children, noting that parental authority is not absolute and can be permissibly restricted if doing so advances the interests of a child's welfare. However, the court noted, "It is cardinal with us that the custody, care and nurturance of the child reside first in the parents, whose primary function and freedom include preparation for obligations the state can neither supply nor hinder" (p. 166).

In *Santosky v. Kramer* (1982), the Supreme Court established that the state may terminate parental rights only by showing "clear and convincing" evidence, rather than the lower standard, "fair preponderance," being applied in some states. The court determined that the fundamental liberty interest of natural parents in the care, custody, and management of their child, as protected by the Fourteenth Amendment, does not "evaporate simply because they have not been model parents or have lost temporary custody of their child to the State" (p. 753). The Supreme Court, however, continues to defer to states to establish and maintain appropriate balancing tests between the state's role, as *parens patriae*, to look after the welfare of children in need and the parents' constitutional rights to the care and control of their children. For example, while the Supreme Court established peripheral boundaries for finding a parent "unfit" (*Santosky v. Kramer*, 1982), ultimately deference is given to the states to establish the definition of "unfit" in the context of parenting.

Federal Legislation Affecting Child Protection

Several federal acts have served to standardize, to some extent, the approach taken by various Child Protective Services (CPS) agencies and by the court systems by providing minimum standards for defining child physical abuse, neglect, and sexual abuse that states must incorporate into their statutory definitions in order to receive federal funds. Through the passage of the landmark Child Abuse Prevention and Treatment Act (CAPTA) of 1974, funding was made available for broad implementation of preventive intervention and for response to existing cases of abuse and neglect. CAPTA required states to adopt laws requiring mandatory reporting to authorities of suspected child abuse, to ensure confidentiality of agency records and court proceedings, and to appoint a guardian *ad litem* for every child in maltreatment proceedings.

In 1980, the Adoption Assistance and Child Welfare Act (AACWA) established a strong preference for the child's biological family as the permanent option. AACWA required funded states to make "reasonable efforts" to serve children in their own homes, prevent out-of-home placement, and facilitate family reunification following placement. Concern arose in the child protection community, however, that the "reasonable efforts" requirement of AACWA meant that child welfare agencies were obligated to return children to unsafe homes (Youth Law Center, 2000). A modification of AACWA in 1997 articulated exceptions to this requirement and obligated states to ensure that children would not languish in foster care when reunification efforts failed or were not practical. A change in the thrust of intervention occurred in 1997 with the passage of the Adoption and Safe Families Act (ASFA, 1997). Enacted to correct perceived problems that stemmed from AACWA, ASFA required states to move foster children more rapidly into permanent homes by terminating parental rights more quickly and encouraging adoptions. With AFSA, the requirement that states make reasonable efforts to preserve and reunify families was continued but, in making decisions about the removal or return home of a child, the child's health and safety were to be paramount.

Child's Best Interest

The idea that society should respect the best interest of the child is seen as fundamental in our culture. Determinations of what is in a child's best interest are made by a legal decision maker (usually a judge) in family and dependency court proceedings. This decision was once guided by the notion of children being "chattel" or possessions of the parent, and thus generally of the father, who was in English common law the owner of all property of the marriage (Mason, 1994). By the end of the 19th century, the "tender years" doctrine, which held that mothers were best qualified to care for their children, emerged and prevailed for a time. With shifting views of sex roles and the advent of "no fault" divorce in the 1960s, courts began to discard the tender years presumption (e.g., *State ex rel. Watts v. Watts*, 1973). It has since been replaced with the best interest of the child standard, which has been adopted by all jurisdictions in the United States (Otto & Edens, 2003).

Today, "best interest" is defined differently in various state statutes (Child Welfare Information Gateway, 2008), and in some states it is determined by case law. The definition is sufficiently indeterminate (Goldstein, Freud, & Solnit, 1979) to require a case-by-case analysis of what is in the child's best interest. In child protection proceedings, generally the concept of best interest is invoked in consideration of disposition, visitation and permanency planning, and termination of parental rights. The Illinois Juvenile Court Act (705 ILCS 405/1-2) reflects many of the elements included in state statutes, such as the child's (a) age and developmental needs, (b) physical safety and welfare, (c) emotional, physical, and mental status or condition, (d) background and ties, including family, culture, and religion, (e) sense of attachments, (f) wishes and long-term goals, and (g) need for permanence, stability, and continuity of relationships, including with siblings.

Overview of Legal Process

Legal procedures in dependency court vary from state to state, but there are some general areas of agreement. Following reports of suspected abuse or neglect to the state child abuse hotline or CPS, an investigation may ensue. In cases of severe or urgent need, the child may be immediately taken into protective custody. Removal of a child from the parent, even temporarily, is an extreme measure, and the law provides certain protections to ensure that it does not occur capriciously. CPS must file a petition for removal and temporary custody that triggers an initial hearing or emergency hearing, the main purpose of which is to determine whether the child should be placed in substitute care or remain with or be returned to the parent pending further proceedings (Child Welfare Information Gateway, 2006).

Adjudicatory hearings, sometimes called *fact-finding hearings* or *jurisdictional hearings*, occur following the initial proceedings and determine whether the child has been maltreated or whether some other legal basis exists for the state to intervene to protect the child. Adjudicatory hearings are followed the same day or within a few weeks by dispositional hearings, when the court decides whether the child can safely return home without further court supervision. Also established are service needs, visitation schedules, and, if in-home services are being provided, an order to formalize the service plan by which CPS will continue to provide in-home follow-up (Child Welfare Information Gateway, 2006). Periodic hearings are held to review whether substitute placement remains a necessity and whether CPS is addressing the child's needs. A final hearing is generally held to formalize return of the child to the parents and cessation of the state's involvement following successful intervention or, when intervention has been unsuccessful, to terminate parental rights (Child Welfare Information Gateway, 2006). Figure 19.1 illustrates stages of child protection proceedings typical to most jurisdictions.

FORENSIC MENTAL HEALTH CONCEPTS
Purpose and Scope of Evaluations

Forensic mental health assessment (FMHA) refers to the objective evaluation of psychological

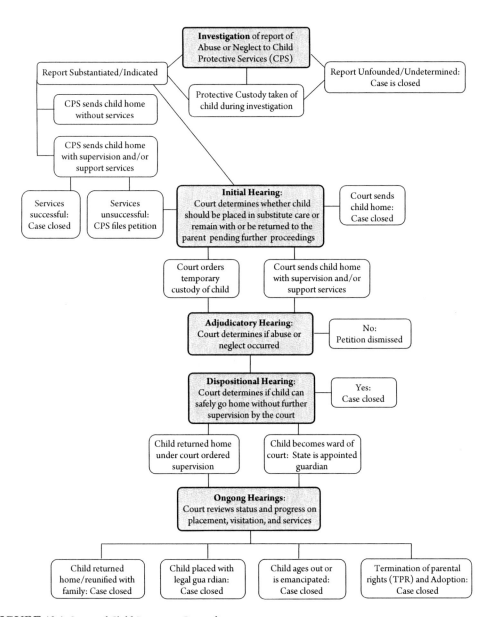

FIGURE 19.1 Stages of Child Protection Proceedings

phenomena conducted for the court or likely to be used in legal proceedings (Heilbrun, Grisso, & Goldstein, 2009). Whether a child protection evaluation is specifically ordered by the court or is requested by a social service agency, there is a high probability that it will be used in court proceedings. For this reason, the assessment should be conceived differently from a clinical or therapeutic assessment. As described in detail by Heilbrun et al. (2009) and by Melton et al. (2007), the FMHA is conducted to assist the legal decision maker by identifying the examinee's functional capacity or impairment directly relevant to the legal issue (Grisso, 2003), rather than to diagnose and treat symptoms. Issues of mental health diagnosis and treatment, which are prominent in clinical and therapeutic evaluations, are usually of less relevance in FMHA. In a child protection context, the functional capacities of interest typically relate to the parent's ability to protect and care for a child. Decisions regarding permanency goals, visitation arrangements, progress toward reunification, and termination of parental rights are the main legal decisions relevant to parenting capability. However, because parenting-capacity assessments may also be used to guide intervention or monitor progress, the scope of the assessment may be broader than typically seen in FMHA, depending on its purpose.

Minimally Adequate Parenting

The intersection between parents' rights and a child's best interest essentially comes down to a judgment about whether a parent's care is "good enough" in the eyes of the law. "Minimally adequate parenting" has been described as "the 'floor' of acceptable parenting sufficient to protect the safety and well being of the child" (Budd, 2001, p. 3). However, no clear operational definition for this term exists either in the law or in the child-development research literature. On the whole, a professional consensus among mental health professionals appears to have emerged (see, e.g., Azar et al., 1995; Budd, 2001, 2005; Jacobsen, Miller, & Kirkwood, 1997) that the evaluator's focus should remain on a "minimal" standard rather than on some higher criterion for which no empirical or legal basis has been established (Budd, 2005). This is consistent with the opinion put forth in *Santosky v. Kramer* (1982) that a parent's retention of parental rights need not be contingent on a display of "model" parenting.

EMPIRICAL FOUNDATIONS AND LIMITS
Parents and Children Involved in Child Protection Proceedings

Although little research exists on the subset of parents referred for FMHAs, general descriptions are available on the incidence of maltreatment and characteristics of parents and children known or alleged to have been involved in maltreatment. A major caveat, however, is that estimates of child maltreatment vary widely depending on the definitions and data-gathering methods used (Feerick et al., 2006; Miller-Perrin & Perrin, 2007). In 2009, an estimated 3.3 million referrals were made on approximately 6.0 million children reported for investigation. Only 62% of the allegations were investigated; the remainder were screened out, mainly for insufficient information. Twenty-five percent of the cases investigated found at least one child to be a victim of abuse or neglect. This amounts to approximately 9.3 victims per 1,000 children annually. U.S. child-abuse statistics show that neglect is the most common form of maltreatment, that young children are most at risk of maltreatment, and that parents, particularly mothers, are the most frequent perpetrators of child maltreatment (excluding sexual abuse) (U.S. Department of Health and Human Services, 2010).

Patterns of maltreatment by racial and ethnic groups are complicated to unravel and have shown disparate findings across databases (Sedlak et al., 2010). Rates of maltreatment for African American children are almost twice as high as those for Hispanic and white children. The rates for other groups (e.g., American Indian or Alaskan Native, Mixed Race, and Pacific Islander) are lower than African Americans but higher than Hispanic and white groups, and Asian Americans are much lower than all others (U.S. Department of Health and Human Services, 2010). Racial and ethnic disparities also have been documented in the number and types of child welfare services provided to families following substantiated abuse or neglect, time spent in care, and outcomes, with less favorable findings for children of color (Courtney et al., 1996). Mental health professionals must also consider contextual factors that are shown to contribute to more minorities entering and remaining in foster care (e.g., poverty, lack of access to services, and biases in service provision) when conducting child protection evaluations.

The U.S. child-abuse data provide a thumbnail sketch of the victims and perpetrators of maltreatment, but this sketch reveals little about the patterns and characteristics associated with its occurrence. Early etiological studies based on clinical descriptions of known abusers pointed to psychological characteristics of adults, such as personality problems and low intelligence, as predictors (Kempe et al., 1962; Steele & Pollock, 1968). Descriptive reports of cases in child protection proceedings based on selected court samples (e.g., Bishop et al., 2003; Taylor et al., 1991) have confirmed an over-representation of parents with psychiatric, intellectual, or substance-abuse problems compared to the general population. However, research suggests that only a small proportion of perpetrators have severe personality or cognitive impairments. Rather, studies have expanded the list of potential antecedents to cover multiple parental characteristics as well as child, family, and environmental factors.

Commonly cited parent factors include individual characteristics (e.g., anger-control difficulties, low self-esteem, mental health problems, alcohol or drug abuse, physical health problems, cognitive impairments, and a history of having been abused as a child) and parenting patterns (e.g., unrealistic expectations, harshness, or rigidity). Child factors include young age, behavioral difficulties, and mental and physical disabilities. Family and environmental factors include single-parent status, low socioeconomic status, unemployment, partner conflict, social isolation, community violence, and sparse resources (cf. Krug et al., 2002; Miller-Perrin & Perrin, 2007; Myers et al., 2002). Importantly, etiological studies have demonstrated that none of these characteristics is determinative of maltreatment, although as the number of risk factors increases, the likelihood of abuse or neglect increases (Brown et al., 1998).

A major responsibility of CPS, in addition to investigating reports of maltreatment, is to provide services to maximize children's safety, promote permanent living arrangements, and facilitate children's development (Haskins, Wulczyn, & Webb, 2007). It is widely acknowledged that states often fall short in meeting the complex needs of children in foster care (Annie M. Casey Foundation, 2009). Problems have included inadequate training and frequent turnover of child welfare staff, a shortage of high-quality foster homes, a dearth of effective intervention services, systemic resistance to implementing promising practices, resource limitations, and ineffective systems of accountability (Kauffman Best Practices Project, 2004).

Cultural Factors Affecting Parenting

All cultures have rules concerning appropriate and inappropriate conduct with children, but beliefs may vary widely regarding what is condoned (Korbin, 1981, 1997). Contextual factors such as racial or ethnic background, region of the country, religiosity, socioeconomic status, and a parent's own experiences of childrearing influence parenting beliefs and practices (Darling & Steinberg, 1993; Harkness & Super, 1996; Kotchick & Forehand, 2002). Further, the impact of parenting behaviors on children's adjustment has been found to differ depending on the contexts in which these behaviors occur. To the extent that parents' punitive discipline practices are culturally normative, they may be seen by children as less rejecting and have a less negative impact on children (Lansford et al., 2005).

Much of the research on parenting and child development has been conducted in the United States and has involved largely middle-class, European American families. Therefore, a basic question arises as to whether the principles and findings drawn from this research hold true across cultures and, particularly for the current discussion, whether they apply to families involved in the child protection system, who often are poor or ethnic minorities. Mental health professionals should bear in mind that cultural, ethnic, and economic differences in normative parenting practices exist and that it is unreasonable to expect parents to achieve or maintain a "best parenting practices" level (APA Committee on Professional Practice and Standards, 2011). Retaining a behaviorally descriptive approach that is sensitive to these differences leaves room for the legal decision maker to determine the societal standard to which parents should be held.

Another pertinent consideration in conducting FMHAs is cultural differences in the interpretation of what constitutes maltreatment. Researchers, legal professionals, and child welfare professionals have struggled with where to draw the line between physical discipline and physical abuse, particularly when it is seen in a cultural context (Lansford et al., 2005; Whipple & Richey, 1997). Some behaviors may be viewed as culturally accepted in one context but become problematic when parents engage in them outside of their normative setting (Hansen,

1997). When families immigrate to the United States, they may engage in practices that were culturally accepted in the family's homeland but that meet local definitions of child abuse or neglect (Gray & Cosgrove, 1985; Levesque, 2000).

Mental health professionals conducting parenting-capacity evaluations are in a position to shed light on the nature of and possible explanations for culturally controversial practices, regardless of whether the actions have been determined by the court to be abusive. They can do this by seeking information regarding (1) the intensity, severity, and context of the parent's behavior; (2) the child's perceptions of his or her treatment and evidence of emotional harm; and (3) the parent's intentions and beliefs about the actions in relation to socialization goals of the family's culture (Korbin, 1981, 1997; Whipple & Richey, 1997). Legal professionals should expect to see this information fleshed out in the report. As there is often not a clear line for determining when a parental practice is appropriate discipline and when it becomes abusive, having a contextual understanding of a parent's actions and the implications for a particular child is important.

Research on Assessment Measures Used in Forensic Practice

Traditional psychological tests have been generally viewed as having varying levels of applicability to forensic assessment. Evidence is lacking to interpret performance on such tests as directly indicative of parenting abilities or deficits. No studies yet have examined the relationship of performance on traditional psychological tests to parenting functioning of individuals undergoing FMHA in a child protection setting. Traditional psychological tests can, however, be useful for measuring characteristics that may explain a parent's caregiving deficits, even though they do not measure parenting capacity itself.

Evolving evidentiary standards have increasingly emphasized the importance of scientific reliability and legal relevance of the testing used in forensic assessment (Heilbrun et al., 2009). *Frye v. United States* (1923) set the initial standard for admissibility of evidence and required that a method used by an expert be generally accepted in that expert's field. In *Daubert v. Merrell Dow Pharmaceuticals, Inc.* (1993), the Supreme Court established as a new standard for admissibility of expert testimony that the methods have demonstrated reliability and scientific

peer review. Tests of intelligence and achievement levels most consistently found to meet these criteria include the Wechsler scales of intelligence and achievement (Wechsler, 1992, 1999, 2008), the Stanford-Binet Intelligence Scale–fourth edition (Thorndike, Hagen, & Sattler, 1986), and the Wide Range Achievement Test–fourth edition (Wilkinson & Robertson, 2006). Tests of personality functioning most consistently found to meet these criteria include the Minnesota Multiphasic Personality Inventory–2 (MMPI-2) (Butcher et al., 2001), the MMPI-2- Restructured Form (Ben-Porath & Tellegen, 2008), and the Personality Assessment Inventory (Morey, 1991). There is controversy about the appropriateness of using the Rorschach Inkblot Method, a subjective test of personality functioning, in forensic settings due to debate in the literature about the validity of the Rorschach scoring system and the normative sample upon which it is based (Garb et al., 2005; Medoff, 2003).

Tests of parenting-related constructs are designed to tap functional characteristics—that is, knowledge, attitudes, beliefs, and behaviors related to childrearing. Despite the plethora of clinical and research measures designed to assess parenting attitudes and behaviors, only two, the Child Abuse Potential Inventory (CAPI) (Milner, 1986) and the Parenting Stress Index (PSI) (Abidin, 1995), have been recommended in forensic reviews as appropriate for FMHAs in child protection cases (Archer et al., 2006; Otto & Edens, 2003; Yanez & Fremouw, 2004). No current tests for assessing parent–child interactions during observations fulfill the criteria necessary for formal forensic use (Otto & Edens, 2003). However, observation of parent-child interactions is recommended whenever possible to provide direct information on parent and child behavior (American Psychological Association Committee on Professional Practice and Standards, 2011). The validity of conclusions increases when drawn from more than one observation, from observations held for longer periods, and from observations conducted in different settings (Azar, Lauretti, & Loding, 1998; Schmidt et al., 2007; Wilson et al., 2008).

The demands of court-ordered testing situations are likely to contribute to parents' motivation to present themselves positively (Carr, Moretti, & Cue, 2005; Stredny, Archer, & Mason, 2006). Of significant concern is that the accuracy of psychological tests may be reduced by response distortions because parents may underreport symptoms or overreport positive qualities in order to appear well adjusted. However, rather than viewing positive presentation bias as a basis for invalidating test results (cf. Carr et al., 2005), Ben-Porath (2009) proposed that evaluators consider the pattern as typical under the circumstances. In that light, legal professionals should expect the evaluator to comment in the report that highly defensive response sets or efforts at positive impression management are frequently observed and understandable in the context of court-mandated assessment and that these response styles may not characterize the individual's responses in general. Any limits to the validity or reliability of information gathered due to such a response style should be discussed.

THE EVALUATION
Finding a Qualified Expert

The educational training of mental health professionals (i.e., psychology, psychiatry, and social work) differs considerably and may equip professionals with distinct skill sets. For example, psychologists are trained in the administration of psychological testing, whereas professionals from other disciplines are not. Psychiatrists, as medical doctors, have extensive training not typical of other disciplines in psychopharmacology and differential diagnosis, particularly when the symptoms could reflect medical conditions. If the referral question requires specialized skills unique to one profession, legal professionals should refer accordingly. However, there is also considerable overlap in knowledge and clinical experience among forensically trained professionals from distinct disciplines. The Guidelines for Psychological Evaluations in Child Protection Matters (hereafter referred to as the Child Protection Evaluation Guidelines) state that "[p]sychologists strive to gain competence sufficient to provide effective and ethical forensic services when conducting child protection evaluations and when addressing case-specific issues that may require specialized professional knowledge, training, or skills" (APA Committee on Professional Practice and Standards, 2011, Guideline II [5]). Such competence may include (1) a background in forensic assessment concepts and methods, (2) familiarity with child protective services and local child welfare practices, and (3) specialized clinical skills, including cultural and linguistic competence, in assessing families involved in the child welfare

system. Most mental health professionals possess a background in only some of these areas, fueling the need for continuing education and training.

Another relevant area of inquiry is the evaluator's relationship, if any, with the individuals to be assessed. The Child Protection Evaluation Guidelines state, "The role of psychologists who conduct child protection evaluations is that of a professional expert who strives to maintain an unbiased, impartial approach to the evaluation" (Guideline II [4]). Conflict may arise when the mental health professional serves as both evaluator and therapist for a parent or child. If a dual relationship cannot be avoided in regions where few qualified forensic professionals are available, mental health professionals should take reasonable precautions to minimize potential negative impact (Committee on Ethical Guidelines for Forensic Psychologists, American Psychology-Law Society and Division 41 the APA, 2011).

Framing the Referral Questions

When making a referral for a parenting-capacity assessment, legal professionals should have a realistic expectation about what the assessment can provide. Table 19.1 lists some general features of what parenting assessments can and cannot do (Budd, 2005; Condie, 2003).

Referrals that delineate specific purposes increase the usefulness of the resulting reports. Legal professionals seeking a parenting-capacity assessment should be prepared to clarify (1) what, specifically, they want to know about the parent's functioning; (2) what problems or events gave rise to the concerns; and (3) what specific outcomes or options will be affected by the findings. Potential referral questions resulting from this process could translate a generic question such as, "What is this parent's caregiving ability and what services are needed?" into the following: (1) "What strengths and weaknesses does this parent have in terms of her or his ability to adequately care for an infant and preschool-age child?" (2) "Given that the parent has a history of bipolar disorder, what, if any, mental health services are recommended?" and (3) "Are there concerns about the children's safety during visitation, and, if so, what factors should be monitored before, during, or after visits?" Ideally, the questions should be written as open-ended rather than yes/no questions.

When an evaluation is sought in relation to a pending legal decision (such as visitation

---

TABLE 19.1 WHAT PARENTING ASSESSMENTS CAN AND CANNOT DO

Parenting Assessments *Can*:

- Describe characteristics and patterns of a parent's functioning in adult and childrearing roles
- Explain possible reasons for abnormal or problematic behavior, and the potential for change
- Identify person-based and environmental conditions likely to positively or negatively influence the behavior
- Describe children's functioning, needs, and risks in relation to the parent's skills and deficits
- Provide directions for intervention

Parenting Assessments *Cannot*:

- Compare an individual's parenting fitness to universal parenting standards (since none exist)
- Ascertain whether or not abuse or neglect occurred
- Determine whether a parent fits a profile of perpetrator characteristics
- Determine whether a parent or child is telling the truth
- Draw conclusions about parenting adequacy based only on indirect measures
- Predict parenting capacity from mental health diagnoses
- Rule out the effects of situational influences (e.g., time limitations, demand characteristics, current stressors, cultural issues) on the assessment process
- Predict future behavior with certainty
- Answer questions not articulated by the referral source

Reprinted with permission from Budd, 2005, p. 436.

arrangements, permanency goal, or other issues), one or more questions should pertain directly to the legal decision (e.g., "What are the risk and protective factors associated with beginning unsupervised overnight visits?" or "What is the likelihood that the mother will make the gains necessary to be able to meet her child's needs and achieve a goal of return home?"). When the pending legal decision is termination of a parent's rights, referral questions may be framed to address the statutory criteria for termination. For example, the Illinois Adoption Act (750 ILCS 50/1 [D (p)]) specifies that parents can be found unfit if they have a current mental condition that renders them unable to discharge parental responsibilities, and if that inability will extend beyond a reasonable time. Questions might be posed that ensure the evaluator identifies the condition of the parent, links that condition to parenting capacity, and specifies the likelihood of change in the future.

In some jurisdictions, *bonding or attachment assessments* are sometimes requested, particularly when children have been in foster care for extended periods and have difficulty relating to their biological parents. Legal professionals may want information about the child's relationship with the biological and/or foster parent in order to determine psychological risks to the child associated with return to the biological parents or removal from the familiar foster parent. The logic for a bonding or attachment assessment in such situations is understandable. The challenge, however, is that validated tools for assessing attachment for children in foster care do not exist. Given the absence of empirical support for these assessments in a child protection context, it may be helpful to reframe the questions to focus on the relevant psychological and legal issues (e.g., how the child's removal from the foster parents may affect the child, the strengths and limitations of the parents in a caregiving role, and positive and negative factors associated with return to the parents).

Data Collection

Common components in FMHA in child protection cases include *reviewing records, interviewing examinees, interviewing collateral or third-party sources, observing parents with their children,* and *conducting testing.* Review of prior records and parent interview are essential to the FMHA, in that they provide basic factual and descriptive material. Collateral interviews and parent–child observation are highly recommended for gauging the reliability of information and broadening the sources and types of data. Testing is often but not always needed, and the nature and extent of the testing depends on the referral concerns and available data sources. Finally, child interviews may be a part of the FMHA when children are old enough to provide independent information and their perspective is relevant. Gathering data from multiple sources and using multiple methods allows the mental health professional to compare and contrast information and draw informed conclusions (Heilbrun et al., 2007). See Table 19.2 for factors to consider when gathering and assessing the reliability and validity of data at each stage of the process.

[table 19.2 near here]

Interpretation

Once data have been collected, evaluators are faced with the challenge of integrating and assigning meaning to the information. Legal professionals should be aware that mental health professionals should adhere to the following principles when interpreting data:

- Consider only data relevant to the referral issue (e.g., information that offers insight into the parent's functioning, probable causes for parenting strengths or deficits, potential benefit from intervention, and the nature of the connection between the parent and child).
- Review data objectively and attend to data that both support and refute working hypotheses. Mental health professionals should not adopt a stance (e.g., for or against a parent's caregiving ability) and attempt to verify or support it with the data, but should strive to let the data inform their opinions.
- Consider the strength and convergence of data across sources and measures in order to draw sound and credible conclusions.
- Note any inconsistencies, gaps, and limitations in the data and the impact of these on the ability to draw conclusions.
- Substantiate opinions or conclusions with information from multiple sources, giving more weight to data from more reliable sources.
- Consider factors at the level of the child, parent, and environment within which the family lives when assessing conditions influencing parenting.
- Use a conservative approach when drawing conclusions. Mental health professionals should avoid offering conclusions not grounded in case-specific facts.

REPORT WRITING AND TESTIMONY
Organization of Report

Considering the high volume of assessment reports prepared for the court and their importance in legal decisions, it is surprising that no specific standards exist for what constitutes an acceptable forensic report. In the absence of accepted standards, scholars (Heilbrun, 2001; Melton et al., 2007) have provided guidelines, which include:

- Write the report in sections, proceeding from data, to inferences, to conclusions.
- Attribute information to specific sources.
- Use plain language and avoid technical jargon.
- Present facts and descriptive material separately from theoretical and clinical inferences.
- Clarify the relationship between data, reasoning, and conclusions and link the clinical data to the legal referral questions.
- Confine the report to topics raised by the referral source and avoid including irrelevant issues.
- Strike a balance between comprehensiveness and efficiency by reporting only findings essential to the clinical formulation.

Because judges and lawyers are accustomed to scanning cases and briefs to look for legal issues most pertinent to their arguments, forensic evaluators have developed a style that facilitates this approach through the use of topical headings that identify different types of information. Samples of assessment reports on parents in child protection cases are available as models (Melton et al., 2007; Oberlander, 2002; Pezzot-Pearce & Pearce, 2004).

Opinions on the Ultimate Issue

There are differing views in the field about whether forensic evaluators should offer an opinion on the ultimate legal issue (i.e., the legal question to be answered by the judge or jury). Some authors have opined that forensic evaluators should *not* do so (Grisso, 2003; Heilbrun, 2001; Melton et al., 2007; Otto & Edens, 2003), arguing that "the ultimate legal question, which includes moral, political, and community values, should not be the focus of the evaluation's conclusion" (Heilbrun et al., 2007,

TABLE 19.2 GUIDELINES AND LIMITATIONS FOR DATA GATHERING
IN PARENTING-CAPACITY ASSESSMENTS

Method	Practice Guidelines	Limits to Validity or Reliability
Review of Records	• Consider records from court, CPS, service providers, and law enforcement • Obtain appropriate authorizations • Seek records from primary sources	• Data from secondary sources • Incomplete or illegible records • Source presents inaccurate or biased information • Source goes beyond scope of expertise
Clinical Interviews	• Review purpose of evaluation and limits of confidentiality • Conduct multiple interviews when possible • Ensure location is private, quiet, and free of distractions • Alter interview style and questioning in response to cognitive limitation, mental illness, or physical disability • Consider potential cultural influences on communication • Use certified translator if examinee's primary language differs from evaluator's	• Single interview • Positive impression management by parent • Concerns about mental status of examinee • Anxiety about being evaluated • Language or cultural barriers
Collateral Contacts	• Consider contact with CPS, service providers, foster parents, sources of support named by examinee • Ask only about areas for which source can provide reliable and unbiased information	• Reluctance to participate • Lack of objectivity • Lack of specific expertise • Suggestibility • Memory loss • Opinions based on limited or incomplete data
Parent–Child Observation	• Consider physical safety and emotional well-being of child when determining whether contact should occur between parent and child • Observe parent with all children in the parent's care • Conduct multiple observations in different settings when possible • Conduct observation in setting familiar to parent and child • Include structured and unstructured activities	• Positive impression management by parent • Concerns about mental status of parent or child • Anxiety about being evaluated • Language or cultural barriers • Coaching of child • Methodological concerns (conducted in unfamiliar situation, short in duration)
Testing	• Use alternative and more direct methods of assessment when possible (e.g., interviews, observations) • Use tests that will provide concurrent data on constructs relevant to parenting capacity • Use tests with standardization sample representative of examinee • Use tests with adequate validity and reliability • Use tests only in the capacity for which they were designed • Use tests with measures of response style	• Lack of ability to generalize from normative group to examinee • Positive impression management by parent • Lack of objective measures of test-taker attitude • Necessity for inferential leap from test results to parenting issues

p. 55). However, as summarized by Budd and Springman (2011), other authors have questioned the practicality of refraining from offering ultimate-issue opinions for several reasons. Notably, they observe that judicial officials prefer to hear specific recommendations from mental health professionals. Further, judges bear the responsibility to weigh ultimate-issue opinions against all available evidence. The authors also observe that mental health professionals have relevant expertise on family dynamics and their opinions may be of assistance to the court. Additionally, when mental health professionals make explicit recommendations, these may facilitate out-of-court settlements. Heilbrun (2001) noted that avoiding conclusions about the ultimate legal issue could lead to exclusion of the entire evaluation or reduction in the weight of the evidence.

The line between the legal decision and the clinical opinion, while distinct in some cases, may not be so in others. For example, the decision by a court to terminate parental rights, while clearly informed by mental health opinion, is guided by statutory criteria, thus limiting the capacity of a mental health professional to make a statement that a parent's rights should or should not be terminated. On the other hand, the decision by a court to grant a parent unsupervised visits is based on the safety and well-being of the child in the parent's care unsupervised, which falls in the range of expertise of a qualified mental health professional.

When legal professionals want mental health professionals to weigh in on ultimate issues, such as whether a parent is "unfit" to parent or what is in the "best interest" of the child, it is best to clarify these questions at the time of referral, as recommended earlier in this chapter. Jurisdictional preferences about evaluators offering opinions on the ultimate issue can be communicated through the referral question, and if there is a specific jurisdictional demand that the evaluator should or should not offer explicit opinion on it, this should be clearly stated. In this way the evaluation can be maximally useful to the judicial process.

Expert Testimony

Whether the evaluator is being proffered directly or the lawyer is preparing cross-examination, there are three critical factors to consider when eliciting testimony: the qualifications of the evaluator and capacity to offer an opinion on the referral issue, the methodology employed to gather data, and the soundness of conclusions drawn by the evaluator. To assess each of these areas, legal professionals can consult Table 19.3 for a checklist of best-practice standards.

[table 19.3 near here]

Lawyers should attempt, whenever possible, to engage in pretrial preparation with the evaluator. This may include discussion of the number of times the evaluator has been qualified as an expert in child protection proceedings; the number of evaluations previously undertaken with similar fact patterns; the extent to which the evaluator relies on referrals from CPS; the nature of any other collaboration between the evaluator and CPS; the number of times the evaluator's testimony has been solicited by parents; and other such questions to explore the neutrality or bias of the evaluator. Also relevant for discussion are the specific questions that will be posed during testimony. Pretrial preparation also allows an opportunity for the evaluator to assist the lawyer in wording questions in a way that will elicit the most useful and relevant information during testimony.

Exploring potential challenges to the admissibility of testimony is also recommended. Evaluators may not fully understand the rules of evidence in legal proceedings and may require assistance understanding legal thresholds to admissibility of expert opinion. For example, if there is to be a challenge to the admissibility of the report because of inclusion of third-party (hearsay) information, the evaluator may need to be prepared to cite professional literature that explicates the importance of third-party sources as an essential component of forensic, as contrasted to clinical, assessment. A challenge to the reliability of test instruments when administered to the parent who belongs to a demographic group not included in the standardization sample would require that the evaluator prepare to explain the standardization samples for the tests used, the ways the evaluator considered the parent's own subcultural affiliation, and the limits to reliability of the findings.

Finally, lawyers may want to cover what the evaluator can expect in the courtroom and during testimony. Especially for evaluators new to the experience, it is helpful to review the stages of

TABLE 19.3 BEST-PRACTICE CHECKLIST FOR PARENTING-CAPACITY
ASSESSMENTS IN CHILD PROTECTION

Qualifications

- Current professional license in field of practice
- Experience conducting evaluations of parents and children involved in CPS
- Knowledge of case law and/or legal standards relevant to the current legal issue
- Familiarity with professional guidelines for FMHA in field of practice (e.g., Ethical Principles of Psychologists
  and Code of Conduct, 2002; Ethical Guidelines for the Practice of Forensic Psychiatry, 2005; Standards for
  Educational and Psychological Testing, 1999; Specialty Guidelines for Forensic Psychologists, 2011; Guidelines for
  Psychological Evaluations in Child Protection Matters, 2011, APA's Record Keeping Guidelines, 2007)

Methodology

- Completed thorough review of records—if no, able to explain why not
- Conducted multiple clinical interviews—if no, able to explain why not
- Conducted collateral contacts with relevant parties—if no, able to explain why not
- Observed the parent and child interact—if no, able to explain why not
- Conducted testing that was valid and reliable for the purposes used

Conclusions

- Based conclusions on data relevant to the issue before the court
- Considered data that supported and refuted working hypotheses when drawing conclusions
- Based conclusions on data from reliable sources
- Described the links between the data and the conclusions
- Acknowledged any inconsistencies, gaps, and limitations in the data
- Substantiated all conclusions with information from multiple sources
- Considered child, parent, and environmental factors in reaching conclusions
- Gave appropriate weight to identified risk and protective factors in formulation of risk
- Did not offer an opinion on the ultimate legal issue if that opinion would require moral or value determinations
  beyond the evaluator's professional expertise

---

testimony, what the evaluator should do if an objection is made during testimony, and the process by which the evaluator may, if needed, refresh his or her memory on details of a case during testimony.

The lawyer whose client is benefited by the mental health professional's findings may assist him or her in preparing for cross-examination by anticipating areas on which cross-examination may focus and discussing those areas. For example, if the lawyer expects that opposing counsel will attack the choice of a particular test, the lawyer may forewarn the mental health professional to be prepared to explain why the test was used, its strengths and limitations, and any controversy in the field about its use in parenting assessment. If there are factual inaccuracies in the mental health professional's report or recent developments in the case that may affect the evaluator's recommendations, this information should also be discussed.

SUMMARY

Although there is growing consensus amongst forensic mental health professionals about what constitutes best-practice standards when conducting evaluations in child protection cases, research has shown that evaluators do not consistently adhere to these standards. Given this, and the substantial impact mental health information can have on court decisions in child protection matters, it is critical that legal professionals are informed consumers when seeking and utilizing mental health information. Possessing knowledge of best-practice standards and key mental health concepts relevant to these specialized assessments is one critical step in achieving this. Also critical is having the skills to assess the qualifications of mental health experts, to assess the utility and credibility of mental health information, and to address the information effectively during testimony.

REFERENCES

Abidin, R. (1995). *Parenting Stress Index manual* (3rd ed.). Odessa, FL: Psychological Assessment Resources.

Adoption and Safe Families Act of 1997. Pub. L. No. 105-89. 42 U.S.C. 675.

Adoption Assistance and Child Welfare Act of 1980. P.L. 96-272, 42 U.S.C.

American Academy of Psychiatry and the Law (2005). *Ethical guidelines for the practice of forensic psychiatry.* Bloomfield, CT: American Academy of Psychiatry and Law.

American Educational Research Association, American Psychological Association, & National Council on Measurement in Education (1999). *Standards for educational and psychological testing.* Washington, DC: American Educational Research Association.

American Psychological Association (2002). Ethical principles of psychologists and code of conduct. *American Psychologist, 57,* 1060–1073.

American Psychological Association (2007). Record keeping guidelines. *American Psychologist, 62,* 993–1004.

American Psychological Association Committee on Professional Practice and Standards (2011). *Guidelines for psychological evaluations in child protection matters.* Retrieved November 9, 2011, from the American Psychological Association Website at http://www.apapracticecentral.org/update/2011/03-17/child-protection.pdf

Annie M. Case Foundation (2009). *Issue brief: Rebuild the nation's child welfare system.* Retrieved on March 12, 2009, from http://www.aecf.org/~/media/PublicationFiles/Child_Welfare_issuebrief2.pdf.

Archer, R. P., Buffington-Vollum, J. K., Stredny, R. V., & Handel, R. W. (2006). A survey of psychological test use patterns among forensic psychologists. *Journal of Personality Assessment, 87,* 84–94.

Azar, S. T., Benjet, C. L., Fuhrmann, G. S., & Cavellero, L. (1995). Child maltreatment and termination of parental rights: Can behavioral research help Solomon? *Behavior Therapy, 26,* 599–623.

Azar, S. T., Lauretti, A. F., & Loding, B. V. (1998). The evaluation of parental fitness in termination of parental rights cases: A functional-contextual perspective. *Clinical Child and Family Psychology Review, 1,* 77–100.

Ben-Porath, Y. S. (2009). *The MMPI-2-RF (Restructured Form): An introduction for forensic psychologists.* Workshop presented at the American Academy of Forensic Psychology, Montreal, QC.

Ben-Porath, Y.S., & Tellegen, A. (2008). *MMPI-2-RF (Minnesota Multiphasic Personality Inventory-2): Manual for administration, scoring, and interpretation.* Minneapolis: University of Minnesota Press.

Bishop, S. J., Murphy, J. M., Hicks, R., Quinn, D., Lewis, P. J., Grace, M., & Jellinek, M. S. (2003). What progress has been made in meeting the needs of seriously maltreated children? The course of 200 cases through the Boston Juvenile Court. *Child Abuse & Neglect, 24,* 599–610.

Brown, J., Cohen, P., Johnson, J. G., & Salzinger, S. (1998). A longitudinal analysis of risk factors for child maltreatment: Findings of a 17-year prospective study of officially recorded and self-reported child abuse and neglect. *Child Abuse & Neglect, 22,* 1065–1078.

Budd, K. S. (2001). Assessing parenting competence in child protection cases: A clinical practice model. *Clinical Child and Family Psychology Review, 4,* 1–18.

Budd, K. S. (2005). Assessing parenting capacity in a child welfare context. *Children and Youth Services Review, 27,* 429–444.

Budd, K. S., Connell, M., & Clark, J. R. (2011). *Evaluation of parenting capacity in child protection.* New York: Oxford University Press.

Budd, K. S., & Springman, R. E. (2011). Empirical analysis of referral issues and "ultimate issue" recommendations for parents in child protection cases. *Family Court Review, 49,*34–45.

Butcher, J. N., Graham, J. R., Ben-Porath, Y. S., Tellegen, A., Dahlstrom, W. G., & Kaemmer, B. (2001). *Minnesota Multiphasic Personality Inventory-2 (MMPI-2): Manual for administration, scoring, and interpretation* (Rev. ed.). Minneapolis: University of Minnesota Press.

Carr, G. D., Moretti, M. M., & Cue, B. J. H. (2005). Evaluating parenting capacity: Validity problems with the MMPI-2, PAI, CAPI, and ratings of child adjustment. *Professional Psychology: Research and Practice, 36,* 188–196.

Child Abuse Prevention and Treatment Act of 1974, Pub. L. No. 93-247.

Child Welfare Information Gateway (2006). *Court hearings for the permanent placement of children: Summary of state laws.* Retrieved November 2, 2008, from U.S. Department of Health and Human Services, Administration for Children and Families, Administration on Children, Youth, and Families, Children's Bureau website: http://www.childwelfare.gov/systemwide/laws_policies/statutes/planningall.pdf.

Child Welfare Information Gateway (2008). *Determining the best interests of the child.* Retrieved from Child Welfare Information Gateway website March 15, 2009, at http://www.childwelfare.gov/systemwide/laws_policies/statutes/best_interest.cfm. Washington, DC: U.S. Department of Health and Human Services, Administration for Children and Families, Administration on Children, Youth, and Families, Children's Bureau, Office of Child Abuse and Neglect.

Committee on Ethical Guidelines for Forensic Psychologists, American Psychology-Law Society and Division 41 of the APA (2011). *Specialty guidelines for forensic psychology.* Retrieved November 9, 2011, from the AP-LS website http://www.ap-ls.org/aboutpsychlaw/SGFP_Final_Approved_2011.pdf.

Condie, L. O. (2003). *Parenting evaluations for the court: Care and protection matters.* New York: Kluwer Academic/Plenum.

Courtney, M. E., Barth, R. P., Berrick, J. D., Brooks, D., Needell, B., & Park, L. (1996). Race and child welfare services: Past research and future directions. *Child Welfare, 75,* 99–137.

Darling, N., & Steinberg, L. (1993). Parenting style as context: An integrative model. *Psychological Bulletin, 113,* 487–496.

Daubert v. Merrell Dow Pharmaceuticals, 509 U.S. 579 (1993).

Feerick, M. M., Knutson, J. F., Trickett, P. K., & Flanzer, S. M. (Eds.). (2006). *Child abuse and neglect: Definitions, classifications, & a framework for research.* Baltimore: Paul H. Brookes Publishing Co.

Frye v. United States, 293 F. 1013 (D.C. Cir. 1923).

Garb, H. N., Wood, J. M., Lilienfeld, S. O., & Nezworski, M. T. (2005). Roots of the Rorschach controversy. *Clinical Psychology Review, 25,* 97–118.

Goldstein, J., Freud, A., & Solnit, A. J. (1979). *Before the best interests of the child.* New York: Free Press.

Gray, E., & Cosgrove, J. (1985). Ethnocentric perceptions of childrearing practices in protective services. *Child Abuse & Neglect, 9,* 389–396.

Grisso, T. (2003). *Evaluating competencies: Forensic assessments and instruments* (2nd ed.). New York: Kluwer Academic/Plenum Publishers.

Griswold v. Connecticut, 381 U.S. 479 (1965).

Hansen, K. K. (1997) Folk remedies and child abuse: A review with emphasis on *caida de mollera* and its relationship to shaken baby syndrome. *Child Abuse & Neglect, 22,* 117–127.

Harkness, S., & Super, C. M. (Eds.) (1996). *Parents' cultural belief systems: Their origins, expressions, and consequences.* New York: Guilford.

Haskins, R., Wulczyn, F., & Webb, M. B. (2007). Using high-quality research to improve child protection practice. In R. Haskins, F. Wulczyn, & M. B. Webb (Eds.), *Child protection: Using research to improve policy and practice* (pp. 1–33). Washington, DC: Brookings Institution Press.

Heilbrun, K. (2001). *Principles of forensic mental health assessment.* New York: Kluwer Academic/Plenum.

Heilbrun, K., Grisso, T. & Goldstein, A. M. (2009). *Foundations of forensic mental health assessment.* New York: Oxford University Press.

Heilbrun, K., Maraczyk, G., DeMatteo, D., & Mack-Allen, J. (2007). A principles-based approach to forensic mental health assessment: Utility and update. In A. M. Goldstein (Ed.), *Forensic psychology: Emerging topics and expanding roles* (pp. 45–72). Hoboken, NJ: Wiley.

Ill. Comp. Stat. Ch. 705, § 405/1-2; Ch 750, § 50/1

Jacobsen, T., Miller, L.J., & Kirkwood, K.P. (1997). Assessing parenting competency in individuals with severe mental illness: A comprehensive service. *Journal of Mental Health Administration, 24,* 189–199.

Kauffman Best Practices Project (2004). *Closing the quality chasm in child abuse treatment: Identifying and disseminating best practices.* Charleston, SC: National Crime Victims Research and Treatment Center.

Kempe, C. H., Silverman, F. N., Steele, B. F., Droegemuller, W., & Silver, H. K. (1962). The battered-child syndrome. *Journal of the American Medical Association, 181,* 17–24.

Korbin, J. E. (1981). *Child abuse and neglect: Cross-cultural perspectives.* Berkeley: University of California Press.

Korbin, J. E. (1997). Culture and child maltreatment. In M. E. Helfer, R. S. Kempe, & R. D. Krugman (Eds.), *The battered child* (5th ed., pp. 29–48). Chicago: University of Chicago Press.

Kotchick, B. A., & Forehand, R. (2002). Putting parenting in perspective: A discussion of the contextual factors that shape parenting practice. *Journal of Child and Family Studies, 11,* 255–269.

Krug, E. G., Dahlberg, L. L., Mercy, J. A., Zwi, A. B., & Lozano, R. (2002). *World report on violence and health.* Geneva: World Health Organization.

Lansford, J. E., Chang, L., Dodge, K. A., Malone, P. S., Oburu, P., Palmérus, K., Bacchini, D., Pastorelli, C., Bombi, A. S., Zelli, A., Tapanya, S., Chaudhary, N., Deater-Deckard, K., Manke, B., & Quinn, N. (2005). Physical discipline and children's adjustment: Cultural normativeness as a moderator. *Child Development, 76,* 1234–46.

Levesque, R. J. R. (2000). Cultural evidence, child maltreatment, and the law. *Child Maltreatment, 5,* 146–160.

Mason, M. A. (1994). *From father's property to children's rights: A history of child custody.* New York: Columbia University Press.

Medoff, D. (2003). The scientific basis of psychological testing: Considerations following Daubert, Kumbo, and Joiner. *Family Court Review, 41,* 199–212.

Melton, G. B., Petrila, J., Poythress, N. G., & Slobogin, C. (2007). *Psychological evaluations for the courts: A handbook for mental health professionals and lawyers* (3rd ed.). New York: Guilford.

Meyer v. Nebraska, 262 U.S. 390, 399 (1923).

Miller-Perrin, C. L., & Perrin, R. D. (2007). *Child maltreatment: An introduction.* Thousand Oaks, CA: Sage.

Milner, J. S. (1986). *The Child Abuse Potential Inventory manual* (2nd ed.). DeKalb, IL: Psytec Inc.

Morey, L. C. (1991). *Personality Assessment Inventory professional manual.* Lutz, FL: Psychological Assessment Resources.

Myers, J. E. B., Berliner, L. Briere, J., Hendrix, C. T., Jenny, C., & Reid, T. A (Eds.) (2002). *The APSAC handbook on child maltreatment* (2nd ed.). Thousand Oaks, CA: Sage.

Oberlander, L. B. (2002). Case 1: Principle: Obtain appropriate authorization. In K. Heilbrun, G. R.

Marczyk, & D. DeMatteo (Eds.), *Forensic mental health assessment: A casebook* (pp. 350–375). New York: Oxford University Press.

Otto, R. K., & Edens, J. F. (2003). Parenting capacity. In T. Grisso, *Evaluating competencies: Forensic assessments and instruments* (2nd ed., pp. 229–307). New York: Kluwer/Plenum.

Otto, R. K., & Melton, G. B. (1990). Trends in legislation and case law on child abuse and neglect. In R. T. Ammerman & M. Hersen (Eds.). *Children at risk: An evaluation of factors contributing to child abuse and neglect* (pp. 55–83). New York: Plenum.

Pezzot-Pearce, T. D., & Pearce, J. (2004). *Parenting assessments in child welfare cases: A practical guide.* Toronto: University of Toronto Press.

Pierce v. Society of Sisters, 268 U.S. 510, 535 (1925).

Prince v. Massachusetts, 321 U.S. 158, 166 (1944).

Santosky v. Kramer, 455 U.S. 745, 752-754 (1982).

Schmidt, F., Cutress, L. J., Lang, J., Lewandowski, M. J., & Rawana, J. S. (2007). Assessing the parent-child relationship in parenting capacity evaluations: Clinical applications of attachment research. *Family Court Review, 45,* 247–258.

Sedlak, A. J., Mettenburg, J., Basena, M., Petta, I., McPherson, K., Greene, A., & Li, S. (2010). *Fourth National Incidence Study of Child Abuse and Neglect (NIS–4): Report to Congress, Executive Summary.* Washington, DC: U.S. Department of Health and Human Services, Administration for Children and Families.

State ex rel. Watts v. Watts, 77 Misc. 2d 178, 350 N.Y.S. 2d 285. (1973).

Steele, B., F., & Pollock, C. B. (1968). A psychiatric study of parents who abuse infants and small children. In R. E. Helfer & C. H. Kempe (Eds.), *The battered child* (pp. 89–133). Chicago: University of Chicago Press.

Stredny, R. V., Archer, R. P., & Mason, J. A. (2006). MMPI-2 and MCMI-III characteristics of parental competency examinees. *Journal of Personality Assessment, 87,* 113–115.

Taylor, C. G., Norman, D. K., Murphy, J. M., Jellinek, M., Quinn, D., Poitrask, F. G., & Goshko, M. (1991). Diagnosed intellectual and emotional impairment among parents who seriously mistreat their children: Prevalence, type, and outcome in a court sample. *Child Abuse & Neglect, 15,* 389–401.

Thorndike, R. L., Hagen, E. P., & Sattler, J. M. (1986). *Stanford-Binet Intelligence Scale Fourth Edition: Technical manual.* Chicago, IL: Riverside.

U.S. Department of Health and Human Services, Administration for Children and Families, Administration on Children, Youth and Families, Children's Bureau. (2010). *Child Maltreatment 2009.* Available from http://www.acf.hhs.gov/programs/cb/stats_research/index.htm#can.

Wechsler, D. (1992). *Wechsler Individual Achievement Test manual.* San Antonio, TX: Psychological Corporation.

Wechsler, D. (1999). *Wechsler Abbreviated Scale of Intelligence.* San Antonio, TX: Psychological Corporation.

Wechsler, D. (2008). *Wechsler Adult Intelligence Scale—Fourth Edition.* San Antonio, TX: Psychological Corporation.

Whipple, E. E., & Richey, C. A. (1997). Crossing the line from physical discipline to child abuse: How much is too much? *Child Abuse & Neglect, 21,* 431–444.

Wilkinson, G. S., & Robertson, G. J. (2006). *Wide Range Achievement Test—Fourth Edition.* Lutz, FL: Psychological Assessment Resources.

Wilson, S. R., Rack, J. J., Shi, X., & Norris, A. M. (2008). Comparing physically abusive, neglectful, and non-maltreating parent during interactions with their children: A meta-analysis of observational studies. *Child Abuse & Neglect, 32,* 897–911.

Yanez, Y. T., & Fremouw, W. (2004). The application of the Daubert standard to parental capacity measures. *American Journal of Forensic Psychology, 22,* 5–29.

Youth Law Center (2000). *Making reasonable efforts: A permanent home for every child.* Retrieved December 19, 2008, from http://www.ylc.org/pdfs/children-makingreason.pdf. San Francisco CA: Youth Law Center.

INDEX

Note: Page numbers followed by "*f*" and "*t*" refer to figures and tables, respectively.